T0355600

‘Secularism has airbrushed the role of religion from the formation and motivation of our Prime Ministers. This book demonstrates the conclusive and increasing importance of faith in the lives of the twentieth-century premiers.’
Jeremy Black, Emeritus Professor of History, University of Exeter

‘Do Christian beliefs, values and prayer have a place in contemporary politics? What have we to fear if they don’t? This timely study reveals the surprising extent to which the Prime Ministers of the past century were influenced by their Christian upbringing and faith – and suggests how their successors could benefit from a similar ethical foundation.’
Tim Farron, MP, leader of the Liberal Democrats, 2015–17

‘This carefully researched and well-written study reveals the religious faith of our Prime Ministers, or lack of it, in vivid colours. Prepare to be shocked and surprised as the author lays bare their souls.’
Sir Anthony Seldon, biographer of the Prime Ministers

‘A brilliant, fascinating, surprising, sometimes touching parade of nineteen believers, heretics, agnostics, atheists, mystics, astrologers, bigots and Bible-thumping pagans: enlightening and entertaining from start to finish.’
Brendan Walsh, Editor, *The Tablet*

Mark Vickers was born in Lincolnshire in 1966. He read History at Durham and practised with one of the City law firms. After studying at the English College, Rome, he was ordained in 2003 and is currently a parish priest in west London. His previous books include *St Eustace White* (2002), *By the Thames Divided* (2013) and *Reunion Revisited* (2017).

GOD IN NUMBER

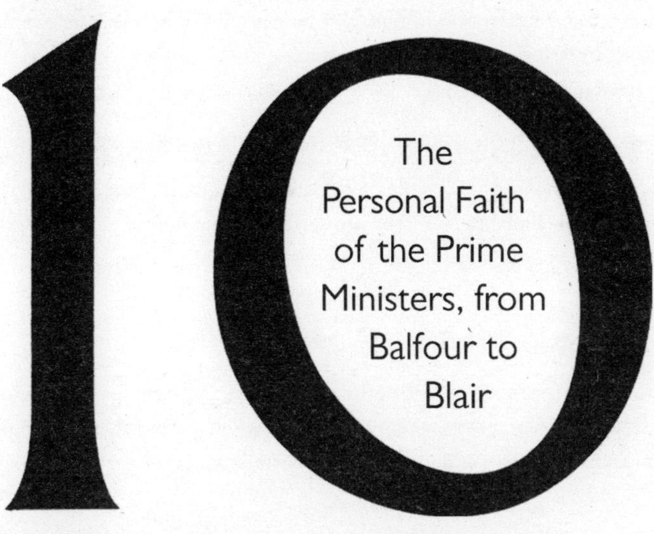

Mark
Vickers

First published in Great Britain in 2022

Society for Promoting Christian Knowledge
36 Causton Street
London SW1P 4ST
www.spck.org.uk

British Library Cataloguing-in-Publication Data
A catalogue record for this book is available from the British Library

ISBN 978-0-281-08728-0
eBook ISBN 978-0-281-08730-3

1 3 5 7 9 10 8 6 4 2

Typeset by Manila Typesetting Company
First printed in Great Britain by Clays

eBook by Manila Typesetting Company

Produced on paper from sustainable sources

Contents

Plates

10 Anthony Eden, Prime Minister (1955–7), with the Queen at the Royal Opera House, Covent Garden, London, 27 October 1955 (PA Images/Alamy Stock Photo).

11 Macmillan 'should have been a cardinal in the Middle Ages, under a strong Pope' (Anthony Eden): Harold Macmillan, Prime Minister (1957–63), at an audience with Pope John XXIII at the Vatican, 23 November 1960 (PA Images/Alamy Stock Photo).

12 Alec Douglas-Home, Prime Minister (1963–4), and Elizabeth Douglas-Home with the Revd John Brewis at St James's Church, Piccadilly, 20 October 1963 (John Twine/ANL/Shutterstock).

13 Harold Wilson, Prime Minister (1964–70, 1974–6), and Mary Wilson at Kirby Baptist Church, Liverpool, 2 February 1969 (Trinity Mirror/Mirrorpix/Alamy Stock Photo).

14 Liberal leader Jeremy Thorpe, Edward Heath, Prime Minister (1970–4), and former Prime Ministers Alec Douglas-Home and Harold Macmillan attend the unveiling of a statue of Winston Churchill by Oscar Nemon at the House of Commons, 1 December 1969 (Fox Photos/Hulton Archive/Getty Images).

15 James Callaghan, Prime Minister (1976–9), speaks at the Labour Party annual conference in Brighton, 5 October 1966. Harold Wilson sits to the left (Rolls Press/Popperfoto via Getty Images).

16 Margaret Thatcher, 'Sermon on the Mound': Margaret Thatcher, Prime Minister (1979–90), addresses the General Assembly of the Church of Scotland in Edinburgh, 21 May 1988 (Trinity Mirror/Mirrorpix/Alamy Stock Photo).

17 Margaret Thatcher and John Major, Prime Minister (1990–7) attend the Armistice Day service at Westminster Abbey on 11 November 2009 (Indigo/Getty Images).

18 'Vicar of St Albion's': Tony Blair, Prime Minister (1997–2007), at St Saviour's and St Olave's School, Bermondsey, south London, on 8 May 2001 (John Stillwell/PA Images/Alamy Stock Photo).

Preface

'We don't do God'

At the age of twelve, I had life planned. Following graduation, I would practise law for a few years before entering Parliament, beginning in earnest the ascent of the greasy pole. Others affirmed my aspirations. Unbidden, Tony Benn sent me a photograph of himself. Shirley Williams, one of the leaders of the newly founded SDP, inscribed a copy of her book 'to a budding politician'. Marcus Kimball, one of the last, great huntin' and shootin' Tory squires, took me around Parliament for the first time in July 1979. Everything fell into place: a history degree, law school and a career with a City law firm. I fought a local government election in 1990 and was called for interview for a parliamentary constituency prior to the 1992 general election.

Man proposes and God disposes. My family were practising Christians in an understated sort of a way. I continued that practice without much serious reflection through school and university. As it was for Harold Macmillan, the faith was brought to life for me in glorious technicolour by the unfamiliar delights of Anglo-Papalism. The lure of politics receded. Unlike Macmillan, for me, it was only a hop, skip and a jump to Rome, figuratively and literally. It was not what I had intended, but the day after Tony Blair's 1997 election victory I was attending the selection conference to train to be a priest for the Diocese of Westminster. Accepted by Cardinal Hume, I was sent to the English College, Rome, and ordained in 2003. The subsequent years have been spent in parish ministry and university chaplaincy work. I have no regrets.

Once politics enters the bloodstream, however, one is never entirely immune from its siren blandishments. Even viewed from the perspective of a 'higher' calling, it is difficult to resist analysing the most recent opinion poll or Cabinet reshuffle and to avoid staying up far too late to watch the results on election night.

Preface

On holiday in the USA in 2014, I was browsing a friend's bookshelves for reading material for a flight and alighted on Barbara Tuchman's *The Proud Tower*, an account of Western society on the eve of the First World War.[1] I was fascinated by her account of Arthur Balfour. I prided myself on a fair knowledge of British modern political history and politicians but had no idea of the Christian faith in which Balfour was raised, the books he wrote and the lectures he gave on philosophy and natural theology. If I was ignorant of Balfour's religious background and beliefs, what was there to be discovered with respect to other twentieth-century Prime Ministers? I began to research the point at which my two passions met.

A new generation has become familiar with the Prime Ministers of the second half of the twentieth century through the royal drama series, *The Crown*.[2] Millions watched the monarchy and nation convulsed by speculation as to whether Princess Margaret might marry the divorcee Peter Townsend. How accurate was the portrayal of the characters? To what extent were they guided by the Christian teaching on marriage? What were the role and beliefs of Anthony Eden, the divorcee Prime Minister, called on to advise the Queen? Margaret Thatcher is seen drawing on the sermons of her father while devising the economic and social policies that reshaped Britain in the 1980s. Clearly the Prime Ministers' faith was relevant to some of the most important events of recent times. Systematic, original research was necessary to establish the nature and consequences of that faith.

On being told the subject matter of that research – the personal faith of the twentieth-century Prime Ministers – one wag retorted that it was bound to be a small book. Initially, I shared that fear. Alistair Campbell had notoriously declared with respect to Blair: 'We don't do God.'[3] It is easy to project that assumption into the past. (Campbell later explained his interjection as not a rejection of religious faith on behalf of politicians but rather a desire to ensure that faith remained part of the politician's private life, strictly demarcated from the public sphere.[4])

1 Barbara Tuchman, *The Proud Tower: A portrait of the world before the war, 1890–1914* (London: Hamish Hamilton, 1966).

2 *The Crown* (Netflix, 2016–).

3 Alistair Campbell, cited Tom Bower, *Broken Vow: Tony Blair – the tragedy of power* (London: Faber & Faber, 2016), p. 330.

4 Alastair Campbell, *Diaries: Outside, inside, 2003–2005*, Vol. 5 (London: Biteback Publishing, 2016), pp. 492–3.

Many of our recent Prime Ministers held deep and sincere religious beliefs. Some did not. In both cases, however, it is impossible to understand them apart from their religious context. For most of the twentieth century, Britain was in name – and to a significant degree in reality – a Christian country. Almost all the Prime Ministers came from practising Christian families. They attended Christian schools and universities. They were surrounded by those who were theologically literate and who practised their faith. Family members and friends were ordained. Religion continued to have an impact on political discourse. Due to the delightful anomalies of the British constitution, whether practising Anglicans or not, they were involved in the appointment of Church of England bishops and senior clergy. Even where they rejected faith, it is important to know why this happened and what they were rejecting, or thought they were rejecting. Yet religious formation and belief are noticeably absent from political biographies written in a more secular age.

At the time he was Prime Minister, Gordon Brown was not known to possess a strong religious faith. He later regretted not having revealed more of the beliefs that constituted and motivated him:

> More personally, how can a public figure who holds convictions that are religious in origin be authentic if we do not state what influences what we say and where we are coming from? A religious conviction cannot be equated with a private preference, such as a liking for sports or a taste in food or music: it is something that shapes your life, public as well as private . . . To expect those of us with strong convictions to leave them at the door of the House of Commons or No. 10 is to require us to bring an incomplete version of ourselves into the public arena.[5]

Whether the result of self-censorship exercised by politicians or the hermeneutic of a secular age, we are left with 'an incomplete version' of our Prime Ministers when serious reference to their religious background, faith and practice is omitted.

5 Gordon Brown, *My Life, Our Times* (London: The Bodley Head, 2017), p. 429.

Books have been written on the faith of modern world leaders and articles on the faith of the more recent Prime Ministers. Works have been attempted on the religion of Churchill and Blair. Thatcher's faith has been used as the introduction for a study of the relationship between the Conservative Party and the Established Church. Yet no one has attempted a systematic examination of the personal faith of the twentieth-century Prime Ministers.

An obvious and immediate question is how an individual's most private beliefs can ever be known with certainty. Writing of Blair's religion, his biographer, John Rentoul, reflected that there are 'always realms of the inaccessible in the mind of the subject of any biography'.[6] Margot Asquith, the second wife of the Prime Minister H. H. Asquith, was never reticent in proffering an opinion. Invited by William Booth, the founder of the Salvation Army, to pray with him in a railway carriage on a journey between Paddington and Swindon, she commented subsequently: 'I think there is something morally vulgar in trying to get too familiar with men's souls.'[7] Many of her contemporaries would have agreed. Fortunately for posterity, they frequently failed to practise what they preached. In their diaries and private correspondence, politicians in the earlier part of the century were more than willing to commit to paper their own religious views and spiritual struggles, and to speculate on those of others – never dreaming that such musings would one day be accessible to the private researcher and the general public.

Another difficulty is how to judge the authenticity of an individual's professed beliefs and religious practice. Again, Margot Asquith identified the dilemma. Whether the realist or the cynic, she described the ruling classes: 'They acquiesce, rather than believe, in religious observances, and go to church merely as an example to their servants.'[8] Of course, the converse can also be true. The fact that a politician does not regularly attend church is not necessarily evidence that they are devoid of religious belief. An individual's beliefs might – and did – change over the course of their life or remain unformulated. It is necessary to balance public utterances and private

6 John Rentoul, 'The Mystery of Blair the Convert', *The Independent*, 23 December 2007.

7 Margot Asquith, *The Autobiography of Margot Asquith*, Vol. 1 (London: Thornton Butterworth, 1920), p. 222.

8 Margot Asquith, *More Memories* (London: Cassell & Co., 1933), p. 265.

sentiments, study the politician's life as a whole and listen to the judgements of their peers. In most cases, a coherent picture emerges.

Researching this book has been both rewarding and challenging. The sheer quantity of primary and secondary material relating to the British Prime Ministers is truly voluminous. (There are said to be a thousand biographies of Winston Churchill alone.) Up to and including Macmillan, the Prime Ministers' papers are generally available to the researcher. From the 1960s, one relies on biographies, published diaries, press articles and interviews. Any assessment, especially of the later Prime Ministers, will change as further material is made public. Fitted into spare moments from parish ministry, my research could not be exhaustive. The COVID-19 pandemic brought its own challenges – more time for writing; less access to archives and libraries.

For a few holders of the office, the material is thin – reflecting a relative lack of interest in religion or the subject's reticence. For the great majority, however, there is abundant material to advance firm conclusions as to the personal faith of the eighteen men and one woman who occupied 10 Downing Street during this period. In some cases, it is a matter of gathering scattered references to arrive at a comprehensive picture. In others, there are real discoveries and surprises – brushes with the occult and mystical visions or genuine religious commitment – passed over by political biographers. There are Prime Ministers who drew consolation from a deeply held Christian faith in times of national crisis or personal conflict. Poignantly, there are others who sought and failed to find spiritual succour or an intellectual rationale from faith. For all, it casts a new perspective on every holder of the highest political office in the realm.

I have received enormous kindness, encouragement and practical help in the production of this work. I was pleasantly surprised by the enthusiasm with which, on the whole, the families of past Prime Ministers have greeted the project. I wish to thank the following who assisted with my enquiries: Dr Clyde Binfield, Dr Francesca Bugliani Knox, the late Lord Coleraine, Joy Crispin-Wilson, John d'Arcy, Canon Jeremy Davies, Professor David Dilks, Lord Home, Christopher Howse, Iona Kielhorn, Sir Edward Leigh, Sir John Major, the Revd Tom McReady, Charles Moore, Archbishop Mark O'Toole, Sir Anthony Seldon, Lord Stockton and Mgr John Walsh. I acknowledge the unfailing professionalism and courtesy of the staff of the following archives and libraries: the Bodleian Library, the British Library, the Cadbury Research Library in the University of Birmingham, Cambridge University Library, Churchill College Archives Centre, Lambeth Palace Library, the National Archives, the National Library of Wales, the National Records of Scotland, the Parliamentary Archives, Dr Williams's Library and the Worcestershire Archive & Archaeology Service. I am grateful for accommodation and hospitality provided on my travels by Mgr Patrick Burke, Fr Michael Dolman, Fr Paul Keane, Canon Brian McGinley, Richard Murray, Lord and Lady Oxford and Fr John Saward. Dr Iestyn Daniel kindly undertook the translation from the original Welsh of material relating to David Lloyd George. I owe a particular debt of gratitude to Michael Hodges for the loan of books, effecting various introductions, and his reading of the draft text. I am extremely grateful to Tom Cull, my agent, and Alison Barr of SPCK, without whom the fruits of several years of research and writing would never have materialized.

This book is dedicated to Richard Whinder, Nicholas Schofield and Marcus Holden, comrades-in-arms from seminary days in Rome. To varying degrees, all were interested in the political world. All, however, heard and answered the call of God to the priesthood. For that, and for their friendship, I am eternally grateful.

Mark Vickers

Acknowledgements

The author and publishers gratefully acknowledge the following for permission to reproduce copyright material:

The Trustees of the Bonham-Carter/Asquith Papers for extracts from the papers of H. H. Asquith, Earl of Oxford and Asquith, and Margot, Countess of Oxford and Asquith, held at the Bodleian Library; Christopher Osborn for extracts from the diaries of Margot, Countess of Oxford and Asquith; the Avon Trustees for extracts of the papers of the Earl of Avon; the Worcestershire Archive & Archaeology Service for extracts from the Baldwin Family Papers; the Syndics of Cambridge University Library for extracts from the papers of Earl Baldwin; Michael Brander for extracts from the papers of Earl Balfour held at National Records of Scotland; Lambeth Palace Library for extracts from the papers of Bishop George Bell; the Chamberlain family for extracts from the papers of Neville Chamberlain; the National Library of Wales for extracts from the papers of D. R. Daniel; Lambeth Palace Library for extracts from the papers of Archbishop Lord Fisher; the Beaverbrook Foundation for extracts from the papers of Andrew Bonar Law; the National Library of Wales for extracts from the papers of David Lloyd George; his grandchildren for extracts from the diaries and papers of James Ramsay MacDonald and his correspondence in the papers of Lady Margaret Sackville; the Macmillan Book Trust for extracts from the Macmillan Papers held at the Bodleian Library; Lambeth Palace Library for extracts from the papers of Archbishop Lord Ramsey; Lambeth Palace Library for extracts from the papers of Archbishop William Temple; and the Margaret Thatcher Foundation for extracts from the papers from the Estate of the late Lady Thatcher.

Every effort has been made to trace the rights holders of Mary Wilson's poem 'The Manse'. Acknowledgement will be made in future editions if their identities are established.

Note: all emphases in quotations, primary or secondary, are original.

Abbreviations

ABL	Bonar Law
ADH	Alec Douglas-Home
AE	Anthony Eden
AJB	Arthur Balfour
AP	Avon Papers
BL	British Library
CB	Henry Campbell-Bannerman
CCAC	Churchill College Archives Centre, Cambridge
CRA	Clement Attlee
CRL	Cadbury Research Library, Birmingham
CSM	Christian Socialist Movement
CSU	Christian Social Union
CUL	Cambridge University Library
EEC	European Economic Community
EH	Edward Heath
HHA	Herbert Henry Asquith
HM	Harold Macmillan
HW	Harold Wilson
JC	James Callaghan
JM	John Major
JRM	Ramsay MacDonald
LG	David Lloyd George
LPL	Lambeth Palace Library
MS	manuscript
MT	Margaret Thatcher
NC	Neville Chamberlain
NLW	National Library of Wales
NRS	National Records of Scotland
PA	Parliamentary Archives
SB	Stanley Baldwin

SPR	Society for Psychical Research
TB	Tony Blair
WAAS	Worcestershire Archive & Archaeology Service
WSC	Winston Churchill

Arthur Balfour (1902–1905)

The Foundations of Belief

Born at Whittingehame in East Lothian on 25 July 1848, Arthur James Balfour was the eldest son of James and Lady Blanche Balfour. He was educated at Eton and Trinity College, Cambridge.

Balfour was the Conservative MP for Hertford (1874–85), Manchester East (1885–1906) and the City of London (1906–22). Created Earl of Balfour, he sat in the House of Lords from 1922. A skilled parliamentary debater, Balfour was appointed President of the Local Government Board (1885) and Secretary of State for Scotland (1886–7). He surprised many as a vigorous and ruthless Chief Secretary for Ireland (1887–91), pursuing a policy of coercion and reform. He was Leader of the Commons (1891–2 and 1895–1902) and leader of the Conservatives in the Commons (1891–1911).

As Prime Minister from 12 July 1902, Balfour failed to provide clear leadership as the government tore itself apart on the issue of tariff reform. He remained in office to improve Britain's defence and diplomatic position following the weaknesses and isolation exposed by the Boer War, finally resigning on 4 December 1905. In the ensuing general election, the Conservative Party suffered its worst defeat of modern times. Balfour himself lost his seat. As leader of the Opposition, he fought Lloyd George's 'People's Budget' of 1909 and the subsequent proposals for House of Lords reform. Two indecisive general elections in 1910 led to mounting internal criticism, and he resigned as party leader on 13 November 1911.

Balfour joined the War Council on the outbreak of the First World War and was appointed First Lord of the Admiralty (1915–16) in Asquith's coalition government. As Foreign Secretary (1916–19) in Lloyd George's coalition government, he issued the Balfour Declaration, often viewed as the genesis of the future state of Israel. Attending the Versailles Peace Conference, he left the conduct of British policy largely in the hands of Lloyd George. He served finally as Lord President of the Council (1919–22 and 1925–9).

Balfour died at his brother's home near Woking in Surrey on 19 March 1930.

* * *

'The last grandee'

Having served as Prime Minister for more than 13 years, Lord Salisbury finally relinquished the seals of office on 11 July 1902. There was a new monarch; the Boer War had concluded. The Victorian era and the nineteenth century were definitively ended. Salisbury's successor was his nephew, Arthur Balfour. Accusations of nepotism were inevitable, but few doubted Balfour's intellectual ability or his political experience.

A committed Anglican, Salisbury was a man of deep faith. Religion was prominent in his nephew's life too. Few British politicians have written so prolifically or spoken so publicly on philosophy and natural theology.[1] Yet Balfour's personal beliefs puzzled contemporaries and have exercised his biographers. Was he an agnostic? How does one account for his involvement in spiritualism? Was he a Christian or simply a theist? To which Christian denomination did he belong? Those closest to him drew very different conclusions. Balfour's intellect, charm and wit delighted many. Yet he was deeply reserved in matters of emotion and personal belief, stating: 'I am more or less happy when being praised: not very uncomfortable when being abused, but I have moments of uneasiness when being explained.'[2]

Balfour was born into a world of privilege and political power. Named after his godfather, the Duke of Wellington, his maternal uncle was Robert Gascoygne-Cecil, the future Marquess of Salisbury and Prime Minister. His father was a Tory MP. The family fortune derived from East India Company contracts. There were extensive estates in Scotland, a London home in St James's Square and a neoclassical mansion at Whittingehame. When he came of age, Balfour was one of the wealthiest men in the country.

1 The philosophical investigation of the bases for belief from human reason and empirical evidence, but excluding divine revelation.

2 Sir Ian Malcolm, *Lord Balfour: A memory* (London: Macmillan & Co., 1930), p. 95.

Balfour's father died when he was just seven. A forceful figure, Lady Blanche Balfour dominated the lives of all her children, especially her eldest son. She was a woman of faith, praying 'that I may guide with the love and wisdom which are from above the religious education of my children'.[3] To understand her son, it is necessary to know something of the mother's religious belief and practice.

Initially a committed Evangelical, Lady Blanche developed a more Broad Church position, disturbed by thoughts of predestination to eternal punishment. Although she eschewed partisan churchmanship, she allowed herself a 'dread' of everything High Church, believing that it weakened religion as a vital, spiritual force, diverting it into futile controversies of theology and ritual. The family insisted, however, that there was nothing dour about their mother's Protestantism.

Arthur was baptized within a week of his birth at the Episcopalian (Anglican) chapel at Haddington. Lady Blanche had no qualms practising as a Presbyterian north of the border, regarding the Church of England and the Church of Scotland as the established Protestant churches in their respective spheres. In 1864 she ensured the appointment of Dr James Robertson as the Church of Scotland minister at Whittingehame. His long incumbency encompassed most of Balfour's life. An Evangelical, Robertson maintained a certain openness to modern biblical criticism and reunion among the Protestant churches. Considering Presbyterian services too lengthy, Lady Blanche did not take the children to church regularly during their earliest years. Thereafter, they were communicants in both the Church of England and the Church of Scotland.

Not 'ecclesiastically minded', Lady Blanche 'attached more importance to private prayer and bible reading than to church services'. Scripture readings after breakfast developed into a conversation between mother and children. The emphasis was invariably on the Old Testament. (At Eton, Balfour expressed astonishment at his fag's ignorance of King David's genealogy.) Lady Blanche, however, awarded herself a surprising degree of latitude in her interpretation of the Bible. Contrary to the scriptural evidence,

3 Revd James Robertson, *Lady Blanche Balfour: A reminiscence* (Edinburgh: Oliphant, Anderson & Ferrier, 1897), cited p. 62.

she maintained that those unfit for heaven are annihilated rather than endure the pains of hell – because she found this the more comforting option.

Her theological library comprised the works of mainstream Protestant authors, who extolled 'simple devotion to duty and simple trust in God, and acquiescence in troubles and difficulties'. Her religion was practical. Accompanied by her children, Lady Blanche distributed material aid to those in need on the family estates and further afield.[4]

Lady Blanche died in 1872, aged 47, when Arthur was only 23. Yet with one significant proviso, almost everything said of his mother's religious beliefs and practice could be applied to her son throughout the course of his life.

'A "Christian" of a queer undefined sort'

Aged 11, Balfour was sent to The Grange, Hoddesdon, a Hertfordshire prep school. The headmaster, the Revd Charles Chittenden, recalled Balfour being 'amenable to *reason* to a greater degree than any boy with whom I ever had to do'.[5] At Eton too, he was taught by Anglican clergy. There were daily prayers in his house. On Sundays, saints' days and other holidays, the school assembled in the chapel for both morning service and afternoon service. The preaching was often inaudible and invariably dull. Services were relieved by music sung by the school choristers and lay clerks from St George's, Windsor.[6] Balfour was confirmed as an Anglican while at Eton.

At Cambridge, he studied the new discipline of Moral Sciences (Philosophy and Political Economy). Chapel was compulsory. Balfour attended Trinity College Chapel five times a week, including twice on a Sunday.

While Cambridge fellows were still required to subscribe to Anglican formularies, actual belief varied, with a tendency to scepticism. Henry Sidgwick, Balfour's future brother-in-law, resigned his fellowship in Balfour's final year, unable to reconcile orthodox Christian doctrine with

4 Eleanor Sidgwick, 'Some Things I Remember about My Mother', October 1922, NRS, Balfour Papers, GD 433/2/145/1; Evelyn Rayleigh, 'My recollections of my mother', September 1922, NRS, Balfour Papers, GD 433/2/145/2; Robertson, *Lady Blanche Balfour*, p. 25.

5 Revd C. G. Chittenden, 'Notes on AJB's Time at Hoddesdon', NRS, Balfour Papers, GD 433/2/195/2/3.

6 A. C. Ainger, *Memories of Eton Sixty Years Ago* (London: John Murray, 1917), pp. 65, 67–8.

scientific enquiry. John Maynard Keynes commented: Sidgwick 'never did anything but wonder whether Christianity was true and prove it wasn't and hope it was'.[7] Although Sidgwick enjoyed a considerable reputation as a moral philosopher, Balfour insisted: 'I was never a disciple of his.'[8]

Contemporaries recollected that, as an undergraduate, Balfour maintained an unfashionable religious conservatism – but qualified their judgement:

> At Cambridge when all the 'intellectual' set was agnostic, Arthur used to be looked upon as a curious relic of an older generation, with affectionate pity . . . Arthur's opinions have not varied. He was then a 'Christian' of a queer undefined sort, and in that faith he has abided.[9]

Balfour's religious practice was entirely conventional. He was a habitual late riser – except on Sundays, when he came down to breakfast in his Sunday best. Then the house was off to Whittingehame parish church. Mary Gladstone, a High Church Anglican, found the services 'dreary', the music 'bad, very'. His Presbyterian sister-in-law, Lady Frances Balfour, was more sympathetic: 'The services were simple, the singing unaccompanied.' (Communion services were only quarterly. In this respect, the Church of Scotland resembled most Anglican parishes of the period.) The family returned to the house, discussing the merits of the sermon and the setting of the psalms.

Sunday was strictly observed at Whittingehame. Meals were served cold. Card-playing and, in earlier years, tennis were prohibited. In the evening, Balfour led prayers for the household.

> They consisted of the Lord's Prayer, the General Confession, and prayers from the Anglican liturgy, including often the Collect for the Sunday, and a chapter from the Bible, which he always chose himself;

---

7 Cited Kenneth Young, *Arthur James Balfour: The happy life of the politician, prime minister, statesman and philosopher, 1848–1930* (London: George Bell & Sons, 1963), p. 20.

8 Arthur James Balfour to Mary Elcho, 29 August 1900, cited ed. Jane Ridley and Clayre Percy, *The Letters of Arthur Balfour and Lady Elcho, 1885–1917* (London: Hamish Hamilton, 1992), p. 173.

9 Reginald Brett to Duchess of Sutherland, 11 February 1894, cited ed. Maurice V. Brett, *Journals and Letters of Reginald Viscount Esher*, Vol. 1 (London: Nicholson & Watson, 1934), pp. 182–3.

> Isaiah, or the Psalms, or St Paul's Epistles were perhaps drawn upon most . . . His reading was rather slow, without dramatic emphasis, but bringing out every inherent shade of beauty and meaning. It deeply impressed all his hearers.

The remainder of the evening could be spent in hymn-singing.

In London too, Balfour was a regular churchgoer. In the 1870s his preferred destination was St Anne's, Soho, which enjoyed a considerable choral reputation. Later, forays were made to hear the fashionable preachers at St Paul's Cathedral, Westminster Abbey and the Temple Church.

For one of integrity and with decided views in such matters, it is unlikely that lifelong practice was simply a matter of habit and social convention. Yet the family were not surprised in the spring of 1930, as he drew close to death, that Balfour sought no consolation from the rites of the Church.[10]

Immersed in an endless round of house parties, cycling, golf and tennis, Balfour was perceived as detached, flippant and languid. His election as MP for Hertford in 1874 seemed the inevitable consequence of his connection to the Cecils. Two brothers and two brothers-in-law were fellows of Trinity. His own second-class degree precluded an academic career. Discussing the possibility of dedicating himself to philosophical studies, his mother advised: 'Do it if you like, but remember you will have nothing to write about by the time you are forty.'[11] Ignoring her advice, Balfour wrote and lectured on philosophy for 50 years.

'The so-called "conflict between religion and science"'

Balfour rejected the traditional undergraduate degrees in Mathematics or Classics to study more 'modern problems'. To his mind, there was

---

10 Mary Gladstone, 'Recollection of Mr Balfour', u/d [1918], BL, Mary Gladstone Papers, Add. MS 46270, ff. 174–200; Lady Frances Balfour, *Ne Obliviscaris: Dinna forget*, Vol. 1 (London: Hodder & Stoughton, 1930), p. 359; Vol. 2, p. 263; Blanche Dugdale, *Arthur James Balfour: First Earl of Balfour, KG, OM, FRS, 1848–1905* (London: Hutchinson & Co., 1939), pp. 145, 42; Blanche Dugdale, *Arthur James Balfour, First Earl of Balfour, KG, OM, FRS, 1906–1930* (London: Hutchinson & Co., u/d), p. 300.

11 Dugdale, *AJB, 1848–1905*, p. 17.

only one modern problem: 'the so-called "conflict between religion and science"'. Balfour arrived at Cambridge during a period of spiritual turmoil. Many of the educated classes suffered a crisis of faith as a result of modern biblical criticism and recent scientific discoveries.

Balfour referred specifically to the influence of the German biblical scholar David Strauss, a liberal Protestant theologian who distinguished the Jesus of history from the Jesus of faith. Strauss maintained the former had little connection to the latter which, together with the miracles and divinity of Christ, were constructs of the early Church. Balfour also cited Ernest Renan. Initially his *Life of Jesus* was welcomed as a rebuttal of Strauss's scepticism, though if anything Renan was more dangerous.[12] Making a pretence of impartiality, he wrote beguilingly, drawing on his personal knowledge of the Holy Land. Christ was presented as an attractive ethical model – at the expense of his divinity, of the miraculous and the supernatural.[13] A former seminarian hostile to Catholic doctrine and ritual, Renan appealed to Protestant England. Intellectually compelling answers to Strauss and Renan were lacking in Cambridge in the 1860s. The 'foolish tracts and dull sermons' provided no assistance to those attempting to clarify their 'way of thinking about God'.[14]

With his reverence for science, the apparent 'conflict between religion and science' exercised Balfour greatly. His passion for technology was more than the curiosity of an uninformed observer. His brother-in-law, John Strutt, Lord Rayleigh, won the Nobel Prize for Physics. His brother, Francis Balfour, was a pioneering embryologist. Balfour corresponded with these and other eminent scientists. Both as a statesman and private benefactor, he promoted national scientific research.

Charles Darwin's *On the Origin of Species* popularized the theory of evolution, leading many to think the Bible mistaken in claiming humanity as God's unique creation.[15] If wrong on this, could the Bible be considered authoritative on any other matter? Sir Charles Lyell's geological

12 Ernest Renan, *Histoire des origines du christianisme, tome 1: Vie de Jésus* (Paris: Michel Lévy frères, 1863); *Life of Jesus*, trans. Charles E. Wilbour (London: Trübner, 1863).

13 A. J. Balfour, *Chapters of Autobiography* (London: Cassell & Co., 1930), pp. 54, 18.

14 AJB to Betty Balfour, 13 September 1915 (copy), BL, Balfour Papers, Add. MS 49831, ff. 120–1.

15 Charles Darwin, *On the Origin of Species by Means of Natural Selection, or the Preservation of Favoured Races in the Struggle for Life* (London: John Murray, 1859).

discoveries, disproving notions that the earth had been created in the space of six days a few thousand years ago, were similarly problematic.

Balfour neither ignored the problems nor took refuge in 'bad science'. Arguments had to be examined and tested. He could not conceive of life without religion. Simultaneously, he looked

> to science more than anything else as the great ameliorator of the human lot in the future. If I had to believe that those two great powers were, indeed, in immutable and perpetual antagonism, it would be impossible for me to avoid that hopeless despair that makes effort impossible, which deprives labour of all its fruit for the future.[16]

He had no interest in abstract speculation for its own sake. His thought and his writing concerned 'the ground-work of living beliefs'.[17]

Frustrated with Anglican clergy unable to guide the laity in their religious perplexities,[18] Balfour set out to investigate these issues for himself and to elucidate them for others, addressing himself to

> the man who is troubled about miracles, the man who stumbles over the Higher Criticism, the man who is repelled by the traditional forms in which religion is enshrined, or wearies of the well-worn phrases in which it is familiarly expounded.[19]

A Defence of Philosophic Doubt

His first book, *A Defence of Philosophic Doubt: Being an essay on the foundations of belief*, was published in 1879. Thereafter public life restricted his time for writing. His second work, *The Foundations of*

16 AJB, Speech to Pan-Anglican Congress, 22 June 1908, cited ed. Wilfrid Short, *Arthur James Balfour as Philosopher and Thinker: A collection of the more important and interesting passages of his writings, speeches and addresses, 1879–1912* (London: Longmans, Green & Co., 1912), p. 504.

17 A. J. Balfour, *Theism and Humanism: Being the Gifford Lectures delivered at the University of Glasgow, 1914* (London: Hodder & Stoughton, 1915), p. 138.

18 AJB to Bishop Edward Talbot, 6 February 1903 (copy), BL, Balfour Papers, Add. MS 49789, f. 195.

19 A. J. Balfour, *Theism and Thought: A Study in familiar beliefs – being the second course of Gifford Lectures delivered at the University of Glasgow, 1922–23* (London: Hodder & Stoughton, 1923), p. 13.

Belief: Being notes introductory to the study of theology, published in 1895, was written during a spell in opposition. The Gifford Lectures at the University of Glasgow were endowed by the Scottish lawyer, Lord Gifford, 'to promote and diffuse the study of Natural Theology in the widest sense of the term – in other words, the knowledge of God'. Balfour gave ten lectures in 1914. A second series was delayed by the First World War until 1922–3. The two series were published as *Theism and Humanism* and *Theism and Thought*.

Balfour was a central figure of the intellectual and aesthetic group known as the 'Souls'. (It was alleged that the group was continually discussing the state of their souls.) He was caricatured in an anonymous verse of the period:

Playful little Arthur, he
Plays with things so prettily
To him everything's a game
Win or lose it's all the same
Plays with politics or war
Trivial little games they are –
Plays with souls and plays at golf –
This must never be put off.
Plays with deep philosophies,
Faiths and minor things like these,
Plays with praise and plays with blame
Everything is but a game
Win or lose, it's all the same.
Playful little Arthur, he
Cannot take things seriously.[20]

Those who reduced Balfour to a series of frivolous aphorisms underestimated the man. With Wilfrid Ward, he founded the Synthetic Society in 1896 'to consider existing Agnostic tendencies, and to contribute towards a working philosophy of religious belief'. Evolution, formerly seen as an obstacle to belief, was viewed as giving 'new meaning and perhaps new

---

20 Cited ed. Ridley and Percy, *The Letters of Arthur Balfour and Lady Elcho*, p. 20.

promise to the attempt to construct... a basis for beliefs'. Avoiding confessional controversies, believers and sympathetic sceptics sought common ground for 'a philosophical basis for religious belief'.[21] Unsurprisingly, few definitive conclusions were produced. Balfour regularly contributed papers and, when the Society was wound up in 1908, he paid for the proceedings to be bound and copies distributed to members.

Despite this exhaustive output, Balfour revealed remarkably little of his own personal beliefs and doubts. Everything was treated dispassionately. Only occasionally did his guard drop to give a glimpse of his soul.

He made little impact in the Commons during his first Parliament. His attendance at the Congress of Berlin in 1878 as his uncle's private secretary was not a demanding commitment. He accounted the publication of his first book as being of far more personal significance. He began writing after the death in March 1875 of May Lyttelton, whom, he declared, he had intended to marry. Grief focused his mind on eternal realities. Lord Salisbury persuaded him to change his original title, *A Defence of Philosophic Scepticism*, fearing that he would be labelled a religious sceptic. Instead, the book was entitled *A Defence of Philosophic Doubt*. His publisher, John Morley, claimed 'that he could not understand a word of it'.[22] Others were similarly perplexed by Balfour's works. There was nothing on Christian doctrine, precious little in the earlier books on the existence of God and no indication that Balfour subscribed to any specific creed. One critic concluded that he sought not so much to defend 'particular beliefs, as *the right to believe*'.[23]

Although requiring application and attention on the part of the reader, Balfour wrote with clarity. Barely 30, he did not lack confidence, taking to task such intellectual giants of the Victorian age as John Stuart Mill and Herbert Spencer. He challenged 'advanced thinkers' who ascribed certainty to scientific knowledge while dismissing religious knowledge as 'superstition and untrue'.[24] He attacked the position he

21 Rules of the Synthetic Society adopted at the Preliminary Meeting, 28 February 1896, cited ed. A. J. Balfour, *Papers Read before the Synthetic Society, 1896–1908* (London: Spottiswoode & Co., 1908), pp. 1–2.

22 AJB, *Chapters of Autobiography*, p. 64.

23 Desmond MacCarthy, *Portraits* (London: Putnam, 1931), p. 24; emphasis original.

24 A. J. Balfour, *A Defence of Philosophic Doubt: Being an essay on the foundations of belief*, 2nd edn (London: Hodder & Stoughton, 1920), pp. 299–300.

termed 'naturalism' – 'the assertion that empirical methods are valid, and that others are not'.[25] Balfour argued not against science per se but against those who sought to employ scientific methods outside their proper sphere. Science was not competent to opine on the existence of God and a spiritual realm.[26] Scientists were unjust in demanding from religion a standard of proof science itself could not satisfy. Science too was grounded on predications incapable of empirical proof. Balfour applied philosophical doubt, maintaining that the law of universal causation and the uniformity of nature were incapable of proof by scientific means.[27]

How helpful was this – arguing that religion *might* lack a firm basis for belief, but so too did science? Even sympathetic readers found his methodology problematic. Edward Talbot, a future Anglican bishop, was troubled by *The Defence of Philosophic Doubt*, inferring that Balfour felt there were no rational grounds for faith.[28] H. G. Wells encountered Balfour at country house parties and shared Talbot's analysis. Balfour

> argued sceptically on behalf of religion. His way of defending the Godhead was by asking, What can your science know for certain? and escaping back to orthodoxy under a dust cloud of philosophical doubts . . . enabled him to accord a graceful support to the Church of England – which might be just as right or wrong about ultimates as anything else.[29]

'Any constructive conclusion'?

Balfour acknowledged that many would find his work 'purely destructive' in character, 'a mere dialectical puzzle'.[30] He was stung, however, when this proved to be exactly how it was interpreted, insisting: 'I am not trying

25 A. J. Balfour, *The Foundations of Belief: Being notes introductory to the study of theology* (London: Longmans, 1895), p. 134.

26 AJB, *The Foundations of Belief*, p. 293.

27 AJB, *A Defence of Philosophic Doubt*, p. 303.

28 Talbot to AJB, 6 May 1879, BL, Balfour Papers, Add. MS 49789, ff. 13–20.

29 H. G. Wells, *Experiment in Autobiography* (London: Victor Gollancz, 1934), p. 773.

30 AJB, *A Defence of Philosophic Doubt*, p. 296.

to establish one set of beliefs by throwing doubt upon another.'[31] In 1924 he conceded that it had taken 40 years for his 'methodological doubt' to attain 'any constructive conclusion'.[32]

His second book, *The Foundations of Belief*, was intended for a more general audience. It received considerable attention and ran through several editions. Balfour himself thought his earlier book 'more satisfactory because a more definite piece of work than *Foundations of Belief* – and this precision in the work of destruction is always easier than in the work of construction'.[33] Yet the same negative and tentative tone is also apparent in the later work. He was incapable of committing himself definitively.

Matter, he argued, is not its own explanation: 'Nature we must treat not as the source of intelligence but its instrument.'[34] A greater, non-material cause was needed: purpose, a mind, a spiritual dimension. Reason 'must be regarded not merely as a product of evolution, but as its guide. It must be above Nature and before it, as well as in it. It must be transcendent.'[35] The order and complexity of the universe were not random. That would be 'a coincidence more astounding than the most audacious novelist has ever employed to cut the knot of some entangled tale'.[36] *The Foundations of Belief* argued that the world 'was the work of a rational Being, Who made *it* intelligible, and at the same time made *us*, in however feeble a fashion, able to understand it'.[37] God is necessary.

Balfour refused to contemplate a universe devoid of reason, love and moral law.[38] In the Gifford Lectures he maintained that our spiritual dimension, the 'soul', was apparent from our certainty of our own existence: 'It is this "soul" which remembers the past and expects the future. It is this soul that hopes, and this soul that fears.'[39] Later he expressed himself more

---

31 AJB, *Theism and Thought*, p. 64.

32 AJB to Professor Andrew Seth-Pringle-Pattison, 7 February 1924, cited Young, *AJB*, pp. 58–9.

33 AJB to Oliver Lodge, 15 April 1899 (copy), BL, Balfour Papers, Add. MS 49798, f. 88.

34 AJB, *Theism and Thought*, p. 235.

35 AJB, 'Familiar Beliefs and Transcendent Reason', 1925 lecture to British Academy, 1925, cited Young, *AJB*, p. 430.

36 AJB, *The Foundations of Belief*, pp. 69–70.

37 AJB, *The Foundations of Belief*, p. 301.

38 AJB, *The Foundations of Belief*, pp. 83–6.

39 AJB, *Theism and Thought*, pp. 202–3.

forcefully: observation and experiment 'cannot explain the mind. No man really supposes that he personally is nothing more than a changing group of electrical charges . . . eliminating the spiritual is not only hazardous but absurd.'[40]

The credibility of the Bible

Balfour also acknowledged the problem of modern biblical criticism, which he dealt with more sparingly, feeling himself less qualified. He sought to avoid theological controversy and the ire of a Bible-reading Protestant nation, recognizing the risk of giving 'great offence to much genuine religious opinion'.[41] Yet the credibility of the Bible was pertinent to his investigations, something on which he commented in lectures and private correspondence.

He welcomed modern scholarship's ability to situate Scripture in a specific historical and cultural context, lending it a new interest and reality for 'the more learned'. He admitted that the Bible was inspired, but not *infallible* 'in the sense commonly attributed to that word'.[42] He allowed, somewhat condescendingly, that Scripture was for 'the unlearned a source of consolation, of hope, of instruction'.[43] He too derived solace from Scripture's capacity to fulfil a human need and provide a point of contact with the transcendent.

Was the Bible objectively true in its capacity to teach supernatural truth, to relay historical and scientific fact? Here Balfour struggled. He could not consider the Bible literally true in all its utterances. How then could one preserve its inspired character? He did not despair of a solution, but felt the contemporary failure to treat the subject convincingly was the greatest impediment to 'educated opinion accepting Christianity'. Until a credible theory of biblical interpretation was developed, he thought 'no thoroughly coherent view of revealed religion is possible'.

---

40 AJB, 'Introduction', in ed. Joseph Needham, *Science, Religion and Reality* (London: Sheldon Press, 1925), pp. 15–16.

41 AJB to Mary Drew, December 1891 (copy), BL, Mary Gladstone Papers, Add. MS 46238, ff. 34–8.

42 AJB, 'Introduction', in ed. Needham, *Science, Religion and Reality*, p. 10.

43 AJB, Speech to British and Foreign Bible Society, 6 March 1903, cited ed. Short, *AJB as Philosopher and Thinker*, p. 60.

'An unresolved dualism'

Balfour welcomed the improved state of relations between science and religion towards the end of his life, aided by a non-fundamentalist approach to Scripture. Theologians no longer read the Bible for geological data. Balfour had never considered himself bound by a literalist interpretation of creation. He rejoiced that 'the theological experts' now accepted that the book of Genesis was not written as a science manual.[44]

Balfour maintained: 'I rest the belief in God on a belief in science.'[45] Scientific discoveries made it easier to believe in a 'rational and benevolent Creator'.[46] Provided religion respected science's legitimate autonomy, science was in no way harmed by the existence of a spiritual realm.[47] Indeed, science required a metaphysical basis:

> If our system of knowledge is to include science (as, of course, it must), it cannot avoid incoherence unless it also transcends science and assumes a Rational Cause beyond the non-rational causes which for science constitute the ultimate terms of possible explanation.[48]

Balfour was too intellectually honest to pretend that all difficulties, such as the question of miracles, had been resolved. He trod cautiously, not relying on immediate divine intervention to account for physical phenomena science was unable to explain. Speaking of the efficacy of prayer, he believed 'that every change in the material world is theoretically capable of a complete mechanical explanation'.[49] Yet he hedged. He refused to exclude the possibility of miracles. Common sense and practical living require we assume 'the uniformity of nature'; that is, that the material

44 AJB, *A Defence of Philosophic Doubt*, p. 333n. While the footnotes were added only to the 1920 edition, in the Preface Balfour suggests they were based on his notes that were largely contemporaneous with the original 1879 work.

45 AJB, *Theism and Humanism*, p. 253.

46 AJB, Speech to Pan-Anglican Congress, 22 June 1908, cited ed. Short, *AJB as Philosopher and Thinker*, p. 502.

47 AJB, 'Introduction', in ed. Needham, *Science, Religion and Reality*, p. 6.

48 AJB, Paper delivered to the Synthetic Society, 25 March 1896, cited ed. AJB, *Papers Read before the Synthetic Society*, p. 5.

49 AJB, Paper delivered to the Synthetic Society, 25 May 1900, cited ed. AJB, *Papers Read before the Synthetic Society*, pp. 329–30.

world operates consistently according to the laws of science. It is not, however, a logical necessity. Balfour, neatly sidestepping the question, cited the example of the human being as a personal, spiritual agent: 'We can certainly act on our environment . . . It constitutes a spiritual invasion of the physical world – it is a miracle.' He made no reference to the resurrection, on which Christianity depends.

Balfour acquiesced 'in an unresolved dualism'.[50] He fought shy of definitions and conclusions, preferring to live with unresolved tensions rather than hazard a potentially mistaken proposition. He acknowledged: 'I am a mystic in some matters, I don't pretend to understand all I believe.'[51]

He distinguished 'metaphysical' and 'religious' concepts of God. God could be accepted as the necessary cause of all existence and the source of rationality, without any practical consequence for daily life and without eliciting a spiritual response. Which God did Balfour believe in? In his Gifford Lectures he opted for the 'religious' God, a God who could be loved and worshipped. He professed himself perplexed as to how the two concepts could be harmonized, while recognizing they could not be treated separately:[52] 'Personally, I accept *both* aspects of the one God, and believe both are necessary. But I have never seen any purely rational way of completely fusing them, so that I remain in this matter something of a mystic.'[53]

In these lectures, Balfour came closest to proclaiming his own creed:

> when . . . I speak of God . . . I mean a God whom men can love, a God to whom men can pray, who takes sides, who has purposes and preferences, whose attributes however conceived, leave unimpaired the possibility of a personal relationship between Himself and those whom He has created.[54]

50 AJB, 'Introduction', in ed. Needham, *Science, Religion and Reality*, p. 16.

51 Lady Frances Balfour, Diary, 1895, cited Lady Frances Balfour, *Ne Obliviscaris*, Vol. 2, p. 274.

52 AJB, *Theism and Humanism*, p. 19.

53 AJB to Professor Andrew Seth-Pringle-Pattison, 13 January 1914 (copy), BL, Balfour Papers, Add. MS 49798, f. 74.

54 AJB, *Theism and Humanism*, p. 21.

Religion existed to give us 'communion with God'. Balfour provided criteria for judging the authenticity of religion: 'Does it offer consolation to those who are in grief, hope to those who are bereaved, strength to the weak, forgiveness to the sinful, rest to those who are weary and heavy laden?'[55]

Balfour was no mere deist with an intellectual belief in a Creator indifferent to his creation. He defended the existence of a personal God who relates to and cares for his creatures, in whom the values of truth and love and beauty are grounded. This personal God 'was rational, moral, spiritual, conscious, exercising will and purpose'.[56] This alone, however, does not make Balfour a Christian.

'Personal immortality'

Cynthia Asquith knew Balfour from her childhood. She observed: 'He was one of the very, very few people I have known who professed never to suffer an instant's doubt about personal immortality.'[57] Balfour affirmed his conviction that religion in its highest forms 'involves a belief in personal immortality'.[58]

In what did this belief in life beyond earthly death consist? Balfour had the opportunity to elaborate when writing to the bereaved – not the occasion for intellectual subtleties. Inferences may be drawn from silence. His intimate friend Mary Elcho, Cynthia Asquith's mother, lost a son in infancy. Balfour concluded that death is a transition 'from life to life', but his counsel is opaque:

> Of death indeed, and of what death means to those left behind to mourn, there is nothing to be said. And howsoever familiar it may be to our thoughts, it always comes with a shock of horror seemingly unmitigated by either knowledge, faith or hope.[59]

55 AJB, 'The Religion of Humanity', Address delivered to Church Congress, Manchester, 2 October 1888, in A. J. Balfour, *Essays and Addresses*, 2nd edn (Edinburgh: David Douglas, 1893), p. 314.

56 AJB to Betty Balfour, 13 September 1915 (copy), BL, Balfour Papers, Add. MS 49831, ff. 119–20.

57 Cynthia Asquith, *Remember and Be Glad* (London: James Barrie, 1952), p. 32.

58 AJB, Paper delivered to the Synthetic Society, 29 April 1898, cited ed. AJB, *Papers Read before the Synthetic Society*, p. 328.

59 AJB to Mary Elcho, 9 January 1893, cited ed. Ridley and Percy, *The Letters of Arthur Balfour and Lady Elcho*, pp. 89–91.

Lady Desborough's two sons were killed in the First World War. Death, he wrote to her, is a source of tremendous pain, the separation of the living from the dead. This separation, however, is not permanent:

> I entertain no doubt whatever about a future life. I deem it at least as certain as any of the hundred and one truths of the framework of the world, as I conceive the world . . . I am as sure that those I love and have lost are living today, as I am that yesterday they were fighting heroically in the trenches . . . death cannot long cheat us of love.[60]

How is this personal survival achieved? Extraordinarily for an intelligent churchgoer, a noted 'Christian' philosopher, there is no mention of Christ's atoning death, his resurrection nor his promise of eternal life. It is difficult to avoid the conclusion that Balfour ultimately shared the scepticism of Strauss and Renan with respect to the resurrection. Otherwise, why not mention it to those in most need of consolation?

His belief in personal immortality seems to stem rather from blind faith, a refusal to contemplate the alternative. Hence his comment to Margot Asquith: 'If there is no future life this world is a bad joke; and whose joke?'[61] Bishop Talbot challenged Balfour. He felt that Balfour resented inquiry into his thoughts on the nature of existence beyond death. The bishop admitted limits to our knowledge, but reminded his friend that Christian belief in this matter was informed by hope in a loving God and his gifts to his children.[62]

Balfour's ghosts

Balfour looked elsewhere for evidence. Many of his contemporaries felt that science disproved Christianity. Yet they were unwilling to accept the materialist claim that human existence ends with earthly death. They turned instead to spiritualism for confirmation of personal survival. In the late nineteenth and early twentieth centuries, spiritualism was not

60 AJB to Lady Desborough, 5 August 1915, cited Dugdale, *AJB, 1906–1930*, pp. 218–19.

61 Margot Asquith, *The Autobiography of Margot Asquith*, Vol. 2 (London: Thornton Butterworth, 1922), p. 109.

62 Talbot to AJB, 24 July 1928, BL, Balfour Papers, Add. MS 49789, f. 276.

viewed as the preserve of the eccentric or deluded. Anglican clergy and Nobel Prize winners, including Marie Curie and Balfour's brother-in-law Lord Rayleigh, looked to spiritualism to provide scientific proof of personal immortality.

Encouraged by Henry Sidgwick, Balfour's interest in spiritualism dated back to his undergraduate days, when he seems to have joined the Ghost Society, founded by the future Archbishop of Canterbury, E. W. Benson. Sidgwick and others believed ghost stories and the paranormal more susceptible to rational investigation than the Gospels. Sidgwick met his wife, Nora Balfour, at a séance in Balfour's London home in the 1870s.[63] There would be many more séances over the course of half a century, including in Downing Street itself.[64] These were often organized by his brother, Gerald, a 'true believer' and lover of Winifred Coombe Tennant, who operated as the medium 'Mrs Willett'. (The two had a child, whom they believed the Messiah.)

What induced Balfour to become involved? At the time of the earlier séances there was emotional rawness, as he grieved for his mother and May Lyttelton. He was unconvinced by the results, but continued to be a willing participant. The spirit world was not politically neutral. In the feverish days prior to the First World War, Balfour's ghosts were protectionists and pro-suffragette. They urged that the return of a Conservative government under Balfour was essential to save the Crown from revolution.[65]

Those who had passed over were insistent in making contact at times of national significance. Balfour had a sitting with Mrs Willett on 22 April 1915, just after he returned from a tour of the Western Front. He was with her immediately following an audience with the King on 19 June 1916 after the Battle of Jutland when, as First Lord of the Admiralty, Balfour was criticized for his unduly negative communiqué.[66] In 1922, Mrs Willett was a delegate at the League of Nations conference in Geneva attended by

63 A. Sidgwick and E. M. Sidgwick, *Henry Sidgwick: A memoir* (London: Macmillan & Co., 1906), pp. 346–7, 302.

64 R. J. Q. Adams, *Balfour: The last grandee* (London: John Murray, 2008), p. 114.

65 BL, Balfour Papers, Add. MS 49832, ff. 119–23, cited Max Egremont, *Balfour: A Life of Arthur James Balfour* (London: Phoenix, 1998), p. 248.

66 Trevor Hamilton, *Arthur Balfour's Ghosts: An Edwardian elite and the riddle of cross-correspondence automatic writings* (Exeter: Imprint Academic, 2017), pp. 105–9.

Balfour. Messages from May Lyttelton flooded in as other delegates spoke.[67] Throughout the 1920s, Lady Blanche, Frank Balfour and May Lyttelton all sought to make their voices heard.

The Society for Psychical Research (SPR) was founded in 1882; Sidgwick was its first president. Balfour himself served as such in 1894 when leader of the Conservatives in the Commons, brushing aside potentially negative consequences for his 'political reputation'.[68] The SPR aimed to determine scientific grounds for the existence of psychical phenomena. It also sought to shed light on the credibility of biblical miracles. Balfour never accepted unreservedly the claims of spiritualism (his belief in personal immortality pre-dated his involvement with psychical research),[69] nor did he dismiss them out of hand. He subjected psychical phenomena to inquiry and experimentation, and while lending telepathy a certain credence, was otherwise sceptical: 'To begin with there is the difficulty of fraud . . . We have come across, and it is inevitable that we should come across, cases where either deliberate fraud or unconscious deception makes observation doubly and trebly difficult.'[70]

Balfour and his contemporaries turned to spiritualism because they lacked faith in the Christian teaching on eternal life. Their dalliance with the spirit world was clearly at variance with scriptural prohibitions. Margot Asquith expressed a more orthodox, common-sense approach: 'I don't at all believe in spiritualism. The idea that the existence of God either outside or within one can be proved by a few stray boxes on the ear after dark, is to me repugnant.'[71]

'A strong Churchman'

When Christian doctrine sat so lightly with him, one might have expected Balfour to have had little time for the Church. That was not the case.

67 Egremont, *Balfour*, p. 249.

68 AJB to Henry Sidgwick, 21 November 1892, cited Young, *AJB*, p. 146.

69 Young, *AJB*, p. 449.

70 AJB, Presidential Address to the Society for Psychical Research, 26 January 1894, cited ed. Short, *AJB as Philosopher and Thinker*, p. 427.

71 Margot Asquith, Diary, 24 June 1915, cited M. Brock and E. Brock, *Margot Asquith's Great War Diary, 1914–1916: The view from Downing Street* (Oxford: Oxford University Press, 2004), p. 160.

A Lowland Scot like herself, Margot Asquith knew Balfour was, therefore, eminently sensible. He 'avoided the narrowness and materialism of the extreme High Church; but he was a strong Churchman'.[72]

Balfour appreciated that 'religion, if it is to be of any value, must come from the heart.' He acknowledged, however, that it must necessarily have an institutional form: 'Religion works, and, to produce its full results, must needs work, through the agency of organized societies. It has, therefore, a social side, and from this its speculative side cannot, I believe, be kept wholly distinct.' He remained his mother's son; faith was to be practical:

> A Church is something more than a body of more or less qualified persons engaged more or less successfully in the study of theology . . . It is an organization charged with a great practical work. For the successful promotion of this work unity, discipline and self-devotion are the principal requisites.[73]

This 'great practical work' included education and charity, inculcating in humanity the values of love and truth and beauty.

There were limits to Balfour's belief in the practical application of faith. He was no proponent of 'a social gospel', criticizing the bishops' tendency of 'to mix themselves up in political questions'. Bishops might hold and express views as private citizens, but as 'clergy, however, their business is with religion'.[74] The Church had no role in the public square:

> It is this direct appeal to the individual soul which is the proper business of the Christian Churches . . . it is the business of the Church, as I conceive it, to appeal to the individual, to seek out his particular weakness, to remedy his particular misfortunes, to raise him from his own particular quagmire.[75]

---

72 Margot Asquith, *The Autobiography of Margot Asquith*, Vol. 1 (London: Thornton Butterworth, 1920), p. 170.

73 AJB, *The Foundations of Belief*, pp. 273, 259, 274.

74 AJB to Talbot, 1 February 1904 (copy), BL, Balfour Papers, Add. MS 49789, f. 220.

75 AJB, Speech to the Church Army, 10 December 1908, cited ed. Short, *AJB as Philosopher and Thinker*, p. 79.

In 1866, Lady Blanche set her 17-year-old son an essay on church governance. Balfour's views remained constant for the next 60 years. He had no time for the authority of tradition: 'I would reject all arguments founded on the supposed precept or example of the Apostles or the precedent of the early Church.' The nineteenth century was utterly dissimilar from the first; the Church must adapt, particularly so when her founders 'were probably neither wiser nor better than ourselves, and . . . certainly less experienced'. It did not occur to the young Balfour that the Church had a divine founder. Church government existed 'to provide suitable religious instruction and worship to people of similar religious tastes and opinions'. The Church was at the service and whim of vastly different cultures and ages. There is no suggestion that she had a mission to convert and form them. It followed that the Church was analogous to political government: each sect had the right to choose 'that form of government best suited to its tastes and opinions'.[76]

Unsurprisingly, Balfour was not unduly troubled by the disunity of Christians:

> One race, many nations, a universal Church, many ecclesiastical organizations – those are the facts we have got to take and make the best of . . . I have no hope that these divisions among us will be healed by being abolished.

He looked forward to the evangelization of the Far East and further divisions as Asians adopted forms of Christianity appropriate to themselves: 'Christendom is and must remain divided.' Christians should be members of their respective denominations, while belonging to 'that greater whole', the universal Church which existed at a spiritual level.[77]

Supporting individuals' right to choose the form of church governance that best suited them, Balfour opposed Erastianism, state control of the Church.[78] In 1905, as his government fell apart over the issue of protectionism, he legislated to give full autonomy to the Church of Scotland. He

76 AJB, Essay on Church Government, 2 March 1866, NRS, Balfour Papers, GD 433/2/195/2/22.

77 AJB, Speech to City Temple, 19 June 1906, cited Dugdale, *AJB, 1848–1905*, p. 218.

78 AJB to George Talbot, 16 February 1899 (copy), BL, Balfour Papers, Add. MS 49853, ff. 45–6.

contemplated similar 'spiritual independence' for the Church of England. (He saw no inconsistency between this and the principle of Establishment.) He believed, however, that the Church of England was insufficiently homogenous; that autonomy would lead to schism along the 'immemorial lines of cleavage'.[79]

Balfour identified as a Protestant. The Reformation was a necessary good. Despite his collaboration with Wilfrid Ward and other Catholics in the Synthetic Society, he viewed Roman Catholicism as restrictive of intellectual freedom and scientific inquiry. His sister described the prejudice typical of their class and age:

> We talked about Roman Catholics and the way they had taken the part of forgery and injustice in the Dreyfus case. [Arthur] expressed his loathing of all their ways – and declared that he was getting bigoted in his old age. They had always been unscrupulous controversialists, using lies and every unfair weapon.[80]

Beyond this, Balfour deplored the desire to overdefine and categorize. This did not mean he favoured a lowest-common-denominator form of Christianity. He declared himself no 'advocate for that colourless thing known as the nondenominational creed'. All were at liberty to determine their own specific beliefs provided they respected those of others and were willing to cooperate with them in the practical work of the Church.[81]

He described himself as a practising member of both the Church of England and the Church of Scotland, considering them 'two branches of the Universal Church'.[82] Mary Gladstone was bemused that the press labelled Balfour a 'Presbyterian': 'One sometimes does not feel quite as if you judged the Church from inside.'[83] His niece too considered him

---

79 AJB to Archbishop Randall Davidson, 9 January 1914 (copy), BL, Balfour Papers, Add. MS 49788, ff. 273–4.

80 Lady Rayleigh, Diary, 24 September 1899, cited Egremont, *Balfour*, p. 123.

81 AJB, Speech marking the Union of the Free and United Presbyterian Churches of Scotland, 15 January 1901, cited ed. Short, *AJB as Philosopher and Thinker*, p. 72.

82 AJB, *Chapters of Autobiography*, p. 18.

83 AJB to Mary Drew, 26 March 1903, BL, Mary Gladstone Papers, Add. MS 46238, ff. 42–3; Mary Drew to AJB, 4 April 1903, BL, Balfour Papers, Add. MS 49794, f. 197.

more at home in the Church of Scotland. While the Church of England infuriated Balfour, he retained a genuine affection for its comprehensive character and was deemed a good friend to it in troubled times. Talbot judged Balfour's parliamentary leadership providential.[84] After the Liberal landslide of 1906, the Archbishop of Canterbury, Randall Davidson, looked to him to use the Tory majority in the Lords to protect Anglican schools and see off threats of disestablishment.[85]

'Theological prejudice'

Given his general sympathy for religion but distaste for extremism, it is ironic that Balfour's tenure of office was marked by intense conflict between the denominations and within the Church of England. Balfour blamed an inefficient educational system for the loss of Britain's economic advantage. He steered the 1902 Education Act through Parliament in the face of extraordinary opposition. Nonconformists objected to the use of public funds to support faith (mainly Anglican) schools and resorted to passive resistance; some High Anglicans and Catholics opposed any local authority control over their schools. Balfour was exasperated by what he viewed as irrational obstinacy in the face of moderate and necessary reform. The strength of feeling he encountered at one point led him to 'hate both religion and education'.[86]

At least educational reform obviously concerned the national interest. A huge amount of political acrimony and parliamentary time was expended on the Ritualist crisis, for which Balfour saw no justification. The growing influence of the High Church party, especially its more advanced members, led many to fear ritual and doctrines that would lead to submission to Rome. Asserting that Anglican bishops were unwilling or unable to discipline dissident clergy, Protestants clamoured for parliamentary action against the Ritualists. Balfour attempted to insert some rationality into the debate:

---

84 Talbot to AJB, 5 February 1899, BL, Balfour Papers, Add. MS 49789, ff. 98–9.

85 Davidson to AJB, u/d [April 1906], BL, Balfour Papers, Add. MS 49788, ff. 258–9.

86 Lady Rayleigh, Diary, 10 July 1902, cited Adams, *Balfour*, p. 170.

> We are Protestants . . . There is little real danger to Protestantism, but there may be danger to the Church if Protestants forget in their zeal the character for charity, toleration and comprehension which ought always to distinguish the National Church.[87]

Illegal ritualistic practices should be stopped. Even legal practices should be avoided if they caused conflict between clergy and their congregations. Yet he rejected any action harmful to the comprehensive character of the Church of England:

> This is not because I have any predilection for High Church doctrine any more than for ritualistic practices, but simply because I am convinced that, if you narrow down the English Church to any particular school of religious thought, you would do it incalculable injury; and I should hold this opinion even if that school of thought happened to be my own.[88]

Bishops, not politicians, were responsible for church governance, and Balfour was frustrated by their failure to enforce discipline.

The Church of England was fortunate that he blocked calls for legislation that might have had devastating effects. He himself was pessimistic:

> I confess to entertaining the gloomiest apprehensions as to the future of the Church of England. I can hardly think of anything else. A so-called 'Protestant' faction, ignorant, fanatical, reckless, but every day organizing themselves politically with increased efficiency. A 'ritualist' party, as ignorant, as fanatical and as reckless, the sincerity of whose attachment to historic Anglicanism I find it quite impossible to believe. A High Church Party, determined to support men of whose practices they heartily disapprove. A laity, divided from the clergy by an ever deepening gulf . . . I will not pursue the

87 AJB, Speech in Bristol, *The Times*, 30 November 1998, cited Bethany Kilcrease, *The Great Church Crisis and the End of English Erastianism, 1898–1906* (London: Routledge, 2016), p. 129.

88 AJB to Evelyn Cecil, 5 August 1898 (copy), BL, Balfour Papers, Add. MS 49853, ff. 5–6.

> subject; my sheet of paper is finished and I should weep for very soreness of spirit if I went on![89]

Confronted by 'theological prejudice',[90] Balfour was hamstrung by his own moderation. If he did not believe in certain supernatural realities, or their immediate relevance to daily life and worship, others certainly did. He was unable to appreciate the strength of their belief. Some felt passionately that a mediating priesthood, sacraments and church tradition were ordained by God and essential for full access to him. For others, this constituted pure idolatry. So tentative in his other positions, why should Balfour infer that he was correct simply to deplore Protestants and Ritualists in equal measure?

Ecclesiastical preferment

Throughout the twentieth century, Prime Ministers were accorded an official role in the appointment of Anglican bishops and senior clergy. In the early period it was a question of balancing the opinions and interests of the Crown, Lambeth Palace and Downing Street. Often who prevailed pivoted on personality. Most Prime Ministers, regardless of their own theological beliefs and background, were conscientious in exercising this role.

Balfour was no exception. He could advance – unsuccessfully in the case of the Diocese of Winchester – the claims of friends such as Edward Talbot, but Talbot's intellect and spirituality amply qualified him for high office. Balfour recommended Randall Davidson to Edward VII when Canterbury fell vacant. These two moderate, practical Scots struck up a good working relationship in the educational and Ritualist crises. Despite his own views, Balfour was willing to promote High Churchmen, but equally proposed an Evangelical for Manchester, when circumstances suggested this. Generally, he deferred to Davidson in matters of ecclesiastical preferment.

---

89 AJB to Talbot, 6 February 1903 (copy), BL, Balfour Papers, Add. MS 49789, f. 195.

90 AJB to Archbishop Frederick Temple, 15 December 1900 (copy), BL, Balfour Papers, Add. MS 49788, f. 41.

The eugenicist

Balfour was held to be a moral man, intolerant of personal injustice and irresponsible gossip. Yet in common with many of his peers, he was a proponent of eugenics. (Winston Churchill was another enthusiast.) British shortcomings in the Boer War were blamed on 'degeneracy'. Members of the upper and middle classes sought to protect the purity of the race and the better elements of society. Balfour was a member of the Eugenics Education Society founded in 1907 to campaign for sterilization and marriage restrictions for 'the feeble-minded'. He supported the Mental Deficiency Act of 1913, which sought to legislate for these objectives. He was active in founding and funding a Chair of Eugenics at Cambridge.

Balfour addressed the First International Eugenics Conference in London in 1912. Elsewhere he had argued that the possibilities of modern science should be subject to the ethical imperatives of religion, but not here:

> I am one of those who base their belief in the future progress of mankind, in most departments, upon the application of scientific method to practical life . . . The whole point of eugenics is that we reject the standard of mere numbers. We do not say survival is everything. We deliberately say that it is not everything; that a feeble-minded man, even though he survive, is not so good as the good professional man, even though that professional man is only one of a class that does not keep up its numbers by an adequate birth-rate. The truth is that we ought to have the courage of our opinions, and we must regard man as he is now, from this point of view – from the point of view of genetics – as a wild animal.[91]

At the time, the Catholic Church and, less consistently, the Church of England, strongly opposed the evils of eugenics. If a convinced Christian, why was Balfour unable to see that all humans are created equal by God, endowed with infinite dignity, and that particular care and compassion are due to the vulnerable?

---

91 AJB, Speech at International Eugenics Congress, 24 July 1912, cited ed. Short, *AJB as Philosopher and Thinker*, pp. 215–17.

'Belief or unbelief'?

Blanche Dugdale, his niece, and Ian Malcolm, his former private secretary, wrote biographies fiercely protective of Balfour's reputation. They rounded on those who queried his religious beliefs, urging readers to look to his published works to refute any suggestion that he was an agnostic or guilty of 'some other fantastic form of belief or unbelief'.[92]

Margot Asquith and Bonar Law knew Balfour well; both were theologically literate. Breakfasting in Downing Street in 1914, Margot surprised Law by asserting that Balfour was 'a deeply religious man'. Even if true, Law queried whether Balfour was an orthodox Christian. Margot responded: 'I should say yes: orthodox is a very awkward word, and conveys different things to different people; but I should say, taken in its widest form, Arthur Balfour's religion is orthodox.'[93] He puzzled his contemporaries, and he continues to puzzle.

Balfour was not an agnostic. He had a definite belief in a personal God. Did he, however, believe in the Christian God? Much of his thought was directed towards disproving other belief systems. His early work was an attack on 'naturalism'. In 1888, as Chief Secretary for Ireland, Balfour was engaged in his programme of repression and reform. Yet he found time to speak on positivism, Auguste Comte's secular 'religion' devoid of any supernatural element. Balfour's critique was devastating, but Mary Gladstone complained – not entirely correctly – that his speech was 'thin' and that 'he never used the word Christianity'.[94] Balfour's riposte was: 'Positivism, not Christianity, is my subject.'[95] He was very good at explaining what he did not believe, and why he did not believe it. Quite naturally, people asked what, if anything, he did believe.

The Foundations of Belief purported to adopt a more positive approach. Balfour noted: 'It is true, of course, that the immediate reason for accepting the beliefs of Revealed Religion is that the religion *is* revealed';[96] that is,

92 Dugdale, *AJB, 1906–1930*, p. 81; Malcolm, *Lord Balfour*, pp. 95–6.

93 Margot Asquith, Diary, 5 September 1914, cited Brock and Brock, *Margot Asquith's Great War Diary*, p. 34.

94 Mary Drew, Diary, 2 October 1888, cited ed. Lucy Masterman, *Mary Gladstone (Mrs Drew): Her diaries and letters* (London: Methuen & Co., 1930), p. 24.

95 AJB, 'The Religion of Humanity', in AJB, *Essays and Addresses*, p. 311.

96 AJB, *The Foundations of Belief*, p. 177.

one accepts Christianity because one believes that Jesus Christ is the Son of God and thus able to teach the truth with authority. Balfour never disclosed whether he in fact accepted this.

Mary Elcho gave a copy of the book to her children's governess, who was obviously no fool:

> I turned to the end and fell upon the page which sums up rather shortly what a vivid realization of Christianity does for people who have faith. I did not feel as I had got much myself just then, but I did feel that page had been written with faith.[97]

Balfour had written:

> What is needed is such a living faith in God's relation to Man as shall leave no place for that helpless resentment against the appointed Order so apt to rise within us as the sight of undeserved pain. And this faith is possessed by those who vividly realize the Christian form of Theism. For they worship the One Who is no remote contriver of a universe to whose ills He is indifferent. If they suffer, did not He on their account suffer also?[98]

He argued that only the Incarnation allows us to understand 'that, in the sight of God, the stability of the heavens is of less importance than the moral growth of a human spirit'.[99] It is claimed on the basis of this passage that Balfour was a believing Christian; that his faith informed his entire approach to life.

Yet Balfour's argument is objective and impersonal. There is no statement of personal belief. What did he mean by the Incarnation? Nowhere did he state his acceptance of the claim that a divine person, the second person of the Trinity, entered creation, taking a human nature to himself. H. G. Wells was adamant that Balfour rejected the doctrine of the

97 Charlotte Jordain to Mary, Lady Elcho, 1903, cited Nicola Beauman, *Cynthia Asquith* (London: Hamish Hamilton, 1987), p. 27.

98 AJB, *The Foundations of Belief*, p. 354.

99 AJB, *The Foundations of Belief*, pp. 347–8.

Trinity.[100] Balfour allowed that Christ suffered, leaving us an example. There is no mention of the cross and the resurrection offering humanity forgiveness and eternal life. Nothing in Balfour's writings is inimical to Renan's presentation of Christ solely as a good man and a moral reformer.

If his contemporaries thought that *The Foundations of Belief* proved Balfour's Christianity, it contains some very opaque passages too. It could be asked, for example, what he meant when he wrote:

> the sense of Reconciliation [to God] connected by the Christian conscience with the life and death of Christ seems in many cases to be bound up with the explanations of the mystery which from time to time have been hazarded by theological theorists. And as these explanations have fallen out of favour, the truth to be explained has too often been abandoned also.

Was he rejecting Christian doctrine or just certain formulations of it? Accepting the existence of a personal God interested in humanity, Balfour appeared to view Christianity only as a provisional, albeit possibly the highest, expression of this. He wrote that the 'spiritual experience . . . of Reconciliation with God' was incomparably greater than all the speculation, including 'the central facts of the Christian story'.[101]

Janet Oppenheimer argued that 'Balfour's theology was grounded, not on sublime certainty, but rather on the conviction of man's spiritual needs.'[102] Religion as satisfying a human need is a constant refrain of his work. It is there in *The Foundations of Belief*: 'We desire, and desire most passionately when we are most ourselves, to give our service to that which is Universal, and to that which is Abiding.'[103] It is there in the Gifford Lectures: 'Theism of a "religious" type is necessary, if the great values on which all our higher life depend are to be reasonably sustained.'[104]

---

100 Wells, *Experiment in Autobiography*, p. 777.

101 AJB, *The Foundations of Belief*, p. 354.

102 Janet Oppenheim, *The Other World: Spiritualism and psychical research in England, 1850–1914* (Cambridge: Cambridge University Press, 1988), p. 131.

103 AJB, *The Foundations of Belief*, p. 31.

104 AJB, *Theism and Thought*, p. 258.

Balfour's approach is not without merit. If religion fails to address our deepest yearnings it is of little practical value. We long to know how 'we are able to face the insistent facts of sin, suffering and misery'[105] – other than with ignorant despair. Yet those human needs are only effectively met if faith is objectively true. Otherwise, the atheists are right: religion is merely a placebo. Balfour knew this. He was desperate to give an adequate basis for faith – and he never entirely succeeded. He remained a theist, not a Christian.

Caroline Jebb was the American wife of a Cambridge academic. Meeting Balfour, she discerned astutely:

> I think the sadness arises partly from the fact that the spirit of the age prevents him, a naturally religious man, from being religious, except on the humanitarian side . . .
>
> All the Balfour family take hold of the end of religion they can be sure of, the helping of people here. Their mother, Lady Blanche, belonging to a different generation, was absorbed in dogmatic religion, and they inherit her unworldly nature, without the power of her unquestioning faith, so they miss her happiness.[106]

It is difficult to improve on that assessment.

Balfour declined a state funeral in Westminster Abbey, choosing to be buried with Presbyterian simplicity at Whittingehame. The service was conducted by the parish minister, the Revd Marshall Lang, brother of the Archbishop of Canterbury. Lang's tribute to Balfour was generously and amply phrased: 'The truths of our holy religion were the possession of his inmost soul.'[107]

---

105 AJB, 'The Religion of Humanity', in AJB, *Essays and Addresses*, p. 290.

106 Caroline Jebb to her sister, 25 July 1880, cited Mary Reed Bobbitt, *With Dearest Love to All: The life and letters of Lady Jebb* (London: Faber & Faber, 1960), pp. 160–1.

107 Cited Malcolm, *Lord Balfour*, p. 124.

Henry Campbell-Bannerman (1905–1908)

'I must just trust in Him'

Henry Campbell[1] was born at Kelvinside, then outside the city of Glasgow, on 7 September 1836. He attended Glasgow High School, Glasgow University and Trinity College, Cambridge.

Campbell-Bannerman was elected as the Liberal MP for Stirling Burghs in 1868, representing the constituency for the rest of his life. He served as a junior minister in William Gladstone's governments, as Financial Secretary at the War Office (1871–4 and 1880–2) and Parliamentary and Financial Secretary to the Admiralty (1882–4). Campbell-Bannerman entered the Cabinet as Chief Secretary for Ireland (1884–5). As Secretary of State for War (1886 and 1892–5), he gained the respect of both the Army and the Royal Family. He was knighted in 1895.

In 1899, Campbell-Bannerman was unanimously elected leader of the Liberals in the Commons, regarded as the only candidate capable of uniting a party divided between Imperialists and Little Englanders. Under his leadership, the Liberals lost the 1900 'Khaki' election, but not as badly as many had feared. Campbell-Bannerman's opposition to the Unionist government's conduct of the Boer War was enormously unpopular at the time, but people later came to appreciate his principled objections.

With the Unionists in turn hopelessly divided on the question of tariff reform, Balfour resigned office, and Campbell-Bannerman was appointed Prime Minister on 5 December 1905. The Liberals proceeded to win a massive Commons majority in the general election held the following month. The government enacted certain reforms but found itself in conflict with the Unionist majority in the House of Lords. Campbell-Bannerman's

1 The hyphenated 'Bannerman' was added reluctantly in 1872 to comply with a conditional bequest from a maternal uncle. For convenience, contemporaries referred to him colloquially as 'CB'.

generous political settlement in South Africa reconciled moderate Boers to their position within the British Empire.

After a prolonged period of ill health, Campbell-Bannerman's resignation was accepted on 5 April 1908. He died shortly afterwards, on 22 April.

* * *

Glasgow Presbyterians

The Liberal landslide victory in the general election of January 1906 led some to believe that the country stood on the verge of political – and possibly religious – revolution. There were more Nonconformist MPs in Parliament than at any time since the days of Oliver Cromwell. They came with a list of grievances for which they expected redress: an end to public funding of denominational education and the Anglican near-monopoly on rural schools, disestablishment (the separation of Church and state), and restrictions on the drinks trade.

There may have been fewer dukes and more lawyers in the new Cabinet but it was still dominated by peers, landowners and professionals. Only Lloyd George and John Burns would have struck a discordant chord in Balfour's Cabinet. A number of the new Liberal Cabinet ministers socialized with their Unionist predecessors in a perpetual round of town and country house parties.

Superficially, there also appeared to be continuity in the persons of the two Prime Ministers. Both were wealthy men whose family fortunes derived from trade. Both were graduates of Trinity College, Cambridge. Both were Scots Presbyterians. Temperamentally, however, they were polar opposites. The new Prime Minister was affable and indolent. He lacked his predecessor's intellectual gifts and debating skills but his practical wisdom, honesty and simple decency resonated with the electorate. Balfour, by contrast, was perceived as brilliant but flippant and ineffectual. The Unionists suffered the electoral consequences of his inability to unite and lead MPs bitterly divided between protectionists and free traders.

Campbell-Bannerman was not born of radical stock. His father, the Tory Lord Provost of Glasgow, twice contested the city constituency (unsuccessfully) and was knighted in 1841. For a generation, Campbell-Bannerman faced his elder brother across the House of Commons, where the latter sat as a Conservative.

Their father and uncle, James and William Campbell, arrived in Glasgow from central Scotland in 1805. Self-made men, they amassed a fortune in the draper's trade, including the sale of newly fashionable tartans. They were also devout Presbyterians. Anecdotally at least, they owed their wealth to their religious observance. Having heard a Sunday sermon roundly denouncing the system of haggling as manifestly unjust to the poor, the two brothers resolved to change their business practice. In future all goods in their shops were sold at a fixed, marked price. Transparency and certainty were rewarded with a huge upturn in business.[2] It was not the only occasion when the brothers allowed their faith to determine commercial decisions: in 1842 they announced they would boycott the Edinburgh and Glasgow Railway if that company ran Sunday trains.[3]

James Campbell married Janet Bannerman in 1822, in the church that later became Manchester Cathedral. She was the daughter of a Perthshire farmer who had established himself in the Lancashire cotton industry. The couple settled in Glasgow, where they raised their six children, of whom Henry was the youngest.

A month after his birth, Campbell-Bannerman was baptized into the Church of Scotland in the city's Barony Church. During his childhood, the family joined many of Glasgow's mercantile class in attending St George's parish church. The minister, the Revd James Craik, was one of Scotland's leading educationalists and took a personal interest in the future Prime Minister's education. The young Campbell-Bannerman was a frequent visitor to the manse.[4] He first attended Glasgow High School, before entering the University of Glasgow at the age of 14.

European tour

Between high school and university, Campbell-Bannerman undertook a ten-month European tour in the company of his brother and cousin. Throughout their travels the three young Scots were meticulous in their

2 T. P. O'Connor, *Sir Henry Campbell-Bannerman* (London: Hodder & Stoughton, 1908), p. 12.

3 David Murray, Memorandum of the History of Glasgow, 14 February 1923, BL, Campbell-Bannerman Papers, Add. MS 41252, f. 253.

4 J. A. Spender, *Life of the Right Hon. Sir Henry Campbell-Bannerman, GCB*, Vol. 1 (London: Hodder & Stoughton, 1923), p. 36.

religious observance. Each week saw them attending Sunday service – often in the morning and again in the afternoon. Generally they went to the 'English' (Anglican) church but would attend the 'Scotch' (Presbyterian) service when the opportunity arose. Writing home, Campbell-Bannerman commented on the sermons heard for the benefit of his sister.

There was nothing narrow about the religious experience of these travellers. They attended Mass and vespers in Catholic churches, sat in on a nun's profession, engaged in conversation with seminarians and inspected relics. Campbell-Bannerman noted that in Milan 'we went into the Cathedral and heard High Mass performed. We had never heard it before and were much struck with it.' He was likewise impressed by the eloquence of the preacher and the numbers present in Narni Cathedral. The party stayed three months in Rome. The Papal Mass was 'uncommonly fine'; Pope Pius IX was 'a kindly pleasant looking old gentleman' – not the judgement expected from a spiritual son of John Knox confronted by the embodiment of Catholic reaction! Campbell-Bannerman was, however, in no danger of being seduced by the errors of Rome. He discovered not 'the smallest particle of devotion' among the congregation at Pontifical High Mass and found 'degrading' the sight of pilgrims ascending on their knees the Scala Santa – by tradition the steps from Pontius Pilate's praetorium climbed by Christ during his Passion and subsequently brought to Rome. Campbell-Bannerman's reaction to the Capuchin friars' 'bone chapel' is understandable: 'Horrid!'[5]

A religious education 'of no substantial value'

Without graduating from Glasgow, Campbell-Bannerman proceeded at the age of 18 to Trinity College, Cambridge, where he read Classics. From a later intervention in a Commons debate on university reform, we know precisely what the undergraduate thought of the state of religion in Cambridge in the 1850s. It was not flattering.

5 Cited ed. Lord Pentland, *Early Letters of Sir Henry Campbell-Bannerman to His Sister Louisa* (London: T. Fisher Unwin, 1925), pp. 43, 91, 102–5, 117.

It was not a Presbyterian's objection to Anglican forms of worship. Campbell-Bannerman's fulminations were far more wide-ranging. Oxford and Cambridge were held up as the epitome of sound learning and religious education. In his experience, however, the learning was not very sound nor the religion very learned. Campbell-Bannerman queried whether a young man's moral character genuinely benefited from compulsory chapel attendance. He recalled that the examinations in the Gospels that undergraduates at the time were required to sit treated Scripture solely as classical literature, giving no account 'to dogmatic teaching or moral training'. The use of Paley's *Evidences of Christianity* he felt to be a historical exercise only, unworthy of the attempt to address his contemporaries' intellectual doubts. His verdict was damning: 'I venture to submit that this so-called religious education has no substantial value.' He concluded that religious education was 'better received at home and at an earlier period of life'.[6]

Campbell-Bannerman might have been critical of the state of religious education prevailing in Cambridge, but his approach differed entirely from that of Balfour a decade later. While Balfour peered into the abyss of unmitigated materialism and devised arguments to reconcile the claims of religion and science, Campbell-Bannerman busily noted anecdotes and doggerel in his commonplace book:

> Why is a High Church parson like a hunted fox? He is a tracked 'airy un.

> A certain man returning from the official sacrament he was obliged to take, was observed to be looking perplexed; on being asked why, he said 'There was an old woman there, taking the sacrament and I can't make out for what office she can have been qualifying.'

> The Ladies praise our Curate's eyes:
> I cannot see their light divine;
> For when he prays he shuts his eyes.
> His sermon closes mine.

6 Campbell-Bannerman, House of Commons, 29 June 1869, cited Spender, *Life*, Vol. 1, pp. 35–6; William Paley, *A View of the Evidences of Christianity in Three Parts*, 2 vols (London: R. Faulder, 1794).

The humour was poor and unsophisticated but these are not the rantings of an atheist or militant anti-clericalist, rather the musings of one entertained by the human foibles of the churchmen around him. One jotting appears to strike a particular chord with the undergraduate:

> What Religion are you of, Mr Rogers?
> Of the Religion of all sensible men, Madam.
> What Religion is that?
> Madam, all sensible men keep that to themselves.[7]

Graduating with a Third – the result of lack of application rather than of ability – Campbell-Bannerman returned to Glasgow to work for the family firm. There too his lack of application was noted. In 1860 he married Charlotte Bruce, a Major General's daughter, in All Souls, Langham Place. Although childless, the marriage was extremely happy. The couple moved between homes in London, Kent and Perthshire, and travelled extensively in Europe. Possibly Charlotte supplied the application her husband lacked. Her family, and his own reading, encouraged Campbell-Bannerman beyond the conventional Conservativism of his family. At the second attempt he was elected as a Liberal MP in 1868. Indeed, he was viewed as a radical.

A very broad faith?

And not only in politics – some suspected him of radicalism in religion too. According to his friend, the Irish Nationalist MP, T. P. O'Connor, the consensus was that Campbell-Bannerman was rather a sceptic in matters of faith, sharing 'something of the detached spirit of the French authors he loved'. (O'Connor found that analysis inaccurate; for him, Campbell-Bannerman's faith, 'whatever it was, was probably very broad'.)[8]

Campbell-Bannerman gave some justification to those who suspected him of agnosticism. In the 1860s he devoured the writings of Charles Darwin and Herbert Spencer. Much neglected today, Spencer was one of

7 CB, Commonplace book, 1855, BL, CB Papers, Add. MS 41248A.

8 O'Connor, *Sir Henry Campbell-Bannerman*, pp. 160–1.

the most influential European philosophers of the mid-nineteenth century. (Balfour went to some length to refute him.) Self-taught, Spencer was an evolutionist who coined the term 'survival of the fittest' and was perhaps best known for his theory of 'social Darwinism', applying the naturalist's arguments to human society. Unlike Darwin, he believed that evolution had purpose and direction; that progress tended towards human perfection. Spencer rejected his Christian faith in his teens. Never a militant opponent of religion, he hoped for some synthesis between faith and science. Yet he had no belief in a personal God, possibly only in a deity who was altogether unknowable. At other times, Spencer seemed to veer towards materialism.

In 1907, Campbell-Bannerman was awarded the freedom of the City of Glasgow. Given that Spencer was now dead and intellectually unfashionable, it was odd that the Prime Minister should use his acceptance speech to acknowledge his intellectual debt to him:

> When I entered Parliament . . . I was a diligent student of Mr Herbert Spencer's philosophy. I am not sure that a good deal of it was not absorbed and does not lurk somewhere in my system today. In truth, I hope it is so.[9]

Such a statement should not be taken too seriously. Campbell-Bannerman delighted in mischievously challenging the prejudices of others – his speech proceeded to cite not the philosopher's agnosticism but his views on municipal government, drains and pavements! He might have read advanced authors but he was not a systematic thinker in the manner of Balfour. Nor were his reading habits necessarily indicative of his religious beliefs.

Unlike Balfour, Campbell-Bannerman wrote or spoke very little about philosophy or theology. It is more telling to examine his practice. We have his travel journals for tours of France, Switzerland, Italy and Spain in the early 1860s. This time he was no longer in the company of his cousin and elder brother, who had organized his earlier schedule for him. Nevertheless, Campbell-Bannerman diligently continued to attend the 'English service'

9 CB, Speech, 25 January 1907, cited Spender, *Life*, Vol. 2, p. 320.

in whichever town he was staying. This appeared to be more than social convention. He commented intelligently, if often critically, on the preaching and music. His particular ire was reserved for a sermon in Geneva dedicated to an appeal for money.[10] When at their Perthshire home, he and Lady Campbell-Bannerman were regular attenders at Meigle parish church.

Parsons and psalms

The company someone keeps is instructive. Campbell-Bannerman's early European tours were undertaken with Charles Oldfield, a fellow student at Trinity College, who became an Anglican clergyman and Prebendary of Lincoln Cathedral. He was also fond of another Trinity contemporary, George Browne (later Bishop of Stepney, then Bristol), who was a regular guest in Scotland, Paris and Marienbad.[11] There were letters of congratulation on Campbell-Bannerman's appointment as Prime Minister from various country parsons.[12] None of this proves the nature of his religious beliefs; nor does it suggest an ingrained antipathy towards the Church and her ministers.

Campbell-Bannerman's childhood formation in the Shorter Catechism and his knowledge of Scripture ran deep. They were never entirely rejected; it was something he drew on in his later years. If he lacked Balfour's philosophical turn of mind, that may have made it easier to live with the perceived inconsistencies and doubts that troubled more academic contemporaries.

When Lady Campbell-Bannerman died in Marienbad in August 1906, the Prime Minister was devastated. Writing to his Cabinet colleagues, however, he expressed his thanks to God and confidence that she was 'now at rest after her long years of suffering'.[13] He brought her coffin home to Scotland for burial. On her grave he had inscribed: 'My trust is in the tender mercy of God for ever and ever.'[14]

---

10 BL, CB Papers, Add. MS 41248B, C and D.

11 G. F. Browne, *Recollections of a Bishop* (London: Smith, Elder & Co., 1915), p. 176n.

12 Spender, *Life*, Vol. 1, p. 19.

13 CB to Lord Ripon, BL, Ripon Papers, Add. MS 43518, f. 104; John Wilson, *Campbell-Bannerman: A life of Sir Henry Campbell-Bannerman* (London: Constable, 1973), cited p. 567.

14 Wilson, *CB*, p. 568.

In June 1907, Cambridge bestowed on him an honorary degree. Staying at his old college, it seemed to him the most natural thing in the world to engage in conversation with the Master, Montagu Butler, on Psalm 107. Campbell-Bannerman confided 'that he was not always in his element in academic circles, but whoever shared his enthusiasm for his favourite Psalms or his favourite passages of Scripture was a kindred spirit'.[15] Later that year he spent time convalescing at Biarritz. Reading a commentary on Isaiah, he acknowledged that it allowed him to understand the prophet properly for the first time.[16]

Church and state

Campbell-Bannerman was naturally tolerant, but politicians could not avoid religious controversies. He was obliged to address the vexed question of the funding of denominational schools. His preference was to relieve the state of any role in the religious education of children, which he maintained should be left to the home and the churches.[17] As a Scots Presbyterian, his approach differed from that of English and Welsh Nonconformists. Personally, he believed it no business of the government's to impose 'a statutory common creed', which he thought as objectionable as a compulsory denominational creed imposed on pupils of another denomination.[18] He had no principled objection to allowing Catholics their own schools within the state system, nor to giving all clergy access to schools to offer instruction to such as wished for it. He was sufficiently pragmatic, however, to appreciate that the real issue was the grievance nursed by Liberal-supporting Nonconformists against the near-monopoly of rural education by the Anglican vicar – 'our own familiar friend who because he is so near to us is dangerous'.[19]

Campbell-Bannerman was a proponent of disestablishment in both Scotland and England. This was not always reflected in his actions and attitudes. In 1905 he opposed Balfour's move to extend the measure of spiritual

15 Spender, *Life*, Vol. 2, pp. 343–4.

16 Spender, *Life*, Vol. 2, p. 375.

17 CB, Speech, 27 February 1871, cited Spender, *Life*, Vol. 1, p. 38.

18 Spender, *Life*, Vol. 2, p. 274.

19 CB to James Bryce, 29 December 1903, cited Spender, *Life*, Vol. 2, p. 133.

independence enjoyed by the Church of Scotland. He trusted laymen and politicians above pastors and priests to protect the Protestant character of the Church. In an early speech as leader of the Opposition he stated his preference for 'a free Church in a free State'. Yet while the Church of England remained the state church, he insisted it should comply, even in matters of doctrine and liturgy, with the will of Parliament and the civil courts.[20] Had they taken note of that speech, contemporaries might have been less surprised that Campbell-Bannerman took such a keen interest in the exercise of his powers of patronage in the Church of England when he entered 10 Downing Street.

'The real sacerdotal lot'

Campbell-Bannerman was the first Prime Minister not to be even formally a member of the Church of England.[21] This caused less comment than might have been anticipated. After all, his predecessor had claimed membership of both the Church of England and the Church of Scotland, two recent Archbishops of Canterbury had been raised as Presbyterians, and monarchs moved between the two Communions depending on which side of the border they found themselves. High Church Anglicans might have expressed unease about a Presbyterian's role in the appointment of bishops, but most Low Churchmen and Nonconformists would rather have had a Presbyterian exercising this role than an Anglican Ritualist, who might harbour secret Roman sympathies.

Claiming himself unable to distinguish a rural dean from a reredos, Campbell-Bannerman feigned ignorance of church affairs, preferring to leave such matters to his private secretary, Henry Higgs. He knew a great deal more than he admitted – Higgs was simply 'his eyes and ears'. The Prime Minister sought advice from others, including the ultra-Protestant Lady Wimborne (Churchill's aunt), to achieve his

20 CB, Speech, 8 March 1899, cited <www.britishpoliticalspeech.org/speech-archive.htm?-speech=8>, accessed 05.08.22.

21 In making this observation, Randall Davidson defined an Anglican as one confirmed according to the rites of the Church of England. Davidson, Evidence to the Church Assembly Committee on the Appointment of Bishops, 29 July 1924, LPL, Bell Papers, 118, f. 25.

objectives.[22] Accustomed to Balfour's laissez-faire approach, the Archbishop of Canterbury was not amused and urged the Crown to suggest that the Prime Minister consult Lambeth before making episcopal recommendations.[23]

Another not amused by Campbell-Bannerman's exercise of ecclesiastical patronage was the left-leaning parson Percy Dearmer. He complained bitterly that the last two Conservative governments had appointed more reform-minded bishops than this Liberal one.[24] This was not an oversight on the part of Downing Street. Campbell-Bannerman candidly acknowledged his predicament:

> I am to appoint Liberals but to avoid extreme Ritualists – that is what I am told. But all the new school of Church Liberals are Sacerdotalists; while all the Evangelicals of mark are pronounced Tories. What is a poor devil to do?[25]

Faced with a clear conflict between politics and religion, he opted for religion, not because he was disinterested or thought the secular power should defer to the spiritual but because of his own religious beliefs. As Prime Minister he considered the particular needs of a Diocese but he would always advance a Conservative Evangelical in preference to a Liberal Ritualist.

The qualities Campbell-Bannerman sought in bishops were a capacity for clear preaching, hard work among the poor and the ability to enforce ecclesiastical discipline against the Ritualists. The force and consistency with which he expressed himself demonstrates he was no mere cypher for the Nonconformists and Low Churchmen sitting on the Liberal benches behind him. He vented his views vigorously on the fact that Anglican prelates were drawn from a narrow social background:

22 Henry Higgs, Memorandum, 29 December 1919, BL, CB Papers, Add. MS 41252, ff. 146–50.

23 Davidson to Sir Francis Knollys, 22 November 1907 (copy), LPL, Davidson Papers, 10, f. 33.

24 Percy Dearmer, *Commonwealth* (October 1907), cited Graham Neville, *Radical Churchman: Edward Lee Hicks and the New Liberalism* (Oxford: Clarendon Press, 1988), p. 123.

25 CB to Robert Spence Watson, 13 July 1907 (copy), BL, CB Papers, Add. MS, 41242, f. 254.

> I have no patience with professors of a religion founded by fishermen who think that the higher posts in the Church must be preserved for the highly born and the highly educated. I have little doubt that St Peter dropped his h's and that Our Saviour's Sermon on the Mount was uttered in the broadest Galilean dialect.

He chose an Evangelical bishop for Newcastle because he thought him capable of evangelizing the pitmen in his Diocese.[26] This was not a sceptical premier indifferent to the claims of religion but a believer wanting to ensure the faith was transmitted more effectively to society at large.

Campbell-Bannerman emphatically opposed 'the real sacerdotal lot'. Had the Prime Minister lived a few months longer, Cosmo Lang would not have been appointed Archbishop of York. He suspected Lang's High Church tendencies and reproached his fellow Scot for his alleged refusal to enter his own father's Presbyterian church.[27] Notwithstanding his intellectual and spiritual gifts, Henry Scott Holland was similarly blocked because he too displayed 'the sacerdotal spirit', which Campbell-Bannerman regarded as inimical to the Protestant Reformation:[28]

> What I dislike intensely is the idea of a mediating priesthood, standing between the individual and his Creator, claiming to reserve sacraments, and to have the right of introducing the laity to the Deity as if they were a privileged caste.[29]

The Prime Minister's religious beliefs remained those of the Church of Scotland youth raised in Glasgow some 60 years earlier.

'The tender mercy of God'

Following his wife's death, Campbell-Bannerman suffered a number of heart attacks and was taken seriously ill in November 1907. After a period

26 CB, cited Higgs, Memorandum, 29 December 1919, BL, CB Papers, Add. MS 41252, f. 150; CB to Robert Spence Watson, 13 July 1907 (copy), BL, CB Papers, Add. MS, 41242, f. 254.

27 CB to John Sinclair, 29 September 1907 (copy), BL, CB Papers, Add. MS 41230, f. 195.

28 Higgs to Davidson, 22 April 1907, LPL, Davidson Papers, 10, f. 23.

29 CB, cited Higgs, Memorandum, 29 December 1919, BL, CB Papers, Add. MS 41252, f. 150.

of convalescence in France, he returned to London in spring 1908 but his health declined rapidly. From the end of March, the Archbishop of Canterbury, Randall Davidson, visited the dying Prime Minister in Downing Street almost daily. The offer, made by the Archbishop, had been accepted cheerfully and immediately. Campbell-Bannerman's contemporaries expressed surprise when these visits became public knowledge. Perhaps they were unaware that he had invited Davidson to visit him in Perthshire after his wife's death 18 months earlier.

It helped that both men were practical, no-nonsense Scots raised as Presbyterians. Davidson talked about past times. The Prime Minister appreciated the Archbishop's approach: 'He is a most sensible man,' Campbell-Bannerman opined. 'I say sensible because he thinks just as I do.'[30] Sitting by his bedside, Davidson read from the book of Ecclesiasticus and spoke of his own serious illness when 'he could not rise to the heights of spiritual feelings or to the clear apprehension of doctrine, but found himself repeating things which his mother had taught him, lines of hymns, the Scottish Paraphrases, of the Psalms and simple texts.' The approach was pastorally sensitive and effective. The Prime Minister replied that was his experience too, how his own belief was best expressed by that verse from the Psalms he had had inscribed on his wife's tomb: 'My trust is in the tender mercy of God for ever and ever.' In his final days he repeated: 'There is One watching over us who will arrange things for the best and we can trust Him. If one had the management of it all oneself, one would make a hopeless mess of it.'[31]

None of this was said simply for the benefit of the Archbishop of Canterbury. Political colleagues found the Prime Minister in the same frame of mind. He spoke to Asquith, the Chancellor of the Exchequer, of the text from the Psalms he had chosen for his own grave and the arrangements made for his funeral.[32] Three days later it was the turn of the Scottish Liberal MP, Tom Buchanan. Campbell-Bannerman confided:

30 Arthur Ponsonby to Davidson, 23 April 1908, LPL, Davidson Papers, 5, f. 81.

31 Spender, *Life*, Vol. 2, pp. 385–6.

32 Margot Asquith, Diary, 27 March 1908, cited Margot Asquith, *The Autobiography of Margot Asquith*, Vol. 2 (London: Thornton Butterworth, 1922), p. 89.

> I am a very weak man and God is very strong and I must just trust in Him . . . You know Tom, I was (or we were) brought up on 'O God of Bethel'[33] and that religion and that is what we have to trust to.

Buchanan had indeed been brought up in that religion and responded: 'In Thee, O Lord, have I trusted, let me never be put to confusion.'[34]

There was a return to the simple faith of his childhood – one suspects never entirely abandoned. Did Campbell-Bannerman have an orthodox understanding of Trinitarian theology or the divinity of Christ? We cannot know. These matters did not trouble him as they did Balfour. His faith was scriptural, drawing heavily on the Old Testament. He trusted in the providence and mercy of God, believed in the resurrection of the dead and left it at that.

Edward VII was reluctant to accept his incapacitated Prime Minister's resignation, fearing it would disrupt his holiday arrangements in Biarritz. Eventually, however, the King bowed to the inevitable and officially received the resignation on 5 April 1908. Campbell-Bannerman never left Downing Street, where he died less than three weeks later. The Archbishop of Canterbury acted as a pall-bearer and conducted the funeral service in Westminster Abbey. At the express wish of the family, Davidson also assisted the Presbyterian minister at the Church of Scotland burial service in Perthshire the following day.[35]

---

33 The hymn by the eighteenth-century Nonconformist minister, Philip Doddridge, very much in an Old Testament vein with no reference to Christ.

34 Tom Buchanan, Diary (copy), 30 March 1908, BL, CB Papers, Add. MS 52520, f. 97.

35 Ponsonby to Davidson, 23 April 1908, LPL, Davidson Papers, 5, f. 81.

H. H. Asquith (1908–1916)

'My husband was never an atheist'

Herbert Henry Asquith[1] was born on 12 September 1852 at Morley in the West Riding of Yorkshire. He was educated at the City of London School and Balliol College, Oxford.

Elected Liberal MP for East Fife in 1886, he represented the constituency until his defeat in the 'Coupon' election of 1918. He returned to the Commons at a by-election at Paisley in 1920 and held that seat until 1924.

Asquith developed a reputation as a powerful intellect and effective speaker. Gladstone appointed him Home Secretary (1892–5). After the Liberals returned to power, he served as Chancellor of the Exchequer (1905–8).

When Henry Campbell-Bannerman resigned, Asquith's succession as leader of the Liberal Party and Prime Minister was unquestioned. He travelled to Edward VII's hotel in Biarritz, where the King appointed him Prime Minister on 6 April 1908.

Asquith continued his predecessor's reforming legislative programme. The 'People's Budget' of 1909 proposed redistributive tax increases to pay for old-age pensions and naval rearmament, leading to a stand-off with the House of Lords and a constitutional crisis. Only after two inconclusive general elections in 1910 and the King's promise to create sufficient new peers to give the Liberals a majority in the Upper House did the Lords accept the loss of their legislative veto. Deprived of his Commons majority, Asquith relied on Irish Nationalist and Labour MPs to keep him in office. The price for Nationalist support was Irish Home Rule, and a further bitter political crisis ensued. The government also had to contend with industrial

1 Like his predecessor, Asquith also changed his name. Unlike Campbell-Bannerman, this change was not effected in law. Known by his family as 'Herbert' or 'Bertie', Asquith's second wife decided that 'Henry' was more appropriate for a senior statesman. In adult life, however, few knew him by his Christian name. To most he was 'Asquith' or 'HHA'.

unrest. Opposed to female suffrage, Asquith was a particular target of the suffragettes.

Only the outbreak of the First World War brought an end to domestic conflict. Asquith secured Britain's entry into the war on 4 August 1914 with a minimal number of resignations from the government. The failure of the Gallipoli campaign and a shortage of munitions led to the formation of a coalition government with the Unionists in May 1915, Asquith continuing as Prime Minister. The protracted and costly nature of trench warfare, delays over the introduction of conscription, criticism of Asquith's relaxed style of leadership, and machinations by Lloyd George and the press led to calls for the effective management of the war to be transferred into other hands. Declining to be a figurehead leader, Asquith resigned on 6 December 1916.

He continued as leader of the Liberals, leading the opposition to Lloyd George's coalition government. Divisions between Asquithian and Coalition Liberals continued beyond the war and proved fatal to the party as an effective political force, allowing Labour to emerge as the main opposition to the Conservatives.

Having lost his Commons seat, Asquith was created Earl of Oxford and Asquith in 1924. He resigned as leader of the Liberal Party in 1926, and died on 15 February 1928.

* * *

'One of us'

'My husband was never an atheist' – society was accustomed to Margot Asquith's strident statements, but why did she feel compelled to defend her husband's religious beliefs after his death? Rumours had circulated during his life. Some had sought to dissuade her from marrying Asquith in 1894 on precisely these grounds.[2] In 1905, J. P. Alderson wrote a curious biography of Asquith. It reads like a manifesto for the position of Liberal party leader, although there was no vacancy. Alderson claimed that

2 Margot Asquith, *More Memories* (London: Cassell & Co., 1933), p. 156.

both Asquith and his wife 'are religious, and both work out their religion in their daily lives'.[3] Where does the truth lie?

The Liberal landslide of 1906 owed much to Nonconformist votes. In the person of the new Chancellor of the Exchequer, it seemed that English Nonconformity finally had one of its own in high political office. Two Protestant missionaries were delighted when they chanced upon Asquith in Naples. One determined to introduce himself:

> He's one of us. If we were at home we should be among his political followers. Besides, he used, when a boy, to collect money for the *John Williams* [a Protestant missionary ship in the South Pacific]. I'm going to speak to him.

The poor missionary rapidly discovered that shared religious roots counted for nothing with Asquith. For his pains, he was brusquely dismissed: 'Would you like me to give you a bit of advice? Well, go off back to New Guinea and get on with your work.'[4]

Those missionaries were not mistaken as to Asquith's origins. The town of Morley never took to Anglicanism after the Reformation, rather it was a stronghold of the Congregationalists, those independent Protestants who held that the Church of England was compromised in doctrine, liturgy and governance by its Catholic past. Congregationalism in Morley fractured with the arrival of a new minister in 1763, and the Prime Minister's forebears were among those who took themselves off to found the new Rehoboth Chapel. At the time of Asquith's birth, it was a major concern. The chapel accommodated 800; there was a flourishing Sunday school.

His father, Joseph Dixon Asquith, was a moderately prosperous wool merchant. His mother, Emily Asquith, was the daughter of William Willans, who had contested his home town of Huddersfield as a Liberal in 1851. Asquith recalled that his 'parents were active workers and devout worshippers', and 'every Sunday [we] went in our best clothes to Rehoboth

3 J. P. Alderson, *Mr Asquith* (London: Methuen & Co., 1905), p. 221.

4 Arthur Porritt, *More and More of Memories* (London: George Allen & Unwin, 1947), pp. 125–6.

Chapel.'[5] Joseph taught Bible classes to the young men, and Emily, an invalid from youth, 'was deeply religious'.[6] The family were related to various Congregational ministers and prominent laymen. They were part of a national Nonconformist network that acquired wealth in the Industrial Revolution, valued education and was determined to flex its political muscle.[7]

'Visions of hell fire'

Asquith listened to innumerable sermons in his youth; the impression he retained was not comforting. The Puritanism in which he was raised presented an uncompromisingly binary view of eternity. Forty years on he could still conjure up 'the visions of hell fire which used to haunt our piously educated childhood'.[8] The alternative destiny, described in the 'lurid lines of a hymn', equally haunted him in childhood:

> Where Congregations ne'er break up
> And Sabbaths have no end.

Understanding heaven as a physical location not dissimilar to his Yorkshire chapel, it was as unappealing as the netherworld.[9]

When he was only seven, disaster struck with the premature death of his father. Emily returned with her three young children to Huddersfield. Asquith recalled his grandfather's home as a sanctuary for 'the big guns of the Congregational pulpit'.[10] He attended Huddersfield College, then a poor, rough Moravian boarding school near Leeds.[11]

---

5 Herbert Henry Asquith, *Memories and Reflections, 1852–1927*, Vol. 1 (London: Cassell & Co., 1928), p. 3.

6 Margot Asquith, *The Autobiography of Margot Asquith*, Vol. 1 (London: Thornton Butterworth, 1920), p. 263; Margot Asquith, Diary, 16 October 1895, Oxford, Bodleian Libraries (Bodleian), Margot Asquith MS, Eng. d. 3200.

7 Clyde Binfield, 'Asquith: The formation of a Prime Minister', *Journal of the United Reformed Church History Society*, Vol. 2, No. 7, April 1981, pp. 204–42.

8 HHA to Frances Horner, 10 August 1892, private collection.

9 HHA to Edith Scott, 24 February 1916, CUL, Kennet Papers, 109/1/34.

10 HHA, *Memories and Reflections*, Vol. 1, p. 230.

11 Margot Asquith, Diary, 16 October 1895, Bodleian, Margot Asquith MS, Eng. d. 3200.

Emily moved to St Leonards-on-Sea on health grounds in 1864. Asquith and his brother were sent to the City of London School, founded by the Corporation of London in the 1830s and popular with Jews and Nonconformists for its lack of religious tests. With a reputation for academic excellence, numerous boys went on to Oxford and Cambridge. Asquith's headmaster was the Revd Edwin Abbott, a Broad Church Anglican who had begun life as a Methodist. Abbott was 'a powerful and suggestive preacher, but there was nothing sectarian or denominational in his presentation of religion to his pupils'.[12] He had written a commentary on John's Gospel and works on early Christianity. In 1878 he published a fictionalized life of Jesus anonymously, fearing that his metaphorical treatment of miracles and the resurrection might cost him his headship.[13]

Initially, the two brothers lived with a maternal uncle in Islington. When he returned to Yorkshire, they lodged with Congregationalist families in Islington and Pimlico. Asquith attended Dr Henry Allon's fashionable Union Chapel in Islington, but also visited other Congregationalist chapels, and 'from time to time listened to the most popular Nonconformist preacher of that era – Spurgeon of the Metropolitan Tabernacle . . . His theology was of the straightest and most uncompromising type of Puritan orthodoxy.'[14] The schoolboy ventured further afield ecclesiastically to hear a good sermon, but was critical of Archdeacon Wordsworth's 'impudence' in defending the Anglican establishment in Ireland in Westminster Abbey.[15]

Asquith cited approvingly the Nonconformist sermons and addresses he heard. He wrote to his mother in the most conventional terms on her fortieth birthday:

> I trust and pray that those [years] which remain may attain to the same reward of joy without an equal trial of suffering. But though no earthly treasure has been laid up – though health and pleasure have been in great measure denied – there is still that treasure to

12 HHA, *Memories and Reflections*, Vol. 1, p. 8.

13 Daniel L. Pals, *The Victorian 'Lives' of Jesus* (San Antonio, TX: Trinity University Press, 1982), pp. 108–10.

14 Pals, *The Victorian 'Lives' of Jesus*, p. 230.

15 HHA to Emily Asquith, 20 May 1868, cited J. A. Spender and Cyril Asquith, *Life of Herbert Henry Asquith, Lord Oxford and Asquith*, Vol. 2 (London: Hutchinson & Co., 1932), p. 29.

> enjoy which is laid up where neither moth nor rust doth corrupt, and where thieves do not break through and steal – there is still that rest to enter upon which remaineth for the people of God – and there is still His 'Well done' to be heard, whom not having seen, we love. The assurance of these as it grows more strong and more full makes all other objects recede into nothingness.[16]

Two things happened to change Asquith's early piety. First, he discovered that life had more to offer than the restricted pursuits and pleasures previously allowed, and made an illicit foray into another world:

> I remember vividly the guilty sense of adventure with which I slipped out early one evening to pay my first visit to the theatre, and the care I took to cover my tracks on my return. We had been brought up to regard the theatre as one of the devil's most damnable haunts; I am sure that my mother never entered one in her life, and her scruples were fully shared by the old Puritan couple – a dispensary doctor and his wife – with whom I lodged. I must have been quite 16 when I took this plunge.[17]

Playing cards was another forbidden activity Asquith embraced with relish. He first diverged from Nonconformity not on doctrinal grounds but over its ethical expression and practical consequences. He conceded that the Puritanism in which he was bred 'had its uses, but it tends to make people intolerant and censorious'.[18]

'Platonism flavoured with a little Christian charity'

If London undermined his faith on pragmatic considerations, Oxford destroyed it intellectually. Asquith won a Classical Scholarship to Balliol

16 HHA to Emily Asquith, 3 May 1868, Spender and Asquith, *Life of HHA*, p. 29.

17 HHA to Venetia Stanley, 20 February 1915, cited ed. M. Brock and E. Brock, *H. H. Asquith, Letters to Venetia Stanley* (Oxford: Oxford University Press, 1982), p. 441.

18 HHA to Venetia Stanley, 22 February 1915, cited ed. Brock and Brock, *HHA, Letters to Venetia Stanley*, p. 443.

in 1870. It might be assumed that Oxford remained secure in its Anglican traditions and practice. Contemporary accounts paint a different picture, at least outside the High Church bastions. Another Congregationalist recalls:

> *Supernatural Religion* was read by undergraduates, who scored it and underlined it to show how the old dogmas, the truth of miracles, the infallibility of the Bible, the claims of supernatural revelation were entirely discredited among the thinkers, and those 'true religious leaders of the day', the men of science . . . Thus undergraduates in Hall sneered at the Hebrew mythology, and if any scholar of Balliol or a University prize man was a Christian, or contemplated taking Orders, he was regarded as a freak.[19]

Asquith was asked by George Eliot 'whether the Church has still much hold on the intellectual elite of young Oxford. I replied that it had very little, and that little was on the wane.'[20]

When he arrived at Balliol, the rebuilding of its medieval edifices had been three years in progress. There was a new master of the college. A 'heretic' and 'bogeyman' to Evangelicals and High Churchmen alike, Benjamin Jowett had contributed to the condemned *Essays and Reviews*. For Asquith, he was nothing of the kind, rather 'an extinct volcano, and even a bit of a reactionary'. Asquith shared Jowett's boredom with 'the infinite pettiness of Tractarian controversy' and acknowledged his contribution to Oxford life: 'to let some fresh air into the exhausted atmosphere of the common rooms, and to widen the intellectual horizon of the place'.[21]

Jowett rejoiced that Balliol now welcomed non-Anglicans. He argued for voluntary chapel attendance and modified the liturgy to meet the needs of the age, dropping the Apostles' Creed. Religious practice was to be informed by rational enquiry. Conceiving Balliol as the nursery for Victorian statesmen, civil servants and imperial administrators, Jowett determined

---

19 Robert Forman Horton, *An Autobiography* (London: George Allen & Unwin, 1917), p. 13; ref. Walter Richard Cassels, *Supernatural Religion: An inquiry into the reality of divine revelation* (London: Longmans, Green & Co., 1874).

20 HHA, *Memories and Reflections*, Vol. 1, p. 36.

21 HHA, *Memories and Reflections*, Vol. 1, pp. 14, 15; HHA to Frances Horner, 19 May 1892, private collection.

to formulate an appropriate religion. It required Christian morality, not miracles and mysticism. Drawing inspiration variously from Plato, Saint John, Kant and Hegel, Jowett's thought was not systematic. He retained vestiges of his Evangelical upbringing, a genuine sense of personal friendship with Christ, known through the pages of Scripture. He clung tenaciously to an early morning celebration of Holy Communion each Sunday.

Asquith thought Jowett had ceased to be the 'great formative influence' he once was. As master, he no longer taught undergraduates.[22] His impact, however, remained considerable. Twice each term Jowett preached kindly, paternalistic advice to the college. One of the first sermons Asquith heard at Balliol was an exhortation not to waste time on futile doctrinal disputes, to concentrate rather on moral improvement:

> The question that a young man has really to answer is not 'What is the true doctrine of the Sacrament', but how shall he make the best use of his time, how shall he order his expenses, how shall he control his passions . . . how can he live to God and the truth instead of living to pleasure and to himself?

Former 'religious divisions' were 'ridiculous', to be replaced by practical cooperation. Jowett held that 'men are to be judged not by their opinions but by their lives.'[23]

He argued for the reformulation of religious ideas. Was he also arguing for change to the underlying teachings? He advised his charges they could quietly reject passages of Scripture that did not sit easily with the modern conscience. Placing little emphasis on the Church and sacraments, it is difficult to see how Jowett understood believers effected real contact with Christ. Not all undergraduates were impressed. One conceded the beauty of Jowett's style while savaging the substance: 'It was just Platonism flavoured with a little Christian charity; Christianity is gutted by him: it becomes perfectly meaningless, if it is only an attempt to take some useful moral hints from.'[24] Asquith thought otherwise. Jowett offered a form

22 HHA, *Memories and Reflections*, Vol. 1, p. 18.

23 Benjamin Jowett, *College Sermons* (London: John Murray, 1895), pp. 55, 74–5, 293.

24 Henry Scott Holland, January 1869, cited Peter Hinchcliffe, *Jowett and the Christian Religion* (Oxford: Clarendon Press, 1987), p. 116.

of Christianity very different from his own family's Puritanism. He cited approvingly Jowett's 'horror of one-sidedness', his distaste for 'dogmatic statements' and refined disdain for fanaticism.[25] Asquith took this with him from Oxford, and continued to visit Jowett until his death in 1893.

'Imposing and half-understood phrases'

If Jowett's star was waning it was being replaced by his erstwhile disciple, T. H. Green. Some interpreted a cooling in their relationship as an older man's jealousy of a younger's success. Asquith felt that unfair – Jowett had reason to be 'a little afraid and mistrustful of Green's influence'. Jowett was intellectually eclectic, not caring greatly what position his students adopted provided they brought an enquiring mind and rigorous rationality to the subject. Green was far more systematic, and Jowett feared undergraduates were accepting his advanced views uncritically. Asquith shared that analysis: 'Men swallowed Green's formulas without digesting them, and imagined that they had got the key to the universe, when in fact they had only stored their memories with a collection of imposing and half-understood phrases.'[26]

Both Jowett and Green were influenced by German idealist philosophy and biblical scholarship. A better philosopher, and a significant lay theologian, Green assimilated this more methodically. He rejected any orthodox understanding of the divinity of Christ. Even the historical existence of Christ was less important than the idea he represented. Christ possessed to a supreme degree a consciousness of God that all men have potentially. Green extolled Saint Paul because his faith was independent of Christ's historical existence or any objective reality on the road to Damascus. (He did great violence to the apostle, for whom the reality of Christ, the cross and the resurrection was everything.) Green rejected miracles and ecclesiastical authority, equating doctrinal Christianity with heresy, in that both reduced 'Christianity to a theory'. He taught his students a belief in God 'who lives in our moral life, and for whom we live in living for the brethren'.[27] Asquith

25 HHA to Frances Horner, 19 May 1892, private collection.

26 HHA to Margot Asquith, 10 August 1891, Bodleian, Margot Asquith MS, Eng. c. 6685, f. 45.

27 Ed. R. L. Nettleship, ed., *Works of Thomas Hill Green*, Vol. 3 (London: Longmans Green & Co., 1911), pp. xxxix, 189, 232, 171, 221.

recalled that, for Green, prayer was less a petition made to an objective deity and more about creating a subjective 'mood, a highly spiritualized and sublimated state' within the one praying.[28]

Asquith counted Green 'undoubtedly the greatest personal force in the real life of Oxford'. Writing half a century later, he claimed that he had never 'worshipped at the Temple's inner shrine'. It is difficult, however, to overestimate Green's influence on Asquith. He judged Green's 'lectures on St Paul's Epistles . . . the best I ever heard' and considered his writings 'food fit for the gods'. This 'militant and contagious propaganda' was enormously appealing.[29] Green claimed to reconcile religion and historical criticism. Here was a creed worthy of modern humanity. Green himself displayed an attractive spiritual demeanour, leading a moral and selfless life. It was, however, Christianity without Christ. Asquith left Oxford having, consciously or otherwise, absorbed much of this approach. Then and subsequently he held 'the two greatest thinkers and teachers [to be] Plato and Kant'.[30]

Hampstead Liberal

Elected a fellow of Balliol, Asquith remained in residence for a further year but decided against academic life. Called to the Bar in 1876, he supplemented his income with journalism. From his schooldays, Asquith had spent his holidays with his invalid mother in St Leonards-on-Sea. He dutifully became a member of her Congregational church there in 1867 – but tellingly did not renew his membership.[31] It was in those Congregationalist circles, as an Oxford undergraduate, that he met Helen Melland, the daughter of a wealthy Manchester doctor. They were married at Rusholme Congregational church in 1877. It is unclear how deeply the Congregationalism of the Mellands ran. Asquith noted that his father-in-law by

28 HHA to Margot Asquith, 13 August 1891, Bodleian, Margot Asquith MS, Eng. c. 6685, f. 56.

29 HHA to Frances Horner, 19 May 1892, private collection.

30 HHA, *Memories and Reflections*, Vol. 1, p. 19, 18; HHA to Margot Asquith, 10 August 1891, Bodleian, Margot Asquith MS, Eng. c. 6685, f. 45.

31 Binfield, 'Asquith: The formation of a Prime Minister', p. 242.

the time of his death was virtually an atheist, the minister struggling to explain why he was being accorded a Christian funeral.[32]

The young couple lived conventionally in Hampstead with their five children. With other members of the Hampstead intelligentsia, each Sunday morning the family attended the large Congregational church in Lyndhurst Road designed by Arthur Waterhouse and opened in 1884. It ought to have been the perfect place of worship for Asquith. He was among the 200 members of the congregation who had petitioned R. F. Horton to be their full-time minister. The first Nonconformist fellow at Oxford, Horton sought to recreate collegiate life in north London, forming a church literary society and inviting academics to speak. He preached a social gospel and adopted an increasingly liberal position with respect to biblical criticism and inspiration. Yet Horton 'confessed that he always regarded it as the great failure of his ministerial life that he was not able to hold Mr Asquith faithful to his Congregational traditions'.[33]

Although Asquith conformed outwardly, religion sat lightly with him. His sons Raymond and Herbert erected an altar to Zeus in the garden and offered there a libation of claret, scandalizing their Nonconformist nurse. By contrast, their father found the incident highly amusing.[34] When Asquith returned to the Lyndhurst Road Congregational church in 1901, it was as a Liberal politician rather than a fellow Nonconformist. There was little of the gospel in his address: 'The message of the old Evangelical preacher was, "Save yourself," while the message of his successor is, "Save others" . . . [Asquith approved this new endeavour] to carry to their neighbours the spirit of community and comradeship.'[35]

A successful QC and promising young Liberal politician, he was essentially a practical man of action, not a speculative thinker. A Cabinet colleague recalled: 'There was nothing metaphysical about Asquith . . . His powerful brain operated directly upon questions as they arose before him,

32 HHA to Venetia Asquith, 23 January 1911, cited ed. Mark Bonham Carter and Mark Pottle, *Lantern Slides: The diaries and letters of Violet Bonham Carter, 1904–1914* (London: Weidenfeld & Nicolson, 1996), p. 255.

33 Porritt, *More and More of Memories*, p. 125.

34 Herbert Asquith, *Moments of Memory* (London: Hutchinson & Co., 1937), p. 17.

35 HAA, Address, October 1901, cited Alderson, *Mr Asquith*, p. 214.

and he never seemed to go in search of them.'[36] In this, he enjoyed a fair degree of self-knowledge: 'There are too few nooks and crannies and unexpected hiding places in my nature: it is constructed like an Italian building – regular, rectangular, and not very interesting.'[37] He was no Gothic cathedral, no spires pointing heavenwards, no darkened recesses where the mysterious might dwell.

'My only preacher and priestess'

Asquith's functional approach to life was, however, challenged early in 1891. At a parliamentary dinner he suddenly became aware of, and was strongly attracted to, Margot Tennant, the daughter of a wealthy Scottish industrialist. He wrote frequently to Margot and saw her often. While remaining faithful to Helen, Asquith experienced a passion and an intellectual frisson in his dealings with Margot he had not known with any other woman. Whatever else she might have been, Margot was a person of faith, enjoying a vibrant, personal relationship with Christ, pitying those who lacked her spiritual sense. She expressed herself strongly on the subject of religion, as she did on every other subject. She would not permit Asquith to avoid the question of belief in God.

That question became urgent after Helen's death from typhoid during a family holiday on Arran in September 1891. Three weeks later, Asquith was assuring Margot of his deep and passionate love for her. She admired his noble character but agonized as to the future, weighing the claims of other suitors, balking at the prospect of five young stepchildren. They met frequently and corresponded daily. Part of the attraction was intellectual. Asquith sought to extend Margot's knowledge of literature and the classics. Twelve years his junior, she in turn sought to educate the newly appointed Home Secretary. One year after they first met, Asquith acknowledged:

> You have taught me more than 'all the sages' of the real meaning of life: the proof of which is that I see and understand as I never did

36 Augustine Birrell, *Things Past Redress* (London: Faber & Faber, 1937), pp. 249–50.
37 HHA to Margot Asquith, 14 May 1892, Bodleian, Margot Asquith MS, Eng. c. 6686, f. 46.

> before the key that is given to its secrets by poetry and by religion. Your imagination has swept me up to a higher point of view, and has revealed, if it has not created, for me a new heaven and a new earth.[38]

Quite some confession.

Margot had no inhibitions in speaking of her own spiritual life nor in attempting to create or develop one for Asquith. He professed himself a willing disciple. His response was candid, indicating the competing claims of love for the divine and for the human:

> how sweet and how good you were to me, as you told me what prayer means to you, and tried to teach me to pray. I have striven since to do what you told me, and though I find it hard to pray for myself I can pray every night for you. The thought of you softens and purifies me, and brings me nearer to the presence in which both you and I believe. Theories and dogmas and forms count for little . . . but God, however we try to define or conceive him, remains an enduring foundation of our higher life. You are my only preacher and priestess – the only human being who has power to draw the veil and give me a glimpse of what lies behind.[39]

Asquith's letters to Margot soon carried regular references to a personal faith. He reassured her on a bereavement: 'We feel that God will not destroy what he has created, and that in a real sense it is true that of such is the Kingdom of Heaven.'[40] Again on her mother's death in 1895: 'What can we any of us do but fall back on our old trust in the infinite purposes of God? But for that faith we might well despair.'[41] He learned quickly. By December 1892, Asquith was recognizing the need for external 'modes of worship and visible sacraments'.[42]

38 HHA to Margot Asquith, 8 February 1892, Bodleian, Margot Asquith MS, Eng. c. 6686, f. 4.

39 HHA to Margot Asquith, 28 February 1892, Bodleian, Margot Asquith MS, Eng. c. 6686, ff. 19–20.

40 HHA to Margot Asquith, 10 May 1892, Bodleian, Margot Asquith MS, Eng. c. 6686, f. 43.

41 HHA to Margot Asquith, 19 January 1895, Bodleian, Margot Asquith MS, Eng. c. 6688, f. 9.

42 HHA to Margot Asquith, 23 December 1892, Bodleian, Margot Asquith MS, Eng. c. 6686, f. 175.

Nor were these tentative graspings after faith restricted to a few phrases in private letters. He accompanied Margot to church, most frequently to evensong at St Paul's Cathedral, noted for its preaching and music, but also for its High Church proclivities. Asquith treasured in his pocket book the message Margot had scribbled on an early visit together: 'Be still and know that I am God.'[43] When Margot finally consented to marry him, Asquith, for a while at least, took to attending St Paul's by himself on the Sundays when Margot was out of London – a token of his good intentions.

Was Asquith's conversion sincere or simply a strategy for wooing Margot? Writing to Margot on the day Helen died, his letter is couched in the language of faith: 'So end twenty years of love and fourteen of unclouded union. I was not worthy of it, and God has taken her. Pray for me.'[44] The tone of his letter to Frances Horner was very different:

> it is hard for me, even yet, to believe that so much life and light has been suddenly put out – not to be re-kindled. But so it is, and there is nothing more to be said or done, but to accustom oneself to the darkness and the solitude.[45]

Writing to Frances Horner a year later on the anniversary of Helen's death, however, Asquith's phraseology was that of conventional late Victorian religiosity:

> She was an angel from Heaven, and God took her back from this miry world with unstained feet and an unspotted heart. Her garments did not need to be washed before she took her place in the 'solemn troops and sweet societies' of the saints.[46]

Of course, he sought to please his beloved, but throughout his life Asquith prided himself on his intellectual integrity. He did not hide his doubts and

43 HHA to Margot Asquith, 3 February 1894, Bodleian, Margot Asquith MS, Eng. c. 6687, f. 117.

44 HHA to Margot Asquith, 11 September 1891, Bodleian, Margot Asquith MS, Eng. c. 6685, f. 64.

45 HHA to Frances Horner, 22 September 1891, private collection.

46 HAA to Frances Horner, 11 September 1892, private collection.

difficulties from Margot. The pleasures of life and his studies at Balliol had changed his religious belief and practice, but at no point was he an avowed atheist. Contact with Margot produced, at least for the moment, genuine development, a focusing of vague beliefs in divinity and immortality:

> I am more and more convinced every day that what is revealed to us by imagination and by spirit, which is only another name for spiritual vision, is more real because more permanent and indestructible, than what we see and hear and infer by reason and argument. Once get to that point of view and one is on solid ground. God, the soul, immortality cease to be unprovable and nebulous hypotheses, and life is transfused with the 'light which never was on sea or shore'. As you can see, I am slowly working my way: you must help me both by your counsel and your prayers . . . I swear that I will be true to you and try to be worthy of you by living closer to that which is unseen and eternal.[47]

It remains reminiscent of Green's idealism. At no point in his voluminous correspondence with Margot did Asquith make substantive reference to the person of Jesus Christ.

The couple were married at St George's, Hanover Square, on 10 May 1894, the Bishop of Rochester, Randall Davidson, and Henry Scott Holland of St Paul's Cathedral officiating. Wondering whether she had made a huge mistake, Margot described their wedding night: 'After a little while he knelt down and said his prayers holding my hand near his forehead . . . I prayed not to be too unhappy and thanked God for all he had done for me.'[48]

'The worst thing Asquith had ever done'

Gradually Margot came to appreciate her husband's love for her and even accepted her role as stepmother. She was horrified to discover that the two youngest children, Violet and Cyril, were not baptized:

47 HHA to Margot Asquith, 14 August 1892, Bodleian, Margot Asquith MS, Eng. c. 6686, ff. 83–4.

48 Margot Asquith, Diary, 10 May 1894, Bodleian, Margot Asquith MS, Eng. d. 3199.

> I don't know why Helen Asquith did not have them christened but though I am not very particular I think it is a drawback for children not to be of their parents' church and I wish them to be confirmed and I was going to say buried like other people.[49]

It was easily arranged. Asquith talked it over with Davidson, now Bishop of Winchester. The family went to stay at the episcopal residence at Farnham Castle, and Davidson baptized the children in the Bishop's Chapel there on 2 August 1896.[50] The children's spiritual status was regularized. What of Asquith himself? There is no record of his own baptism. Was he the only twentieth-century Prime Minister – with the exception of the Unitarian, Neville Chamberlain – not to be baptized?

Congregationalists recognized infant baptism but were not consistent in its practice. This seems to have been the case in Asquith's own family. His father and brother were baptized as infants at the Rehoboth Chapel in Morley – but his sisters, including two who died in infancy, appear not to have been. Evidence suggests that Asquith mother's family (and the Mellands) tended towards a more doctrinally liberal Congregationalism (some having Unitarian associations), which would all point to baptism being viewed as less of a priority.[51]

This is pertinent to the question of Asquith's own denominational allegiance. Many years later, Lloyd George expressed himself strongly:

> The worst thing Asquith had ever done had been to join the Church of England . . . He had not joined because of principle but, L.G. could only suspect, because of society. He thought this was one of the meanest things Asquith ever had done and had always held him in contempt for doing it.[52]

---

49 Margot Asquith, Diary, 2 August 1896, Bodleian, Margot Asquith MS, Eng. d. 3201.

50 HHA to Davidson, 28 July 1896, Lambeth Palace Library (LPL), Davidson Papers, 523, ff. 109–10.

51 Information provided by Dr Clyde Binfield.

52 Sylvester, Diary, 30 July 1936, cited ed. Colin Cross, *Life with Lloyd George: The Diary of A. J. Sylvester, 1931–45* (London: Macmillan, 1975), pp. 143–4.

There was no love lost between the two men after Lloyd George ousted Asquith from the premiership, but what truth is there in this statement and the imputed motivation?

Certainly, at an early stage in his relationship with Margot, Asquith ceased attending Nonconformist chapels – unless duty demanded. Instead he went with reasonable regularity to Sunday services in the Church of England. He now mixed in a socially smarter set, whose members were more likely to belong to the Established Church. To attribute Asquith's transfer to the Church of England simply to reasons of social pretension, however, is to do him a disservice. With good taste and emotional reserve, he did not care for extempore worship, uneducated preachers or Puritan mores. He and his family referred to his love of the dignity of the Anglican liturgy. His daughter recalled: 'Afterwards he gravitated to the Anglican Church, the Church of England, which he infinitely preferred. He loved the beauty of the words in the Church of England service.'[53]

Was this simply an informal move to Anglicanism based on personal preference and marriage to Margot? The evidence suggests something more. There was nothing to prevent a Protestant Nonconformist attending Church of England services. Margot, however, specifically mentions both of them receiving Holy Communion at St Paul's Cathedral.[54] This may seem unremarkable today but, in the late nineteenth century, sacramental discipline was taken very seriously. Anglicans did not receive Holy Communion until they were confirmed, and many were not confirmed. Some parson in a remote parish might have turned a blind eye to administer the sacrament to a prominent Liberal politician. However, this is scarcely to be imagined at St Paul's with its High Church tendencies and the likelihood of publicity. It is probable that Asquith himself would wish to observe proprieties; Margot certainly would.

Asquith is unlikely to have received Holy Communion as a Protestant Nonconformist – still less if unbaptized. Again, he had at least one godchild, Henry Tennant, Margot's nephew,[55] and being a godparent

53 Norman St John Stevas, 'Conversation with Lady Violet', *Times Saturday Review*, 15 November 1969.

54 Margot Asquith, Diary, 28 July 1895, 23 February and 2 August 1896, Bodleian, Margot Asquith MS, Eng. d. 3200 and 3201; Margot Asquith to Evelyn Lyttleton, CCAC, Chandos Papers, CHAN I/5/1.

55 HHA to Sylvia Henley, 2 June 1917, Bodleian, Asquith Papers, Eng. 542, f. 896.

presupposed his own baptism. It is possible that the Rehoboth Chapel records are incomplete or that Asquith was baptized elsewhere. That still fails, however, to explain his becoming a communicant at St Paul's.

It may be impossible to prove conclusively, but a more convincing answer is that Asquith was baptized and confirmed as an Anglican later in life. Lloyd George might have been correct in implying that he formally defected from Nonconformity. It is only supposition, but Davidson might well have been involved. Asquith had little regard for him personally, dismissing him subsequently as 'a commonplace man'.[56] As a former royal chaplain, however, Davidson moved easily in society and made himself useful there. A fellow Lowland Scot, he was a house guest of Margot's parents, he married her and Asquith, and took to calling at their home in Cavendish Square. It is natural that she turned to this helpful bishop to have the children discreetly baptized. By 1895, Davidson was sharing with Margot his view that Asquith was destined for the highest political office – no doubt he wished to secure him for the Established Church.[57]

Unsettled on discovering her husband was not baptized, it is entirely possible Margot persuaded him to make good this omission. If this is what occurred, perhaps Asquith was baptized and confirmed in the bishop's private chapel. Asquith himself would have deprecated publicity, keenly aware that Nonconformist voters would have ill-received such a move. In the light of these sensitivities, details may never have been entered in the registers.

Only three people are likely to have known the truth: Davidson, Margot and Asquith himself. Subsequently, Davidson made two ambiguous statements. Writing to Margot after Asquith's death, he recalled 'the baptisms' at Farnham and the talks he had had with Asquith 'about *that*'.[58] Would the baptism of children have necessitated a series of conversations between a bishop and a senior statesman? Was Davidson alluding to Asquith's own baptism? In 1924, Davidson gave a brief synopsis of the religious affiliation of the Prime Ministers he had known. He equivocated

56 HHA to Frances Horner, 28 December 1902, private collection; HHA to Sylvia Henley, 4 August 1915, Bodleian, Asquith MS, Eng. 542, f. 299.

57 Margot Asquith, Diary, 26 June 1895, Bodleian, Margot Asquith MS, Eng. d. 3200.

58 Davidson to Margot Asquith, 15 February 1928, Bodleian, Margot Asquith MS, Eng. d. 3285, f. 31.

when he came to Asquith: 'He believed that Mr Asquith would in a general way describe himself as a member of the Church of England.'[59] Davidson could, and perhaps so intended, be understood either as referring to Asquith's informal transfer of allegiance, or as alluding to his possible reception as an Anglican. On balance the latter is more consistent with Asquith's behaviour. Baptized or not, the Archbishop was under little illusion as to Asquith's level of spiritual zeal, describing him as 'a doubtful Anglican' in later life.[60]

'A marvellous piece of writing'

For almost two decades following his marriage to Margot, Asquith's religious practice was conventional, if not fervent. He said his prayers nightly. He attended church regularly but certainly not every Sunday. He sought dignity and simplicity in the liturgy. It was the sermon and, to a lesser extent, the music that interested him. Good preaching would take him beyond the confines of the Church of England. He went to hear the eclectic Dr Orchard (a Congregationalist who later converted to Catholicism). Despite the lack of scriptural content, Asquith praised Orchard: 'He knows what argument means and talks excellent English.'[61] With Margot he attended Church of Scotland services north of the border, where he found the standard of preaching higher than in the Church of England. Asquith was happy reading the lesson when called on to do so. He led a prayer service at home for the servants after Margot's final miscarriage.

His level of practice fell off with the start of a series of romantic friendships with younger women, beginning with Venetia Stanley in 1912. In 1915 he wrote to another younger female friend, Venetia's sister, Sylvia Henley: 'The womankind have all gone off to morning Church.'[62] Asquith himself remained at home on Sundays, reading and penning letters.

---

59 Davidson, Evidence to the Church Assembly Committee, 29 July 1924, LPL, Bell Papers, 118, f. 25.

60 Davidson, Memorandum, 12 August 1923, LPL, Davidson Papers, 14, f. 220.

61 HHA to Hilda Harrison, 22 December 1919, cited ed. Desmond MacCarthy, *H.H.A., Letters of the Earl of Oxford and Asquith to a Friend: First series, 1915–1922* (London: Geoffrey Bles, 1933), p. 118.

62 HHA to Sylvia Henley, 12 June 1915, Bodleian, Asquith MS, Eng. 542, f. 114.

Rebutting allegations of his supposed atheism, Margot maintained that her husband 'knew and read his Bible'.[63] His Congregational upbringing is evident from the scriptural quotations and allusions in his social correspondence. It was not uncommon for him to read Shakespeare, Boswell's *Life of Johnson* or the Scriptures late into the night. On his final night in Downing Street, Margot found him reading the Bible in bed – it was the crucifixion narrative.[64] The epistles remained an enduring favourite – a legacy of Green's Balliol lectures. He told Hilda Harrison, another young confidante: 'I find a very occasional dose of St Paul interesting and stimulating.'[65] He held Romans 8 to be 'a marvellous piece of writing'.[66] And that is the point – there is little indication in later life that Asquith read Scripture for spiritual guidance or doctrinal truth. Rather, he regarded the King James Bible 'as standing alone among the masterpieces of literature'.[67]

'Provincial prejudice'

Although he might have dropped the precepts and practice of Congregationalism, Asquith retained its prejudices. He maintained a distaste for clergy in general and a loathing of Catholicism in particular. He approved the scriptural 'exploits of Doeg the Edomite – a man after my own heart. He "fell upon the priests" and in a single day "slew fourscore and five persons that did wear a linen ephod (1 Sam. 22)." Almost a record bag.'[68]

Asquith's contact with Roman Catholicism was limited. His prejudice derived from folk memories of the Armada and the fires of Smithfield, the Protestant Englishman's sense of superiority and the reading of anti-Catholic novels, which he devoured 'with greedy Protestant gusto'.[69] He objected to the Blessed Sacrament procession proposed for the 1908 Eucharistic Congress: 'This gang of foreign cardinals taking advantage of

63 Margot Asquith, *More Memories*, p. 156.

64 Margot Asquith, *Off the Record* (London: Frederick Muller, 1943), p. 33.

65 HHA to Hilda Harrison, 11 May 1917, cited ed. MacCarthy, *H.H.A., Letters . . . to a Friend: First series*, p. 21.

66 HHA to Sylvia Henley, 8 August 1915, Bodleian, Asquith MS, Eng. 542, f. 318.

67 HHA, 'The English Bible', Address, 29 March 1911, cited HHA, *Occasional Addresses, 1893–1916* (London: Macmillan & Co., 1918), p. 130.

68 HHA to Hilda Harrison, May 1924, cited HHA, *Memories and Reflections, 1852–1927*, Vol. 2, p. 212.

69 HHA to Sylvia Henley, 20 August 1918, Bodleian, Asquith MS, Eng. 542, ff. 1056–7.

our hospitality to parade their idolatries through the streets of London: a thing without precedent since the days of Bloody Mary.'[70] Lack of personal knowledge may have accounted for his hatred of religious life, 'that foul institution *Monkery*'.[71]

His eldest son, Raymond, had even less time for religion but was bemused by his father's anti-Catholicism. When Asquith made a courtesy call on the Vatican, Raymond wrote to his wife: 'I see that the P.M. has been having a crack at the Pope. I hope he contrived to fight down his provincial prejudice against the Papacy and keep a civil tongue in his head.'[72] The Catholic Church was not greatly disadvantaged by Asquith's antipathy. His daughter-in-law and grandchildren converted in the 1920s. (Today his descendants are committed Catholics with a Catholic chapel in the grounds of their home.) Violet recalled the 'great suffering' their conversion caused her father.[73]

Asquith did not reserve his censure solely for Catholics. He was equally scathing of Judaism: that 'narrow, sterile, tribal creed'. His hope that his views in this respect were 'detached and impersonal'[74] is difficult to sustain. The outburst was provoked by the decision of Venetia Stanley, with whom he was enamoured, to marry his Jewish ministerial colleague, Edwin Montagu, and convert to Judaism.

'Curiously interested in bishops'

Writing immediately after his appointment as Chancellor of the Exchequer, Lavinia Talbot, wife of the Bishop of Southwark, noted that Asquith was 'curiously interested in Bishops and matters ecclesiastical'.[75] For all Asquith's jibes directed against the clerical caste, her observation was correct. It was borne out by Davidson's experience. Asquith endeav-

70 HHA to Lord Crewe, 10 September 1908, cited Roy Jenkins, *Asquith* (London: Collins, 1964), p. 191.

71 HHA to Hilda Harrison, 5 June 1923, cited ed. Desmond MacCarthy, *H.H.A., Letters of the Earl of Oxford and Asquith to a Friend: Second series, 1922–1927* (London: Geoffrey Bles, 1934), p. 118.

72 Raymond Asquith to Katherine Asquith, 3 April 1916, cited John Jolliffe, *Raymond Asquith: Life and letters* (London: Collins, 1980), p. 254.

73 Violet Bonham Carter to Archbishop Michael Ramsey, 9 December 1964, LPL, Ramsey Papers, Vol. 3, f. 177.

74 HHA to Sylvia Henley, 30 May 1915, Bodleian, Asquith MS, Eng. 542, f. 27.

75 Lavinia Talbot to Mary Drew, 11 December 1905, Mary Gladstone Papers, BL, Add. MS 46236, f. 341.

oured 'to look at ecclesiastical appointments from the standard of one who had the best interests of the Church of England at heart. The pains he took in regard to nominations were immense.'[76] In the exercise of this duty, he sought the Archbishop's advice but did not feel constrained to follow it. Instead he might rely on personal contacts and independent enquiries.

Asquith's ecclesiastical appointments surprised some and dismayed many of his own political supporters. They hoped for a continuation of Campbell-Bannerman's policy of preferring Evangelicals. Instead Asquith translated Cosmo Lang to York, Edward Talbot to Winchester and Charles Gore to Oxford – in the eyes of Nonconformists and Low Churchmen, three of the most dangerous members of the bench of bishops. He considered promoting Scott Holland, an object of similar suspicion. By no means were all Asquith's appointments High Churchmen. In 1912 he was responsible, against the wishes of the bishop, for the appointment of the heterodox Hensley Henson as Dean of Durham. Henson's Erastianism recommended itself to Asquith. Both were determined to retain political control over episcopal appointments rather than allow the Church itself to exercise this power.

Above all Asquith sought scholarly bishops, regretting the perceived intellectual decline in the episcopacy in recent years. In retrospect he was pleased with his achievements: 'I was always disposed to favour the great schoolmaster if you could get him . . . I think on the whole we kept a good standard, a very good standard, of scholarship and learning.'[77] Asquith saw the importance of maintaining a balance of churchmanship, but one qualification invariably disposed the Prime Minister towards a candidate: if he could say of him, he 'was at Balliol in my time'.[78]

'Realizing the real self'

So was Asquith an atheist? He was not one of those militant materialists whose opprobrium against the faith was fired by the scientific discoveries

76 Davidson, Evidence to the Church Assembly Committee, 29 July 1924, LPL, Bell Papers, 118, f. 25.

77 HAA, Evidence to the Church Assembly Committee, 6 May 1926, LPL, Bell Papers, 118, f. 62.

78 HHA to Davidson, 15 May 1908, LPL, Davidson Papers, 10, f. 40.

of Charles Darwin and others. Asquith understood and agreed with Balfour's exposure of 'the uncertainty of the supposed certainties of science'.[79] He affirmed this a generation later: 'One may be as sceptical about so-called Science [in this case Huxley's evolutionism] as about so-called Religion.'[80]

Consoling grieving friends and relatives, Asquith asserted the existence of a spiritual nature, which survived death. He wrote to Margot on the death of her mother:

> the starting point of all religion is resignation and trust in God, but it takes and taxes all one's faith to be able to feel in the presence of approaching death that after all, as Wordsworth says, it is but this: 'That man is from God sent forth, Doth yet again to God return?' Nothing is lost – neither life nor love; it flows back to its source, and even the weariest river winds somewhere safe to the sea?[81]

His message to Frances Horner was similar: 'The memories, which are more than memories, of companionship, and of love given and received, have become an indestructible fact of one's own being and are beyond the power of death.'[82] All this, however, is very vague, unconnected to specific religious belief. When Raymond was killed on the Western Front, Asquith experienced none of the consolations of faith, writing bleakly: 'In him and his future I had invested all my stock of hope. That is all gone, and for the moment I feel bankrupt.'[83]

Contemporaries and biographers referred to Asquith's 'Roman' character, comparing him to the great public figures of the Roman Republic. He was held to possess nobility of character, detachment, an impressive intellect – in contrast to the businessmen who followed him, who had profited from the war. G. K. Chesterton wrote on Asquith's departure from office:

---

79 HHA to Frances Horner, 20 November 1891, private collection.

80 HHA to Venetia Stanley, 20 February 1915, cited ed. Brock and Brock, *HHA, Letters to Venetia Stanley*, p. 441.

81 HHA to Margot Asquith, 20 January 1895, Bodleian, Margot Asquith MS, Eng. c. 6688, f. 13.

82 HHA to Frances Horner, 24 June 1898, private collection.

83 HHA to Sylvia Henley, 20 September 1916, Bodleian, Asquith MS, Eng. 542, f. 748.

> I think Mr Asquith will be the last of the true Prime Ministers . . . He represents the older world, notably, for instance, in the fact that he is very much a scholar and is one of a family of scholars. It is that pagan but humane love of learning which has accompanied the English oligarchy since the Renaissance.[84]

Asquith approved Chesterton's analysis. While complimentary, it identified a pre-Christian, or non-Christian, ideal.

That classical ideal of detachment could readily degenerate into aloofness, a purely practical mindset, a supercilious disdain for others, a reliance on self alone. Churchill saw in Asquith a 'sense of a scorn, lightly and not always completely veiled, for arguments, for personalities and even for events which did not conform to the pattern he had with so much knowledge and reflection decidedly adopted'.[85] It is an attitude not easily reconcilable to faith, with its requirement for humility, an openness to the other, a recognition of personal inadequacy. Asquith sought inspiration in the classics rather than the church fathers. His fondness for Edward Gibbon's *History of the Decline and Fall of the Roman Empire* is unsurprising. He cited approvingly the 'irony . . . of a very detached and mocking outsider'[86] that Gibbon employed in his Enlightenment account of the early history of the Church.

In his courtship of Margot, Asquith genuinely sought to rekindle the Christian faith of his childhood. This did not occur in any substantive or permanent form. He confided that he sat 'pretty loosely to some of the orthodox tenets' such as the Trinity.[87] His travels in Palestine in 1924 evoked none of the responses expected from a believer visiting the sites associated with the Incarnation and Redemption. In Nazareth he was captivated not by the 'mythical "objects of interest"' but rather the 'very good-looking'

84 G. K. Chesterton press cutting sent by HHA to Sylvia Henley under cover of his letter of 26 December 1916, 542, f. 815.

85 W. S. Churchill, *Great Contemporaries* (London: Thornton Butterworth, 1937), p. 137.

86 HHA to Hilda Harrison, 5 September 1917, cited ed. MacCarthy, *H.H.A., Letters . . . to a Friend: First series*, p. 30; Edward Gibbon, *The History of the Decline and Fall of the Roman Empire*, 6 vols (London: Strahan & Cadell, 1776–88).

87 HHA to Hilda Harrison, 18 February 1918, cited ed. MacCarthy, *H.H.A., Letters . . . to a Friend: First series*, p. 60.

local women.[88] The Holy Land left Asquith unmoved; it was simply 'an arid, rocky, hummocky, treeless expanse'.[89]

He himself identified the fundamental problem back in the 1890s:

> I do not believe in, and never preach, the doctrine of self-sacrifice in the monkish sense of self-mortification. There is no merit or use, per se, in cutting off the right hand or plucking out the right eye. But (as Green used to teach us) it is (not in sacrificing) but in realizing the real self that true life consists.[90]

Asquith's approach was one of practical humanism. A denial of sacrifice, suffering voluntarily accepted and the cross was effectively a rejection of Christ and Christianity.

Margot maintained that her husband 'believed that we were put into this world for a purpose'.[91] He probably entertained some vague belief in a Creator, a Supreme Being or Mind. This, however, had no relation to the Christian belief in the definitive revelation of God in Jesus Christ. Asquith valued Christianity as a formative influence on Western civilization, the source of some useful moral teaching – but it went little further. He noted that 'the mass of mankind' conceived of God in anthropomorphic terms:

> They pray because God is to them a Judge who can be asked for mercy – a King who can be petitioned for favours (special providences, etc.) – a Father whose heart can be touched by entreaties and who can be persuaded and (as it were) coaxed into indulgence.[92]

88 HHA to Hilda Harrison, 1 December 1924, cited HHA, *Memories and Reflections*, Vol. 2, p. 112.

89 HHA to Hilda Harrison, 26 November 1924, cited HHA, *Memories and Reflections*, Vol. 2, p. 219.

90 HHA to Margot Asquith, 22 May 1891, Bodleian, Margot Asquith MS, Eng. c. 6685, f. 20.

91 Margot Asquith, *More Memories*, p. 156n.

92 HHA to Margot Asquith, 13 August 1891, Bodleian, Margot Asquith MS, Eng, c. 6685, ff. 55–6.

Christians may nuance that a little but, yes, they do believe in a personal God who has been revealed as a Judge, King and Father. The implication is that Asquith did not share their belief.

Uncertainty as to ultimate realities never concerned Asquith. His son recalled:

> I rarely heard him discuss a problem of philosophy. During these later years I remember one occasion when the conversation suddenly turned to the subject of psychical research and the value of the evidence it had supplied on the question of the survival of the soul: he seemed to listen with interest, but he did not take much part in the discussion, and at the end of it he suddenly lifted his head and said that he thought we were 'not meant to know' what happened on the other side of death.[93]

Asquith discouraged conjecture as to his interior life: 'My own opinions on these high matters have never been more than those of an interested amateur, and are of no importance to anyone but myself.'[94]

And yet, in dying, we often return to earlier beliefs and associations. In the weeks before his death on 15 February 1928, Asquith slipped in and out of consciousness. At one moment he turned to Margot and said:

> 'They have come to take me away from you . . . you are Margot Tennant and you won't let them take me', and broke a long silence by saying:
>
> 'Kneel down beside me . . . do you see all those people kneeling on the open road? . . . they are on their way to Calvary. Look at the crowd! – they are all praying.'[95]

He was buried, as he wished, with great simplicity in the village churchyard at Sutton Courtenay.

93 Herbert Asquith, *Moments of Memory*, p. 376.
94 HHA, *Memories and Reflections*, Vol. 1, p. 19.
95 Margot Asquith, *More Memories*, pp. 271–2.

David Lloyd George (1916–1922)

'The Welsh Wizard'

David George[1] was born in Manchester on 17 January 1863. He was educated at Llanystumdwy National School.

As a young solicitor, Lloyd George narrowly won the constituency of Caernarvon Boroughs for the Liberals at a by-election in 1890. He held the seat continuously until 1945, when he was created Earl Lloyd George.

A quick-thinking and witty speaker, Lloyd George established a reputation as a radical espousing Welsh separatism and social reform. His opposition to the Boer War earned him extreme opprobrium at the time. Nevertheless, Campbell-Bannerman appointed him President of the Board of Trade in 1905. His energy and efficiency, his capacity for settling industrial disputes, gained him the respect of employers and employees alike. When Asquith became Prime Minister in 1908, Lloyd George succeeded him as Chancellor of the Exchequer. His controversial 'People's Budget' in 1909 sought to redistribute wealth, taxing the rich to pay for old-age pensions. The budget passed only after two general elections and the curtailing of the Lords' veto. Lloyd George continued to legislate for social reform, including National Insurance, providing for the payment of workers during periods of ill health.

Prior to the declaration of hostilities, Lloyd George opposed Britain's entry into the First World War. But from the moment Germany invaded Belgium, his support for the war effort was unwavering. Following an outcry against ammunitions shortages, Lloyd George was made Minister for Munitions in the 1915 coalition government, and then succeeded Earl Kitchener as Secretary of State for War in 1916. He presided over a

1 'Lloyd' was added to his surname as a mark of respect to his maternal uncle, Richard Lloyd, who helped raise the young family after their father's premature death.

massive increase in the production of shells and was a leading voice calling for the introduction of military conscription. Mounting dissatisfaction with Asquith's leadership led to his resignation, and Lloyd George became Prime Minister of a Unionist-dominated coalition on 6 December 1916. He increased military cooperation with the French and gave the Dominions a role in the direction of the war, but struggled to assert political control over the generals. His energy, organization and optimism helped boost national morale.

Lloyd George capitalized on the Allied victory by calling a general election on 14 December 1918 – the first in which (some) women could vote. Coalition candidates were awarded a 'coupon' as evidence of their endorsement by Lloyd George's government, their opponents denounced as unpatriotic. The result was an overwhelming Coalition victory at the expense of the Asquithian Liberals, but the post-war economic downturn severely curtailed funding for further social reforms. Unionist backbenchers grew restless as Lloyd George granted independence to the Irish Free State, profited from the sale of honours and threatened war with Turkey. They voted to fight the next election as a separate party from the Coalition Liberals and Lloyd George resigned as Prime Minister on 19 October 1922. The Unionists went on to win the subsequent general election.

His opponents feared Lloyd George as a potent political force throughout the 1920s and 1930s. Lacking, however, significant parliamentary backing, and with the Liberals divided, his anticipated return to power never materialized. He served as leader of the Liberal Party between 1926 and 1931 but illness prevented his involvement in the formation of the National government. He died on 26 March 1945.

* * *

A Bible-thumping pagan?

During his lifetime and subsequently, Lloyd George aroused intense and conflicting reactions. He was a man of tremendous energy and ability, as well as immense charm. To some he was 'the man who won the war', who laid the foundations of the welfare state on which the government of Clement Attlee built 40 years later. To others he was simply an unprincipled opportunist, financially and sexually immoral, responsible for the destruction of his own party and the corruption of public life. Where does religious faith sit in all this?

Teasing out the truth concerning personal faith is complex for most politicians but especially so for Lloyd George. David Daniel, secretary of the local quarrymen's union and a close friend from the 1880s, recognized the conundrum future biographers would face: 'There will doubtless come a day that will see much dispute as to what in fact was the religious belief of the man who came from the Nonconformist cottage to be one of Britain's leading statesmen.'[2] In public, Lloyd George appeared the devout Nonconformist. In private, he expressed himself more freely but there remained inconsistencies and puzzles. His brother and his nephew acknowledged his doubts and difficulties but maintained he was a deeply religious man and strongly rejected claims he lacked a sense of the transcendental.[3] Lloyd George's own children were divided on the subject. To his daughter, Olwen, he was unquestionably a sincere, if understated, believer. His elder son, Richard, thought him 'one of the greatest Bible-thumping pagans of his generation'.[4] Admittedly, Richard had a tempestuous relationship with his father, but others shared his analysis, viewing any display of religiosity as politically motivated and bordering on the fraudulent. Starting with the facts of his early life, is it possible to say anything meaningful concerning Lloyd George's mature religious convictions?

His birth in England was the consequence of the temporary appointment of his father, William George, to a school in Manchester. No one, however, disputed Lloyd George's Welsh identity. The family returned to Wales when he was just a few weeks old. His father was a teacher who came from Pembrokeshire farming stock. The Georges were orthodox Baptists. Lloyd George's biographers imply that his father was a freethinker,

2 D. R. Daniel, 'D. Lloyd George: Chancellor of the Exchequer' (1908), NLW, D. R. Daniel Papers, 2,912, f. 8.

3 W. R. P. George, *The Making of Lloyd George* (London: Faber & Faber, 1976), p. 109; cf. John Grigg, *The Young Lloyd George* (London: Eyre Methuen, 1973), pp. 33–5.

4 Olwen Carey-Evans, *Lloyd George was My Father: The autobiography of Lady Olwen Carey-Evans* (Llandysui: Gomer Press, 1985), pp. 70–1; Richard Lloyd George, *Lloyd George* (London: Frederick Muller, 1960), p. 10.

influenced by rationalists, socialists and the Unitarian, James Martineau.[5] William himself admitted as much, but also declared his return to a more orthodox stance:

> Your opinion of the value of the Bible as a religious textbook appears to be lower than mine now is. I was at one time prejudiced against it by the writings of the Socialists and controversies etc, with which I now have little sympathy indeed. I . . . am getting back into the old opinion that as a source of instruction on the spiritual nature and destiny of man, there is no book in the world to be compared to it.[6]

Whether or not he held to Trinitarian theology and the divinity of Christ, he commended the Lord Jesus to his pupils as the exemplar of the injunction to do good.[7]

William George's religious beliefs were, however, largely irrelevant to his son. He died when Lloyd George was less than 18 months old. Far more momentous was the decision of his mother, Elizabeth, to return to the home of her mother and bachelor brother, Richard Lloyd, at Llanystumdwy in Caernarvonshire. This was to ensure that Lloyd George was raised in the most intensely religious environment of any twentieth-century Prime Minister.

A 'strange little sect'

The Lloyds considered themselves part of the wider Baptist denominational grouping. They belonged, however, to a 'strange little sect' known variously as the Disciples of Christ, the Church of Christ or Campbellites, founded by Alexander Campbell, a Scots emigrant to the USA. Lloyd George summarized its position: 'It has no paid preachers and no dogma. Its members take the Bible as it stands, and everyone is entitled to

5 Grigg, *The Young LG*, p. 25; ed. Kenneth O. Morgan, *Lloyd George Family Letters, 1885–1936* (Oxford: Oxford University Press, 1973), p. 7.

6 William George to unknown schoolmaster, *c.*1859, cited W. R. P. George, *The Making of LG*, p. 55.

7 William George, Farewell address to Pwllheli school, 1861, cited W. R. P. George, *The Making of LG*, p. 58.

interpret it for himself.'[8] They permitted themselves no ritual other than that found in the New Testament; practised baptism and administered, with great simplicity, Holy Communion every Sunday. In later life, Lloyd George was rather vague as to the detail. In fact candidates had to confess their belief in God, the Father, Son and Holy Spirit, and declare their willingness to follow Jesus throughout their life before being baptized by immersion and admitted to membership of the church.[9] Although numerically significant in the USA, there were only a tiny number of Disciples of Christ in Wales. The Lloyds were proudly conscious of their minority status in an area dominated by Calvinistic Methodism.

Wales, especially North Wales, was overwhelmingly Nonconformist. The privileges of the Established Church were deeply resented, especially the fact that many Nonconformist parents were compelled to educate their children in Anglican schools. Between 1866 and 1878, Lloyd George attended Llanystumdwy National (Anglican) School. Although fewer than 20 per cent of the pupils were Anglican, the school day opened and closed with prayers from the Book of Common Prayer and the children were taught the Anglican Catechism.

For Lloyd George, it was an injustice demanding redress, and at the age of eleven he commenced his career as a champion of radical causes against oppressive authority. Each year, as the headmaster brought the rector, inspectors and neighbouring gentry into the classroom, the older children stood to recite the creed. This year, at Lloyd George's instigation, the visiting party was greeted by sullen silence. The headmaster implored his charges to comply with his request, but for the moment there was a standoff. Eventually, feeling sorry for the headmaster, the boycott was broken – by his younger brother, William, to whom Lloyd George subsequently administered a thrashing for his lack of solidarity. The point, however, had been made. There were no repercussions for Lloyd George himself; recitation of the creed was omitted in future years. Nor was he punished for playing truant on those feast days when the school was marched into the Anglican parish church.[10]

8 LG, August 1918, cited Lord Riddell, *War Diary, 1914–1918* (London: Ivor Nicholson & Watson, 1933), p. 350.

9 William George, *My Brother and I* (London: Eyre & Spottiswoode, 1958), p. 74.

10 William George, *My Brother and I*, p. 42; Grigg, *The Young LG*, p. 35.

In fact there is little evidence that authority was unduly oppressive at Llanystumdwy National School. Lloyd George received a good education. The headmaster wanted both him and William to remain as pupil teachers – a path to educational and social advancement at a time when opportunities were limited. This, however, would require their conformity to Anglicanism. Visiting the family to argue the case, the rector offered to relax the conditions. He thought 'it would be quite sufficient if [Lloyd George] went to Church *once* on Sunday' but failed to appreciate the strength of Nonconformist feeling. The family summarily dismissed the offer. Years later Lloyd George mused how different his life might have been had his uncle accepted: 'I might have become a respectable curate by this time – who knows?' The brothers did, however, act as voluntary pupil teachers on various occasions – and thoroughly enjoyed the privilege.[11]

'Uncle Lloyd'

The future Prime Minister's knowledge of Scripture was supplemented by lessons from his 'beloved patron',[12] 'Uncle Lloyd'. Over a long life, Richard Lloyd held faithfully to the tenets of the Disciples of Christ. An unpaid minister preaching every Sunday at the Penymaes Chapel one and a half miles from their home, he supported himself, his mother and his sister's family as a self-employed cobbler. Uncle Lloyd seems to have been eminently sensible, well able to account for his faith. Challenged by William that the family's frequent chapelgoing seemed more akin to Old Testament legalism than the freedom of the gospel, he had no difficulty dismissing his nephew's argument:

> I am afraid that you have quite a wrong idea as to the meaning of the freedom which all who are in Christ enjoy. It does not mean freedom to do what you like. Our freedom in that sense is far less than that of the man of the world or of the Jew in olden times. The Christian's daily prayer is that not his own but that God's will be done on earth

11 William George, *My Brother and I*, p. 50; Frances Stevenson, Diary, 15 May 1926, cited ed. A. J. P. Taylor, *Lloyd George: A diary by Frances Stevenson* (London: Hutchinson & Co., 1971).

12 Daniel, 'D. LG', NLW, D. R. Daniel Papers, 2,912, f. 25.

> as it is in heaven. The difference between the Jew and the Christian on this point is that the Jewish code was part of the law of the land, and liable to be enforced accordingly, whilst obedience under the Christian dispensation is purely voluntary, enforceable only by such sanctions as are embodied in the Law of God.

A man of deep prayer, a teetotaller and a non-smoker, Richard Lloyd was 'calm and optimistic', living 'a perfectly normal life', never making 'a parade of his religion'.[13]

Richard Lloyd kept himself abreast of current theological thought. The German rationalists' assertion of the superiority of human reason to Scripture he compared to the attempt to hold a candle to the sun,[14] but generally he avoided controversy in preaching. Rather he spoke, often for the better part of an hour, on the Scriptures themselves, especially the New Testament and the Psalms, and their practical application to his congregation's lives. He began calmly and quietly, building up to an ecstatic climax, carrying his audience on a flood of emotion. The 17-year-old Lloyd George summarized one such sermon:

> there were the most startling hits, and the peroration swept everything before. The audience feelings drowned in tears . . . He asked outsiders not to go to hell if it was only for the sake of those who are already there, as it added to the misfortunes (if possible) of the unhappy wretches, and he quoted Dives' infernal ejaculation 'Tell my brothers not to come here.' Then to crown all he said 'We are going to the everlasting rest, come with us.'[15]

The preaching was powerful, but in their personal relations Lloyd George did not recall 'his uncle ever talking to him about religion with a view to influencing him'.[16]

13 William George, *My Brother and I*, pp. 33–4.

14 LG, Diary, 7 January 1883, NLW, Lloyd George Papers, MS 4, ff. 3–4.

15 LG, Diary, 12 December 1880, NLW, LG Papers, MS 4, f. 46.

16 A. J. Sylvester, Diary, 4 April 1932, cited ed. Colin Cross, *Life with Lloyd George: The diary of A. J. Sylvester, 1931–45* (London: Macmillan, 1975), p. 74.

‘I was in hell’

Lloyd George was baptized by his uncle on 7 February 1875. The baptism was by immersion in the stream running beside Penymaes Chapel.[17] A few years later Lloyd George scandalized his co-religionists, denying baptism as necessary, or indeed even desirable, for eternal life. Like Balfour, he believed that humanity had progressed in spiritual matters; there was nothing immutable about ‘the Christian ordinances’. Whatever the effect baptism had at the time instituted by Christ, it did not have the same effect ‘in this country and this age’. For Lloyd George, ‘principles only were eternal’ – giving no indication as to what those principles were nor how they might be determined.[18]

Was this scepticism a reaction against his adolescent experience of chapel or the result of a questioning mind fed by rationalist literature? The evidence suggests both, but also the consequence of an event occurring far earlier in Lloyd George’s life – the source of some controversy. Lloyd George spoke later to intimate friends about his recollection of the complete loss of his faith as a child. It was a traumatic experience. Yet one biographer, B. B. Gilbert, disputes whether such an event ever occurred. He cites inconsistencies in the accounts and the lack of any reference in Lloyd George’s diary to any ‘agony of the soul, or . . . any detestation of religious services’. Gilbert implies that Lloyd George was less concerned to give a factually accurate account of his early life than he was to impress others, giving free rein to ‘his general tendency for self-dramatization’.[19]

Revisiting the evidence, it is difficult to conclude that Lloyd George invented a spiritually significant and dark experience in his early life. He recounted it on several occasions to Frances Stevenson (his secretary, mistress and subsequently second wife), to Charlie Masterman (a fellow Liberal politician) and ‘many times’ to David Daniel. Those accounts are remarkably consistent. In all of them, Lloyd George experienced this

---

17 Sylvester, Diary, 18 January 1945, cited ed. Cross, *Life with LG*, p. 337.

18 LG, Diary, 30 May 1886, NLW, LG Papers, MS 6, f. 66; 16 December 1883, NLW, LG Papers, MS 4, f. 176; 13 July 1884, NLW, LG Papers, MS 5, f. 78.

19 B. B. Gilbert, *Lloyd George: A political life – the architect of change, 1863–1912* (Columbus, OH: Ohio State University Press, 1987), p. 36.

phenomenon at the age of eleven. (Daniel also states that Lloyd was eleven, but has it occurring on the night of his baptism, when Lloyd George was already twelve.) All except one have Lloyd George in bed at night. Frances Stevenson's autobiography written in old age has Lloyd George on the road, 'walking to chapel from Llanystumdwy to Criccieth'. Her earlier diary entries, however, agree with the other accounts.

What happened? Masterman's description is essentially the same as the others:

> At the age of eleven he woke up one night and as he lay awake he realized in a sudden flash that he did not believe one word of all the religion that was being taught to him either in church or chapel, that he regarded it all as fiction. It had not been produced by any special reading but by the sudden breaking of something in his brain.

Daniel has Lloyd George reflecting on his baptism earlier that day:

> He was musing on what he had done and professed, his eyes looking into the darkness, when he saw the whole heaven of his earlier religious instruction and imagination being shut in front of him like the covers of a book, everything disappearing in a flash. The image he used was that of a building collapsing in a heap, leaving a pile of messy ruins before his mind's eye. He sat up in his bed at dead of night and testified with his tongue and with the words 'Nothing of the sort exists, everything taught me and which I professed are baseless imaginings. God and everything I was taught about him is a dream.'

The effect on a child from a devoutly religious home can only be imagined. Lloyd George confided to Masterman: 'From that time on, I was in hell. I saw no way out!' He told Frances Stevenson:

> He was in mental distress on the subject of religion – he felt like a man who had suddenly been struck blind, and is groping for the way but can find no support . . . the thought was horrible to him that the universe should be under no direction, with no purpose, no supreme control.

It took three years to summon up the courage to raise the matter with his uncle, who to his surprise expressed neither shock nor anger but 'seemed to understand perfectly well'. In the Masterman account, Uncle Lloyd simply told his nephew 'he would come back to it all again. And so I have, Ll. G. said, in a sort of a way.'[20]

Gilbert is correct that Lloyd George's diary contains no reference to these events. That diary, however, only commenced three years later. It was a contemporary record of his daily life in which he was not given to retrospective reflection. But he is incorrect in asserting that the diary provides no evidence of Lloyd George's dissatisfaction with religious services – there is evidence in plenty. Over a decade, Lloyd George recorded his religious practice and thought.

'The way to the heart'

Chapelgoing was central to the life of the Lloyd home in Llanystumdwy. Lloyd George attended three times on a Sunday: for a service at midday, another in the early evening and also for Sunday school. He was in chapel again on Wednesday evenings for prayer and hymn-singing. Nor was he there just as an observer – the young Lloyd George was called on to read from Scripture, lead the hymns, play the organ and teach at Sunday school.

He had no sacramental understanding of the Christian faith and dismissed the practice of his own sect: 'Then comes that ceremony they call the sacrament or the breaking of bread or what you will. This imposing farce having been gone through or dragged through by John Davies we sang an anthem and filed out.'[21] His sole criterion for a religious service was the quality of the preaching; this was determined by the preacher's oratorical skills rather than the doctrinal content.[22] His uncle always scored highly in this respect but Lloyd George could be very critical of others.

20 Stevenson, Diary, 22 November 1915 and 31 October 1934, cited ed. Taylor, *LG*, pp. 77, 286; Frances Lloyd George, *The Years that are Past* (London: Hutchinson, 1967), p. 19; Lucy Masterman, *C. F. G. Masterman: A biography* (London: Nicholson & Watson, 1939); Daniel, 'D. LG', NLW, D. R. Daniel Papers, 2,912, ff. 8–10.

21 LG, Diary, 8 May 1881, NLW, LG Papers, MS 3, f. 15.

22 Daniel, 'D. LG', NLW, D. R. Daniel Papers, 2,912, f. 19.

Curiously, given that his intellectual appreciation of the faith was developing along entirely rationalistic lines, he expected religion to satisfy his emotional needs. He was susceptible to the various revivalist movements that periodically swept the chapels of North Wales and described one scene of 'ecstasy': 'Women screaming, men shouting ['Hallelujah'] etc., etc. Standing on their feet, great part of the audience and the preacher vociferating might and main – an exciting but (query) edifying scene.'[23] And he returned for more:

> Much the same as when I heard him before – a mixture of nonsense and striking refined comment bordering upon eloquence – he is quite a study. His influence upon the people is quite inexplicable. In fact a hardened sinner like me not much addicted to wringing my hands over my sins – I feel an occasional electric shock running through my constitution . . . The secret of the man's success is this: he has found the way to the heart.[24]

His tragedy is he never effected a synthesis of heart and mind in his spiritual quest.

Given the prominence of preaching in Welsh society and his veneration for his uncle, it is not surprising that Lloyd George considered becoming a preacher:

> As a boy, I admired and revered the great preachers; I was never tired of listening to them. But the difficulty was that in our sect you could not become a preacher unless you were able to support yourself by your private means or earnings. The preachers in the sect are not allowed to make any charge for their services. Consequently, as I had to earn my living, I was unable to fulfil my ambition. Otherwise who knows? I might have become one of the leading preachers of the day![25]

23 LG, Diary, 21 April 1883, NLW, LG Papers, MS 4, f. 58; the '(query)' is LG's.

24 LG, Diary, 1 September 1883, NLW, LG Papers, MS 4, f. 124.

25 LG quoted in Riddell, Diary, August 1918, cited Riddell, *War Diary*, p. 350.

His rhetorical gifts were to be employed for the benefit of the courtroom and the House of Commons rather than the chapel.

His uncle encouraged Lloyd George's ambition, suggesting they might lead the services at the Penymaes Chapel on alternate Sundays.[26] The offer did not appeal to his nephew but he did take to the pulpit occasionally, most notably joining John Roberts, a lay preacher, in leading a mission to Penmachno in 1882–3. Preaching a simplified and perhaps not entirely orthodox Christianity, he explained his motivation to a benefactress:

> As one of many of us, who have taken an oath before heaven and earth, to be a good soldier of Him, who died for us, I could not rest from doing my part without betraying my trust . . . It is very selfish and unworthy of a kind man to be content to inherit life eternal for himself, while allowing others he knows to drown in death . . . I believe – rather I hope – I would feel happy, not miserable, when I'm subjected to contempt because I'm given an opportunity to do some small work for Jesus.[27]

Lloyd George enjoyed success but was not comfortable in the role.

On another occasion, having addressed a weekday evening congregation, he wrote:

> I was much praised afterwards that the matter was excellent and the delivery more natural than ever. But I really cannot speak effectively in chapel – the subjects I must necessarily speak on are not those upon which I feel deeply and earnestly, and you are ashamed somehow at appearing so awfully good.[28]

Fear of the charge of hypocrisy hung heavily over him. When he spoke in chapel in those early days he tended to restrict himself to the social concerns of Nonconformity, such as temperance, education and disestablishment of the Anglican Church.

26 LG, Diary, 30 December 1885, NLW, LG Papers, MS 5a, f. 122.
27 LG to Sydney Roberts, Summer 1883, cited W. R. P. George, *The Making of LG*, pp. 107–8.
28 LG, Diary, 2 July 1884, NLW, LG Papers, MS 5, f. 75.

'So full of boredom'

Lloyd George most resented the Sunday-school attendance required of adults as well as children. He was contemptuous of teachers unable to answer his questions and had no hesitation in disparaging them before the class – the presence of the young, combative lawyer was a considerable trial for them. He pursued his points ruthlessly: the contradictions he found between various passages of Scripture, his refusal to believe that God could use suffering as a means of conversion and sanctification.[29] A major confrontation concerned the efficacy of prayer:

> I maintaining boldly that the notion that it had any effect in changing the predetermined schemes of the Almighty was a thorough absurdity. This was my argument: God is all wise – he knows what is best for us. God is all good – he will do what is best for us. If he changes his schemes at our dictation and petition he is wrong and erratic either in intention or consummation.

No one was able to explain that, being eternal, God was not *subsequently* changing his mind in response to human prayer. Rather, teacher and class 'were all dumbfounded' by Lloyd George's arguments.[30] He found teaching only marginally less irritating than being a pupil.[31] After introducing 'rank heterodoxy' and Unitarianism, little more is heard of his involvement with the Sunday school.[32]

Much as Asquith's had been, Lloyd George's views on eternity were coloured by his childhood experience of chapelgoing:

> When I was a boy, the thought of Heaven used to frighten me more than the thought of Hell. I pictured Heaven as a place where there would be perpetual Sundays with perpetual services, from which there would be no escape, as the Almighty assisted by the cohorts

29 LG, Diary, 30 March and 6 April 1884, NLW, LG Papers, MS 5, ff. 35, 39; LG, Diary, 9 and 16 November 1884, NLW, LG Papers, MS 5, ff. 124, 126.

30 LG, Diary, 31 August 1884, NLW, LG Papers, MS 5, f. 98.

31 LG, Diary, 13 May 1883, NLW, LG Papers, MS 4, f. 69.

32 LG, Diary, 26 July 1885, NLW, LG Papers, MS 5a, f. 154.

> of angels, would always be on the look-out for those who did not attend. The conventional Heaven with its angels perpetually singing, etc., nearly drove me mad in my youth and made me an atheist for ten years.[33]

The two premiers were probably not alone in this respect.

Lloyd George told Frances Stevenson that religion had made his childhood 'so hard to bear and so full of boredom. He could not feel that he had a part in it, and yet he was unable to get away from it.'[34] There were times when only the walk to and from chapel relieved the terrible tedium of his adolescent Sundays.[35] He maintained that communing outdoors with the God of nature alone constituted true worship. A Sunday walk through the Welsh country convinced him 'of the scandalous waste of opportunities involved in a chapel-huddling religion of pseudos – the calm and beauty of the scenery breathed far more divinity than all the psalmodies and prayers of a million congregated churches.'[36] He shared his anguish with his brother:

> Felt miserable in Chapel. Can't stand this sort of nonsense much longer. After Chapel walk with [William] discussing these religious difficulties. [William] inclined to concur in many points. His ambition appears to be to become a moral reformer, mine to be a social reformer.[37]

While sympathizing with his brother's plight, William went on to become a conventional Baptist lay preacher.

'Challenging his Creator'

Lloyd George's antipathy to organized religion is well documented. As his brother and nephew were quick to point out, this was not the entire story.

33 LG quoted in Riddell, Diary, 3 September 1919, cited Lord Riddell, *Lord Riddell's Intimate Diary of the Peace Conference and After, 1918–1923* (London: Victor Gollancz, 1933), pp. 122–3.

34 Stevenson, Diary, 22 November 1915, cited ed. Taylor, *LG*, p. 77.

35 Stevenson, Diary, 19 July 1934, cited ed. Taylor, *LG*, p. 276.

36 LG, Diary, 12 October 1884, NLW, LG Papers, MS 5, f. 114.

37 LG, Diary, 27 September 1886, NLW, LG Papers, MS 6, f. 118.

His involvement in the Penmachno mission was voluntary and sincere. At the same time, aged 19, he composed 'an imaginary epistle to the Welsh churches stimulating them to greater activity'. To his uncle's immense pride, it was published in the *Christian Advocate.*[38] This was not the work of a sceptic:

> There are two great armies in the world engaged in mortal combat – the army of the Lord and that of the Prince of Darkness. Every Christian is a recruiting sergeant in his Master's service. What progress are we making as regards recruiting in Wales?[39]

In October 1882, in a similar vein, he began an essay, *Amcan Bywyd* ('The Purpose of Life'), which he delivered to the Porthmadog Debating Society. He condemned atheism's 'mistaken attitude concerning the true purpose of life', arguing that humanity's purpose is to glorify the Creator:

> by going about doing good, by diminishing man's misery in every respect and by promoting his happiness. In this respect Jesus Christ is the *great model.* He consecrated his life on earth to do the will of his Father in heaven.[40]

How are such fervent assertions and his preaching a mission to be reconciled with Lloyd George's insistence on his complete loss of faith several years earlier and his denunciation of the reality of Welsh Nonconformity? Faith is seldom a constant over the lifetime of a believer. At any given time, an individual's attitudes and actions may be inconsistent when measured both internally and against the standard of doctrinal Christian orthodoxy. Within the space of a week, Lloyd George was able to write both of his willingness to resist the devil – 'Thanks to omnipotent love, there is yet another who is far more winsome and attractive, and he may

38 LG, Diary, 1 September 1882, NLW, LG Papers, MS 3, f. 133; LG, Diary, 25 February 1883, NLW, LG Papers, MS 4, f. 30.

39 LG, Epistle, cited George, *My Brother and I*, p. 6.

40 LG, *Amcan Bywyd*, cited W. R. P. George, *The Making of LG*, p. 109.

yet lead me' – and tentatively condemn 'this impostorship (???) Christianity'.[41] Clearly, he was in the throes of an interior spiritual conflict.

Speaking of his loss of faith at the age of eleven, Lloyd George clarified that, in an absolute sense, this loss was not permanent. In *Amcam Bywyd* he wrote:

> By challenging his Creator, when he is young, a man does not perhaps suffer any pangs of conscience; but when he grows older he starts to suffer from the damage he has done to his spirit. He has deeply wounded his spiritual personality and the signs of ill health manifest themselves.[42]

Would it be wrong to detect an autobiographical overtone here? Is he describing his own return to some form of faith?

Gilbert claims that 'there was little inquiry or reflection'.[43] Lloyd George's diary demonstrates ample evidence of inquiry and reflection in his late teens and early twenties. He was reading avidly. At the age of 17 he was rescued from the abyss of unbelief by Thomas Carlyle's *Sartor Resartus.*[44] In obscure fashion, told through the analogy of a philosophy of clothes, Carlyle recounts the quest for spiritual truths. Lloyd George 'felt strengthened in his mind, for the purpose of things had been revealed to him to some extent, and his vision was cleared'.[45] He was so taken by *Sartor Resartus* that he gave William a copy for his birthday.[46] Although couched in the language of faith, the book was anything but a defence of traditional Christianity. Lloyd George was struck by the sentence: 'Let us take these outworn vestments to bind the sore and bleeding wounds of humanity.'[47] He could breathe more easily, retaining, he supposed, a belief in the transcendent without being burdened by miracles, the supernatural

---

41 LG, Diary, 5 and 9 February 1883, NLW, LG Papers, MS 4, ff. 20, 23; the triple question marks are LG's.

42 LG, *Amcan Bywyd*, cited W. R. P. George, *The Making of LG*, p. 109.

43 Gilbert, *LG: A political life*, p. 37.

44 Thomas Carlyle, *Sartor Resartus* (Oxford: Oxford University Press, 2008; first published 1833–4).

45 Stevenson, Diary, 22 November 1915, cited ed. Taylor, *LG*, p. 77.

46 LG, Diary, 23 February 1881, NLW, LG Papers, MS 3, f. 6.

47 Masterman, *C. F. G. Masterman*, p. 209.

and corporate worship. But it was a human construct. Doctrine was replaced by social action. *Amcan Bywyd* betrays his debt to Carlyle. For Lloyd George, Christ is not the divine Saviour and Redeemer, but rather 'the *great model*' encouraging us to relieve human suffering.

Other works encouraged him in the same direction. Like Balfour and James Ramsay MacDonald, he read and discussed Ernest Renan's *Life of Jesus*.[48] This 'too gave him consolation and peace of mind, for he was able to see things from a broader point of view'. That the author was an atheist was of less interest to Lloyd George than that Renan portrayed Christ as 'a living being, a hero, a perfect man'.[49] Among his reading material are other books by Carlyle, F. W. Farrar's *Early Days of Christianity*[50] and even the Qur'an. Lloyd George was emboldened to articulate his thoughts, 'asserting my latitudinarianism and rationalism in society of my religious friends'.[51] In Sunday school he rejected the Baptist belief in a literal interpretation of the Bible, doubting the historicity of much of the Old Testament.[52] In autumn 1887 he proclaimed his religious independence by joining the Congregationalists in Porthmadog, but did not persevere in his intention.[53]

Maggie Owen

By the mid-1880s, Lloyd George's fascination with religious controversy was waning, replaced by his interest in law, politics and women. In 1888 he married Margaret ('Maggie') Owen, a forceful figure in her own right. She was the daughter of a prosperous farmer, a deacon in the Calvinistic Methodist chapel. Maggie herself was a lifelong believing and practising Methodist, with a 'complete and absolute faith and trust in her God'.[54] From the beginning, Lloyd George was utterly frank with respect to his own 'sceptical vagaries . . . I told her emphatically the other

48 Ernest Renan, *Histoire des origines du christianisme, tome 1: Vie de Jésus* (Paris, Michel Lévy frères, 1863); Life of Jesus, trans. Charles E. Wilbour (London: Trübner, 1863).

49 Stevenson, Diary, 22 November 1915, cited ed. Taylor, *LG*, pp. 77–8.

50 F. W. Farrar, *The Early Days of Christianity*, 2 vols (London: Cassell, 1882).

51 LG, Diary, 16 December 1883, NLW, LG Papers, MS 4, f. 176.

52 LG, Diary, 29 August and 4 September 1887, NLW, LG Papers, MS 7, ff. 14–15, 19.

53 LG, Diary, 18, 23 and 28 September 1887, NLW, LG Papers, MS 7, ff. 23–5.

54 Viscount Gwynedd, *Dame Margaret: The life story of his mother* (London: George Allen & Unwin Ltd, 1947), p. 253.

day that I could not, even to win her, give them up, and that I would not pretend that I had. They were my firm convictions.'[55] He resented what he deemed 'religious bigotry' and 'sectarian pride'. He furiously accosted Maggie when she objected to his associating with Baptist girls from his own chapel:

> one of the few religious dogmas of our creed I believe in is fraternity with which you may couple equality. My God never decreed that farmers and their race should be esteemed beyond the progeny of a fishmonger and strange to say Christ – the founder of our creed – selected the missionaries of his noble teaching from amongst fishmongers.[56]

Lloyd George, a known flirt, was protesting a little too much. Yet it was obviously a sore point. The slightest provocation in future years would have Lloyd George railing to his wife against Methodist 'Pharisaism'.[57]

Maggie's parents disapproved of her marriage to a Baptist, then insisted that it be celebrated in their chapel.[58] Eventually they compromised on a Methodist chapel near Lloyd George's home, the service being conducted by both a Methodist minister and Uncle Lloyd. After the marriage, another source of conflict was Maggie's continued attendance at her Methodist Sunday school, rather than accompanying her husband to the Baptists.[59] The couple compromised in baptizing their five children alternately as Baptists and Methodists (Richard and Olwen chose to practise as Baptists, Mair, Gwilym and Megan as Methodists). Their father never required the children to attend chapel; it was their mother who insisted.[60]

Doing the rounds of the London chapels

From his twenties, Lloyd George was increasingly in London on legal business and then as an MP. If his chapelgoing had been simply to

55 LG, Diary, 9 January 1888, NLW, LG Papers, MS 9, f. 7.
56 LG to Margaret Lloyd George, u/d, 1887?, NLW, LG Papers, MS 20404C/64/1.
57 LG to Margaret Lloyd George, 21 August 1897, NLW, LG Papers, MS 20419C/823.
58 LG, Diary, 1 October 1886, NLW, LG Papers, MS 6, f. 120.
59 LG, Diary, 12 February 1888, NLW, LG Papers, MS 9, f. 24.
60 Carey-Evans, *LG was my Father*, p. 17.

appease the expectations of his family and community, one would have expected it to have ceased in the anonymity of the metropolis. This was not the case, at least in the early years. Sitting legal exams in 1881 and 1884, he did the rounds of the London chapels. Adopting again as his criteria the quality of the preaching and the emotional response this evoked, Lloyd George tended to patronize the capital's Welsh chapels. It helped further if the sermon coincided with his political opinions. He was particularly effusive about Hugh Price Hughes' preaching on 'Christ as a Socialist'.[61]

Most frequently Lloyd George attended the Welsh chapels in Castle Street and Charing Cross Road, but he spread his favours, visiting the City Temple and the Metropolitan Tabernacle to listen to the great Nonconformist preachers of the day. (As he made his political reputation, these preachers increasingly sought Lloyd George out, asking him to speak and write for them.) On hearing the Baptist Charles Spurgeon, he recognized many of traits familiar from North Wales – 'the same superstitious notion of religion, the melody pitched in the same minor key'. And yet it made an impression: 'He almost galvanized my dead faith into something like transient somnolence if not life.'[62] David Daniel noted the same reaction when they visited the City Temple:

> When we entered, the congregation was on its feet singing jubilantly to the organ and sound of trumpets. He instantly joined in and said between two stanzas, 'This is it, Daniel, after all.' His nature is so spirited, so Celtic and Welsh that an appeal to some emotion touches him mightily.[63]

The Welshman was not impressed by an initial visit to St Paul's Cathedral: 'The service was a fraud . . . He read his sermon. He was not an orator . . . Gesticulating too much and the gestures far from natural.'[64] Three years later he was more favourably impressed by the 'splendid' singing

61 LG, Diary, 29 January 1888, NLW, LG Papers, MS 9, f. 17.

62 LG, Diary, 30 April 1884, NLW, LG Papers, MS 5, f. 50.

63 Daniel, 'D. LG', NLW, D. R. Daniel Papers, 2,912, f. 20.

64 LG, Diary, 13 November 1881, NLW, LG Papers, MS 3, f. 47.

and Canon Henry Liddon's sermon. The approval was qualified – Liddon was only:

> a good speaker as English pulpiteers go. But he has the same way as all the English preachers and lacks that impassioned, appealing oratory which seems to be characteristic of Welsh preachers . . . *English preachers don't know how to speak.*[65]

Lloyd George crossed confessional boundaries to hear good preaching. In 1899 he attended Catholic High Mass and wrote approvingly of 'the power ful sermon by the Cardinal's brother's homily on the Catholic attitude towards the Bible'.[66]

As in Wales, Lloyd George would not allow others to dictate the practice of his faith. When Maggie scolded him for taking a Sunday river trip to Kew rather than attending chapel, he rounded on her:

> there is a great deal of difference between the temptation to leave your work for the pleasure of being cramped up in a suffocating malodorous chapel listening to some superstitious rot I have heard thousands of times before and on the other hand the temptation to have a pleasant ride on the river in the fresh air with a terminus at one of the loveliest gardens in Europe.[67]

Richard Lloyd George recalls how his parents worshipped for more than half a century at 'the little Welsh Chapel in Castle Street, a quiet backwater within a stone's throw of Oxford Circus'. His father was formally received as a member of the chapel. Yet Richard admits that his practice came to constitute little more than annual attendance at the chapel's Flower Day Service, when he would always give a rousing speech in Welsh.[68] By the 1890s, the theatre was assuming a greater prominence in Lloyd George's life, and after the turn of the century there is little

65 LG, Diary, 27 April 1884, NLW, LG Papers, MS 5, f. 48.

66 LG to William George, 1899, NLW, William George Papers.

67 LG to MLG, 13 August 1890, NLW, LG Papers, MS 20407C/126/1.

68 Gwynedd, *Dame Margaret*, p. 6.

reference to consistent chapelgoing – at least during the regular periods of separation from Maggie.

'Not one atom of comfort'

As he passed through his thirties and into his forties, there was no particular crisis, just a gradual drift away from the religious practice of his youth. On attaining high office, however, two events throw light on the practical application, or lack thereof, of his faith. Lloyd George was particularly fond of his daughter, Mair. She died suddenly and unexpectedly on 30 November 1907, aged only 17, after an unsuccessful operation for appendicitis. Driven by grief to the verge of insanity, Lloyd George was affected to a far great degree than Maggie. Richard explained: 'This was not at all because she had loved Mair less than he, nor because she was less desolated by a feeling of irretrievable loss. It was merely because my mother shared Mair's faith in the goodness of God.'[69]

William noted the effect of Mair's death on his brother, whom he visited in London:

> For the time being, at all events it shook his faith in God Himself... [He] could not understand why he should have been deprived of his daughter's understanding love and companionship at such a critical juncture in his career.[70]

William wrote subsequently, urging him to 'make a point of activating the spiritual side of your nature a little more'.[71] Daniel, who also visited after Mair's death, was more explicit:

> there was not for him one jot of comfort to be had from the wells from which his fully believing compatriots drink in similar straits. 'Some hand from the dark' had seized his heart's beloved, and 'she

69 Gwynedd, *Dame Margaret*, pp. 211–12.

70 William George, *My Brother and I*, p. 216.

71 William George to LG, 31 December 1907, PA, LG/I/2/2/8.

was no more, she's gone' were his words, and for him there was not the least delight in trying to follow her on wings of imagination.

Carlyle and Renan, having stripped Christ of his divinity, were no help in Lloyd George's hour of need. He gained no consolation from the doctrine of the resurrection: 'His position was an entirely *rationalistic* one. In the evening discussion at Ashley Gardens he admitted to me that he took not one atom of comfort in that direction.'[72]

A virtual bigamist

If religion did not inform Lloyd George's thought and action in moments of sorrow, nor did it in moments of pleasure. Frances Stevenson, the daughter of a Scots father and a Franco-Italian mother, was a teacher who had been Mair's contemporary at Clapham High School. In 1911, Lloyd George invited her to tutor his younger daughter, Megan. Maggie was rightly suspicious. By 1913, Frances had become Lloyd George's secretary and lover. Richard took his mother's part: 'This young lady with the magnetized heart and disturbed judgment became a permanent fixture in our home . . . He had hurt mother repeatedly and needlessly.'[73] There had been other affairs, but this was different. Lloyd George moved Frances into a house in Walton Heath in 1915. In 1922 he built a home for himself in Churt, Surrey. Initially, careful scheduling ensured that wife and mistress were not in residence simultaneously, but eventually Maggie withdrew. There was no formal separation and certainly no divorce. Lloyd George continued to appear with Maggie in London and Wales but the greater part of his time was spent with Frances at Churt. In 1929 they had a daughter, Jennifer.

Only after Maggie's death were Lloyd George and Frances married, in the Guildford Register Office in 1943. For Frances, this was a mere formality – 'Our real marriage,' she wrote, 'had taken place thirty years before.'[74] The solemn vows with Maggie before God, the Christian teaching on marriage, the pain he caused his family, seemed to count for nothing

72 Daniel, 'D. LG', NLW, D. R. Daniel Papers, 2,912, ff. 12–13, 18.

73 Richard Lloyd George, *LG*, p. 209.

74 Frances Lloyd George, *The Years that are Past*, p. 272.

with Lloyd George. In the eyes of his private secretary, A. J. Sylvester, he was guilty of something more than adultery:

> He lived virtually as a bigamist, continuing relationships with both his wife and his mistress. This was in flat contrast to his public role as a spokesman for Welsh nonconformity and British nonconformity in general, and as a family man.[75]

Choosing 'his words with precision'

When Lloyd George entered 10 Downing Street in December 1916, he was Britain's first Nonconformist Prime Minister. (Campbell-Bannerman had been a member of the established Church of Scotland; Asquith, raised a Congregationalist, to the extent that he practised faith, did so as an Anglican.) Although past its high-water mark of 1906, Nonconformity was still a potent force in British politics. Lloyd George happily addressed both national and local events, presenting himself as one of their own, engendering a sense of pride and community. In this spirit, and with tongue firmly in cheek, he addressed a Nonconformist gathering in the prelude to the January 1910 general election. Combining political opportunism with personal sentiment, he declared he came before them 'not as a Liberal Minister or member of a political party', but only as 'a quiet and retiring Free Churchman taking counsel with his fellow-members of the Free Churches'.[76]

Initially Lloyd George cautiously welcomed Balfour's 1902 Education Bill as an attempt at necessary reform. Quickly perceiving its confessional implications, however, he used opposition to the legislation to harness Nonconformity to the Liberal Party. It proved his path to national prominence. He might have been in a north Welsh pulpit as he spoke across the country:

> Teach religion in the schools, give the children the Bible. Let Him speak to them in His own words, so simple that a child can

75 Ed. Cross, *Life with LG*, pp. 16–17.

76 LG, Address to Free Church demonstration, Queen's Hall, 16 December 1909, cited Stephen Koss, *Nonconformity in Modern British Politics* (London: B. T. Batsford, 1975), p. 104.

> understand them – not confused and perplexed by these theologies which priests have for years and years defined, until no man of ordinary intelligence can comprehend them. No; let all this din and clamour of priests and the schools subside. Let the children hear for themselves the voice of the best friend they ever had, and the most dangerous foe the priest could ever encounter.[77]

The battle lines were not always as clearly drawn. He confessed his dilemma to Maggie when Lord Salisbury's government proposed a grant to the Catholic school in Caernarvon in the face of fierce opposition from the local school board. Nonconformists would expect his unwavering backing. Yet the newly elected MP in this marginal constituency was fully aware that 'my best supporters are Roman Catholics'.[78]

David Daniel marvelled that Lloyd George, with all his rationalist ideas regarding religion, remained for so long 'an idol to multitudes and to Wales's Nonconformist leaders'. Daniel was unstinting in his praise – the more so given Lloyd George, at least when speaking about religion, never resorted to hypocrisy:

> Although skilful in not placing emphasis on any idea that is part of revealed religion, which sometimes almost amounts to casting a cloak over his thought, I have to admit, in spite of listening to him attentively enough many a time, that I have never once caught him using a sentence of which it could be said that he communicated through it to his listeners an idea or belief that he did not actually hold . . . He has considered what is relevant and chosen his words with precision from the outset of his public career.

As a Welshman, close to his audience in 'heart and feeling', Lloyd George was able to conceal difference in doctrinal belief.[79] He employed the same technique soliciting Nonconformist support for the war effort. Speaking in the City Temple in 1915, he drew readily on the Christian concepts of

77 LG, Speech, Lincoln, 10 December 1902, *Lincoln Leader*, 13 December 1902, cited Gilbert, *LG A Political Life*, p. 226.

78 LG to Margaret Lloyd George, 31 July 1890, NLW, LG Papers, MS 20407C/119.

79 Daniel, 'D. LG', NLW, D. R. Daniel Papers, 2,912, ff. 4–7.

sacrifice, judgement and redemption to sway his listeners, without once giving an indication whether this represented his personal faith.[80]

Although his lack of regular practice was noticed, and there were rumours of a mistress, a love child and financial irregularities, there was no public denunciation of Lloyd George. (His willingness to litigate was sufficient to see off any such threat.) Yet by the 1930s, Nonconformist leaders were tired of being taken for granted. The Conservative and Labour Parties were attractive alternatives for many Nonconformist voters. When Lloyd George appealed to the Free Church Council to support his Council of Action, his proposal for a New Deal for Britain, the response was distinctly underwhelming.

'Church of England never'

Lloyd George was no admirer of Anglicanism – 'Atheist he might become, but Church of England never'.[81] Its privileges, real or perceived, produced in him the reactions of the underdog, a burning desire to right injustices. He cut his political teeth campaigning for Welsh disestablishment and never missed an opportunity to take a crack at Anglican social pretensions, commenting cynically on claims to apostolic succession:

> Some virtue from Peter has been transmitted through ages and generations and is now running in the veins of Welsh parsons . . . [Yet if Saint Peter] had turned up to the Church Congress the other day, there is not a prelate or a prebendary or a dean amongst them who would not have shunned him.[82]

He asserted that since the Reformation, medieval endowments given for the relief of the poor had been appropriated 'by the bishops and their clergy'.[83] He objected to the liturgy too: 'He despised parrot-like incantations,

80 John Grigg, *Lloyd George: From peace to war, 1912–1916* (London: Methuen, 1985), p. 185.

81 Masterman, *C. F. G. Masterman*, p. 211.

82 LG, Speech, Rhyl, 10 November 1891, cited Grigg, *The Young LG*, pp. 111–12.

83 LG, Speech, Shrewsbury, 22 February 1893, *Shrewsbury Chronicle*, 24 February 1893, cited Grigg, *The Young LG*, pp. 131–2.

mere conditioning of faith.'[84] Predictably, Lloyd George reserved his greatest scorn for High Church Anglicans, disapproving of all the bobbing up and down that took place 'in this chanting shop'.[85] Anglican Ritualism, he quipped, was the attempt 'to substitute for the Protestant doctrine of justification by faith a system of salvation by haberdashery'.[86]

So often, however, Lloyd George's response was personal rather than principled. He approved of Charles Gore, Bishop of Oxford and highest of Anglicans – 'a very attractive fellow . . . [a] great priest of the old type' – because he sensed that Gore 'sympathized with the people'.[87] Many churchmen despised Lloyd George for his attacks on their schools during the Education Bill debates. He struck up, however, an unlikely and enduring friendship with Alfred Edwards, Bishop of St Asaph and later first Archbishop of Wales. Lloyd George was touched by the bishop's writing to him at Mair's death, sympathizing with him in his sorrows and promoting a 'rational' basis for faith.[88] In turn, the politician invited Edwards to accompany him on a holiday to Italy. Lloyd George spent the night before Winston Churchill's wedding as Churchill's guest discussing the doctrine of the atonement with Edwards, Hugh Cecil and F. E. Smith.[89] It is probably fair to surmise that there was no meeting of minds.

Lloyd George was an occasional weekend guest at the Bishop's Palace at St Asaph. His brother recalled the controversy in Nonconformist circles when one 'Sunday morning he attended service and received Holy Communion at the Bishop's hands'.[90] The controversy was not only on the Nonconformist side. Lloyd George was present at Edwards's enthronement as Archbishop of Wales in 1920: the Archbishop of Canterbury recalled his surprise, but not disapproval, when Lloyd George 'and his wife appeared at the Early Service in the Cathedral [and communicated]'.[91] High Church Anglicans were less pleased – 'distress and bewilderment' were the

84 Richard Lloyd George, *LG*, p. 22.

85 LG to William George, [11 Aug 94], NLW, William George Papers, 270.

86 LG, House of Commons, 23 March 1898, Hansard, cited Grigg, *The Young LG*, p. 215.

87 LG to William George, 1 May 1912, NLW, William George Papers, 2586.

88 Bishop Alfred Edwards to LG, 12 and 22 December 1907, PA, LG/B/1/2A/1 and LG/B/1/2A/2.

89 LG to William George, 12 September 1908, NLW, William George Papers, 2101.

90 William George, *My Brother and I*, p. 216.

91 Archbishop Randall Davidson, Journal, 27 June 1920, cited G. K. A. Bell, *Randall Davidson: Archbishop of Canterbury*, 3rd edn (Oxford: Oxford University Press, 1952), p. 990.

reactions of the *Church Times* and its readers.[92] Untroubled by doctrinal and sacramental scruples, Lloyd George had simply acted as seemed right to him at the moment.

A religion 'for women and children'

His reaction to Catholicism was similarly complex. By upbringing and sentiment, every instinct should have militated against Rome. Certainly there were occasions when this response was uppermost – especially when there was also a political dimension. Reading that the Church supported Franco in the Spanish Civil, Lloyd George reverted to type:

> 'One principle I have is my Protestantism', he said, and went on to show how the priests in Spain . . . were wallowing in riches, expensive jewellery and fine vestments, all of which were obtained from grinding down the poor peasant and worker.[93]

He had shared the same prejudice with his friend years earlier: 'I hate a priest, Daniel, whenever I find him.'[94] Lloyd George believed strongly that the individual should have a direct relationship with God – regardless of whether he enjoyed such a relationship himself – mediated neither through a priest nor anyone else.

And yet he was fascinated by an institution so universal and ancient that made such extravagant claims. Something in the Catholic Mass appealed to his emotional needs. In Rome in 1897 he expressed the desire to attend a Papal Mass. If Nonconformist sentiment was disturbed when Lloyd George received Communion from an Anglican bishop, the political consequences of his presence at Leo XIII's Christmas Mass, if known, would have been devastating. The Pope and the beauty of the Mass captivated him:

> Candidly, I have never been present at a more impressive ceremony. Somehow, one could not fail to feel 'the Presence'. There

92 *Church Times*, 11 June 1920.

93 Sylvester, Diary, 8 November 1936, cited ed. Cross, *Life with LG*, p. 159.

94 Cited ed. Morgan, *LG Family Letters*, p. 7.

> was something about that service I would not have believed possible, something which one felt but could not describe.[95]

Attending the Marquis of Ripon's Requiem Mass in Westminster Cathedral in 1909, Lloyd George delighted in riling the Anglican Charlie Masterman: 'This knocks chunks off anything your Church can do!'[96] He was similarly impressed by the Catholic art in the Vatican.[97] Lloyd George admired Catholicism's grasp of human psychology, its treatment of the saints, the 'practical common sense' of the season of Lent.[98]

As always, however, he lacked consistency. He reacted against the Oberammergau Passion play – 'This is not *my* Christ. This is the Christ of the theologians.' Present at the liturgy in Monaco in 1911, his attention focused rather on the good looks of a girl in the congregation. Catholicism, he declared, was a religion 'for women and children, whom he appeared to regard as an inferior order of beings'.[99]

To reflect all aspects

Inevitably, there were concerns as to how Lloyd George, a Baptist, would exercise his powers of patronage in the Church of England. On becoming Prime Minister:

> the Cecils and other high churchmen went to see him to protest about his appointing bishops. L.G. said: 'Would you like Bonar Law to make the appointments?' (Bonar Law was a Scottish Presbyterian.) 'No' was the answer. 'Then would you like your Chief Whip to make the bishops?' (Lord Edmund Talbot was a Roman Catholic.) Again 'No' was the answer.[100]

95 A. J. Sylvester, *The Real Lloyd George* (London: Cassell & Co, 1947), p. 63.

96 Masterman, *C. F. G. Masterman*, p. 169.

97 LG to Margaret Lloyd George, 29 December 1897, Rome, NLW, LG Papers, MS 20419C/868.

98 Sylvester, Diary, 5 September 1935, cited ed. Cross, *Life with LG*, p. 129; LG to Labour leaders, Stevenson Diary, 7 December 1916, cited Grigg, *LG: From peace to war*, p. 479.

99 Masterman, *C. F. G. Masterman*, p. 180.

100 Sylvester, Diary, 17 November 1936, cited ed. Cross, *Life with LG*, pp. 161–2.

His critics were disarmed. Lloyd George's appointments proved unremarkable – save for his first, which provoked major controversy. The Dean of Durham, Hensley Henson, appealed to Lloyd George, as he had to Asquith, as a noted preacher and a scholar. In 1917 the Prime Minister proposed his name for the Diocese of Hereford. The problem was Henson's doctrinal heterodoxy, his doubts about the virgin birth and the resurrection. Having promised the Archbishop of Canterbury that he would welcome his advice on such matters, Lloyd George subsequently ignored it and persisted with Henson's nomination. The objections of his Anglican Unionist colleagues equally failed to move him, as he argued:

> With the Church an established body it [was] essential that all aspects should be reflected in its government: were the Church merely a sect, or a private and unofficial corporation, it would be possible and it might even be right that aspects such as those Henson reflected should be excluded or suppressed. The little man stated his case with incomparable lucidity and humour, carrying the sympathy of those who heard him.[101]

Henson proved a conservative presence on the episcopal bench, and three years later Lloyd George was able to translate him to Durham almost without comment.

Lloyd George's lack of time and interest posed a greater problem than any theological bias. Praising the decisions eventually arrived at, his private secretary recalled: 'It was always difficult to get L.G. to attend to ecclesiastical matters; he invariably put off his decisions for as long a time as possible.'[102] Dissatisfaction with the Hereford appointment led to Lloyd George agreeing in 1918 to the appointment of an Advisory Committee comprising four Anglican laymen and a cleric. They were not to suggest candidates themselves, simply to comment on those proposed. They met on ten occasions and had two amicable interviews with Lloyd George, but he simply ceased to consult them after a couple of

101 Lord Crawford, Diary, 18 January 1917, cited John Grigg, *Lloyd George: War leader, 1916–1918* (London: Allen Lane, 2002), p. 363.

102 Sylvester, *The Real LG*, p. 45.

years.[103] There was no ambiguity. He informed the Archbishop of Canterbury that he had no intention of surrendering the Prime Minister's 'well-established responsibility' of tendering advice to the Crown on ecclesiastical appointments.[104]

'A man of many parts'

What of Lloyd George's personal faith during his premiership and beyond? Associates, staff and guests painted a consistent picture of his religiosity. It was commonplace for an evening to end with a rousing rendition of Welsh hymns – often accompanied by Frances Stevenson. Lloyd George would regale the company with stories of the great preachers of the past. At other times, hymn books to hand, the household gathered around the radio for a broadcast service. He proposed writing a book on eighteenth- and nineteenth-century Welsh preachers, and did contribute a preface to a new hymn book, *Hymns of Western Europe*.[105] Despite his resentment of the restrictions of his Puritan upbringing, Lloyd George continued to observe some of these – such as declining to play golf on Sundays.[106] In Wales he continued to present himself as the practising Baptist:

> We all went to Berea Chapel . . . L.G. is indeed a most remarkable man. Today he has been the devout Nonconformist. At Berea this morning he and his family walked up to the front seat, which had been reserved. During the singing, he turned round and faced the audience. It was a sight to see L.G., who is at heart a true pagan if ever there was one, singing loudly and apparently feelingly. He is indeed a man of many parts.[107]

Every year he invited Nonconformist leaders to stay at the house he had built at Criccieth, and to preach at the local chapel.[108]

103 Lord Phillimore, Memorandum re Appointment of Bishops Committee, 11 February 1924 (copy), LPL, Bell Papers, 118, ff. 8–9.

104 LG to Davidson, 21 February 1920 (copy), LPL, Bell Papers, 118, f. 209.

105 Frances Lloyd George, *The Years that Are Past*, pp. 248, 231.

106 Riddell, *War Diary*, p. 11.

107 Sylvester, Diary, 28 August 1938, cited ed. Cross, *Life with LG*, p. 215.

108 William George, *My Brother and I*, p. 273.

In Churt too he could present a similar image. Another private secretary reminisced:

> to see him standing with his harmonium on a Sunday in his own house, singing hymns, you would think he was absolutely inspired by Christian ideals and based himself on the highest code of Christian morality. It was wonderful to hear him . . . even I . . . was almost persuaded that he was an inspired angel.[109]

Lloyd George was emotionally attached to the externals of his childhood faith – the preaching and the hymn singing. His private secretaries and others were conscious, however, that this was not borne out by his lifestyle nor – outside Wales – his religious practice.

'No conscience at all'

Two areas of his life in particular belied the claim to interior Christian faith. The first was conscience and morality. Richard Lloyd George is not an impartial source, but he claimed that his father's entire adult life was 'a series of affairs with women',[110] of which that with Frances Stevenson was only the most enduring. In February 1915, Frances believed she was pregnant. The birth of an illegitimate child could have spelled the end of a political career dependent on Nonconformist votes. Frances wrote: 'The idea of our love-child will have to go for the time being.' There was no birth. A. J. P. Taylor, editing her diary, delicately circumvented the subject: perhaps Frances had a miscarriage or simply miscalculated her periods.[111] John Grigg was more robust: the obvious explanation was that Frances had an abortion. Indeed, he claims that Frances subsequently told their daughter Jennifer that she had two abortions during the early years of her affair with Lloyd George.[112]

109 Horace Hamilton, cited Robert Rhodes James, *Memoirs of a Conservative: J. C. C. Davidson's memoirs and papers, 1910–37* (London: Weidenfeld & Nicolson, 1969), p. 42.

110 Richard Lloyd George, *LG*, p. 42.

111 Ed. Taylor, *LG*, p. 5.

112 Grigg, *LG: From Peace to War*, p. 224.

Just as shocking was the one-sided suicide pact he made Frances promise him in April 1917. If Lloyd George were to die first, and there were no children of the partnership to care for, then Frances was to commit suicide. Lloyd George could not contemplate the possibility of Frances finding happiness and a husband after his death, even though she was a generation younger than he was. 'I shall go too,' she recorded, 'and his end shall be my end.'[113] Lloyd George dreaded the loss of his faculties and, disregarding the Christian prohibition, contemplated suicide in this eventuality, selecting barbiturate acid as his preferred method of dispatch.[114]

Not only were Lloyd George's attitudes concerning sexual morality and the dignity of human life the subject of severe criticism, so were his financial dealings. As Chancellor of the Exchequer, together with the Attorney General and the Chief Whip of the Liberal Party, he was accused of insider dealing in Marconi shares in 1912. As Prime Minister, his sale of honours was notorious. Such a practice was not unique, but whereas others tended to use the proceeds to fund political parties, Lloyd George treated them as his personal property to dispose of as he chose.

All Christians are deeply conscious of their failure to live fully the precepts of their faith, but in Lloyd George's case there so often seemed no attempt to do so, no evidence of any internal dilemma – no indication of remorse, repentance or amendment of life. He chose to define Jesus as the supreme example whom we should follow, but an example limited to social reform, not touching on personal morality – despite the clear teaching of Scripture. His private secretary wrote: 'He seems to have no conscience at all.'[115]

'No one at the other end'

If Lloyd George recovered his faith in his late teens as a result of reading Carlyle and Renan, it did not involve any personal contact with God. Christ, as a historical figure, constituted an example for us. There was no sense in which he was a living person with whom we could communicate.

113 Stevenson, Diary, 23 April 1917, cited ed. Taylor, *LG*, p. 153.

114 Sylvester, Diary, 23 January 1938, cited ed. Cross, *Life with LG*, p. 172.

115 Sylvester, Diary, 5 February 1933, cited ed. Cross, *Life with LG*, p. 91.

Lloyd George told David Daniel that he ceased to pray when he lost his faith at the age of eleven and never resumed the practice. If he attempted to pray, a feeling of 'peculiar estrangement . . . came over him when, after shutting his eyes, he would hear his own voice resounding in the emptiness while he addressed nothingness'.[116] He described the same experience differently to his son Richard: 'There have been times when I have prayed – prayed desperately; but there seemed to be no one at the other end of the telephone.'[117] Again, his private secretary discounted any suggestion that Lloyd George was religious: 'He never says his prayers. He never prays, although he goes through the form of praying in chapel.'[118] If he did not believe in orthodox doctrine and if he did not seek contact with God through prayer, it is difficult to see in what sense Lloyd George could be described as a practising Christian.

Lloyd George once remarked 'how much he would like to lead the opposition in Heaven: what fine material there would be for him to make an attack'. It was a comment made in jest. Nevertheless, it may indicate a significant truth as to why he, and other politicians, have an ambiguous relationship with religion. Christian faith does not sit well with the individual's desire always to be centre stage, continuously in control.[119]

Margot Asquith demonized Lloyd George after he replaced her husband in 10 Downing Street, but in autumn 1915 relations were still good. She felt that the Welshman had 'an odd kind of faith in an undefined God'.[120] She was correct that Lloyd George did not believe in the God of Christian revelation. In the period around 1882–3 his writings and mission work indicated a degree of religious fervour and a personal relationship with Jesus Christ. These were not sustained – whether the consequence of his modernist reading material, the company he kept, his experience of chapelgoing or the temptations that came his way. There was no dramatic crisis as there had been in his childhood, just a gradual move away from Christianity.

116 Daniel, 'D. LG', NLW, D. R. Daniel Papers, 2,912, f. 10.

117 Richard Lloyd George, *LG*, p. 20.

118 Sylvester, Diary, 5 February 1933, cited ed. Cross, *Life with LG*, p. 91.

119 Sylvester, Diary, 6 December 1931, cited ed. Cross, *Life with LG*, p. 61.

120 Margot Asquith, Diary, 15 November 1915, cited M. Brock and E. Brock, *Margot Asquith's Great War Diary, 1914–1916: The view from Downing Street* (Oxford: Oxford University Press, 1920), p. 213.

Cultural loyalty and political necessity meant he never formally defected from the Baptists:

> He held no great belief in their doctrines, but he had been brought up amongst them, and having progressed among them, he would never have it thought that, once he had made his position, he had let them down by transferring to some other faith.[121]

What, if anything, remained? Writing after Mair's death, William was conscious that his brother's faith had been weakening over the years, that politics were the dominant force in his life. As a consequence, in William's view, he lacked the resources to face this personal tragedy:

> I know there is no one more religious than you in a true and deep sense. But in the stress of the great conflict in which you have been engaged from childhood against actual wrongs, you have perhaps forgotten to keep the direct line of communication that should exist between every warrior and his Captain as clearly as they should be.[122]

While disavowing any interest in conventional piety, there were occasions when Lloyd George claimed for himself that 'he had the religious sense strongly developed'.[123] Frances had no illusions. There was nothing of the mystic in Lloyd George; he was the consummate realist, interested in this world only: 'What religion he has is purely emotional, and not spiritual.'[124] That emotional response manifested itself in his reaction to the externals of religion, to good preaching and rousing hymns.

His private secretary was forthright in his assessment: 'He is not deeply religious, as so many think he is. He is not religious at all. He is essentially pagan.'[125] 'Pagan' was an adjective frequently applied to Lloyd George,

121 Sylvester, Diary, 30 July 1936, cited ed. Cross, *Life with LG*, p. 144.
122 William George to LG, 31 December 1907, PA, LG/I/2/2/8.
123 Riddell, Diary, 30 March 1918, cited Riddell, *War Diary*, p. 334.
124 Stevenson, Diary, 9 February 1917, cited ed. Taylor, *LG*, pp. 142–3.
125 Sylvester, Diary, 5 February 1933, cited ed. Cross, *Life with LG*, p. 91.

occasionally by himself.[126] It was used not necessarily to indicate an atheist but rather a non-Christian. Lloyd George did have some perception of a supreme mind controlling human destiny, conveniently corresponding with his self-understanding of his own prominence in the workings of providence. After Mair's death he wrote to Maggie of the 'multitudes [to] whom God has sent me to give a helping hand out of misery and worry'.[127] He made a similar statement to the newspaper proprietor George Riddell six years later: 'I am myself convinced that nothing will be allowed to happen to me until I have accomplished some great work for the performance of which I have been singled out.'[128] Lloyd George's belief in himself was considerably stronger than his belief in God. John Grigg's summary is essentially correct: 'His true position was that of a secularist with a sentimental colouring of Christianity.'[129]

'Who will lead me to the strong city?'

Lacking Christian faith in the resurrection, it is no surprise that Lloyd George did not do death well. Friends feared for his sanity when Mair died. He refused to see her mortal remains, or those of Maggie or anyone else.[130] While critically ill in 1931, he 'had no more thought of religion (he himself admits it) than a pagan'.[131] As he approached the ultimate realities, however, it was a little different. He returned to his roots, living for the final months of his life with Frances, to whom he was now married, at the house he had had restored and extended at Llanystumdwy. Towards the end he asked her to play the hymn 'Who will lead me to the strong city?' The last verse began: 'Christ will lead me to the strong city.' As he was dying, he whispered to her: '"It is the sign of the Cross," [she] asked what his meaning was, but he only repeated: "It is the sign

126 Sylvester, Diary, 26 January 1941, cited ed. Cross, *Life with LG*, p. 287.

127 LG to Margaret Lloyd George, 4 December 1907, NLW, LG Papers, MS 20429C/1303/2.

128 G. A. Riddell, Diary, 21 May 1913, cited ed. J. M. McEwen, *The Riddell Diaries, 1908–1923* (London: Athlone Press, 1986), p. 65.

129 Grigg, *LG: War Leader*, p. 359.

130 Sylvester, Diary, 21 January 1941, cited ed. Cross, *Life with LG*, p. 286.

131 Stevenson, Diary, 8 November 1934, cited ed. Taylor, *LG*, p. 288.

of the Cross.'"[132] He died in the presence of Frances and his daughter, Megan, on 26 March 1945.

Lloyd George had already dismissed the possibility of a funeral and burial at Westminster Abbey. It was not his style; he anticipated controversy, possibly concerning his beliefs or personal life. Nor did he want to be buried in a cemetery.[133] Instead, on Good Friday 1945 he was laid to rest, as he wished, by the River Dwyfor at Llanystumdwy, the site marked not by a gravestone but by a boulder.

132 Frances Lloyd George, *The Years that Are Past*, pp. 278, 252.

133 Masterman, *C. F. G. Masterman*, p. 142; Tom Jones, Diary, 23 August 1922, cited Thomas Jones, *Whitehall Diary, Vol. 1, 1916–1925* (London: Oxford University Press, 1969), pp. 206–7.

Bonar Law (1922–1923)

'Deep and solemn sadness'

Andrew Bonar Law[1] was born on 16 September 1858 at Kingston (subsequently renamed Rexton), New Brunswick, in the days before Canadian federation. He was educated at Glasgow High School.

After a successful career as a Glaswegian iron merchant, Law was elected as the Unionist MP for Glasgow Blackfriars in 1900. Losing the seat to Labour in 1906, he was returned to the Commons shortly afterwards at a by-election at Dulwich. In the December 1910 general election he took the fight for tariff reform to the heartlands of the free-trade cause, contesting Manchester North West. Narrowly defeated, Law was elected for Bootle at a by-election in 1911. Finally, he represented Glasgow Central from 1918 until his death.

With his business background and a prestigious memory used to effect in marshalling facts in Commons debates, Law was appointed Parliamentary Secretary to the Board of Trade in 1902. A capable advocate of fiscal reform and a doughty opponent of Irish Home Rule, he was nevertheless the surprise victor in the 1911 Unionist leadership contest when his opponents withdrew from the field. Personally kind and moderate, he adopted a far more combative strategy in the fight against Home Rule and the proposal that Ulster be coerced into accepting rule from Dublin. During the period preceding the First World War, political life became increasingly bitter, and civil war in Ireland was feared.

At the outbreak of war with Germany, Law pledged Unionist support to the Liberal administration. When Asquith formed a coalition government in 1915 he entered the Cabinet as Colonial Secretary. With the press, Lloyd George and many Unionists clamouring for a more vigorous prosecution

1 Named after the Revd Andrew Bonar, Moderator of the General Assembly of the Free Church of Scotland, Law was always known by his second Christian name.

of the war effort, George V invited Law to form a government in December 1916. When Asquith refused to serve under him, Law declined the offer. Instead he served under Lloyd George as Chancellor of the Exchequer, Leader of the House of Commons and, effectively, deputy Prime Minister. It was a successful partnership. Law raised the necessary finance and attended to parliamentary business, freeing Lloyd George to coordinate the push for victory.

Having worked extraordinarily hard, Law emerged exhausted from the war. He accepted the less onerous position of Lord Privy Seal, while continuing to lead the Unionists in the Commons until his resignation on health grounds in 1921. Law was coaxed from retirement to lend his support to those Unionist MPs seeking withdrawal from the coalition government. Their success led to Lloyd George's immediate resignation. Law was re-elected leader of his party and appointed Prime Minister on 23 October 1922.

Law promptly called, and won, a general election. Ironically, one of his first tasks was to oversee the final enactment of legislation giving constitutional reality to the Irish Free State. His premiership was dominated by post-war tensions in Europe and the renegotiation of Britain's war debts to the USA – and his own ill health. Lung cancer forced him to resign on 20 May 1923.

Law died on 30 October 1923.

* * *

A transatlantic premier

As the dignitaries left Westminster Abbey following Law's funeral, Asquith reputedly quipped that it was fitting to bury the Unknown Prime Minister next to the Unknown Soldier. Known or otherwise, various claims can be made on Law's behalf. At 211 days, his was the shortest premiership of the twentieth century. He was the first, and until Boris Johnson's appointment in 2019, the only Prime Minister born outside the British Isles. A non-graduate from neither the landed classes nor an English public school, he is claimed as the first *modern* leader of the Conservative Party. He was the only twentieth-century Prime

Minister to be a son of the manse and, until Gordon Brown and Theresa May, the only one born to a clergyman of any denomination. Law was the first Prime Minister to be cremated.

What is known of his religion, other than the assumption by those close to him that he had none? His father, the Revd James Law, an Ulsterman of Scots descent, was for 32 years the Free Church of Scotland minster of St Andrew's Church, Kingston. A graduate of Glasgow University, he was for a short while minister at Coleraine in Ulster before emigrating to Canada. Presumably he baptized Bonar Law at St Andrew's soon after his birth. (Records for the period do not survive.) Bonar Law's mother, Elizabeth Annie Kidston, who came from a Glaswegian mercantile family, died when he was just two. Her sister, Janet Kidston, travelled to New Brunswick to keep house for her brother-in-law and help raise five young children.

Parishioners remembered James Law as a popular minister and a fine preacher, who delivered fervent and lengthy extempore prayers. He was able to overcome – at a local level – the divisions between the Established and Free churches that beset the Church of Scotland for much of the nineteenth century.[2] The Sabbath was kept with severity and the scattered Scottish community travelled great distances to attend St Andrew's, where services lasted four hours. James Law resorted to locking his family into a barn on Sundays – an act not of Calvinist cruelty but of parental kindness – he wished his children to be free to play away from prying Presbyterian eyes. There was, however, a darker side. Preparing for his Sunday duties caused Law great mental anguish. There were periods, sometimes lasting weeks, when he withdrew entirely within himself. There is little to substantiate Robert Blake's suggestion that this was the result of religious doubt.[3] Living in an isolated outpost of empire, he seems to have suffered from clinical depression. Whatever the cause, it was crippling: 'For the last five years of his life he had been the victim of a despondency so great as to amount almost to insanity.'[4]

2 Anon., 'The Background of the Rt. Hon. Andrew Bonar Law', PA, BL/118/9/29.

3 Robert Blake, *The Unknown Prime Minister: The life and times of Andrew Bonar Law, 1858–1923* (London: Eyre & Spottiswoode, 1955), p. 20.

4 Tom Jones, Diary, 28 January 1921, cited Thomas Jones, *Whitehall Diary, Vol. 1, 1916–1925* (London: Oxford University Press, 1969), p. 127.

Presbyterian respectability

Bonar Law spent six years in local schools before it was decided he would benefit from an education among his maternal relatives in Scotland. Separated from his father and siblings, the upheaval for a young boy must have been immense – leaving the remote Canadian Atlantic coast for a hub of commerce and industry, the second city of the British Empire, and going from relative poverty to the affluence of upper-middle-class Glaswegian life. Law lived with an aunt in Helensburgh, a wealthy commuting settlement on the northern bank of the Clyde, where the Sabbath was observed with even greater rigour than in New Brunswick. He resorted to reading Walter Scott's novels under his bed in semi-darkness. Initially he joined cousins at Gilbertfield House, a new preparatory school at Hamilton, Lanarkshire, 'for the board and education of young gentlemen'. Run by a clergyman, it was not a success.[5] From there, Law spent three years at Glasgow High School, which produced two Prime Ministers to Eton's one during the first 50 years of this study, when English public schools reputedly exercised an iron grip on the upper echelons of government.

Leaving Glasgow High School at the age of 16, Law joined the family merchant bank. Reading voraciously in his free time, he played golf, tennis, bridge and chess. Out of office hours he attended the lectures at the University of Glasgow designed for the improvement of young professional men such as himself. Having no direct male heirs, the Kidstons sold their firm to the Clydesdale Bank, providing Law with the means to become managing partner of a Glasgow iron merchant, trading in metals. Working hard, he prospered. The profits from this enterprise, together with family bequests, gave him the financial independence to enter politics. In 1891 he married Annie Robley, the daughter of another Glasgow merchant, at Helensburgh Free Church. They had six children and the family was extremely happy. The couple conformed to the expectations of their age and class. Every Sunday they attended Helensburgh Free Church, where Law taught at the Sunday school for a time. Later, in

5 H. A. Taylor, *The Strange Case of Andrew Bonar Law* (London: Stanley Paul & Co., u/d), pp. 24–5.

London, he attended St Columba's Church of Scotland church in Pont Street, where he was an elder.

Youthful musings

A file in the Bonar Law Papers contains a number of his essays, undated, but apparently written during his school years and subsequently. They provide an insight into his religious beliefs. The earliest is a life of John Knox, 'one of the noblest of Scotland's sons'. It is conventional stuff, with Law repeating the prejudices heard in the home and from the pulpit. Knox is presented uncritically as freeing 'the word of God' from the oppression and abuses of the Church. Law made no attempt to spare 'the Romish Church':

> The face of the country was darkened by swarms of priests and friars of every description who devoured the substance of the people while their only influence was derived from a superstition of the grossest character. The lives of the clergy who, in this country enjoyed an exceptional degree of wealth and power, were of the most shameful nature.[6]

There was a definite change, however, by the time Law attempted a biographical sketch of Oliver Cromwell. He had no time for the supposed Romanizing tendencies of Charles I, but reserved his strongest censure for 'a stern and unbending Puritanism'. Protestantism, he believed, had degenerated. The 'joyousness' and 'strength' displayed at the time of the Reformation had been replaced by a certain 'bitterness'. Law deplored the fact that Puritans had 'turned to the Old Testament rather than to the New for comfort and consolation'. Therefore he praised the intervention of Cromwell and the army to prevent the imposition of Presbyterian conformity and the persecution of the sects that proliferated in the 1640s: 'Other men had preached toleration, Cromwell practised it; and there was greater religious liberty at this time than there had ever been before.'[7] (Irish Nationalists

6 Andrew Bonar Law, 'The Life of Knox', PA, BL/13/4.

7 ABL, 'Oliver Cromwell', PA, BL/13/4.

understandably objected vociferously when Law advanced Cromwell as a model of religious tolerance in parliamentary debates in 1906.)

Then there is a profile of Blaise Pascal. Law bestowed unconditional praise on this seventeenth-century French Catholic who, from the time of his conversion, 'devoted himself entirely to the service of God'. Law admired Pascal's ability to place scientific and religious knowledge 'within the comprehension of everyone', contrasting him favourably with 'the obscure phraseology and endless verbosity of the [scholastics]'. Of course, it helped that Pascal had defended the Jansenists against the Jesuits – not that Law held any brief for Jansenism. Its 'gloomy ascetism' seemed too similar to the Scottish Calvinism in which he had been raised. In the essay, Law employed the term 'every Christian' and implicitly placed himself within that category. For example, he concluded: '[Pascal's] last words were a prayer – a prayer well-suited to the life of every Christian – "My God never abandon me!"'[8]

Carlyle's anti-Christian influence

Law's historical interpretation may be questionable but his essays provide a rare insight into his youthful mind. There was a movement from uncritical support for Presbyterianism to a rejection of its more austere and gloomy manifestations. But there is no suggestion of a general repudiation of Christianity and its central doctrines. Something happened subsequently. As a politician, Law was portrayed, and was happy to portray himself, as a man of business, practical and successful – 'this most unphilosophical of statesmen'.[9] As a wartime Chancellor of the Exchequer, he was the man who managed the money and the business of the House of Commons, freeing Lloyd George to devise strategy and inspire the nation. Law had, however, been willing and able to think philosophically as a young man: he attended Professor Edward Caird's lectures in Moral Philosophy, and his final essay takes a philosophical subject.

8 ABL, Glasgow, 'Pascal', PA, BL/13/4.

9 R. J. Q. Adams, *Bonar Law* (London: John Murray, 1998), p. 70.

While occupying the government front bench in Asquith's coalition government, Law turned to Augustine Birrell, the Irish Chief Secretary, and told him that 'his faith in Christian Revelation, as recorded in the Gospels, and embedded in the Apostles' Creed, or "Belief" as it was once called, was destroyed in his young days by Thomas Carlyle's books, which he read with breathless interest'.[10] Law was not given to making flippant or inconsequential statements.

He wrote his essay on the principle motivating human life, noting that much religious teaching is 'simply a careful calculation of profits and losses giving this as net result: Be good and you will be happy!' Businessman though he was, he rejected this 'prosperity gospel'. It was natural, Law believed, for the young to seek for meaning in life. Yet as they grow old they become satisfied with the mundane: 'They wake and sleep, they eat and drink, they buy and sell as if these more than any realities would last for ever.' Even a 'great tragedy' only temporarily disturbs their complacency, and they return rapidly to former diversions. A few – the great – seek for more. Law dismissed those 'who are tempted to fly from the world altogether to bury themselves in cloisters'. Instead he praised those who seek a higher goal than happiness: 'blessedness'.

This sounds promising material from a Christian perspective. However, rather than explore the Sermon on the Mount and the gospel of Jesus Christ, Law chose to extol 'Carlyle's gospel'. For the philosopher and historian Carlyle, 'blessedness' was attained through work and devotion to duty (both of which Law fulfilled to an exemplary degree): '"Man's highest and sole blessedness," [Carlyle] says, "is that he toil, and know what to toil at; not in ease, but in united victorious labour, which is at once evil and the victory over evil, does his freedom lie."'[11]

Law's favourite book was Carlyle's *Sartor Resartus* – supposedly a defence of religion but only at the expense of abandoning revelation and its transmission. According to the protagonist, 'the Letter of Religion' (objective truth) had to be dispensed with in order that 'the living Spirit of Religion' (subjective experience) might take its place. 'Jesus of Nazareth' is simply a religious symbol, albeit the highest. 'The Ideal' lies within the

10 Augustine Birrell, *Things Past Redress* (London: Faber & Faber, 1937), p. 275.
11 ABL, Untitled essay, PA, BL/13/4.

individual subject. Nietzsche concluded: 'At bottom, Carlyle is an English atheist who makes it a point of honour not to be one.'[12] Birrell was of a similar opinion: 'Carlyle's influence in the long run, though not obviously so at first, must be reckoned as distinctly *Anti-Christian*.'[13]

It was not the conclusion the young Law drew in his essay:

> Carlyle's true glory seems to be that in an age of materialism and of practical atheism he was able to make it possible for men to believe that the world is in reality spiritual, not material, that it is founded in God and not on chaos.

Although by no means alone among his contemporaries in doing so, it is difficult to see how Law arrived at this position. Even granted that Carlyle retained some form of deist belief, there is nothing in his God that can be known, loved or of assistance to humans on their earthly journey. Tellingly, Law approved of the fact that, out of consideration for her feelings, Carlyle hid 'from his old mother that his belief in God was altogether different from the Calvinistic Christianity in which he had been [raised]'.[14] Law was introduced to Carlyle at similar age to Lloyd George. In Law's case, acquaintance with his thought was even more transformative – and destructive.

'No special adherence to any denomination'

Publicly, Law presented himself as an observant Presbyterian. The Archbishop of Canterbury, Randall Davidson, who shared a similar background and, through personal contact, was in a position to assess his faith. Speaking only months after Law's death, he chose his words carefully: Law 'certainly called himself a Presbyterian though perhaps he gave no special adherence to any denomination'.[15] It was the closest he could come to calling a recent Prime Minister an agnostic or atheist. Law came from the Free Church tradition within Presbyterianism – those who objected to

12 Thomas Carlyle, *Sartor Resartus* (Oxford: Oxford University Press, 2008; first published 1833–4), p. xxviii.

13 Birrell, *Things Past Redress*, p. 275.

14 ABL, Untitled essay, PA, BL/13/4.

15 Davidson, Evidence to Church Assembly Committee, 29 July 1924, LPL, Bell Papers, 118, f. 26.

civil interference with the affairs of the Church, including in the matter of appointments. Yet following the union of the Free Church with the United Presbyterian Church in 1900, Law put the minister in Helensburgh on notice of his intention to join the established Church of Scotland, stating his preference for 'the principle of the State recognition of religion'.[16]

Since he was Prime Minister for less than a year, Law was responsible for only one – entirely unexceptional – episcopal appointment within the Church of England: that of Arthur Headlam to the Diocese of Gloucester on the recommendation of his predecessor.

Of Ulster descent and raised in the West of Scotland, Law grew up in an uncompromisingly Protestant environment. On his election as leader of the Unionist Party, there were fears of the possible consequences on the highly volatile situation in Ireland. Law reassured a Catholic correspondent:

> I think I can sincerely say that there is no one who less likes to arouse religious bigotry than I do, and I do not think I have said a word in any of my speeches which would be open to the charge that I attacked your religion.

With respect to Ireland, he argued, his position would be just the same if he were defending a Catholic minority against a Protestant majority.[17] To an Anglican, he maintained that his opposition to Home Rule had nothing to do with any form of 'attack upon the Roman Catholic religion'.[18] Law refused to address Orange lodges if required to wear their quasi-religious insignia.[19] He was similarly unambiguous with his constituents in Bootle: 'I am not fond of talking about religion. When I came down here as your candidate, I was told that I must not talk politics, that I must abuse my Roman Catholic fellow-subjects. I do not believe it.'[20] And while Law was initiated as a Freemason in 1900 when membership

16 ABL to Revd William Leitch, 18 November 1911 (copy), PA, BL/12/2/3.

17 ABL to Lady Ninian Crichton-Stuart, 7 October 1912 (copy), PA, BL/33/4/57.

18 ABL to Sir Charles Cripps, 7 October 1912 (copy), PA, BL/33/4/58.

19 Adams, *BL*, p. 392n.

20 Taylor, *The Strange Case of ABL*, p. 166.

was almost de rigueur in certain Protestant circles, there is no evidence he was ever active.[21]

His profession of tolerance was not limited to the public and political sphere. He employed as his children's governess a staunch Catholic, Miss Duggan. Of course, he was no crypto-Catholic. For Law, one form of revealed religion was as good, or as lacking in credibility, as any other. He told against himself the story of a time when Lloyd George was Prime Minister and he Chancellor of the Exchequer: 'A deputation came to Downing Street, carrying a banner bearing the inscription, "God will see right done!" BL's Roman Catholic governess remarked, "That banner is no good. They don't know God in this street."'[22] Miss Duggan was a very outspoken and astute lady.

'Man's highest and sole blessedness is that he toil, and know what to toil at'

In March 1921, Law addressed the University of Glasgow, where he had been appointed rector. In concluding, he returned to a familiar theme: the importance of work and the praise of Carlyle. He even used the same quotation cited in his earlier essay on Carlyle: 'Man's highest and sole blessedness is that he toil, and know what to toil at; not in ease, but in united victorious labour, which is at once evil and the victory over evil, does his freedom lie.' But there was a difference: as a young man he had praised Carlyle as a defender of religion and a bulwark against atheism; at the end of his life, Law made no such claim. Indeed, he made it clear that this position was distinct from, if not necessarily opposed to, religion, which he defined as 'a man's relations with his Maker'.[23]

In the decades between his youthful essay and his rectorial address, Law had known much sorrow. In 1909 his beloved wife, Annie, died suddenly at the age of 42. He never remarried nor enjoyed again any form of personal intimacy. Two sons were lost in the First World War: one while fighting against the Ottoman Turks; the other in the Royal Flying Corps,

21 <www.pglglasgow.org.uk/Andrew-Bonar-Law.html>, accessed 21.12.17.

22 George Riddell, Diary, 10 September 1919, cited Lord Riddell, *Lord Riddell's Intimate Diary of the Peace Conference and After, 1918–1923* (London: Victor Gollancz, 1933), p. 126.

23 ABL, Rectorial Address, Glasgow University, 11 March 1921, PA, BL/17/5/7.

who was shot down over France. Devastated, Law was able to draw no consolation from the Christian faith, from the hope of personal survival and eternal life. Condolences poured in after his wife's death. Not one letter made reference to Law's faith.[24] With those to whom he was familiar, he made no pretence of a faith he did not possess. Contemporaries acknowledged his 'scepticism, lack of faith'.[25]

Carlyle's philosophy might have appeared intellectually compelling in youth, but stripped of any belief in revelation and a personal God, it offered no comfort in the hour of need. Law had spoken accurately in his essay: 'The whole of [Carlyle's] view of life rests upon a foundation of deep and solemn sadness.'[26] No one can accuse Law of inconsistency. Following these crushing bereavements, as Carlyle had advised, he lived only for work and the fulfilment of public duty. He collapsed from exhaustion just two days after delivering the address in Glasgow.

Law was an inveterate smoker; lung cancer forced his final retirement from office and claimed his life shortly afterwards. He had requested that he be buried alongside his wife in Helensburgh. His fellow Scots Canadian and friend, the press magnate Lord Beaverbrook, persuaded his family and the authorities that a public funeral in London was more appropriate. Law was cremated at Golders Green Crematorium in north London on 3 November 1923. The ashes were taken to St Columba's for a private service before a state funeral and interment at Westminster Abbey two days later. Tom Jones, Deputy Secretary to the Cabinet, attended with his wife:

> Rene and I at St Columba's and then at the Abbey at Bonar Law's funeral . . . All these prayers and hymn singing very alien to the B.L. known to me. He once remarked to me that L.G. still had some sort of belief in a future life and clearly implied that he, B.L., had none whatever.[27]

So passed one of the saddest, most conscientious and least believing of Prime Ministers.

---

24 PA, BL/123.

25 J. M. Keynes, *Essays in Biography* (London: Macmillan & Co., 1933), p. 43.

26 ABL, Untitled essay, PA, BL/13/4.

27 Tom Jones, Diary, 5 November 1923, cited Jones, *Whitehall Diary, Vol. 1*, p. 254.

Stanley Baldwin (1923–1924, 1924–1929 and 1935–1937)

'Chosen as God's instrument'

Stanley Baldwin was born in Bewdley, Worcestershire, on 3 August 1867. He was educated at Harrow and Trinity College, Cambridge.

After two decades working for the family business, Baldwin unsuccessfully contested Kidderminster as the Unionist candidate in the 1906 general election. Two years later he was returned unopposed for his father's former constituency of West Worcestershire, a seat he held until his retirement in 1937, when he was created Earl Baldwin of Bewdley.

Baldwin went largely unnoticed at Westminster until appointed Parliamentary Private Secretary to Bonar Law in 1916 and Joint Financial Secretary to the Treasury in 1917. He entered the Cabinet as President of the Board of Trade in 1921. Baldwin disliked intensely Lloyd George's presidential style and alleged corruption, fearing that he would split the Conservative Party as he had the Liberals. Threatening resignation if Lloyd George took Britain to war with Turkey and if the Conservatives fought another election in coalition with him, he persuaded Law to return to political life and support the backbench Tory rebellion against their coalitionist leaders. In October 1922, Baldwin was appointed Chancellor of the Exchequer in Law's government. He had only limited success in renegotiating the terms of Britain's wartime debt to the USA and struggled to convince Law to accept his deal.

When Law resigned as Prime Minister, George V controversially appointed Baldwin as his successor on 22 May 1923. (Lord Curzon, his rival, was held to be disqualified because he was a peer.) Baldwin was elected leader of his party a few days later. Despite the Conservatives having won a parliamentary majority the preceding year, he called a general election on 6 December 1923, seeking a mandate for protectionism. He miscalculated. The Conservatives lost their majority and were defeated when the Commons reassembled. He resigned on 22 January 1924, to be replaced by Ramsay MacDonald, who led the first (minority) Labour government. Baldwin was unperturbed, determining to educate Labour as a responsible party of government.

MacDonald's government survived only nine months. In the general election of 29 October 1924, the Conservatives won a majority of more than two hundred. Although a moderate, Baldwin was determined to defeat the unions in the 1926 General Strike, which he perceived to be a threat to constitutional democracy. He quietly prepared resources and public opinion, and the strike quickly collapsed. In the latter half of the Parliament, Baldwin appeared unfocused. The general election of 30 May 1929 produced another hung Parliament, with Labour emerging as the largest party. In opposition, Baldwin's position was threatened by the right wing of his own party and the press, who thought his leadership insufficiently robust and favoured a policy of imperial preference. He saw off the challenge, portraying the press barons as just as unconstitutional as the Trades Union Congress.

In an attempt to reassure the markets and avoid financial collapse, the Conservatives entered a National government on 23 August 1931. MacDonald remained Prime Minister, but given the government's dependence on Conservative votes, effective control passed to Baldwin, who took office as Lord President of the Council. That reality was emphasized by the general election of 27 October 1931, when the National government won a massive majority, 471 of its MPs being Conservatives. Exchanging roles with MacDonald, Baldwin became Prime Minister for the third time on 7 June 1935. Under his leadership the National government won another large majority in the general election of 14 November 1935. Overseas, the clouds gathered. Against a background of economic depression, dictators had assumed power in Germany and Italy; civil war divided Spain. Soviet Russia was an uncertain presence on the international stage. Lacking diplomatic support and fearing to push Mussolini into the arms of Hitler, Baldwin failed to respond effectively to the Italian invasion of Abyssinia. At home he skilfully managed the abdication crisis of 1936, finally stepping down on 28 May 1937 after the coronation of George VI.

Baldwin retired to popular acclaim. Although infuriating colleagues with his indecision and occasionally erratic actions, he read and articulated the public mood brilliantly, seeking the national rather than the narrowly partisan interest. Trusted as a force for stability and moderation in a troubled world, Baldwin attracted many former Liberals and established the Conservatives as the dominant political force of the interwar period. That popularity vanished during the Second World War, for which he was blamed. Such accusations were unjust, particularly when emanating from former opponents of his policy of limited rearmament. Rather, perhaps, he deserves credit for ensuring Britain entered the war as a strong democracy and united nation.

Baldwin died during the night of 13–14 December 1947.

* * *

'My Nonconformist ancestry'

When Windham Baldwin wrote about his father's life in the 1950s, his primary objective was to refute claims that Stanley Baldwin had been an appeaser who left the country unprepared for the Second World War. In matters of religion, he expected to say that his father was entirely conventional; that is, in a very English sort of a way he believed in God, accounted himself a Protestant and attended church, at least during some periods of his life. As he read his father's papers, however, Windham realized he knew him less well than he thought and needed to reassess the nature and depth of his father's religious beliefs.[1]

For the two decades preceding 1923, the premiership had been dominated by those from the Celtic fringes and those of ambiguous religious beliefs. With Baldwin's appointment, it appeared that 10 Downing Street was occupied by an uncomplicated English churchman for the first time since 1902. The reality was more complex.

Stanley Baldwin was the only child of Alfred Baldwin and his wife Louisa (née Macdonald). The Baldwins had farmed and worked metals in Shropshire and Worcestershire for generations. Alfred transformed the failing family firm into a highly profitable conglomerate of metalworking and mining interests. A Unionist MP, he was also chairman of the Metropolitan

1 A. W. Baldwin, *My Father: The true story* (London: George Allen & Unwin, 1956), p. 326.

Bank and the Great Western Railway. On his mother's side, Stanley was pure Celt – Highland Scot with a dash of Irish and Welsh. Louisa Macdonald introduced the solidly commercial Baldwins to the world of art and literature. A published author herself, her sisters married Rudyard Kipling's father and the artistic baronets Edward Burne-Jones and Edward Poynter.

Stanley was baptized on 9 September 1867 at St Leonard's, Ribbesford, near the family's Bewdley home. At the time, both parents were recent and rather uncertain members of the Church of England. Baldwin later acknowledged his great debt 'to my Nonconformist ancestry'. He referred to 'a Quaker strain' that went all the way 'back to the earliest days of the Quakers'.[2] More significantly, both sides of his family were Wesleyan Methodists. A paternal great-grandfather had been President of the Wesleyan Methodist Conference. His maternal great-grandfather had been ordained by John Wesley himself, while both his maternal grandfather and his uncle were prominent Wesleyan ministers.

There was a reality to the family's Christian faith, a readiness to apply it to daily life and to speak of it without inhibition. Alfred's Wesleyan mother wrote to him on his tenth birthday:

> as soon as you awake offer praise and prayer to your heavenly father, praise for all his mercies to you, and prayer that he will guide and direct you through life, that he may help you in your studies so that you may learn and improve in all, that you may be able to fill, if your life be spared, a respectable and useful station in society, not in the world but in the Church; but above everything else pray that you may become a child of God made his by adoption while yet a child.

Alfred and Louisa happily addressed Stanley in similar terms.

Alfred parted company with the Methodists soon after leaving school – the consequence of unease with 'certain forbidding aspects of' Methodism.[3] He detailed the dramatic spiritual journey of his youth. In rapid succession he had been 'a strong dissenter, a Methodist [and] a rationalist'. Alfred confessed to being a 'queer young dog' who always had 'some bit

2 Stanley Baldwin, Speech to Nonconformist Unionist League, 8 April 1924, cited Stanley Baldwin, *On England and Other Addresses* (London: Philip Allen & Co., 1926), p. 269.

3 Cited A. W. Baldwin, *The Macdonald Sisters* (London: Peter Davies, 1960), pp. 184–6.

of theology rampant'. At one point he 'was much drawn' to Catholicism. Dr Pusey's writings resolved his doubts as to Anglican claims to apostolic succession.[4]

Charles Kingsley convinced Alfred that the Church of England was indeed his spiritual home. Kingsley's emphasis on the love of God, the centrality of the person of the Christ in the life of the individual believer and the need for faith to inform one's dealings with the world was decisive. Alfred wrote his profession of faith for Louisa:

> what I hope is the very root of all my beliefs, that GOD is really and indeed the King of this earth; and that He as truly governs this England of ours as He did the Jews of old . . . my belief is that all is GOD's – that we are holding all that we have for the advancement of His glory and the good of His Church . . . it seems to me to follow that a man's daily labour, whatever it be, if only honest, is holy . . . He should strive to do his duty in that estate of life in which GOD has placed him. The harm is not in riches nor in influence but in the way that they are used.[5]

Alfred put this into practice. Despite his growing wealth, he continued to live by the foundry, knowing his workmen by name and tithing his income. The example was not lost on his son.

'An extreme High Churchman'

Alfred became an Anglican at the age of 19. Louisa followed him into the Church of England on their marriage in 1866. He looked to the Church for reverent liturgy, preferably with good music and intelligent, orthodox preaching. When St Leonard's, Ribbesford, failed to provide this, the couple remained at home on most Sundays. Louisa occasionally ventured to the Methodist chapel – a journey Alfred was not prepared to make.

4 Alfred Baldwin to Louisa Macdonald, 14 October 1865 and 24 December 1865, WAAS, Baldwin Family Papers, 705:775/8229/6/ii.

5 Alfred Baldwin to Louisa Macdonald, 13 October 1865, WAAS, Baldwin Family Papers, 705:775/8229/6/ii.

Surprisingly, however, he followed her example in twice attending the Quakers' meeting. The Baldwins were saved for Anglicanism by Bishop Henry Philpott of Worcester, who gradually drew the young industrialist into the life of the Church.[6]

Philip Williamson, one of the few political biographers to take seriously his subject's religious faith, seeks to dispel one claim: the classification of Alfred and Stanley Baldwin as High Anglicans. This misunderstanding, he maintains, arises from a misreading of Alfred's declaration to Louisa that he was 'an extreme High Churchman'. Williamson argues that he meant this statement to be 'not absolute but relative – that of a former Nonconformist addressing the daughter of a Nonconformist minister'.[7] This is not an accurate representation of Alfred Baldwin's beliefs.

In his younger days, Alfred read extensively, including the works of Herbert Spencer, Thomas Carlyle and the controversial Bishop John Colenso.[8] Charles Kingsley, Frederick Maurice and the Tractarian John Keble, however, became firm favourites. Keble's *Christian Year* was his model for sober devotion and the practical application of faith. Alfred punctiliously observed the Church's liturgical calendar and ritual. He admired the French Dominican, Lacordaire, but was puzzled how one could be both 'a devoted Romanist and a strong liberal'.[9] His frequent return to John Henry Newman's works suggests that he found them spiritually beneficial.[10]

From the 1870s, there was a pronounced shift towards a definite High Church position. It mattered that liturgy was 'ritually correct'; sermons had to be 'clear, sound, dogmatic'.[11] When staying in London, Alfred was increasingly attracted to St Paul's Cathedral and, from the later 1870s, to All Saints, Margaret Street, St Thomas's, Regent Street, and St Alban's,

---

6 Alfred Baldwin, Diary, 31 January, 7, 21 and 28 February, 4, 11 and 25 April, 15 August, 24 October 1869, WAAS, Baldwin Family Papers, 705:775/8229/1/vi.

7 Philip Williamson, *Stanley Baldwin: Conservative leadership and national values* (Cambridge: Cambridge University Press, 1999), p. 104; Alfred Baldwin to Louisa Macdonald, 14 October 1865, WAAS, Baldwin Family Papers, 705:775/8229/6/ii.

8 Alfred Baldwin, Diary, 21 November 1869, WAAS, Baldwin Family Papers, 705:775/8229/1/vi.

9 Alfred Baldwin to Louisa Baldwin, 20 July 1869, WAAS, Baldwin Family Papers, 705:775/8229/6/ii.

10 Alfred Baldwin, Diary, 7 February 1875, 7 October, 4 November 1877 and 24 November 1878, WAAS, Baldwin Family Papers, 705:775/8229/2.

11 Alfred Baldwin to Louisa Baldwin, 24 December and 12 February 1882, WAAS, Baldwin Family Papers, 705:775/8229/6/ii.

Holborn.[12] These were among the most 'advanced' London parishes, in which no moderate Anglican would risk his Protestant soul. St Thomas's became the family's preferred London parish, where they often attended matins, 'the High Celebration' of Holy Communion and evensong on the same Sunday. Louisa too came to revel in High Church liturgy.

When travelling in Europe it was not uncommon for English Protestants to visit Catholic churches to satisfy their curiosity and taste for spectacle. With the Baldwins it was different. In Belgium and France, Vienna and Prague, they returned to Catholic churches Sunday after Sunday for Mass, vespers, sermons and processions.[13] They were greatly moved by the 1878 Corpus Christi procession in Vienna, fully conversant with what they were witnessing.[14] In Brittany in 1888, the local parish priest 'stroked our eyes [including those of the 20-year-old Stanley] with the holy relic of the finger of St John', the family returning for Mass two days later.[15]

'Not to give people the idea that we are only Sunday religionists'

With exacting standards regarding liturgy and music, Alfred built and paid for his own church, All Saints, Wilden – a fine Arts and Crafts building. The Burne-Jones stained glass depicted a young Stanley setting out on the journey of life accompanied by his guardian angel. On the evening of the church's consecration, Alfred wrote: 'The work is done; thanks be to GOD; and may His blessing be on me and mine and the whole Church. O Lord, remember me for good.'[16] Alfred frequently attended three services on a Sunday and was present during the week as well. He commended the

12 Alfred Baldwin, Diary, 28 March, 12 and 18 July 1875, 14 April, 25 June, 9 July and 19 November 1876, 1 April 1877, WAAS, Baldwin Family Papers, 705:775/8229/2; 3 and 10 February, 16 March, 22 June, 27 July, 16 November 1884, WAAS, Baldwin Family Papers, 705:775/8229/3.

13 Alfred Baldwin, Diary, 8 and 10 September 1876, 7 July 1878, WAAS, Baldwin Family Papers, 705:775/8229/2; 15 and 22 August 1886, WAAS, Baldwin Family Papers, 705:8229/3.

14 Louisa Baldwin to SB, 20 June 1878, CUL, Baldwin Papers, 235/2/21; Alfred Baldwin, Diary, 20 June 1878, WAAS, Baldwin Family Papers, 705:775/8229/2.

15 Louisa Baldwin, Diary, 6 and 8 July 1888, WAAS, Baldwin Family Papers, 705:775/8229/8.

16 Alfred Baldwin, Diary, 4 May 1880, WAAS, Baldwin Family Papers, 705:775/8229/2.

practice to his son: 'I hope you will be able sometimes to run in to matins or evensong, so as to not to give people the idea that we are only Sunday religionists; matins is a good beginning of a day.'[17]

This is the world in which Stanley Baldwin was raised: a world of bishops and fashionable preachers from St Paul's Cathedral visiting Wilden, and of conversations dominated by Church appointments, music and liturgical colours. Theirs, however, was no superficial faith. It was sustained by prayer and manifest in actions of charity and justice to workmen and villagers.

After his baptism, Stanley next attended church at the age of two. Thereafter he regularly joined his parents and was familiar with Anglican liturgy and clerical company from his earliest years. There was daily prayer and Scripture reading in the home. Alfred recorded his pride in his seven-year-old son: 'Heard Stan repeat his Catechism which he got through with scarcely an error.'[18] His mother wrote to Stanley at his preparatory school in Slough:

> Don't forget our little custom of reading a few verses daily. It would be a good place to read a little of the daily Psalms. Never forget God is as near to you at Slough as at Wilden, and loves you and cares for you, and it is He who makes us love each other.[19]

Stanley complained that the school's liturgical life fell short of the standards set by Wilden:

> I wish more than ever that we could have a proper service here. We have one hymn each service. No anthem. Plain chants for everything. No services for the canticles. No cassocks. It is such a pity I think, don't you?[20]

Stanley proceeded to Harrow in 1881. There too the school chapel met with disapproval. Even by the norms of the age, his interest in matters ecclesiastical was pronounced. He wrote to his father on the subject of

---

17 Alfred Baldwin to SB, 2 August 1888, CUL, Baldwin Papers, 235/3/1.

18 Alfred Baldwin, Diary, 7 February 1875, WAAS, Baldwin Family Papers, 705:775/8229/2.

19 Louisa Baldwin to SB, 9 May 1878, CUL, Baldwin Papers, 235/2/6.

20 SB to Alfred Baldwin, 5 June 1881, Slough, CUL, Baldwin Papers, 236/1/9.

Church appointments, his reading material was the *Church Times* and he spent his allowance on editions of Gregorian chant.[21] Alfred confided his hopes for his son as he was confirmed in the school chapel in March 1884: 'May GOD bless him and bring him through "the dangers and temptations and ignorances of his youth" and "may he never run into folly and the evils of an unbridled appetite".'[22] During school holidays, Stanley accompanied his parents on Sundays to All Saints, Wilden, High Church parishes in London and the Catholic Mass during their travels in Europe.

Holy orders?

In October 1888, Baldwin went up to Trinity College, Cambridge, to read Classics. Before the end of the first week he had written home announcing his intention to seek ordination. His father noted laconically that he was not surprised.[23] Nothing further is mentioned of the possibility of a priestly vocation, but it was certainly not a question of Baldwin losing his faith as an undergraduate. He spent one Easter vacation at the college mission in Camberwell and took his father to visit on another occasion.[24]

Tom Jones, Deputy Secretary to the Cabinet, shared Baldwin's Christian faith and became a close friend. Jones believed that Baldwin 'had been influenced at Cambridge by Cunningham'.[25] The Revd William Cunningham was Chaplain of Trinity, a position he combined with that of Vicar of Great St Mary's during Baldwin's final year. He lectured in English Economic History and was a Tory tariff reformer. Raised a Scots Presbyterian, he converted to Anglicanism, attracted by the liturgy and, like Alfred Baldwin, by F. D. Maurice, who taught him at Cambridge. Cunningham's preference for moderate High Church worship and daily public prayer gave Baldwin a ready point of reference. He joined and contributed to Cunningham's Sunday Essay Society, where a range of religious subjects were discussed. It may have been Cunningham's emphasis on the social application

21 SB to Alfred Baldwin, 7 December 1884, CUL, Baldwin Papers, 236/1/17.

22 Alfred Baldwin, Diary, 18 March 1884, WAAS, Baldwin Family Papers, 705:775/8229/3.

23 Alfred Baldwin, Diary, 5 October 1885, WAAS, Baldwin Family Papers, 705:775/8229/3.

24 Alfred Baldwin, Diary, 21 July 1888, WAAS, Baldwin Family Papers, 705:775/8229/3.

25 Tom Jones, Diary, 22 December 1923, cited Thomas Jones, *Whitehall Diary, Vol. 1, 1916–1925* (London: Oxford University Press, 1969), p. 262.

of Christian faith that caused Baldwin to reconsider his vocation. He was a welcome guest at Wilden.

On graduation, Baldwin returned to Worcestershire to work in the family firm. His parents' pride in their son on his twenty-first birthday was evident:

> What makes me most thankful of all is, that I believe by the goodness of God, you have taken the right side at the very beginning of life, with Christ for your guide and leader. To Him I have commended you at every step of your life, and shall do so to the end, in the certainty that His love will never fail you.[26]

He was invariably present at All Saints, Wilden on Sundays, occasionally on weekdays too, teaching in the parish Sunday school. His ecclesiastical opinions continued to reflect those of his parents. He rated Salisbury Cathedral poorly; the service there was 'sloppy'.[27] In March 1893 he wrote to his mother expressing his appreciation of certain sermons and giving a lengthy interpretation of a passage from Saint Paul's Letter to the Romans, citing the church fathers and various commentaries.[28] It was the last such letter he was to write.

'My wife and I are one'

By the mid-1890s, his church attendance had fallen off considerably, limited to appearances at Christmas and Easter, baptisms, weddings and funerals. Sunday mornings were given over to walking and correspondence. What caused such a radical change?

Windham Baldwin maintained that his father ceased attending church during his years in public office 'for reasons of very necessary rest and privacy'.[29] It is true that during much of this period Baldwin was exhausted, living on the edge of his nerves and coming close to a breakdown in the summer of 1936. Yet for a believer accustomed to traditional religious

26 Louisa Baldwin to SB, 2 August 1888, CUL, Baldwin Papers, 235/3/2.
27 SB to Louisa Baldwin, 27 September 1892, CUL, Baldwin Papers, 236/2/50.
28 SB to Louisa Baldwin, 11 March 1893, CUL, Baldwin Papers, 236/2/56.
29 A. W. Baldwin, *My Father*, p. 326.

observance, one might have expected him to find spiritual strength and peace in the Church's liturgy and sacraments. There is another difficulty with this explanation: Baldwin ceased attending church two decades before appointment to government office and a decade before election to Parliament. The reason must be sought elsewhere.

Through his Burne-Jones cousins in Rottingdean, Sussex, Baldwin met his future wife, Lucy ('Cissie') Ridsdale. Her father was a scientist, a Liberal and an agnostic. The couple were married on 12 September 1892 at Rottingdean parish church, where Cunningham officiated. It was a long and happy marriage. Lucy Baldwin was a force to be reckoned with – 'Formidable and overwhelming in laying down the law'[30] is how Tom Jones recalled her. Despite her father's scepticism, she was a decided believer. The Swedish Ambassador put the question directly to her at Lord Curzon's funeral in 1925:

> 'You are a believer, Mrs Baldwin', I whispered to her. 'I am indeed,' she replied, 'and I must tell you that every morning when we rise we kneel together before God and commend our day to Him, praying that some good work may be done in it by us. It is not for ourselves that we are working, but for the country and God's sake. How else could we live?' She looked at me sincerely and naturally and I realized the simple earnestness of their conception of life.[31]

It was, however, a very different faith from that in which her husband had been raised.

Lucy Baldwin was never baptized. She believed in a deity and the power of prayer, but it is uncertain whether this was the Christian God of Jesus Christ. She had little time for Church or creed. The difference was apparent on the death of Tom Jones's wife. Whereas Stanley wrote of 'the inscrutable will of God', Lucy referred rather to 'the Highest Spirit'.[32] She was

30 Tom Jones, Diary, 26 March 1944, cited Thomas Jones, *A Diary with Letters, 1931–1950* (London: Oxford University Press, 1954), p. 515.

31 Baron Erik Pamstierna memoirs, cited ed. Philip Williamson and Edward Baldwin, *Baldwin Papers: A Conservative statesman, 1908–1947* (Cambridge: Cambridge University Press, 2004), pp. 497–8.

32 SB to Tom Jones, 1 July 1935, NLW, Thomas Jones Papers, A.6/90/1–2; Lucy Baldwin to Tom Jones, 25 June 1935, NLW, Thomas Jones Papers, A.6/89.

highly selective as to which church services she would attend with her husband – if he went to Communion, he went alone. Allergic to ritual and sacraments, she pronounced 'symbolism and adornment and other parts of the English church worship to be "pagan"'.[33] On the fourth Sunday of the month, the children were excused church attendance 'because the service was full of Athanasian creeds and things, and these were wrong'. Instead, in their mother's presence, they 'recited the Lord's Prayer and the Thanksgiving, even then leaving out a few phrases at the end'.[34]

Stanley and Lucy were often at Wilden on Sundays. For the first year of their marriage he was generally at matins and Holy Communion with his parents, but Lucy chose to stay away. After 1893 there is little evidence of either attending. In political life, Baldwin would be criticized for being insufficiently assertive and failing to take the initiative. It seems to have been the case in the religious life of the family too. Baldwin insisted on the children's baptism but little else.

'My wife and I are one.'[35] No one doubted Baldwin's claim that his marriage was a partnership. Marriage changed his religious practice – his early High Church belief and practice were clearly not as deeply rooted as that of his parents.[36]

'Such vivid expectations of meeting him again'

Abandonment of participation in public worship is often the external manifestation of an inner disengagement from all matters spiritual. That was not true for Baldwin. For him, Christian faith was essential to effect 'the individual transformation of character', a character 'formed on the model of Our Lord and Master'. In his opinion it was through the influence of such lives, rather than the churches, 'that some day the Kingdom

33 A. W. Baldwin, *My Father*, p. 326.

34 Oliver Baldwin, *The Questing Beast: An autobiography* (London: Grayson & Grayson, 1932), p. 7.

35 Jones, Diary, 22 May 1936, cited Jones, *A Diary with Letters*, p. 205.

36 Baldwin's withdrawal from the liturgy of the Church was not absolute. A cricketing enthusiast, having watched a game, he would on occasion cross the River Severn to attend evensong at Worcester Cathedral, a building he knew and loved all his life.

of Heaven will come on earth'.[37] Baldwin did not reject the churches but wished them to 'cultivate their own garden – the garden of religious life. This is their own peculiar field, and within it they should strive to grow the finest fruits of the spirit.'[38]

His faith remained orthodox and scriptural. There was no flirtation with Modernism. He lectured the Salvation Army on the reality of the human condition: 'We have banished the word "sin" from the dictionaries. You may expunge the word as much as you like, but the ugly fact remains, and will remain.'[39] He had similarly robust advice for a family member, telling her to banish 'silly thoughts and suspicions back to where they came from – the Devil!'[40] The emphasis was, however, on divine love and guidance: 'The personality of our Lord' exercised a 'universal appeal to mankind.'[41] He was recognized as an 'earnest and unquestioning Christian'. On his appointment as Prime Minister one political journalist wrote:

> Mr Baldwin . . . conserves at the depths of his personality something that is now regarded by numerous people as superstition. He believes that men may be used by the invisible forces of the universe as instruments for the good and elevation of mankind.[42]

The resurrection and personal survival beyond death were for him less intellectual beliefs than experienced realities. Baldwin apologized to his mother for not speaking more of the past after his father's death. He felt it unnecessary:

> To me father exists so much more in the present and in the future. I mean that I feel his spirit so often with me – at Paddington, in the City – anywhere and everywhere – and I have such vivid expectations

37 SB, Address to the National Free Church Conference, 'Christian Ideals', 12 March 1925, cited SB, *On England*, pp. 206, 210, 211.

38 SB, Address to the Bible Society, 'The Bible', 2 May 1928, cited Stanley Baldwin, *This Torch of Freedom: Speeches and addresses* (London: Hodder & Stoughton, 1935), p. 91.

39 SB, 'William Booth', Address to the Salvation Army, 10 April 1929, cited SB, *This Torch of Freedom*, p. 108.

40 SB to Monica Baldwin, 3 June 1942, CUL, Baldwin Papers, 236/3/19.

41 SB, 'The Bible', cited SB, *This Torch of Freedom*, p. 91.

42 A Gentleman with a Duster [Edward Harold Begbie], *The Conservative Mind* (London: Mills & Boon, 1924), pp. 8, 13.

of meeting him again – where or in what shape I know not – and earning possibly a 'Well done' from him.

These things are not easy to explain: perhaps you will understand.[43]

There was a moment of mystical experience during the funeral of his cousin, Sir Ambrose Poynter:

> I had an extraordinary feeling in the church that the coffin contained nothing but a discarded shell and I seemed to know with a certainty beyond any earthly knowledge that Ambo was with his mother and that all the apparent failure of his life was clear to him. I could see the whole thing and it gave me a strange confidence that all was well and that it was an occasion for profound thanksgiving. The feeling – or rather the vivid sense of it – passed, but it was the realest thing yesterday and the sense of it was abiding.[44]

This was very different from the faltering hope or downright scepticism of his immediate predecessors and successors in 10 Downing Street.

Belief was borne out by practice. The Sabbath was still observed, simply not in church. The Canadian Prime Minister, Mackenzie King, noted that for Baldwin, Sunday was sacrosanct, given over to 'reflection'.[45] There was an increasing dependence on a life of prayer. Each day he prayed for 'ability to do [his work], whatever and wherever it is, and to do it with cheerfulness'.[46] Bible reading was part of daily life. Tom Jones's eye was drawn to 'a pocket edition of the Parables of Jesus' on the Prime Minister's desk at Chequers.[47] Baldwin's morality too was explicitly Christian:

> To elevate every desire, however obscene, into a good because it is desired may be the way of all flesh, but it is not the way of the cross. And the moral anarchy which is said to pervade our youth . . . is not

43 SB to Louisa Baldwin, 12 February 1916, CUL, Baldwin Papers, 236/2/421.

44 SB to Louisa Baldwin, 3 June 1923, CUL, Baldwin Papers, 236/2/579.

45 Mackenzie King, Diary, 1 October 1923, cited ed. Williamson and Baldwin, *Baldwin Papers*, p. 113.

46 SB to Joan Dickinson, 11 December 1916, cited ed. Williamson and Baldwin, *Baldwin Papers*, p. 27.

47 Jones, Diary, 30 September 1923, cited Jones, *Whitehall Diary, Vol. 1*, p. 244.

going to be countered by lowering the demands of religion, but by insisting on them.[48]

'It was during the war that I found my soul'

When Alfred Baldwin died unexpectedly in 1908, his funeral at Wilden was attended by five thousand people. His son and nephews kept vigil beside his coffin the preceding night. Representing the constituency vacated by his father's death, Stanley's entry into Parliament was inspired more by filial piety than a passion for politics or the pursuit of power. After eight years on the back benches he questioned his presence there. He felt he was 'no use to God or man'. Then came the moment of spiritual awakening: 'It was during the war that I found my soul. There came to me by degrees a changed sense of values, and I began to feel that I might be used for some special work. I didn't know what.' It began with personal action. Baldwin was deeply conscious both that his business interests had profited massively from the war and that he had been spared the tragic loss of family members in the slaughter of the trenches. He proceeded to give away about £200,000 (some £4 million in current values). In an anonymous letter to *The Times*, he urged men of substance to follow his example.[49]

Finally appointed to ministerial office as he was approaching the age of 50, Baldwin wrote to his mother, discerning the hand of divine providence:

> We both believe there is guidance in these things. I never sought a place, never expected it, and suddenly a way opened and an offer of wider service was made. If one tackles public life in the right spirit, it is unselfish service.[50]

He began to plan for the kind of world he wished to see when peace returned. With others, he was bitterly disappointed by the subsequent social inequality and industrial unrest: 'Since the last war the manifest forces of

48 SB, 'The Bible', cited SB, *This Torch of Freedom*, pp. 83–4.

49 SB, 'Note for Cousin', Margaret Mackail (copy), misdated (?) 6 October 1937, CUL, Baldwin Papers, 236/7/1.

50 SB to Louisa Baldwin, 11 February 1917, CUL, Baldwin Papers, 236/2/436.

Satan have been conspicuously at large.'[51] He was not reticent in identifying the source of the moral malaise affecting the body politic. Baldwin had a visceral hatred of Lloyd George. He despised the tainting of the honours system, the corrosive influence of the press barons and Lloyd George's presidential style of government. With real moral indignation, he led the opposition to the leadership of his own party. To their surprise and perhaps his own, he prevailed, and Lloyd George was gone.

Baldwin never overestimated his own ability but neither did he doubt the purpose behind his promotion to high office. He saw his life to date as a preparation for this moment:

> The problem was to get at the soul of the working people. I found that those long quiet years at Wilden had given me a knowledge of them that few men in politics had. The lines of my policy grew clear, and I *knew* that I had been chosen as God's instrument for the work of the healing of the nation.[52]

In his own understanding at least, his political career from this point on was to be just as vocational as the ordained ministry considered at Cambridge 35 years earlier. He explained his motivation in terms simultaneously political, moral and religious: 'My job is to try and educate a new democracy in a new world and to try and make them realize their responsibilities in their possession of power, and to keep the eternal verities before them.'[53] This was not just for private consumption. Baldwin declared publicly that if he felt his work was not advancing the kingdom of God, 'I could have no hope, I could do no work, and I would give over my office this morning to anyone who would take it.'[54]

Philip Williamson contends that Baldwin's speeches became more explicitly Christian as the 1930s progressed.[55] That is true, but faith was

51 SB, 'Religion and Politics', Address to Wesleyans, 11 February 1926, cited SB, *On England*, p. 196.

52 SB, 'Note for Cousin', 6 October 1937, CUL, Baldwin Papers, 236/7/1.

53 SB to Monica Baldwin, 22 December 1935, CUL, Baldwin Papers, 236/3/5.

54 SB, 'The Bible', cited SB, *This Torch of Freedom*, p. 93.

55 Philip Williamson, 'The Doctrinal Politics of Stanley Baldwin' in ed. Michael Bentley, *Public and Private Doctrine* (Cambridge: Cambridge University Press, 1993), p. 200.

there from the beginning of his premiership. He conceived of the nation's problems in spiritual terms:

> It was obvious that the first thing to be done was to pull the country together: to make them realize the brotherhood of the human family. It seemed simple and obvious, but how to do it? The bitterness in the country was of the devil.[56]

He formulated the solution in spiritual terms too:

> There is nothing this country needs as much as another Wesley or Whitefield . . . I confess I am not sure, if a Wesley or a St Francis arose today, that to found a body of preaching friars would not be the best thing they could do for the world.[57]

To be authentic, religion was 'an affair of Christians in politics, in diplomacy, in trade, in industry, in school, in sport'.[58] On his retirement he summarized his political philosophy:

> Use men as ends and never merely as means; and live for the brotherhood of man, which implies the Fatherhood of God. The brotherhood of man today is often denied and divided and called foolishness but is in fact one of the foolish things of the world which God uses to confound the wise . . . That is the message that I have tried to deliver as Prime Minister, in hundreds of speeches.[59]

Baldwin's motivation was apparent to others from the outset. Harold Begbie wrote: 'He is in Parliament for no other purpose under heaven than to do his duty as an Englishman, and . . . his definition of a statesman would

---

56 SB, 'Note for Cousin', 6 October 1937, CUL, Baldwin Papers, 236/7/1.

57 SB, 'Religion and Politics', Address to Wesleyans, 11 February 1926, cited SB, *On England*, p. 195.

58 SB, 'Religion and National Life', Address to the Annual Assembly of the Congregational Union, 12 May 1931, cited SB, *This Torch of Freedom*, p. 81.

59 SB, Speech, Empire Rally of Youth, 18 May 1937, cited Stanley Baldwin, *Service of Our Lives: Last speeches as Prime Minister* (London: Hodder & Stoughton, 1937), pp. 166–7.

be "a politician who tries to do the Will of God"'.[60] Few knew him better than Tom Jones, who judged: 'He was more preacher than statesman. He had no profound faith in politics as a cure for man's miseries.'[61] The former editor of the Liberal *Daily News* arrived at the same conclusion: '"He has none of the attributes so common to the politician;" rather "he belongs to the pulpit . . . and raises grave issues in the spirit of the preacher rather than of the statesman."'[62]

Within his own party there were those critical of Baldwin's approach. At least one minister protested:

> A Prime Minister ought not to be tempted, by lack of competition, to stray too far into the regions of morals and imagination; and Baldwin yielded too easily to this temptation. To a Cornish mass-meeting he liked to talk of Wesley rather than of statesmanship.[63]

The *Financial Times* was even more disparaging: 'He was the first revivalist produced by the Tory party, and we greatly hope that they will not produce another.'[64] Did his references to religion harm Baldwin politically? His electoral record and personal popularity strongly suggest otherwise. He told George VI 'that the average working man' might not attend church himself, but he was 'glad to know' that his monarch did.[65] In the interwar years, 'the average working man' probably had similar expectations of his Prime Minister – provided he was neither divisively sectarian nor given to affecting moral superiority. Baldwin avoided both pitfalls.

'Give peace in our time, O Lord'

'I want to be a healer,' Baldwin declared on entering 10 Downing Street. He identified two areas where the need was acute: relations between social

60 A Gentleman with a Duster [Begbie], *The Conservative Mind*, p. 30.

61 Jones, *A Diary with Letters 1931–1950*, p. xxxii.

62 A. G. Gardiner, cited Williamson, *SB*, p. 337.

63 Eustace Percy, *Some Memories* (London: Eyre & Spottiswoode, 1958), p. 204.

64 *Financial Times*, 10 November 1952, cited A. W. Baldwin, *My Father*, p. 168.

65 Earl of Crawford to Lord Tweedsmuir, 1 December 1937, cited ed. Williamson and Baldwin, *Baldwin Papers*, pp. 445–6.

classes and industrial relations. To that end he indicated that he would employ both resolute conviction and spiritual generosity:

> If there are those who want to fight the class war we will take up the challenge and we will beat them by the hardness of our heads and the largeness of our hearts. I want to leave this country, when my term ends, in better heart than it has been for years.[66]

He was willing to face down his own party as well as his political opponents, refusing to allow Conservatives to reverse concessions won by trade unionists. In doing so, he appealed to a nonpartisan shared faith:

> Although I know that there are those who work for different ends from most of us in this House, yet there are many in all ranks and all parties who will re-echo my prayer. '*Give peace in our time, O Lord*.'[67]

A similar stance characterized Baldwin's response to the General Strike of May 1926: 'I am a man of peace. I am longing and working and praying for peace, but I will not surrender the safety and security of the British Constitution.'[68] The strike led to a temporary realignment of confessional sympathies. Archbishop Davidson and other Protestant leaders irritated Baldwin, seeming to place the government and strikers in a position of moral equivalence. Instead, he thanked Cardinal Bourne, the Catholic Archbishop of Westminster, for his unambiguous condemnation of the strike. Subsequently, Baldwin appeared less focused, his magnanimity less evident. Yet at the end of his political career he felt he had been called by God for this purpose: 'I believe that my work has not been in vain: I believe that the feeling in industry is better than it has ever been.'[69]

Baldwin was Prime Minister on the last occasion when Parliament was convulsed by the internal affairs of the Church of England. For a generation, the Anglican hierarchy had struggled to revise the 1662 Prayer Book

66 SB, Edinburgh, July 1923, cited Kenneth Young, *Stanley Baldwin* (London: Weidenfeld & Nicolson, 1976), p. 45.

67 SB, House of Commons, 6 March 1925, cited Young, *SB*, p. 66.

68 SB, Radio broadcast, cited Young, *SB*, p. 74.

69 SB, 'Note for Cousin', 6 October 1937, CUL, Baldwin Papers, 236/7/1.

in a manner acceptable to all shades of churchmanship, seeking to prevent unauthorized forms of worship. In December 1927, the Church laid its proposed solution before the House of Commons. A compromise measure, it satisfied few. It was opposed by the more extreme Anglo-Catholics, whose liturgical practices it sought to curb, while Protestant opinion was enraged by concessions to moderate Anglo-Catholics.

Baldwin had been raised on the Book of Common Prayer but was unmoved by the controversies surrounding its revision. He voted for the proposal, but his speech was neither a ringing endorsement nor a clear indication of his own position. He claimed to be 'entirely independent' of those who supported the change and those who opposed it. He disavowed any attempt to influence MPs who saw this as a matter of conscience. He simply asked those with no strong views to consider the consequences of rejecting the measure. It would, he claimed, weaken the Church and be interpreted as a lack of trust in its capacity to put its own house in order. The only people who would rejoice at such a rejection would be 'the men who have been in rebellion in the Church'; that is, the extreme Ritualists. Rejection would produce 'a state of chaos' and calls for disestablishment. That Baldwin deplored, because he felt it would reintroduce sectarian bitterness to party politics and undermine the comprehensive nature of the Church of England.[70] Such a pragmatic approach, while eminently reasonable, cut little ice in a debate where passions ran high. The proposal was defeated.

The measure was reintroduced to Parliament the following year. Lambeth Palace asked William Bridgeman, Baldwin's friend and Cabinet colleague, to assist its passage. Bridgeman, in turn, advised the Prime Minister that if he were prepared to speak in favour of the measure, it might secure its success and defeat the unattractive elements of Protestant bigotry. To no avail. The revised Prayer Book was rejected a second time. Bridgeman wrote disconsolately to his wife: 'I'm afraid the P.M. cannot have taken much trouble to let his views be known.'[71] Unlike his father, Baldwin possessed no appetite for doctrinal and liturgical controversies.

70 SB, House of Commons, 15 December 1927, Hansard, Vol. 211, cols 2531–655.

71 William Bridgeman to SB, 30 May 1928; William Bridgeman to Caroline Bridgeman, 15 June 1928, cited ed. Philip Williamson, *The Modernization of Conservative Politics: The diaries and letters of William Bridgeman, 1904–1935* (London: The Historians Press, 1988), p. 214.

The abdication crisis: 'He has no religious sense'

At a personal level, Baldwin liked Edward VIII but doubted his judgement and stability. The Prime Minister was reluctant to intervene in the King's private life, hoping that Wallis Simpson was a passing infatuation. However, his hand was forced in October 1936 as the American press reported the Simpsons' divorce proceedings and the King declared his intention to marry the woman he loved. Baldwin posed as a neutral umpire, placing various options before the King, promising to gauge what might be acceptable to Parliament and public opinion in the UK and the Dominions. Publicly at least, he made little reference to the religious and moral implications of the King, as Supreme Governor of the Church of England, marrying a divorcee. That way he minimized his own political risk and positioned himself to effect healing after a constitutional crisis. When the King abdicated on 10 December 1936, Baldwin told the Commons that he 'had left nothing undone' to avoid that eventuality. He evinced nothing but sympathy for the plight of his former monarch: 'There is not a soul here today that wants to judge. We are not judges.'[72]

Were, however, Baldwin's role and motivation quite that straightforward? His private comments and the statements of others indicate otherwise. He was certainly no moral prude. Initially he suggested to the King that he keep Wallis Simpson as his mistress, out of the public eye.[73] Nor was he the entirely impartial observer he sought to portray himself as, with no objective other than to be helpful to the various parties and steer the ship of state through choppy waters. Alan Don was chaplain to Archbishop Lang and the Speaker of the House of Commons. He referred to the Speaker's visit to Chequers, where he 'had found [Baldwin] roused about HM's behaviour. [Baldwin] is evidently determined to do all in his power to prevent a marriage between the King and Mrs. S.'[74] Edward VIII floated the possibility of a morganatic marriage, whereby he might marry a divorcee but

72 SB, Statement to House of Commons, 10 December 1936, cited SB, *Service of Our Lives*, p. 80.

73 Monica Baldwin, Diary, 7 October 1937, cited ed. Williamson and Baldwin, *Baldwin Papers*, p. 421.

74 Revd A. C. Don, Diary, 16 November 1936, LPL, MS 2864, f. 108.

neither Mrs Simpson nor any children would enjoy royal status. Baldwin doubted its constitutional feasibility; it also offended his sense of the integrity of Christian marriage: 'Is this the sort of thing I've stood for in public life? If I have to go out, then I'd be quite ready to go out on this.'[75]

He was generally a tolerant man, taking others as he found them. While he empathized with the King in his predicament, he was also profoundly disturbed:

> What rather shocked me if I may say such a thing, was that there seemed to be no *moral* struggle *at all* . . . He had *no* spiritual conflict *at all*. There was no *battle* in his will . . . He is extraordinary in the way he has no spiritual sense: no idea of sacrifice for duty . . . He has no religious sense. I have never in my life met anyone so completely lacking in any sense of the – the – what is beyond . . . There was simply no moral struggle, and it appalled me.[76]

The evening before the abdication he packed his bags and was ready to spend the night with the King, wrestling for his soul. In the event he was not required.

The coronation of George VI stirred up a variety of emotions:

> His thoughts frequently turned to the Duke of Windsor and Mrs Simpson, and how as the service proceeded he felt such a service would have been blasphemous with them and impossible for him and the Archbishop. He and Mrs Baldwin have a profound feeling of Divine guidance.[77]

Baldwin interpreted the abdication crisis in religious and moral terms, and acted accordingly.

Robert Beaken has revealed how Cosmo Lang, Archbishop of Canterbury, opposed to divorce and remarriage as contrary to the teachings of Christ, played a more decisive role in the abdication crisis than formerly

75 Jones, Diary, 25 November 1936, cited Jones, *A Diary with Letters*, p. 288.

76 Monica Baldwin, Diary, 7 October 1937, cited ed. Williamson and Baldwin, *Baldwin Papers*, pp. 421–2.

77 Jones, Diary, 20 May 1937, cited ed. Williamson and Baldwin, *Baldwin Papers*, p. 437.

appreciated.[78] Baldwin and Lang collaborated more closely than previously thought. It would have been unthinkable that the Prime Minister and the Archbishop of Canterbury were not in contact given Edward VIII's role as Supreme Governor of the Church of England and the established status of the Anglican Church. Lang noted that the two 'kept in close contact'. Over a period of six weeks, they enjoyed several long talks, in person and by telephone, devising a joint strategy. The Archbishop recorded: '[The Prime Minister] realized *my* difficulty in intervening at *present*, and agreed it would be best to leave the matter in his hands at present.'[79] Lang was referring to the King's antipathy for clergy in general, and himself in particular. It is also likely that Baldwin wished to protect the Church from any reaction if seen to be placing pressure on the King.

After the abdication, Baldwin's statement to the Commons spoke of regret and sympathy. Lang adopted a very different tone in his broadcast to the nation, criticizing Edward VIII for surrendering 'a high and sacred trust' and acting inconsistently 'with the Christian principles of marriage'.[80] In doing so, he offended the British sense of fair play due to their departed monarch and he received a hostile mailbag. Among his letters of support, however, Lang prized one above all others. It was from Baldwin:

> You said just what was wanted and, if I may say so, just what you ought to have said. I know how difficult a task you had, but you triumphed over all difficulties and you were indeed the voice of Christian England.[81]

The Church reciprocated the praise: 'We may well thank God for Stanley Baldwin – at times of crisis he is magnificent.'[82] Baldwin and Lang may have used different means and language, but they shared the same values and faith.

78 Robert Beaken, *Cosmo Lang: Archbishop in war and crisis* (London: I. B. Tauris, 2012), pp. 86–142.

79 Lang, Memorandum, 'The King's Matter', u/d, LPL, Lang Papers, 318, ff. 80–93.

80 Lang, Broadcast, 13 December 1936, cited Beaken, *Cosmo Lang*, p. 244.

81 Baldwin to Lang, 14 December 1936, cited Beaken, *Cosmo Lang*, p. 123.

82 Don, Diary, 11 December 1936, LPL, MS 2864, f. 125.

The dignity of the 'child of God'

Critics asserted that Baldwin paid insufficient attention to foreign affairs, but here too his outlook was informed by faith. His Christianity made him essentially a man of peace, arguing that 'it is hard to equate the gospel of human brotherhood with embattled nations engaged in mutual slaughter'.[83] The threat to peace was a spiritual threat. The attack on 'revealed religion' created the conditions 'for that diabolical hatred without which Communist triumph and supremacy could not be achieved'.[84] The distinction between the Anglo-Saxon democracies and the totalitarian regimes was essentially a spiritual one:

> The Christian State proclaims human personality to be supreme. The servile State denies this. Every compromise with the infinite value of the human soul leads straight back to savagery and the jungle. Expel that truth of our religion and what follows? The insolence of dominion and the cruelty of despotism. Denounce religion as the opiate of the people and you swiftly proceed to denounce political liberty and civil liberty as opium.[85]

Baldwin reiterated his message on the eve of the Second World War:

> I would always stress the spiritual rather than the political foundations . . . It is a recognition of the dignity of man and of his individuality, and that [this] dignity and individuality are his as a child of God [which] is the unbridgeable gulf between democracy and the isms that . . . for the time being control so great a part of Europe.[86]

---

83 SB, 'Religion and National Life', Address to the Annual Assembly of the Congregational Union, 12 May 1931, cited SB, *This Torch of Freedom*, p. 84.

84 SB, Speech to the Primrose League, 4 April 1930, cited Williamson, *SB*, p. 329.

85 SB, Speech, Empire Rally of Youth, 18 May 1937, cited SB, *Service of Our Lives*, p. 165.

86 SB, 16 August 1939, New York, cited Williamson, *SB*, p. 330.

'I cannot change the direction of my life'

In the quest for peace and opposition to Nazism, one organization in particular sought to enlist Baldwin in their ranks. Frank Buchman is little known today but in the 1930s he exercised an international influence. An American Protestant evangelist, his non-denominational call for 'a Christian awakening, a rebirth of spiritual power' struck a chord with Oxford undergraduates, leading to his disciples being known as the Oxford Group. 'Moral rearmament' was the solution to class warfare and industrial unrest; it was viewed as 'the only assurance of a lasting peace' between nations. Interested parties and influential figures were invited to house parties 'to discover the secret of spiritual power'.[87] Not only students were attracted by Buchman; senior Conservatives were also sympathetic: Lord Salisbury, Lord Halifax, Lord Davidson (the former party chairman) and his wife, and Lady Bridgeman.

Tom Jones poured cold water on a proposed letter to the press that Baldwin was invited to sign. He objected to the content, 'which screeched and jarred', but also advised against signing because to do so 'would be to label him and diminish the influence he has with all sorts and conditions of men'. Jones knew Baldwin well, and the threat of spiritual classification was well calculated. Baldwin was anxious to avoid promoting himself as a spiritual leader: 'If people responded to the appeal he would not know what to do. He was not St Francis.'[88] Baldwin did, however, sign an amended letter to *The Times*:

> The real need of the day is therefore moral and spiritual rearmament... God's Living Spirit calls each nation, like each individual, to its highest destiny, and breaks down the barriers of fear and greed, of suspicion and hatred . . . 'Thy will be done on earth,' is not only a prayer for guidance, but a call to action. For His Will is our Peace.[89]

87 Invitation to Oxford Group House Party, 13–23 March 1936, PA, Davidson Papers, DAV/226.

88 Jones to Lady Griggs, 1 August 1938, cited ed. Williamson and Baldwin, *Baldwin Papers*, p. 453.

89 SB, Salisbury et al. to Editor, *The Times*, 10 September 1938, cited ed. Williamson and Baldwin, *Baldwin Papers*, p. 456.

Baldwin sympathized with the Oxford Group's objectives and met privately with Buchman. He could not, however, 'get over a certain distrust of Group methods'.[90] Principal among these was its reputed practice of public confession – something he was not prepared to contemplate: 'We have all done things of which we are ashamed but I cannot imagine the Almighty wants us to add to the world's misery by confessing it to all and sundry. He'll be content if we repent to Him.'[91] In old age, Baldwin increasingly returned to the traditional Anglicanism of his youth. He thanked his cousin, Margaret Mackail, for her invitation to join the Oxford Group, but firmly rebuffed her: 'I cannot change the direction of my life at any suggestion from others however deep my respect and love for them.'[92]

Moderation all round

Archbishop Davidson found Baldwin 'delightful to deal with' when it came to ecclesiastical appointments. As a believing Anglican, Baldwin possessed 'a background of general knowledge and traditional interest', which Campbell-Bannerman, Lloyd George and Law lacked. The Archbishop was gratified too that he was inclined to act on his recommendation.[93] Baldwin made it clear that, generally speaking, 'anything the Church thought fit to do would be the right thing to do'. Nevertheless, he would pursue his own enquiries among bishops and leading laymen, 'and then use his own judgment'. Conscious of his duty to both Church and Crown, he had no intention of relinquishing his role in appointments.[94]

Baldwin's style was decidedly casual, as William Temple discovered when translated to York:

> The two Archbishops [Davidson and Lang] had put my name first, but had urged Baldwin to enquire himself and make his own choice;

90 SB to Lord Davidson, 20 August 1941, PA, Davidson Papers, DAV/283.

91 Jones to Lady Griggs, 1 August 1938, cited ed. Williamson and Baldwin, *Baldwin Papers*, p. 453.

92 SB, 'Note for Cousin', 6 October 1937, CUL, Baldwin Papers, 236/7/1.

93 Davidson, Memorandum, 12 August 1923, LPL, Davidson Papers, 14, ff. 220–1.

94 SB, Evidence to Church Assembly Committee on the Appointment of Bishops, 18 March 1927, LPL, Bell Papers, 118, ff. 142–57.

it was not to be said that he had merely accepted the advice of the Archbishops.

The Prime Minister came and the Archbishop left me alone with him. He at once said: 'I think that the Archbishop has told you what I want to see you about.' I said: 'Yes.' He stared and looked in my face, saying 'Well?' And that was the extent of his formal offer.[95]

Baldwin often lacked a sense of urgency or efficiency when it came to filling vacancies. Experience taught Davidson that matters were better expedited by a personal interview than by correspondence.[96]

The Prime Minister was not without his own views on such matters – as in the political sphere, his preference was for moderation. Geoffrey Fry, his private secretary who dealt with Church appointments, told Davidson: 'Mr Baldwin's great anxiety in the matter of higher preferment is to maintain so far as may be possible a fair and just balance between the various points of view.'[97] Baldwin expressed his aim to keep 'preferment in a particular Diocese to men whose views would not violently conflict with what might be the prevailing views in a Diocese'.[98] It is clear, however, he had an aversion to extreme High Churchmen, making known his inclination for clergy 'belonging in the large sense to the Evangelical section'.[99] Davidson advised him to extend the pool of potential candidates: 'You would not wish that the reasonable High Churchmen or the reasonable Evangelicals should feel that they have been passed over or that all the emphasis had been laid elsewhere than on their friends.'[100]

Given Lang's High Church reputation and supposed Anglo-Catholic sympathies, his appointment to Canterbury in succession to Davidson might appear surprising. Baldwin recognized Lang, however, as the candidate of 'the Court' and so calculated that this was 'the line of least resistance'. Consulting the High Churchman Edward Wood was unlikely to

95 William Temple, Memorandum, 2 August 1928, LPL, W. Temple Papers, 46, f. 281.

96 Davidson to Stamfordham, 24 November 1926 (copy), LPL, Davidson Papers, 11, f. 124.

97 Geoffrey Fry to Davidson, 30 November 1926, LPL, Davidson Papers, 11, f. 125.

98 SB, Evidence to Church Assembly Committee on the Appointment of Bishops, 18 March 1927, LPL, Bell Papers, 118, f. 142.

99 Davidson to Fry, 25 October 1923 (copy), LPL, Davidson Papers, 11, f. 83.

100 Davidson to SB, 18 July 1928 (copy), LPL, Davidson Papers, 11, f. 138.

have persuaded him otherwise.[101] In the event, Lang's tenure at Lambeth was as moderate as Baldwin could have wished for.

Baldwin's objections could be political as well as theological. He considered the bishops' intervention during the General Strike and its aftermath naïve, playing into the hands of 'the atheist bolshevists'.[102] Temple's socialist tendencies were well known. When proposed for York, Baldwin's initial reaction was, 'Temple can wait', and advanced the candidacy of Thomas Strong, Bishop of Oxford.[103]

'A Churchman in little more than name'?

If these factors influenced Baldwin in his exercise of church patronage, what of his own churchmanship? He had no desire to deceive others. He told the House of Commons: 'Although I was born and baptized a member of the Church of England, I belong to no party in that Church.'[104] He went further in private correspondence: 'I fear I am a Churchman in little more than name.'[105] Not all Anglicans appreciated Randall Davidson; they found him cold and uninspiring. Baldwin recognized other qualities in the Archbishop: 'his realization of the breadth of the Church and his determination that so far as lay in his power during his Primacy there should be nothing in the way of heresy hunting'.[106] Baldwin acknowledged that the Church of England appeared illogical to many. He felt, however, that the attempt to overdefine was responsible for the divisions among Christians. Overrationalizing was unhelpful:

> Instead of accepting the Sacrament . . . you get into your difficulties and begin to see lines of division and demarcation . . . To my mind,

101 SB to Edward Wood, Lord Irwin, 15 September 1927, Halifax Indian Papers, cited ed. Williamson and Baldwin, *Baldwin Papers*, p. 202.

102 Tom Jones, Diary, 21 July 1926, cited Thomas Jones, *Whitehall Diary, Vol. 2, 1926–1930* (London: Oxford University Press, 1969), p. 63.

103 Jones, Diary, 21 November 1927, cited Jones, *Whitehall Diary, Vol. 2*, p. 117.

104 SB, House of Commons, 15 December 1927, Hansard, Vol. 211, cols 2531–655.

105 SB to Lady Bridgeman, 24 October 1932, cited ed. Williamson and Baldwin, *Baldwin Papers*, p. 302.

106 SB, Speech, Harrow Association Dinner, 12 July 1928, cited SB, *This Torch of Freedom*, p. 226.

> the glory of our Church is its comprehensiveness in having men of different types in the same Church.[107]

This did not make Baldwin a liberal Anglican. He was pleased to discover that his son, Oliver, had recovered some form of belief and had written a life of Christ. However, finding that Oliver rejected the divinity of Christ, he put the book to one side because 'he did not wish anything to disturb his faith which was most orthodox C of E'.[108] Baldwin believed in heaven and hell, in sin and salvation, and in the resurrection. Prayer and Scripture were fundamental. He was profoundly conscious of the presence of God in the wonders of creation. He enjoyed a personal relationship with Christ. Avoiding partisan classification enabled Baldwin to speak of Christian faith to a wider Protestant constituency. Many Nonconformists responded to this: he was welcomed by the National Free Church Council in a manner impossible for previous Conservative leaders. He appealed explicitly to church and chapel: 'They . . . had both been, and are, and will be great social forces with great political consequences.'[109] He was fully aware of the political advantages of detaching Free Church members from their allegiance to the Liberal Party, but there was nothing insincere in the religious content of his speeches.

He was sufficiently generous to credit authentic faith, and its practical consequences, wherever he encountered it. Thus the two religious figures mentioned most frequently in his speeches were John Wesley and Saint Francis of Assisi. He loved to draw parallels between the two: 'Had Wesley been born four centuries earlier, he would have been Wesley just the same, but he would have worn a rough robe girded with a cord and have founded a great body of preaching friars.'[110] The Salvation Army evinced a similar spiritual simplicity and vibrancy: 'It did not come from Canterbury. The Franciscans did not come from Rome . . . It sprang – where all these things have sprung from – it sprang from the very heart of the people.'[111]

107 SB, House of Commons, 15 December 1927, Hansard, Vol. 211, cols 2531–655.

108 Oliver Baldwin, Memoirs, cited ed. Williamson and Baldwin, *Baldwin Papers*, p. 483.

109 SB, Speech, Tregrehan, 23 June 1927, cited Williamson, *SB*, p. 287.

110 SB, Address to Wesleyans, 'Religion and Politics', 11 February 1926, cited SB, *On England*, p. 195.

111 SB, Address, 'Political Education', 27 September 1923, cited SB, *On England*, pp. 148–9.

(The Holy Spirit and Pope Innocent III might query Baldwin's analysis of the origins and growth of the Franciscans.)

Baldwin had his very own Franciscan-inspired Anglican at hand in Worcestershire in the person of Fr William Sirr. Combining ascetic severity with full Anglo-Catholic ritual, he founded a one-man monastery, others being unable to endure the austerity. Baldwin liked to call by on occasion, to savour the peace and ruminate over 'the eternal verities' with Fr William of Glasshampton. It was, he said, 'good to feel there was a man of prayer in the neighbourhood'.[112] Robert Beaken reports anecdotal evidence of Baldwin serving Fr William's Mass at St Mary at the Cross Monastery, Glasshampton, but wisely cautions against uncritical acceptance of the claim.[113]

What of Baldwin's own High Church past? On occasion he reminisced fondly about Tractarian preachers and authors. It had, however, become a foreign country. Finding himself in London for Easter 1910, he attended All Saints, Margaret Street, for the first time in 20 years. The experience perplexed him. It was all much 'more ornate' than he remembered.[114] In autumn 1932, Caroline Bridgeman asked him to speak at a church gathering at the Queen's Hall in Langham Place. References suggest it was to be the centenary congress of the Oxford Movement the following year. Baldwin was having none of it:

> The movement may be a good one and I think it is, but I am not in it, nor am I likely to be . . . I should not feel I should be honest either to myself or to the audience if I stood up and addressed them.[115]

The establishment, his wife and his own personal preferences had taken him some way from the religion of his youth.

His attitude to Roman Catholicism also differed significantly from that of his parents. High Mass and Corpus Christi processions did not feature

112 Jones, Diary, 10/12 July 1944, cited Jones, *A Diary with Letters*, p. 524.

113 Ed. Robert Beaken, *Faithful Witness: The confidential diaries of Alan Don, Chaplain to the King, the Archbishop and the Speaker, 1931–1946* (London: SPCK, 2020), p. 133n.

114 SB to Louisa Baldwin, 29 March 1910, CUL, Baldwin Papers, 236/2/265.

115 SB to Lady Bridgeman, 24 October 1932, cited ed. Williamson and Baldwin, *Baldwin Papers*, p. 302.

during his lengthy sojourns in France. At times, Baldwin displayed anti-Catholic prejudice:

> Events in this war [i.e. the First World War] are bringing home to some of us an understanding of the attitude of our rude forefathers to the Church of Rome.
>
> If the hopes of an Irish settlement are broken it will be owing to the Roman bishops, i.e. the Vatican . . . The Vatican influence has been against us in Europe all the time . . . A plausible theory is that the Vatican hopes by busting the Irish Convention to bring Lloyd George down, thus paving (as they think) the way to an early and German peace.[116]

While Baldwin opposed Catholicism in the abstract, he was more tolerant towards individuals. Monica Baldwin was the orphaned daughter of cousins; Baldwin was her trustee. Prior to the First World War, Monica told him of her desire to become a Catholic and a nun. Baldwin sought to dissuade her, sending her to see Arthur Galton, who had converted to Catholicism himself and briefly been a Catholic priest (then, as an Anglican vicar, waged a personal campaign against the Catholic Church). When Galton failed to dissuade Monica, however, Baldwin placed no further obstacles in her path.[117] He showed great kindness, visiting her in Bruges and England, and welcoming her into his home when she left her convent – but not the Church – a generation later.

'Led till the end'

Baldwin's colleagues and associates were aware that he was unlike other politicians. Lord Halifax wrote 'of the romantic, almost mystical, streak to his composition'.[118] Neville Chamberlain's wife detected something similar: 'these other qualities – of a mystic and a poet – whatever one

116 SB to Louisa Baldwin, 30 January 1918, CUL, Baldwin Papers, 236/2/455.

117 SB to Louisa Baldwin, 27 and 29 January 1914, CUL, Baldwin Papers, 236/2/384, 386.

118 Lord Halifax, *Fullness of Days* (London: Collins, 1957), p. 168.

may call it'.[119] Baldwin's prayer life deepened over the years: 'As one grows old, one's prayers became shorter – just sighs and ejaculations.'[120] He revealed only glimpses to family and friends. There was no hint of spiritual pride. One day Baldwin commented to his daughter 'upon the phrase "The peace of God which passeth all understanding," with the words: "I am afraid that I am a long way from that."' On another occasion

> he was discovered in his library studying a small book. 'Look,' he said, and pointed to a page. The words were the Lord's prayer, and the clause, 'Thy will be done.' 'It's taken me all my time and energy to achieve it,' he said.[121]

He was exhausted when he retired in 1937. But it was only then that he 'could say with deep conviction: "Use me as Thou wilt or throw me away. Thy will be done." But I took a long time to get to that point!'[122]

In his final years, Baldwin's reading material was primarily of a religious nature.[123] Without in any way being precious or excessively pious, he was conscious of God's presence – in his own spiritual life and that of the nation as well. It is worth quoting extensively from his letter to Halifax after the fall of France:

> With millions of others I had prayed hard at the time of Dunkirk, and never did prayer seem to be more speedily answered to the full. And we prayed for France and the next day she surrendered. I thought much and when I went to bed I lay for a long time, vividly awake. And I went over in my mind all that had happened, concentrating on the thoughts that you had dwelt on; that prayer, to be effective, must be in accordance with God's will and that by far the hardest thing to say from the heart, and indeed the last lesson we learn (if we ever do) is to say and mean it, 'Thy will be done.' And I thought what mites we

119 Anne Chamberlain to Neville Chamberlain, 10 October 1930, cited Peter Marsh, *The Chamberlain Litany: Letters within a governing family from empire to appeasement* (London: Haus Publishing, 2010), p. 227.

120 Cited Young, *SB*, p. 118.

121 A. W. Baldwin, *My Father*, p. 326.

122 SB, 'Note for Cousin', 6 October 1937, CUL, Baldwin Papers, 236/7/1.

123 Oliver Baldwin, Memoirs, cited ed. Williamson and Baldwin, *Baldwin Papers*, p. 483.

> all are and how we can never see God's plan, a plan on such a scale that it *must* be incomprehensible.
>
> Then suddenly, for what must have been a couple of minutes, I seemed to see with extraordinary and vivid clarity, and to hear someone speaking to me. The words at the time were clear, but the recollection of them had passed when I seemed to come to, as it were, but the sense remained and the sense was this. 'You cannot hope to see the plan,' then, 'Have you not thought there is a purpose in stripping you, one by one, of all the human props on which you depend, that you are being left alone in the world? You have now one upon whom to lean and I have chosen you as my instrument to work with my will. Why then are you afraid?' And to prove ourselves worthy of that tremendous task, is our job.[124]

To his cousin, Baldwin wrote: 'I believe that in my public life I have been increasingly led, and I mean to be led till the end.'[125] Historians continue to debate his political legacy; he himself would have attributed everything beneficial in it to his Christian discipleship.

His long years of absence from church can therefore appear puzzling. He was sustained by prayer, Scripture and a strong personal faith, but these had been transmitted to him through the Church in the person of his parents and the sacramental practice of his youth. In his final years, both his sons noticed a change. He resumed his practice of receiving Holy Communion every Sunday – normally at his own parish of St Peter's, Astley, and on occasion at All Saints, Wilden.[126] While his wife still declined to accompany him to Communion services, for Baldwin, the spiritual life had come full circle.

In his final years his thoughts turned to the venue for his funeral and burial. Both his predecessor and successor as Conservative leaders were buried in Westminster Abbey, and that option was open to Baldwin. He wanted nothing so 'splendid and solemn' – 'A country churchyard', or

---

124 SB to Halifax, 23 July 1940, cited Keith Middlemas and John Barnes, *Baldwin: A biography* (London: Weidenfeld & Nicolson, 1969), pp. 1058–9.

125 SB, 'Note for Cousin', 6 October 1937, CUL, Baldwin Papers, 236/7/1.

126 A. W. Baldwin, *My Father*, p. 326; Oliver Baldwin, Memoirs, cited ed. Williamson and Baldwin, *Baldwin Papers*, p. 483.

even the garden, would satisfy him.[127] There was, however, another concern. Lady Baldwin was not baptized, and as the two wished to be buried together, he thought there might be trouble with the abbey.[128] They decided on Worcester Cathedral, where Baldwin had donated the High Altar and its furnishings. Following cremation, his ashes were mingled with those of his wife, who had predeceased him by two and a half years, and interred beneath the cathedral nave.

127 SB to Louisa Baldwin, 31 July 1919, CUL, Baldwin Papers, 236/2/489; Oliver Baldwin, Memoirs, cited ed. Williamson and Baldwin, *Baldwin Papers*, p. 483.

128 Why Baldwin thought this is uncertain. Being unbaptized had not prevented Chamberlain's burial at the abbey.

Ramsay MacDonald (1924 and 1929–1935)

'Celtic mysticism'

James Ramsay MacDonald[1] was born in Lossiemouth, Moray, in north-eastern Scotland on 12 October 1866. He was educated close by, at Drainie Parish School.

He contested Southampton in 1895 and Leicester in 1900 as the Independent Labour Party candidate, going on to win Leicester in 1906. After he was defeated for Leicester West in the 1918 'Coupon' election, he fought the Woolwich East by-election in 1921 before being elected for Aberavon in 1922. In 1929, MacDonald transferred to the safe seat of Seaham Harbour. However, standing as the National Labour candidate in 1935, he lost to the official Labour Party candidate. Returned to Parliament at a by-election in January 1936, he represented the Combined Scottish Universities until his death the following year.

A capable organizer and compelling orator, MacDonald was unanimously elected leader of the Parliamentary Labour Party in 1911. He resigned at the outbreak of the First World War when most Labour MPs supported Britain's entry into the war. Not a strict pacifist himself, he opposed the war, which he felt was being waged not for reasons of national security but to maintain autocratic regimes like Tsarist Russia. His stance made him one of the most unpopular men in the country.

On emerging from the 1922 general election as the largest opposition party, Labour promptly re-elected MacDonald as its leader. Following the inconclusive 1923 election, Baldwin was defeated in the Commons and

1 Later in life MacDonald was surprised to discover he had been registered at birth as 'James McDonald Ramsay'. Known as 'James' or 'Jamie' by the family, he took to calling himself 'Ramsay' to distinguish himself from another James MacDonald in the Labour Party.

MacDonald was appointed Prime Minister and Foreign Secretary of the first Labour government on 22 January 1924. Lacking a parliamentary majority, and a convinced internationalist, MacDonald focused on foreign affairs: granting recognition to the Soviet Union, promoting disarmament and seeking to modify the terms of the Versailles Peace Treaty. The government fell when the Liberals withdrew their support over its handling of a prosecution against a communist for alleged incitement to mutiny. The Conservatives won the ensuing general election on 29 October 1924, but Labour increased its share of the popular vote. MacDonald resigned as Prime Minister on 4 November 1924, having established in the minds of many Labour's reputation for moderation and competence, a party capable of government.

Labour won the most seats in the 1929 general election, and MacDonald became Prime Minister (but not Foreign Secretary) for a second time on 5 June 1929. Once more he focused on foreign affairs and disarmament. The financial crash of 1929 led to a trade depression and mass unemployment. Relying on orthodox fiscal measures, the Labour government's response appeared uncertain and impotent. Most of the Labour Party refused to contemplate the severe public spending cuts demanded as the condition for the international loans required to support sterling. So too, initially, did MacDonald. A sense of duty and pressure from George V persuaded him otherwise. When the majority of the Cabinet resigned on 24 August 1931, MacDonald remained as Prime Minister of a National government comprised mainly of Conservatives and Liberals.

The 1931 general election returned a majority of more than five hundred for the National government, although the overwhelming number of its MPs were Conservatives. Despite his expulsion from the Labour Party, MacDonald continued to view himself as a good socialist. There was great bitterness as he campaigned against former colleagues, who regarded him as a traitor influenced by aristocratic friends and personal vanity. Despite the slow economic recovery, MacDonald's final years in Downing Street were an unhappy period. He was compelled to accept the Conservative predominance in government while deteriorating health impaired his capacity. On 7 June 1935 he stood down as Prime Minister, swapping office with Baldwin. He resigned as Lord President of the Council on 28 May 1937.

After setting out for a tour of South America, MacDonald died at sea on 9 November 1937.

* * *

'A world of mystery and beauty'

For 15 years, from the early 1920s, national political life appeared to be dominated by people of faith – for the first time since the late nineteenth century. Even if not a regular churchgoer during his time in office, there is no doubting Baldwin's Christianity. What, however, of the man who faced him across the dispatch boxes and then served alongside him in the National government? Extravagant claims were made for the first Labour Prime Minister. The journalist Harold Begbie thought him an 'earnest and unquestioning' Christian.[2] Arthur Porritt, editor of the Nonconformist *Christian World*, agreed: 'Mr Ramsay MacDonald was, I think, the most religious Prime Minister we have had since Gladstone. M. Maisky, the Russian Ambassador, said MacDonald impressed him with religious fervour.'[3] The Oxford historian and Labour peer, Godfrey Elton, was tutor and friend to MacDonald's son, Malcolm. Writing the father's biography, he concluded that MacDonald was 'a deeply religious man'.[4] Are these assessments correct?

His religious antecedents were clear. He was descended from a line of small farmers 'who worshipped God and reverenced men'.[5] His immediate forebears were 'Wee Frees', members of the Free Church of Scotland who had separated from the established Scottish Church, resenting state interference and rejecting the appointment of ministers by lay patrons.

MacDonald was born in a small cottage in Lossiemouth and raised by his mother and grandmother. He never hid the fact that he was illegitimate.

2 A Gentleman with a Duster [Edward Harold Begbie], *The Conservative Mind* (London: Mills & Boon, 1924), p. 25.

3 Arthur Porritt, *More and More of Memories* (London: George Allen & Unwin, 1947), p. 131.

4 Lord Elton, *The Life of James Ramsay MacDonald, 1866–1919* (London: Collins, 1939), p. 14.

5 James Ramsay MacDonald, Memorandum, *c.*1900, cited ed. Jane Cox, *A Singular Marriage: A Labour love story in letters and diaries* (London: George G. Harrap, 1988), p. 3.

His mother, Anne or Annie Ramsay, had been in service at a local farm, where his father, John Macdonald, was the foreman. The couple had been engaged to be married. For whatever reason, the engagement was broken off, and the father played no part in MacDonald's life. On 14 December 1866, both parents appeared before the Kirk Session, where they 'professed their sorrow and their desire to be forgiven and led in the way of divine commandment'. Consequently, they were 'absolved from Church censure and . . . restored to Church privileges'.[6] No doubt among the reasons for that appearance and the 'Church privileges' referred to was MacDonald's baptism, which is likely to have been celebrated in St James's Free Kirk in Lossiemouth. Neither the church building of the time nor the baptismal registers survive.

Both his mother and grandmother were seamstresses. While Annie supplemented the family income by working in the fields and with the herring catch, MacDonald was often left with his grandmother, Isabella or Bella Ramsay. A forceful figure, she was a committed member of the Free Kirk. Her brother, who had been a minister, died of pneumonia contracted preaching outdoors in the snow. Bella attended St James's every Sunday without fail. She was an intelligent woman. MacDonald nostalgically recalled her library:

> A great three-volumed Brown's Bible in sheepskin, a huge *Life of Christ* which I could not lift but whose back in green polished leather always attracted me, some collections of Sermons and a few books bound in black on theology and Church history.[7]

She was his first teacher in the ways of faith, reading the Bible to him in bed:

> What matters it, however, whether I understood or not? . . . I was being taught to feel, to wonder, to know that there was a world of mystery and beauty . . . I was taught the Shorter Catechism and the

6 Kirk Session Minute Book, 14 December 1866, Alves Free Kirk, cited David Marquand, *Ramsay MacDonald*, 2nd edn (London: Jonathan Cape, 1977), p. 5.

7 JRM, cited Elton, *The Life of JRM*, p. 24.

> Psalms of David in Metre – every one of which including the CXIX I committed to memory.[8]

It is suggested that Annie Ramsay was more secular than her mother, but her early letters at least were full of prayers for God's guidance and blessing. She wrote to her prospective daughter-in-law:

> We propose but God disposes and many a dark day have I spent since then but God has given me more than I ever thought of – a good son . . . And I do trust that God will make you both happy.[9]

Behind the conventional picture of Calvinist doctrine, kirk and Bible, preaching and prayer, something else is hinted at. Bella Ramsay relayed fairy stories and ancient folklore to her grandson. Family tradition maintains that she had 'the sight', the capacity to foresee the future.[10] This struck a romantic chord in the adult MacDonald, who proclaimed his spiritual affinity with

> the people who have not lost communion with the mystic things of life, the people of witcheries, the people who see in the dark, the people who are only half born into the delusion which men call Time and Space.[11]

At his grandmother's instigation, MacDonald initially attended the Lossiemouth Free Kirk School. He was withdrawn due to the intrusion of the state and of board schools into local education. Rather than suffer this, he walked the four-mile round trip each day to Drainie Parish School.[12] The schoolmaster, his namesake, the Revd James MacDonald, was a Church of Scotland minister passionate in his desire to impart learning. MacDonald acknowledged his debt to the school and teacher: 'The machinery was as

8 JRM, Memorandum, *c.*1900, cited Cox, *A Singular Marriage*, p. 4.

9 Annie Ramsay to Margaret Gladstone, 27 July 1896, NA, James Ramsay MacDonald Papers, 30/69/775.

10 Iona Kielhorn, JRM's granddaughter, letter to the author, 14 March 2020.

11 JRM, cited Elton, *The Life of JRM*, p. 14.

12 JRM to Margaret Gladstone, 14 July 1896, cited Cox, *A Singular Marriage*, pp. 91–2.

old as Knox; the education the best ever given the sons and daughters of men.'[13] His praise, however, did not extend to his religious education. He had no objection to the chapter of the prophet Isaiah, psalm and hymn recited daily.[14] Years later, however, he recalled that he had been taught 'all about the Kings of Israel and the succession of the prophets, and when we studied the life of Paul we were told only of the number of places he had visited, and the number of churches he founded'. He felt it worse than useless 'to teach this skeleton of religion in the name of religion'. As a parent and a politician, he was to argue that religion should be taught only in the home if it was not to descend to mere formalism.[15]

MacDonald also recalled the gloomier aspects of his Calvinist upbringing. It 'was a religion based on awe', emphasizing the failings of human nature: 'Our deeds were wicked, our efforts of no avail . . . The only path of approach to [God] was contrition. At every thought of him our spirit groans in its unworthiness.'[16] That note of criticism is lacking, however, in MacDonald's teenage diary. He was in the kirk every Sunday morning, attended the afternoon Sunday school and read extensively from the Scriptures at home. He had fulsome praise for the preaching. His praise, however, was not reserved for the sermons – his eye was drawn to the girls present in church.[17] Forty years later, he remembered fondly those who had caused his heart to flutter Sunday by Sunday in Lossie Free Church.[18]

Re-evaluating Christian beliefs

In his final four years at Drainie Parish School, MacDonald acted as a pupil-teacher but looked increasingly beyond the school and kirk to satisfy his desire for knowledge and its practical application. At 17, he was already a speaker and committee member of the Lossiemouth Mutual

13 James Ramsay MacDonald, *Wanderings and Excursions* (London: Jonathan Cape, 1925), p. 24.

14 JRM, Diary, 1880, NA, JRM Papers, 30/69/772.

15 JRM, *Hansard* (1906), Vols 155 and 156, cited Marquand, *Ramsay MacDonald*, pp. 98–9.

16 JRM, Lecture, u/d, f. 10, NA, JRM Papers, 30/69/1587.

17 JRM, Diary, 1880, NA, JRM Papers, 30/69/772.

18 JRM, Diary, 11 July 1926, NA, JRM Papers, 30/69/1753/1, f. 239. Quotations from MacDonald's diary are required to carry a note to the following effect: 'The contents of this Diary are meant as notes to guide and revive memory as regards happenings and must on no account be published as they are, J. Ramsay MacDonald.'

Improvement Association, the local debating society. There he launched an attack on the superstition inimical to 'social progress and scientific research'. He denounced 'over-scrupulous religion', 'hero or saint worship' and 'bigotry in any moral device or thought'. There was no condemnation of Christianity, only a plea for education.[19] Indeed, the association met at the United Presbyterian church hall; there were clergy on the committee. His political radicalism was expressed in the Lossiemouth Democratic Association. This too solemnly refused to call God 'unjust and improvident'. Rather, it demanded human action to achieve a more equitable distribution of the fruits of God's gift of land and sea.[20]

In 1883, MacDonald founded the Lossiemouth Field Club, for which he organized scientific excursions and papers. He realized early that the discoveries of Charles Darwin and others called for a certain re-evaluation of Christian beliefs. One no longer needed to look to God to explain secondary causation. The creation account in the book of Genesis could not be taken literally.

MacDonald never argued that modern science obviated the need for the Christian faith. He admired his father-in-law, Dr John Gladstone, Professor of Chemistry at the Royal Institution and fellow of the Royal Society:

> When the discoveries regarding human origins and unwritten history were frightening the pulpits and giving birth to the vainest and most absurd defenders of the faith, he wrote and spoke frankly, accepting the discoveries and whole-heartedly embracing theories like evolution, but denying either one or the other made a dent on the Christian shield . . . he annexed science for his Christian Evidence lectures and pamphlets.[21]

MacDonald readily conceded that there were questions modern science struggled to answer: the origins of life and matter, and human

19 JRM, 'Debate – Is Superstition Natural or Acquired?', 1883, NA, JRM Papers, 30/69/771.

20 Manifesto of the Lossiemouth Democratic Association, 'Digest of a Speech Delivered to the Association', early 1880s, NA, JRM Papers, 30/69/771.

21 James Ramsay MacDonald, *Margaret Ethel MacDonald*, 2nd edn (London: Hodder & Stoughton, 1912), p. 5.

self-consciousness. He concluded that the existence of God, more perfectly understood, remained a logical necessity.[22]

As with other political contemporaries, MacDonald's adherence to orthodox Christianity was less affected by Darwin's *On the Origin of Species*[23] than by modern biblical criticism.[24] His reading of Ernest Renan and German scholars such as Johann Gottfried Herder, Friedrich Schleiermacher and David Strauss led him to question the authority of Scripture and the divinity of Christ.

In the early summer of 1885, MacDonald responded to an advertisement in the press placed by the Revd Mordaunt Crofton of St Stephen's Church, Bristol, seeking an assistant for the Boys' and Young Men's Guild he was founding there. It is not known how he replied to Crofton's inquiries as to his religious and political convictions but, armed with references from the clergy at the kirk and Drainie Parish School, he was appointed to the position. What did MacDonald and his new employer have in common? Only in his twenties himself, Crofton was an Oxford graduate and the son of an Irish baronet. There is no evidence that MacDonald's duties extended to religious instruction. Rather, he was lecturing youth like himself, away from home, with a view to their self-improvement.[25]

MacDonald wrote: 'We had all the enthusiasm of early Christians in those days. We were few and the Gospel was new.'[26] Unfortunately, he was not describing his employment. With respect to that, he confided: 'I went to Bristol to help a clergyman in some work. This turned out to be a lamentable failure.'[27] MacDonald was inspired rather by the Bristol branch of the Social Democratic Federation, the newly formed first socialist party in Britain, the platform of which was Marxist and atheist. Whether for this or other reasons, his connection with Crofton was swiftly terminated and MacDonald was back in Lossiemouth by the end of the year.

22 JRM, Sermon, 16 April 1893, NA, JRM Papers, 30/69/1587.

23 Charles Darwin, *On the Origin of Species by Means of Natural Selection, or the Preservation of Favoured Races in the Struggle for Life* (London: John Murray, 1859).

24 JRM, Lecture, 4 December 1893, NA, JRM Papers, 30/69/1587.

25 JRM, Outline lecture, 22 July 1885, NA, JRM Papers, 30/69/1585.

26 JRM, cited Elton, *The Life of JRM*, p. 47.

27 JRM to Margaret Gladstone, 1 July 1896, cited Cox, *A Singular Marriage*, p. 11.

The Ethical Society

In 1886 he tried his fortune in London. Temporary clerical work was interspersed with periods of unemployment until he established himself as a freelance journalist and lecturer. All the time, MacDonald was involved with various socialist societies. He attended the South Place Chapel in Finsbury, which a century earlier had begun life as a Nonconformist congregation denying the doctrine of eternal punishment. During the nineteenth century, its tenets were Unitarian, rejecting the Trinity. By the time of MacDonald's arrival in London, its stance was increasingly that of secular humanism. Under its American minister, Stanton Coit, it changed its name from the South Place Religious Society to the South Place Ethical Society.

In the 1890s, MacDonald spoke at South Place and other branches in east London and Croydon, and wrote regularly for its journal, *Ethical World*. He was a signatory to the 1898 manifesto, which declared: 'Ethical societies are founded upon a conviction that the good life is desirable for its own sake, and rests upon no supernatural sanction.'[28] Another future Labour politician described the Ethical movement as 'a religion of morality without theology'.[29] Members were free to retain their own confessional traditions but the society itself rejected all dogma. These ethical societies retained much of the phenomena of Christianity – services, hymns, sermons and sometimes even the title 'church' – but they spurned its doctrinal content. The message was the love of the good rather than the love of God.

There were many similar societies, often with relatively small, interconnected and fractious memberships. The Fellowship of New Life was founded in 1883 by another Scot, Thomas Davidson, as a 'society for people interested in religious thought, ethical propaganda and social reform'. The Fabian Society seceded from it in 1884, advocating a more political programme of social action, while the Fellowship emphasized the moral and spiritual development of the individual. It also promoted communal living. MacDonald came into contact with the Fellowship in 1890 and was elected its secretary two years later. He resided in its Bloomsbury house. After

28 Society of Ethical Propagandists, Manifesto, 1898, cited Elton, *The Life of JRM*, p. 94.
29 Lord Snell, *Men, Movements and Myself* (London: J. M. Dent & Sons, 1936), p. 160.

his flirtation with the Social Democratic Federation, he consistently rejected class conflict, promoting a moderate and *ethical* socialism. This is what he sought in the Fellowship of New Life: 'Political change is not desirable for its own sake, but rather for its effect on human well-being . . . The Fellowship therefore aims at a reform of the ideals of the individual.'[30] His experience of the Ethical Society and the Fellowship influenced much of MacDonald's subsequent religious and spiritual thought.

'Two red revolutionaries'

In May 1895, MacDonald received a donation to his Southampton election expenses from a social worker four years his junior, Margaret Gladstone. She contrived to meet him the following month; romance rapidly ensued. Both were committed to radical social reform; both came from Scottish Presbyterian families. Margaret's maternal grandfather was a Presbyterian minister, first in Glasgow, then in Westbourne Park, London. There, however, similarities of background ceased. The Gladstones were middle class, professional and prosperous.

Her mother having died shortly after her birth, Margaret was raised by her father, an eminent scientist and practising Christian, active in social and religious works. He was a founder of the YMCA and conducted Bible classes in the family's Bayswater home every Sunday afternoon. Family prayers were said morning and night. MacDonald wrote approvingly of the faith he found there:

> The home in Pembridge Square breathed religion . . . Its traditions, its activities, its connections, were religious – Nonconformist in all their modes of expression and yet unbounded by sectarianism of any kind. It was a religion of prayer and praise, of faith mingled with works.[31]

Dr Gladstone was untroubled by his prospective son-in-law's heterodox belief and practice. Margaret assured MacDonald that her father had no

30 JRM, 'The New Fellowship', *Seedtime* (April 1892), cited Marquand, *Ramsay MacDonald*, p. 25.

31 JRM, *Margaret Ethel MacDonald*, p. 45.

objection to his broad religious views nor the fact that he played golf on Sundays rather than attending church.[32]

By her mid-twenties, Margaret had travelled some distance in her own spiritual journey. Devout from her earliest years, she had attended church, read the Scriptures and prayed. Yet she was not baptized until 1887; after her birth, only a dedication ceremony had been celebrated. Her commitment to more formal religious practice was the result of an attachment to a curate at St Mary Abbots, Kensington. She went frequently to Communion (with the Presbyterians as well as the Anglicans), taught at the Sunday school and helped the boys' club at St Mary Abbots. She was also an occasional visitor to the Westbourne Park Chapel to hear the Baptist preacher Dr John Clifford, who became a family friend.

This conventional late-Victorian piety did not last. The ritual and the social exclusivity of the congregation troubled her. She wanted to teach socialism and universalism – the claim that all are saved and none damned – to her Sunday-school pupils. Forbidden by the clergy to do any such thing, she resigned. Her religion became one of 'simple purity of spirit and trust in God'.[33] Denomination meant nothing to her:

> I can worship just as well with RCs or Jews, as with any Protestants, so long as whoever they are they seem to be in earnest; and I can get some spiritual good from the writings of Buddhists or Atheists or anyone who looks beyond the superficial life. I never now regularly read the Bible or kneel down regularly to pray.[34]

What mattered most was faith's expression in practical charity and a passion for social reform.

The spiritual positions of husband and wife were, therefore, very similar when they married on 23 November 1896, in the neo-Gothic splendour of St Mary Abbots. The officiant was the Revd A. L. Lilley, a socially progressive and well-connected clergyman from Chelsea, assisted by the vicar, the Hon. Revd Carr Glynn, a chaplain to the Queen and the son-in-law of a duke. Margaret made light of the situation: 'It would be such a joke to have

32 Margaret Gladstone to JRM, 2 July 1896, NA, JRM Papers, 30/69/778.

33 JRM, *Margaret Ethel MacDonald*, p. 56.

34 Margaret Gladstone to JRM, 2 July 1896, NA, JRM Papers, 30/69/778.

[Glynn] pairing off two red revolutionaries.'[35] MacDonald insisted that the ritual be pared to the minimum and that no sermon be preached.[36] His radical friends remained unimpressed. One accused him of hypocrisy because MacDonald had refused to attend her own marriage 'on principle'.[37]

The marriage was a union of hearts and minds. Margaret, like her husband, saw in socialism 'not only the economic organization of society which she deemed to be necessary, but the love of the brethren which was involved in her love of God, the Father'.[38] The couple had six children, one of whom died young. None were baptized as infants, suggesting the parents' rejection of any sacramental practice. (At least one child chose to be baptized as an adult.)[39] Dr Clifford conducted a service of dedication in the MacDonalds' home for their son, Alister.[40] Church attendance was not a regular feature of family life, except during holidays in Lossiemouth. On Sundays, MacDonald might read to the family from the Bible. The girls were sent to a Quaker Sunday school.[41] The boys boarded at Bedales, a nondenominational public school which, unusually for the period, had no chapel.

This is how the couple chose to express their religious beliefs and spiritual needs, but there are suggestions that Margaret did not find it altogether fulfilling. MacDonald wrote of her unsatisfied 'yearning for social worship'.[42] She died prematurely at the age of 41 on 8 September 1911. As death approached, MacDonald

> asked her if she desired to see anyone who would speak to her of what was to come. 'That would be but a waste of time,' she replied, 'I have always been ready. Let us praise God together for what has been. He has been very good to me in giving me my work, my friends, and my faith. At the end of the day I go gladly to Him for rest and shelter.'[43]

35 Margaret Gladstone to JRM, 16 September 1896, cited Cox, *A Singular Marriage*, p. 135.

36 JRM to Margaret Gladstone, 18 November 1896, cited Cox, *A Singular Marriage*, p. 175.

37 Enid Stacey to JRM, 24 July 1896, cited Cox, *A Singular Marriage*, p. 106.

38 JRM, *Margaret Ethel MacDonald*, p. 135.

39 Iona Kielhorn, letter to the author, 14 March 2020.

40 Sir James Marchant, *Dr John Clifford: Life, letters and reminiscences* (London: Cassell, 1924), p. 130n.

41 JRM, Diary, 25 December 1916, NA, JRM Papers, 30/69/1753/1, f. 36.

42 JRM, *Margaret Ethel MacDonald*, p. 61.

43 JRM, *Margaret Ethel MacDonald*, pp. 62–3.

Margaret's body was cremated at Golders Green Crematorium and her ashes buried in Spynie churchyard near Lossiemouth. MacDonald was devastated by her death.

A Unitarian lay minister

During their courtship, the couple wrote of their respective religious beliefs. MacDonald assured Margaret that he was no materialist: 'I call myself a Christian.'[44] Elaborating, he said that he was a Unitarian. Margaret imagined she was too – at least she omitted those articles of the creed proclaiming the divinity of Christ.[45] The reference to Unitarianism is unremarkable. Many of the religiously curious, especially the politically radical like Lloyd George, were expressing interest in it. What is remarkable, and has gone largely unnoticed, is the extent and depth of MacDonald's commitment.

On 8 May 1892, MacDonald led the service at Canterbury Unitarian Church.[46] We do not know how he came to be there. It may have been through connections in the Ethical Society or the Fellowship of New Life, or possibly through contacts in Dover, where he spoke for the Labour candidate in the general election. We do know that he served as a Unitarian lay minister and preacher for the next 11 years in at least a dozen different churches, predominantly in Kent and south London. He was most active in the period 1893–6, but also had significant involvement in 1897, 1898 and 1900, possibly supplying for absent ministers.

On 9 February 1895, MacDonald took up a three-month appointment as the 'temporary minister' of the newly formed Ramsgate and Margate Unitarian Circle of Religious Fellowship.[47] For up to 15 shillings a week, he conducted Sunday morning and evening services and weekday evening lectures held in hotels, assembly rooms and private homes. He 'spoke with great force and earnestness'. On his departure the congregation expressed their thanks for 'his talents . . . the high tone of his teaching . . . [and] the

44 JRM to Margaret Gladstone, 21 November 1895, cited Cox, *A Singular Marriage*, p. 55.

45 Margaret Gladstone to JRM, 2 July 1896, NA, JRM Papers, 30/69/778.

46 I am grateful to the Revd Thomas McReady, who first drew my attention to this.

47 *Christian Life and Unitarian Herald*, 9 February 1895, cited McReady, 'Introduction: The Unitarian Sermons of James Ramsay MacDonald', <www.revtom.co.uk/ramsay-mac-research.html>, accessed 02.09.19.

uniform help, courtesy and forbearance he has shown them in their difficulties'.[48] From an envelope of his sermon and lecture notes in his papers at the National Archives, we know the content of many of his sermons and lectures delivered at Ramsgate, Margate and elsewhere. It constitutes the single most important source on MacDonald's religious beliefs.

He asserted his 'spiritual' credentials, simultaneously raising questions as to his interpretation of faith and revelation:

> Man is religious by nature, for what more can we mean by religion than the sense of the growing perfection of man and of the excellence of the world that is becoming; and an assurance that through our individual lives we contribute something to the fulness of God's purposes.[49]

He distinguished Christianity from 'the Christian spirit'. By the former, he meant 'theories of original sin, damnation and claims of pretentious clericalism', welcoming its replacement by 'the growth of ethical and religious thought'.[50]

MacDonald claimed to embody progress in religious thought. He rejected anthropomorphic concepts in which human qualities were projected on to God. Instead, he preached God as pure mind who revealed himself to imperfect human minds down the ages.[51] To this extent, he presented authentic Christianity. However, faith for MacDonald did not mean

> belief in a self-existent perfect God with a will which interferes with the human conscience, but a belief in spiritual growth towards a perfection shadowed in these higher glimpses and yearnings for a moral life which man cannot yet for a while live. Faith is not a belief in a life apart from man, but a belief in the growth of the spirit of man.

48 *Christian Life and Unitarian Herald*, 9 February and 27 April 1895, cited McReady, 'A Socialist's Salvation: A theological reflection on the Unitarian sermons of James Ramsay MacDonald', <www.revtom.co.uk/ramsay-mac-research.html>, accessed 02.09.19.

49 JRM, Sermon, 31 December 1893, NA, JRM Papers, 30/69/1587, f. 2.

50 JRM, Sermon, 1 September 1895, NA, JRM Papers, 30/69/1587, f. 4.

51 JRM, Sermon, 16 April 1893, NA, JRM Papers, 30/69/1587, f. 11.

If he is simply purifying some primitive notions of God, he does the church fathers and scholastics a disservice when he condescends to say: 'Had these dogmatics known of the laws of growth as we do, they would have searched their own hearts for God and found him there.'[52]

At times, MacDonald suggested that God is only immanent and subjective. He told the Canterbury Unitarians: 'Our gods do not create us, we create our gods.'[53] Elsewhere he acknowledged the mysterious transcendent God, the Creator of the universe who is worthy of our worship. He accepted that God was, in principle, capable of performing miracles. However, he was unable to imagine him ever exercising such a power.[54] The omnipotent God denies himself the possibility of revelation to his creatures. The Revd Tom McReady is a Unitarian minister whose research has cast light on MacDonald's religious thought and ministry. He notes that, although a Unitarian, MacDonald made no direct assault on Trinitarian dogma.[55] He composed prayers addressed to 'the Father', made in the name of the Son, Jesus Christ. There were references to the Holy Spirit. In these prayers, he conceived of God in personal terms, requesting spiritual help from him, confessing sin to him. There was a lack of consistency. Naturally intelligent and widely read, MacDonald was not a systematic theologian – and made no claim to be.

Influenced by Renan

An early sermon employed surprisingly traditional Christological titles: Jesus is the king of Zion and the second Adam. He is the fulfilment of the Messianic prophecies. Jesus is 'identical' with God the Father.[56] However, MacDonald rejected orthodox Christianity, including the divinity of Christ. Influenced by Renan, he gave a contentious reading of Scripture: descent from David and the virgin birth were invented by the evangelists;[57] 'Christ simply was a man of extraordinary spiritual force and

52 JRM, Sermon, 16 February 1894, NA, JRM Papers, 30/69/1587, f. 14.

53 JRM, Sermon, 12 November 1893, NA, JRM Papers, 30/69/1587, f. 4.

54 JRM, Sermon, 29 September 1895, NA, JRM Papers, 30/69/1587, ff. 3–4.

55 McReady, 'Blessed Is the Peacemaker: The religious vision of James Ramsay MacDonald', p. 2, <www.revtom.co.uk/ramsay-mac-research.html>, accessed 02.09.19.

56 JRM, Sermon, 19 March 1893, NA, JRM Papers, 30/69/1587, ff. 5, 6.

57 JRM, Sermon, 5 June 1893, NA, JRM Papers, 30/69/1587, f. 8.

consequently magnetic personality and simplicity of character';[58] he was our elder brother, the last of the prophets and an example to be followed, not a divinity to be worshipped. Jesus

> came on the one hand to show us the Father and on the other to show us ourselves . . . Between the two existences Jesus of Nazareth stood and reconciled them. He held up a new type of human excellence.[59]

MacDonald discounted literal interpretations of the resurrection and Ascension. Rather, they were to be understood as the eternal triumph of ideas. A divine Christ was the creation of politicians and priests, and separated us from the real Christ. When he could not avoid Christ's claims to supernatural powers or a special relationship to his heavenly Father, he argued confusion on Christ's part.[60] In these instances, we were to ignore Christ's teaching and simply follow his example.[61] MacDonald failed to give reasons why such a selective interpretation of the gospel was permissible.

Taking his cue from Renan, MacDonald accorded Saint Paul a pre-eminent position in his pantheon of spiritual villains. Paul was not an apostle but rather the leader of a school of Greek philosophy.[62] MacDonald argued that to his immediate contemporaries, Jesus was merely a reforming rabbi seeking to lead Israel back to the purer spirituality of the later prophets and the psalms. Paul's writings were responsible for subverting this with modern Christian theology.

Denying the truth 'of orthodox salvation dogma'

The doctrine to which MacDonald took greatest exception, and to which he returned repeatedly in his sermons, was that of the atonement: the belief that there is sacrificial merit in Christ's death capable of winning

58 JRM, Sermon, 11 March 1894, NA, JRM Papers, 30/69/1587, f. 5.
59 JRM, Sermon, 7 September 1895, NA, JRM Papers, 30/69/1587, f. 12.
60 JRM, Sermon, 5 June 1893, NA, JRM Papers, 30/69/1587, f. 13.
61 JRM, Lecture (?), 4 December 1898, NA, JRM Papers, 30/69/1587, f. 13.
62 JRM, Sermon, 16 February 1894, NA, JRM Papers, 30/69/1587, f. 1.

salvation for those who believe in him. MacDonald aimed to lead his congregation 'from that black cloud of curses in which theologically minded men desire to dwell and go out with joyful heart into the wide fields and free air of Christian life'. We do not know what curses might have been hurled against MacDonald and his mother when he was born in illegitimacy in a stern Calvinist community. Their involvement in the life of the kirk does not suggest any enduring stigma. MacDonald rightly maintained that Christ 'did not come to appease the wrathful displeasure under which a violated Law is supposed to have held us'.[63] Any distortion of the Christian doctrine of salvation and failure to emphasize the mercy of Christ ought to have invited a return to a more faithful tradition, not the rejection of Christianity's central tenets.

That, however, was MacDonald's response: 'I denied the truth of the whole fabric of orthodox salvation dogma.'[64] He did so on two grounds. First, he claimed that modern science made it impossible to accept the doctrine of original sin – the belief that sin, separation from God, is imputed to the human race by virtue of our first ancestors' wrong exercise of free will. He was not alone in struggling with the implications of recent scientific discoveries. He failed to distinguish, however, between Genesis's poetic account of the origins of the universe and its theological truths of the origins of evil and the transmission of humanity's wounded nature. MacDonald offered no convincing alternative explanation for the reality of evil. Second, he asserted that 'there is nothing in the gospels to support this theology [of salvation]'. That argument cannot be sustained. All four Gospels contain statements by Christ, indicating that he clearly understood his death to have salvific value for his disciples. MacDonald weakly contradicted himself by maintaining that such statements 'were used metaphorically by Christ'.[65]

MacDonald countered potential criticism by declaring that while rejecting traditional notions of the atoning merit of Jesus' death, he did not disallow any atoning value to his life.[66] In his opinion, that value comprised assistance in this life rather than a changed state in any future one. Christ gave us an example as to how to endure suffering that provided 'consolation

63 JRM, Sermon, 7 September 1895, NA, JRM Papers, 30/69/1587, ff. 4, 10, 11.

64 JRM, Sermon, 31 March 1895, NA, JRM Papers, 30/69/1587, f. 3.

65 JRM, Sermon, 17 March 1895, NA, JRM Papers, 30/69/1587, ff. 5, 6.

66 JRM, Sermon, 7 September 1895, NA, JRM Papers, 30/69/1587, f. 10.

and inspiration' for his disciples. It is a very impoverished notion of Christian hope. MacDonald preached that salvation 'is not primarily a mental but a moral attitude'.[67] No Christian would dispute that. Salvation is not simply assent to an intellectual proposition; it requires the response of love towards God and neighbour.

'I do not want to go to heaven'

MacDonald did not believe in eternal life in the orthodox Christian sense. He had made it plain to Margaret during their courtship:

> Personally I do not want to go to heaven and I hope they will not send me to hell. I cannot form a conception of your idea of compensation without passing judgment on its immorality, so I cannot hold it. It is very pleasant to think of meeting one's dear friends again, but it is more pleasant to think of the end of Peace that is coming, and we can meanwhile enshrine the memories of friends so that they are always with us.[68]

Both refused to believe that God created people only to condemn them to eternal damnation and punishment. Neither considered that such a possibility was only the consequence of our own actions. MacDonald's claim that Christ's teaching contains no reference to eternal reward and eternal punishment[69] is not borne out by a cursory reading of the Gospels. A generation on, he was a little less dogmatic: 'I have no opinions about what "cometh after death," but the use to which faith in this matter is put repels me from the quality of mind which seems to believe in it.'[70]

He eschewed a purely material view of humanity, but it is difficult to define how he understood the survival beyond physical death – nowhere did he express belief in the resurrection of the body. He no longer believed in 'Heaven as a kingdom, as a paradise, flowing with love, resplendent

67 JRM, Sermon, 17 March 1895, NA, JRM Papers, 30/69/1587, ff. 7, 9.

68 JRM to Margaret Gladstone, 21 November 1895, cited Cox, *A Singular Marriage*, p. 55.

69 JRM, Sermon, 11 March 1894, NA, JRM Papers, 30/69/1587, f. 5.

70 JRM to Lady Margaret Sackville, 10 September 1918, NA, Margaret Sackville Papers, RW/1/4/9.

in grandeur'.[71] He wrote that 'future life to me is, what I believe Christ taught, the resurrection of God in the race.'[72] He did not specify where Christ taught this. His own position at times resembled pantheism or Hegel's 'world spirit'. There was a breezy lack of precision: 'What am I when I am gone? . . . I live nevertheless in other men . . . quiet fruitful action may send a flow of sunshine and life into another soul.' Finally, there was a prudential hedging of bets: 'It may even be in addition to all this there is something awaiting us akin to the hopes of the Christian.'[73]

'Preaching the fatherhood of God and the brotherhood of man'

Unitarianism afforded MacDonald the space to develop and articulate his beliefs. He argued that Unitarians retained spiritual truths while discarding archaic creeds.[74] Acknowledging that they were few in number, he justifiably claimed for them an extensive influence:

> We are not small because our opinions are those of but a peculiar people, but because they have become the general beliefs of Christians; we are not quiet because the opposition with which we meet is too powerful, but rather because it is no opposition in principle at all.[75]

MacDonald sought to advance religion from formalized conduct to 'a real sense of relationship with everything from the lowest to the highest and a permanent attitude of mind'.[76] He aimed to heighten a sense of spiritual awareness and moral responsibility, of the oneness of humanity.[77] It is difficult to find an objective foundation for these noble ideals. Revelation, ecclesiastical authority, even conscience orientated towards something external to itself, were subordinated to 'every pure impulse that comes from the

71 JRM, Sermon, 12 November 1893, NA, JRM Papers, 30/69/1587, f. 2.

72 JRM to Margaret Gladstone, 21 November 1895, cited Cox, *A Singular Marriage*, p. 55.

73 JRM, Lecture, u/d, NA, JRM Papers, 30/69/1587, ff. 15, 22.

74 JRM, Sermon, 31 March 1895, NA, JRM Papers, 30/69/1587, f. 7.

75 JRM, Sermon, 11 March 1894, NA, JRM Papers, 30/69/1587, f. 4.

76 JRM, Lecture (?), 4 December 1898, NA, JRM Papers, 30/69/1587, f. 4.

77 JRM, Lecture, u/d, NA, JRM Papers, 30/69/1587, f. 12.

thoughts of men, the voice of nature, or the whisperings of our own souls'. The end justified the means: 'If reason makes you give up prayer, give it up. The giving of it up *is* prayer. If reason makes you reject parts of your Bible, reject them; the rejection is a sacrifice to God.'[78] His optimistic humanism was based on a predication of the inevitable forward march of progress. That might have appeared plausible when science, democracy and social reform seemed to promise the continual betterment of the human condition. It could not be sustained in the experience of the First World War and the authoritarian regimes of the twentieth century.

From the turn of the century, MacDonald's preaching engagements diminished and then ceased completely. There is no reason to suspect this was due to anything more than increasing political and family commitments, nor that there was any significant change in his religious beliefs. Yet something about his experience as a Unitarian preacher requires explanation. McReady rightly states that it is extraordinary that such a major part of his life has gone virtually undocumented. It might almost be doubted whether those sermons in the National Archives were actually preached by MacDonald, were it not substantiated by contemporary references in the local and religious press. During the 1895 election campaign in Southampton, his opponents slandered MacDonald as 'an irreligious and illiterate man'. A supporter set the record straight: 'For three months previous to his campaign here he was conducting religious services and preaching the fatherhood of God and the brotherhood of man twice every Sunday, in connection with religious bodies at Ramsgate and Margate.'[79]

It is more than political biographers' lack of interest in other spheres of their subject's life. MacDonald willingly spoke and wrote about himself at length. He and Margaret corresponded constantly prior to their marriage. There is the one reference where he had told her he was a Unitarian, but no mention of the preaching and lecturing occupying so much of his time. Nor was there after their marriage, nor in their letters to others. Nor in MacDonald's later diaries. It is as if he systematically erased the whole episode. Did he find it politically and socially more advantageous to be a

78 JRM, Sermon, 23 June 1895, NA, JRM Papers, 30/69/1587, ff. 11–12.

79 C. A. Woodland, press cutting, July 1895, cited Cox, *A Singular Marriage*, p. 50.

lapsed Presbyterian than a practising Unitarian? It is a question unlikely to be answered satisfactorily.

MacDonald's socialism was unquestionably the expression of his religion. He distinguished British socialism from its European counterparts, rejecting claims that the movement was inherently atheistic. He saw nothing incongruous in the fact that some socialists happened to be atheists. Far more illogical, in his view, was the fact that many Christians were doctrinaire individualists.[80] For MacDonald, faith and politics were inseparable: 'The love of man leads us to the love of God, and the desire to alleviate human suffering ultimately throws us back upon God's strength.' For socialists, the principle of solidarity was the motivating force of social reform. Such solidarity would be more willingly embraced where there was a 'consciousness of a common Father'.[81] MacDonald acclaimed the Sermon on the Mount as the most sublime manifesto ever issued. He employed hyperbole, however, when he interpreted the Beatitude, 'Blessed are the meek, for they shall inherit the earth', as Christ implying that the meek would control the means of production.[82]

His internationalism, his belief in the common brotherhood of man, led MacDonald to oppose armed conflict between nations. His stance against the Boer War and the First World War was principled and courageous. He articulated it using Christian terminology, predicting that when peace returned, conscientious objectors would be able to 'confront the world with faces unashamed, and . . . say to posterity, "We await your verdict." And the verdict will be: "Blessed is the peacemaker, for he shall be called the child of God."'[83] The First World War marked the moment of his darkest disillusionment with the traditional churches: 'The war and the conduct of clergymen have all but shattered belief in anything but popularity and irrationality.' He remarked that, if he did pray, it would be that the Lord preserve him from despair and cynicism.[84]

80 JRM, Draft letter to press, u/d, NA, JRM Papers, 30/69/771.

81 JRM, Sermon, 20 September 1895, NA, JRM Papers, 30/69/1587, f. 4.

82 JRM, Sermon, 7 April 1895, NA, JRM Papers, 30/69/1587, f. 16.

83 JRM, Speech, Briton Ferry, March 1916, cited Marquand, *Ramsay MacDonald*, p. 185.

84 JRM, Diary, 12 September 1915 and 13 January 1916, NA, JRM Papers, 30/69/1753/1, ff. 19, 27.

'Quiet communion with the mind of God'

It might be supposed that, as an adult, Ramsay MacDonald was not a regular churchgoer save for holidays in Lossiemouth, where he reverted to his childhood practice of kirk on Sundays and family prayers.[85] The reality was more complex. He attended and led Unitarian services for a decade from 1892. For the most part, he had little time for formal organized worship. He was critical of the House of Commons service at St Margaret's, Westminster, on the anniversary of the outbreak of the war: 'Better employed at home when I set aside some minutes thinking of the suffering, the dead, and the sorrowing women and children of both armies and all nations.'[86] He and Margaret went occasionally to Dr Clifford's Baptist Church in Westbourne Park.[87] Christmas observance was limited to the Quaker services at his daughters' Sunday school.[88] Later MacDonald sporadically took himself to the Temple Church, where he appreciated the music.[89] During weekend house parties, he was not averse to attending Anglican matins, inviting his fellow guests to share the consolation of peace he derived from the service.[90] While never a committed churchgoer after his Unitarian period, neither was he a principled opponent.

Regular Bible reading was another practice dropped after his departure from Scotland. There are occasional references to his reading of Scripture. He turned to the Old Testament prophets and Wisdom literature for a sense of peace.[91] Christ and the Gospels did not feature.

Recognizing that prayer consisted of more than the recitation of formal phrases, MacDonald urged its practice as 'one of the holiest avenues by which we may approach the divine presence', through which we might enjoy 'quiet communion with the mind of God'. To what extent did he expect

85 JRM to Margaret MacDonald, June 1911, cited Cox, *A Singular Marriage*, p. 369.

86 JRM, Diary, 4 August 1918, NA, JRM Papers, 30/69/1753/1, f. 114.

87 Porritt, *More and More of Memories*, p. 132.

88 JRM, Diary, 25 December 1916 and 24 December 1917, NA, JRM Papers, 30/69/1753/1, ff. 36, 84.

89 JRM to Sackville, 24 June 1915, NA, Margaret Sackville Papers, RW/1/2/12; JRM, Diary, 29 November 1936, NA, JRM Papers, 30/69/1753/2, f. 157.

90 JRM, Memo for Cosmo Lang, 20 February 1935, Lambeth Palace Library (LPL), Lang Papers, 139, f. 100; JRM, Diary, 21 April 1935, NA, JRM Papers, 30/69/1753/2, f. 21.

91 JRM, Diary, 23 February and 20 March 1919, 12 October 1927, NA, JRM Papers, 30/69/1753/2, ff. 127, 130, 252.

to be challenged and changed by dialogue with a transcendent other? He rejected prayer of petition – at least regarding the material order – as requiring a false belief in a God who intervened in creation. In spiritual matters he recommended prayer to God 'in his mercy and love to perfect what he has planned'. At times, prayer seemed to be simply the mental effort to imitate what we admire: 'Our prayer is answered as we make it.' He spoke in elevated tones:

> Prayer becomes an exercise of the devout spirit and a privilege of the aspiring soul. It brings us to the secret place of the most high and leading (*sic*) us through the gates of humility; it supports us in the steep ascent of the hill of aspiration from the slope of which we get ever widening glimpses of the land of perfect love and joy.[92]

It is difficult to detect any substance to this. Sadly, in his greatest need, when mourning the loss of family, MacDonald found no comfort in prayer.

Lady Margaret Sackville

The biographies of MacDonald are as unforthcoming about his romantic life after his wife's death as they are about his spiritual life. Marquand refers only obliquely to 'warm friendships with a number of women'.[93] There were several of varying duration and degrees of intensity, mostly with younger, well-born women. One of the most passionate was with Lady Margaret Sackville, daughter of Earl De La Warr, a socialist, poet and Catholic. MacDonald protested that he cared little for convention:

> I have always thought that of all the constitutional absurdities which mankind have placed in the temple of morality to protect it from the eye of reason the love of man and woman who do not marry is one of the greatest.[94]

92 JRM, Sermon, 29 September 1895, NA, JRM Papers, 30/69/1587, ff. 8–11, 13.

93 Marquand, *Ramsay MacDonald*, p. 135.

94 JRM to Sackville, 18 September 1915, NA, Margaret Sackville Papers, RW/1/2/27.

His letters do not bear out this bravado. He desperately wanted to marry. Sackville refused, citing friends' lack of sympathy and understanding for the institution of marriage.[95] As they pursued their affair, MacDonald wrote that he would always consider her to be his wife. As with Lloyd George, one must ask the extent to which the moral life influenced the life of faith.

'A pagan Presbyterian'

MacDonald was unequivocally a child of the Reformation, wanting the individual believer to have access to Christ free from priestly mediation. When seeking 'the Nazarene carpenter' in the Holy Land, his impressions were very mixed: 'out upon the hills of Judea, the road to Jericho, the way-sides of Samaria . . . [he was able] to feel the Presence'; by contrast, he sought to escape the places 'desecrated by lies and superstition'. He took especially against Bethlehem: 'There, three rival sects light altar lamps with curses . . . I wonder what he, in whose memory the lamps are kept lit, thinks of it all.'[96]

While welcoming the impulses that led to the Reformation, MacDonald was not uncritical of its consequences. Protestants simply replaced one set of doctrines with another. The Reformation also produced an 'individualist standpoint and philosophy' inimical to state intervention and social reform.[97]

He brought a similarly nuanced approach to the Presbyterian faith in which he was raised, lamenting that the Westminster Confession of Faith, adopted by the Church of Scotland as its doctrinal constitution in 1647, had not died with a previous generation of believers but continued to be worshipped 'with the devotion of relic worshippers'.[98] Two years later he praised the 'stern' character of Calvinism in preference to 'humanism and flabbiness'.[99] John Knox exercised an enduring fascination. At one moment, MacDonald was decrying this dour man;[100] at another, extolling him

95 JRM to Sackville, 21 September 1915, NA, Margaret Sackville Papers, RW/1/2/29.

96 JRM, *Wanderings and Excursions*, pp. 157, 186.

97 James Ramsay MacDonald, *Socialism and Society*, 6th edn (London: Independent Labour Party, 1908), pp. 75–7.

98 JRM, Sermon, 20 January 1895, NA, JRM Papers, 30/69/1587, f. 3.

99 JRM, Sermon, 11 June 1897, NA, JRM Papers, 30/69/1587, f. 15.

100 JRM, Diary, 1 January 1919, NA, JRM Papers, 30/69/1753/1, f. 123.

in fulsome terms: 'What a great, rude, rugged character he was, what a massive intelligence, how childlike did he display the weakness of his magnificence. I revel in the Confession of Faith and the Book of Discipline.'[101] His proposed biography of the Scottish reformer never materialized.

For all his previous commitment, MacDonald never described himself as a Unitarian after the 1900s. Denominational labels sat lightly with him, but from the early twentieth century, he consistently identified as a Presbyterian – invariably qualifying that. He described himself to his wife as 'a Quaker Presbyterian'.[102] Later in life, in correspondence with his friend Princess Marthe Bibesco, he called himself 'a pagan Presbyterian'.[103] In his official dealings as Prime Minister with the Anglican hierarchy, he presented himself as an uncomplicated, if non-practising, Presbyterian.

At one level, there was never any separation from what was best in the kirk. MacDonald retained an abiding affection for 'the simple Presbyterian services unsullied by gaudy display and conscious effort'.[104] He maintained good relations with the Presbyterian ministers in Lossiemouth and would walk over from his country cottage in Buckinghamshire to visit Dr Alexander Whyte, a noted preacher and retired Moderator of the General Assembly of the Free Church of Scotland. For MacDonald, Whyte embodied authentic Presbyterianism: 'simple calm and . . . the Christian spirit of loveable simplicity'.[105] The politician thrilled to listen to the octogenarian as he read and expounded the prophet Isaiah with enthusiasm and fervour.[106]

'In the Labour Party, we have the spirit that used to animate your souls'

Although describing himself as a Free Churchman by prejudice and inclination,[107] MacDonald's relationship with English Nonconformity was

101 JRM to Sackville, 9 September 1918, NA, Margaret Sackville Papers, RW/1/4/8.

102 JRM, *Margaret Ethel MacDonald*, p. 61.

103 JRM to Marthe Bibesco, 20 March 1932, cited Marquand, *Ramsay MacDonald*, p. 687.

104 JRM, *Margaret Ethel MacDonald*, p. 61.

105 JRM, Diary, 2 September 1917, NA, JRM Papers, 30/69/1753/1, f. 64.

106 JRM, Diary, 10 February 1918, NA, JRM Papers, 30/69/1753/1, f. 88.

107 JRM to Revd Thomas Law, 20 June 1905, cited Stephen Koss, *Nonconformity in Modern British Politics* (London: B. T. Batsford, 1975), p. 149.

problematic. His dealings with Nonconformist leaders could be cold and tense. It has been suggested that they were suspicious of his Unitarian heterodoxy.[108] Yet MacDonald was more critical of the Free Churchmen than they were of him. The Congregationalist newspaper *Christian World* noted that his 1924 Cabinet 'includes a very large proportion of Free Churchmen, and has perhaps a more definite religious complexion than any Cabinet in recent years'. Its praise for his second government was equally effusive, awarding him 'high marks for packing his administration with Free Churchmen'.[109] Another Nonconformist paper spoke hopefully of the first Labour administration: 'Whether we agree with his political ideas and dreams or not, the present Prime Minister is a Christian, and brings to the great task a Christian outlook and spirit which he believes to be the expression of his faith.'[110]

MacDonald thought that too many Nonconformists, having achieved respectability and prosperity, betrayed the cause of political and social reform, seduced by Baldwin's Utopian speeches on fraternal love.[111] He voiced his fears for the political and religious consequences of the path Nonconformity had chosen to tread:

> The future of Nonconformity as a living and inspiring force in Wales is trembling in the balance. More, religion is truly democratic, and its inspiration is mainly working-class. The good soul I meet of an evening dispensing spiritual comfort and wealth to his neighbours in sorrow, I meet next day black in face going home from the pit. He cannot separate religion from life because it is life, and when he finds a tightening of materialistic interests upon his chapel, it is of his very faith that he doubts.[112]

108 Graham Dale, *God's Politicians: The Christian contribution to 100 years of Labour* (London: HarperCollins, 2000), pp. 60–1.

109 Koss, *Nonconformity in Modern British Politics*, pp. 170, 183.

110 Revd Thomas Nightingale, *British Weekly*, 31 January 1924, cited Koss, *Nonconformity in Modern British Politics*, p. 170.

111 JRM, Diary, 18 May 1925, NA, JRM Papers, 30/69/1753/1, f. 220.

112 JRM, Aberavon, 1918, cited JRM, *Wanderings and Excursions*, pp. 114–15.

He was equally direct addressing a Nonconformist audience in England: 'In the Labour Party, we have the spirit that used to animate your souls, widened, brightened and heightened.'[113]

The Society of Friends, the Quakers, were excluded from MacDonald's strictures against Nonconformity. He admired their belief in the priesthood of all believers, their simplicity of worship. He sent his daughters to a Quaker Sunday school; his sons boarded at Bedales, a school popular with Quakers. His attitude was reflected in a diary entry: 'Marriage at Society of Friends, so simply beautiful and natural, man at his best and God at his nearest.'[114] He praised their pacificism during the First World War but found their stance in the 1930s naïve:

> Your Quaker friends' thoughts are godly but our own experience of the last two years show them to make war inevitable. It is not God but the Devil who is in charge of the international situation and those who are working for God in it are poor servants if all they do is worship God and neglect their duty to circumvent the Devil.[115]

'I shall do my duty to the Church'

MacDonald appreciated Anglican liturgy when he found simplicity, good preaching and good music. His contact with the Church of England, however, consisted principally in the exercise of his powers of ecclesiastical patronage. From the outset, he made clear his strong opinion that this ought not to be part of the Prime Minister's functions: 'Why I, a Presbyterian, who call the Church Episcopalian, should be bothered with Bishops, I know not. A self-respecting Church would not allow me to interfere. I shall do my duty to the Church and damn pressure.'[116] Most Anglicans agreed that he did indeed do his duty to their Church. His fellow Scot, Archbishop Randall Davidson, took to him immediately and

113 JRM, Speech, Sheffield, 21 October 1924, cited Koss, *Nonconformity in Modern British Politics*, p. 173.

114 JRM, Diary, 12 April 1921, NA, JRM Papers, 30/69/1753/1, f. 148.

115 JRM to Helen Robertson, 1934, cited Marquand, *Ramsay MacDonald*, pp. 750–1.

116 JRM, Diary, 18 June 1924, NA, JRM Papers, 30/69/1753/1, f. 185.

was 'immensely impressed by his thoughtfulness and care'. He found that in the matter of Church appointments, MacDonald 'took more pains than anybody since Mr Asquith'.[117]

MacDonald knew a number of Anglican clergy involved in the Labour Party and wished to send out a 'sign that high preferment in the Church is not confined to any one class nor inaccessible to priests of [their] political outlook'.[118] A candidate for Leicester in 1900, he had been hosted by 'the Red Vicar', Lewis Donaldson, who maintained: 'Christianity is the religion of which socialism is the practice.' MacDonald allowed Donaldson's politics to trump his Ritualism, appointing him a canon of Westminster Abbey in 1924.

Two of MacDonald's episcopal appointments attracted criticism. He knew Ernest Barnes, a former Master of the Temple Church, through the Union of Democratic Control (a peace movement formed during the First World War), but he was not his first choice for the vacant see of Birmingham. Both Anglo-Catholics and Evangelicals fiercely opposed Barnes's Modernist theology. MacDonald refused to back down, writing to one critic: 'My only interest is to put men in high position in the Church who really believe in Christianity and who regard it as a spiritual power influencing thought and conduct.'[119] The other controversy concerned the successor for an Anglo-Catholic bishop in Truro. MacDonald took a personal interest, seeing it as his duty to check the influence of those whom he judged to be imposing an 'illegal' ritual on the Church of England. He interviewed his preferred candidate, Joseph Hunkin, the son of a Methodist lay preacher, advising him what his policy should be in Truro,[120] and saw through his appointment despite objections to his Modernist views.

MacDonald had an abhorrence of Catholic dogma and practice, whether encountered in the Anglican or Roman Communions. He wrote to Archbishop Cosmo Lang of his 'horror' at the 'very high ritual' he endured in

117 Davidson, Memorandum, 23 March 1924, LPL, Davidson Papers, 14, f. 370; Davidson, Assembly Committee on the Appointment of Bishops, 29 July 1924, LPL, Bell Papers, 118, f. 44.

118 JRM to Davidson, 15 February 1924, LPL, Davidson Papers, 11, f. 103.

119 JRM to Sidney Dark, 13 August 1924, cited John Barnes, *Ahead of His Time: Bishop Barnes of Birmingham* (London: Collins, 1979), p. 148.

120 JRM, Diary, 20 March 1935, NA, JRM Papers, 30/69/1753/2, f. 10.

one Sussex church.[121] He feared that the irrelevance and declining influence of Nonconformity was resulting in the country being lost to Catholic influences.[122] He mocked the doctrine of Purgatory, offering to pay sixpence to a priest to pray Margaret Sackville's soul into heaven.[123] Yet MacDonald's personal experience of Roman Catholicism was minimal. He attended his first Catholic service at the age of 51, when present at the Requiem Mass for the Irish Nationalist John Redmond. He thought the music beautiful and Westminster Cathedral impressive but found the liturgy distracting, lacking simplicity.[124] He admitted to 'prejudices against Romanism',[125] retaining the Free Church of Scotland conviction that 'the only head of the Church is Christ',[126] and assumed that the papacy, episcopacy and priesthood militated against this. He was utterly opposed to elaborate ritual and ceremonial. Such things, he feared, risked reason being overwhelmed by emotion.[127]

A 'strange message . . . through the veil'

For all his claims to strict rationality in religion, MacDonald required a release for his own emotional needs. The death of his mother, five-year-old son David and wife left him completely bereft. In his grief, he derived no comfort from the faith he had taught as a Unitarian. Time and again, he found himself wondering 'if [Margaret] was or was not, if she cared, or knew, or what'. Like many others of his generation, he turned to spiritualism: 'From time to time I have been reading spiritualist literature, automatic writing, etc. but it repels me on the whole.'[128]

MacDonald's interest in the occult pre-dated Margaret's death. His horoscope had been cast in 1910, foretelling, with astounding inaccuracy, five years of good fortune.[129] Not discouraged, he returned to astrology in 1915.

121 JRM, Memorandum to Lang, 20 February 1935, LPL, Lang Papers, 139, f. 100.
122 JRM to Porritt, cited Porritt, *More and More of Memories*, p. 131.
123 JRM to Sackville, 30 May 1928, NA, Margaret Sackville Papers, RW/1/8/1.
124 JRM, Diary, 8 March 1918, NA, JRM Papers, 30/69/1753/1, f. 93.
125 JRM to Sackville, u/d, NA, Margaret Sackville Papers, RW/1/9/59.
126 JRM, House of Commons, 16 June 1913, cited Elton, *The Life of JRM*, p. 143.
127 JRM, Sermon, 11 June 1897, NA, JRM Papers, 30/69/1587.
128 JRM, Diary, 12 September 1915, NA, JRM Papers, 30/69/1753/1, f. 19.
129 T. D. Benson to JRM, 22 July 1910, NA, JRM Papers, 30/69/815.

Again he was assured that the future was set fair, including a second marriage.[130] (Lady Margaret Sackville was less willing to have her matrimonial prospects determined by the stars.[131]) It is unclear whether it was this horoscope or another that described MacDonald as 'a dreamer of beautiful dreams', predicting that 'all mystic subjects will have a special fascination and interest for you . . . a love of the metaphysical is deeply buried with your nature'.[132] On another occasion, MacDonald had his destiny prophesied 'by automatic writing from the other side'.[133]

In 1924, within days of leaving Downing Street, a palm reader foretold 'a great disaster'.[134] The following year he attended his first séance. The American medium George Valiantine, using his luminous trumpet, conjured up the spirit of the recently deceased Lord Curzon, who urged MacDonald to use every endeavour to prevent future wars that would destroy civilization. The next spirit to be summoned, that of a close family member, spoke 'personal messages of love' to the leader of the Opposition.[135] Valiantine was exposed as a fraud in 1931.

In seeking evidence for personal survival, MacDonald's receptivity to communications from the spirit world became known in certain circles. As Britain headed towards financial crisis in the summer of 1931, the airwaves were positively buzzing. 'Effie' from Watford wrote to tell him of the 'strange message' she had received for him 'through the veil'.[136] More substantive messages were received through the Wembley medium Grace Cooke. MacDonald's wife was extremely loquacious. She reminded her husband:

> We used to speak of things spiritual. We always knew the great reality of the invisible spiritual universe . . . One of the very first experiences I had on my awakening over here was the great realization of the *one* all-pervading consciousness of *God*. I knew then what life meant.

---

130 Anon., Notes on Horoscope, 1915, NA, JRM Papers, 30/69/815.

131 JRM to Sackville, u/d, NA, Margaret Sackville Papers, RW/1/9/45.

132 Notes on Horoscope, u/d, NA, JRM Papers, 30/69/815.

133 JRM to Sackville, u/d, NA, Margaret Sackville Papers, RW/1/9/35.

134 JRM, Diary, 28 November 1924, NA, JRM Papers, 30/69/1753/1, f. 215.

135 H. Dennis Bradley, *The Wisdom of the Gods* (London: T. Werner Laurie, 1925), pp. 402–3.

136 Euphemia Johnson to JRM, 10 August 1931, NA, JRM Papers, 30/69/834.

The spirit world did not restrict itself to the hereafter – it had plenty to say about the 1931 general election and internal divisions within the Labour Party.[137]

Biographies have noted MacDonald's interest in the occult but downplayed his credulity. None appreciated the sheer range and duration of his involvement. It is impossible to reconcile this behaviour with the youth who solemnly denounced all forms of superstition or with the Unitarian preacher who proclaimed a purely rational faith commensurate with modern science and progress.

'His religion is agnostic and yet he is evidently seeking out a faith'

Of all the twentieth-century Prime Ministers, it is most difficult to discover a consistent line of development in the religious beliefs of Ramsay MacDonald. Without questioning his sincerity, he led a highly compartmentalized life. His political contemporaries recognized a genuine religious sensibility and fervour. The economist Harold Laski commented that MacDonald's speeches 'state great platitudes with an almost theological enthusiasm. Indeed, it might well be argued that Mr MacDonald's hold over the populace is essentially that of a lay preacher, with an immense power of moral fervour.'[138]

One senses the sadness of someone searching for something never quite attained. In the 1890s, MacDonald spoke of the Scottish poet John Davidson. He might have been speaking of himself:

> His religion is agnostic and yet he is evidently seeking out a faith . . . there is too much Celtic mysticism in him ever to allow him to settle down quietly in the cold calm of a scientific (narrowly-speaking) creed.[139]

137 Grace Cooke to JRM, 10 September and 5 November 1931, 25 and 28 February [1932], NA, JRM Papers, 30/69/815.

138 Harold Laski, cited Anne de Courcy, *Circe: The life of Edith, Marchioness of Londonderry* (London: Sinclair-Stevenson, 1992), p. 183.

139 JRM, Lecture, 1897?, NA, JRM Papers, 30/69/1585.

MacDonald can appear remarkably contemporary, the sort of person who identifies himself as 'spiritual, but not religious'. It brought him little comfort or sense of fulfilment.

Exhausted on his retirement from politics in 1937, MacDonald, together with his daughter, Sheila, set off for South America in search of recuperation. He died of a heart attack on the Atlantic on 9 November 1937. The coffin was brought back to Britain by the Royal Navy. Following a public funeral service in Westminster Abbey on 26 November, his body was cremated at Golders Green Crematorium and the ashes were taken by train to Scotland. There was a brief service at his Lossiemouth home the next day before his ashes were buried next to those of Margaret, who had died 26 years earlier.

Neville Chamberlain (1937–1940)

'A reverent agnostic'

Arthur Neville Chamberlain was born in Edgbaston, Birmingham, on 18 March 1869. He was educated at Rugby and Mason College, Birmingham.

After managing a failed family investment in the Bahamas, Chamberlain's involvement in two Birmingham metalworking firms was considerably more successful. Following family tradition, he pursued a programme of social reform in local politics, serving as Lord Mayor of Birmingham in 1915–16. Success in local government led to his appointment as Minister of National Service in 1916, with a brief to coordinate conscription and the industrial manpower required for the war effort. It was not a happy experience. Chamberlain's relationship with Lloyd George was marked by acrimony and he resigned after less than a year.

Elected as the Unionist MP for Birmingham Ladywood in 1918, Chamberlain transferred in 1929 to the safer seat of Birmingham Edgbaston, which he held until his death in 1940.

The break-up of the Conservative–Liberal coalition government in 1922 saw Chamberlain's dramatic rise to political prominence. Bonar Law appointed him Postmaster General and then Minister of Health in 1923. After Baldwin became Prime Minister, Chamberlain succeeded him as Chancellor of the Exchequer. His tenure at the Treasury was brief as Baldwin lost the 1923 general election. Some were surprised when Chamberlain returned to the Ministry of Health after the Unionist victory in 1924, but it was the role he sought. The department enjoyed far wider responsibilities than subsequently, including pensions, roads, housing, town planning and local government. He was recognized as an efficient administrator and principled social reformer.

In opposition, he was Chairman of the Conservative Party. During the 1931 financial crisis, he led negotiations with the Labour Party that resulted in the formation of the National government. Briefly Minister of Health again, he returned to the Treasury as Chancellor in November 1931. Chamberlain pursued a policy of tariff reform, cheap money and sound finance. Economic recovery and his role as deputy to both Ramsay MacDonald and Baldwin meant he was the obvious successor when Baldwin finally retired from 10 Downing Street.

Chamberlain was appointed Prime Minister on 28 May 1937. He exercised a much firmer control over the government than either of his two immediate predecessors. More partisan than Baldwin, he was popular with wide sections of the Conservative Party.

His record in office is, of course, associated with his policy of appeasement. Chamberlain was under no illusion as to the threat posed by the dictatorships in Germany, Italy and Japan. Opposed to everything they represented, he sought simultaneously to avoid at all costs a repeat of the carnage of the First World War. Hailed as the saviour of world peace for the Munich Agreement, which he negotiated with Hitler during the Czechoslovak crisis of 1938, Chamberlain was later vilified when Germany invaded first Prague and then Poland. His preference for informal contact with the dictators was ill-advised; he massively overestimated his own capacity to contain them. There can be no doubting, however, Chamberlain's sincerity. His policy failed but Britain entered the Second World War united, unambiguously in the moral right and with the crucial advantage of an extra year's rearmament.

Chamberlain was not a successful war leader. He lacked breadth of vision and the capacity to inspire the nation. After the failure of the Norwegian campaign, the Labour opposition and Conservative rebels forced his resignation on 10 May 1940. He continued to serve in the War Cabinet under Churchill as Lord President of the Council and as leader of the Conservative Party until a few weeks before his death.

Chamberlain died of bowel cancer on 9 November 1940.

* * *

Birmingham Unitarians

With the possible exception of Asquith, Chamberlain was the only twentieth-century Prime Minister not to be baptized. His sister, Hilda, expressed her indignation on returning from a baptism: 'A barbarous ceremony . . . Nothing can reconcile me to the idea that the poor innocent baby should be regarded as steeped in sin until the magic ceremony has taken place.'[1] As Unitarians, the Chamberlains rejected the historic Christian churches' belief that humanity's fallen nature is transmitted from our first parents; that reconciliation to God is affected by Christ through the sacrament of baptism.

Chamberlain was not the first Prime Minister to have been a Unitarian. The third Duke of Grafton had embraced their tenets, but only after he left office in 1770. As young men, Lloyd George flirted with Unitarianism and MacDonald counted himself among their number. In England, Unitarianism had tended to develop out of Presbyterianism, attracting other Nonconformists too. In a scientific and rationalist age, it appealed to those who found the doctrines of the Trinity, the divinity of Christ and original sin intellectually implausible. There was something of a fissure within Unitarianism in the nineteenth century as James Martineau developed a more emotionally satisfying form of romantic mysticism. The Chamberlains remained adherents of the original rationalism.

Neville was the son of Joseph Chamberlain and his second wife, Florence (née Kenrick). Joseph moved from London to Birmingham, where he made a fortune manufacturing screws. He became one of the most iconic and divisive politicians of his day. A social reformer and radical, he was critical of the Established Church and the monarchy. At Westminster, he first split the Liberal Party over Irish Home Rule and then the Conservatives over his policy of tariff reform. His religious background was an advantage in his adopted city, dominated as it was by Quakers and Unitarians. There is little evidence Joseph Chamberlain was ever particularly devout, but in his early years he conformed in terms of public worship.

Joseph attended the Church of the Messiah, where he encountered the leading members of the city's Unitarian community, including the Kenricks. The attraction was less the liturgy and doctrine but more the Unitarians' commitment to education and social reform. Both Joseph and Florence taught in Unitarian Sunday schools. The commitment was

1 Hilda Chamberlain to Neville Chamberlain, 3 April 1936, CRL, NC18/2/965.

to imparting secular rather than religious knowledge to disadvantaged children.

The Church of the Messiah in Broad Street was completed seven years before Neville's birth. Despite the determination to teach a religion fit for the modern age, the architecture harked back to a medieval past, with tower, spire and gabled aisles. Although the building could seat 950, the congregation never exceeded half that number. The minister in charge until his death in 1893 was William Crosskey, a noted geologist who preached an intelligent form of liberalism much to the taste of those present. Crosskey had become rather tired by the end. In 1894, Neville's sisters welcomed the arrival of the new minister, hoping he would 'bring some new life into the old institutions'. They approved of his sermons, his intention 'to make the Church a centre of work' and the fact 'he is very broad, yet he has some religion left'.[2]

For all his financial and political success, Joseph was acquainted with personal tragedy. He was paralysed by a stroke in the prime of his public life. His first two wives died young. John Morley relayed the following account to Asquith:

> When his first wife died, Joe became very religious, was assiduous at his chapel and in his good works, and began to teach zealously in the Sunday school. He married again and, after a time, the second wife died also. This was too much for Joe, and he not only renounced his faith and became a pronounced unbeliever, but by way of doing what he could to punish the God in whom he had ceased to believe, he swore that he would never enter a chapel again and discontinued all his subscriptions![3]

Morley exaggerated; Joseph's Sunday-school teaching pre-dated his first bereavement; his financial support of the Unitarians survived the second. It is true, however, that he was devastated by the death of Neville's mother, and this was reflected in his religious practice.

2 Beatrice Chamberlain to NC, 31 October 1894, CRL, NC1/13/2/39; Hilda Chamberlain to NC, 17 October 1894, CRL, NC1/15/3/27.

3 Asquith to Margot Asquith, 23 May 1892, Oxford, Bodleian Libraries, Margot Asquith MS, Eng. c. 6686, f. 60.

Florence Chamberlain died when Neville was not yet six. His younger sister's only memory of their mother was the rustling of her skirts as she knelt for bedside prayers with Neville and herself.[4] Florence's funeral was extremely simple: no church service; prayers in the family home led by Crosskey; a burial service at the graveside.[5] Joseph was distraught. Crosskey attempted to console him:

> Those who know you . . . can only pray that you may be able to trust the Unseen Goodness, which has been veiled in so fearful a shadow and that the peace which may be hoped to follow the devotion and self-surrender of a noble heart may not be denied you.[6]

With no reference to the resurrection, eternal life nor even the Christian God, this rationalist faith brought Joseph neither comfort nor hope. He had too much integrity to pretend otherwise:

> [This life] is a hideous business and our conception of its beginning and meaning is thoroughly unsatisfying . . . I refuse to try and buy comfort by forcing myself into insincere conviction.[7]

Joseph remarried a third time, an American, Mary Endicott, a practising Episcopalian. He recovered a measure of happiness but not his religious faith. Yet he was never aggressively anti-religious. Neville remembered him during those years:

> He was not what is called a religious man and I cannot recollect his going to church in Birmingham, but his attitude towards religion is best described in his own words to me one evening. 'I am,' he said, 'a very reverend agnostic.' He never scoffed at religion and became less inclined to disbelieve anything as he grew older.[8]

4 Peter Marsh, *The Chamberlain Litany: Letters within a governing family from empire to appeasement* (London: Haus Publishing, 2010), p. 6.

5 Press cutting, 18 February 1875, CRL, NC1/6/4/18.

6 Revd H. W. Crosskey to Joseph Chamberlain, 18 February 1875, CRL, NC1/6/4/6.

7 Joseph Chamberlain to John Morley, 7 December 1875, cited Peter Marsh, *Joseph Chamberlain: Entrepreneur in politics* (London: Yale University Press, 1994), p. 92.

8 Neville Chamberlain, Account of Joseph Chamberlain, 6 July 1914, CRL, NC/1/6/11.

Joseph never repudiated his Unitarian roots; he was proud of the Unitarians' social and political achievements:

> In the great struggle for political liberty, which has now been going on for some 100 years, that body, small though it is, has always been on the side of progress, and on the side of the people; and, further, I can say of that body what can be said of few other sects, that its men, when they become rich, do not cease to be liberal.[9]

Although Joseph's funeral included a service at the Church of the Messiah, the private family element was minimalistic: a couple of hymns after dinner before the coffin in the library.[10] Yet long after the doctrine had been discarded, all the Chamberlains retained a strong sense of public duty, personal morality and charitable giving.

In the Birmingham society in which the Chamberlains moved, it is surprising how rapidly the content of faith disappeared. Rationalism was quickly replaced by outright scepticism. Neville's half-sister, Beatrice, recorded a Quaker dinner party that concluded with a game of charades: 'Someone asked if the Bible was allowed. "Oh yes," said Mrs Wilson King, "Miss Chamberlain included fiction!"' One of the family suggested an advertising strategy for the Unitarians: 'Just stick up on a board: "Last in, first out. No hell and no devil." You'd fill the place."'[11]

The fact that Joseph sent his sons to Rugby, an Anglican foundation, suggests a certain indifference as to the religious instruction they received. When Austen, Neville's elder half-brother, started at the school, Joseph confirmed that he was happy for him to attend the chapel and receive the same Bible teaching as the other boys. When Neville arrived at Rugby, he and another Unitarian boy entered a token protest against the established religion by refusing to face east in the school chapel during the creed. The extent of their rebellion was limited. Both volunteered to accompany the hymns at Sunday evening prayers.[12]

---

9 Joseph Chamberlain, 1868, cited Marsh, *JC*, p. 7.

10 NC, Diary, 6 July 1914, CRL, NC2/20.

11 Beatrice Chamberlain to NC, 31 December 1895, CRL, NC1/13/2/83.

12 David Dilks, *Neville Chamberlain: Pioneering and reform, 1869–1929* (Cambridge: Cambridge University Press, 1984), pp. 19, 23.

A devoted disciple of Darwin

It was intended that Austen follow his father into public life. Neville, by contrast, was destined for business, returning to Birmingham for two years of vocational and technical studies at Mason College. About this time he began reading Charles Darwin. He judged Darwin the greatest Englishman who ever lived – together with Shakespeare and his own father. Not that Joseph Chamberlain encouraged Neville's enthusiasm. He was firmly of the view 'that it was a waste of time discussing questions as to which we did not and could not know the answer'.[13]

For Neville, however, it was a lifelong passion, one he shared with his sisters and later his wife. He and his sisters read and discussed Darwin and also subsequent commentaries and developments, which seemed to them to contain 'the most thrilling possibilities'.[14] His admiration was unbounded; he kept Darwin's photograph in his study. Darwin provided answers to the mysteries of the natural world in which Neville thrilled:

> [He was] the most ultra-modern of all great men . . . with his power of continually chewing over and revolving a subject, coupled with a never-ceasing speculation round and round it, till in the end he left nothing out of consideration that could be known, and had weighed and balanced everything till every factor had its weight.[15]

At one point, Neville was teaching Darwinism to the Sunday-school children at the Church of the Messiah. He returned continually to the works of Darwin with profit and delight.

Did Darwin's theories, calling into question a literal interpretation of the Bible, cause or increase Chamberlain's religious scepticism? There is no evidence of a strong religious faith before he encountered Darwin. He resented unintelligent criticism of Darwin, recalling 'the atmosphere of prejudice and bigotry which existed',[16] especially that articulated by churchmen

13 Ida Chamberlain, Memoir of NC, 1941, CRL, NC9/2/10, f. 9.

14 Hilda Chamberlain, Memoir of NC, 1941, CRL, NC9/2/9, ff. 1–2.

15 NC, cited Keith Feiling, *The Life of Neville Chamberlain* (London: Macmillan, 1946), p. 234.

16 NC to Hilda Chamberlain, 6 September 1936, CRL, NC18/1/975.

'defending dogmatic assertions of creation'.[17] His relationship with an Anglo-Catholic clergyman in the Bahamas was almost destroyed at the outset when he spoke flippantly of Darwin:

> Strolling into my room he picked up *The Origin of the Species* and after remarking that he had spent much time over it he went on, 'But after all there's a good deal to be said for poor old Darwin's theory. You know the reason why he kept on hammering after this missing link was because he was so exactly like a monkey that he felt there must be some connection.' I could have kicked him or knocked him down. Such a mixture of ignorance, conceit and profanity is contemptible to the last degree.[18]

This veneration of Darwin was the closest Chamberlain came to a sense of the sacred. He looked to Darwin to provide answers to the natural world, however, and was unconcerned by any theological implications of his writings.

Chamberlain was a member of the Birmingham and Edgbaston Debating Society. As president, he took as the subject of his address 'Human Development under Natural Selection'. Although a strong patriot, he did not subscribe to crude theories of racial superiority. Perceived advantages, he felt, derived from educational opportunities. Other comments were, however, less attractive. He opposed the 'feeble-minded' having children of their own.[19] He expressed similar views as Minister of Health: 'I inspected Monyhull where 1,100 [mentally deficient] men and women and children are in residence . . . it leaves me very depressed after seeing all those mistakes and misfits.'[20] Such sentiments placed Chamberlain in the company of Balfour and Churchill, representing the gospel of Charles Darwin, or at least of the social Darwinists, not the gospel of Jesus Christ.

---

17 NC to Hilda Chamberlain, 25 February 1934, CRL, NC18/1/861.

18 NC to Ida Chamberlain, 6–10 December 1891, CRL, NC1/16/2/10.

19 NC, Address to the Birmingham and Edgbaston Debating Society, 28 September 1910, CRL, NC9/1/1.

20 NC, 10 October 1926, cited ed. Robert Self, *The Neville Chamberlain Diary Letters: The reform years, 1921–27* (Aldershot: Ashgate, 2000), p. 368.

'I wish all the reverends in the Bahamas were at the bottom of the sea'

Joseph Chamberlain grew alarmed at the increasing expense of his political and social life, and in 1891, in the hope of replenishing the family fortune, sent the 22-year-old Neville to the Bahamas. He was to set up and manage a venture producing hemp from the sisal plant. It was a complete failure. Neville remained for six years, isolated from educated society, but it was a formative experience. He used the opportunity to read voraciously and educate himself. His books included Darwin, Shakespeare and, at least as a work of reference, the Bible. Like Lloyd George and Law, he read Thomas Carlyle but, unlike them, escaped his influence: '[Carlyle's musings are] very mystical and often unintelligible to me. This much however I can clearly make out: that I myself am a miserable, hollow, shallow, paltry, trivial, but fortunately temporary phantasm on this divine-infernal earth – which is cheerful.'[21] Theology and spirituality did not feature among his reading material.

In Birmingham, Chamberlain's exposure to religion had been controlled and limited. That was not an option in the Bahamas. Even in his comparative isolation, religion was apt to intrude at every turn. He expressed his frustration on his arrival: 'On Sunday I was obliged to lie idle at Mastic Point as all my men had scruples about working on the Sabbath.'[22] His Sundays were spent on correspondence, fishing and in pursuit of the local flora and fauna. He was exasperated by the number of new churches built by missionaries and the disputes between competing denominations.

Chamberlain was singularly unimpressed by the clergy he met: 'I wish all the reverends in the Bahamas were at the bottom of the sea.'[23] The tedium was such, however, that he was prepared occasionally to attend religious services by way of diversion:

> On Sunday I amused myself by going to the Roman Catholic chapel where the priest with perspiration running down his cheeks and

21 NC to Beatrice Chamberlain, 27–29 November 1892, CRL, NC/1/13/3/15.

22 NC to Joseph Chamberlain, 6 June 1891, CRL, NC1/6/10/16.

23 Cited Feiling, *The Life of NC*, p. 25.

> hands bid us think of the excruciating torments of the damned in hell and the 'poor souls in purgatory'. I thought if there were as many mosquitos there as in the chapel they must be having a very bad time indeed.[24]

There was no intellectual or spiritual engagement with the concepts or practices he encountered.

Father Matthews was the Anglo-Catholic priest whose frivolous comments on Darwin incurred Chamberlain's wrath. Improbably, the two men came to hold each other in mutual respect and remained in contact after Chamberlain's return to England. Chamberlain acknowledged Matthews's human qualities: his conversation, engagement with modern technology and medical skill.[25] He found all this difficult to reconcile with the priest's religious views and practice: 'It gave me quite a shock to see [Matthews] waving the incense before the altar. He is so sensible on everyday matters.'[26]

Chamberlain and Matthews viewed each other as allies in advancing social conditions, much as the Church of the Messiah saw its role in Birmingham. Matthews attributed the progress against alcoholism to Chamberlain's firm action and noted a change of attitude: 'He seems very favourably disposed towards the Church.'[27] At this practical level, Chamberlain was willing to support the missionaries, and he and his father sent donations to help rebuild churches destroyed by a hurricane.

Annie: 'A devout member of the Church of England'

Back in Birmingham, Chamberlain proved himself a successful businessman. Active in local government and civic life, his hobbies included shooting and fishing, ornithology and botany. He had resigned himself

24 NC to Austen Chamberlain, 17 June 1891 (copy), CRL, NC1/19/28.

25 NC to Ida Chamberlain, 22–23 October 1891, CRL, NC1/16/2/8.

26 Cited Feiling, *The Life of NC*, p. 29.

27 Revd F. B. Matthews to Archdeacon Wakefield, 28 February 1894, CRL, NC3/7/24.

to a bachelor existence when at the age of 41 he met Anne ('Annie') de Vere Cole. Fourteen years his junior, Annie was Irish, pretty, vivacious, disorganized and, at times, highly strung. She and her family were also religious. Her mother was heiress to her uncle, Sir Stephen de Vere, an Anglo-Irish MP who had converted to Catholicism in 1847. 'A devout member of the Church of England',[28] Annie attended church most Sundays. The two were married on 5 January 1911 at St Paul's, Knightsbridge, the High Church parish close to Annie's Sloane Street home. It was a loving and successful marriage.

Chamberlain made no objection to an Anglican marriage service and insisted that their children, Dorothy and Frank, be baptized, confirmed and educated as Anglicans – 'Unitarianism', he commented, 'is so bleak.'[29] Not that the family were sternly pious. Chamberlain recorded the scene at Frank's baptism:

> Dorothy kept us in convulsions of suppressed laughter while Frank was being christened last week. Archdeacon Owens performed the ceremony, gabbling over the service at a great rate. [Dorothy] called out in the middle, 'Who is the man talking to?' and after hushing and whispering from Emma, 'I mustn't talk while the man talks.'[30]

Chamberlain employed Miss Leamon, a committed Anglican, as the children's governess, giving her free rein regarding their religious instruction. Annie described the consequences:

> I heard a familiar sort of deep murmur coming from the glass room, and as I approached, two rather uncertain looking children explained as they rose from their knees 'we're playing at Church' . . . They said, 'Go away and leave us' and they returned to their knees. Afterwards Dorothy came in and announced, 'Frank gave a *charming* service'! and on further questioning I hear he had given a most interesting sermon.[31]

28 Revd A. C. Don to Revd A. J. Meek, 20 February 1940 (copy), LPL, Lang Papers, 175, f. 122.

29 Hermione Hammond to David Dilks, 16 January 1976 (copy).

30 NC, Diary, 30 April 1914, CRL, NC2/20.

31 Anne Chamberlain to NC, 9 June 1919, CRL, NC1/25/47.

'A matter which must be left to his own conscience'

Chamberlain found himself asked to act as godfather to the children of friends and associates, including to the family of Alfred Greenwood, private secretary to the Governor of the Bahamas. Could a Unitarian act in such a capacity given the Unitarians' rejection of the Trinity and the doctrine of original sin, the very basis of the sacrament of baptism? Theological considerations did not feature in Greenwood's request nor Chamberlain's acceptance.[32] In any event, Chamberlain assumed his responsibilities in absentia, a proxy making the Christian vows on his behalf.

The issue might have passed unnoticed in the 1890s. It was a different matter in 1940 when Chamberlain was Prime Minister. The Archbishop's chaplain had to pen a careful response to an irate Nottinghamshire clergyman:

> There were of course special reasons why Lord Dunglass [Alec Douglas-Home] and Mr Lennox Boyd should wish to have the Prime Minister as godparent to their children. They are both closely associated with the Prime Minister in the work of the government. If the Prime Minister in these circumstances is prepared conscientiously to undertake the duties and responsibilities of a godparent that is a matter which must be left to his own conscience.
>
> I may add that I have spoken to the Archbishop of Canterbury on the subject and what I have just said may be taken to represent his opinion in a case of this kind where, as I understand, there were other godparents whose qualifications from a strict Church of England point of view were beyond question.[33]

There is no attempt at theological justification. Lambeth appears to have been reluctant to challenge a Prime Minister who had acted in sincerity.

32 NC to Alfred Greenwood, 12 June 1898, CRL, NC7/5/41.

33 Don to Meek, 20 February 1940 (copy), LPL, Lang Papers, 175, ff. 121–2.

Warming to Anglicanism

As Minister of National Service, Chamberlain met with the Archbishops of Canterbury and York. He was conscious of the irony: 'It does make me smile when I think how I used to hate the Church.'[34] He had been brought up 'to hate' the Established Church and its privileges, which had excluded Unitarians and others from higher education and public life.

Chamberlain attended his stepmother's second marriage to Canon William Carnegie:

> I had never been present at a communion service before and was scandalized to see the priest go and drink up the remains of the wine when he thought no one was looking, just like waiters after a party. But Ivy explained to me that you mustn't leave any and that those remains are the priest's 'perks'. She didn't use that word but that's what I understood. Doesn't it strike you as rather 'rum' to have Isaac and Rebecca dragged into a modern marriage service? I always wonder whether the congregation will know who they were.[35]

By describing the requirement to consume the consecrated elements in such a way, Chamberlain unwittingly revealed his scant knowledge of Anglican practice despite his time at Rugby. Neither Chamberlain nor his half-brother liked the proposal for Prayer Book revision brought before the Commons in December 1927, but they voted for it, thinking, as non-Anglicans, that 'it was not for us to refuse what the Church through constitutional and democratic means had asked for'.[36]

Chamberlain's disposition towards the Church of England warmed on better acquaintance with Archbishop Cosmo Lang. The Chamberlains were members of the same house party in January 1935 and 'found him very good company and were glad to have him in the house'.[37] Lang made good use of the time. Two months later they stayed with him in Canterbury. He 'liked' the Archbishop; she 'adored' him. Chamberlain drew the line at accompanying

34 NC to Hilda Chamberlain, 27 January 1917, CRL, NC18/1/99.

35 NC to Hilda Chamberlain, 6 August 1916, CRL, NC18/1/73.

36 NC, 17 December 1927, cited ed. Self, *NC Diary Letters: The reform years*, p. 437.

37 NC to Ida Chamberlain, 6 January 1935, CRL, NC18/1/900.

his wife to early service but was happy enough for Lang to give him a private tour of Canterbury Cathedral.[38] In his final illness, he wrote to Lang:

> Your generous and affectionate letter was a source of great pleasure and encouragement to me. You know how much I value your good opinion, and I always thought that you had pre-eminently that political sense which is notoriously rare amongst the clergy and the civil service![39]

Significantly, he praised Lang's political judgement, not his spiritual counsel.

When attending state occasions, such as George V's Silver Jubilee service and funeral, Chamberlain was impressed on patriotic not spiritual grounds: 'As I gazed across to the ambassadors on the other side I thought "This'll show 'em."'[40] That constituted the limit of his religious practice. Unlike his wife, Chamberlain only once attended the Ellesborough parish church near Chequers – for the first official Day of National Prayer.[41] With no sacramental understanding, he was simultaneously bemused and irritated by Lord Halifax's insistence on a Communion Service at Ellesborough when staying at Chequers on a Sunday.[42]

Strictly speaking, the Unitarians were not Christians because they rejected the faith's fundamental doctrines. Both Austen and Neville, however, self-identified as belonging to the broad spectrum of Protestant Nonconformity.[43] Others were similarly willing to classify Chamberlain. He acted as Vice-President of the Nonconformist Unionists but was concerned lest they ask him to speak. The 1916 Congregationalist annual assembly was not to his taste:

38 NC to Ida Chamberlain, 30 March 1935, CRL, NC18/1/911.

39 NC to Lang, 1940, LPL, Lang Papers, 191, f. 302.

40 NC to Hilda Chamberlain, 12 May 1935; NC to Ida Chamberlain, 1 February 1936, cited ed. Robert Self, *Neville Chamberlain Diary Letters: The Downing Street years, 1934–40* (Aldershot: Ashgate, 2005), pp. 132, 172.

41 Revd Norman White to David Dilks, 17 July 1973 (copy).

42 Notes of conversation, Stephen and Dorothy Lloyd with David Dilks (copy).

43 Austen Chamberlain to Hilda and Ida Chamberlain, 23 December 1927, cited ed. Robert Self, *The Austen Chamberlain Diary Letters: The correspondence of Sir Austen Chamberlain with his sisters Hilda and Ida, 1916–1937* (Cambridge: Cambridge University Press, 1995), pp. 322–3; NC, 17 December 1927, cited ed. Self, *NC Diary Letters: The reform years*, p. 437.

> We got let in for a regular revivalist meeting with stories of the drunken boxer's reformation and the death bed reconciliation of the aged father and the prodigal son. We were both feeling very sick and were quite finished off when a gentleman from Boston U.S.A. said that after the war the Christian soul of England would go out to the Christian soul of Germany![44]

Unlike Baldwin, Chamberlain was never comfortable in the company of Nonconformists.

'A great thing for her to have gone Roman'

With his Unitarian background and allergy to clergy, one would have expected Chamberlain to react badly to Catholicism. That was true in the Bahamas. When taken to Benediction, he thoroughly disapproved:

> [The priest] went through many performances before the altar, unlocking a cupboard and taking out some relic, waving incense to it, bowing, showing it to the congregation while a bell was struck, and finally replacing it. Truly it is a barbarous religion.[45]

Later his attitude was more nuanced. Even co-religionists of Cardinal Francis Bourne, the Archbishop of Westminster, found the clergyman difficult; not the Chamberlains. When they lunched with him in 1926, they

> both took to him immensely. He has just the face you so often find among eminent R.C. ecclesiastics, wise and kind and humorous and intelligent, and in conversation he was eminently sensible and vigorous. Such a contrast to Ch. of Eng. Archbishops![46]

When Catholicism affected the Chamberlains more nearly than this, they were curiously relaxed. In 1916, Annie's stepsister and her husband converted to Catholicism. Chamberlain simply remarked:

44 NC to Hilda Chamberlain, 8 October 1916, CRL, NC18/1/83.
45 NC, Diary, 14 June 1891, cited Dilks, *NC*, p. 47.
46 NC, 3 July 1926, CRL, NC18/1/534.

> Annie does not mind her family turning R.C. a bit. She herself hasn't much sympathy with the Church now and though she is not in the least attracted by the R.C. she is broad enough not to mind what Church people belong to if they believe in it.[47]

Hilda, Chamberlain's sister – she who took such exception to infant baptism – was also remarkably understanding:

> There is no doubt that some people are much happier when they come to see things in that light and I think her [Annie's] mother may be one of them. All the artistic side, if I can call it so, as well as the emotional, would appeal to her very much. They do understand the use of beauty as no other church does.[48]

This was prescient: Chamberlain's mother-in-law followed the example of her uncle and daughter and became a Catholic in 1921. Then Chamberlain's niece, Hilda Mary, converted to Catholicism in 1934. Again, brother and sister agreed that she would benefit from that faith. He thought it 'a great thing for her to have gone Roman'.[49] Both were sufficiently detached from Protestantism to view the matter objectively: the niece was 'one of those who feel the need for unity of faith and certainty of dogma which can only be found in the Roman Church'.[50]

Ecclesiastical appointments

Not all Anglicans were so dispassionate when a Unitarian Prime Minister exercised church patronage. With characteristic hyperbole, Lord Hugh Cecil told the Church Assembly: 'If we lived in the reign of Henry VIII a Unitarian would not be in Downing Street. He would be burned at Smithfield.' He followed this up in February 1938 with a letter to *The Times*:

---

47 NC to Hilda Chamberlain, 3 December 1916, CRL, NC18/1/91.
48 Hilda Chamberlain to NC, 1 December 1916, CRL, NC18/2/42.
49 NC to Hilda Chamberlain, 18 May 1936, CRL, NC18/1/961.
50 Hilda Chamberlain to NC, 1 June 1934, CRL, NC18/2/879.

'I (still) think it unseemly that a Unitarian should have the predominant voice in the appointment of Bishops.'[51]

It did not deflect Chamberlain from his exercise of ecclesiastical power. Generally, he did so diligently and impartially. The only one of Archbishop Lang's preferred candidates whom Chamberlain blocked was Neville Talbot to the Diocese of Sheffield, and then Rochester. Lang intimated that Talbot might have been too High Church, while Chamberlain sought an Evangelical.[52] The Prime Minister possibly objected more to Talbot's commitment to the Youth Peace Campaign and 'the system of collective responsibility' the League of Nations was intended to embody. Incongruously, it was the Unitarian Prime Minister who challenged Lang's recommendation of Geoffrey Fisher to the Diocese of London. Chamberlain did not doubt Fisher's 'intellectual and administrative' skills; rather, he queried his 'spiritual' qualities. He dropped his opposition when Lang assured him that Fisher did a nice Confirmation service.[53]

'A cause that surely has the blessing of Almighty God'

Chamberlain assured Lang how he felt sustained by 'all the heartfelt prayers that were going up for the success of [his] efforts'[54] during the terrible stress he endured during the 1938 Munich Crisis. His pronouncements on the outbreak of the Second World War were couched in religious language. On 1 September 1939 he told the Commons that he had *prayed* that it would never fall to him to take the country to war.[55] Two days later he had to tell the nation that his efforts to maintain peace had failed:

> Now may God bless you all and may He defend the right. For it is evil things that we shall be fighting against, brute force, bad faith,

51 <http://uudb.org/articles/nevillechamberlain.html>, accessed 18.10.19.

52 Lang, Memoranda, 27 March, 12 July and 14 July 1939, LPL, Lang Papers, 169, ff. 239, 241 and 258.

53 Lang to Jasper Rootham, 31 March 1939, LPL, Lang Papers, 169, f. 241.

54 NC to Lang, LPL, Lang Papers, 191, f. 275.

55 Robert Self, *Neville Chamberlain: A biography* (London: Routledge, 2016), p. 378.

> injustice, oppression, and persecution. And against them I am certain that the right will prevail.[56]

The next month he was venting his hatred of Hitler: 'We have to kill one another just to satisfy that accursed madman. I wish he could burn in Hell for as many years as he is costing lives.'[57] After his resignation as Prime Minister, Chamberlain broadcast to the nation: 'We shall be fighting . . . with the conviction that our cause is the cause of humanity and peace against cruelty and wars; a cause that surely has the blessing of Almighty God.'[58] Possibly he was simply using conventional terms to inspire a Christian nation. However, he was a man of great integrity. He was not prepared to attend church services just for the sake of form. Even at a time of national emergency, it is unlikely he would have said anything he did not sincerely believe. Of course, it is noticeable that his statements were not explicitly Christian.

Chamberlain said less about his personal beliefs perhaps even than Law. The Archbishop of Canterbury's chaplain was left to surmise:

> He was brought up as a Unitarian and so far as I am aware he has never formally severed his connection with that body, though to the best of my knowledge he is not in the habit of attending any Unitarian place of worship now-a-days. He is, however, a God-fearing man of high Christian principles whose life and example [put] to shame many orthodox Churchmen.[59]

'The inner sanctuary of his spirit'

After Chamberlain's death, Lang spoke of 'the door of the inner sanctuary of his spirit which doubtless he kept closed'. That probably is where any discussion of the matter would have ended had the Archbishop not discreetly invited his widow to comment on Chamberlain's religious belief. Lang was 'sure that in the shrine of that sanctuary he came increasingly

56 NC, Radio broadcast, 3 September 1939, cited Feiling, *The Life of NC*, p. 416.

57 NC, 15 October 1939, cited Feiling, *The Life of NC*, p. 419.

58 NC, Radio broadcast, 30 June 1940, cited Feiling, *The Life of NC*, p. 449.

59 Don to Meek, 20 February 1940 (copy), LPL, Lang Papers, 175, ff. 121–2.

as anxieties and responsibilities grew to rely upon the help of God and the guidance of his Spirit'. Annie agreed: 'I think that door *was* closed, as far as *words* went, except to me.' Both Annie and the Archbishop realized they were clutching at straws in claiming Chamberlain for the Church. That is not to say there was no appreciation of spiritual values, 'an inward light . . . [and] as anxieties and responsibilities grew, so his reliance on it grew. It was that that gave him his assurance and strength.'[60] Understood in this way, Annie felt that even though she was the churchgoer, her religion lacked 'the strength and vitality of his. It was like a well of living water, and one saw things true and clear.'[61]

She commented further on their religious practice:

> Though he did not go to church himself as some people do – he always – ever since I knew him – liked me to go – and especially these last dark years.
>
> When I went to the early Service – the Communion Service at the Abbey – I went for him as well as for myself.
>
> I used often when he was working late to go into his room and say (it became sort of an amusing formula) 'Shall I go to church tomorrow or shan't I? I can't bear to get up so early.' And he always replied, 'That's for you to decide.' And I knew he wanted me to go.

She recalled a conversation during a car journey in the early 1930s when they were 'talking of all sorts of things including a spiritual law'. It was at that point that Chamberlain, echoing his father a generation earlier, described himself as 'a reverent agnostic'. Lang replied that he 'felt the stress should be laid on the word reverent'.[62]

'He was happy in his soul'

Chamberlain was diagnosed with bowel cancer in the summer of 1940. He died six months after leaving Downing Street. For an agnostic, he had

60 Anne Chamberlain to Lang, 4 November 1941, LPL, Lang Papers, 191, ff. 323–4.

61 Anne Chamberlain to Lang, 2 March 1942, LPL, Lang Papers, 191, f. 327.

62 Anne Chamberlain to Lang, 4 November 1941 and 2 March 1942, LPL, Lang Papers, 191, ff. 324–5, 327.

a surprisingly Christian death, reading the book of Job before he underwent surgery.[63] In his final days, Annie read to him from Scripture, including Luke's Gospel: 'Father, if Thou be willing remove this cup from me. Nevertheless, not my will but Thine. And there appeared an angel from heaven strengthening him.' As the end approached, Annie spoke of her faith:

> Happy talk. Told him of belief in future and meeting. Talked of spirit – loving and cherishing which was with him, the spirit that made him bold and beautiful . . . Felt happiness of soul in him. Sat by bed holding his hand all the time. I had felt God with him loving and comforting him and me.

She described the final moments:

> Before he went to sleep I held his hand and we talked or didn't talk. I reminded him of the Psalm, The Lord is my shepherd, and he said, 'I am not afraid to die' . . . He was glad to go. He was happy in his soul.[64]

Chamberlain died on 9 November 1940. He was cremated at Golders Green Crematorium on 13 November with no ceremony and only two mourners present. (Cremation was not chosen for any religious motive but rather encouraged by Westminster Abbey, given lack of space.) The ashes were taken to the abbey for the funeral service the following day. Not publicized for security reasons, it was a bleak affair. The mourners froze beneath the abbey's unglazed windows. Chamberlain's ashes were buried next to those of Law.

63 Anne Chamberlain, Notebook, u/d, CRL, NC11/2/5.
64 Anne Chamberlain, Diary, 4, 6 and 9 November 1940, CRL, NC11/2/3.

Winston Churchill (1940–1945 and 1951–1955)

'A flying buttress'

Winston Leonard Spencer-Churchill was born on 30 November 1874 at Blenheim Palace in Oxfordshire. He attended Harrow School and the Royal Military Academy, Sandhurst.

Churchill contested 20 parliamentary elections – with a very chequered record. Having lost a by-election there in 1899, he was elected as a Unionist for Oldham in the 1900 'Khaki' election. He defected to the Liberals in 1904 in protest against protectionism. Although he had won Manchester North West in 1906, Churchill lost the by-election in 1908 occasioned by his appointment to ministerial office. Returned for Dundee at another by-election, he was defeated there in 1922. He lost as a National Liberal free trader at Leicester West in 1923 and as an anti-socialist in the 1924 Westminster Abbey by-election. Churchill finally won Epping as a 'Constitutionalist' in the 1924 general election, subsequently representing the seat as a Conservative until 1945. Following boundary changes, he was the MP for Woodford until his retirement in 1964.

Churchill was appointed Undersecretary of State for the Colonies in 1905, entering the Cabinet as President of the Board of Trade in 1908. With Lloyd George, he promoted a programme of social reform. Home Secretary from 1910, the following year he was transferred to the Admiralty. A dynamic and popular First Lord, he prepared the Royal Navy for war with Germany. He was, however, blamed for the failure of the Gallipoli campaign. His dismissal was a Unionist condition for entry into the coalition government of 1915. Initially remaining in office as Chancellor of the Duchy of Lancaster, Churchill resigned in November 1915 to fight in the trenches on the Western Front.

In 1917, Lloyd George brought him back into the government, where Churchill oversaw the reorganization of the Ministry of Munitions and the production of the first tanks. In 1919 he was appointed Secretary for War and Air, and was responsible for demobilization. Controversially, he supported military intervention against Bolshevik Russia. His final position as a Coalition Liberal was as Colonial Secretary from January 1921; he administered Britain's new responsibilities in the Middle East and helped to negotiate the treaty that led to the partition of Ireland.

Baldwin astonished many Conservatives by appointing Churchill to the Exchequer in 1924. As Chancellor he cut income tax and defence spending, and returned Britain to the Gold Standard. He spent the 1930s in the political wilderness, opposing the party leadership over proposals for Indian self-government. He was among the first to recognize the threat posed by Nazi Germany and was a bitter opponent of appeasement.

The outbreak of the war in September 1939 compelled Chamberlain to include Churchill in the Cabinet as First Lord of the Admiralty. The failure of the Norwegian campaign and Labour's refusal to serve in a coalition under Chamberlain or Halifax led to Churchill's appointment as Prime Minister on 10 May 1940, and he replaced the dying Chamberlain as party leader on 9 October 1940. As the Germans overran the Low Countries and France, British forces were evacuated from Dunkirk. There were to be further defeats in the Mediterranean, North Africa and South-East Asia. While Britain stood alone and others contemplated a negotiated peace, Churchill never abandoned the objective of ultimate victory. Acting as his own Minister of Defence, he coordinated the war effort. His speeches, energy and resolve inspired the nation through the Battle of Britain and the Blitz. Having entered into an alliance with the Soviet Union and the USA, Churchill celebrated victory in Europe.

With an end to the war in sight, however, Labour withdrew from the coalition and Churchill formed a caretaker Conservative government on 23 May 1945. In the ensuing general election, the electorate distinguished between the Prime Minister and the party he led. To Churchill's surprise, Labour won a landslide victory. He resigned as Prime Minister on 26 July 1945.

Much rethinking of Conservative policies, largely by others, was undertaken in opposition. The party fought the general election of 23 February 1950 accepting the welfare state and nationalization as political facts. Labour narrowly retained office, but in the general election of 25 October

1951 the Conservatives were returned to power with a majority of 17. The following day Churchill became Prime Minister and (until 1952) Minister of Defence again.

Domestically and overseas there was much continuity with the policies of Attlee's government. Gradually, post-war austerity and rationing were relaxed, new homes were built and living standards improved. In June 1953, Churchill suffered a stroke, a fact concealed from the public. To the frustration of colleagues, he clung to office, finally resigning on 5 April 1955. He refused a peerage but was created a Knight of the Garter in 1953.

Churchill was no stranger to controversy or criticism, but when he died in his London home on 24 January 1965 he was recognized as one of the greatest Britons of his age. After a state funeral at St Paul's Cathedral, he was buried in the churchyard at Bladon, close to his birthplace.

* * *

Nanny Everest

This summarizes only one aspect of an extraordinary life. In addition to being a politician and statesman, Churchill was a soldier, journalist, author, artist, racehorse-owner, gambler and bricklayer. Where did faith fit into all of this? There have been those who have maintained that Churchill was an agnostic, even an atheist. More recently, American Protestant pastors and his own great-grandson have claimed him as a committed Christian, or at least the providential instrument of God.

Winston Churchill was born at Blenheim Palace, the ancestral home of his grandfather, the seventh Duke of Marlborough. Both property and title were the gift of a grateful nation to John Churchill for his victories over the armies of Louis XIV. Winston was baptized at Blenheim on 27 December 1874 by his grandfather's chaplain. The furnishings and imagery of the family chapel speak more of the apotheosis of 'the Great Duke' than of the house of God.

Churchill did not inherit faith from his parents – not that the wider family were devoid of religion. His great-uncle, Ignatius Spencer, was a noted convert to Catholicism, a Passionist priest, now on the path to canonization.

Cousins on both sides of the family, the ninth Duke of Marlborough and Sir Shane Leslie, also converted to Catholicism. To provide ecclesiastical balance, Churchill's aunt, Cornelia, was an anti-Catholic bigot, who founded and funded Lady Wimborne's Protestant League to combat Ritualism in the Church of England.

His father, Lord Randolph Churchill, a younger son of the Duke of Marlborough, pursued a brief, brilliant and self-destructive political career. His mother, the society beauty Jennie Jerome, was the daughter of an American financier. The couple were engaged within three days of being introduced by the Prince of Wales and married not in church but in the British Ambassador's residence in Paris. Churchill doted on both parents but saw little of either during his childhood.

The Jeromes were French Huguenots by origin. Convention dictated that they worshipped at the South Brooklyn Presbyterian Church, but Jennie's father had renounced organized religion when his own father smashed his violin for playing on a Sunday. Political expediency required that Lord Randolph defended the privileges of the Established Church in national life, but there is no indication of personal faith. During their engagement, he wrote to Jennie of his religious indifferentism and profound boredom induced by church services.[1]

Churchill's real introduction to Christianity came through his nanny, Elizabeth Everest, to whom he was devoted. If his parents were doctrinally indifferent, Mrs Everest possessed very decided views. She was a Low Church Protestant, a stance she instilled into the young Churchill. He recalled how with 'her dislike of ornaments and ritual, and generally her extremely unfavourable opinion of the Supreme Pontiff, [she] had prejudiced me strongly against that personage and all religious practices supposed to be associated with him'.[2] Mrs Everest held the Pope responsible for Fenian outrages – of which the Churchills were very conscious given his grandfather's position as Lord Lieutenant of Ireland. Churchill's childhood adulation of his nanny did not, however, prevent him from provoking her by threatening

1 R. F. Foster, *Lord Randolph Churchill: A political life* (Oxford: Oxford University Press, 1981), p. 66.

2 Winston S. Churchill, *My Early Life: A roving commission* (London: The Reprint Society, 1944), p. 20.

to 'worship idols'.[3] At the age of 20, he was impressed how her simple faith enabled her to approach death without fear. Churchill made the funeral arrangements and paid for the upkeep of her grave throughout his life.

His early acquaintance with Anglican clergy was not encouraging. Aged eight, he was sent to a preparatory school, St George's, Ascot, run by an unpleasant sadist, the Revd H. W. Sneyd-Kynnersley, who beat the boys mercilessly. Churchill was further prejudiced against him by the 'High Church character' of the chapel services. Withdrawn from St George's, he was sent to a more kindly establishment, Brunswick School in Hove, run by two spinster sisters, the Misses Thomson. Here too, however, his religious principles were tested. The school attended the Chapel Royal, Brighton, where the congregation turned to face east for the Apostles' Creed. Churchill decided that it was his conscientious duty to testify to his Protestant beliefs by refusing to rotate. He prepared to endure martyrdom on his return to school, and was puzzled when nothing was said. Seated in an eastward-facing pew the next Sunday, he resolved that it would be perverse to make any further protest. He gratefully acknowledged the tenderness with which the Misses Thomson had treated his religious scruples: 'Not being resisted or ill-treated, I yielded myself complacently to a broad-minded tolerance and orthodoxy.'[4]

'I might have gone into the Church'

In 1888, Churchill arrived at Harrow, where chapel attendance was required three times on a Sunday, in addition to daily prayers, morning and evening, through the week.[5] Being in his house, Churchill came to know the headmaster, the Revd James Welldon, better than most. Churchill approved of him as 'an able man and a great scholar and not only this but also a man of the world, and no foolish priest – narrow minded and dogmatical'.[6] Welldon was more than an ambitious, worldly minded cleric. A serious theologian, he wrote on the immortality of the soul, defending the

3 A. L. Rowse, *The Later Churchills* (London: Macmillan, 1958), p. 327.

4 WSC, *My Early Life*, pp. 20, 22.

5 WSC, *My Early Life*, p. 20, 22.

6 Winston S. Churchill to Jennie Churchill, 18 November 1896, cited Randolph S. Churchill, *Winston S. Churchill: Companion Vol. 1, Part 2, 1896–1900* (London: Heinemann, 1967), p. 703.

orthodox position on judgement, the divinity of Christ and the mission of the Church. He recognized the different genres Scripture employed to convey truth and praised both the Protestant emphasis on the primacy of conscience and the Catholic practice of prayer for the dead.[7] The paths of headmaster and former pupil crossed again in India, where Welldon was Bishop of Calcutta. Having read a collection of his sermons, Churchill wrote of his 'pleasant memories of Harrow Chapel'.[8]

There was a moment of religious awakening, possibly of enthusiasm, at Harrow. In June 1891 he was commenting to his father on episcopal appointments.[9] The following month, he wrote to his mother as to his future career: 'Really I feel less keen about the Army every day. I think the church would suit me much better.'[10] It is impossible now to gauge the sincerity of the proposal; but the idea was mooted. Churchill later speculated that, had he failed his Army exams, 'I might have gone into the Church and preached orthodox sermons in a spirit of audacious contradiction to the age.'[11] His son Randolph's imagination was even more heated: had his father been ordained in the Church of England, he envisaged him crossing the Tiber, being created a Cardinal and returning to Anglicanism before reconciling Rome and Canterbury; Cardinal Churchill was elected Pope in the conclave of 1940, accepted the restoration of the Papal States from a grateful Mussolini and ensured the happy political union of Europe 'under the double leadership of Britain and the Church of Rome'.[12]

Back in 1891, Churchill's spiritual horizons were more limited. Of his own volition, he requested Confirmation. Nanny Everest was delighted. His mother commented cynically that she supposed that Confirmation classes excused him from more onerous duties elsewhere.[13] The schoolboy's religious fervour did not survive. Churchill told his cousin, Shane

7 J. E. C. Welldon, *The Hope of Immortality* (London: Seeley & Co., 1898).

8 WSC to Rt Revd J. E. C. Welldon, 22 February 1899, cited Randolph S. Churchill, *WSC: Companion Vol. 1, Part 2*, p. 1010.

9 WSC to Lord Randolph Churchill, 8, 9 and 10 June 1891, cited Randolph S. Churchill, *WSC: Companion Vol. 1, Part 1, 1874–1896* (London: Heinemann, 1967), p. 240.

10 WSC to Jennie Churchill, 14 July 1891, cited Randolph S. Churchill, *WSC: Companion Vol. 1, Part 1*, p. 259.

11 WSC, *My Early Life*, p. 35.

12 Randolph S. Churchill, *WSC: Vol. 1, Youth, 1874–1900* (London: Heinemann, 1966), p. 155.

13 Jennie Churchill to Lord Randolph Churchill, 6 November 1891, cited Randolph S. Churchill, *WSC: Companion Vol. 1, Part 1*, p. 284.

Leslie, that he had been confirmed and received Communion once – presumably around this time – and never again.[14]

The only member of staff at Harrow who interested himself in Churchill's spiritual welfare was the Revd Frederick Searle, assistant housemaster in Welldon's house. Perturbed by Churchill's pursuit of pleasure and daredevil adventures, he made a pitch for his soul:

> You must once for all realize that to please God must be the ground work of your life. Up to this time you have not set this before you. You have been content to take the world as you find it, getting out of it as much so called amusement as you could. Such a life is not a happy one – it has no worthy aim and can give no lasting satisfaction. Then, my dear Churchill, do turn and decide once for all that you will set the pleasing of God and the service of other men before you as the object of life.[15]

The plea went unheeded. Churchill opted for a commission in a fashionable cavalry regiment.

'A violent and aggressive anti-religious phase'

Churchill left for India in September 1896, a conventional Anglican. For the preceding 14 years, he had attended institutions where Sunday worship was an obligation. Even at home during the holidays he went to church weekly. He 'dutifully accepted everything [he] had been told'.[16] In a rather desultory manner, religion was debated in the mess. Officers discussed 'Whether we should live again in another world when this was over?' 'Whether we have ever lived before?' 'Whether we remember and meet each other after death or merely start again like the Buddhists?' and 'Whether some higher intelligence is looking after the world or whether

14 Randolph S. Churchill, *WSC: Vol. 1, Youth*, p. 158.

15 Revd Frederick Searle to WSC, 3 March 1893, cited Randolph S. Churchill, *WSC: Companion Vol. 1, Part 1*, p. 370.

16 WSC, *My Early Life*, pp. 122–3.

things are just drifting along anyhow?' The consensus was that religion was a good thing for women and 'the lower orders' but ought not to be pursued to excess. It really did not matter what one believed provided one did one's duty, was faithful to one's friends and kind to the less fortunate.[17]

His complacent acceptance ceased when Churchill discovered himself at an intellectual disadvantage to his contemporaries who had been to university. With time on his hands in the East, he determined to give himself a thorough education and read voraciously. Starting with history, he progressed to philosophy, economics and the classics. Like many of his generation, he was captivated by the elegant cynicism of Edward Gibbon's *History of the Decline and Fall of the Roman Empire*,[18] a work that appealed all the more when he discovered it had been a favourite of his father. Gibbon's secularism was reinforced by William Lecky's *History of European Morals from Augustus to Charlemagne* and *History of the Rise and Influence of the Spirit of Rationalism in Europe*.[19]

His Harrovian religious education challenged, Churchill initially inclined towards disregarding these disturbing new ideas. He was persuaded, however, by William Winwood Reade's *The Martyrdom of Man*, recommended by his colonel, the dashing Anglo-Irishman John Brabazon. *The Martyrdom of Man* is a contentious account of human history, dismissive of all revealed religion. According to Winwood Reade, Christianity was invented by Saint Paul and Platonic philosophers in Alexandria, and the doctrine of the Trinity was appropriated from Egyptian mythology. It was 'the creed of the uneducated people', 'never the religion of a scholar and a gentleman'. Like Gibbon, he held Christianity responsible for the downfall of the Roman Empire. The book is crammed with crude characterizations. Priesthood is portrayed as 'the doctrine that men who adopt a particular profession are invested with magical powers which stream into them from other men's finger ends'. It was repugnant to Winwood Reade that simple folk might inherit the kingdom of heaven while the learned might be excluded. His conclusions were stark: 'Supernatural Christianity is false.

17 WSC, *My Early Life*, pp. 123–4.

18 Edward Gibbon, *The History of the Decline and Fall of the Roman Empire*, 6 vols (London: Strahan & Cadell, 1776–88).

19 William Edward Hartpole Lecky, *History of the Rise and Influence of the Spirit of Rationalism in Europe*, 2 vols (London: Longmans, Green, 1865); *History of European Morals from Augustus to Charlemagne*, 2 vols (London: Longmans, Green, 1869).

God-worship is idolatry. Prayer is useless. The soul is not immortal. There are no rewards and there are no punishments in a future state . . . [Christianity] ought to be destroyed.'[20]

With no Christian apologist at hand to rebut these charges, Churchill recalled: 'I was indignant at having been told so many untruths, as I then regarded them, by the schoolmasters and clergy who had guided my youth . . . I passed through a violent and aggressive anti-religious phase.'[21] Even at the time, he was not uncritical of Winwood Reade. He recognized that he was not an original thinker. Although fascinated by the thought and agreeing with the arguments summarized in *The Martyrdom of Man*, Churchill still felt it a mistake to commit them to print. There would come a time when humanity would develop to the extent that it no longer required the assistance of religion. Then, but only then, 'Christianity will be put aside as a crutch which is no longer needed, and man will stand erect on the legs of reason.' For the moment, however, it was 'wicked' to deprive people of their 'pleasant hopeful illusions'.[22]

The combination of Winwood Reade, Gibbon and Lecky had its impact on Churchill's belief system. He shared his new-found position with his mother: 'I expect annihilation at death. I am a materialist – to the tips of my fingers.'[23] He reiterated this a few months later: 'I do not accept the Christian or any other form of religious belief.'[24] There is no evidence that his mother was unduly perturbed by her son's loss of faith.

Three decades later, Churchill noted that his atheism had been a passing 'phase'. Personal experience caused him to modify his stance. His attention was diverted from religion and philosophy to military campaigns, journalism and politics. Reflection on organized religion, however, continued to betray the influence of Winwood Reade:

20 William Winwood Reade, *The Martyrdom of Man* (London: Trubner & Co., 1872), pp. 242, 349, 523, 525.

21 WSC, *My Early Life*, p. 124.

22 WSC to Jennie Churchill, 14 January 1897, cited Randolph S. Churchill, *WSC: Companion Vol. 1, Part 2*, p. 725.

23 WSC to Jennie Churchill, 31 March 1898, cited Randolph S. Churchill, *WSC: Companion Vol. 1, Part 2*, p. 907.

24 WSC to Jennie Churchill, 24 August 1898, cited Randolph S. Churchill, *WSC: Companion Vol. 1, Part 2*, p. 969.

> All great movements, every vigorous impulse that a community may feel, become distorted and perverted as time passes, and the atmosphere of the earth seems fatal to the noble aspirations of its peoples . . . The fear of God produces bigotry and superstition. There appears no exception to this mournful rule, and the best efforts of men, however glorious their early results, have dismal endings.[25]

Easy words for a young man eager to make his name in the world to write, but was it a worthwhile system by which life could be lived? Churchill records: 'My poise was restored during the next few years by frequent contact with danger.'[26]

'My prayer . . . was . . . answered'

Churchill believed he was created for some supremely important mission. He made no attempt, however, to avoid material dangers to ensure his survival to fulfil that mission. In 1899, the *Morning Post* sent him as their correspondent to cover the Boer War. When his train was derailed by the enemy, Churchill promptly took command and directed operations. His action allowed a number of British troops to escape, but he himself was captured. Having no intention of remaining a prisoner of war in Pretoria, he simply hopped over the fence one night. Outside the prison, his difficulties had only just begun. Deep in enemy territory, he lacked supplies, assistance and a plan of action. One option only was open to him:

> I found no comfort in any of the philosophical ideas which some men parade in the hours of their ease and strength and safety. They seemed only fair-weather friends. I realized with awful force that no exercise of my own feeble wit and strength could save me from my enemies, and that without the assistance of that High Power which interferes in the eternal sequence of causes and effects more often than we are prone to admit, I could never succeed. I prayed long and

25 WSC, *The River War: An historical account of the reconquest of the Soudan*, Vol. 1 (London: Longmans, Green & Co., 1899), pp. 57–8.

26 WSC, *My Early Life*, pp. 124–5.

> earnestly for help and guidance. My prayer, as it seems to me, was swiftly and wonderfully answered.[27]

By 'chance', Churchill stumbled on the one friendly house in the neighbourhood, that of a British mining engineer, and so made his escape to freedom.

'Lacking in the religious sense'

This 'miraculous' deliverance did nothing to persuade Churchill of the benefits of regular prayer, but it did confirm his belief in some form of destiny or providence guiding and protecting him, though he did not care to define it too closely. In the trenches of the First World War, he narrowly avoided death, summoned to an aborted meeting as his dugout suffered a direct hit. He wrote to his wife:

> It is all chance or destiny and our wayward footsteps are best planted without too much calculation. One must yield oneself simply and naturally to the mood of the game: and trust in God which is another way of saying the same thing.[28]

When he finally entered 10 Downing Street in May 1940, Churchill concluded: 'I felt as if I was walking with Destiny, and that all my past life had been but a preparation for this hour and for this trial.'[29] His Evangelical apologists argue that 'Churchill did not regard Providence as an impersonal force; he saw it as the guiding hand of God.'[30] This contention cannot be sustained. Churchill might have understood something more than blind fate being at play but there is no sense of any interpersonal relationship, still less the intervention of the Christian God of Jesus Christ.

---

27 WSC, *My Early Life*, p. 290.

28 WSC to Clementine Churchill, November 1915, cited Andrew Roberts, *Churchill: Walking with destiny* (London: Allen Lane, 2018), p. 119.

29 WSC, *The Second World War: The gathering storm* (Boston: Houghton Mifflin Co., 1948), p. 667.

30 Jonathan Sandys and Wallace Henley, *God and Churchill: How the great leader's sense of divine destiny changed his troubled world and offers hope for ours* (London: SPCK, 2016), p. 197.

His contemporaries remarked on Churchill's lack of interest in matters spiritual. Having sat next to him at dinner, Beatrice Webb's judgement was: 'No notion of scientific research, philosophy, literature or art, still less of religion.'[31] That was not entirely fair. Churchill had a good working knowledge of Christian doctrine and vocabulary but focused exclusively on his political career and the policies he planned. He conceded the point in an interview with the journalist A. G. Gardiner: 'Yes, I have read James' *Immortality.* I have read it three times. It impressed me deeply. But finally I came to the conclusion that I was lacking in the religious sense, and put it away.' He might not have possessed 'the religious sense' himself but he was deeply respectful of those who did.[32]

In the early twentieth century, religion could still raise the political temperature across a range of issues. With no strong views himself, Churchill attempted to bring a moderating rationalism to bear on contested questions. It won him few friends. The payment of tithes to Anglican clergy was a divisive issue in the 1899 Oldham by-election. Supporting the retention of tithes, Churchill suggested that they be shared pro rata between all denominations. The proposal might have appeared 'fair, logical, reverent and conciliatory' to him but it failed to convince others.[33] He upset the Archbishop of Canterbury and Protestant sentiment by supporting Sunday trading in large towns. His views on denominational education placed him at odds with most Tories: while allowing for the possibility of religious education in state schools, he believed this should not extend beyond 'the Bible without comments – hymns ancient and modern with a few exceptions'; schools should be staffed by 'secular instructors appointed by the Government' – anything more should be taught by parents at home.[34]

The very possibility of eternal salvation Churchill found doubtful, particularly that it might be mediated exclusively through Christ. He clashed with his former headmaster on the desirability of Christian missionary

31 Beatrice Webb, Diary, 8 July 1903, cited ed. Norman and Jeanne Mackenzie, *The Diary of Beatrice Webb, 1892–1905*, Vol. 2 (London: Virago, 1983), p. 288.

32 A. G. Gardiner, *Prophets, Priests and Kings* (London: Alston Rivers, 1908), p. 107; ref. William James, *Human Immortality: Two supposed objections to the doctrine* (Boston and New York: Houghton Mifflin Co., 1897).

33 WSC, *My Early Life*, p. 235.

34 WSC, Notes, 1897, cited Randolph S. Churchill, *WSC: Companion Vol. 1, Part 2*, p. 759 and Martin Gilbert, *Churchill: A life* (London: Pimlico, 2000), p. 70.

activity in India. Showing a faulty grasp of the origins and spread of the faith, he argued that Christianity originated 'among *white* men' and was 'adapted to the spiritual needs of the European inhabitants of the North Temperate Zone'.[35] Influenced by social Darwinism, he held that religions, like races, evolved. As a member of the Liberal government elected by Nonconformist votes, Churchill found it expedient to deliver the opening address to the 1908 London Missionary Society Exhibition. He appeared to have reversed his earlier position, extolling Protestant missionary work. The object of his praise, however, was social and educational reform and the advancement of the British Empire as much as Christian evangelization.[36]

During the Second World War, Churchill offended his orthodox Anglican secretary: 'The P.M. came out with the supreme blasphemy that "every nation creates God in its own image".'[37] Churchill was an early supporter of the eugenics movement and argued for the forced sterilization of the feebleminded. With other leading politicians, he was a member of the first international Eugenics Conference held in London in 1912.

Churchill's astrologer

Those in public life are liable to be contacted by all manner of oddities. Spiritualists felt no hesitation in writing to politicians at the turn of the twentieth century with messages 'from the other side'. Churchill received communications purporting to be from his father in 1909 and from his mother in the early 1920s. The latter – and the poet Shelley – urged him not to visit Ireland on account of the risk to his life from a personal attack.[38]

More persistent was the correspondence he received from an astrologer in Norwich called R. G. Hickling. Hickling was not an educated man. His political information was limited to the parliamentary reports in the daily papers. Yet over a period of four years, on the basis of the movement of the

35 WSC to Welldon, 10 December 1896 (copy), cited Randolph S. Churchill, *WSC: Companion Vol. 1, Part 2*, p. 714.

36 Geoffrey Scott Smith, *Duty and Destiny: The life and faith of Winston Churchill* (Grand Rapids, MI: Eerdmans, 2021), pp. 65–6.

37 John Colville, Diary, 2 April 44, cited John Colville, *The Fringes of Power: Downing Street diaries, 1939–1945* (London: Hodder & Stoughton, 1985), p. 482.

38 Edith K. Harper, London, to WSC, 17 February 1909, CCAC, Churchill Papers, CHAR 2/39/20; Shirley Carson Jenney to WSC, 7 June [1922], CCAC, Churchill Papers, CHAR 2/123/3–10.

planets, he advised Churchill on government policy relating to industrial disputes and diplomatic crises.

Churchill's response was curious. He acknowledged Hickling's letters but also circulated them, as from 'my astrologer', to Asquith, Sir Edward Grey and, less frequently, Lloyd George. Understandable once or twice for the entertainment value maybe, but Churchill persevered. His colleagues made gentle fun of him – Asquith suggested perhaps one did not need to refer 'to celestial bodies' to explain a change of heart on the part of the miners. And on the eve of the outbreak of the First World War, Churchill wrote to the Prime Minister stating he was making his travel arrangements in accordance with Hickling's advice: 'He has been right every time so far.'[39] It would be extraordinary, having rejected revealed religion, if Churchill was willing to give credence to the stars. Many years later, however, his private secretary noted that he was prone to superstition.[40]

A God 'of pity, self-sacrifice, and ineffable love'

Religion did not feature large in married and family life. Churchill married Clementine Hozier at St Margaret's, Westminster, on 12 September 1908. (The ceremony was delayed for two hours by the procession of 20,000 children, part of the Catholic Church's International Eucharistic Congress.) The couple were married by the Bishop of St Asaph, Alfred Edwards, whom Lloyd George had introduced to Churchill; Welldon preached the sermon. Clementine took faith more seriously than her husband – in adolescence she had displayed a certain Anglican piety. She questioned Winston as to whether he found himself thinking of Christ in the trenches. Throughout their long marriage, she practised her faith sporadically, though she did so more actively after her husband's death. The children were baptized as a matter of course. Political, not spiritual considerations determined the choice of godparents. Their daughter, Mary, is clear that she owed her Christian faith to her nanny, not her parents.

39 WSC to Asquith, 3 Aug [1914], CCAC, Churchill Papers, CHAR 2/64/9.

40 Colville, Diary, 25 June 1940, cited *The Fringes of Power*, p. 170.

The historian Andrew Roberts, in his 2018 biography, makes the point that in the five million words of Churchill's speeches, 'Christ' only occurs once and 'Jesus' never.[41] The results would have differed, however, had Roberts included recorded conversations, correspondence and published works, and searched instead for 'God', 'the Almighty', 'Jehovah', 'Supreme Being' and 'Higher Power'. Churchill's choice of vocabulary is indicative of his relationship to Christianity but also demonstrates that religion was not entirely absent from his thought.

Religion was at the forefront of Churchill's mind in the early 1930s in a way that was not true of other periods. It is difficult to say why. He had suffered the bereavements of his mother and his four-year-old daughter, Marigold, but these occurred a decade earlier. Possibly it was related to the fact that after 1929 he was out of office for ten years, in the political wilderness, and had yet to discover his calling to alert the nation to the perils associated with the rise of the dictators. Momentarily, he allowed himself to focus on eternal truths.

In 1930, Churchill published the memoirs of his first 26 years, *My Early Life*. It contains a surprisingly frank and lengthy account of his religious beliefs, detailing how he came to espouse atheism – and his subsequent disenchantment with it. It was followed by two extraordinary essays both originally published in the *Strand Magazine* in 1931. In 'Fifty Years Hence', Churchill speculated on future scientific advances. His imagination outpaced actual developments, foreseeing aerial and germ warfare, nuclear energy, genetically modified food, test-tube babies and human robots. He pleaded for scientific progress to be controlled by 'the laws of a Christian civilization' and 'moral philosophy' (and makes no reference to his own earlier support of eugenics). He concluded that the purpose of existence was to 'answer simple questions which man has asked since the earliest dawn of reason – "Why are we here? What is the purpose of life? Whither are we going?" No material progress . . . can bring comfort to his soul.'[42]

In 'Moses' he expounded his views on the Jewish Old Testament leader. Like most other early twentieth-century Prime Ministers, he had been swayed by Ernest Renan's Modernism. Churchill sought to explain away

41 Roberts, *Churchill*, p. 43.

42 WSC, 'Fifty Years Hence', in WSC, *Thoughts and Adventures* (London: Thornton Butterworth, 1932), pp. 269–80.

the miracles of Exodus, but then to redeem himself in the eyes of believers: 'All these purely rationalistic and scientific explanations only prove the truth of the Bible story.' Individual 'miraculous' events are irrelevant, he argued, when set beside the truly miraculous fact that the Jewish people alone in the ancient world were monotheists. They alone believed in the

> one God, a universal God, a God of all nations, a just God, a God who would punish in another world a wicked man dying rich and prosperous; a God from whose service the good of the humble and of the weak and poor was inseparable.

Having extolled Moses, he proceeded to look forward to the new revelation in Christ when God would be revealed:

> as the God not only of Israel, but the God of all mankind who wished to serve Him; a God not only of justice, but of mercy; a God not only of self-preservation and survival, but of pity, self-sacrifice, and ineffable love.[43]

The battle for Christian civilization

The more fanciful Evangelicals portray Churchill in the role of a fully committed Christian crusader during the Second World War:

> For Churchill, the primary issue of the war was faith. He firmly believed that World War II was a battle between Christendom and the sinister paganism of Adolf Hitler and throughout the War he replenished his unusual moral courage in worship and prayer.[44]

No one can know with certainty the nature of Churchill's prayer life, but the reference to regular worship is pure fantasy.

43 WSC, 'Moses', in WSC, *Thoughts and Adventures*, pp. 283–94.

44 Stephen Mansfield, *Never Give In: The extraordinary character of Winston Churchill* (Nashville, TN: Cumberland House Publishing Inc., 1996), p. 48.

Churchill might couch his rousing wartime orations in religious imagery. He was not hypocritical in doing so. Broadcasting to the nation after entering Downing Street, he paraphrased the first book of Maccabees:

> Today is Trinity Sunday. Centuries ago words were written to be a call and a spur to the faithful servants of Truth and Justice: 'Arm yourselves, and be ye men of valour, and be in readiness for the conflict; for it is better for us to perish in battle than to look upon the outrage of our nation and our altar. As the Will of God is in heaven, even so let it be.'[45]

The following month he told the House of Commons: 'I expect that the Battle of Britain is about to begin. Upon this battle depends the survival of Christian civilization.'[46] Churchill was too good a historian not to appreciate that Western civilization is indeed founded on Christianity. In 1938 he had reminded the American people:

> Since the dawn of the Christian era a certain way of life has slowly been shaping itself among the Western peoples, and certain standards of conduct and government have come to be esteemed. After many miseries and prolonged confusion, there arose into the broad light of day the conception of the right of the individual; his right to be consulted in the government of his country; his right to invoke the law even against the State itself.[47]

He proclaimed the same message in the British Parliament: 'There can never be friendship between the British democracy and the Nazi power, that power which spurns Christian ethics, which cheers its onward course by a barbarous paganism.'[48]

45 WSC, Broadcast, 19 May 1940, cited Roberts, *Churchill*, p. 535.

46 WSC, Speech, 18 June 1940, cited Roberts, *Churchill*, p. 563.

47 WSC, Radio broadcast to USA, 16 October 1938, cited Sandys and Henley, *God and Churchill*, p. 93.

48 WSC, Speech during the Munich Debate, 5 October 1938, cited Sandys and Henley, *God and Churchill*, pp. 91–2.

Churchill accepted the primacy of Christian ethics, even while he did not believe in the underlying doctrine. With the Blitz still in progress, he enunciated his vision for the post-war world order:

> When the war was over there would be a short lull during which we had the opportunity to establish a few basic principles, of justice, of respect for rights and property of other nations, and indeed of respect for private property so long as its owner was honest and its scope moderate. We could find nothing better than Christian ethics on which to build and the more closely we followed the Sermon on the Mount, the more likely we were to succeed in our endeavours.[49]

He repeated his conviction during the Cold War: 'The flame of Christian ethics is still our highest guide. To guard and cherish it is our first interest, both spiritually and materially. The fulfilment of spiritual duty in our daily life is vital to our survival.'[50]

'Hopelessly out of his depth in such matters'

Churchill was baptized and confirmed into the Church of England. He remained a nominal Anglican throughout his life. To claim, however, that he was 'a devoted son of the Anglican church'[51] is nonsense. Violet Asquith knew Churchill well from her youth and wrote, 'Winston knew few, if any, parsons, and felt little, if anything, about them.'[52] The second half of that statement is correct – and Churchill probably thought he knew too many parsons during his schooldays. He acknowledged there were, of course, good and kind clergy but he believed, sadly, that a large proportion were hypocrites, neither practising nor believing what they preached.[53]

The clergy of the Established Church were expected to conform to Churchill's views, and he was vocal in his criticism of those who espoused

49 Colville, Diary, 26 January 1941, cited Colville, *The Fringes of Power*, p. 346.

50 WSC, Speech, 31 March 1949, MIT, Boston, cited ed. Richard M. Langworth, *Churchill by Himself* (London: Ebury Press, 2008), p. 461.

51 Mansfield, *Never Give In*, p. 213.

52 Violet Bonham Carter, *Winston Churchill as I Knew Him* (London: Eyre & Spottiswoode and Collins, 1965), p. 161.

53 WSC to Jack Churchill, 7 December 1896, CCAC, Churchill Papers, CHAR 28/152A/75–6.

socialism or pacificism. William Temple, the Archbishop of Canterbury, aroused his ire on the former grounds, and when he died in October 1944 'His demise caused the P.M. no sorrow. In fact he was quite ribald about it.'[54] Hensley Henson, the former Bishop of Durham, was Churchill's model prelate. At the Westminster Abbey service marking the first anniversary of the outbreak of the Second World War, Henson 'preached an eloquent fighting sermon, containing much alliteration, many fiery denunciations, a good deal of politics and no Christianity – which was what Winston had come to hear'.[55]

Errant bishops excepted, Churchill held no animosity towards the Church of England. Harold Macmillan recounted the tale of Clementine 'reproaching Winston for non-churchgoing: "Ah you, my dear Clemmy" – replied Winston – "are like a great pillar, you support the church from the inside! But I am like a flying buttress; I support the Church from the outside!"'[56] It was a line too good to be wasted; Churchill employed it to effect on numerous occasions.

To the extent that Churchill expressed opinions on ecclesiastical affairs, they were Low Church and Erastian. He addressed the Ritualist controversy in the 1899 Oldham by-election, praising the Church of England for 'her comprehensive toleration'. He would have no hesitation in supporting parliamentary intervention if 'extremists' persisted in 'introducing certain ceremonies and practices which are wholly contrary to her spirit, and antagonistic to her welfare'.[57] He disliked the Prayer Book revision proposed in 1928 as taking the Church of England in a more Catholic direction, but felt compelled to vote for the measure to avoid 'a period of chaos' its rejection would entail.[58] His objections to reform, however, were as likely to be based on aesthetic grounds and innate conservatism as on principled Protestantism. Innovation generally he bemoaned: 'As for the Revised Version of the Bible and the alterations in the Prayer Book and especially the Marriage Service, they are grievous.'[59]

54 Colville, Diary, 22 December 1944, cited Colville, *The Fringes of Power*, pp. 526–7.

55 Colville, Diary, 3 September 1940, cited Colville, *The Fringes of Power*, p. 239.

56 Alistair Horne, *Macmillan, 1957–1986* (London: Macmillan, 1989), p. 611.

57 WSC, Election Address, 24 June 1899, cited Randolph S. Churchill, *WSC: Companion Vol. 1, Part 2*, p. 1030.

58 WSC, Speech, 14 June 1928, Hansard, Vol. 218, cols 1264–70.

59 WSC, *My Early Life*, p. 32.

In matters of Church history, Churchill endorsed the Whig school of historiography in his *History of the English Speaking Peoples*. Starting with the reaction to Augustine's mission in the sixth century, he detected an anti-Roman character in British Christianity. He traced the pedigree of the Anglican hierarchy all the way back to those days with no break in continuity. The reformers of the sixteenth century were only reasserting the true English character of the national Church. Race and religion were inextricably intertwined. The survival and salvation of the English people 'were bound up for ever with the victory of the Reformed Faith'. The King James Bible was 'a splendid and lasting monument . . . to the genius of the English-speaking peoples'.[60]

Churchill had no interest in the exercise of Church patronage unless a candidate of 'advanced' political views or a critic of the government's war policy was suggested. He hesitated to support William Temple's proposed translation from York to Canterbury on the grounds that 'he went about talking of Christian revolution and stuff of that kind'.[61] He eventually approved the move, remarking to Attlee that Temple 'was the only half-a-crown article in a sixpenny bazaar'.[62] Churchill blocked George Bell's appointment to the Diocese of London because of his vocal opposition to the RAF's bombing campaign of Germany. The Anglican establishment was critical of Churchill, maintaining that he 'is hopelessly out of his depth in such matters and is consequently liable to be stampeded by bright suggestions which, on further enquiry, are found to be fantastic'.[63] The Archbishop of Canterbury, Geoffrey Fisher, later opined: 'Winston Churchill knew nothing.'[64] The hierarchy complained of the delay in appointments. Not unreasonably, Churchill responded just before D-Day: 'I hope that you will understand that my time is so much occupied with our urgent and immediate affairs.'[65]

60 WSC, *A History of the English Speaking Peoples: The New World*, Vol. 2 (London: Cassell & Co., 1974), pp. 144, 123.

61 Lord Moran, Diary, 9 January 1942, cited Lord Moran, *Churchill at War, 1940–45* (London: Robinson, 2002), p. 23.

62 Cited Keith Harris, *Attlee* (London: Weidenfeld & Nicolson, 1982), p. 218.

63 Revd A. C. Don, Diary, 28 April 1941, LPL, MS 2869, ff. 24–5.

64 Archbishop Geoffrey Fisher, Memorandum, 'Appointment of Bishops', [1956?], LPL, Fisher Papers, Vol. 165, f. 235.

65 WSC to Archbishop William Temple, 22 May 1944, LPL, W. Temple Papers, Vol. 11, f. 362.

Initially, Churchill took advice on ecclesiastical appointments from Brendan Bracken, an agnostic and lapsed Irish Catholic who was briefly his Parliamentary Private Secretary. John ('Jock') Colville, Churchill's Anglican secretary, did not think this was necessarily a bad thing: Bracken 'feels very strongly the importance of good appointments and of deeply spiritual and saintly men being encouraged to enter the Church. We need Saints, he says, not good administrators.'[66] Fisher subsequently congratulated himself that the normal processes had been restored and that he was able to effect his own choice of bishops through a quiet word with Anthony Bevir, the Prime Minister's appointments secretary.[67]

'Priestly rule and ascendancy'

Churchill's reaction to the Catholic Church was complex. He never entirely discarded the Protestant prejudice transmitted by Nanny Everest and the English establishment. He deprecated what he saw as the Papacy's tendency to interfere in politics and stifle opposition:

> Priestly rule and ascendancy will always I trust encounter staunch resistance from free and enlightened men . . . the Catholic Church has ruined every country in which it has been supreme, and worked the downfall of every dynasty that ruled in its name.[68]

As an Englishman raised on the Whig interpretation of history, the Catholic Church would always be associated with 'foreign influence' and 'the fires of Smithfield, the Massacre of St Bartholomew's Day, the Spanish Armada, and the Gunpowder Plot'.[69]

Yet Churchill was essentially a fair man, opposing unjust discrimination. As Home Secretary, he withstood strong pressure from Edward VII and gave permission for the consecration of Westminster Cathedral to proceed with full Catholic ceremonial. He acknowledged that in Britain and

66 Colville, Diary, 28 July 1940, cited Colville, *The Fringes of Power*, pp. 203–4.

67 Fisher, Memorandum, 'Appointment of Bishops', [1956?], LPL, Fisher Papers, Vol. 165, f. 235.

68 WSC to Clementine Churchill, 5 June 1911, cited Randolph S. Churchill, *WSC: Companion, Vol. 2, Part 2, 1907–1911* (London: Heinemann, 1969), pp. 1088–9.

69 WSC, *A History of the English Speaking Peoples*, Vol. 2, pp. 77, 291.

Ireland, the Catholic Church sought to alleviate the condition of the poor. A family member was assured he had no time for 'Romish practices',

> [but simultaneously he sympathized with working men] for their aching longing for something not infected by the general squalor and something to gratify their love of the mystic, something a little nearer to the 'all-beautiful' – and I find it hard to rob their lives of this one ennobling aspiration – even though it finds expression in the burning of incense, the wearing of certain robes and other superstitious practices.

Catholicism brought comfort, he conceded, but at the expense of economic growth and industry.[70]

As a soldier, Churchill recognized the efficacy of the Catholic Church. During the Boer War, his article in the *Morning Post* caused consternation, contrasting 'a ridiculous discourse' by an Anglican chaplain to a brigade about to go into battle with the 'gallant' ministry of Catholic chaplains he had encountered.[71] As a historian and a romantic, he admired the sheer antiquity of the Catholic Church: 'He felt that there must be something in a faith which could survive so many centuries and had held captive so many men.'[72] As a politician, he welcomed the Catholic Church as an ally against authoritarian dictatorships. Notwithstanding Catholicism's failings, he praised John Fisher and Thomas More as defenders of 'all that was finest in the medieval outlook' against Henry VIII's despotism. In his own day, he praised the fact that 'the Catholic Church raises her immemorial authority against secular tyranny'.[73] He was received in audience by Pius XI in 1927 and by Pius XII in 1944; on both occasions, Churchill established common cause with the Pope, sharing their concerns on the threat posed by Communism.[74]

---

70 Cited Gilbert, *Churchill*, p. 102.

71 WSC, *My Early Life*, p. 348.

72 Moran, Diary, 23 August 1944, cited Moran, *Churchill at War*, p. 211.

73 WSC, *A History of the English Speaking Peoples*, Vol. 2, pp. 52, 291.

74 Roberts, *Churchill*, p. 325; Moran, Diary, 23 August 1944, cited Moran, *Churchill at War*, p. 211.

'The most precious possession of mankind'

Lord Randolph Churchill was unusual among his aristocratic contemporaries in having many Jewish friends. Winston shared his admiration for the Jewish people. His father's friends, the Rothschilds and Cassells, extended their patronage to Churchill at the beginning of his career. He in turn opposed anti-Semitism wherever he encountered it – at a time when such prejudice was acceptable, even fashionable. Lord Alfred Douglas alleged that Churchill had falsified reports during the First World War to allow his Jewish friends to engage in highly lucrative speculation and was rewarded for his role. (Douglas was imprisoned for the libel.) Churchill was a consistent supporter of Zionist aspirations for a national homeland in Palestine. From its earliest stages, he denounced Nazi persecution of the Jews.

Why did Churchill hold the Jews in such high esteem? He respected their intellectual and artistic achievements, their commercial acumen and their success in the face of adversity. He also recognized, however, that as citizens of many nations they were defined by religion. At the time of his visit to Jerusalem as Colonial Secretary in 1921, he declared:

> We owe to the Jews a system of ethics which, even if it were entirely separated from the supernatural, would be incomparably the most precious possession of mankind . . . On that system and by that faith there has been built out of the wreck of the Roman Empire the whole of our existing civilization.[75]

The point was that, even if he himself did not subscribe to the creed, faith and ethics could not be separated: 'This wandering tribe, in many respects indistinguishable from numberless nomadic communities, grasped and proclaimed an idea of which all the genius of Greece and all the power of Rome were incapable.'[76] The Judaeo-Christian concept of a universal God who bestowed a moral code, who rewarded men in eternity according to their conduct in this world, underpinned Western civilization. Churchill

75 Cited Roberts, *Churchill*, p. 278.

76 WSC, 'Moses', in WSC, *Thoughts and Adventures*, p. 292.

later presented a copy of his essay on Moses to the Israeli Prime Minister, David Ben Gurion. The two argued who was the greater, Ben Gurion taking the part of Christ and Churchill that of Moses.[77]

'A militant and proselytizing faith'

In 2014, the press carried sensationalist headlines that a century earlier Churchill had been on the brink of conversion to Islam. There was no substance to the story save for a recently discovered letter from Churchill's sister-in-law, pleading: 'Please don't become converted to Islam; I have noticed in your disposition a tendency towards orientalism, pasha-like tendencies.' Like other members of the ruling class who revelled in the trappings of Empire, Churchill might have occasionally affected the dress and manners of Britain's Eastern subjects, but he was never attracted to the tenets of Islam.[78]

Even if he did not engage with them systematically, Churchill was the first twentieth-century Prime Minister to have personal experience of non-Judaeo-Christian world religions. In India, Sudan and the Middle East, he saw Islam at first hand, and he was not impressed. In his account of the campaigning on India's north-west frontier, he wrote:

> The Mahommedan religion increases, instead of lessening, the fury of intolerance. It was originally propagated by the sword, and ever since its votaries have been subject, above the peoples of all other creeds, to this form of madness . . . civilization is confronted with militant Mahommedanism. The forces of progress clash with those of reaction. The religion of blood and war is face to face with that of peace. Luckily the religion of peace is usually the better armed.[79]

Having fought in Sudan, he acknowledged that

---

77 Ed. Langworth, *Churchill by Himself*, p. 363.

78 Lady Gwendoline Bertie to WSC, 27 August 1907, cited Warren Dockter, *Churchill and the Islamic World: Orientalism, empire and diplomacy in the Middle East* (London: I. B. Tauris, 2015), p. 12.

79 WSC, *The Story of the Malakand Field Force* (London: Thomas Nelson & Sons, 1916), pp. 58–9.

> individual Moslems may show splendid qualities . . . but the influence of the religion paralyses the social development of those who follow it. No stronger retrograde force exists in the world. Far from being moribund Mohammedism is a militant and proselytizing faith.[80]

During the Second World War, Churchill approved plans and funding for what would become the London Central Mosque – in the face of some Christian criticism. His motivation, however, was to sway Arab opinion in the Middle East.[81]

'Not a Christian'

It is possible to evaluate Churchill's own religious beliefs with some degree of accuracy, while discounting the various witticisms he regularly articulated. For example, he speculated that heaven might be a constitutional monarchy, in which case he hoped 'that the Almighty might have reason to "send for him"'.[82] On his seventy-fifth birthday, 'asked if he feared death, he said, "I am ready to meet my Maker. Whether my Maker is prepared for the great ordeal of meeting me is another matter".'[83] Churchill might be frivolous but he was never dishonest. He never pretended, for reasons of respectability or otherwise, to any form of belief he did not possess.

He enjoyed an intellectual curiosity about philosophy and eternal truths that was largely lacking in, for example, Attlee and Anthony Eden. His son recalled that

> [he] frequently speculated on the mysteries of the universe – why we were here, what we were supposed to be doing and where we were going. Frequently the author heard him say that the reason why we were here was to find out why; but that when we did find out,

80 WSC, *The River War: An historical account of the reconquest of the Soudan*, Vol. 2 (London: Longmans, Green & Co., 1899), pp. 249–50.

81 Scott Smith, *Duty and Destiny*, p. 90.

82 Colville, *The Fringes of Power*, p. 128.

83 Cited Roberts, *Churchill*, p. 914.

> the world would come to an end, as we would have achieved our objective.[84]

In late-night conversation Churchill often turned to his companions, questioning them about their religious faith and asking them to justify it. His doctor, Charles Wilson, remembered being interrogated:

> At length he said: 'I suppose that you believe in another life when we die?' When I did not answer he pressed me: 'You have been trained in logic. Tell me why you believe such things.' I had a feeling that he, too, wanted desperately to believe in something, but from what he said he did not find it easy.[85]

After his descent into scepticism in India, Churchill seldom attended church except for national occasions and baptisms, weddings and funerals. Presumably he did not feel the need. President Roosevelt took him to morning service with the Methodists on Christmas Day 1941. Churchill raised no objection: 'I am glad I went. It's the first time my mind has been at rest for a long time. Besides, I like singing hymns.'[86] He was well versed in Scripture from his youth. Towards the end of his life, his doctor saw a Bible in Churchill's room: '"Do you read it?" I asked. He did not answer for some time. Then he said: "Yes, I read it; but only out of curiosity."'[87]

Desmond Morton was a soldier, confidant and personal assistant of Churchill. He was also well versed in theology, and summarized Churchill's beliefs:

> I know that he used to claim with sincerity that although he was not a Christian, since to name himself such would be dishonest, he firmly believed in the existence of God. A sort of Unitarian outlook. He said he was not a Christian since he could not believe that Christ

84 Randolph S. Churchill, *WSC: Vol. 1, Youth*, p. 158.

85 Moran, Diary, 17 August 1944, cited Moran, *Churchill at War*, p. 208.

86 Moran, Diary, 25 December 1941, cited Moran, *Churchill at War*, p. 13.

87 Moran, Diary, 7 March 1958, cited Lord Moran, *Churchill: The struggle for survival, 1945–65* (London: Robinson, 2006), p. 427.

was God, though he recognized him as the finest character that ever lived.[88]

In conversation with Field Marshal Montgomery in 1952, Churchill maintained that 'Christ's story was unequalled and his death to save sinners unsurpassed, moreover the Sermon on the Mount was the last word in ethics.'[89] It is difficult to accept this as a recognition of Christ's mission as Saviour. Churchill is not known to have made any similar statement and was probably simply referring objectively to the content of the Christian creed. In 1953, when asked to read the lesson at the Commonwealth Thanksgiving Service in St Paul's Cathedral, Churchill rejected the text proposed as containing too many references to Jesus Christ. He claimed that he had not led a sufficiently good life to read this with conviction. More likely he was unwilling to articulate doctrine of which he was unconvinced. A less dogmatic passage of Scripture was substituted.[90]

'Is there nothing beyond?'

Did Churchill believe in life after death? That is less easy to determine. His comments on the subject were inconsistent. He was non-committal in the letter he wrote to his wife to be opened in the event of his death on a planned visit to the Dardanelles in 1915: 'Death is only an incident, and not the most important which happens to us in this state of being . . . If there is anywhere else I shall be on the lookout for you.'[91]

Jock Colville was in close contact with Churchill throughout most of the Second World War, and an astute observer of spiritual matters. He recorded how in the early days of the war Churchill had said that he thought often of death, not 'that I believe much in personal survival after death, at

88 Desmond Morton to R. W. Thompson, 10 October 1962, cited R. W. Thompson, *Churchill and Morton: The quest for insight in the correspondence of Major Sir Desmond Morton and the author* (London: Hodder & Stoughton, 1976), p. 190.

89 Colville, Diary, 18 May 1952, cited Colville, *The Fringes of Power*, p. 648.

90 Anthony Eden, Diary, 29 March 1953, CRL, AP 20/1/29.

91 WSC to Clementine Churchill, July 1915, cited Roberts, *Churchill*, p. 222.

least not of the memory'.[92] Colville thought, however, that Churchill's beliefs changed:

> As regards religion he was an agnostic who, as the years went by, and I think more particularly as a result of the Battle of Britain, slowly began to conceive that there was some overriding power which had a conscious influence on our destinies . . . he unquestionably developed in his later years a conviction that this life was not the end.[93]

Colville's judgement appeared to be borne out by Churchill's tribute to the Duke of Kent after his death in 1942: 'Only faith in a life after death in a brighter world where dear ones will meet again – only that and the measured tramp of time can give consolation.'[94] Closer examination of his words, however, suggests more aspiration than personal conviction. On various occasions, Churchill contemplated, generally with a degree of equanimity, the divine judgement he would face in an afterlife for his sanctioning British bombing raids on Germany and his role in the development of the atomic bomb.[95]

His doctor recalled the note of uncertainty in Churchill's voice when he almost died of pneumonia in North Africa in 1943: 'He asked me rather abruptly: "Do you believe that when you die it is the end of everything? Is there nothing beyond?"'[96] After his stroke in 1953, uncertainty turned to despair, or at least acceptance of oblivion: 'Winston spoke of death. He did not believe in another world; only in "black velvet" – eternal sleep.'[97] Morton recalled that Churchill was wont to quote Hamlet on death: 'Sleep, perchance to dream.'[98]

Towards the end of his life, Churchill invited Lord Hailsham to dinner. With eternity weighing heavily on his mind, he asked: 'Do you believe in the afterlife?' Hailsham, a committed Anglican, replied that he did. Churchill was silent and Hailsham sensed that he was troubled. He

92 Colville, Diary, 24 January 1941, cited Colville, *The Fringes of Power*, p. 341.
93 Colville, *The Fringes of Power*, p. 128.
94 WSC, Speech, House of Commons, 8 September 1942, Hansard, Vol. 383, col. 78.
95 Scott Smith, *Duty and Destiny*, pp. 5, 121–5.
96 Moran, Diary, 23 August 1944, cited Moran, *Churchill at War*, p. 212.
97 Moran, Diary, 2 July 1953, cited Moran, *Churchill: The struggle for survival*, p. 129.
98 Morton to Thompson, 11 July 1961, cited Thompson, *Churchill and Morton*, p. 162.

reminded Churchill about the passage in *My Early Life* where he spoke of his prayers having been answered in his escape from Boer captivity. It was clear, however, that Churchill now lacked any form of spiritual solace. Hailsham felt that 'his soul [was] clad with dust and ashes'. On returning home, he wept silently at the great man's desolation.[99]

Churchill had also written in *My Early Life* about the fine surplus he had accumulated 'in the Bank of Observance' on account of the number of church services attended during his youth. He treated the subject humorously, acknowledging that he did not make 'too close enquiries about the state of my account', fearing that he might find it in overdraft.[100] Like many Englishmen of his age and class, he had regarded faith as a possession to be stored rather than a relationship to be lived. It left him bereft of spiritual comfort and strength when he stood most in need of it.

'A religion of the Englishman'

It is difficult to categorize Churchill in party-political terms. Some contemporaries were perplexed, many infuriated by his lack of tribal loyalty as he twice crossed the floor of the House of Commons. His capacity to combine extreme reaction with surprising radicalism led some to classify him as an eighteenth-century Whig. There was something of the eighteenth century about Churchill's religion as well as his politics. Morton wrote:

> Winston did believe in God, though he was not Christian, on his own argued confession and admission. His God was akin to 'the Lord of the Jews', but further away and completely incomprehensible to Man. It was the Theistic belief common to the period of the great John Duke of Marlborough. A God who did create the world and all that is, but who is so detached therefrom that no access is possible.[101]

That rather comfortless position is probably the most accurate precis of Churchill's religious belief.

---

99 Lord Hailsham, *A Sparrow's Flight: Memoirs* (London: Fontana, 1991), p. 225.

100 WSC, *My Early Life*, p. 123.

101 Morton to Thompson, 11 July 1961, cited Thompson, *Churchill and Morton*, p. 162.

Many strange meetings have taken place in 10 Downing Street but few more curious than the encounter on 25 May 1954 between the elderly Prime Minister who had led Britain through its darkest hour to ultimate victory in the Second World War, and a Kansas farm boy. The evangelist Billy Graham had led a 12-week crusade in London, attracting hundreds of thousands. Just before his departure from London, Graham received an invitation to Downing Street. Churchill changed his schedule to accommodate the young American.

It was in the days before politicians felt the need to associate with celebrities. The private meeting took place behind closed doors. There was genuine curiosity on Churchill's part. (Press reports that Graham was anti-socialist and pro-bomb probably helped.) He was interested in how the clergyman filled the arena night after night. Graham had no doubts: 'I think it's the Gospel of Christ. People are hungry to hear a word straight from the Bible.' Churchill referred to the perilous nature of world affairs. Time and again, he referred to his sense of hopelessness. Graham seized the opportunity: 'Are you without hope for your own soul's salvation?' Churchill replied: 'Frankly, I think about that a great deal.' The pastor took out his New Testament and preached an extempore sermon on salvation through Jesus Christ. Churchill was 'receptive, if not enthusiastic'. Finally, Graham asked if they might pray. Keeping the Duke of Windsor waiting for his lunch appointment, Churchill agreed: 'Most certainly. I'd appreciate it.'[102] Later Evangelicals claimed that Churchill said: 'I do not see much hope for the future unless it is the hope you are talking about young man. We must have a return to God.'[103] Graham's autobiography, based on his contemporaneous notes, contains no such statement. Rather, the overwhelming impression is one of sadness, with Churchill unable to share Graham's fervent convictions.

Churchill died in his London home, 28 Hyde Park Gate, on 24 January 1965, just weeks after his ninetieth birthday. A third of a million people filed past his coffin as he lay in state in Westminster Hall for three days. Then he was granted the first state funeral accorded to a commoner for more than a century. The ceremony in St Paul's Cathedral on 30 January

---

102 Billy Graham, *Just As I Am: The autobiography of Billy Graham* (London: HarperCollins, 1997), pp. 235–7.

103 Mansfield, *Never Give In*, p. 193.

was rich in military pageantry, accompanied by the rousing hymns he so enjoyed.

Broadcasting to the nation at the beginning of the lying-in-state, Michael Ramsey, Archbishop of Canterbury, elegantly sidestepped the question of Churchill's own religious beliefs. He asked his fellow countrymen to thank God for the gift of Churchill's life:

> What a gift it was of our good God, and what a gift it is . . . Thank God for him tonight, and let your heart go out to God . . . For Winston Churchill there is the sure Christian hope of life after death.[104]

His predecessor, the retired Archbishop Geoffrey Fisher, subsequently preached a less tactful but more honest sermon. Churchill, he said, had his religion,

> but it was a religion of the Englishman. He had a very real belief in Providence; but it was God as the God with a very special care for the values of the British people. There was nothing obscure about this; it was utterly sincere, but not really at all linked on to the particular beliefs which constitute the Christian faith and the life which rests on it.[105]

Churchill had previously requested that he be buried under the croquet lawn at Chartwell, his home in Kent, but changed his mind. Seventy years earlier, he had visited his father's grave in the Oxfordshire churchyard of St Martin's, Bladon, close to Blenheim:

> The service in the little church was going on and the voices of the children singing all added to the beauty and restfulness of the spot . . . I was so struck by the sense of quietness and peace as well as by

104 Archbishop Michael Ramsey, BBC broadcast, January 1965, LPL, Ramsey Papers, Vol. 74, ff. 226–7.

105 Fisher, cited W. F. Purcell, *Fisher of Lambeth: A portrait from life* (London: Hodder & Stoughton, 1969), p. 110.

> the old world air of the place – that my sadness was not unmixed by solace.[106]

It was here that he chose to be buried. After all the pomp in London, he was laid to rest alongside his parents with great simplicity.

106 WSC to Jennie Churchill, 23 June 1895, cited Randolph S. Churchill, *WSC: Companion Vol. 1, Part 1*, p. 579.

Clement Attlee (1945–1951)

'Can't believe the mumbo jumbo'

Clement Richard Attlee was born on 3 January 1883 in Putney in south-west London. He was educated at Haileybury College and University College, Oxford.

After graduating and completing his legal training, he quickly discovered that the law held no attractions for him and undertook social work in London's East End. He saw action in Gallipoli, Mesopotamia and France during the First World War. After his discharge from the Army, Major Attlee returned to the East End and local government politics. Elected Labour MP for Limehouse in 1922, he held the seat until its abolition in 1950. He then represented West Walthamstow until 1955.

Ramsay MacDonald made Attlee his Parliamentary Private Secretary. He was appointed Undersecretary of State for War in the first Labour government in 1924. From 1927 to 1930, he served on the Simon Commission into the governance of India. He was appointed Chancellor of the Duchy of Lancaster in May 1930 and Postmaster General in March 1931. Already critical of the Labour government's inadequate response to the economic crisis, Attlee resigned office in September 1931 rather than remain in MacDonald's National government.

As one of only three Labour MPs with ministerial experience to survive the 1931 general election, Attlee became deputy leader of the parliamentary party, and was elected leader on 26 November 1935. Acknowledged as quietly efficient and a team player, few would have predicted he would be leader for the next 20 years. Recognizing the threat posed by the European dictators, Attlee and the majority of the Labour Party gradually came to support a policy of rearmament.

Attlee's refusal to serve in a proposed coalition under Chamberlain sealed the latter's fate. Instead, on 11 May 1940 he joined Churchill's

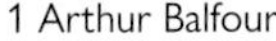

1 Arthur Balfour

2 Henry Campbell-Bannerman

3 H. H. Asquith

4 David Lloyd George (centre)

5 Bonar Law

6 Stanley Baldwin (left) and Neville Chamberlain

7 Ramsay MacDonald (left)

8 Winston Churchill (right)

9 Clement Attlee (left)

10 Anthony Eden

11 Harold Macmillan

12 Alec Douglas-Home (left)

13 Harold Wilson (centre)

14 Edward Heath (centre)

15 James Callaghan (right)

16 Margaret Thatcher

17 John Major

18 Tony Blair

coalition as Lord Privy Seal, effectively acting as Churchill's deputy. It was a successful partnership – they complemented each other, and Attlee committed his party wholeheartedly to the war effort. He was Dominions Secretary from 1942 to 1943, Lord President of the Council from 1943 to 1945 and officially Deputy Prime Minister from 1942. The coalition government came to an end on 23 May 1945.

Few expected Labour's landslide victory in the general election of 5 July 1945. The result was delayed as the votes of overseas troops were counted, but three weeks later Attlee formed the first majority Labour government. He also acted as Minister of Defence until 20 December 1946. Although the country was physically and financially exhausted after six years of war, the government introduced a sweeping programme of radical reform. The mines, steel and other industries were nationalized. The National Health Service was created. The process of decolonization was begun. Despite sectarian violence, the transfer of power to India and Pakistan was viewed as a personal success for Attlee. In foreign affairs and defence matters, there was continuity: commitment to the Western alliance and NATO; an increasingly firm stance against Soviet Russia; and the establishment of the UK's independent nuclear deterrent.

Fuel and food shortages, and a sterling crisis, led to a revival in the Conservatives' electoral fortunes and in the general election of 23 February 1950 the Labour majority was reduced from 146 to just 5. The outbreak of the Korean War in June 1950 further strained national finances and party unity. Another election was called on 25 October 1951. Although the Labour Party won the popular vote, Churchill's Conservatives gained a parliamentary majority of 17 and Attlee resigned as Prime Minister on 26 October 1951. He remained Labour leader and leader of the Opposition, fighting the 1955 election in which the Conservatives increased their majority. Attlee resigned as party leader on 6 December 1955, entering the House of Lords as Earl Attlee.

Attlee died on 8 October 1967. His funeral service was held at the Temple Church and his ashes were buried in Westminster Abbey.

* * *

Suburban Anglicanism

Clement Attlee succeeded Churchill as Prime Minister on 26 July 1945. The contrast between the two could not have been greater. Churchill was born in a ducal palace; Attlee in suburban London. In his early years, Churchill saw action in the campaigns at the high noon of empire, participating in cavalry charges and escaping from an enemy prisoner-of-war camp. Attlee escaped the drudgery of a legal apprenticeship for the world of municipal politics. Churchill never denied himself the consumption of life's luxuries; Attlee practised moderation in all aspects of his private life. Whereas Churchill was expansive and grandiloquent, Attlee was clipped and abrupt. And yet their religious convictions – or lack thereof – were very similar. Attlee was delighted to learn of Churchill's quip that he was not a pillar of the Church, rather a buttress, supporting it from the outside.[1] How could these two, so different in background and temperament, arrive at a similar position?

By family tradition and childhood practice, Attlee was immersed in the Church of England – more so even than Harold Macmillan, often regarded as the Anglican paradigm of twentieth-century Prime Ministers. Attlee was born into the social and financial security of a professional, middle-class family. Henry Attlee, his father, was a City solicitor who went on to become senior partner of his firm, President of the Law Society and Deputy Lieutenant of London. An uncle was an Anglican clergyman in the Diocese of Worcester. An elder brother, Bernard, was also ordained. His sister, Mary, followed female cousins in becoming a missionary, spending much of her life in South Africa.

The Attlees settled in Putney, already far advanced along the path of transformation from Surrey village to London suburb, close to the family home of his mother, Ellen Bravery Watson, in Wandsworth. The former Prime Minister recalled a certain fluidity in the family's churchmanship: they were 'at first Evangelical, later inclined to be more High Church'.[2] Possibly this accounts for the fact that the eight children were baptized in four different churches. The family initially practised at the ancient riverside

1 Clement Richard Attlee to Tom Attlee, 9 November 1940, Oxford, Bodleian Libraries (Bodleian), Attlee MS, Eng. c. 4793, f. 9.

2 CRA, Draft autobiography, CCAC, Attlee Papers, ATLE 1/7.

parish of St Mary's, Putney, but then spread their favours to encompass All Saints, Wandsworth, and St Stephen's, Clapham Park. By the time Clem and the younger children arrived, Holy Trinity, West Hill, Wandsworth, was their preferred place of worship. Attlee was baptized there on 18 February 1883. It was an imposing church on the Portsmouth Road built in the Decorated Style two decades earlier, and subsequently extended.

At the time and in his subsequent recollections, the thought of Sundays in his early years filled Attlee with foreboding. The day 'was kept very strictly when we were children. Everyone wore their best. Father a top hat, etc.' The family attended Holy Trinity in the morning; Attlee and his siblings were sent back for an afternoon children's service. The Attlees frequently also attended an evening service at St Stephen's, Clapham Park, or St Anne's, Wandsworth (a severe, neoclassical preaching box that was renovated in the early 1890s to facilitate more High Church practices). In the affluent suburbs of late Victorian London, the churches were filled to capacity.

From his earliest years, Attlee was driven to distraction by all this churchgoing, devising mind games to help pass the time: 'I used to try to work out routes whereby one might climb up into the roof or I would attempt to fit the pieces of coloured glass in the West Window together. I used to be very bored.'[3] Games were prohibited on Sundays and only reading of a religious nature permitted. Walks were the only opportunity to escape this strict sabbatarian discipline, although the regime was relaxed somewhat in later years.[4] Kenneth Harris maintains that it was this unhappy childhood experience of church attendance that turned Attlee against Christianity for life.[5] But the biographer and daughter-in-law of his brother, Tom, makes the reasonable point that the rest of the family were raised in the same religious environment and remained committed Christians.[6]

3 CRA, Draft autobiography, CCAC, Attlee Papers, ATLE 1/7.

4 C. R. Attlee, *As It Happened* (London: William Heinemann, 1954), p. 4.

5 Kenneth Harris, *Attlee* (London: Weidenfeld & Nicolson, 1982), p. 7.

6 Peggy Attlee, *A Quiet Conscience: Thomas Simmons Attlee* (London: Dove & Chough Press, 1995), p. 4.

Religion was not reserved for church. Attlee subsequently wrote: 'England in the nineteenth century was still a nation of Bible readers.'[7] That was true of his own home. The day began with family prayers with the servants. After the Lord's Prayer, there was a Bible reading for five or ten minutes, then another prayer. Lessons after breakfast commenced with more Scripture. Each child had their own copy of the Bible and took turns to read a verse until the passage was completed. During term-time, they worked their way through the Gospels and the Acts of the Apostles, which they all came to know by heart. The Psalms were studied during the holidays.[8]

Attlee readily conceded that his family's Christianity did not remain at the level of the abstract and the devotional. There was a general atmosphere 'of strict morality' within the home and 'a high standard of duty towards poorer neighbours' beyond. 'There was a strong tradition of social service' in the family: his mother was a district visitor, assisting the clergy in visiting sick parishioners and those in need; his sisters taught in Sunday school and worked for the Girls' Friendly Society, established to help young working women; his brothers assisted with the running of clubs for working class boys, especially in Haggerston, where Bernard was a curate. Attlee recognized that in every case save his own these 'good works' were inspired by his family's Christian faith.[9]

'Fed up with public school religion'

At the age of nine, Attlee joined Tom at Northaw Place, a Hertfordshire preparatory school run by a family friend, the Revd F. J. Hall. He had no time for the religious instruction imparted there, which consisted of memorizing the names of the kings of Israel and Judah and the deeds of the people of Israel recorded in the Old Testament: 'It is incredible the amount of time wasted in acquiring this useless knowledge, for there was no critical exegesis at this time.'[10] The fact that Attlee came first in the Diocese in the Bishop's Examination was viewed by others as a sign of a possible vocation. Attlee was clear that it was merely the consequence of

7 C. R. Attlee, *The Labour Party in Perspective* (London: Victor Gollancz, 1937), p. 27.
8 Harris, *Attlee*, p. 5.
9 CRA, Draft autobiography, CCAC, Attlee Papers, ATLE 1/7–9.
10 CRA, *As It Happened*, p. 5.

a good memory.[11] He had fonder recollections of Sunday evenings in the headmaster's drawing room, the boys singing hymns and carols, accompanied by Mrs Hall on the piano. For Attlee, the 'real religion' of Northaw was cricket.[12]

In 1896 he followed his brothers to Haileybury College, founded to educate the sons of East India Company officials. The headmaster was another cricketing cleric, Canon Edward Lyttelton. Attlee shared Tom's antipathy towards 'the deadly dullness of the Chapel' at Haileybury.[13] 'Decidedly fed up with public school religion',[14] he determined on a formal break. Matters came to a head when he was due to be confirmed. He shared his parents' moral sensibilities and their social concern for the less fortunate, but he concluded that he did not believe in God:

> So far as I was concerned it was mumbo-jumbo. It worked for many of those I most liked and admired, so it was nothing to laugh at or asperse. But it meant nothing to me one way or the other.

He proceeded with Confirmation, to avoid giving unnecessary offence to his family, but at the age of 16 he quietly rejected the Christian faith, and having arrived at this decision he was not easily persuaded otherwise. His housemaster wrote in his final report: 'His chief fault is that he is very self-opinionated, so much so that he gives very scant consideration to the views of other people.'[15]

Adolescent boredom with church services was scarcely a unique phenomenon then, as now. Why, in Attlee's case, did it lead to the rejection of belief? There was, he admitted in a passage from his draft autobiography that did not survive into the published version, an additional reason. Towards the end of his schooldays, he had developed 'a religious scepticism which revolted against the fundamentalist teaching in which I had been brought up'. For Attlee, this was unconnected to any perceived conflict between church teaching and Darwinian theories. His family were relatively

11 Harris, *Attlee*, p. 7.
12 CRA, *As It Happened*, pp. 5–6.
13 Tom Attlee, cited Peggy Attlee, *A Quiet Conscience*, p. 7.
14 CRA, Draft autobiography, CCAC, Attlee Papers, ATLE 1/8.
15 Harris, *Attlee*, pp. 9–10.

advanced on this issue: 'It accepted the need for change and believed optimistically in human progress. It accepted the one time infidel doctrine of evolution.'[16] Given his observation on the lack of critical exegesis, Attlee's difficulties might have been concerned rather with scriptural accounts of the miraculous and the supernatural, or the insistence on the literal accuracy of the Bible. He had a questioning mind. When questions were not permitted or answered, the result was profoundly damaging.

'Religiosity of any kind was most distasteful to me'

Attlee went up to Oxford in 1901 to read Modern History at University College. Undergraduate passions were less readily stirred by religious controversies. He noted that the mid-nineteenth-century Oxford 'violently excited over the Tractarians' seemed far removed from his own generation – the university 'was of course much more clerical in those days'.[17] Not that this could be guessed from the company he kept: 'Five of my closest friends became parsons.' In addition to Charles Bailey and George Day, contemporaries from Haileybury, his 'most intimate friends' included Herbert Holland (later Bishop of Wellington, New Zealand) and Grandage Powell (later suffragan Bishop of Penrith).[18] Closest of all was Hugh Linton, the son of an Australian bishop, who followed his father into ordained ministry in Southwark and Australia.[19] Attlee remained in contact for life with many of them, following their ecclesiastical careers with unfeigned interest. Sundays were often spent with Tom, walking to Wolvercote, where Bernard had recently been appointed vicar.

The clerical circles in which Attlee moved in Oxford were not noticeably different from those of his Putney home. He was respectful of their faith but did not share it: 'I was definitely divorced from religion and as a consequence tended to adopt the somewhat cynical attitude found in

16 CRA, Draft autobiography, CCAC, Attlee Papers, ATLE 1/7.

17 CRA to Tom Attlee, 21 January 1959, Bodleian, Attlee MS, Eng. c. 4794, f. 80.

18 CRA, Draft autobiography, CCAC, Attlee Papers, ATLE 1/7.

19 Michael Jago, *Clement Attlee: The inevitable Prime Minister* (London: Biteback Publishing, 2014), p. 20.

undergraduates.'[20] The Christian Social Union (CSU), committed to social reform, was founded by Henry Scott Holland in 1889. Local groups investigated and discussed social problems and proposed remedies. Tom encountered its Oxford branch and became a committed member. Sympathetic to its aims, Attlee was suspicious of its motivation and membership: 'Most of those interested . . . were either high or low church and religiosity of any kind was most distasteful to me.'[21]

'The Bible is full of revolutionary teaching'

Attlee expressed his views freely on the interaction of religion and social work as he found it in London's East End. The family made no objection when he abandoned the early stages of a legal career to devote himself to alleviating the lot of the poor. It began in October 1905 when he joined his brother, Laurence, in visiting the club his school ran in Stepney, offering cadet training and educational and social opportunities to the boys there. It was a decided advantage for Attlee that, unlike most school and university missions, the Haileybury Club was largely secular. There was 'a voluntary religious class' run by an old lady 'of very wide sympathy', but no clergyman or paid missioner, no religious tests or definite religious teaching.[22] Tom, by contrast, worked for the CSU's Maurice Hostel in Hoxton.

When Attlee began working in the East End, social work was viewed principally as an expression of charity, which, he acknowledged, was primarily a religious concept. At its purest, charity was the love of one's fellow people, which was 'at the root of all vital social work'. Yet too often, he felt, motives were mixed. He was angered when religion was used to reconcile the poor to their lot in this life, and queried the charitable intent of a testator expecting something in return for their largesse, such as prayers for their soul.[23] Some 'charity' appeared to him to be naked bribery: 'There was a good deal of feeling against some of the religious clubs. As one boy said, "They say, 'Come to our service and we'll give a ticket for

20 CRA, Draft autobiography, CCAC, Attlee Papers, ATLE 1/7.

21 CRA, Draft autobiography, CCAC, Attlee Papers, ATLE 1/8.

22 CRA, *As It Happened*, p. 22; CRA, Draft autobiography, CCAC, Attlee Papers, ATLE 1/7.

23 C. R. Attlee, *The Social Worker* (London: George Bell & Sons, 1920), pp. 8–9.

the entertainment' – garn!'"'[24] Attlee equally deplored the influence of religion in education, criticizing its tendency to divert attention from essential needs to petty sectarian squabbles.[25]

He was, however, prepared to award credit where he felt it was due. In the nineteenth century, both Evangelicals and the Oxford Movement had helped to awaken a social conscience. He paid tribute to slum priests: 'Indeed it is the extreme high churchmen who are the most outspoken in their demands for social justice.'[26] Charles Kingsley and F. D. Maurice are singled out for praise in preaching a gospel of freedom, equality and fraternity. Recognition was even accorded to Roman Catholics: their care for poor immigrant parishioners and the social teaching of Pope Leo XIII and Cardinal Manning. Yet Attlee was simply describing observed phenomena. He urged the churches to inspire an ideal of service, encourage the moral life and provide practical help organized around the parish or the chapel. There was no intimation of a supernatural basis for any of this. Attlee's writing reflected his own secular beliefs.

The two Attlee brothers Tom and Clem, close in age and affection, were divided by religion. This manifested itself during the First World War. While Clem was commissioned into the South Lancashire Regiment, Tom was imprisoned as a conscientious objector, citing the Lord's command to love one's enemies. Nothing in Attlee's military service caused him to modify his view of the Church. In the Army, 'the general feeling towards the organized religious bodies especially the C of E is contempt'. This was true even for the minority of officers 'who are most inclined to look on life from a religious point of view'.[27] Attlee's ire was aroused by an 'example of clerical fatuity'. The culprit was Bishop Welldon, Churchill's former headmaster, who had written to *The Times*, complaining that of all the German atrocities, one of the most tragic was an attack launched during Holy Week. Attlee fulminated: 'The most tragic!! as if the loss of a single human life was not infinitely more tragic.'[28]

---

24 CRA, *As It Happened*, p. 22.

25 CRA, *The Social Worker*, p. 47.

26 CRA, *The Social Worker*, p. 164.

27 CRA to Tom Attlee, 20 March 1918, Bodleian, Attlee MS, Eng. c. 4792, f. 12b.

28 CRA to Tom Attlee, 2 April 1918, Bodleian, Attlee MS, Eng. c. 4792, f. 18.

Attlee's experience of East End poverty led him to condemn the failures of capitalism and to embrace socialism. He joined the Independent Labour Party in Stepney in 1908. His socialism was based not on Marxist materialism but on the practical desire to improve the living standards and increase the opportunities of those around him. This, he claimed, was the true position of the British Labour Party, distinguishing it from socialist parties elsewhere:

> I think that the first place in the influences that built up the Socialist movement must be given to religion.
>
> The Bible is full of revolutionary teaching, and it is not surprising that, in a country where thought is free, many men and women have drawn from it the support which they needed for their instinctive revolt against the inhuman conditions which Capitalism brings. I think that probably the majority of those who have built up the Socialist movement in this country have been adherents of the Christian religion – and not merely adherents, but enthusiastic members of some religious body. There are probably more texts from the Bible enunciated from Socialist platforms than from all the other parties.[29]

This was more than a pitch for church and chapel votes. It was Attlee's sincere belief and the position of his family.

Sundays at home

Attlee married late. He met Violet Millar, 13 years his junior and the sister of an Oxford contemporary, on holiday in Italy. Like the Attlees, the Millars were conventional, committed Anglicans. The couple were married at Christ Church, Hampstead, on 10 January 1922. Bernard officiated, assisted by Vi's brother, the Revd Basil Millar. Vi was a regular communicant at the early services in the parish church at Woodford, where the Attlees first made their home, then at Stanmore. Religious differences caused the couple no difficulties. The children were baptized and, when

29 CRA, *The Labour Party in Perspective*, pp. 27–8.

old enough, accompanied their mother to church. One incident displays Vi in a surprising light, although not exceptional for her time and class. Shortly after her husband's landslide victory in 1945, she, her daughter and some friends organized an after-dinner séance in Downing Street. She described it for his benefit. They attempted table-lifting and spelling out messages by means of a moving glass. When one of the company entered a trance, Vi was willing to be convinced: 'I think that it was all too well done to be acting. It was really most uncanny.'[30] Attlee's response is unrecorded.

Attlee spent Sundays at home, reading, walking, playing tennis and engaging in DIY. His churchgoing was limited to baptisms, weddings and funerals, as well as state occasions. When required to attend, however, he was on familiar ground and not afraid to voice his liturgical preferences:

> Today we attended the service of thanksgiving in St Paul's which was quite well done. There was some lusty singing with a good choice of hymns though I always resent the modern bowdlerising of 'Praise my Soul the King of Heaven' by cutting out the somewhat pagan bowing down of the sun and the moon.[31]

Outside service times, he was a systematic visitor of cathedrals and historic churches, but only on the grounds of architectural and aesthetic merit.

'The need for youthful drive'

Attlee was critical of the historical pedigree of the Church of England in which he was raised, lamenting the Crown's seizure at the Reformation of monastic properties that had provided for the sick, poor and homeless. He argued that the position deteriorated further in the eighteenth century, when 'in the main, the country parson became either a sort of squire or a hanger on of the landed classes' and churchmen appeared indifferent to 'the misery and injustice around them'.[32] Matters improved with the

30 Francis Beckett, *Clem Attlee* (London: Richard Cohen Books, 1997), p. 224.

31 CRA to Tom Attlee, 19 May 1943, Bodleian, Attlee MS, Eng. c. 4793, f. 33.

32 CRA, *The Social Worker*, pp. 33, 158–9.

religious revival of the nineteenth century, but he feared that the Church of England remained too associated with just one class.

For a professed non-believer, Attlee devoted an extraordinary amount of time and effort to the exercise of his powers of ecclesiastical patronage. The contrast with Churchill was marked. In August 1945, the new Labour government faced massive problems regarding establishing Britain's role in the new world order and restructuring the economy and society at home in the context of physical and financial exhaustion. Yet Attlee found time to lunch separately with the Archbishops of Canterbury, Geoffrey Fisher, and of York, Cyril Garbett, to discuss ecclesiastical affairs at length.[33] He followed this up with a substantial memorandum to Fisher, setting out lucidly the issues as he saw them and the principles by which he intended to operate.[34] As Prime Minister, he was always available to meet or correspond with bishops.

Fisher later claimed that he found Attlee

> a splendid person to work with. When things occurred, he preferred me to go and talk with him directly, and that I liked. Everything was dealt with speedily, properly and competently, and I knew exactly where I was with him.[35]

It was not always so amicable at the time. Attlee held decided views, although not in terms of party or church politics. In terms of churchmanship, he was eager only to avoid swings from one extreme to another within a Diocese.[36]

Attlee believed that the Church of England stood in need of revitalization. He viewed the candidates proposed for preferment as too elderly, displaying no 'outstanding qualities of leadership with the ability to arouse enthusiasm'. The younger generation, he feared, would be lost 'unless there is a real touch of imagination . . . some boldness, some readiness to take risks and some appreciation of the need for youthful drive rather

33 CRA to Tom Atlee, 30 August 1945, Bodleian, Attlee MS, Eng. c. 4793, f. 53.

34 CRA to Fisher, 28 September 1945, Lambeth Palace Library (LPL), Fisher Papers, Vol. 3, ff. 356–9.

35 W. F. Purcell, *Fisher of Lambeth: A portrait from life* (London: Hodder & Stoughton, 1969), p. 266.

36 CRA to Tom Attlee, 7 November 1950, Bodleian, Attlee MS, Eng. c. 4794, f. 9.

than for elderly safety first'.[37] He was critical of the tendency to translate existing bishops to 'more important' Dioceses on the basis of seniority. Unless there were exceptional circumstances, a bishop should remain in his Diocese to establish pastoral relationships.[38] He resisted Fisher's desire to appoint canonists and technical experts to the bench of bishops.[39] It is difficult to fault Attlee's approach. The perspicacity of his views and his doggedness in pursuing them do not suggest a man who considered the Church an irrelevance.

Attlee had little contact with the Free Churches. He went to the kirk for the first time only in Glasgow in 1941 for a service in memory of the victims of the Blitz, and was taken aback when asked to address a few helpful words to the elders and congregation.[40]

Better Catholic than Communist

An undergraduate visit to Lourdes had elicited an unfavourable reaction. He found the Catholic shrine 'tawdry', rather like an Earl's Court exhibition.[41] On more mature consideration, Attlee was not demonstrably hostile to Roman Catholicism, believing perhaps that the doctrine of one church was no more or less objectionable than another. He approved of priests living close to their people, seeking to improve their plight, and was appreciative of Arthur Hinsley, the down-to-earth and patriotic wartime cardinal.[42] Attlee was also complimentary of the two popes he met in audience – Pius XII ('a gentle idealist') and John XXIII ('a fine fellow').[43] When his great-nephew entered the Jesuit novitiate, Attlee's response was laconic: 'I suppose being a Catholic priest even a Jesuit is better than becoming a Communist.'[44]

---

37 CRA to Fisher, 28 September 1945, LPL, Fisher Papers, Vol. 3, ff. 356, 358.

38 CRA to Fisher, 17 May 1946, LPL, Fisher Papers, Vol. 13, f. 83.

39 CRA to Fisher, 14 December 1945, LPL, Fisher Papers, Vol. 3, ff. 379–80.

40 CRA to Tom Attlee, 7 April 1941, Bodleian, Attlee MS, Eng. c. 4793, f. 10.

41 CRA, *As It Happened*, p. 16.

42 CRA to Tom Attlee, 15 August 1941, Bodleian, Attlee MS, Eng. c. 4793, f. 13.

43 CRA to Tom Attlee, 4 September 1944, Bodleian, Attlee MS, Eng. c. 4793, f. 44; CRA to Patricia Beck, 3 June 1963, Bodleian, Attlee MS, Eng. let. c. 571, f. 38.

44 CRA to Tom Attlee, 24 August 1960, Bodleian, Attlee MS, Eng. c. 4794, f. 92.

'The ethics of Christianity'

What exactly was Attlee's personal position? Harris asserts that following his rejection of the Christian faith at Haileybury, Attlee 'did not give God or the Life Everlasting very much thought'.[45] That is not entirely accurate. Attlee pondered the claims of Christianity in spring 1918, writing to his brother: 'I am less convinced than ever of the truth of the church's teaching.'

A particular problem was 'the doctrine of vicarious sacrifice which is to my mind thoroughly immoral'. Attlee did not elaborate what precisely he found so immoral. Presumably not that Christ in love freely chose to give his life for sinful humanity, though possibly the doctrine of penal substitution, the belief prevalent in certain schools of Protestant thought that God's wrath had to be appeased by the suffering of his Son. Such a doctrine is indeed immoral, attributing Christ's death to a cruel Father rather than the consequence of perfect love confronting pure evil. Sadly, there is no evidence that Attlee discussed his difficulties with anyone qualified to help him. Another problem was the question of 'mysticism', which he dismissed as little more than 'mere sentimentality', although he conceded it was something he had studied little.[46] In this case, more culpability attached to Attlee – an unwillingness to see anything other than pragmatic endeavour as having value.

Lord Longford, one of Attlee's junior ministers, made a sweeping claim: 'In my eyes Clem Attlee was not only the most selfless politician of the first rank that I have known, but the most ethical Prime Minister in the whole of British history.'[47] Attlee's political opponents did not dispute that he was indeed one of the most moral of men, even if they disagreed with Longford's implication that this made him a closet Christian. A Liberal politician wrote of Attlee: 'This man burns with a hidden fire and is sustained by a certain spiritual integrity which enables him to scale the heights.'[48] Attlee himself readily granted the basis of his morality:

45 Harris, *Attlee*, p. 10.

46 CRA to Tom Attlee, 2 April 1918, Bodleian, Attlee MS, Eng. c. 4792, f. 19b.

47 Lord Longford, cited ed. Geoffrey Dellar, *Attlee as I Knew Him* (London: Tower Hamlets Library Service, 1983).

48 Alan Campbell-Johnson, Diary, 6 March 1947, cited Harris, *Attlee*, p. 381.

> Our Western civilization has been built up in the main on the acceptance of the moral standards of Christianity. Even those who find themselves unable to accept Christian dogma accept in the main its ethical standards.[49]

Counting himself among those 'unable to accept Christian dogma', Attlee repeated the sentiment more succinctly in a 1965 interview with Harris: 'Believe in the ethics of Christianity. Can't believe the mumbo jumbo.'[50]

'Lord, who shall dwell in Thy tabernacle'

It was not only his moral behaviour that caused observers to speculate on Attlee's possible faith. He was never a man to court popularity on a false basis or say anything he did not sincerely believe. At the outset of the Second World War, he called on 'spiritual forces' to aid the Allied cause, acknowledging Christianity's great contribution of the value it attributed to 'each individual soul'.[51] Two years later he was equally explicit: 'The fight is not just a fight on the material plane. It is a spiritual contest between good and evil . . . [Hitler aimed to destroy the civilization] built up through the centuries on the teaching of Christ.'[52] When the Japanese surrender finally brought hostilities to an end, Attlee told the House of Commons of 'the feeling of gratitude to Almighty God for this great mercy'.[53] He was not afraid to recall the Church of England to its duty in this conflict:

> During the past ten years the whole basis of moral values has been attacked by the Fascists and to a large extent by the Communists. The material fight has been won, it has yet to be seen whether the spiritual victory will be achieved.[54]

---

49 CRA, Broadcast, January 1940, cited CRA, *As It Happened*, p. 106.

50 Harris, *Attlee*, p. 564.

51 CRA, Broadcast, January 1940, cited CRA, *As It Happened*, pp. 109, 107.

52 CRA, Speech, Liverpool, 22 March 1942, cited Jago, *Clement Attlee*, p. 131.

53 CRA, Speech to House of Commons, 14 August 1945, cited Harris, *Attlee*, p. 269.

54 CRA to Fisher, 28 September 1945, LPL, Fisher Papers, Vol. 3, f. 357.

Attlee could not be claimed for Christianity, but he was neither a materialist nor devoid of spiritual principles.

Harry Snell died in April 1944. An agricultural labourer who became Labour leader in the House of Lords, Snell's religious views also underwent significant change. Rejecting the Protestant fundamentalism of his youth, Snell embraced Unitarianism then secularism before finding a home in the Ethical movement. It fell to Attlee to arrange Snell's funeral. His sense of conventional etiquette was offended by the fact that the cremation service was led by the chairman of the Ethical Society. Attlee sought to redress the balance by choosing 'the psalm, Lord who shall dwell in Thy tabernacle, the lesson St Paul on Charity and Spring Rice's hymn I vow to thee, my country'.[55]

Attlee meticulously planned his own funeral, held in the Temple Church on 11 October 1967. The Scripture reading selected was from Revelation 21: 'I saw the holy city, the new Jerusalem.' Together with Parry's setting of Blake's 'Jerusalem', it harked back to his vision of 'the new Jerusalem' inaugurated on earth, which Attlee had proclaimed on the creation of the welfare state in 1945 – socialism as the ethical successor of Christianity. His ashes were interred at Westminster Abbey the following month at a service Attlee had also carefully devised: two traditional hymns, 'To be a pilgrim' and 'I vow to thee, my country'. But also once more the psalm 'Lord, who shall dwell in thy tabernacle' and an Old Testament passage – read by Harold Wilson – from Ecclesiastes: 'Fear God and keep his commandments: for this is the whole duty of man. For God shall bring every work into judgment, with every secret thing, whether it be good, or whether it be evil.'[56] This was scarcely the manifesto of a sceptic.

'Incapable of religious experience'

Two years earlier, Harris had sought in interview to define Attlee's religious beliefs. The attempt was not overtly successful. The ageing statesman deployed his notoriously abrupt responses and simply confirmed he was not a 'professing Christian'. Asked whether he was an agnostic,

55 CRA to Tom Attlee, 1 May 1944, Bodleian, Attlee MS, Eng. c. 4793, f. 40.
56 Ecclesiastes 12.13–14, KJV.

he replied: 'I don't know', and was no more forthcoming about his belief in the existence of an afterlife: 'Possibly.' At one point, however, Attlee perhaps revealed more than he intended: 'I'm one of those people who are incapable of religious experience.'[57] Are there people *incapable* of religious experience? Attlee clearly thought so.

This seems the key to understanding Attlee. Bored by his experience of church services at home and school, dissatisfied by the intellectually inadequate responses to his questions, he felt nothing towards the version of Christianity he was offered. Possibly he was at fault in terms of a self-sufficiency amounting to pride, but it is unlikely he fundamentally denied the possibility of Christianity's truth. He never mocked the Christian faith – as distinct from some of its ministers or institutions – nor publicly disclaimed it, and not because he was conscious of the electoral implications. He was too honest in his assessment of its impact on the lives of many of those he admired most. At times, there is almost the sense that he wished he shared what they possessed. He did not. Instead he was left with conscience and duty, and fulfilled both in an exemplary manner.

57 Harris, *Attlee*, pp. 563–4.

Anthony Eden (1955–1957)

'A prayer of fear'

Robert Anthony Eden was born on 12 June 1897 at Windlestone Hall, County Durham. He was educated at Eton and Christ Church, Oxford.

Having served in France during the First World War and studied Oriental Languages at Oxford, Eden contested the mining constituency of Spennymoor as a Conservative in 1922. Elected for Warwick and Leamington in 1923, he held the seat until his retirement in 1957. Eden was a One Nation Conservative, promoting a property-owning democracy. He was appointed Private Parliamentary Secretary to the Undersecretary at the Home Office in 1925 and to the Foreign Secretary, Austen Chamberlain, in 1926. In the National government of 1931, Eden was Undersecretary for Foreign Affairs, regularly deputizing for the Foreign Secretary. He made his reputation at the Geneva Disarmament Conference, becoming convinced of the need for collective action against aggressors. As Lord Privy Seal from 1934, he was responsible for matters pertaining to the League of Nations.

When Samuel Hoare was compelled to resign in 1935 for abandoning Abyssinia to Mussolini, Eden replaced him as Foreign Secretary. Confronted by Hitler's occupation of the Rhineland, Japanese aggression in the Far East and civil war in Spain, he came to support a policy of rearmament. Neville Chamberlain's interference in foreign affairs and use of informal channels to conduct diplomacy constituted an increasing source of frustration. Eden dramatically resigned in February 1938, opposing the recognition of the Italian occupation of Abyssinia. Anti-appeasers were disappointed, however, by his failure to provide leadership against Chamberlain.

On the outbreak of the Second World War, Eden returned to office as the Dominions Secretary. In May 1940 he was appointed to the War Office in the coalition government. Churchill promoted him to the Foreign Office in December 1940. Although the two did not always agree on foreign-policy issues, Eden provided loyal and efficient support to the Prime Minister throughout the war. Participating in the conferences of the Allied leaders, he contributed to the planning of the post-war world order. After the 1945 general election defeat, Eden spent much of the next six years deputizing as Conservative leader while Churchill travelled and wrote his memoirs.

When the Conservatives returned to power in 1951, Eden became Foreign Secretary for the third time. He achieved a striking success at the 1954 Geneva Conference, avoiding conflict with Russia in Europe and with China in South-East Asia, a feat recognized in his being created a Knight of the Garter. Acknowledged as the heir apparent, Eden privately fumed at Churchill's reluctance to relinquish office.

Finally appointed Prime Minister on 6 April 1955, Eden immediately sought the dissolution of Parliament. He fought the election on 26 May on the Conservatives' record of peace, prosperity and commitment to the welfare state. With Labour divided, the government increased their majority to 60. Eden's glamorous good looks led many to underrate him. He was capable of great charm but sensitive to criticism and perceived not to be a team player.

A consummate diplomat, Eden's failure to hold any of the great domestic offices of state was reckoned a significant political disadvantage. It is ironic, therefore, that his downfall was occasioned by events overseas. Eden had persuaded a reluctant Churchill to agree to the withdrawal of British troops from Egypt. In July 1956, the Egyptian leader, Gamal Abdel Nasser, nationalized the Suez Canal, of which the British government was a major shareholder. Illness clouded Eden's judgement. He cast Nasser in the mould of the 1930s dictators, misjudged the US response to British action, hesitated over military intervention and misled Parliament over collaboration with the Israelis. American opposition and a threatened economic crisis led to the declaration of a ceasefire within 24 hours of the Anglo-French invasion. The result was national disunity and international humiliation.

Eden's position was further undermined by his subsequent convalescence in the West Indies. Harold Macmillan used that absence to manoeuvre himself as a candidate for succession to the leadership. Eden resigned as Prime Minister on health grounds on 9 January 1957, and as an MP on 11 January. He was created Earl of Avon in 1961.

He died at Alvediston in Wiltshire on 14 January 1977 and was buried in the churchyard there three days later.

* * *

'The tribulations of a baronet'

For centuries, the Edens had been major Durham landowners. With other conservatively minded gentry, they participated in the abortive 1569 Northern Rising, which sought to reverse the Reformation and restore the Catholic faith. Subsequent generations were reconciled to the Established Church. The Prime Minister's grandfather, Sir William Eden, built a chapel at Windlestone in 1868 to house the remains of the six children who predeceased him. The exterior bore the verse *Ego sum Pastor Bonus et agnosco oves meas* ('I am the Good Shepherd and I know My sheep') and images of a child shepherd and the pelican in piety.

His son, also Sir William, made no pretence to piety. His mother lamented: 'I am so grieved no one from the Hall, except the servants, goes to church. It is very sad!'[1] The younger William displayed considerable accomplishments: a horseman, shot and boxer, a collector of modern art and was himself a watercolourist. He was, however, notoriously difficult. His family and friends went in fear of his intemperate outbursts.

He was no better disposed towards God than towards his fellows. Eden wrote of his 'father's frequently expressed agnostic opinions'.[2] His elder brother, Timothy, remembered their father as 'irreligious and a violent and sincere scoffer of angels and archangels and all the hierarchy of heaven, without belief in the continuity of life, without hope beyond the grave'. His atheism, however, Timothy opined, was based less on a strict materialism and more on an 'indignation with the cruelties and injustice of existence'.[3] Religion was used to bait his family. Anthony, when he won the Brinckman Divinity Prize at Eton, explained that this reflected more his prowess

1 Dowager Lady Eden, cited Timothy Eden, *The Tribulations of a Baronet* (London: Macmillan, 1933), p. 27.

2 Anthony Eden, *Another World, 1897–1917* (London: Allen Lane, 1976), p. 49.

3 Timothy Eden, *The Tribulations of a Baronet*, pp. 21–2.

in Greek than any predilection for sermons. His father was having none of it, introducing him to all and sundry 'as "my son who is going into the Church," or sometimes as "my son who is going to be a bishop"'.[4]

Eden's mother, Sybil, Lady Eden, was a society beauty, loved by the estate tenants and all who benefited from her acts of charity. These, however, were wont to exceed her means, and her profligacy caused the family much heartache, contributing to the forced sale of Windlestone in the 1930s.

A believing and practising Anglican, Lady Eden kept her spiritual options open. One son, Jack, was killed in action in October 1914; a second was a prisoner of war. Having attended church that morning, Lady Eden consulted a medium later the same day for assurances from the spirit world. She was not disappointed:

> Jack sent me a message to say he is always near me – that he is perfectly happy – so glad he passed over and he did because it was such a glorious death . . . He told me he was looking after Tim. Oh! Anthony, darling, how near we are really to the spirit world could we but realize it – cleanse ourselves of earthly faults, failings. We put it from us instead of drawing it nearer to us. It is illogical to limit thought-power to the earth sphere.[5]

Anthony's mother prayed that he would be an exemplary Christian – of the type admired by Englishmen of his generation and class: 'Pray God to help you develop into a true, Christian gentleman in the real sense of the word. To help you always do your duty – to live for others – not for yourself alone.'[6]

Institutionalized religion

Eden was baptized at the parish church of St James's, Coundon, on 4 September 1897. His mother celebrated by throwing a party for 300. In his memoirs of his early life, Eden made no substantive reference to religious practice. This, however, reflected more his priorities in later life rather

4 AE, *Another World*, p. 57.

5 Mother to Anthony Eden, 23 May 1915, CRL, AP 22/1/211.

6 Mother to AE, 10 June 1915, CRL, AP 22/1/213.

than the reality of his childhood and youth, when he was at church most Sundays at school or with his mother and siblings in the holidays.

His biographer, D. R. Thorpe, maintains that such early religious sensibilities Eden might have possessed were 'dissipated' by the experience 'of the institutionalized services in Eton College Chapel'.[7] Eden's schoolboy diary contains a number of disparaging references to the services he sat through in the college chapel. As a 15-year-old, he found chapel 'very long and dull and monotonous'. The prayer-boards on which the boys knelt were 'dreadfully uncomfortable'. The following year he referred to an unmemorable sermon preached by 'some weird Bishop or other'.[8]

These were, however, the normal musings of an adolescent, not evidence of an embryonic atheism. Eden critiqued services as he found them. He was as likely to apportion praise as censure. One month he condemned a 'patriotic and idiotic sermon by the Head' (Canon Edward Lyttelton), the next he recorded a 'very good sermon by the Head'.[9] Likewise there was praise for sermons by the Bishops of Zululand and Yukon. Bishop Gore of Oxford was rated excellent.[10] Eden refused on principle to give to the collections for the African missions but was happy supporting those for the more secular causes of hospitals and the blind.[11]

During the school holidays he attended evensong at St Cuthbert's, Darlington, with his family. He found it 'perfectly delightful'.[12] Thorpe suggests that by the age of 16, Eden already suffered doctrinal scruples about presenting himself for Holy Communion.[13] The diary entry does not bear out such an interpretation. Eden found the Communion service difficult because he was exhausted, having seen in the New Year the night before. He invariably received Communion at Easter and Christmas and on a handful of occasions during the year.[14] His practice was therefore similar to that of most other observant Anglicans of the period.

7 D. R. Thorpe, *Eden: The life and times of Anthony Eden, First Earl of Avon, 1897–1977* (London: Chatto & Windus, 2003), p. 30.

8 AE, Diary, 5 February 1913, 26 January 1913 and 19 July 1914, CRL, AP 20/1.

9 AE, Diary, 15 June and 27 July 1913, CRL, AP 20/1.

10 AE, Diary, 16 February 1913, 7 June and 14 December 1914, CRL, AP 20/1.

11 AE, Diary, 19 October 1913 and 28 June 1914, CRL, AP 20/1.

12 AE, Diary, 13 and 27 April 1913, CRL, AP 20/1.

13 Thorpe, *Eden*, p. 30.

14 AE, Diary, 1 January, 12 April and 25 December 1914, AP 20/1.

Prayer in time of battle

From 1916, Eden witnessed at first hand the horrors of the Western Front. His eldest brother had been killed in 1914. His younger brother, Nicholas, was killed at the Battle of Jutland. Eden retrieved the body of his friend and commanding officer, Charlie, Lord Feversham, and read a few lines from the burial service over the grave.[15] His experience of war neither destroyed nor deepened his faith. He expressed his irritation at military chaplains who 'preached to the men as though they were fools'.[16] Armistice Day was marked by a very simple service: a brief address from the General, 'O God our help in ages past', the Lord's Prayer and the French and British national anthems. Eden thought it 'the most impressive service I have ever been at'.[17]

He believed that most soldiers, even the least religious, prayed in time of battle. For many, himself included, it was 'a prayer of fear', an attempt to bargain with God:

> If, Almighty God, you will do this for me, I will promise reform, to obey the commandments scrupulously, or whatever the offer might be. For me the prayer was always at heart the same: Please God, if I am to be hit let me be slightly wounded or killed but not mutilated.[18]

Eden's views on the afterlife were inconsistent. On learning of Nicholas's death, he countenanced only annihilation. He wrote to his sister: 'I can hardly believe that I shall *never* see him again. It seems too cruel. However, there it is, and we can but make the best of it.'[19] (He experienced the same desperate emptiness when his own son was killed in the Second World War.[20]) Later Eden said more hopefully of his brother: 'But perhaps he is happier where he is.'[21] He wrote to Timothy:

---

15 AE, *Another World*, p. 117.

16 AE to mother, 27 February 1916, CRL, AP 22/1/238.

17 AE to sister, Marjorie, Lady Brooke, 15 November 1918 (transcript), CRL, AP 20/2/93.

18 AE, *Another World*, pp. 137–8.

19 AE to sister, 15 June 1916 (transcript), CRL, AP 22/2/35.

20 AE, Diary, 20 July 1945, CRL, AP 20/1/25.

21 AE to sister, 24 December 1916 (transcript), CRL, AP 22/2/50.

> Jack and Nicholas are with us still, with all of us, and around us all, helping in our struggle until our time comes, be it soon or later, when we are called to join them . . .
>
> Should I be killed before I see you again, remember this always – I shall be with Jack, Nicholas, and Daddie, and although I may be for a time here in this earth I shall be with the others. I shall be *so* happy with them, I *know* I shall . . . it all seems so cruel, and yet I know that they are all much happier in paradise.[22]

Intellectual assent to belief in an afterlife appears to have reasserted itself once the immediate emotional shock of grief had subsided.

Islam at Oxford

His studies in Oriental Languages at Oxford introduced Eden to unfamiliar cultures and beliefs. He was taught by the Revd D. S. Margoliouth, an Anglican clergyman and the son of a convert from Judaism. Margoliouth was one of the Western world's foremost Islamic scholars, equally happy lecturing in Arabic in universities in Baghdad and Lahore as he was teaching in Oxford. Eden found Margoliouth kind and delightful. He enjoyed his reading of the Qur'an, although he had less time for medieval commentaries, 'having no taste for theological discourse or controversy'.[23]

'The true nature of marriage declared by Our Lord'

Eden married Beatrice Beckett, the daughter of a Tory MP and banker who was also proprietor of the *Yorkshire Post*. The Becketts were practising Anglicans. Eden attended church and received Communion with them at Kirkdale, their North Yorkshire home, where he admired the Saxon

22 AE to Timothy Eden, cited Robert Rhodes James, *Anthony Eden: A biography* (New York: McGraw-Hill, 1987), p. 41.

23 Anthony Eden, *Full Circle: The memoirs of the Rt. Hon. Sir Anthony Eden, KG, PC, MC* (London: Cassell, 1960), p. 191.

architecture but deplored the quality of the preaching.[24] The marriage took place at St Margaret's, Westminster, on 5 November 1923. Having buried Bonar Law's ashes in Westminster Abbey that morning, Cosmo Lang, the Archbishop of York, officiated. The address was preached by a distant cousin, Rodney Eden, the Bishop of Wakefield.

If not weekly, the Edens initially went regularly to church at St Margaret's and, after moving into their new home, Chelsea Old Church, where their eldest son, Simon, was baptized in February 1925. Eden also attended churches in his constituency.[25] After Simon's birth and a world tour later in 1925, however, the frequency of his churchgoing declined significantly. By 1926 his attendance was limited to little more than Christmas and Easter. Promoted to junior office, Eden was preoccupied with politics and preferred to spend his Sundays reading and writing, gardening and playing tennis and bridge.

Beatrice did not share her husband's political interests. The two gradually drifted apart, separating in December 1946. The divorce was formalized in 1950. On 14 August 1952, Eden married Clarissa Churchill, 24 years his junior and a niece of Winston Churchill, at the Caxton Hall Registry Office. Clarissa was a baptized Catholic. Her Church, in common with most Christians at the time, did not recognize the remarriage of divorcees. The novelist Evelyn Waugh, a friend, wrote her a furious letter:

> Did you never think that you were contributing to the loneliness of Calvary by your desertion? . . . I . . . hoped that if you were seriously tempted to apostasy, you would trust me by asking advice . . . I think you were left in childhood with a conception of the Church as being a sort of club, from which one can resign at any moment if the cooking deteriorates. I don't think you saw it as a complete way of life. As a friend I might have shown you.[26]

Clarissa declined the offer of advice.

---

24 AE, Diary, 5 and 19 August, 2 September and 25 December 1923, CRL, AP 20/1.

25 AE, Diary, 25 November 1923, 3 and 10 February, 2 March, 4 May, 25 December 1924, 28 February, 22 March, 12 April and 24 May 1925, CRL, AP 20/1.

26 Evelyn Waugh to Clarissa Eden, cited Clarissa Eden, *A Memoir: From Churchill to Eden* (London: Weidenfeld & Nicolson, 2007), pp. 114–15.

Eden was the only twentieth-century Prime Minister to divorce and remarry during the lifetime of a former spouse. The *Church Times* thundered:

> It is now apparently to be accepted as a matter of course that those who occupy the highest positions in political and public life may break the Church's law without embarrassment or reproach . . . The world has now openly rejected the law of Christ in this, as in so much else.[27]

There is no evidence of Eden being troubled by religious or moral scruples on his remarriage, nor that the British electorate was unduly censorious.

Geoffrey Fisher, the Archbishop of Canterbury, privately expressed his distress that Eden could 'no longer bear his witness to the true nature of marriage declared by Our Lord and committed to His Church'. Every divorce, he maintained, was objectively a sin. Yet he was sure no 'moral stigma' attached to Eden, given he had been deserted by Beatrice. (His political future might have been less secure had Fisher and others realized that both had carried on affairs and that the divorce was by mutual consent.) Clergy asked Fisher to speak out against Eden's succession as Prime Minister but he was clear this was 'quite impossible' in a democracy and likely to 'cause violent reactions against the Church'. He reminded Eden's critics of his achievements as Foreign Secretary in 'the cause of peace and goodwill among nations . . . a cause very dear to Our Lord and His Church'. He was confident that Eden had been motivated in that by 'a deep sense of Christian duty and, I doubt not, in the strength of Christian prayer'.[28]

'Quite a struggle'

Critics of Eden's remarriage asked how, as a divorcee, he could be expected to exercise his powers of ecclesiastical patronage. Fisher reassured

27 Editorial, *Church Times*, 15 August 1952, cited Bernard Palmer, *High and Mitred: A study of Prime Ministers as bishop-makers, 1837–1977* (London: SPCK, 1992), p. 244.

28 Fisher to Revd W. L. Howlden, 14 June 1955 (copy), Lambeth Palace Library (LPL), Fisher Papers, Vol. 155, ff. 262; Fisher to Peter Winckworth, 8 Oct 1952 (copy), LPL, Fisher Papers, Vol. 99, f. 299; Fisher to Prebendary Harland, 8 April 1954 (copy), LPL, Fisher Papers, Vol. 140, f. 200.

them, asserting that the Prime Minister did not advise the Queen 'in a personal capacity' in such matters and was 'strongly controlled' by the Archbishops. He was certain that Eden's judgement and 'methods of getting advice' in this respect would be 'a hundredfold more reliable' than Lloyd George's.[29]

A number of sees fell vacant during Eden's brief premiership. Assisted by Anthony Bevir, his appointments secretary, Eden took seriously his responsibility in filling them. Fisher had deluded himself over the Archbishops' 'strong control'. When Cyril Garbett died in 1955, Fisher wanted George Bell to succeed him in York. Eden, however, felt strongly that Bell, aged 72 and tainted by his opposition to the RAF's wartime bombing of Germany, was 'most unsuitable'. He was also aware that the Diocese of York preferred Michael Ramsey, the Bishop of Durham.[30] There ensued 'quite a struggle' between Downing Street and Lambeth Palace. Eden prevailed.[31]

Divorce and the princess

Clarissa found it 'bizarre'[32] that her husband, a divorcee, was required to advise the Queen on the potential constitutional crisis that arose when her sister, Princess Margaret, considered marriage to another divorcee, Group Captain Peter Townsend. Townsend proposed to Margaret in 1953. The Royal Marriages Act 1772 required the Queen's permission and she made it clear that, as Supreme Governor of the Church of England, she could not consent to marriage to a divorcee. When she attained the age of 25, however, Margaret could petition the Privy Council for permission to marry in return for renouncing her right of succession, provided Parliament did not object. Despite intense speculation, there was no announcement on the Princess's twenty-fifth birthday on 21 August 1955. When Margaret declared on 31 October that she would not be marrying Townsend after all, many suspected that a conservative establishment in Church and state had thwarted a love match.

29 Fisher to Peter Winckworth, 8 Oct 1952 (copy), LPL, Fisher Papers, Vol. 99, f. 299.

30 Thorpe, *Eden*, pp. 446–7.

31 AE, Diary, 31 December 1955, CRL, AP 20/1/31.

32 Clarissa Eden, Diary, 29 July 1955, cited Clarissa Eden, *A Memoir*, p. 217.

Given the complexities of his own position, what role did Eden play? He recognized popular support for the marriage and, according to Clarissa, 'thought that she should be free to make her own choice'.[33] Flying up to Balmoral on 1 October 1955, he advised the Royal Family that if Margaret was determined to marry Townsend, she should inform the Queen and renounce her right of succession.[34] Had the marriage proceeded, he proposed to tell the Commonwealth Prime Ministers that Margaret's renunciation would not affect her royal status and duties, nor her Civil List allowance. Eden strongly discouraged his Cabinet colleague, the High Anglican Lord Salisbury, from proffering his own, more traditional advice to the Queen and the princess.[35]

There is no evidence that religious and moral considerations entered into Eden's calculations. He wished only to give the correct legal advice – with an eye to any political repercussions that might have had. His practical stance was similar to that he took during the 1936 abdication crisis, when his 'chief concern' had been for clear communication to Parliament and the empire to minimize risks of misunderstanding and division.[36]

Eden did not entertain a high opinion of the clergy. He found Cosmo Lang, who officiated at his marriage to Beatrice, 'a little "smarmy" and a little snobbish'.[37] Nor did Lang's successors at Lambeth fare much better: Eden was appalled by William Temple's views on the Treaty of Versailles and clashed with Geoffrey Fisher over Church appointments and the Suez Crisis.[38] Hensley Henson, the Bishop of Durham from 1920 to 1939, was a different type of prelate. Initially, Eden thought him a 'very well read and interesting man with a splendid brain'. However, he came to see through the flattery, judging Henson too political.[39] Cyril Garbett, Archbishop of York, he genuinely liked.[40]

33 Clarissa Eden, *A Memoir*, p. 219.
34 AE, Diary, 1 October 1955, CRL, AP 20/1/31.
35 AE, Diary, 15 October 1955, CRL, AP 20/1/31.
36 AE, Diary, 5 December 1936, CRL, AP 20/1/16.
37 AE, Diary, 4 May 1924, CRL, AP 20/1.
38 Thorpe, *Eden*, pp. 115, 447.
39 AE, Diary, 4 January 1923, CRL, AP 20/1 and 10 September 1926, CRL, AP 20/1/6.
40 AE, Diary, 31 December 1955, CRL, AP 20/1/31.

'I haven't much love for the Church of Rome'

Allied victories in the Mediterranean led Pope Pius XII in 1943 to articulate his fears of increased British influence in the light of its government's perceived anti-Catholicism. Such prejudice was attributed principally to the person of Eden.[41] The Vatican was well informed.

Anti-Catholicism was the default position of early twentieth-century English Protestantism but Eden took it more seriously than most. It might have been thought a reaction to Catholic criticism of his marriage to Clarissa, but his prejudice pre-dated this by at least a generation. Spanish Catholicism drew his particular ire. In 1927 he attended High Mass at Granada Cathedral on Easter Sunday, approving of the singing but otherwise finding it 'an unimpressive service'.[42] His reaction on visiting the former mosque in Cordoba later that week was barely rational:

> A vulgar cathedral crammed into the midst of the most interesting monument of Spain – and what is left desecrated . . . How I hate the R.C. Church at this work – it drives me to a frenzy and I almost have it in my heart to become a Muslim![43]

Had Eden perhaps been influenced by his study of the Qur'an at Oxford?

His memoirs contain an anodyne account of his audience with Pius XI in 1934, when the Pope graciously referred to him as the 'Apôtre de la Paix'.[44] His diary entry, however, was less guarded: 'Half an hour's appointment with the Pope in his own room, hideously appointed. In front of him a singularly poor figure of Christ. Behind him one of the ugliest modern stained glass windows I have seen.'[45] Eden combined a sense of aesthetic superiority with a residue of popular prejudice. He welcomed the 'No Popery' agitation at the time of the Prayer Book revision debates as 'a healthy sign'.[46]

41 Harold H. Tittmann, *Inside the Vatican of Pius XII: The memoir of an American diplomat during World War II* (New York: Image Books, 2004), p. 197.

42 AE, Diary, 17 April 1927, CRL, AP 20/1/7.

43 AE, Diary, 22 April 1927, CRL, AP 20/1/7.

44 Anthony Eden, *Facing the Dictators: The Eden memoirs* (London: Cassell, 1962), pp. 75–6.

45 AE, Diary, 26 February 1934, CRL, AP 20/1/14.

46 AE, Diary, 15 December 1927, CRL, AP 20/1/7.

The bias occasionally spilled over into his professional life. While Foreign Secretary during the Second World War, he wrote: 'an R.C. Irishman is not a help in our service nowadays'.[47] Catholicism was inimical to his understanding of what it meant to be an English gentleman. Tolerance, for Eden, was the primary virtue: 'For me to be civilized is to be tolerant. That's why I haven't much love for the Church of Rome.'[48]

Tolerance, not dogma

Eden had to contend with a childhood in a broken home, the loss of two brothers in battle and a beloved sister from cancer, the slaughter of the trenches, the premature death of two sons, the failure of his first marriage, prolonged ill health and an ill-fated premiership. He met it all with stern stoicism, neither seeking nor finding spiritual meaning or emotional comfort from religion. From the mid-1920s, his churchgoing was infrequent, but even sporadic attendance should not be dismissed. Politically, it was not necessary for him to attend church at all – his three immediate predecessors were not churchgoers, and they did not suffer electorally as a consequence.

Eden was a social conservative who understood the Church's role as maintaining the fabric of society. He supported Henson as a champion of the Church of England's established status.[49] His son, Nicholas, recalled his traditional tastes, which were reflected in the patriotic hymns and regimental music chosen for his Memorial Service at Westminster Abbey.[50] Eden was a cultured man, sensitive to beauty, who judged church services on aesthetic grounds – the architecture and the quality of the music and preaching. He objected to 'being preached at', any suggestion that the sermon was designed to produce conversion of heart and mind on the part of the congregation.[51] 'Religious frenzy'[52] was to be avoided at all costs.

47 AE, Diary, 5 August 1943, CRL, AP 20/1/23.
48 AE, Diary, 19 January 1951, CRL, AP 20/1/27.
49 AE, Diary, 4 January 1923, CRL, AP 20/1.
50 Thorpe, *Eden*, p. 594.
51 AE, Diary, 12 June 1927, CRL, AP 20/1/7.
52 AE, Diary, 15 December 1927, CRL, AP 20/1/7.

Other than references to his visceral hatred of Catholicism, Eden's reticence regarding his own religious beliefs matched that of Law and Attlee. In 1953 he reread Samuel Butler's semi-autobiographical novel, *The Way of All Flesh*. It chronicled the protagonist's relationship with his sadistic, clerical father, his accepting a career in the Church in deference to parental wishes and subsequent loss of faith. Eden expressed his delight: 'I love his philosophy and views on life. I share his hatred of dogma and that one's religion didn't so much matter as the tolerance – which doesn't mean laxity – with which it is practised.'[53]

Butler provides the best insight into Eden's attitude towards faith. The supernatural claims of Christianity were humbug, but Christian morality retained much of its force. A vague belief in something remained. If zealous intolerance was the greatest evil, then atheism could be as objectionable as belief: 'he is the most perfect saint who is the most perfect gentleman'.

> Christianity was true in so far as it had fostered beauty, and it had fostered much beauty. It was false in so far as it had fostered ugliness, and it had fostered much ugliness. It was therefore not a little true and not a little false; on the whole one might go farther and fare worse; the wisest course would be to live with it, and make the best and not the worst of it.[54]

Eden might have written the passage himself. It was certainly how he conducted his life.

Sixteen months before his death, Eden quoted Horace Walpole in his diary: 'Life is a comedy to those who think, a tragedy to those who feel.'[55] Those are the words of a man who experienced life to be subject to the whims of fate, not the workings of divine providence.

Eden died on 14 January 1977. The small family funeral three days later held at St Mary's, Alvediston, the Wiltshire village to which he retired, was led by the vicar and the retired Bishop of Sherborne. The coffin was laid to rest in the plot in the churchyard chosen by Clarissa and him. It has a commanding view over the valley, a quintessentially English landscape of

53 AE, Diary, 10 February 1953, CRL, AP 20/1/29.

54 Samuel Butler, *The Way of All Flesh* (New York: E. P. Dutton, 1916), pp. 338, 446.

55 AE, Diary, 8 September 1975, CRL, AP, 20/2/20, cited Thorpe, *Eden*, p. 607.

meadows and woodland. The tomb bears no religious inscriptions or imagery, simply a record of offices held and honours and decorations received. A small exhibition on the life of the former Prime Minister is maintained in the church. There is reference to his cattle breeding – but none to his faith or church attendance.

Harold Macmillan (1957–1963)

'One of the most deeply religious souls in politics'

Maurice Harold Macmillan was born on 10 February 1894 at 52 Cadogan Place, just before Chelsea becomes Belgravia. He was educated at Eton and Balliol College, Oxford.

A Guards officer on the Western Front, Macmillan was severely wounded in the First World War. After a spell as aide-de-camp to the Governor General of Canada and time with the family publishing firm, he contested Stockton as a Conservative in 1923, only narrowly losing. For a generation, this north-eastern constituency, which suffered great deprivation between the wars, swung to and fro. Macmillan won the seat from the Liberals in 1924, lost it to Labour in 1929, regained it in 1931, held it in 1935 but was ousted in 1945. He was rapidly returned to the Commons at a by-election for the safe seat of Bromley, which he represented until his retirement at the 1964 general election.

Critical of his own party's economic and foreign policies, Macmillan remained a back bencher until Churchill appointed him Parliamentary Secretary to the Minister of Supply in 1940, and Undersecretary at the Colonial Office in 1942. However, it was from January 1943 as Minister Resident in French North Africa that Macmillan arrived on the international stage, consorting with the Allied leaders. His sphere of responsibility shifted to include Italy, Yugoslavia and Greece. In Churchill's short-lived caretaker government, he became Secretary of State for Air in May 1945.

In opposition, Macmillan was influential in the modernization of the Conservative Party. Churchill, on the party's return to power in 1951, appointed him to the Ministry of Housing, where he exceeded his target of building 300,000 new homes, and in 1954 to the Ministry of Defence. When Eden succeeded to the premiership in April 1955, he made Macmillan Foreign Secretary but transferred him to the Exchequer eight months later. As Chancellor, Macmillan introduced Premium Bonds. Initially among the hawks who urged military action during the Suez Crisis, he reversed his stance when confronted by American opposition and British economic weakness.

Macmillan's languid approach belied shrewd political judgement and keen personal ambition. He manoeuvred himself into the position where he was Eden's natural successor. Appointed Prime Minister on 10 January 1957, he surprised many by remaining so for almost seven years. He was confirmed as leader of the Conservative Party on 22 January 1957.

Macmillan calmly reunited and energized a government badly demoralized by the Suez debacle, and rebuilt the Anglo-American alliance. He was accused by his Chancellor, Peter Thorneycroft, among others, of stoking inflationary pressures. Although beset by industrial conflict, sterling crises and a failure to increase productivity, from the perspective of post-war austerity and the decline of the next two decades, the Macmillan years seemed a halcyon period of prosperity. He encouraged this interpretation, even if his 'never had it so good' speech is often quoted out of context. (Critics later accused his government of a damaging 'stop–go' economic policy.) Campaigning on the Conservatives' record in office, he entreated the electorate not to allow Labour to ruin it, and the government's majority increased to 100 in the general election of 8 October 1959.

Macmillan helped Britain adjust to a new international role after the Second World War. While retaining the UK's independent nuclear deterrent, he used diplomatic means to avoid conflict with the Soviet Union, travelling to Russia in 1959 to meet its volatile leader, Nikita Khrushchev. During the Cuban Missile Crisis in 1962, Macmillan proved a steadying influence. He developed a particularly close relationship with the young American President John F. Kennedy, helping to achieve a partial test ban of nuclear weapons. However, the Anglo-Saxon alliance was viewed askance in Europe: the President of France, Charles de Gaulle, vetoed Britain's application for membership of the European Economic Community (EEC) in 1963. The process of decolonialization created difficulties both with the right wing of his own party and white settlers in Africa. Macmillan was uncompromising, delivering his 'winds of change' speech to the apartheid regime in Cape Town in 1960.

As the Swinging Sixties progressed, the media and a resurgent Labour Party portrayed Macmillan as a relic of a vanished society. A sense of drift and by-election defeats led to a sweeping Cabinet reshuffle in 1962, 'the Night of the Long Knives'. The sense of panic in which it was undertaken destroyed Macmillan's reputation for unflappability. A series of spying and sex scandals, culminating in the Profumo Affair in 1963, further undermined the government's credibility. As the Conservative Party Conference assembled in Blackpool, Macmillan underwent prostate surgery in London. Visiting him in hospital, the Queen accepted his resignation as Prime Minister on 18 October 1963. He enjoyed a long retirement as a publisher, author and elder statesman, and was created Earl of Stockton – on his ninetieth birthday. He died in his Sussex home of Birch Grove on 29 December 1986. The funeral was held on 5 January 1987 at St Giles, Horsted Keynes, and he is buried in the churchyard there.

* * *

Scottish forebears and an American mother

Most twentieth-century Prime Ministers were less religious in belief and practice than their parents. Harold Macmillan was a notable exception. As a politician, he did not wear his soul on his sleeve. However, Margaret Thatcher, whom he first appointed to ministerial office, astutely observed that he 'was a man of masks. It was impossible to tell, for instance, that behind the cynical Edwardian facade was one of the most deeply religious souls in politics.'[1]

Not that religion was lacking in the family. Macmillan venerated his paternal grandfather, who died 37 years before his birth. From crofting stock on the Isle of Arran, Daniel Macmillan sought his fortune in the London book trade. With his brother, he established a publishing house in Cambridge. Thomas Hughes, of *Tom Brown's Schooldays* fame, a Macmillan author, wrote Daniel's biography, a book his grandson read repeatedly in his youth.[2] Hughes was less concerned with his subject's business acumen: 'Daniel Macmillan was before all things a devout Christian, one whose

1 Margaret Thatcher, *The Path to Power* (London: HarperCollins, 1995), p. 91.
2 Harold Macmillan, *Winds of Change, 1914–1939* (London: Macmillan, 1966), p. 49.

faith informed and coloured his whole life, and was not ashamed of letting this be plainly known.'[3]

The Macmillans were originally stern Presbyterians. Arriving in England, Daniel vacillated between dissent and scepticism but never entirely lost a sense of the spiritual: 'Prayer relieved me. Prayer seemed to me a more real thing than ever.'[4] In the 1840s he finally opted for the Church of England, attracted by doctrinal orthodoxy and sacramental liturgy. He wrote of Holy Communion that it 'seemed to me to say more than all other "means of grace", as to how we are united to each other and to God'.[5] His sympathies extended beyond Anglicanism; he read Aquinas and praised John Henry Newman.

Two of the most important influences on Daniel Macmillan – as they would be on Stanley Baldwin's father, Alfred – were Charles Kingsley and F. D. Maurice, who became 'intimate friends'.[6] He wrote of Maurice's *Kingdom of Christ*: 'I found it to be a book I cannot live without.'[7] Their promotion of education and social reform appealed to Daniel, a supporter of their Christian Socialist Movement. Later in life, Harold Macmillan recalled that in his youth, after his own grandfather, none were more respected at home than Maurice and Kingsley.[8] His father, he himself and his son were named Maurice after the former. As a Conservative, Macmillan recognized him as 'a great and good man' but was critical of his 'somewhat confused thinking'.[9] Maurice's emphasis on the social expression of Christianity was noticeably lacking from Macmillan's own faith when for many of his political contemporaries it was all of religion that remained.

Harold's father, Maurice Macmillan, was shy and reserved, wholly committed to his publishing work. He had little of Daniel's spiritual sensibility,

3 Thomas Hughes, *Memoir of Daniel Macmillan* (London: Macmillan & Co., 1883), p. viii.

4 Daniel Macmillan to William Macmillan, 13 September 1833, cited Hughes, *Daniel Macmillan*, p. 38.

5 Daniel Macmillan to Alexander Macmillan, 25 October 1853, cited Hughes, *Daniel Macmillan*, p. 250.

6 HM, *Winds of Change*, p. 39.

7 Daniel Macmillan, cited Hughes, *Daniel Macmillan*, p. 102; F. D. Maurice, *Kingdom of Christ*, 2 vols (London: Rivington, 1838).

8 Harold Macmillan, *The Past Masters: Politics and politicians, 1906–1939* (London: Macmillan, 1978), p. 14.

9 Harold Macmillan to Archbishop Michael Ramsey, 6 June 1963, Lambeth Palace Library (LPL), Ramsey Papers, Vol. 50, f. 214.

seldom speaking of religion. Harold knew nothing of his father's beliefs but suspected 'that he had discarded dogma'. Nevertheless, he observed external proprieties, attending church and every Sunday night reading Evening Service from the Book of Common Prayer to the family.[10]

Nellie Macmillan was the more forceful of Harold's parents. The daughter of a doctor from Indiana, she was fiercely ambitious for her sons, identifying Harold at an early age as the most promising of the three. She was not given to reticence in religion or any other matter. A Methodist by background, her most firmly held belief was anti-Catholic prejudice – and her most damning indictment was to pronounce an argument 'Jesuitical'.[11]

The Macmillans were conventional Anglicans attending church in London and in Sussex, when at their country home, but without 'fervour or even great regularity'.[12] Macmillan was baptized on 23 May 1894 by the Revd F. W. Carnegy at the parish church, Holy Trinity, Sloane Street. Lady Arthur Russell, a friend of his mother, was his godmother. Holy Trinity, paid for by Earl Cadogan, was barely complete at the time of the baptism. A vast shrine to the Arts and Crafts movement, its high liturgy was far removed from the austere simplicity of the Midwestern Methodism in which Nellie was raised. She tolerated the church because of its social respectability, but remained deeply suspicious.

Scripture was a staple of Macmillan's education at home and, from 1903, at Summer Fields, his Oxford preparatory school. In 1906 he proceeded as a King's Scholar to Eton. The religion there, which captured neither his mind nor his heart, was described as the attempt

> to teach the sons of gentlemen the religion in which their mothers believe, and their fathers would like to: a religion without 'enthusiasm', in the old sense, reserved in its self-expression, calculated to reinforce morality, chivalry, and the sense of truth, providing comfort in times of distress and a glow of contentment in declining years; supernatural in its nominal doctrines, yet on the whole rationalistic in its mode of approaching God.[13]

---

10 HM, *Winds of Change*, p. 39.

11 HM, *Winds of Change*, p. 39.

12 HM, *Winds of Change*, p. 39.

13 R. A. Knox, *A Spiritual Aeneid* (London: Longmans, Green & Co., 1918), p. 19.

Macmillan's headmaster was the sporting cleric, Canon Edward Lyttelton, who taught two other future Prime Ministers: Attlee at Haileybury and Eden at Eton.

'If you live with a saint, it's quite an experience'

Nellie withdrew her son from Eton in 1909 on grounds of ill health. He was prepared for Oxford by a series of private tutors, including Dillwyn Knox, a friend of Macmillan's eldest brother, Daniel. It was not a success. An austere atheist, he was replaced by his brother, who was completely otherwise. Ronald Knox was killing time between graduation and Anglican orders and an Oxford fellowship. A brilliant scholar and wit, the product of Summer Fields, Eton and Balliol, son of an aggressively Evangelical Bishop of Manchester, Ronnie Knox ought to have been a safe pair of hands from Nellie's perspective. Within a matter of weeks, however, she had dismissed him on account of his pernicious spiritual influence.

Through his reading, Knox arrived at an Anglo-Catholic position while at Eton, where he took a private vow of celibacy, fasted and frequently attended Holy Communion and evensong. During the holidays, he sampled the illicit pleasures of London's ritualistic churches. His religion became more extreme during his time at Balliol: Mass at Pusey House and with the Cowley Fathers, confession and spiritual direction. By the time of his graduation, Knox was an Anglo-Papalist, believing the Church of England a true member of the Western Catholic Church, sharing the same faith as Rome, from which the English Church had been wrongly separated by the civil power in the sixteenth century.

It was not simply a matter of externals. Beneath Knox's ritual and satire lay a loving heart and the search for sanctity. It was a heady combination for a sensitive adolescent accustomed to a cold, formal religion and a dominant mother. Half a century later, Macmillan wrote that Knox 'had a profound influence upon me, both then and afterwards'.[14] Later still he reminisced: 'He was sweet and he influenced me because he was a saint . . . the only man

14 HM, *Winds of Change*, p. 43.

I have ever known who really was a saint . . . and if you live with a saint, it's quite an experience.'[15] Macmillan's biographers have disputed who influenced whom in their respective spiritual journeys. Confusion is caused by the failure to understand the sense in which the term 'Catholic' was used and to distinguish three distinct periods: Knox's tutorship of Macmillan in autumn 1910 and Macmillan's two spiritual crises in the winter of 1913–14 and the summer of 1915.

It is wrong to suggest that, while acting as his tutor in 1910, Knox engaged in 'a covert campaign to induce Harold to "Pope"'.[16] When an Oxford friend wrote asking whether he was 'making [Macmillan] a Catholic', Knox replied: 'I'm not making him anything yet, but biding my time. I trust that I may be sent some opportunity.'[17] Neither was speaking of conversion to Roman Catholicism but rather the Catholic tradition within the Church of England. Whether due to prejudice or a mother's intuition, Nellie might have foreseen Rome as the ultimate destination, fearing that conversion would preclude her son from high political office and an advantageous marriage.

An ordinand of very pronounced views, it was never likely that Knox would limit his conversation with Macmillan to the Classics. When Knox began to share his conception of the Church of England, Macmillan asked to be taken to Mass at a neighbouring Anglo-Catholic church. He was drawn to the beauty he encountered. It did not end well – Nellie's antennae were finely attuned to such dangers. Having made some discovery, she required Knox 'to promise not to mention religion in private conversation with her son'. He of course refused and promptly left, on 3 November 1910, unable to say a word to Macmillan, of whom he had grown fond.[18]

'The Newman of our time'

Nellie claimed an early victory but it was only the first skirmish in a campaign lasting five years. Going up to Balliol in 1912 and freed from

15 HM, Interview, cited Alistair Horne, *Macmillan, 1894–1956* (London: Macmillan, 1988), p. 18.

16 D. R. Thorpe, *Supermac: The life of Harold Macmillan* (London: Chatto & Windus, 2010), p. 33.

17 Ronald Knox to Edward Kay-Shuttleworth, 10 October 1910, cited Evelyn Waugh, *The Life of Ronald Knox* (London: Chapman & Hall, 1959), p. 106.

18 Knox to Winifred Knox, 4 November 1910, cited Waugh, *Ronald Knox*, p. 106.

maternal supervision, Macmillan re-established contact with Knox, now ordained and a fellow of Trinity. They were heady days. Knox cut a controversial figure in Oxford, sporting the cassock and praying the Roman breviary. He 'began to make proselytes' among the undergraduates attracted to what they called 'Ronnie Knox's religion'.[19] (Knox himself strongly deprecated such personal references; for him, the 'Catholic system' was everything.) They were captivated by the combination of the young priest's charisma, the appeal of Catholic truth and the frisson of youthful rebellion against the establishment.

Prominent among these proselytes were Macmillan and Guy Lawrence. Lawrence arrived in Oxford at the same time as Macmillan to read Classics at Trinity. He was already considering ordination. Handsome, brilliant and highly strung, his charm and religiosity held considerable sway over both Knox and Macmillan.[20]

Knox, regarded by his acolytes as their spiritual director, sought to form them in prayer and a personal relationship with Christ. He was unquestionably the dominant influence in the group at this point. Macmillan and Lawrence served him at the altar at St Stephen's House, the Anglo-Catholic theological college in Oxford. Accompanied by just a server and such others as chose to attend, Knox felt no qualms about using Latin and importing prayers from the Roman missal to conform the Anglican Communion Service as closely as possible to the Catholic Mass. In April 1913, Macmillan was telling Knox he was 'happy about the Faith'; Knox was urging him to adopt the practice of regular confession.[21] It was advice he accepted, according to Knox's biographer, Evelyn Waugh.[22] Macmillan pointed the contrast: 'the Protestantism of the public school life I was brought up in all seemed rather arid'.[23] What he now possessed was enticing and liberating. He was fully alive to the historical precedents: 'I and my generation at Oxford were great sympathizers with Newman. In a sense Ronnie Knox was the Newman of our time.'[24]

19 Knox, *A Spiritual Aeneid*, p. 117.

20 Penelope Fitzgerald, *The Knox Brothers* (Newton Abbot: Readers Union, 1978), p. 20.

21 Knox to HM, 6 April 1913, cited Horne, *Macmillan, 1894–1956*, p. 23.

22 Waugh, *Ronald Knox*, p. 127.

23 HM, Interview, cited Horne, *Macmillan, 1894–1956*, p. 25.

24 HM to Ava, Viscountess Waverley, 12 June 1962, Oxford, Bodleian Libraries (Bodleian), Waverley MS, c. 4779, f. 4.

'The family would be awful if it comes to the point'

'Catholicism' in his first year at Oxford was still understood exclusively within the context of the Church of England. Macmillan's practical contact with Roman Catholicism was negligible. Knox reprimanded him for frivolous criticism of 'our sister church on the continent'. On holiday in France, Macmillan had been unimpressed by the lack of reverence and the speed with which Mass was celebrated.[25]

Circumstances changed dramatically towards the end of 1913, forcing him for the first time to question his spiritual allegiance. It concerned events in a faraway place called Kikuyu in East Africa, where a conference of Protestant missionaries proposed a United Communion Service. The Evangelical bishops of Mombasa and Uganda tentatively sanctioned the possibility of Anglicans sharing pulpits and sacraments with denominations making no claim to episcopal ministry. This led the Anglo-Catholic bishop of Zanzibar to lay charges of heresy against his brother bishops. The reverberations reached Oxford. The Catholic position in the Church of England stood or fell by its claim to apostolic succession. Kikuyu appeared to put paid to that.

Knox was relatively relaxed, willing to wait for the Anglican Communion as a whole to pronounce at the Pan-Anglican Congress scheduled for 1918. His neophytes were less phlegmatic. Lawrence, accompanied by Knox, spent the Christmas vacation on the Italian Riviera for health reasons. He corresponded regularly with Macmillan as the two undergraduates contemplated the doctrinal collapse of the Church of England and formulated their response. It was not simply a handful of students overreacting. Charles Gore, Bishop of Oxford, wrote to *The Times*: 'I doubt if the cohesion of the Church of England was ever more seriously threatened than it is now.'[26]

Lawrence was the more agitated but Macmillan shared his concerns. Seventy years later he minimized the issues at stake as 'rather scholastic

25 Knox to HM, 14 August 1913, cited Horne, *Macmillan, 1894–1956*, p. 25.

26 Bishop Charles Gore, *The Times*, 29 December 1913, cited G. K. A. Bell, *Randall Davidson: Archbishop of Canterbury*, 3rd edn (Oxford: Oxford University Press, 1952), p. 694.

arguments . . . curiously unrelated to life'.[27] That was not how he viewed them at the time. With Lawrence, he envisaged secession to Rome: 'If individual Bishops are to be allowed without official censure to throw overboard these things we have been taught to love and cherish then (and Guy is very strong in this) we have hardly any alternative.' Macmillan saw this as a near inevitability. If not Kikuyu, then some similar crisis would arise. The prospect caused him 'great distress', realizing that 'the family would be awful if it comes to the point'. It was, however, where he felt his duty lay.

The undergraduate conscience was not as fixed as Macmillan had imagined. He assuaged it by firing off a letter of protest to Edward Talbot, Bishop of Winchester.[28] 'No Bishop of my acquaintance is getting a moment's peace,'[29] he proclaimed. The Archbishop of Canterbury deferred any definitive pronouncement, commissioning an inquiry. By March 1914, the immediate crisis had passed, and Macmillan reported that Guy 'has little inclination to "pope"'.[30]

Even in his spiritual turmoil Macmillan displayed a certain detached objectivity. He recognized the inconsistency of their calls to censure the Evangelical bishops when, at the other extreme, Ronnie Knox's ritualism equally flouted Anglican discipline. He articulated

> the view which I've long secretly been inclined to move to, that we are living in our little Oxford group, in rather an unreal, in some ways rather an unhealthy, dreamland of our own . . . inclination, convictions of Faith, and other reasons, would urge us to join the Roman Church. But the (humanly speaking) impossibility of helping England from outside make us feel it our duty to stick to the Anglican Church.[31]

The dilemma was accurately stated; it was not to be resolved on this occasion.

27 HM, Interview, cited Horne, *Macmillan, 1894–1956*, p. 25.
28 HM to F. F. Urquhart, 25 December 1913, Bodleian, Macmillan MS, c. 452, ff. 28–32.
29 HM to Urquhart, January 1914, Bodleian, Macmillan MS, c. 452, f. 36.
30 HM to Urquhart, March 1914, Bodleian, Macmillan MS, c. 452, f. 39.
31 HM to Urquhart, 25 December 1913, Bodleian, Macmillan MS, c. 452, ff. 28–9.

'What does matter is Christ'

It is wrong to see Macmillan as Knox's uncritical disciple obsessed with religious trivia. He discovered 'the Union as a guarantee of a healthy life at Oxford . . . a complete answer to ecclesiasticism'.[32] He found a 'guide and confessor' in F. F. ('Sligger') Urquhart, a Balliol History fellow and Oxford's first Roman Catholic don since the Reformation. Macmillan was a member of the reading party held at his chalet in Savoy in July 1913. Urquhart lacked Knox's intensity and propensity to proselytize. Consequently, Macmillan felt more able to confide in him. At the end of his first term, he was concerned that his studies had suffered from his spiritual agitation: 'But still, that doesn't matter. What does matter is Christ. Cicero must give place to Him and had to give place to Him last term.'[33] Macmillan shared his analysis of Knox with Urquhart. He stood in awe of Knox's 'intellect and his saintliness' but felt that his lack of a normal sense of humour and failure to 'understand other people' prevented him from achieving the influence he deserved.[34]

Knox planned a reading party of his own in Gloucestershire in August 1914. It was to be a spiritual retreat as much as an academic and social gathering. Macmillan was among those invited to 'Ronnie's monastery'. Lawrence urged him to accept, but he hesitated.[35] Writing to Knox, Lawrence was scathing as to the perceived reasons for Macmillan's procrastination:

> Why should [Harold] give any reason whatever for his whereabouts? It's all silly nonsense this truckling to the old-fashioned ignorance of his parents and hanging onto his mother's apron strings. I should like 5 minutes conversation with her on the point.[36]

In the event, Knox went to Gloucestershire by himself. Britain entered the First World War, and his younger friends answered the call to arms.

---

32 HM to Urquhart, December 1913, Bodleian, Macmillan MS, c. 452, ff. 24–5.

33 HM to Urquhart, 10 December 1912, Bodleian, Macmillan MS, c. 452, ff. 5–6.

34 HM to Urquhart, 4 August 1913, Bodleian, Macmillan MS, c. 452, f. 16.

35 HM to Urquhart, August 1914, Bodleian, Macmillan MS, c. 452, f. 63.

36 Guy Lawrence to Knox, u/d, cited Waugh, *Ronald Knox*, p. 128.

Macmillan did not welcome the outbreak of war; he sought a spiritual interpretation for this turn of international affairs: 'How damnable it all is. But I suppose we had to join in in honour and we must put up with this punishment for our sins, as no doubt it is.'[37] Knox, increasingly troubled by his own position in the Church of England, found it difficult to advise others. He visited Lawrence and Macmillan at their training camps and they met up in London during their leave. The two young officers intended remaining as Anglicans as they prepared to go off to battle.[38] However, independent of both his mother and Knox, Macmillan remained far from comfortable in the Church of England. He refused to attend the Anglican church parade, dismissing it as 'quite inexpressibly Protestant'. Instead, he took his Catholic soldiers off to Mass. He found the 'dear Irish priest' infinitely preferable to 'the rather pompous Anglican deans who abound here'. Yet he felt a fraud, unable to answer his men's questions about the Church and allowing the priest to think him one of his flock.[39]

'It would be almost sacrilege to do so'

The second and more serious spiritual crisis came early in the summer of 1915. Writing to another former undergraduate, Knox maintained that his young friends' distress was caused less by the prospect of departure for the Western Front and more by the return of Kikuyu to haunt consciences troubled by the validity of Anglican claims to apostolicity. Such doubts had very much disturbed Lawrence – 'and Harold too'.[40] The Archbishop's Kikuyu Commission reported at Easter 1915. It satisfied no one. Though it ruled it inappropriate to proceed with the United Communion Service in the current circumstances, it found, in principle, no objection to Anglicans sharing pulpits and Holy Communion with those not episcopally ordained. It was no longer an abstract question for Lawrence and Macmillan: their training complete, they faced the prospect of active service and the significant risk of an early death.

37 HM to Urquhart, 9 August 1914, Bodleian, Macmillan MS, c. 452, f. 62.

38 Knox, *A Spiritual Aeneid*, p. 184.

39 HM to Urquhart, January 1915, Bodleian, Macmillan MS, c. 452, ff. 71–2.

40 Knox to Richard Rawstorne, 14 June 1915, Knox Family Papers.

Lawrence visited Knox first, looking for counsel. For himself, Knox was still prepared to wait for the Pan-Anglican Congress of 1918. He recognized, however, that as a combatant, Lawrence was in a different situation. He advised him to follow his conscience and consult Macmillan. Lawrence urged Knox to join him in converting to Rome. Shortly afterwards, it was Macmillan's turn to visit Knox. He did not seek to persuade Knox to become a Roman Catholic but 'he agreed with [Lawrence] that the Anglican situation had become impossible'.[41]

Lawrence had no difficulty in discerning the way ahead. He wrote to Knox on 28 May:

> You told me to act on my own judgement and I've done so. My mind was made up for me this morning. God made it clear to me and I went straight to Farm Street, asked for Father St John and explained all to him. He took me through the faith for a little and then baptized me and received me and heard my confession. It was all done in under one hour . . . I know I am happy and I only long for you to be happy with me. Come and be happy. [Harold] will, I think, follow very soon. I am to see him this afternoon.[42]

Lawrence was sent to Gallipoli days later. Surviving the slaughter for the next three years, he was killed near Arras on 28 August 1918, having intended to try his vocation with the Oratorians, possibly together with Knox.

Macmillan did not 'follow very soon'. Knox wrote that the young officer 'did not find the transition so easy'.[43] Macmillan announced to Urquhart his intention to convert: 'Guy and I have decided to seek admission to your Church.' Why did he not follow through? Lawrence's admission to the Catholic Church was expedited given his imminent departure for active service. Macmillan was to remain in England for a few more weeks and was, therefore, expected to undergo some form of instruction.[44] It provided the opportunity for reflection. He came within a hair's breadth of conversion

41 Knox, *A Spiritual Aeneid*, p. 195.

42 Lawrence to Knox, 28 May 1915, cited Waugh, *Ronald Knox*, p. 139.

43 Knox, *A Spiritual Aeneid*, p. 195.

44 HM to Urquhart, June 1915, Bodleian, Macmillan MS, c. 452, ff. 73–4.

to Catholicism. Had Lawrence remained to hand, it is probable he would have pushed Macmillan over the line.

Just before he left for France in early August 1915, Macmillan wrote to Knox:

> I'm going to be rather odd. I'm *not* going to 'Pope' until after the war (if I'm alive).
>
> 1 My people. Not at all a good reason …
> 2 My whole brain is in a whirl. I don't think God will mind. I mean I've felt at last after a lot of thought and prayer that it would be wrong to go now. Because I can't think things calmly now. And I think somehow now that with my mind as it is, it would be almost sacrilege. If I get through, I'll go away from home and you and everything and try and find God's guidance. But I believe now that I may have to *relearn* everything.
>
> About now, I think I can't go to Mass at a RC performance, and say my prayers and that be all . . . I felt a kind of inspiration that this was right – lately.[45]

His mother's reaction, possibly the loss of his share of the family money, weighed heavily on him. It was, however, something he had been prepared to contemplate 18 months earlier. Political ambition was not an overriding factor at this point. He set out his thoughts more calmly when writing to Urquhart from France. It is clear it was his second point to Knox, the fear of possible sacrilege, that was conclusive. He admitted:

> I have come to feel so confused in thought and everything by this wild nightmare, that I feel I can't do justice to anything. I almost feel as if I had lost the faith altogether – and then again, I seem as sure as ever. So far, then, I have taken no steps to be received. I feel that as I am now it would be almost sacrilege to do so.[46]

---

45 HM to Knox, [23] July 1915, private collection, Knox Papers, X/01/2755.

46 HM to Urquhart, 22 August 1915, Bodleian, Macmillan MS, c. 452, ff. 84–5.

Macmillan did not reject the possibility of future conversion but felt unable to make such a momentous decision while unable to see clearly where God was calling him. He needed time to himself, away from Knox and, probably more so, away from Lawrence.

Others advanced a less charitable interpretation. Lord Hailsham alleged a character flaw. He maintained that, faced with difficult decisions, Macmillan was prone to panic, abandoning his initial resolve, citing Suez and 'the Night of the Long Knives' as examples. Hailsham was not a disinterested party. He blamed Macmillan for pressing him to put himself forward as a candidate for leadership of the Conservative Party in 1963, giving the impression that he was his favoured successor then changing his mind days later. It was, Hailsham argued, 'another of his famous somersaults . . . It was another retreat from the Roman Catholic Church.'[47] A disgruntled Hailsham was projecting back his analysis of Macmillan's character to an incident 50 years earlier, but there may be substance to his claim.

Some allege that 'religious issues' never meant much to Macmillan. Rather, as an undergraduate he had been temporarily intoxicated by a heady mix of incense and intimate friendships.[48] This is not borne out by his correspondence. No doubt after the austerity of home life, Macmillan revelled in the liturgy and the brilliance of the company. His letters to Urquhart, however, evidence a profound and real faith: the centrality of the person of Christ, reference to prayer, his distaste for worldliness and careerism, a concern for purity and his sheer gratitude to God for his kindness to him.[49]

'Ever so grateful to you for all you've been to me'

When Knox entered the Catholic Church in September 1917, Macmillan penned a gracious but melancholy letter to him:

47 Lord Hailsham, *A Sparrow's Flight: Memoirs* (London: Fontana, 1991), p. 356.

48 Simon Ball, *The Guardsmen: Harold Macmillan, three friends and the world they made* (London: HarperCollins, 2004), p. 24.

49 HM to Urquhart, 10 December 1912, 23 December 1912, April 1913, 4 August 1913, 25 December 1913, Bodleian, Macmillan MS, c. 452, ff. 5–6, 11, 15, 17, 32.

> It seems that, for the moment at least, the end of the journey has been reached. Reached that is by you and Guy, while I am still lagging, timid and cowardly and faint. I feel sure you are right. I hope God will bless you and you will be very happy . . .
>
> From a personal point of view, though, it's rather sad. 3 years ago we were a happy party, and all agreeing and ready to continue together. I feel horribly now like a deserter. Only I do hope you and Guy think of me at any rate as an honest 'conscientious objector' – for the moment. What the future will bring, God knows . . . I feel ever so grateful to you for all you've been to me. Honestly, I don't believe it's all been useless. There is left in me at any rate a memory; an experience never forgotten or, I hope, a turn of mind, which but for you I should never have had, remains to me – 'for information and necessary action' if God wills . . .[50]

Macmillan remained open about his reverence and affection for Knox and how close he had come to conversion.[51] The two maintained contact but substantive discussion of religion ceased – 'That was all over, in 1917,' Macmillan declared.[52]

It was not quite all over as far as Knox was concerned. Severely wounded at the Somme in September 1917, Macmillan spent the remainder of the war convalescing in London. His family still feared the influence of Knox and Lawrence, keeping watch over his hospital room to prevent Catholic visitors gaining unsupervised access. However, Knox discovered that, unknown to Macmillan's parents, visitors were allowed at midday, and he advised Urquhart to make use of the opportunity, as he did himself. He still had hopes that, freed from the attention of family and doctors, Macmillan might engage in conducive 'spiritual reflections'.[53] In fact civilian life took him in a different direction.

Macmillan once mused, only half in jest, that had circumstances differed just slightly, Knox might have been Prime Minister and he Monsignor

50 HM to Knox, 4 September 1917, private collection, Knox Papers, X/01/2755.

51 David Dilks, Private Interview, 26 September 2019; HM, *Winds of Change*, p. 43.

52 HM, Interview, cited Horne, *Macmillan, 1894–1956*, p. 33.

53 Knox to Urquhart, 17 March and 29 August 1918, private collection, Knox Papers, X/01/2757.

Macmillan.[54] Knox went on to become Catholic Chaplain at Oxford, a distinguished Scripture scholar, writer and spiritual guide to many. The end was touchingly appropriate. When Knox was dying of cancer, Macmillan invited him to stay in Downing Street for an appointment with his consultant in June 1957. Driving Knox to Paddington Station the following morning, Macmillan said: 'I hope you will have a good journey.' Knox replied: 'It will be a very long one.' To which Macmillan said: 'But Ronnie, you are very well prepared for it.'[55] Macmillan withdrew and wept.[56] Knox died ten weeks later, leaving Macmillan his copy of Kempis's *Imitation of Christ*.[57]

Because religion does not feature prominently in Macmillan's diaries and memoirs, it is easy to infer that it assumed a less important role after Oxford. It seems, rather, that one of the conclusions Macmillan drew from his relationship with Knox and Lawrence was to make faith a more private affair. Allowing his personal beliefs to surface had caused him considerable pain. He was determined it would not happen again. His later diaries were probably written with a view to publication, so that he was very cautious as to what he revealed about the interior life. There are, however, sufficient references in correspondence and elsewhere to demonstrate that Macmillan continued to draw strongly on his Christian faith throughout his life.

His library in the trenches included the classics but also the Bible, the *Imitation of Christ* and Saint Augustine's *Confessions*.[58] He attended church services when possible and read the Bible when not.[59] Good Friday 1916 found him in his dugout reading Saint Luke's account of the Passion and sharing his New Testament with his men.[60] Despite being wounded on several occasions and coming close to death, Macmillan believed that God was sparing his life for a purpose.[61] His strong faith in the resurrection meant he did not grieve at Lawrence's death: 'About Guy there is nothing to wish otherwise. He, with his love of beauty and fine pleasures, gave up

54 HM, Interview, cited Horne, *Macmillan, 1894–1956*, p. 18.

55 HM, *Winds of Change*, p. 43.

56 HM, Diary, 13 June 1957, Bodleian, Macmillan MS, d. 29, f. 64.

57 Terry Tastard, *Ronald Knox and English Catholicism* (Leominster: Gracewing, 2009), pp. 183–4.

58 HM to mother, 10 September 1915, Bodleian, Macmillan MS, d. 1/1, f. 56.

59 HM to mother, 10 July 1916, Bodleian, Macmillan MS, d. 2/1, f. 222.

60 HM to mother, 21 April 1916, Bodleian, Macmillan MS, d. 2/1, f. 38.

61 HM to Urquhart, 3 August 1916, Bodleian, Macmillan MS, c. 452, f. 136.

everything to duty. And God has him now in His keeping.'[62] Yet he was concerned for those less well prepared, writing to his mother: 'I wish that more of the young men who are taking their commissions now realized that in a few months they may be called to meet their God.'[63]

'In doing what was difficult, I had my reward in the end'

With her son surviving the war and secured for the Church of England, Nellie Macmillan appeared triumphant. Macmillan married Lady Dorothy Cavendish, daughter of the Duke of Devonshire, and was elected to Parliament. The wedding on 21 April 1920 was a splendid social occasion. Dorothy's cousin, Canon William Temple (the future Archbishop of York and later, briefly, Canterbury), was assisted by the Revd John Macmillan, a cousin of the groom, subsequently appointed Bishop of Dover and then Guildford. In her own way, Dorothy was a churchgoing Anglican, but her attention was focused on the natural, not the supernatural world.

In 1929, Dorothy commenced an affair with her husband's parliamentary colleague, Robert Boothby, which lasted for the rest of her life. Husband and wife eventually established a modus vivendi and enjoyed mutual affection, but the situation pained Macmillan enormously, especially when Dorothy pressed for a divorce to enable her to marry Boothby. Macmillan refused, not just because of the consequences for his political career but also on religious grounds.[64] He remained faithful to his marriage vows, reflecting at the end of his life: 'In doing what was difficult, I had my reward in the end.'[65]

The abdication crisis, therefore, had a particular poignancy for Macmillan. At its height, he wrote to Baldwin, congratulating him on the position he had adopted:

62 HM to Urquhart, 5 September 1918, Bodleian, Macmillan MS, c. 452, f. 153.

63 HM to mother, May 1915, Bodleian, Macmillan MS, c. 452, f. 294.

64 Thorpe, *Supermac*, pp. 93, 95, 97, 128.

65 HM, Interview, cited Horne, *Macmillan, 1894–1956*, p. 90.

> You are dealing with eternal verities here, from which no deviation is possible without disaster . . . The slightest weakness now would be a shattering blow to the whole basis of Christian morality, already grievously injured during recent years.[66]

Privately, Macmillan reverted to the subject of divorce on numerous occasions. He was not an absolutist, regretting the *Church Times*' attack on Eden's remarriage. In common with most contemporaries, Macmillan assumed that Eden was the innocent party deserted by his wife.[67] Nevertheless, he lamented 'the change in public morality and the attitude towards divorce' as he noted the number of divorced Cabinet colleagues.[68]

'Man longs to adore something or somebody'

Religion went below the radar in the interwar years but it was something to which Macmillan referred in private correspondence. A tour of Soviet Russia in 1932 provided him with much matter for reflection, musing after a visit to Lenin's mausoleum: 'Even under Communism, human nature reasserts itself. Man longs to adore something or somebody. Christ has been taken away, and Lenin put in His place.' He was amused rather than challenged by 'anti-religion museums': exhibits were crude – an attack on superstition, not religion properly understood. Entitlement to abortions in state hospitals he found an unattractive aspect of the regime.

Macmillan believed that Marxist-Leninist materialism would not endure. Once current economic and political difficulties had been resolved, he felt 'some kind of idealist philosophy' would reassert itself.[69] Viewing the Cold War in spiritual terms, he repeated his contention a generation later. Soviet Russia, he asserted, could not avoid indefinitely asking 'the old questions' that define mankind: 'Who made us? Why are we here? What

66 HM to SB, 7 December 1936, CUL, Baldwin Papers, 176/103.

67 HM, Diary, 13–15 August 1952, Bodleian, Macmillan MS, d. 12, f. 18.

68 HM, Diary, 29 June 1959, cited ed. Peter Catterall, *The Macmillan Diaries: Prime Minister and after, 1957–1966* (London: Macmillan, 2011), p. 228.

69 HM to mother, 16 September 1932, Bodleian, Macmillan MS, d. 3/1, ff. 19, 15, 40, 17, 28.

is the purpose of life? Is there right and wrong? Is there sin? Is there God?' It was essential, in the interim, that the free world did not lose its own faith.[70] Macmillan continued to ponder 'the old questions' throughout his life, even if he seldom gave them public utterance.

As Minister Resident in North Africa from 1943, he attended whenever possible the liturgy provided for the servicemen by the Anglican chaplains. His comments betrayed a changed emphasis from his undergraduate preferences. No longer did he seek out extreme ritual and devotions, assuming they were to be found in an Anglican context in a war zone. Instead, he attended matins and evensong, with the occasional Communion service. His praise was reserved for good, short sermons and hymns sung 'with great gusto' – provided no enthusiast substituted 'some new-fangled tune'. He was particularly gratified if the clergy asked him to read the lesson. Nevertheless, he retained a good eye for church furnishings. When the theatre of operations crossed to Italy, the local architecture indulged his taste for the Baroque. As the Allies advanced and his responsibilities increased, his churchgoing tended to give way to official duties or he simply stayed in bed to recover from exhaustion. It was a tendency, however, he deplored.[71]

'A somewhat squirearchical view of the Church'

After he entered 10 Downing Street in January 1957, Macmillan's interest in church affairs was not always welcomed. Relations with the Archbishop of Canterbury were frosty – Macmillan already thought Geoffrey Fisher 'a silly, weak, vain and muddle-headed man'.[72] A meeting in the first month of his premiership did not improve matters. Macmillan complained: 'I try to talk to him about religion. But he seems to be quite uninterested and reverts all the time to politics.'[73] The politician schemed against the

70 HM, Address, June 1958, DePauw University, DePauw University Video Archives.

71 HM, Diary, 11 April 1943, 4 and 18 July 1943, 13 June 1943, 22 August 1943, 25 March 1945, cited Harold Macmillan, *War Diaries: Politics and war in the Mediterranean, January 1943–May 1945* (London: Macmillan, 1984), pp. 60, 140, 155, 121, 188, 723.

72 HM, Diary, 21 July 1956, cited Thorpe, *Supermac*, p. 327.

73 HM, Diary, 8 February 1957, Bodleian, Macmillan MS, d. 28, f. 19.

prelate, enlisting the support of his brother, Arthur, an ecclesiastical lawyer and traditionally minded layman:

> Can you with your expert knowledge, think of a way I might retort? Is there no heresy which he leaves unrebuked, no liberalism lapsing into infidelity of which I could remind him? I should dearly like to counter-attack by invading his territory.[74]

Fisher, in turn, conceded that the Prime Minister 'was a keen and very well-informed churchman; but *au fond* had a somewhat squirearchical view of the Church'.[75]

They had clashed over Macmillan's introduction of Premium Bonds as Chancellor of the Exchequer in 1956. Fisher denounced the scheme as officially sanctioned gambling. At a City livery dinner, Macmillan ribbed the Archbishop on the Church of England's profits on an oil investment, expressing the hope that he now looked more favourably on Premium Bonds.[76]

There was a more significant incident in January 1960. Careless in his choice of words, Fisher warned of the dangers of materialism, fearing that modern Britons in their new-found prosperity 'may become traitors to the truth'. He continued: 'There is a dreadful current phrase. It is indeed dreadful – "We've never had it so good."'[77] Macmillan, whom he had quoted, felt bound to respond. He noted that the Archbishop had cited him out of context. Indeed, he had urged the need to secure material prosperity but also for 'moral and intellectual steadfastness'. Of course, he admitted the primacy of 'spiritual values'. Nevertheless, he had witnessed the human damage wrought by unemployment, low wages and slum dwellings in Stockton in the 1930s. He believed it 'the function of Governments to try to improve material conditions and I have always thought that the Church had supported us in this effort'. That had been the case with Fisher's 'great

74 HM to Arthur Macmillan, 11 February 1957, c. 321, cited Thorpe, *Supermac*, p. 376.

75 W. F. Purcell, *Fisher of Lambeth: A portrait from life* (London: Hodder & Stoughton, 1969), p. 266.

76 Thorpe, *Supermac*, p. 327.

77 Fisher, Sermon, Croydon Parish Church, cited *The Times*, 10 January 1960.

predecessor', William Temple.[78] Fisher replied unconvincingly that he had forgotten 'the parentage of the slogan', but offered no apology.[79]

'We brought it off'

The Prime Minister had to wait only a year for his revenge. Fisher announced his resignation on 17 January 1961. Macmillan acted with a speed and single-mindedness that caught the Archbishop off guard. He used as his excuse the Queen's imminent departure for India. Fisher had hoped to be succeeded by Donald Coggan, the Evangelical Bishop of Bradford. Macmillan had no objection to Coggan personally but wanted a complete change at Lambeth. He conceded Fisher's ability as an 'organizer'. Something different was required in his successor: 'We need now a profound thinker, scholar, Christian apologist.'[80] He is reported to have said: 'I thought we had had enough of Martha and it was time for some Mary.'[81]

Macmillan's candidate was Michael Ramsey, Archbishop of York. He approved of Ramsey's churchmanship – 'a "High" Churchman, but not an extreme Anglo-Catholic'.[82] He rated Ramsey 'a great theologian',[83] having read his recent work, *From Gore to Temple*, a survey of liberal Catholic thought in Anglican theology. Owen Chadwick, Ramsey's biographer, was impressed but felt it unlikely Macmillan would have 'perused every word of the book'[84] – a disservice to his reading capacity and theological knowledge.

Fisher reacted badly. He was '*violently*, even *brutally* opposed to Dr Ramsey'.[85] The two bishops had known each other almost half a century; Fisher had been Ramsey's headmaster at Repton. He felt Ramsey lacked

78 HM to Fisher, 15 January 1960, LPL, Fisher Papers, Vol. 251, ff. 95–7.

79 Fisher to MHM, 28 January 1960 (copy), LPL, Fisher Papers, Vol. 251, f. 99.

80 HM, Diary, 19 January 1961, Bodleian, Macmillan MS, d. 41, f. 47.

81 HM, cited Owen Chadwick, *Michael Ramsey: A life* (Oxford: Oxford University Press, 1991), p. 107.

82 HM, Diary, 19 January 1961, Bodleian, Macmillan MS, d. 41, f. 47.

83 HM to Bishop Mervyn Stockwood, 25 January 1961, c. 330, cited Thorpe, *Supermac*, p. 509.

84 Chadwick, *Michael Ramsey*, p. 105; Michael Ramsey, *From Gore to Temple: The development of Anglican theology between Lux Mundi and the Second World War, 1889–1939* (London: Longmans, 1960).

85 HM, Diary, 15 January 1961, Bodleian, Macmillan MS, d. 41, f. 45.

administrative skills and was suspicious of his churchmanship and lack of enthusiasm for the principle of Establishment. Macmillan told Fisher that he might have been Ramsey's headmaster but he was not his.[86] He left nothing to chance. Writing to Ramsey on the day Fisher announced his resignation, Macmillan declared his intention to recommend Ramsey as his successor, and asked for his response 'as soon as possible', following this up with a phone call. Assuming Ramsey's acceptance, he sought his views on Coggan's suitability for York. (They were favourable.)[87] Everything was settled and announced within the week – the two archdioceses were filled.

Fisher was furious. He objected to Coggan's nomination to York. As Macmillan pointed out, this was perverse as he had been happy to see him go to Canterbury. Fisher deprecated Macmillan's 'natural inclination to think that an Archbishop's opinion is not to be taken very seriously', protesting 'that he had been fair neither to me nor to the church'. It all went to show 'how really Victorian the P.M. is in his regard for the Church as in so many other ways'.[88] It had been a 'drama, even melodrama', Macmillan confided to his diary. 'However, we brought it off.'[89]

'A mistake to bewilder people'

The following month Ramsey was at Downing Street for 'a long talk about the future of the Church and all the episcopal vacancies which are crowding on us'.[90] Sensing a spiritual affinity with Ramsey, Macmillan candidly stated his position:

> He discoursed about his understanding of the Church and said that we had to hold the high and low together but for his part his sympathies were with the high. He added that while the evangelicals had their part in the Church he did not think that on the whole they had the qualities suitable for being bishops.[91]

86 Lord Stockton to the author, 28 May 2020.

87 HM to Ramsey, 17 January 1960, LPL, Ramsey Papers, Vol. 3, ff. 81–3; HM, Diary, 19 January 1961, Bodleian, Macmillan MS, d. 41, ff. 47–50.

88 Fisher to Ramsey, 18 January 1960, LPL, Ramsey Papers, Vol. 3, ff. 93–5.

89 HM, Diary, 19 January 1961, Bodleian, Macmillan MS, d. 41, ff. 47, 50.

90 HM, Diary, 22 February 1961, Bodleian, Macmillan MS, d. 41, f. 67.

91 Ramsey, cited Chadwick, *Michael Ramsey*, p. 104.

Fisher was not entirely wide of the mark when commenting on the Prime Minister's 'Victorian' attitude towards the Church. An avid reader of Anthony Trollope, Macmillan clearly relished exercising powers of ecclesiastical patronage. He did so as a churchman rather than a politician, disconcerting many Conservatives by his nomination of the socialist Mervyn Stockwood as Bishop of Southwark in 1958.[92] He maintained his commitment to a balance on the bench of bishops, agreeing to Ramsey's suggestion of 'a broad and liberal evangelical appointment' to the Diocese of Chelmsford.[93]

Despite his enjoyment of the role Establishment afforded him, Macmillan shared Ramsey's unease at the powers Parliament possessed over the Church of England. He feared that while most 'active Christians in the House of Commons tended to be High Churchmen, the rank and file and also the "indifferents" were sturdily Protestant in outlook'. This had been the reason for the rejection of the revised Prayer Book in 1928 and 'he hoped that the House of Commons would never again be called upon to discuss the Communion Service in detail'.[94] He was relieved when the Ecclesiastical Jurisdiction Measure passed in 1963, limiting the temporal power's disciplinary jurisdiction over the spiritual life of the Church.[95]

In the spring of 1963, Mervyn Stockwood sent Macmillan a 'sincere' and 'challenging' book by his suffragan John Robinson, Bishop of Woolwich. Macmillan read it over 'with great interest' – twice. *Honest to God*[96] sold more than a million copies and was denounced by some as heretical. It was an attempt to protect Christianity against the charge of atheism arising from the popular view of God as 'a being out there'. It is difficult to pin down what Robinson actually believed, hiding as he did behind modern German theologians, whom he cited mostly approvingly, sometimes critically. Whether he accepted the divinity of Christ is unclear, presenting him rather as the supreme witness to unconditional love. Robinson

92 Thorpe, *Supermac*, p. 507.

93 HM to Ramsey, 16 November 1961, LPL Ramsey Papers, Vol. 5, f. 126.

94 Note of conversation between HM, Ramsey and David Stephens, 28 September 1961, LPL, Ramsey Papers, Vol. 13, f. 122.

95 HM, Diary, 18 July 1963, Bodleian, Macmillan MS, d. 49, f. 159.

96 John A. T. Robinson, *Honest to God* (London: SCM Press, 1963).

criticized prayer and liturgy as an attempt to 'find' God, and appeared to reject the natural law and traditional morality.

Displaying considerable theological nuance, Macmillan's response to Robinson was not one of unthinking reaction. There is much in the book he liked – and much he disliked. He accepted that 'it may well be for the youth of today we need different symbols' to represent God. Nevertheless, he felt Robinson 'naïve' in seeking to discredit traditional symbols only to replace them with more modern ones, arguing that 'if we use symbols at all I do not see much more difficulty in imagining God up there than God down there'. He seemed to have a far better grasp of the authentic Christian tradition than Robinson: 'Whether God is represented as God the Father in conventional painting or as a series of triangles and circles, it is still only an attempt to use the material to represent the infinite.' He felt, however, the need 'to strengthen Church discipline' to prevent such 'confusion and uncertainty' entering 'many people's minds'.[97]

Macmillan thought it 'a mistake to bewilder people'. His rereading of the book enabled him to see

> even more clearly the weaknesses of logic and thinking. It is really a very naïve piece of theology and philosophy. It seems a pity that so great a circulation should be obtained by what is really no more than a *succès de scandale* . . . I cannot believe that the Bishop of Woolwich's concepts would help anybody's ordinary life.[98]

He was 'most grateful' for Ramsey's booklet, *Image, Old and New*,[99] which helped settle consciences disturbed by *Honest to God*.[100]

Ramsey was a Liberal in politics and, while there was mutual respect, the Prime Minster and the Archbishop did not agree on all matters. They discussed the morality of the possession of nuclear weapons. Macmillan formulated the theological difficulty: 'These nuclear weapons are by definition so frightful and so indiscriminate that their use by a Christian man can, so it is argued, never be justified in any circumstances.' As a Christian,

---

97 HM to Stockwood, 14 April 1963, LPL, MS 4188, f. 19.

98 HM to Ramsey, 2 May and 6 June 1963, LPL, Ramsey Papers, Vol. 50, ff. 157, 213–14.

99 Michael Ramsey, *Image, Old and New* (London: SPCK, 1963).

100 HM to Ramsey, 2 May and 6 June 1963, LPL, Ramsey Papers, Vol. 50, ff. 157, 213–14.

however, he disagreed, believing in their deterrent value 'to preserve peace and prevent holocaust'.[101]

He 'should have been a cardinal in the Middle Ages, under a strong Pope'

After the First World War, there was never any realistic possibility of Macmillan's conversion to the Catholic Church. Nevertheless, Rome retained an enduring fascination. In his diary he occasionally referred to Whitehall as 'Vatican City' and to Chequers as 'Castel Gandolfo' (the Pope's summer residence).[102] When the Allies reached Rome in 1944, Sir D'Arcy Osborne, British Minister to the Holy See, suggested that Macmillan seek a papal audience. Macmillan protested, unconvincingly, that he was not interested in that sort of thing. At his audience on 18 November, he was so overwhelmed that he was uncharacteristically lost for words and remembered little of the occasion. He reflected simply on 'the queer chance that brought me into the Vatican – a long way from St Martin's Street [the office of the family's publishing business] and further still from Arran!'[103] There were subsequent audiences with Pius XII. Macmillan empathized with his heavy responsibilities and admitted to 'being impressed by his saintliness and goodness of heart'.[104] Conversation flowed more freely. At one audience, Macmillan supposedly told the Pope 'that Christendom lacked the united front presented by Communism, and that he could take the first step towards it by the recognition of Anglican orders. The Pope merely smiled.'[105]

As Prime Minister, he had at least two audiences with Pope John XXIII. Emboldened by his success with archiepiscopal appointments in the Church of England, Macmillan tried his hand with the Church of Rome. He was accompanied at an audience on 2 February 1963 by Edward Heath and told him: 'I want [the Pope] to appoint my man as the new Archbishop

101 HM to Ramsey, 15 July 1963, LPL, Ramsey Papers, Vol. 37, ff. 369–70.

102 HM, Diary, 12 January 1964, Bodleian, Macmillan MS, d. 51, f. 71.

103 HM, Diary, 16 and 18 November 1944, cited HM, *War Diaries*, pp. 584, 586–7.

104 HM, Diary, 25 May 1945, cited HM, *War Diaries*, p. 763.

105 Archbishop Cyril Garbett, Diary, 28 April 1945, cited Thorpe, *Supermac*, p. 203.

of Westminster.' (Cardinal Godfrey, the last incumbent, had died the preceding month.) Possibly the Vatican had been forewarned, but this time he was outclassed. Although dying of cancer, John XXIII spoke for 35 minutes without pausing for breath. Macmillan had no opportunity to state his request and left frustrated. Insisting on seeing the Cardinal Secretary of State, he declared: 'I have a very good man for you to replace the late Cardinal.' The Vatican official countered: 'Prime Minister, all our top men in your country are very good men.'[106] Macmillan might have been able to finesse the Anglican establishment; his writ did not run to Rome. In his diary he alluded to the Pope's loquacity but made no reference to the purpose of his mission and its failure.

Who was the 'very good man' whose cause he was advancing? Other than Knox, who had died six years earlier, Macmillan knew few secular clergy in the Catholic Church. The most likely candidates were the Jesuits Fr Martin D'Arcy and Fr Thomas Corbishley, who moved in similar Oxford and London literary and academic circles to himself. Both shared his admiration and affection for Knox – Corbishley wrote a brief biography in 1964. Macmillan probably preferred Corbishley, an early enthusiast for ecumenism.

Macmillan once referred disparagingly to the 'atmosphere of petty intrigue' at the Vatican.[107] Yet with his sense of history and political wile, it was precisely this that appealed to him. Eden made the telling comment that his successor 'should have been a cardinal in the Middle Ages, under a strong Pope'.[108] Reading about the outcry against the 'papal aggression' of 1850, when the Catholic hierarchy was re-established in England, Macmillan was delighted to discover that the real culprits were *The Times* and a 'very low' government. A century on, nothing had changed, he mused.[109] The machinations of the First Vatican Council (1869–70) and tensions between Newman and Manning likewise beguiled him, though his interest extended to the contemporary Catholic Church. He was charmed by the conversation over a lunch Corbishley hosted at the Jesuits' Mayfair house

106 Edward Heath, *The Course of My Life: My autobiography* (London: Hodder & Stoughton, 1998), pp. 251–2.

107 HM, Diary, 29 July 1944, cited HM, *War Diaries*, p. 494.

108 Cited Robert Rhodes James, *Anthony Eden: A biography* (New York: McGraw-Hill, 1987), p. 617.

109 HM, Diary, 8 September 1963, Bodleian, Macmillan MS, d. 50, ff. 69–70.

in Macmillan's honour after his retirement: 'chiefly very critical of the Curia and enthusiastically in favour of Pope John'.[110]

Ironically, had Macmillan become a Catholic with Knox, the two may well have parted company subsequently. While Knox remained orthodox, Macmillan's sympathies lay more with liberal Catholicism. He strongly approved of John XXIII and his reforms and 'feared that there might be a fundamentalist Pope next time'. Moreover, he wished to acknowledge Pope John's achievements by creating full diplomatic relations with the Holy See during his pontificate.[111] To his disappointment, the proposal was dropped. Ramsey was 'nervous', fearing the Tory government would reap the benefit with Catholic voters, leaving the Church of England to bear the opprobrium of anti-Roman sentiment.[112]

An Anglo-Catholic?

What kind of Anglican was Macmillan? His biographers are unanimous: 'a dedicated Anglo-Catholic'; his spiritual state was 'one of High Anglo-Catholicism'; a 'devout Anglo-Catholic'.[113] This does not, however, quite fit the facts.

His village church, St Giles, Horsted Keynes, became progressively more Anglo-Catholic during his lifetime but not at his instigation. He observed with detached bemusement:

> Our little parson, Mr Eastham, gets gradually higher and higher. Having some knowledge of liturgy (from old Oxford days and Ronnie Knox and so forth) I am amused to see his slow but steady upward progress! We have now dalmatic, alb, but not maniple. We leave out the Collect for the King, but do not yet venture on the Last Gospel.[114]

110 HM, Diary, 19 March 1964, Bodleian, Macmillan MS, d. 51, f. 107.

111 Minutes of meeting of HM, Ramsey and John Hewitt, 6 March 1963, LPL, Ramsey Papers, Vol. 46, f. 184.

112 HM, Diary, 7 March 1963, Bodleian, Macmillan MS, d. 48, f. 101.

113 Horne, *Macmillan*, 1894–1956, p. 34; Thorpe, *Supermac*, p. 59; Charles Williams, *Harold Macmillan* (London: Weidenfeld & Nicolson, 2009), p. 318.

114 HM, Diary, Easter Sunday 1951, Bodleian, Macmillan MS, d. 8, f. 14.

In the country, people may feel obliged to attend the local church regardless of its churchmanship. London affords more freedom. Macmillan did not gravitate towards the capital's Anglo-Catholic 'shrine' churches. Instead, he attended St Peter's, Eaton Square – reminiscent of the 'Edwardian High' at Holy Trinity, Sloane Street, of his childhood – and occasionally evensong at the Guards' Chapel, which was Prayer Book High. However, he also went to St Michael's, Chester Square, close to his London home, which in his day was Establishment Low.[115]

The distinction between 'High' and 'Anglo-Catholic' was one Macmillan himself drew, indicating his preference for the former.[116] A High Churchman would be doctrinally orthodox but without the sacramental or ritualistic emphasis of the Anglo-Catholic. He would be loyal to the Book of Common Prayer against attempts to substitute Romanizing alternatives. This was reflected in Macmillan's insistence on attending matins, despite the rector's desire to suppress the service.[117] He was a devout communicant but, for most of his life, only monthly. His grandson agrees that it is more accurate to describe him as 'a traditional High Churchman'.[118] Macmillan noted the general liturgical trend within the Church of England: 'Even an ordinary service (not High or Anglo-Catholic) today would seem "High" or "Ritualistic" to the Churchmen of 100 years ago.'[119] Yet the victory of the High Church party was for him tinged with sadness, given his opinion 'that the C of E has lost the nation'.[120]

'I don't think a nation can live without religion'

Macmillan enjoyed ecclesiastical intrigue and gossip but they did not define his faith, even if occasionally he used them to deflect what he regarded as intrusive enquiries into intimate aspects of belief. Churchgoing

115 Lord Stockton to the author, 28 May 2020.
116 HM, Diary, 19 January 1961, Bodleian, Macmillan MS, d. 41, f. 47.
117 HM, Diary, 19 January 1964, Bodleian, Macmillan MS, d. 51, f. 78.
118 Lord Stockton to the author, 28 May 2020.
119 HM, Diary, 20 July 1963, Bodleian, Macmillan MS, d. 50, f. 3.
120 HM, Diary, 18 January 1964, Bodleian, Macmillan MS, d. 51, f. 73.

became more routine as he was freed from the cares of office. He savoured declaiming the lessons 'in great style'. During the holidays, he was known to change the Old Testament reading to one more likely to capture the imagination of the grandchildren who accompanied him to matins: 'The school children enjoy a bit of blood and violence, not boring Deuteronomy!' It stood them in good stead when it came to winning Scripture prizes.

He derived spiritual comfort and inner peace from public worship and came increasingly to rely on it. The present Lord Stockton frequently travelled overseas with his grandfather after 1963 and recalls that his priority was to establish the time and venue of Sunday service at the local church. Macmillan also attended divine service on board ocean liners, including the burial at sea of an elderly passenger who had died en route.[121] Towards the end of his life he was extremely frail and in considerable pain, requiring assistance getting in and out of cars, yet insisted on attending church as long as possible. David Dilks, his former research assistant, protested that it was unnecessary at his age to kneel. Macmillan was having none of it: 'My dear boy, it is the only permissible posture in the presence of the Almighty.'[122]

Macmillan shared with others the more entertaining and controversial details of the church histories and biographies he read, but they did not constitute the sum total of his spiritual reading. He took Augustine's *Confessions* with him to India and kept abreast of developments in apologetics, the 'attempt to defend Christianity against or in light of modern science'.[123] Scripture remained a staple. There was a Bible continuously at his bedside, with a booklet of suggested readings.[124] As his eyesight failed, the Bible and spiritual reading formed a large part of his collection of audio books.[125]

Macmillan made few references to prayer – he would have considered it inappropriate – but there is no doubt he was a man of prayer. During the period of spiritual turmoil at Oxford, he sought the prayers of others for enlightenment and the strength to do what was right.[126] Twenty years later

121 Lord Stockton to the author, 28 May 2020.

122 David Dilks, Private Interview, 26 September 2019.

123 HM, Diary, 15 March 1964, Bodleian, Macmillan MS, d. 51, f. 104.

124 Lord Stockton to the author, 28 May 2020.

125 David Dilks, Private Interview, 26 September 2019.

126 HM to Urquhart, 25 December 1913, Bodleian, Macmillan MS, c. 452, f. 32.

and in a more materialistic world, it was being revealed to him in prayer 'that those things our [Oxford] friends cared about were really worthwhile, and have won through in the end'.[127] Although never parading the fact, Macmillan also brought to prayer national and international affairs. He was elated by the news of the success of the partial Test Ban Treaty between the USA and the Soviet Union with respect to nuclear weapons: 'I have prayed hard too for this, night after night.'[128]

In March 1953, Macmillan was admitted to St Thomas' Hospital for the removal of a gallstone. He received Holy Communion from a little altar erected in his room,[129] approving of the hospital's religious character:

> This is a charming place – like a convent. The Anglican tradition is (happily) very strong – chapel morning-evening and (since my little room is near the chapel) a sort of perpetual hum of psalms and hymns and anthems and the exercise we used to know at Eton as 'organ practice' . . . The nuns (or nurses, as I think they like to be called today) are charming.[130]

In October 1963 he was operated on at King Edward VII's Hospital for the swollen prostate that caused him to resign the premiership. In between the surgery and the business of recommending a successor to the Queen, he received Holy Communion and read the Old Testament.[131]

Macmillan knew his *Decline and Fall of the Roman Empire* as well as any early twentieth-century Prime Minister.[132] Yet having read the account of the early Church, he wrote: 'It is such an extraordinary story that it cannot be explained (in spite of all his wit and cynicism) by Gibbon and his followers. It seems to allow of only one explanation.'[133] He never doubted the truth of

127 HM to Urquhart, 26 February 1933, Bodleian, Macmillan MS, c. 452, f. 195.

128 HM, Diary, 27 July 1963, Bodleian, Macmillan MS, d. 50, f. 16.

129 HM, Diary, Easter Sunday 1953, Bodleian, Macmillan MS, d. 13, f. 73.

130 HM to Ava Waverley, 2 April 1953, Bodleian, Waverley MS, c. 4778, ff. 7–8.

131 HM, Diary, 9, 20 and 27 October 1963, Bodleian, Macmillan MS, d. 51, ff. 11, 30, 41.

132 Edward Gibbon, *The History of the Decline and Fall of the Roman Empire*, 6 vols (London: Strahan & Cadell, 1776–88).

133 HM to Ava Waverley, 23 August 1960, Bodleian, Waverley MS, c. 4778, f. 80.

the Christian faith. The 'spiritual background'[134] provided by Ronnie Knox remained for life. Materialism was Western society's greatest threat:

> The unattractive side of the Norwegian 'affluent society' is its increasingly Pagan character. Christianity (they have a Lutheran church) is despised, and a sort of vague, materialistic agnostic creed flourishes (as over a large part of British life).[135]

Religion was the solution. He returned to the theme with increasing insistence in old age:

> I don't think a nation can live without religion . . . if you don't pray every night, and if you don't believe in God, and if you don't think you can serve God eventually, you can't solve all these problems and you can't even survive them . . . When you give up religion, you give up any kind of idealism.[136]

It was not a social gospel. His was an intensely personal faith – with social implications. In 1980 he told the American conservative commentator William F. Buckley: 'If you don't believe in God, all you have to believe in is decency . . . decency is very good. Better decent than indecent. But I don't think it's enough.'[137] Having lived through two world wars and the ideologies of the twentieth century, Macmillan was intensely realistic about human nature – and its need for Christianity.

Any lingering suspicion as to Macmillan's faith is dispelled by the counsel he offered Jacqueline Kennedy after the assassination of her husband:

> I am sure you must say to yourself (as I do) over and over again 'such a waste! such folly! such bad workmanship! can there really be a God, who made or guides the world' . . . when one has this terrible temptation to ask 'Why, oh why?' how terrible must have been the

134 HM to Urquhart, 11 May 1916, Bodleian, Macmillan MS, c. 452, f. 113.

135 HM, Diary, 10 June 1960, cited Catterall, *The Macmillan Diaries*, pp. 306–7.

136 HM, 'Declaration', cited Horne, *Macmillan, 1894–1956*, p. 34.

137 HM, Interview with William F. Buckley Jr, 20 November 1980, cited Horne, *Macmillan, 1957–1986* (London: Macmillan, 1989), pp. xiii–xiv.

> temptation of those simple men who, after the apparent utter failure – of the whole campaign, ending in the meanest possible form of death, by assassination on a cross – somehow managed to get a Faith to carry them on.[138]

The consolations of faith upheld him in his final years: 'I go to Communion as long as I can. At home in the house, I reach for the Bible whenever I can . . . I still find religion a great help.'[139]

Macmillan died at Birch Grove on 29 December 1986. He had been saddened when his brother, Daniel, had been cremated and his ashes scattered two decades earlier.[140] The arrangements he made for his own funeral reflected his traditional Anglican beliefs. That funeral took place on 5 January 1987 at St Giles's, Horsted Keynes, the church where he had worshipped with his family for so many years. The congregation sang the hymns he loved: 'Fight the Good Fight', 'The King of Love my Shepherd is' and 'I vow to thee, my country'.[141] Then he was buried in a corner of the churchyard with Dorothy, next to his parents and the two children who had predeceased him. The graves are notable only for their simplicity – names and dates alone are inscribed.

Six weeks later, on what would have been Macmillan's ninety-third birthday, there was a Memorial Service in Westminster Abbey. His successor as Prime Minister, Lord Home, delivered the address:

> He was always ready to testify that from his Christian faith he drew the strength for the daily round.
>
> For him we may be content that of this he was sure, totally sure, that when the time came to die he would receive at the hands of his Lord and Saviour love, and mercy and justice.[142]

Fitting testimony by one Christian statesman of another.

---

138 HM to Jacqueline Kennedy, 18 February 1964, cited Horne, *Macmillan, 1957–1986*, p. 578.

139 HM, cited Horne, *Macmillan, 1957–1986*, p. 611.

140 HM, Diary, 9 December 1965, Bodleian, Macmillan MS, d. 53, f. 103.

141 Thorpe, *Supermac*, p. 608.

142 Alec Douglas-Home, Address, Westminster Abbey, 10 February 1987, cited D. R. Thorpe, *Alec Douglas-Home* (London: Sinclair-Stevenson, 1996), pp. 467, 469.

Alec Douglas-Home (1963–1964)

'A declaration of faith'

Alexander Frederick Douglas-Home[1] was born at 28 South Street in Mayfair on 2 July 1903. He was educated at Eton and Christ Church, Oxford.

Douglas-Home contested Coatbridge and Airdrie as a Scottish Unionist (Conservative) in the 1929 general election, losing to Labour. Elected for Lanark two years later, he held the seat until 1945 and won it back in 1950. On his father's death on 11 July 1951, he entered the House of Lords as the Fourteenth Earl of Home. Following his appointment as Prime Minister, Douglas-Home disclaimed his peerage and was elected MP for Kinross and West Perthshire at a by-election on 7 November 1963. He represented the constituency until retiring from the Commons at the October 1974 general election.

In 1936, the Chancellor of the Exchequer, Neville Chamberlain, appointed Douglas-Home as his Parliamentary Private Secretary. (He had acted in a similar capacity for junior ministers at the Scottish Office and the Ministry of Labour.) He remained with Chamberlain until his resignation as Lord President of the Council in October 1940. Serving Chamberlain loyally, he suffered by association with the policy of appeasement. Tuberculosis of the spine precluded military service during the Second World War.

In May 1945, Douglas-Home was appointed Undersecretary at the Foreign Office in Churchill's caretaker government. In 1951, Churchill made him Minister of State for Scotland. Perceived as conscientious, hardworking and personable, Douglas-Home entered the Cabinet in 1955 as

1 He was known by a series of names during his long life – a personal essay in the intricacies of British titles. When his father inherited the earldom in 1918, Alec Douglas-Home received the courtesy title, Lord Dunglass. He in turn became the Earl of Home on his father's death in 1951, until he renounced his hereditary peerage in 1963. He was created a life peer, Lord Home of the Hirsel, in 1974. He is referred to as Douglas-Home throughout this chapter, the name by which he was known as Prime Minister. Having been created a Knight of the Thistle in 1962, he was Sir Alec Douglas-Home.

Secretary of State for Commonwealth Relations. His tact and firmness helped preserve Commonwealth unity during the Suez Crisis and disputes over the apartheid regime in South Africa. From 1957, he was also Leader of the House of Lords and Lord President of the Council.

There was surprise and criticism when Macmillan appointed him Foreign Secretary in 1960 – the most reckless appointment since Caligula made his horse a consul, fumed the *Daily Mirror*. The outrage was misplaced. Douglas-Home was single minded in his support of the Western Alliance, countering Soviet influence. With Macmillan, he encouraged the American President, John F. Kennedy, in his calm but firm response during the Cuban Missile Crisis, as the world stared into the nuclear abyss. He supported the UK application for membership of the EEC.

When Macmillan fell ill in October 1963 his most likely successors were deemed to be Rab Butler and Lord Hailsham. There was astonishment when the Queen, on Macmillan's recommendation, called on Douglas-Home to form an administration. It was not an establishment stitch-up – Macmillan had consulted widely; Douglas-Home was felt to be the candidate most capable of preserving party unity. He was elected party leader on 11 November 1963.

An aristocrat entering 10 Downing Street on 19 October 1963 was a gift to those wishing to portray the Tories as the outdated enemies of progress. Douglas-Home was given a difficult job. With their economic competence in question, and tarnished by a series of scandals, the Conservatives massively trailed Labour in the opinion polls. It is testimony to Douglas-Home's integrity and honesty that this gap was largely bridged during his brief premiership. Much of his time was occupied with foreign affairs and the impending general election, held on 15 October 1964. After 13 years of Conservative rule and a sense that it was time for a change, it was a considerable achievement to limit Labour's victory to just four seats. Douglas-Home resigned as Prime Minister the following day.

When it was suggested that his opposition to the Labour government was insufficiently robust, Douglas-Home stood down as leader of the Conservative Party on 22 July 1965, permitting the election of his successor according to the more transparent procedure he had introduced. Douglas-Home served again as Foreign Secretary in Edward Heath's government. One of his first acts was to expel 105 Soviet spies from their London embassy. His second term as Foreign Secretary was dominated by southern Africa, Middle Eastern crises and the UK's successful application for EEC membership. After the October 1974 general election, he returned to the House of Lords as a life peer.

Douglas-Home died at the Hirsel in Coldstream, Berwickshire, on 9 October 1995. His funeral was held at St Mary and All Souls, Coldstream, five days later.

* * *

'We knew that God was looking down on us with a forgiving smile'

As Harold Wilson relentlessly reminded the nation in the approach to the 1964 general election, his rival, Sir Alec Douglas-Home, was the product of privilege: an Old Etonian who had inherited an ancient earldom and extensive estates. He also apparently seamlessly inherited a sincere Christian faith. Youthful rebellion against parental faith is now an expectation. It was the experience of various twentieth-century Prime Ministers, including Asquith, Lloyd George, Bonar Law, Ramsay MacDonald and Attlee. Even the young Macmillan reacted against the form of his parents' religion. Douglas-Home stood in marked contrast to this pattern.

How was this achieved? Ultimately, faith is always a matter of personal response, but for Douglas-Home that choice was made easier because from his earliest years the religion in which he was raised was natural and authentic. It had its boundaries and doctrines but was not defined by restrictions and puritanical prohibitions.

A few weeks after Douglas-Home's birth, the family returned north of the border for his baptism as an Episcopalian. His religion derived from both sides of the family. Maria, his paternal grandmother (great-niece of the Prime Minister Earl Grey), suffering from tuberculosis, was sustained by an intense faith. She retained her own chaplain and built chapels at the family seats at the Hirsel and Douglas (the former, with its own chaplain until the First World War, was demolished after the Second).

A cousin wrote of her: 'She found her real vocation in spiritual devotion. Like a cloistered nun, her soul was steeped in deep inward peace and content.'[2]

Her son inherited her spiritual sensibilities. Alec Douglas-Home recalled:

> My father was the nearest thing to a saint. He could not bring himself to think ill of anyone. When in the last war, my brother Edward was a prisoner of the Japanese in the notorious camp in which so much cruelty was inflicted, someone said to my father, 'Never mind, one day we will have our revenge.' His reply was, 'What would be the point of that?'[3]

His custom of praying aloud caused his wife much embarrassment. '"Go along, you silly little man," she used to say, trying to scotch, entirely unsuccessfully, a habit my father had of offering a prayer every time he left the room.' There was nothing of the 'cloistered nun' about the thirteenth Earl. Arriving for the second service of Sunday morning to discover the parson still preaching at the first, he remarked: 'No use going in yet, Lil, the little devil's still drivelling on.' He had no compunction, between reading lessons, to pause in the nave to discuss estate matters with his tenants. Similar latitude was not extended to his children. Catching the future Prime Minister and his brother pulling faces at one another, he summarily dismissed both from the church. His faith was without affectation:

> My father never treated God as anybody very special, merely as a good friend who, although he never came in person for the shooting or the fishing, was a sportsman none the less. He therefore found it natural to treat Him naturally.[4]

---

2 Louisa, Countess of Antrim, cited Kenneth Young, *Sir Alec Douglas Home* (London: J. M. Dent & Sons, 1970), p. 7.

3 Alec Douglas-Home, *The Way the Wind Blows* (London: Collins, 1976), pp. 22–3.

4 William Douglas Home, *Mr Home Pronounced Hume: An autobiography* (London: Collins, 1979), pp. 16, 19, 26.

Alec's mother was Lady Lillian Lambton. Her faith was expressed rather differently from that of her husband – prayers were said privately in her bedroom. The emphasis was on 'God and individual salvation'. It meant for Douglas-Home: 'From my earliest years I had had my mother's and my father's teaching on Christianity on which to rely.'[5] His brother was similarly grateful:

> We knew that God was looking down on us with a forgiving smile. Thus did the tenor of our lives proceed, though disciplined, in happiness – a happiness transmitted to us from the deep well of our parents' faith in a benign, though sometimes stern, Creator.[6]

His father's standard for Christian living was stated succinctly and frequently. He 'used to din into my head week in and week out that the purpose of life was to give service to other people'.[7] 'Remember to ask yourself before you act, what the likely effect is to be on the other fellow'[8] were words not wasted on his son and heir. Every Sunday evening, his mother gave religious instruction to her children. The message was easily imbibed:

> There was a God. Jesus was His Son. We were all born in His image, and He watched us individually at work and play. He was to be loved and feared, for He would approve of us if we were good and punish us if we were naughty. So my mother taught us the difference between right and wrong as contained in the Christian code of conduct.

Understanding that the punishment was directly connected to the crime and administered fairly left Douglas-Home 'with no lingering sense of guilt and inferiority'.[9]

---

5 ADH, *The Way the Wind Blows*, p. 76.
6 Douglas Home, *Mr Home Pronounced Hume*, p. 26.
7 ADH, cited Young, *Sir Alec Douglas Home*, p. 2.
8 ADH, *The Way the Wind Blows*, p. 23.
9 ADH, *The Way the Wind Blows*, p. 22.

'Prayers and Church were a "must".'[10] Each day, family and servants gathered for formal prayer. Every Sunday, when at the Hirsel, the family attended St Mary and All Souls, the Episcopalian church on the other side of Coldstream. Douglas-Home came to appreciate and strongly support the reasons for Sunday church attendance. In his youth, however, he was not always an enthusiast:

> 'It's funny, Alec,' [his mother] would say, 'how every Sunday you've got the flu or something worse, yet, every Monday morning, you're in the shooting-brake by half-past nine.' 'Good timing, Mamma,' he would answer, grinning at her with that crooked grin.[11]

Christianity: 'an exacting but a happy religion'

Douglas-Home attended preparatory school at Ludgrove. It was not a time of spiritual growth. Worship was entirely routine; there was nothing to stimulate the imagination:

> Every Sunday we went to Church in a crocodile march, and matins was made as dull as it could possibly be . . . the average boy can only have come away with the impression that the Christian religion was at best lifeless and dull, and at worst fearful and forbidding.[12]

His experience at Eton differed considerably, thanks to one man. Cyril Alington had taught at Eton, where he was ordained, before being appointed headmaster of Shrewsbury School. He returned to Eton as headmaster the year before Douglas-Home's arrival in 1917. Ronnie Knox, who knew him at Eton and Shrewsbury, had cause to be grateful to Alington. His preaching, atypical of public schools of the period, was 'at once brilliant and easy of comprehension'.[13] Douglas-Home agreed:

10 ADH, *The Way the Wind Blows*, p. 23.

11 Douglas Home, *Mr Home Pronounced Hume*, p. 28.

12 ADH, *The Way the Wind Blows*, p. 76.

13 R. A. Knox, *A Spiritual Aeneid* (London: Longmans, Green & Co., 1918), p. 217.

'He preached the most remarkable sermons boys have ever heard.'[14] The impact was permanent:

> With his intellectual powers he had a very strong influence on the boys. He had a fine presence – tall, with classic features and a head of white hair, all set off in chapel with the scarlet cassock of a Chaplain to the King. No one who has heard them will ever forget his Holy Week sermons, or the Eton Fables [preached at evensong].[15]

Half a century later, Douglas-Home was recommending others to read Alington's Fables.[16]

Those fables were a series of imagined conversations between inanimate objects: plants, school buildings and church furnishings. They imparted 'truth embodied in a tale'.[17] The language was simple and direct, designed to engage a schoolboy's attention. Douglas-Home was confirmed at Eton. Alington made clear that Confirmation was not a matter of sentimentality. Speaking during the First World War, he employed military imagery: 'You don't join the Army because you feel good, but because you want to do your duty.' This was more than patriotism in a religious guise. Alington stressed a higher reality: 'You are always singing hymns about having a greater King and a better Country somewhere else, and you can't blame us for having supposed you meant it.'[18]

Alington knew the religious mind of his audience: 'The ordinary Englishman has a strong grasp of elementary Christian morality, but fails to see that this inevitably depends on Christian doctrine.' He provided the rational basis for the Christianity practised in the family home, and preached Christ, whose 'purpose was to encourage a certain type of life, based on a certain belief'.[19] Alington's learning and presentation of the evidence 'convinced many a doubter by the weight of the historical facts', while at the same time he avoided trying to prove too much, and admitted that

14 Alec Douglas-Home, cited Young, *Sir Alec Douglas Home*, p. 17.

15 ADH, *The Way the Wind Blows*, p. 55.

16 David Dilks, Private Interview, 26 September 2019.

17 C. A. Alington, *A Dean's Apology: A semi-religious autobiography* (London: Faber & Faber, 1952), p. 65.

18 C. A. Alington, *Shrewsbury Fables* (London: Longmans, Green & Co., 1917), pp. 32, 30.

19 Alington, *A Dean's Apology*, pp. 16, 134.

to be a Christian was an act of faith. The reality of sin and evil were acknowledged, but his starting point was rather the search for union with God, signified by Holy Communion. 'Christianity was an exacting but a happy religion' – Douglas-Home found Alington persuasive; 'Christ was God's personal messenger to man.' As a consequence, 'the gap which was to be bridged by faith is much less daunting'.[20]

Building on the foundations of a Christian home, Alington's teaching had a practical influence on Douglas-Home that was noticed by others. One clergyman wrote to his father that, during his time at Eton, Alec had done much to restore

> moral leadership among the older boys, the absence of which since the war has been one of the chief difficulties of the school . . . [He was] a real Christian in the best sense of the word with real thought in it.[21]

That faith was less prominent at Oxford. Douglas-Home graduated from Christ Church with a Third – the consequence of lack of application rather than lack of intellect. He prioritized cricket over academic study and theology.

Back in Scotland, he put into practice his father's insistence on *noblesse oblige*, entering Parliament in service of the people and the nation. Duty was not restricted to the secular sphere. Like his father, Douglas-Home was an active patron of the Boys' Brigade. Partly Christian youth group, partly cadet force, the brigade had been founded in Glasgow in 1883. Its objectives were 'the advancement of Christ's kingdom among boys' and their formation in 'Christian manliness'. Douglas-Home welcomed them to the Hirsel, as he did the summer camps of the Boys' Club from Edinburgh's Canongate Kirk.[22]

Concerned that the youth were being lost to Christianity, Douglas-Home addressed the Church of Scotland General Assembly: the youth could not be taken for granted; the clergy were taking insufficient interest; deference to parental authority had died with the Victorian age; the

20 ADH, *The Way the Wind Blows*, pp. 77, 80.

21 Very Revd Albert Baillie, Dean of Windsor, to 13th Earl of Home, cited Young, *Sir Alec Douglas Home*, p. 17.

22 D. R. Thorpe, *Alec Douglas-Home* (London: Sinclair-Stevenson, 1996), p. 37.

Church had lost its monopoly in the local community; young people now had many claims on their time and allegiance, not simply secular activities but also atheistic ideologies. Referring to Communism he declared: 'The modern pagan outlook is that if the State says, "Let us prepare for war, then the State is right. Let us be freed from the fetters of Christianity and then we can get ahead."' The young MP's solution, however, appeared amateur and vague: if young people preferred hiking to church attendance, 'Well and good: "If the hiker won't go to the Church, the Church must go to the hiker."'[23]

'A glimpse of the infinite'

Douglas-Home married in Durham Cathedral on 3 October 1936. The celebrant was the dean, his former headmaster and now father-in-law, Dr Alington. Elizabeth Alington shared her husband's deep and practical faith. When she died in 1990, *The Times* noted that her humility derived from 'the spiritual strength she found in true Christianity'. On their wedding day, the couple broke with convention, meeting at 8 a.m. in a side chapel to receive Holy Communion together from the bride's father.

The couple had four children. The baptism of the second, Meriel, caused a minor controversy when Douglas-Home invited his chief, the Unitarian Prime Minister, Chamberlain, to act as godfather. The participation of a non-Christian scandalized more rigorous Anglicans. For Douglas-Home, it was more important that Chamberlain was 'a God-fearing man' of blameless life. Lambeth Palace agreed.[24]

According to their son, their home was Christian in practice and tone but less stern than that of his grandparents. The formal prayers that had begun each day were dropped. Instead of spoken grace before meals, a moment's silence was kept. Douglas-Home never forced his religion on his children. They were expected to attend church but he was no strict disciplinarian.

---

23 ADH, Address to the Church of Scotland Assembly, 27 May 1935, cited Young, *Sir Alec Douglas Home*, p. 44.

24 Revd A. C. Don to Revd A. J. Meek, 20 February 1940 (copy), LPL, Lang Papers, 175, ff. 121–2.

The children were taken to the Three Hours' Devotion on Good Friday – but permitted to go fishing after the second hymn.[25]

Early in his marriage Douglas-Home's physical, mental and spiritual powers were tested to the limit. He was diagnosed with tuberculosis of the spine. In September 1940 he endured six hours' surgery with no guarantee of success. For two years he was encased in plaster, able to move only his forearms. It afforded ample opportunity for reflection. The experience of physical suffering intensified his faith. This reserved aristocrat was not given to 'vivid religious experience[s]', but at this time of illness he 'looked over the edge. A glimpse of the infinite.'[26] He wrote of the transformation effected by his suffering:

> For many years I was content to accept Christianity at second hand . . . I began to concentrate my mind. It was then that I finally became convinced that there must be a God, and if that were so the Christian interpretation of His nature was difficult but not impossible.[27]

'An element of witness'

His family believed that Douglas-Home regarded religion as a private matter, something seldom to be spoken of. His son was therefore 'surprised' that his father had been prepared to speak publicly about his Christian faith.[28] Again, perhaps it was the experience of suffering, and gratitude for recovery, that sharpened his sense of duty. He told the Church of Scotland General Assembly: 'In politics there must be leadership and in the leadership of a Christian nation, there should be an element of witness.'[29] Douglas-Home was almost unique among his political contemporaries in this willingness to be that public witness to Christian faith.

25 15th Earl of Home, Private Interview, 2 August 2020.

26 ADH, cited Young, *Sir Alec Douglas Home*, p. 18.

27 ADH, *The Way the Wind Blows*, p. 78.

28 15th Earl of Home, Private Interview, 2 August 2020.

29 ADH, 'Morals, Politics and the Nation', Address to the Church of Scotland General Assembly, 28 May 1962, cited ed. Eldon Griffiths, *Peaceful Change: A selection of speeches by Sir Alec Douglas-Home* (London: Arthur Baker, 1964), p. 50.

In the 1930s he had urged Christian ministers to go hiking to reconnect with the youth. The ordeal he subsequently endured forced him to clarify his thought and gave him the courage to articulate it. In 1946 he accepted an invitation to the Christian Leadership Conference, a gathering of youth leaders in Edinburgh, where he spoke alongside a Presbyterian and a Catholic on the subject, 'Why I believe in God.'

Douglas-Home's address was coherently argued, bearing rereading in the twenty-first century. He started with the existence of God and man's 'incurably inquisitive' nature. For him, science was not a stumbling block to belief. It was implausible to suggest that an 'ordered evolution' leading up to 'the existence of life and in particular the life of man' with capacity for thought, control of his environment and creation was the product of chance. Science is only possible because the universe is ordered: 'The probabilities lie with a creator and controller; with a Supreme Being, with a God.'

What was the purpose of life? We differ fundamentally from the rest of the animal kingdom. We alone do not act simply on instinct; we alone possess a conscience, the desire for truth and the capacity for free choice. Inanimate matter is incapable of giving rise to this spiritual dimension. Douglas-Home argued that 'the mind is the passport to immortality and that man is the instrument through which God will achieve the purpose of creation.' He concluded with his personal credo:

> I believe in God the Maker of heaven and earth, and in God the Maker of man, the Giver of man's mind, and I believe in a Christian God Who sent Christ into the world to give man the promise that the purpose of creation was Good.[30]

'One has to confess one's faith'

Delivered by a relatively unknown former Tory MP, that address attracted little notice outside Scottish ecclesiastical circles. When he spoke to the

30 ADH, 'I believe in God', Christian Leadership Conference, 21 September 1946, cited ADH, *The Way the Wind Blows*, pp. 78–81; Young, *Sir Alec Douglas Home*, pp. 72–3.

Church of Scotland General Assembly in 1962, however, it was as Foreign Secretary. Superficially less a personal testimony, it still bore witness to his fundamental beliefs. Douglas-Home took as his theme the role of religion in national and political life. He trod cautiously. Acknowledging the Church's primary duty to nurture the relationship between God and humanity, the salvation of souls, he quickly moved to more familiar territory. As we are social creatures, the Church 'must also be concerned with man in society'. It was bound 'to hold before the community the ideal of the good life'.

Could it be said that the British people and their politicians in the 1960s were 'inspired by a Christian ethic'? It would be easy to answer no. Douglas-Home was less certain. How else could one explain the commitment to free education, the concern for peace and disarmament, the fact that legislators found it easier to pass laws if they were morally right rather than merely politically expedient? He argued that in large part it was 'because the teaching "do unto others as you would they should do unto you" has sunk into our national bones'. His conclusion again was an uncompromising call to national witness: 'to discover God and to know God. Then we may yet claim to be a God-fearing Christian country.'[31]

As a self-identified Christian politician in the Swinging Sixties, Douglas-Home received numerous requests to deliver 'homilies, moral stands'. Most he declined, thinking it 'an arrogant thing to do', not wishing to imply that his political opponents were in any way morally inferior. His last major foray into the field was as Shadow Foreign Secretary, addressing Cambridge undergraduates in 1967. He passed on his father's counsel: before acting, ask always the effect it will have on your neighbour. In nine out of ten situations, Douglas-Home maintained, in international affairs, industrial relations and matters of personal morality, 'The answer will be clear and the individual will know what the right answer is.' He argued that Britain could only be understood in terms of Christianity, a faith that science had not disproved. Christ's teaching that our 'heavenly salvation' was connected to our behaviour on this earth remained true.[32]

Occasionally, Douglas-Home also ventured into print. Writing in a Sunday newspaper, he maintained that the best way of coming to know God

31 ADH, 'Morals, Politics and the Nation', cited ed. Griffiths, *Peaceful Change*, pp. 47–50.

32 ADH, Address, Great St Mary's Church, Cambridge, 19 November 1967, cited Young, *Sir Alec Douglas Home*, pp. 260–2.

was through knowledge and tolerance of one's neighbour. His bishop, the Bishop of Edinburgh, 'came down on [him] like a ton of bricks', claiming that Douglas-Home had just inverted Christianity. Knowledge of God was a prerequisite for love of neighbour. Douglas-Home accepted the rebuke but not the premise. He concluded his correspondence with the bishop in stating his belief that he knew no better way of living the Christian faith.[33]

Baldwin excepted, previous twentieth-century Prime Ministers had tended to avoid public references to personal belief. Margaret Thatcher and Tony Blair acknowledged in their autobiographies that they were believing and practising Christians, but references to faith were scattered and not systematic. In 1976, Douglas-Home published his memoirs, *The Way the Wind Blows*. The fifth chapter was entitled, 'A Declaration of Faith.' He began: 'There comes a moment when one has to confess one's faith, and perhaps this is the right place to do so.' He proceeded to give an account of his faith since childhood. There was little by way of dramatic incident, no suggestion of spiritual pride. He simply asserted that he owed his happiness and confidence to his faith in God.[34] In a series of letters to his grandson, Matthew Darby, published subsequently in 1983, he dealt with the Christian response to issues of war and peace, defence and disarmament.

'Religion, service and sacrifice'

What impact did his Christian faith have on his politics? Two months after his arrival in Downing Street, Douglas-Home set out his philosophy. Affluence, by itself, he argued, was an inadequate response to socialism and Communism, and material gain was no substitute for 'religion, service and sacrifice'. Religion was 'still the basic if subconscious influence in the life of the British people', and they responded best to requests for service and sacrifice. Christian teaching provided the best basis for social conduct.[35]

Throughout his political life he resolutely opposed Communism, which he perceived as destructive of 'every other creed and every other way of

33 ADH, *The Way the Wind Blows*, p. 82.

34 ADH, *The Way the Wind Blows*, pp. 76–82.

35 ADH, Personal Minute to Sir Michael Fraser, 30 December 1963, cited Young, *Sir Alec Douglas Home*, p. 188.

life'.[36] He expounded his thought in correspondence to his grandson. The essence of Christian practice, for the individual and for the nation, was 'tolerance and trust, and turning the other cheek to the man next door'. However, having lived through two world wars and the Cold War, he was a realist:

> Dictators place a Christian democracy in a cruel dilemma. We are instructed by our religion to respect our neighbour, and that the meek shall inherit the earth . . . What attitude, however, does a Christian society take when the crunch comes and everything, including its religion, is in imminent danger of forcible take-over by alien arms and an alien doctrine?

He did not doubt the sincerity of pacifists. Christianity counselled conciliation and 'restraint in the use of power'. However, 'I can find nothing in the Christian teaching which denies to me or to my companions in democracy, the right to defend life and the basic values which make it worth living, against those who aim to destroy them.' Nor did his faith require him to relinquish the nuclear deterrent, which restrained 'a potential aggressor by making the risk of war too high'.[37]

It was not simply political theory. Travelling to Moscow to sign the Test Ban Treaty in August 1963, Douglas-Home ensured that there was a church service in the British Ambassador's residence on the Sunday. He chose and read the lesson, from Mark 9: 'have peace with one another'. (Heath, the Lord Privy Seal, played the harmonium.)[38] This was supposed to have impressed the Soviets, though how many were aware of this act of Christian witness? The power of prayer was less easy to quantify.

Macmillan delighted in the exercise of ecclesiastical patronage, pitting his wits against obdurate prelates. Such an approach was distasteful to Douglas-Home. He was there to do his duty by Church and country. The Lambeth Palace files demonstrate his inclination to accept the recommendations proffered him. There was relief, as well as gratitude, in

36 ADH, *The Way the Wind Blows*, p. 250.

37 Lord Home, *Letters to a Grandson* (London: Collins, 1983), pp. 9, 21–3, 123–4.

38 Thorpe, *ADH*, p. 265.

Archbishop Michael Ramsey's letter written on Douglas-Home's departure from Downing Street:

> I am so grateful for all the trouble and care which you gave to church matters which came to you, and I have a feeling that you enjoyed that part of your task! You certainly could not have helped me more.[39]

'The simple message of Christ'

Douglas-Home was not uncritical of the Church. He lectured the Church of Scotland General Assembly in 1962:

> If I dared to offer advice, I believe the Church would increase its influence if it paid less attention to forms of worship and more to the simple basic teachings of Christ. Too often they are overlaid by doctrine and dogma against which intelligence revolts. There must of course be rules and discipline . . . Do not allow the pure teaching of the 'Good Neighbour' to be overlaid.[40]

Accepting that others would consider him naïve, he had no interest in liturgy or denominational disputes: 'I was, and am, impatient of the muddle and confusion and division which the Churches have made of the simple message of Christ.'[41] Issues of real substance separated Christians but they did not trouble the Prime Minister. He felt able to maintain a personal relationship with his God without having to consider or resolve such matters.

One biographer claimed that Douglas-Home's 'Christianity was of the heart, not of the pew'.[42] The quintessential countryman, whose passions were racing, shooting and fishing, he cheerfully acknowledged:

39 Michael Ramsey to ADH, 28 October 1964, cited Thorpe, *ADH*, p. 375.

40 ADH, 'Morals, Politics and the Nation', cited ed. Griffiths, *Peaceful Change*, p. 49.

41 ADH, *The Way the Wind Blows*, p. 78.

42 Thorpe, *ADH*, p. 62.

> It is in nature that I find myself in perfect tune with creation, and can discover and rediscover peace of mind. Beauty in its purest form I find in the beasts and the birds, the butterflies and the flowers. Nothing can take that away, and surely perception of it must be at least a part of the passport to the heart of the Creator?[43]

Yes, nature as a pathway to God but, as he says, only in part. Douglas-Home strongly advocated Sunday church attendance. Its decline saddened him. He recognized that earlier generations might have attended for mixed motives, but they had derived some benefit:

> At its highest it was good for the spirit; at its lowest it was no bad thing for at least once a week to subordinate one's wishes to those of others . . . With the decline of religious observance I believe that some virtue has departed from the British people.[44]

Douglas-Home practised what he preached and went to church every Sunday without fail. The necessity of forming a Cabinet during his first weekend in Downing Street did not prevent him attending St James's, Piccadilly, on the Sunday morning.[45] When at the Hirsel he was present at St Mary's, Coldstream. In London his preference was for the Guards' Chapel and later Chelsea Old Church.[46] His Christianity was encapsulated in Psalm 23, 'The Lord's my Shepherd', and the hymn, 'Come down, O Love Divine'.[47]

Given his preference for traditional, mainstream Anglican worship, it is surprising to discover that Douglas-Home was friends with, and influenced by, the American evangelist Billy Graham. They first met in 1960 as houseguests of the Governor General of Southern Rhodesia and remained in contact. Initially, Douglas-Home was nervous. When Graham called on Downing Street, the Prime Minister summoned his brother for moral support, fearing that otherwise 'he might ask me to get down on my knees and

43 ADH, *The Way the Wind Blows*, p. 284.
44 ADH, *The Way the Wind Blows*, p. 280.
45 Thorpe, *ADH*, p. 321.
46 15th Earl of Home, Private Interview, 2 August 2020.
47 ADH, *The Way the Wind Blows*, pp. 82–3.

say a prayer, or something'. The two brothers succeeded in restricting conversation to racing.[48]

Douglas-Home candidly admitted that he was not 'particularly attracted by the spectacular stage-management of his Christian circus', but readily conceded that Graham 'got results'. He approved the 'plain simplicity of his message'. What mattered was that Graham 'spread the hope and joy of Christianity'.[49] When the American threw a dinner party in London, the guests included Douglas-Home, Cliff Richard and a member of the royal family. They spent the evening discussing Christianity, 'especially the deity of Jesus Christ'.[50]

Douglas-Home never claimed that virtue resided exclusively in any one denomination, but he did not doubt the truth of the Christian faith: 'No religion, he thought, presented any better rules for social conduct than Christianity.'[51] He did not despair because, as the truth, 'it will in due time once more command the allegiance of man'.[52] One of his final political acts was to lobby during the passage of the 1988 Education Bill for the centrality of Christianity in the teaching of religious education in schools.

'The hope of a God who is a Redeemer'

When Douglas-Home died, a private funeral was held on 14 October 1995 at St Mary's, Coldstream. He was buried nearby in Lennel churchyard, alongside his wife and close to the banks of his beloved Tweed. Services of Thanksgiving were held in St Giles's Cathedral, Edinburgh, on 4 December 1995 and in Westminster Abbey on 22 January 1996.

A Cabinet member advised an early biographer: 'Don't search for an answer to an enigma – there isn't an enigma.'[53] That was as true spiritually as it was politically. Douglas-Home was arguably the least complex and most

48 Douglas Home, *Mr Home Pronounced Hume*, p. 103.

49 ADH, *The Way the Wind Blows*, p. 77.

50 Billy Graham, *Just As I Am: The autobiography of Billy Graham* (London: HarperCollins, 1997), p. 688.

51 Young, *Sir Alec Douglas Home*, p. 190.

52 ADH, *The Way the Wind Blows*, p. 280.

53 John Dickie, *The Uncommon Commoner: A study of Sir Alec Douglas-Home* (London: Pall Mall Press, 1964), p. vii.

decent occupant of Downing Street in the twentieth century. His faith was inherited from his family, nourished by an exceptional headmaster and strengthened by the experience of physical suffering. Life, for him, was 'only lived by the grace of God'.[54] He concluded his autobiography:

> I am glad that I was brought up in the Christian faith and provided with the hope of a God who is a Redeemer . . . My belief may not be rational. It may be intuitive. It cannot be proved. But it is for me, today, for tomorrow, and I trust for always, 'The way the wind blows.'[55]

54 ADH, *The Way the Wind Blows*, p. 280.
55 ADH, *The Way the Wind Blows*, p. 285.

Harold Wilson (1964–1970 and 1974–1976)

'A man without religion?'

James Harold Wilson was born in Cowersley, near Huddersfield, on 11 March 1916. He was educated at Royds Hall Grammar School, Huddersfield, Wirral Grammar School and Jesus College, Oxford.

After time as an Oxford don and war work as a Civil Service economist, Wilson was elected as the Labour MP for Ormskirk in 1945. Following boundary changes, he represented Huyton from 1950 until his retirement from the House of Commons in 1983.

Immediately upon his election, Wilson was appointed Parliamentary Secretary at the Ministry of Works. Promotion came quickly. Made Secretary for Overseas Trade in March 1947, he entered the Cabinet later the same year as President of the Board of Trade. There he oversaw increasing exports and the ending of various wartime rations and restrictions. He resigned in 1951 in protest against NHS prescription charges introduced to fund military expenditure during the Korean War.

Wilson entered the Shadow Cabinet in 1955, speaking on trade matters. Hugh Gaitskell, the newly elected party leader, appointed him Shadow Chancellor later that year. Opposing Gaitskell's attempt to drop Labour's commitment to nationalization, he unsuccessfully challenged him for the Labour Party leadership in 1960. He served as Shadow Foreign Secretary from 1961. After Gaitskell's unexpected death, Wilson stood again and, benefiting from a split in the vote on the Right, was elected on 14 February 1963. He was an effective leader of the Opposition, fighting a tired Conservative administration beset by scandal. Avoiding contentious issues that divided the Labour Party, he campaigned on a platform of modernization, technological development and investment.

The result of the general election on 15 October 1964 was surprisingly close. The Labour Party won an overall majority of just four, and Wilson was appointed Prime Minister on 16 October. His dynamism and studied moderation were rewarded at the general election of 31 March 1966, when the government majority increased to 97.

The newly created Department for Economic Affairs announced a National Plan to coordinate all areas of development over a five-year period. Many economic objectives, however, were sacrificed to the defence of sterling, ultimately unsuccessfully – the currency was devalued in November 1967. Wilson's 'pound in your pocket' broadcast, claiming that the public would be unaffected by devaluation, severely damaged his reputation for economic competence. He sought to reform industrial relations but proposals outlined in the paper 'In Place of Strife' were rejected by both the unions and the Labour Party.

Wilson prevented British involvement in the Vietnam War but reliance on American financial support limited his scope to criticize US action. Withdrawal from military bases east of Suez was a recognition of economic realities and Britain's diminished status as a world power. Wilson was a hesitant supporter of the UK's second application for membership of the EEC, which was blocked in 1967 by the French President, Charles de Gaulle, who thought the UK still too closely allied to the USA.

Although Wilson focused on economic and foreign affairs, arguably the greatest changes effected by the 1964–70 government were social. Access to tertiary education was expanded with the foundation of new universities and polytechnics. Comprehensive schools increasingly replaced selective education. The death penalty was abolished and laws relating to abortion, homosexuality, divorce and censorship were relaxed. Legislation against racial discrimination was enacted. Wilson portrayed himself as the embodiment of a new classless and egalitarian society.

After a series of disastrous by-elections and opinion polls, living standards and the balance of trade improved significantly from 1969. Wilson felt confident in calling a general election on 18 June 1970. However, he underestimated Edward Heath, who led the Conservatives to an unanticipated victory. Wilson resigned as Prime Minister on 19 June.

In the dire economic circumstances resulting from the 1973 oil crisis and the miners' strike, Heath called a general election on 28 February 1974 on the question of who governed Britain. The Conservatives were widely expected to win but Wilson managed to broaden the debate and present

Labour as the party of moderation. Gaining fewer votes than the Conservatives, Labour nevertheless won four more seats. When Heath failed to form a coalition with the Liberals, Wilson was appointed Prime Minister of a minority government on 4 March. He promptly settled the strike on terms favourable to the miners and appealed to the country again on 10 October 1974, this time winning a three-seat majority.

Wilson, seeking to resolve party divisions, called a referendum on 5 June 1975, on continued membership of the EEC, to which the UK had only finally acceded in January 1973. He achieved a decisive majority for continued membership, while maintaining Labour unity. His final period in office was marred by industrial disputes, scandals involving those around him and paranoia about an alleged 'dirty tricks' campaign by the media and security services. The unexpected announcement of his resignation on his sixtieth birthday led to speculation as to his motivation. He left Downing Street on 5 April 1976. Wilson was viewed by some as an unprincipled opportunist, yet he effected significant change during his long tenure of office and led Labour to four general-election victories – in sharp contrast to its electoral record in the 1950s and 1980s.

He was created a Knight of the Garter in 1976. Leaving the Commons in 1983, he entered the House of Lords as Baron Wilson of Rievaulx.

Wilson died on 24 May 1995. His funeral service was held at St Mary's Church in the Scilly Isles.

* * *

'Making a reality of Christian principles'

Harold Wilson had a quick mind and a reputation for pragmatism. He recognized that the roots of the British Labour Party lay more in Methodism than Marxism. Great numbers, he wrote, 'had joined Labour because they believed that socialism was a way of making a reality of Christian principles in everyday life'.[1] Politically astute, he was fully aware that in

1 Harold Wilson, *Memoirs: The making of a Prime Minister, 1916–64* (London: Weidenfeld & Nicolson, 1986), p. 182.

the early 1960s, moderate opinion within the party and the wider electorate was still largely Christian in sympathy if not always in practice. At the 1962 Party Conference, he quoted the nineteenth-century American poet J. R. Lowell:

> Man is more than Constitutions; better rot beneath the
> sod,
> Than be true to Church and State while we are doubly
> false to God!
> We owe allegiance to the State; but deeper, truer, more,
> To the sympathies that God hath set within our spirit's
> core.[2]

Wilson knew how to invoke Christian sentiments and vocabulary. To what extent was it reflected in his own convictions and practice? Even political colleagues claimed that references to Labour's religious roots amounted to no more than cynical opportunism.

Like Asquith 60 years earlier, Wilson was the product of Yorkshire Congregationalism. Originally farmers from Rievaulx in the North Riding, the Wilsons had been Nonconformist in religion and radical in politics since the seventeenth century. Religious independence was equated with social justice, educational opportunities and, as Wilson noted, the application of Christian principles. His father was fond of quoting the phrase 'What is morally wrong can never be politically right.'[3]

Wilson's paternal grandfather, James, had moved to Manchester. Wilson remembered him as 'a deeply religious man who believed that politics represented the nation's application of religious principles'. His maternal grandfather, William Seddon, was a deacon, treasurer and Sunday-school superintendent of the Lees Street Congregational Chapel in Openshaw, Manchester. As with the Wilsons, there was no separating his religion and politics. To celebrate the Liberal landslide in the 1906, Seddon announced

2 J. R. Lowell, 'On the Capture of Fugitive Slaves near Washington', *The Complete Poetical Works of James Russell Lowell* (Boston and New York: Houghton Mifflin Co., 1896), p. 82.

3 HW, *Memoirs*, p. 34.

the singing of the hymn, 'Sound the loud timbrel o'er Egypt's dark sea! Jehovah hath triumphed, his people are free.'[4]

The Lees Street Chapel featured large in the life of the family. Wilson's parents, Herbert and Ethel, taught in its Sunday school. They were married there by the Revd Robert Sutton, who had married Ethel's own parents a generation earlier. He baptized Ethel and then Wilson's elder sister, Marjorie. The Wilsons left Manchester in 1912 when Herbert found employment as a chemist in the textiles industry in Huddersfield. They returned to Openshaw, however, so that Harold too could be baptized by Sutton.[5]

The Wilsons were typical of the early twentieth-century English lower middle classes in that the Christian faith underpinned their lives, and yet was seldom explicitly mentioned in the home. There the practice of the faith was limited to the saying of grace before meals and the singing of hymns with friends around the piano on Sunday evenings. Old-fashioned Protestant sabbatarianism still made itself felt.[6] Wilson was in his fifties before he could 'sit down on a Sunday night, say, pick up a book, a biography or some historical essays, and sit back without any feeling that [he] *oughtn't* to be doing it'. It left a lasting impact: 'I can't say I admire conventional puritan morality.'[7]

Chapel and the Scouts

The outward manifestation of religion was regular chapel attendance. The Wilsons and the Seddons were Congregationalists, but with no chapel of their own denomination close by, the family went each Sunday to the 10.30 a.m. service at Milnsbridge Baptist Church. The minister, the Revd W. H. ('Pa') Potter, was a considerable figure in the locality. Wilson and his sister returned in the afternoon for Sunday school, where he was remembered for asking, and answering, a great many questions. Both parents taught at the Sunday school. His father was secretary of the Church Amateur Operatic Society, his mother the founder of the Women's Guild.

4 HW, Interview with Kenneth Harris, *The Observer*, 1966, cited Kenneth Harris, *Conversations* (London: Hodder & Stoughton, 1967), p. 266.

5 Leslie Smith, *Harold Wilson: The authentic portrait* (London: Hodder & Stoughton, 1964), p. 15.

6 Smith, *HW*, pp. 17–8.

7 HW, *The Observer*, 1966, cited Harris, *Conversations*, p. 273.

Potter's sermons failed to capture Wilson's imagination. This created problems back home when his housebound grandfather quizzed him on the content. In order to pass muster, Wilson resolved to memorize them systematically in future.[8]

In 1960, Wilson reminisced about his early years: 'Life revolved around the chapel', he wrote, adding significantly, 'and for me the Scout troop, which met in the basement below the chapel building.'[9] His official biographer remarked: 'Scouting and religion fused in Harold's mind, scouting taking on a semi-mystical significance, religion being a matter of practical good deeds.'[10] The identification of faith with the Scout movement is unsurprising. Potter was also the Scoutmaster, and ran the troop as an extension of the chapel. Prayer and an exhortation to Christian living formed part of each meeting; Sunday-school attendance was a condition of membership. Potter was a more effective youth leader than a preacher. Regarded with genuine affection by the Scouts, he held advanced views for his age, happily discussing any issue they wished to raise, including questions of sex and morality.

Wilson's father went on to become the District Commissioner for the Scouts, his mother a Guide Captain.[11] He himself became a Patrol Leader in the 3rd Colne Valley Milnsbridge Baptist Scouts.[12] He relished the practical outreach, the outdoor activities and the authority their hierarchical structure offered him.

The Scouts were also responsible for Wilson's continuing attachment to Christianity. Annually, on Scout Sunday, Potter handed over the service at the Baptist Church, including delivery of the sermon, to the Scouts. One of the Rovers, who had never set foot in the pulpit previously, proved a more persuasive preacher than the minister. He took as his text 'He hath made of one blood all the nations of the earth' (Acts 17.26). Wilson was struck; for the first time he recognized that Christianity had a relevance and coherence. An address on Scout Sunday the following year on the text 'I have

8 Smith, *HW*, pp. 17, 30.

9 HW, 'Why I Believe in God', *Sunday Express*, 4 December 1960.

10 Philip Ziegler, *Wilson: The authorised life of Lord Wilson of Rievaulx* (London: Weidenfeld & Nicolson, 1993), p. 6.

11 Smith, *HW*, pp. 28–9, 17.

12 HW, *Memoirs*, p. 16.

come that ye may have life and have it more abundantly' (John 10.10) made a similar 'indelible impression'. He later claimed: 'Those two texts – more than any other – gave me my philosophy and an inspiration which led me into political life. They still hold for me the key to all the complicated issues of domestic and world politics.'[13] He did not elaborate on the claim.

After a period of unemployment, Herbert Wilson found work in Cheshire and the family moved to the Wirral in 1932, where Harold attended Wirral Grammar School. The staff were practising Christians, and for the first time he was challenged to think seriously about matters of faith. The family were able to worship at a church of their own denomination, enrolling as members of the Highfield Road Congregational Church in Rock Ferry, Birkenhead. Built in 1870–1, it is an imposing stone structure with spire, stained glass and a series of vestries and lecture halls. In one respect at least, the minister, Mr Patterson, scored higher in Wilson's estimation than 'Pa' Potter, and he rated Patterson 'a very fine preacher'.[14]

Wilson's attention, however, might not have been exclusively focused on the preaching at the Rock Ferry church. He met Gladys Mary Baldwin[15] at the local tennis club in 1934. They quickly discovered that they belonged to the same church, but had never met because his family attended the morning service while Mary went in the evening. Wilson rapidly changed his churchgoing habits and proceeded to walk Mary home afterwards.[16] The two were to be together for the next 61 years.

Religion was a rather intense affair in Mary's childhood home. For the Wilsons, the chapel was the venue for various practical and secular activities. The Baldwins took the doctrinal content of faith more seriously. Mary's father, the Revd Daniel Baldwin, was a Congregational minister. He featured in the poetry Mary wrote later in life:

> Within the study, where the sunlight never falls
> My father writes his sermon, hooded eyes down-bent;
> He shapes each phrase, deploys each argument
> And turns from time to time instinctively

13 HW, 'Why I Believe in God'.

14 HW, *Memoirs*, pp. 30–1.

15 Wilson's wife only chose to be known by her middle name, Mary, in the 1950s.

16 Smith, *HW*, p. 65.

To the great Bible open on his knee.[17]

Mary had been required to commit whole passages of Scripture to memory, attending chapel as often as five times on a Sunday.[18] She recalled: 'I had been brought up in a tradition in which showing-off was frowned upon, and in which the Bible was taken literally.'[19] The fundamentalism and fervour had receded by the time the couple met, but Mary continued to believe and practise her faith. Their shared Nonconformist background informed the couple's values on matters of social equality and justice.

Oxford: Congregationalism, the Christian Union and the Oxford Group

Winning an exhibition to read History at Exeter College, Oxford, Wilson later transferred to Philosophy, Politics and Economics. There was no rejection of his northern Nonconformity, and he attended church every Sunday during his undergraduate years. On his first Saturday in Oxford, Wilson visited Dr Nathaniel Micklem, Principal of Mansfield College, at the time a Congregational theological training college. Wilson found him 'a really nice fellow'. Micklem differed from the ministers Wilson had known previously. From a family of Liberal gentry, he moved effortlessly between the worlds of religion, scholarship and politics. For many years, he was President of the Oxford Liberal Association. Attacked by conservative Congregationalists for teaching Thomistic philosophy to his students and promoting a more formal style of worship, he was also criticized by modernists for his defence of the revealed content of faith. Unlike those ministers Wilson knew from home, Micklem was not a strict teetotaller.

His urbane liberality appealed to Wilson, flattered by the courteous interest shown in him. He 'thoroughly enjoyed the services' at Mansfield and resolved to attend every Sunday. Micklem put him in contact with the Dale Society, a Congregationalist student discussion group, which met on

17 'The Old Manse', Mary Wilson, *Selected Poems* (London: Hutchinson, 1980), p. 52.

18 Ben Pimlott, *Harold Wilson* (London: HarperCollins, 1992), p. 30.

19 Mary Wilson, *The Guardian*, 10 May 1976.

Sunday afternoons.[20] Wilson listened to speakers explaining the connection between faith and action, including on matters of race relations and Third World development, and often spoke himself.

His religious involvement was not limited to Mansfield. He attended evensong in his own college chapel and occasionally went to Balliol for Sunday evening organ recitals given by a young Edward Heath. Eric Sharpe was a college contemporary who later became a Baptist minister. He accompanied Wilson to some of those services and judged that 'there was a deeply religious element in his make-up'.[21]

For students seeking spiritual novelty, 1930s Oxford abounded with opportunity. Wilson was unimpressed by the Christian Union, which he found 'shallow and, more important, definitely run by the Anglican element, and worse than that, by the Anglo-Catholics at Pusey House'.[22] Frank Buchman's Oxford Group was noted for its forceful recruitment of the privileged and the promising. In his first month, Wilson was befriended by an older undergraduate, who invited him to meals to explain the group's aims and activities. The emphasis on a Christian reawakening and moral rearmament transcending denominational divisions possessed a certain appeal. With its camps and regime of physical exercise, the group bore more than a passing resemblance to the Scouts. Wilson wrote to his family that 'it's the only thing I have seen more than skin deep'.[23] He attended a few of their meetings but did not persevere. Possibly he was influenced by Micklem's antipathy for the Oxford Group. In turn, group members within Mansfield did not hesitate to point out 'the moral and spiritual inadequacies of their Principal'.[24]

In the course of his studies, Wilson spent 'long hours grappling with the world's greatest philosophers, Plato, Aquinas, Descartes, Leibnitz, Spinoza, Kant'. But the engagement seems to have been exclusively academic, not spiritual. Nor did the 'memorable hours [spent] listening to some of

20 HW to Marjorie Wilson, October 1934, cited Wilson, *Memoirs*, pp. 33–4.

21 Pimlott, *HW*, pp. 40–1.

22 HW to Marjorie Wilson, 17 October 1934, cited Ziegler, *Wilson*, p. 17.

23 HW to parents and sister, 31 October 1934, cited Ziegler, *Wilson*, p. 17.

24 Nathaniel Micklem, *The Box and the Puppets* (London: Geoffrey Bles, 1957), p. 77.

the greatest philosophers and theologians of our day' create any greater impression on his personal beliefs and practice.[25]

There is little mention of religion in his autobiography after his undergraduate days. Wilson later referred to a 'rebellious' phase in his early twenties. He conducted an acrimonious dispute in the correspondence pages of the *Christian World*, a respected and influential Nonconformist newspaper: 'I felt that the Church was too obsessed with personal vices such as drink and not concerned enough with social evils such as unemployment and poverty.' The real reason for Wilson's disengagement from organized religion was more mundane: he was a workaholic with little time for anything deemed non-essential. Even family life suffered from his desire to achieve practical results in the fields of economics and politics. Joining the University Labour Party in the late 1930s, he became increasingly committed to politics as the means for 'applying values which we take for granted in personal life, such as being good neighbours, to the bigger broader problems of the group, and national, and international relationships'.[26]

Harold and Mary married in Mansfield College chapel on 1 January 1940. Dr Micklem officiated, assisted by Mary's father. The couple's two sons, Robin and Giles, were both baptized, Giles in the Crypt of the House of Commons. He was named after Wilson's close friend, Giles Alington, Dean of University College, Oxford, who was Alec Douglas-Home's brother-in-law and one of the godparents. Clement and Violet Attlee were two others.

'No Christian can ever be far from politics'

During the Second World War, Wilson lived in Richmond, where he attended the Vineyard Congregational Church. After much commuting between London and Oxford, the family settled in Hampstead Garden Suburb in 1948. There they enrolled at the Free Church. Founded in 1910, it was the first interdenominational church in the country. The church building was designed by Lutyens. Its foundation stone declared: 'God is larger than the Creeds.' The minister might be from any denomination

25 HW, 'Why I Believe in God'.

26 HW, *The Observer*, 1966, cited Harris, *Conversations*, p. 267.

– provided he was neither an Anglican nor a Catholic. When the Wilsons arrived, a Congregationalist had been the minister for the preceding generation.

Defending his friend from the charge of religious scepticism, the journalist Ernest Kay recorded that the Wilson family attended the Free Church 'regularly'.[27] The emphasis seems to have been on the *family*. Increasingly, that meant Mary and the boys, while Harold remained at home. Robin and Giles were duly allowed to decide for themselves whether they wished to accompany their mother.[28] The Free Church was not averse, however, to having a prominent member of the Labour Party deliver addresses, and on occasion Wilson preached from their pulpit.

As President of the Board of Trade, Wilson returned to the Milnsbridge Baptist Church in 1948 to preach at their Sunday-school anniversary service. He called the congregation to emulate 'the faith and principles' of the Sunday-school founders, without specifying what that might entail. Several times he insisted that 'personal goodness' of itself was insufficient: 'Every Christian must take his principles out of his own life and into the world. It is my belief that no Christian can ever be far from politics.'[29] There had been little development in Wilson's religious thought since he had left the area as a teenager. Vague praise of Christianity by a Cabinet Minister no doubt pleased the Milnsbridge Baptists, but involved no commitment on his part. There was no indication of how that faith and those principles were to be discerned and transmitted; no suggestion that this might involve prayer, worship and conversion of life – simply engagement in public life.

From the 1950s, the Wilsons regularly took their holidays on the Scilly Isles off the Cornish coast, later buying a property there. They attended both St Mary's Anglican church and the Methodist church. Again, Mary was the more committed, but the tradition developed that Harold read the lesson in the parish church every Easter Sunday morning.[30]

Wilson referred often to the Labour Party's ethical origins. When interviewed by Kenneth Harris, he remarked that the party was full of

27 Ernest Kay, *The Pragmatic Premier: An intimate portrait of Harold Wilson* (London: Leslie Frewin, 1967), p. 8.

28 Ziegler, *Wilson*, p. 61.

29 HW, Address, Milnsbridge Baptist Church, 1948, cited Smith, *HW*, p. 37.

30 Kay, *The Pragmatic Premier*, p. 168.

'second-generation nonconformist-radicals . . . men and women whose approach to politics stems from the religious values their parents planted in them'. He quickly remembered to add: 'There are a lot of first generations, too.'[31]

Wilson told delegates at the 1962 Labour Conference: 'This party is a moral crusade or it is nothing.'[32] The allusions were always to morality, never to doctrine; they concerned generalizations not personal conviction. Were they translated into action? When it was insinuated during the 1951 election campaign that he was sympathetic to Communism, Wilson replied that he was a committed member of the Parliamentary Christian Socialist Group. Following the Labour victories of 1964, 1966 and 1974, he asked for a 'service of dedication'. The first was led by Mervyn Stockwood, the radical Bishop of Southwark, and Donald Soper, former President of the Methodist Conference and another Labour supporter. Cabinet Ministers greeted the initiative with cynicism. The services were not well attended.[33]

Christian teaching and social liberalism

If Wilson was proud of Labour's roots in Britain's chapel communities, what part did he play in the liberalization of legislation relating to personal morality occurring during his premiership in the 1960s – a period, critics would claim, that saw the decisive separation of UK law and Christian teaching? It is difficult to tell. Wilson was a committed proponent of racial equality and opponent of the death penalty, but he said remarkably little about the liberalization of laws relating to divorce, abortion and homosexuality. That silence is instructive but what was the motivation for his reticence?

No doubt there was a pragmatic aspect to his approach. Wilson was conscious of his Catholic constituents in Huyton and the social conservatism of the electorate at large in and beyond the Swinging Sixties. He sought to avoid a political backlash on issues on which he probably did not hold strong personal views, persuaded that it was better to allow the Commons

31 HW, *The Observer*, 1966, cited Harris, *Conservations*, p. 267.

32 Cited Jeremy Nuttall, 'Wilson and Social Change', in eds Andrew Crines and Kevin Hickson, *Harold Wilson: The unprincipled Prime Minister?* (Biteback Publishing, 2016), p. 31.

33 Ziegler, *Wilson*, pp. 95, 177.

to debate them at an early stage rather than have them returning ever closer to a general election.[34] He also strove to maintain party unity – a significant number of his own MPs shared their constituents' distaste for much of this legislation. By temperament he was far happier pursuing economic measures than promoting a liberal social agenda.

Left to himself, it is doubtful whether Wilson would have initiated any of these measures. They were the result of private members' bills, the enthusiasm of his young Home Secretary, Roy Jenkins, and the scheming of the parliamentary business managers Richard Crossman and John Silkin. Wilson was the product of his background. Rejecting the harsher elements of puritanism did not make him an advocate of the permissive society. Bernard Donoughue, later head of Wilson's Policy Research Unit, commented: 'He remained middle class, middlebrow, provincial in the best sense of the word, and a Nonconformist, grammar school, "Little Englander."'[35]

Crossman, Leader of the House of Commons, believed that Wilson 'has a number of moral convictions . . . he's against the legal reforms to deal with homosexuality or abortion'.[36] Wilson was absent or abstained from the votes for the liberalization of divorce and made no reference to any of this legislation in his hefty account of the 1964–70 government. Given the book was published after his resignation, electoral considerations were no longer an issue. It is reasonable to surmise that his Nonconformist upbringing continued to colour Wilson's views on such matters. Yet the fact remains that he appointed Jenkins to the Home Office in 1965 knowing his liberal credentials, and allowed the changes to proceed.[37]

'An oasis of peace'

Exposed to broader ecclesiastical influences in southern England, Wilson rapidly overcame the anti-Anglican prejudice he displayed on arriving in Oxford. He was soon comfortably worshipping according to the rites of

34 Richard Crossman, Diary, 27 October 1966, cited Crossman, *The Diaries of a Cabinet Minister*, Vol. 2 (London: Hamish Hamilton, 1976), p. 97.

35 Bernard Donoughue, *Downing Street Diary: With Harold Wilson in No. 10* (London: Jonathan Cape, 2005), p. 11.

36 Crossman, Diary, 11 December 1966, cited Crossman, *The Diaries of a Cabinet Minister*, Vol. 2, pp. 159–60.

37 Peter Dorey, 'Social and Sexual Liberation', in eds Crines and Hickson, *HW*, pp. 170, 176.

the Established Church in his own College chapel and later in the Scilly Isles. The Archbishop of Canterbury, Michael Ramsey, himself the son of a Congregationalist, found that Wilson retained an understanding of matters of faith from his Nonconformist upbringing. He regretted, however, that his style of government was opportunistic rather than principled.[38]

Never disavowing his Nonconformist roots, Wilson accepted the need to act in the interests of the Established Church and the nation with regard to Church appointments. He took those duties 'most seriously'.[39] Indeed, he enjoyed this aspect of his role – poring over the files prepared by the appointments secretary provided 'an oasis of peace' amid the strife of government.[40] Not being an Anglican himself did not inhibit him from disagreeing respectfully with Ramsey, including on the identity of his successor at Canterbury. Ramsey favoured John Howe, a theologian whose work as Secretary General of the Anglican Communion gave him an international perspective. Wilson, who consulted widely, rejected the socialist Mervyn Stockwood, who would not have been 'the right man', and was probably closer to mainstream Anglican opinion than Ramsey. Eventually, he recommended Donald Coggan, the long-serving Archbishop of York, who enjoyed a greater national profile.[41]

Wilson spoke of extending ecclesiastical representation in the House of Lords to include all denominations, even the Quakers. Other than his nomination of Donald Soper for a life peerage in 1965, nothing came of the suggestion.[42]

A future cardinal saving 'the day for a future prime minister'

Mary's outlook was equally ecumenical after her strict Congregationalist childhood. But there were limits to her tolerance. When the couple visited

38 Owen Chadwick, *Michael Ramsey: A life* (Oxford: Oxford University Press, 1991), p. 136.
39 Wilson to Sir Malcolm Knox, 5 June 1974, cited Ziegler, *Wilson*, p. 417.
40 Harold Wilson, *The Governance of Britain* (London: Weidenfeld & Nicolson, 1976), p. 108.
41 Ziegler, *Wilson*, pp. 417–18.
42 Kay, *The Pragmatic Premier*, pp. 166–7.

Pope Paul VI in the Vatican, she recorded, '[I] felt my back turn cold, I really did.'[43] Wilson had to be more nuanced in his relations with Rome. Huyton contained the highest proportion of Catholics of any British constituency and he was mindful of the views of working-class Catholic voters generally.

In the 1951 general election, Bishop Heenan of Leeds had warned of Marxist infiltration of the Labour Party. Local Conservatives in Huyton capitalized on this. The 'agitated' young Labour candidate contacted the bishop, who helpfully produced a letter expressly excluding Wilson from his condemnation of Marxists. Wilson published that reply and held the seat by a small majority. Heenan claimed that he 'had helped to save the day for a future prime minister'. Wilson repaid the favour with the support he gave to Catholic schools.[44] As Archbishop of Westminster, Heenan visited Wilson in Downing Street to express Catholic opposition to proposals to liberalize the abortion laws. On that occasion, however, he received no more than a sympathetic hearing.

In 1977, the Wilsons retired to a flat in Ashley Gardens, literally in the shadow of Westminster Cathedral. He was photographed on his balcony observing the visit of Pope John Paul II in 1982.[45] As his health declined, Wilson spent long hours on that balcony observing the thousands of worshippers crossing the Cathedral Piazza and pondering their purpose. He did so in 'the long, lonely farewell which is Alzheimer's disease'.[46]

'Why I believe in God'

The religious affairs coverage of the *Sunday Express* for the period typically consisted of vicars marrying nubile young parishioners, nuns selling their prayers and priests financing their parishes with the proceeds of gambling. The series of articles announced in autumn 1960 marked a significant departure. Various public figures were asked to write on the

43 Cited Cherie Booth and Cate Haste, *The Goldfish Bowl: Married to the Prime Minister, 1955–97* (London: Chatto & Windus, 2004), p. 138.

44 John C. Heenan, *A Crown of Thorns: An autobiography, 1951–1963* (London: Hodder & Stoughton, 1974), pp. 33–4, 248–9.

45 Ziegler, *Wilson*, p. 493.

46 Archbishop Derek Worlock, Homily, Closing Mass of Westminster Cathedral Centenary.

subject of 'Why I believe in God'. When Wilson heard that Lord Hailsham was writing for the Conservatives, he was concerned. He looked up and down the Opposition front bench, wondering which Labour politician might pen an appropriate piece, but concluded it would be best if he wrote it himself.[47]

He began in informal fashion:

> I will be quite frank. I have never really made myself think this question out fully until now. Perhaps there are millions more who had taken the answer for granted, who would have said, '*Of course I believe in God*,' but who did not know why, or even remember how their belief in God began.

Making reference to the West Riding chapel he had attended, he continued to engage his audience's sympathy as he shared his experience of a son's grief: 'Two years ago I saw my mother die. At a time like that one summons every reserve of philosophy and tortuous argument in an attempt to understand, to explain.'

Then the tone changed – the *Sunday Express* readers were treated to a discourse on 'epistemological arguments'. Wilson conceded that, ultimately, 'belief in God is a matter of faith'. He argued, however, that faith is justified. In doing so, he demonstrated that he was not a materialist. Every human being, he maintained, 'has a soul, a mind, a consciousness of itself that cannot be explained in physical terms. The creation of that soul requires an explanation that no physical scientist can give.' His mother's death clarified for him the conviction that earthly death was a purely physical event. It 'does not and cannot mean the obliteration of everything one has loved in the person who has died'. 'The soul, the real self' survives.

If one believed, as Wilson evidently did, in the existence of the soul, then one had also to believe 'in the Creator of the soul'. It did not concern him 'that we cannot in this life know anything of the ultimate destination of the soul', apparently forgetting the clear gospel teaching on the subject he would have received in chapel and Sunday school. Wilson developed rather

47 John Cole, 'James Harold Wilson', in eds John Taylor and Clyde Binfield, *Who They Were in the Reformed Churches of England and Wales, 1901–2000* (Donington: Shaun Tyas, 2007), pp. 248–9.

the argument of another dimension or sense of which we may not be fully conscious in this world: Handel's *Messiah* possesses a beauty and power even though a deaf person cannot appreciate it; the flower does not lack beauty even though a person may be blind. 'To understand God', Wilson asserted, we simply needed to move into a world of additional dimensions. Personally, he had no difficulty accepting that our human faculties were currently limited, but that such a world existed.[48]

'He did not think much about wider religious questions'

Two years later, Wilson was a candidate for leadership of the Labour Party. Supporters of his rival, George Brown, alleged that Wilson was 'a man without religion'. Such tactics may well have been counterproductive in their effect on MPs.[49] Ernest Kay sought to refute such accusations, pointing to the fact that Wilson retained his membership of the Congregationalist Church and attended the Hampstead Garden Suburb Free Church: 'If he is not religious he is surely misusing his precious time.'[50] But Wilson was only an occasional worshipper; and not everyone in church is a believing Christian. Is it possible to form a more accurate assessment based on the evidence?

Interviewed by Kenneth Harris for *The Observer* in 1966, Wilson referred to his *Sunday Express* article, which he had clearly reread. Many of his responses repeated the earlier piece. Yes, Wilson replied, he had 'religious beliefs', which 'have very much affected my political views'. Harris pressed him as to whether his religious beliefs excluded notions of God. Wilson was emphatic: 'Oh no!' In the *Sunday Express* he had argued strongly for the spiritual nature of humanity and personal survival after death, but he had failed to connect this in any significant way to the Christian faith and the doctrine of the resurrection:

48 HW, 'Why I Believe in God'.

49 Kay, *The Pragmatic Premier*, pp. 126–7; Kenneth O. Morgan, *Callaghan: A life* (Oxford: Oxford University Press, 1997), p. 182.

50 Kay, *The Pragmatic Premier*, p. 127.

> The Jewish believer has visions of the soul being welcomed by Abraham, the Christian of a Heaven beyond the skies, the Buddhist of an absorption in the stream of life divine. If this is one's faith, one cannot be shaken by the mocking sceptic.

Equating faiths in this way scarcely denotes a committed Christian. His objective in *The Observer* was similar – to prove personal survival after death. He continued: 'And if there is an afterlife, then the idea of God, and then of Christ, is relatively easy to accept.'[51]

His biographer, Leslie Smith, commented that it was 'difficult to persuade Wilson to talk about his religion'. Smith asked him outright whether he regarded himself as a practising Christian. He received an ambiguous response:

> One Christian's job may be to help to redeem an individual, another to be a prison visitor, maybe. I'm not doing as much as the dedicated Christian who goes to relieve poverty or loneliness among old people. There has to be a division of labour and I'd use my abilities to improve old-age pensions to help two million people. I think everybody has a job to do, and it is a Christian duty to try to do it well.[52]

Bernard Donoughue knew Wilson well. He concluded: 'He was not religious in any spiritual sense. But the Christian Chapel tradition of good works inspired his early politics.'[53] Mary Wilson shared that assessment: 'Religion was part of his tradition. He never questioned it, but he did not think much about wider religious questions. When he did, he believed that people should translate Christianity into good works.'[54]

Wilson never rejected the Christian faith and, at one level, probably continued to accept it. Nonconformist ethics of justice and equality helped form his political views. He believed in the soul, an afterlife and, in some sense, God. 'A man without religion?' No; yet his religious beliefs had little

51 HW, *The Observer*, 1966, cited Harris, *Conversations*, p. 267; HW, 'Why I Believe in God'.

52 Cited Smith, *HW*, p. 215.

53 Lord Donoughue, Lord Speaker's Lecture, 6 March 2018, <www.parliament.uk/globalassets/documents/lords-information-office/2018/Lord-Donoughues-Lecture.pdf> accessed 17.07.22.

54 Mary Wilson, cited Pimlott, *HW*, p. 41.

discernible impact in adult life in terms of an interior spiritual life or engagement with organized religion. He was a pragmatist dedicated to improving the material lot of his fellows in this world.

Wilson died in London on 24 May 1995. His funeral service was held at St Mary's parish church in the Scilly Isles on 6 June. It was a traditional Anglican funeral liturgy, in which the local Methodist minister participated, with Scripture readings and hymns. His coffin was carried out of St Mary's by teams of lifeboatmen, oarsmen and firemen to the graveyard of the Old Town Church, where he was buried overlooking the sea.

Edward Heath (1970–1974)

'Coming through the valley of bewilderment'

Edward Richard George Heath[1] was born at St Peter's-in-Thanet, close to the Kentish coastal town of Broadstairs, on 9 July 1916. He was educated at Chatham House Grammar School, Ramsgate, and Balliol College, Oxford.

After service with the Royal Artillery during the Second World War and a variety of positions subsequently, Heath won Bexley for the Conservatives in 1950. He remained an MP until his retirement in 2001. Boundary changes led to the seat being renamed Sidcup in February 1974 and Old Bexley and Sidcup in 1983.

Heath served in the Whips' Office between 1951 and 1959. As Chief Whip from 1956, he helped restore party unity after the Suez crisis. Briefly Minister of Labour, Heath was appointed Lord Privy Seal in 1960, speaking on foreign affairs in the Commons. Entrusted with responsibility for negotiating UK membership of the EEC, Heath was passionately committed to joining as a means of avoiding future conflict and advancing national interests. Veto of the application by the French President, Charles de Gaulle, in no way reflected badly on Heath, and Douglas-Home appointed him President of the Board of Trade in 1963. When the Conservatives lost the 1964 general election he became Shadow Chancellor, organizing an effective campaign against the 1965 Finance Bill.

When Conservative MPs elected their party leader for the first time on 27 July 1965, Heath, the meritocratic modernizer, succeeded the aristocrat, Douglas-Home. It did not provide the immediate fillip the Tories hoped for; they were decisively defeated by Harold Wilson's Labour Party in the 1966 general election. Despite the government's economic difficulties, Heath's

1 'Teddy' to his family and Oxford contemporaries, Heath emerged from his wartime service in the Army as 'Ted'.

period as leader of the Opposition was an unhappy time, in which he was frequently outwitted by Wilson on the floor of the Commons. However, he led the Conservatives to a surprise 30-seat majority victory in the election on 18 June 1970 and was appointed Prime Minister the following day.

Almost immediately Heath reopened negotiations for membership of the EEC. With de Gaulle no longer in office the application was successful, and the UK became a member state on 1 January 1973. The government fared less well elsewhere, confronted by exceptionally difficult circumstances: terrorism in the Middle East; escalating troubles in Northern Ireland; industrial strife leading to declarations of states of emergency; and an energy crisis caused by soaring oil prices. Having been elected to reduce the size of the state and tackle inflationary wage increases, the government appeared to perform a U-turn in 1972. Pursuing more interventionist and expansionist policies, the focus switched from tackling inflation to reducing unemployment.

When the miners went on strike, Heath introduced a three-day working week and called a general election on 28 February 1974 on the question of who governed Britain, the elected government or the trade unions. Though he was initially favoured to win, his chances of success faded as the accuracy of the government's case against the miners was questioned, support for the Liberals surged and Enoch Powell urged voters to support Labour for the chance to leave Europe. Although the Conservatives polled more votes than Labour, they won four fewer seats. Heath remained in Downing Street as he sought to reach an understanding with the Liberals. The approach having failed, he resigned as Prime Minister on 4 March 1974.

Wilson consolidated Labour's position in the general election on 10 October 1974. Heath had lost three elections out of four; a challenge to his leadership was inevitable. He paid the price for his electoral record and failure to cultivate his own backbenchers when Margaret Thatcher defeated him in the first ballot on 4 February 1975. Heath resigned immediately but never reconciled himself to the result. There were genuine political and personal differences between him and his successor but he did himself no favours as he maintained his 'long sulk' during Thatcher's years of leadership.

Never offered a Cabinet office by Thatcher, Heath remained active in politics, playing a prominent role in the successful Yes campaign in the

1975 referendum on continued membership of the EEC. He travelled extensively promoting peace, aid for the developing world, improved relations with China and the release of British hostages in Iraq. He was created a Knight of the Garter in 1992.

Heath died in his Salisbury home on 17 July 2005. His funeral took place in Salisbury Cathedral, where his ashes were later interred.

* * *

'Brought up in a Christian home'

Most British Prime Ministers of the twentieth century were reluctant to discuss religion. Bonar Law, Chamberlain and Attlee were notoriously reticent. Heath was equally taciturn, but in his case silence did not necessarily indicate unbelief. A choirboy and organist, a former journalist on the *Church Times*, he possessed the credentials of the ultimate Anglican insider, apparently a committed churchman in the mould of his Conservative predecessors, Macmillan and Douglas-Home. Yet like many aspects of Heath's personal life, his convictions and feelings in matters of faith are difficult to ascertain.

There was nothing complex in terms of Heath's religious antecedents. His father, William Heath, was a carpenter and later a self-employed builder. He had no religion and was not a churchgoer. Heath was upset when, after his mother's death in 1951, his father married a divorcee in a registry office, though it did not prevent him attending the ceremony.[2]

Heath was very close to his mother, Edith, a former lady's maid. He recalled that she 'had the spiritual sense of her Christian faith. Not that she was at all ethereal about it – she kept our feet on the ground.'[3] Her husband put it more pithily: 'Teddy's mother was a churchwoman. I wouldn't say she went to church every Sunday, but she was certainly a churchwoman.'[4]

2 John Campbell, *Edward Heath: A biography* (London: Jonathan Cape, 1993), p. 81.

3 Heath, Interview with Kenneth Harris, *The Observer*, 16 January 1966, cited Kenneth Harris, *Conversations* (London: Hodder & Stoughton, 1967), p. 255.

4 William Heath, cited George Hutchinson, *Edward Heath: A personal and political biography* (London: Longman, 1970), p. 6.

Anglican tradition was sufficiently engrained that after the birth, Edith went to the parish church of St Peter to be churched and to have Heath baptized.[5]

Edith became a regular churchgoer later in life. Heath made excuses on her behalf for his childhood years when 'she was generally too busy to worship regularly herself'. She deemed her religious duties fulfilled by ensuring that her children 'went to church without fail'. Nor was she particular as to which 'church' that might be. Shortly after his birth, Heath's family moved to Crayford, where his father found wartime work, remaining there until 1923. His parents were 'delighted' when neighbours offered to take the young Heath with them each Sunday to the Christadelphian chapel. It was the most exotic period of Heath's spiritual life. The Christadelphians were a mid-nineteenth-century sect who rejected the Trinity and emphasized Christ's Second Coming. Heath maintained that he adopted no part of their creed but admired 'their orderly, well-mannered approach to life' and 'vigorous singing'.[6]

Propriety was restored at the age of five as Heath entered the Anglican school at Crayford. When the family returned to Thanet, he continued his education at St Peter's school there. The school was not only geographically close to the parish church: the headmaster was one of the churchwardens and began each school day with prayers, and the clergy were regular visitors in the classroom.[7]

St Peter-in-Thanet was an active parish, with a number of curates and retired clergy assisting the vicar at the parish church and the chapel of St Andrew's. In 1930 there were three Communion services every Sunday as well as a schools' service, matins, children's service and evensong.[8] St Peter's was vaguely High without being Anglo-Catholic. It was one of the first parishes to introduce the *English Hymnal*. Heath remembered the vicar, the Revd C. H. S. Matthews, as 'a remarkable man', 'a forceful preacher and something of a radical'.[9] He had spent his early ministry with the Brotherhood

5 Marian Evans, *Ted Heath: A family portrait* (London: William Kimber, 1970), p. 45.

6 Edward Heath, *The Course of My Life: My autobiography* (London: Hodder & Stoughton, 1998), pp. 4–5.

7 EH, *The Course of My Life*, p. 7.

8 G. M. Hogben, *The History of St Peter-the-Apostle Church in Thanet* (Margate: Aurelian, 2017), pp. 216, 270.

9 Edward Heath, *Music: A joy for life* (London: Sidgwick & Jackson, 1976), p. 16.

of the Good Shepherd. This 'Bush Brotherhood' evangelized the Australian outback but was viewed with suspicion by Evangelicals in Sydney on account of the semi-monastic vows taken by its members. Matthews was able to attract a number of prominent preachers to Thanet. Heath listened to the Revd Studdert Kennedy, 'Woodbine Willie', known for his ministry in the trenches of the First World War, and Canon Dick Sheppard, a pacifist, early religious broadcaster and Dean of Canterbury. Matthews left St Peter's to become the chaplain at Marlborough College.

Heath was prepared for confirmation at the age of 14 by the new vicar, the Revd Kenneth Percival Smith. A contemporary recalled his impact:

> I think that the vicar was the first man to have a very considerable influence on Heath. He opened our eyes to religion, to Christianity, and from that point on Teddy took his religion very seriously. I believe that it's a deep-seated sense of religion which may – rightly or wrongly – make him think he's a man of destiny.[10]

Regardless of whether religion gave Heath a sense of destiny, much of his adolescent life revolved around the church. He attended the parish youth club and played tennis in the vicarage garden.

Music: A joy for life

St Peter's also introduced Heath to his lifelong passion for music. The parish took choral music very seriously. The choir of 12 male voices and 24 boys sang a wide repertoire, firmly within the Anglican musical tradition. Heath joined the choir at the age of eight and became a treble soloist. It was a significant commitment – he was expected to sing at matins and evensong on Sundays and at the monthly Choral Communion Service. The boys rehearsed by themselves during the week and with the men on Friday evenings. When his voice broke at the age of 14, Heath joined the men's voices and took up playing the organ at St Peter's.[11]

---

10 Ronald Whittell, cited Hutchinson, *EH*, p. 10.

11 EH, *The Course of My Life*, p. 9; EH, *Music*, p. 14.

He won a scholarship to Chatham House Grammar School in Ramsgate, where he was active in the school debating society, speaking in favour of motions for the abolition of Sunday cinema and the death penalty.

'I did not feel a true calling'

In 1935, Heath went to Oxford to read Philosophy, Politics and Economics at Balliol. His attendance at the college chapel was unremitting though not necessarily an indication of religious fervour. As an organ scholar, Heath was required to play at the daily service at 8 a.m. each weekday morning and at evensong on Sundays. A friend and contemporary did not rate the spiritual fare offered in the chapel, which few undergraduates attended. Neither was he impressed by the chaplain, the Revd T. W. Pym, whom he found 'a little too intimate'. The liturgy was not edifying: 'I have never known Holy Communion taken with less feeling and so much in a drone.' Heath greatly admired the Master, A. D. ('Sandy') Lindsay, a socialist who integrated his Christian faith into his political philosophy. Lindsay lacked a liturgical presence in the chapel, however, simply reading his sermon at evensong.[12]

Increasingly engaged in student politics as a 'One Nation Conservative', Heath was elected President of the Oxford Union. Discarding convention, he introduced the first ever theological motion to the Union: 'That a return to religion is the only solution to our present discontents.' It passed comfortably.

Many of Heath's undergraduate friends were, like himself, committed Anglicans: Freddy Temple and Stephen Verney went on to become bishops, George Hood a missionary in the Far East. Heath's mother entertained hopes he might also pursue a vocation within the Church, though he was more realistic:

> It was certainly an exciting time for the Church of England. However, despite a deeply held faith and a considerable interest in ecclesiastical affairs, I did not feel a true calling nor would such a career have

12 Freddy Temple to his parents, October 1935, cited Christopher Dobb, *Freddy Temple: A portrait* (Calne: Rooftop Publishing, 2006), p. 36.

> provided me with the opportunity I sought to shape the affairs of my country.[13]

His mother's enthusiasm cooled when she discovered how badly the clergy were paid.

'Relevant – when very few others were'

Heath met Freddy Temple at the Balliol Freshers' Dinner and they immediately struck up a friendship. The grandson of one Archbishop of Canterbury and nephew of another, Temple was raised in the heart of the Anglican establishment. Temple and Heath were part of a group who debated matters of theology, morality and politics into the small hours of the night.

As Temple's parents were stationed in India, he often stayed with his uncle, Archbishop William Temple of York, at Bishopthorpe. Temple wrote to his uncle asking him to resolve points of dispute among the Balliol undergraduates.[14] In turn, the Archbishop paid frequent visits to his nephew in Oxford. Freddy was not entirely uncritical: 'Uncle William preached a good and very amusing sermon at St Mary's, but I was very surprised when he descended to mere attacks on political parties, extremely funny though they were.'[15]

Heath credited the Archbishop with providing the Christian foundations for his own political beliefs: 'Temple's impact on my generation was immense',[16] he wrote, and acknowledged his debt to Freddy in helping him appreciate the true stature of his uncle. When Heath arrived at Oxford, the Archbishop's student mission of 1931 was still being spoken of. 'It is to be recognized', the Archbishop had said, 'that sex is holy as well as wholesome . . . it is the means by which we may cooperate with God in bringing into the world children of His own destined for eternal life.'[17] An unremarkable statement today but considered contentious 90 years ago.

13 EH, *The Course of My Life*, pp. 66–7.

14 EH, *The Course of My Life*, p. 46.

15 Freddy Temple to his parents, 7 May 1938, cited Dobb, *Freddy Temple*, p. 39.

16 EH, *The Course of My Life*, p. 33.

17 Archbishop William Temple, cited John Kent, *William Temple* (Cambridge: Cambridge University Press, 1992), p. 185.

It was this attempt to make the Church of England relevant to the general population, the desire to move beyond what he viewed as arid theological debates and Church politics, that appealed to Heath:

> William Temple was foremost among the leaders of the nations, temporal or spiritual, in posing challenging, radical questions about the nature of our society and its economic basis at a time of world recession, massive unemployment and social despair . . . whatever the answers to his questions might prove to be, they had to be founded, he insisted, on a moral code. Most important of all, he propounded with lucidity and vigour his understanding of the Christian ethic in its application to the contemporary problems which engrossed us all . . . In short, for us he was relevant – when very few others were.[18]

He was grateful to Temple for propounding 'a view of morality which was not preoccupied with sexuality, but which was relevant to the myriad problems besetting the individual in the personal, professional and social spheres'.[19]

Heath claimed, not entirely fairly, that Temple failed to give sufficient emphasis to personal freedom and to appreciate the limitations socialism imposed on freedom. Nevertheless, he applauded Temple's desire to construct a fairer society on a firm moral basis, outlined in his seminal work, *Christianity and Social Order*, published in 1942,[20] for which Heath wrote the preface in a 1976 edition. This book, Heath contended, did more than anything else to bring about the welfare state. Heath agreed with Temple: it was not the Church's business to devise a specific programme of action.[21] Others were better placed to formulate practical solutions but 'only the Church can provide the contemporary teaching, the enunciation of principle, on which all else must be founded'.[22]

18 Edward Heath, 'Foreword', William Temple, *Christianity and Social Order*, reprint of 1st edn (London: SPCK, 1976), p. 1.

19 EH, *The Course of My Life*, p. 34.

20 William Temple, *Christianity and Social Order* (Harmondsworth and New York: Penguin, 1942).

21 EH, Interview, *The Observer*, 1966, cited Harris, *Conversations*, p. 264.

22 EH, 'Foreword', Temple, *Christianity and Social Order*, pp. 2–3.

'Bored stiff at the *Church Times*'

In February 1948, to his family's surprise, Heath was appointed news editor of the *Church Times*, then an Anglo-Catholic weekly newspaper. The position was no indication of his churchmanship; it simply paid a considerably higher salary than the civil service work he had undertaken since demobilization. He himself admitted: 'I was not a High Anglican, nor did I have much experience of journalism. Further, although I cared deeply about Church affairs, my strictly theological knowledge was limited.'[23]

The year he worked for the paper was not a happy one. He had a difficult relationship with the editor, Hugh Beevor, a left-wing Anglo-Catholic. His coverage of the 1948 Anglo-Catholic Congress and Bishop Wand's London mission was rated professionally competent, demonstrating a capacity 'to master the most abstruse and highly theological arguments'.[24] However, Heath's heart was not in the work, and he made mistakes. To the amusement of his colleagues, he managed to transpose the 'YMCA' for the 'UMCA', never having heard of the Universities' Mission to Central Africa.[25] 'He was', a friend recalled, 'bored stiff at the *Church Times*.'[26]

Christian principles and individual liberty

Heath's memoirs are similar to Wilson's in that there is no substantive reference to his personal religious beliefs and practice after his undergraduate days. The emphasis is on music, sailing and interior design – and, of course, politics. Political life, however, is never without at least a moral dimension. Like Wilson, Heath had to take, or avoid taking, a stance on the changes to social legislation in the late 1960s, though he was more willing to nail his colours to the mast. His reputation as a modernizer extended to this area of political life:

> Some older members of the Conservative Party like to trace all Britain's problems to the social reforms of [the 1960s] but I generally

23 EH, *The Course of My Life*, p. 121.

24 John Trevisick, cited Hutchinson, *EH*, p. 62.

25 EH, *The Course of My Life*, p. 121.

26 Cited Hutchinson, *EH*, p. 61.

> supported Roy Jenkins' spell as Home Secretary, although I had some reservations about the pace of change.[27]

Speaking at a Westminster Cathedral centenary lecture, he argued that there were relatively few matters in politics that required the application of the values of faith, and he made it clear he would always favour tolerance and individual liberty over enforcement of Christian principles.[28]

At a Vatican audience in 1972, Pope Paul VI urged the British government to align UK law with traditional Christian teaching with respect to abortion and homosexuality. Heath listened politely – and did nothing.[29] On two ethical questions, he appeared to support the Christian position on the sanctity of human life: he opposed the death penalty and euthanasia. In both cases, however, his opposition stemmed less from an acceptance of the objective value of all human life than from reluctance to ask any individual to administer such actions.[30]

'A fairly understanding churchman'

Heath had no qualms of self-doubt concerning his role in the appointment of Anglican bishops. He later noted that he had been responsible for the recommendation of 45 diocesan and suffragan bishops during his term of office, and complimented himself on the appointments: 'They were also often – I shall probably be excommunicated for saying this – better than they would have been had they been left entirely to the Church, with no involvement from No. 10.'[31] Others thought his appointments at best safe but lacking in imagination.[32]

---

27 EH, *The Course of My Life*, p. 284.

28 Edward Heath, 'Christian Values in Politics', in eds Edward Stourton and Francis Gumley, *Christian Values* (London: Hodder & Stoughton, 1996), pp. 135–6.

29 Philip Ziegler, *Edward Heath: The authorised biography* (London: HarperCollins, 2010), p. 325.

30 EH, *The Course of My Life*, p. 103; Douglas Hurd to Catherine O'Brien, 9 November 1970, Heath Papers, 3 2/14, cited Ziegler, *EH*, p. 589.

31 EH, *The Course of My Life*, p. 314.

32 Campbell, *EH*, p. 492.

The Archbishop of Canterbury found Heath 'a man of integrity . . . a fairly understanding churchman'.[33] Heath had sufficient interest in the matter and confidence in his own judgement that he was willing, on occasion, to pass over the first choice of the Archbishop of Canterbury, Michael Ramsey, for a vacancy and recommend his own preference. His most controversial appointment was that of the establishment candidate Gerald Ellison to London, rather than the Anglo-Catholic Graham Leonard. Heath might have upset the Diocese in the process, but in this instance he was following Ramsey's advice. In order to know the bishops better, Heath instituted a series of dinners for them and their wives at Downing Street. He felt the innovation such a success that he proposed something similar for the Catholic bishops. Elements of the Anglican establishment were aghast, but Heath persisted.[34]

Heath was not an uncritical churchman. He deplored antiquarianism. When it was suggested that a suffragan see of Winchester be called Silchester, he intervened, arguing that Basingstoke was far more appropriate for 1970s Britain.[35] He supported the ecumenical movement and interfaith dialogue.[36] His perennial concern for the Church's relevance implies a genuine care for its mission. There was a real need, he argued, to reinterpret 'permanent Christian principles for a new generation'. He felt the Church's problem was 'to explain what the Christian basis of morality actually is *today*. I'm not sure the Church as a whole does enough in the way of real instruction in the tenets of its faith.'[37]

William Temple remained Heath's hero in this regard. He regretted that the Church had failed to follow his lead:

> Young people today, as well as many of their elders, are clamouring for an intellectual justification for belief and for the presentation of a morality which is not preoccupied with sexuality but which

33 Archbishop Michael Ramsey, cited Owen Chadwick, *Michael Ramsey: A life* (Oxford: Oxford University Press, 1991), p. 137.

34 Bernard Palmer, *High and Mitred: A study of Prime Ministers as bishop-makers, 1837–1977* (London: SPCK, 1992), pp. 271–3.

35 Ziegler, *EH*, p. 321.

36 EH, 'Christian Values in Politics', in eds Stourton and Gumley, *Christian Values*, pp. 133, 135.

37 EH, Interview, *The Observer*, 1966, cited Harris, *Conversations*, p. 264.

> is relevant to the myriad problems besetting the individual in his personal, his family and his communal activities.[38]

He conveniently ignored the fact that Christianity's founder had rather a lot to say on sexual ethics. In the 1990s he was decrying even more forcefully the Church's inability to explain 'the basic tenets of the faith', especially in schools, preferring to engage in political and social polemics rather than presenting 'the basic characteristics of our faith'.[39] Here, at least, he shared common ground with Thatcher.

Heath frequently critiqued the institutional Church, but what of his own faith? It seems he continued to practise that faith, although due to the pressures of office, more intermittently between the Second World War and retirement. As far as he was concerned, it was no one else's business. He was less willing to be photographed on his way to church than Wilson. Yet he did attend. When staying with his family, who had moved to Broadstairs, he attended Holy Trinity, which was very much in the Anglo-Catholic tradition.

Heath once said: 'I don't think there should be too much talk about religion and politics.'[40] It was an approach he adopted consistently. His Westminster Cathedral centenary lecture, 'Christian Values in Politics', was a general talk on the geopolitical situation, with no mention of God or Jesus and no real reference to Christian values. It would be easy to assume that his attachment to the Christian faith was shallow, lacking any reflection. Heath regaled the Salisbury Cathedral clergy, his neighbours in retirement, over the dinner table with 'a repertoire of stories concerning clerical personalities'. They surmised, however, 'that this superficial level of interest in the politics and personalities of religion was something of a smokescreen to disguise a more substantial interest in religious matters'.[41] Courtesy dictated that the conversation remained at this level. Fortunately, journalists were able to probe deeper.

38 EH, 'Foreword', Temple, *Christianity and Social Order*, p. 2.

39 EH, 'Christian Values in Politics', in eds Stourton and Gumley, *Christian Values*, p. 134.

40 EH, Interview, *The Observer*, 1966, cited Harris, *Conversations*, p. 264.

41 Canon Jeremy Davies to the author, 23 August 2020.

'I believe in God'; 'I believe in prayer, and I pray'

'His religion' was 'not a thing one talks about very much, but it has a secure hold,' Heath admitted to James Margach of the *Sunday Times* in 1965.[42] A few months later Kenneth Harris of *The Observer* asked him to describe his 'basic beliefs as a Christian'. Heath affirmed the central tenets of Christianity:

> I believe in God. Very much the kind of God, I would say, that most ministers of the Church of England believe in. I believe in Christ and in the divinity of Christ. I believe in an after-life. I believe in the significance and the meaning, the lesson, of the crucifixion.

He qualified his credo in two respects. Referring to John Robinson's book *Honest to God*,[43] he stated: 'I don't accept some of the images of Christianity, some of the terms and some of the institutions . . . I don't see God as a kind old man in the sky.'[44] This in no way detracts from his orthodoxy. But given his professed belief in 'an after-life', his comment 30 years later with reference to his mother's death ('You realize that you will never see them again'[45]) does raise the question of what he thought belief in the resurrection entailed.

In a 2000 documentary directed by Bryan Forbes, Heath was asked about prayer. He was at his most terse. Did he pray? 'Yes.' Did he find it helpful? 'Yes.' Why? 'Because it is spiritual communion.'[46] Providing no illumination as to the nature of that prayer life, it was nevertheless a clear affirmation that Heath believed prayer provided access to God. He had been more forthcoming with Kenneth Harris:

---

42 EH, Interview with James Margach, *Sunday Times*, 30 October 1965.

43 John A. T. Robinson, *Honest to God* (London: SCM Press, 1963).

44 EH, Interview, *The Observer*, 1966, cited Harris, *Conversations*, p. 264.

45 Michael Cockerell, Documentary, *A Very Singular Man* (Blakeway Productions, 1998).

46 Bryan Forbes, Documentary, *Sir Edward Heath: A life beyond politics* (Bryan Forbes, 2000), cited Ziegler, *EH*, pp. 8–9.

> I believe in prayer, and I pray. By prayer, I don't mean asking God to send you a Telex telling you whether to increase the Bank Rate or not or whether Mr Jones is a good man or a bad man. I mean trying in one's mind to see one's problems in terms of the guidelines provided by the essentials of the Christian faith.[47]

It was something he preferred to keep hidden, but Heath clearly believed in and was a practitioner of prayer with a mature understanding of Christian prayer.

In terms of personal intimacy, others remarked how Heath expressed himself more fluently in music than in words. Spiritually, it was similar. From the beginning, Christianity was, for Heath, linked to music, first when he was a choir boy then as an organist. The Salisbury Cathedral clergy felt that 'music was one of Ted Heath's paths to spiritual vision and enlightenment'.[48] Liturgically, he could be a traditionalist. He regretted that the Catholic Church had adopted the vernacular, admiring the 'resonance and authority' of Latin, and believed that Christmas carols provided a similar sense of universality for Anglo-Saxons: 'We can still feel that we are celebrating Christ's birthday together, in the same way and in the same tongue.'[49] For 40 years, he conducted a carol concert at Broadstairs.

Church music was one of the attractions that drew Heath to Salisbury when he acquired a home in the Cathedral Close in 1985. Typically, he was not afraid to give offence to those willing to take it: he compared the sound of Salisbury's choir unfavourably with that of Winchester and was characteristically robust in venting his views to the dean when the cathedral ended the practice of centuries and introduced girls into the choir: 'We don't want bloody women.'[50] Nevertheless Heath was an enthusiastic supporter of Salisbury Cathedral and an active fundraiser for its fabric and music. He was also a devout communicant, attending the Eucharist each Sunday.[51] Confined to a wheelchair from 2003, the Cathedral was one of the few places he visited regularly in the last two years of his life.

47 EH, Interview, *The Observer*, 1966, cited Harris, *Conversations*, p. 264.
48 Canon Jeremy Davies to the author, 23 August 2020.
49 EH, *Music*, pp. 192, 67.
50 Cited Ziegler, *EH*, p. 543.
51 Canon Jeremy Davies to the author, 23 August 2020.

Making peace with his Maker?

Heath liked to give the impression that his spiritual journey had been serene: one smooth development through the entirety of his life, untroubled by doubt or crisis. Talking about his faith, he told Harris in 1966: 'It's been the same all along. I was brought up in a Christian home, as they say in obituaries, and at Oxford – well, I just went on, as I do today.'[52]

His private papers reveal something rather different. He confided to his diary:

> The only principles I have ever had firmly implanted have been religious but these never had any intellectual backing. I never even realized what the grounds of belief are and how they compare with anything else. The result was that the religious beliefs I had were undermined at Oxford. I felt that they were silly, that I couldn't defend them against other people. Only now am I beginning to realize their justification. I may be slowly coming through the valley of bewilderment.[53]

Heath hated being made to appear foolish and intellectually ill-prepared. In some ways it is perhaps surprising that his faith survived as there is little evidence he did much to inform himself systemically of the intellectual basis for belief. It accounts for his reticence in discussing matters of faith – and his appeal to the Church for a more convincing apologetic.

Did he come 'through the valley of bewilderment'? The fact that he remained a practising Anglican suggests so. He found consolation in both prayer and music, though unlike other Prime Ministers of his period, there is no reference to his reading Scripture. But was he untroubled? Henrietta Mayhew was a secretary in his private office from 1990. When she heard that he had died on 17 July 2005, she mused: 'I wish I'd been to see him recently and told him to make his peace with his Maker. Did he? I wonder.'[54] It was a reasonable question. Could anyone be entirely at peace with

52 EH, Interview, *The Observer*, 1966, cited Harris, *Conversations*, p. 264.

53 EH, Diary, January 1940, Heath Papers, 1 1/15, cited Ziegler, *EH*, p. 29.

54 Henrietta Mayhew, Diary, 17 July 2005, cited Michael McManus, *Edward Heath: A singular life* (London: Elliott & Thompson, 2016), p. 285.

the Creator when so notoriously difficult in his relations with most of his creatures?

Heath's funeral took place in Salisbury Cathedral on 25 July 2005. Involving the bishop and dean, it was a mixture of simplicity and magnificence. The coffin was wheeled on a traditional funeral handcart the short distance from his home and placed beneath the Spire Crossing. His private secretary, Robert Burn, read the lesson from Ecclesiasticus 44 and Lord Armstrong, Principal Private Secretary during his Downing Street days, read from 1 Corinthians 15. 'The choir and the organ [were] at their glorious best.'[55] It was reported that Heath had planned every detail of the service. In fact he had been reluctant to discuss anything pertaining to the preparations for his death. The order of service was largely the work of Canon Jeremy Davies, Precentor of the Cathedral. He suggested propers and music of which he knew Heath approved. Heath simply consented to the proposals.[56]

The funeral was followed by a private cremation service. His ashes were subsequently interred in the South Crossing of the Cathedral.

55 Ziegler, *EH*, p. 590; Robert Key, cited McManus, *EH*, p. 286.

56 Canon Jeremy Davies to the author, 23 August 2020.

James Callaghan (1976–1979)

'A Christian upbringing'

Leonard James Callaghan[1] was born in Portsmouth on 27 March 1912. He was educated at Portsmouth North Secondary School. On leaving school, he worked as a tax officer and later as a trade union official. He served in the Royal Navy during the Second World War.

Callaghan was elected MP for Cardiff South in the 1945 general election. Following boundary changes, he represented Cardiff South East from 1950 to 1983 and Cardiff South and Penarth from 1983 to 1987. Appointed Parliamentary Secretary to the Undersecretary at the Dominions Office, Callaghan resigned in December 1945 over the terms of the US loan replacing the Lease-Lend arrangement. He served as Parliamentary Secretary to the Ministry of Transport from 1947 and as Parliamentary and Financial Secretary to the Admiralty from 1950. In opposition, Callaghan was the Labour Party spokesman on transport, fuel, education and Commonwealth and colonial affairs. From 1961 he was Shadow Chancellor. He contested the Labour leadership in 1963 but came third behind Harold Wilson and George Brown.

When Labour won the 1964 general election, Callaghan was appointed Chancellor of the Exchequer. It was a difficult period. There was tension with the newly created Department of Economic Affairs, and he inherited an overheated economy with a balance of trade deficit and pressure on sterling. Callaghan was forced to raise interest rates, cut public spending and impose an import surcharge. He also introduced Capital Gains Tax and Corporation Tax. The government was unable to withstand market pressures, however, and was compelled to accept a humiliating devaluation of the currency in November 1967.

1 Known by his family and early friends as 'Leonard' or 'Len', on entering political life Callaghan opted to be called by his middle name.

Shortly afterwards Callaghan moved to the Home Office, where he pursued a less radical liberalizing agenda than his predecessor, Roy Jenkins. He promoted anti-race discrimination legislation, prison reform and children's welfare, but was criticized by the Left for restricting immigration. Callaghan responded firmly to the outbreak of the Northern Irish Troubles, sending in the Army to protect the Catholic minority in 1969. His opposition to Barbara Castle's trade union reform proposals incurred Wilson's displeasure and suspicion.

Again in opposition, Callaghan acted as Shadow Home Secretary from 1970 to 1972 and Shadow Foreign Secretary from 1972 to 1974. Appointed Foreign Secretary when Labour returned to power in March 1974, he renegotiated the terms of the EEC Accession Treaty prior to the 1975 referendum. Four years older than Wilson, he had discounted the possibility of the premiership until the Prime Minister resigned unexpectedly in March 1976. A candidate of the Centre-Right with strong links to the trade unions, Callaghan was perceived as a safe pair of hands, a repository of practical common sense. In the third round of voting, he defeated Michael Foot on 5 April and was appointed Prime Minister the following day.

Almost immediately the Labour government lost its tiny parliamentary majority and was kept in office thanks to an arrangement with the Liberals – the 'Lib-Lab pact' – between March 1977 and August 1978. Callaghan experienced an unpleasant sense of déjà vu as a trade deficit and government borrowing once more brought sterling under tremendous pressure. In December 1976, the Chancellor, Denis Healey, was forced to accept an International Monetary Fund loan conditional on significant spending cuts. Callaghan strove, successfully, to maintain Cabinet unity during the crisis.

Although the episode was politically damaging, the economy improved significantly in 1977–8. To the surprise of many, Callaghan hesitated to go to the country in the autumn of 1978. It was a decision he came to regret. The government's incomes policy, seeking to control inflation, led to conflict with the public-sector unions. The 'winter of discontent' saw massive disruption as the government appeared unable to control union militancy. Referenda in Scotland and Wales failed to gain the necessary majorities for devolution. The government lost a vote of confidence in the Commons on 28 March 1978. Viewed as decent and honest by the public, Callaghan could be forceful, even menacing towards colleagues, opponents and journalists. Despite his personal popularity, Labour was decisively defeated by Margaret Thatcher's Conservatives in the general election on 3 May 1979. He resigned as Prime Minister on 4 May 1979.

Callaghan retired as Labour Party leader on 15 October 1980. He was created a Knight of the Garter in 1987. Retiring from the Commons in the same year, he entered the House of Lords as Lord Callaghan of Cardiff.

He died in Sussex on 26 March 2005.

* * *

Choosing 'between the Church and my mother'

Edward Heath once said that over the course of a long parliamentary career, no member of the public had ever asked him about his faith. Popular interest in such matters, he concluded, was 'almost nil'.[2] The experience of other twentieth-century Prime Ministers was similar. Of course, the situation might have been otherwise had they not all been drawn from mainstream Protestantism. Even the Unitarian Chamberlain identified with this constituency.

In at least one part of the country, however, religion retained the capacity to arouse controversy well into the century. Seeking nomination as the Labour candidate for Cardiff South, Callaghan was asked pointedly whether he was a Catholic. Only after he had reassured his questioner that he was in fact a Baptist was he able to secure her support. Given his surname, others made similar assumptions about his religious affiliation – until he pointed out their error, the *Catholic Herald* listed him among the Catholic Members elected to the Commons in 1945.[3] What were the facts about his confessional roots and personal convictions?

His father served as chief petty officer on the royal yacht, based in Portsmouth. Callaghan was unaware of his paternal family ancestry until the

2 Edward Heath, 'Christian Values in Politics', in eds Edward Stourton and Francis Gumley, *Christian Values* (London: Hodder & Stoughton, 1996), p. 133.

3 James Callaghan, *Time and Chance* (London: Collins, 1987), p. 61; Kenneth O. Morgan, *Callaghan: A life* (Oxford: Oxford University Press, 1997), p. 51.

Sun undertook research early in his premiership. His great-grandfather was an Irish Catholic weaver who emigrated to Britain at the time of the famine. His grandfather, a West Midlands silversmith, married a Jewish woman, Elizabeth Bernstein, though their ten children were raised Catholic. His father was born James Garoghan in 1877. Running away to sea, he changed his name on enlisting in the Royal Navy to avoid detection by his family.

The young petty officer met Charlotte Speare (née Cundy) in Plymouth. She was already a widow, her first husband, another sailor, having been killed in a naval accident. He proposed marriage but there was a difficulty: as a Catholic, he required permission to marry a non-Catholic, and the Catholic naval chaplain refused it. Callaghan's father was incensed, declaring 'that if he had to choose between the Church and my mother, then he would have nothing further to do with the Church'. He was as good as his word. The couple were married outside the Catholic Church in 1903.[4]

The requirement for permission to marry a non-Catholic was designed to ensure that the Catholic spouse continued to practise their faith, and baptized and raised any children as Catholics. We cannot know whether the naval chaplain in question was simply reiterating a policy decision or had specific concerns about Callaghan's fiancée. The Cundys had a long naval connection. They were also staunch Baptists. Did he fear that the petty officer's Catholic faith would be no match for the evangelical fervour of this Devonian Protestant? In any event the couple and their children – Callaghan and his elder sister Dorothy – all practised as Baptists.

'To me it was a dreadful prospect'

Charlotte was a 'deeply religious and fundamentalist' woman.[5] She was certainly the predominant spiritual influence on her children by virtue of her forceful personality and because her husband was frequently away from home and in fact died young. Callaghan recalled praying every night at her knee, including for the safety of his father at sea. The ritual concluded with his singing the hymn he remembered 75 years later:

4 JC, *Time and Chance*, p. 22; Morgan, *Callaghan*, pp. 5, 7.

5 JC, *Time and Chance*, p. 25.

Lord, keep us safe this night,
Secure from all our fears.
May angels guard us while we sleep
Till morning light appears.[6]

Callaghan was first interviewed by the press at the age of two and a half. The evangelical magazine *Ashore and Afloat* quoted him at the outset of the First World War praying for the safe return of his father: 'Please Jesus bring my daddy safe home again for Leonard, Mamma and Dorothy. Amen.'[7]

Charlotte Callaghan's belief in the imminent Second Coming of the Lord made a particular impression on her young son. At his coming, those who were worthy would literally ascend to heaven. He recognized that this dogma of faith 'enabled her to bear her present troubles' but he did not share her joyful sense of expectation.

> To me it was a dreadful prospect. Only God and I knew what terrible sins I had committed: *I* knew that I was unworthy to be taken up to heaven with all those who were saved; and what shame my mother would feel when she ascended to heaven but I was left on earth as unworthy. To a seven-year-old the fear was real and tangible. I came home one day from school to find the house empty and silent and I knew at once what had happened. The Second Coming had taken place, my mother had been taken up to Heaven and I had, as I had always feared, been rejected. For a moment near-panic set in and then, with a relief almost too great to describe, I heard the sound of my mother's voice.

He was never able to confide this boyhood fear to his mother but felt it responsible for the sense of guilt he carried into adult life.[8]

---

6 Cited Michael Cockerell, Documentary, *James Callaghan: Looking back at age 80* (BBC, 1992).

7 *Ashore and Afloat* (December 1914), cited Morgan, *Callaghan*, p. 8.

8 JC, *Time and Chance*, p. 25.

'A strict religious home'

Every day in Callaghan's home began with a brief Bible reading before the children left for school: 'It was a strict religious home.'[9] Grace before meals was a given. Card playing was forbidden in the house, as were Sunday newspapers. The only secular reading permitted was the *Children's Encyclopaedia*.

Life revolved around the chapel. In Portsmouth, the Callaghans attended the London Road Baptist Church, a solid brick building with a tower and stone tracery. Virtually the whole of Sunday was spent there. Sunday school at 9.30 a.m. was followed by morning service at 11. There was time only for a cold lunch back home before Sunday school resumed at 2.30 p.m. There might be a Sunday-school tea and then evening service at 6.30 p.m. Nor was chapel limited to Sundays. The Band of Hope Union, warning children of the evils of drink, met on Monday evenings, while on Tuesday evenings Christian Endeavour encouraged young people to pray and read the Bible aloud. There was a prayer group on Thursday evenings and a youth choir on Fridays.[10]

Callaghan's father was wounded at the Battle of Jutland. After his discharge from the Navy, he worked as a coastguard in Brixham, Devon, until his death in 1921. The annual Harvest Festival of the Sea in Brixham Baptist Church provided a little local colour. Callaghan recalled the chapel decorated with fishing nets, oars, sails and lobster pots; the area superintendent preached in a frock coat, and green and red lanterns hung either side of the pulpit.[11]

The London Road Sunday school was a major concern, with 100 teachers and 600 'scholars'. Young students were required to memorize long passages from Scripture. (Callaghan would take both the title and opening quotation of his memoirs from the Bible.) Later they sat written exams, being awarded prizes depending on the results. Entering his teenage years, Callaghan began to challenge what he was being taught. The authorities responded by appointing him a Sunday-school teacher himself at the age of 14. The following year he was baptized. Some activities were of

9 Cited Cockerell, Documentary, *JC*.

10 JC, *Time and Chance*, p. 25.

11 JC, *Time and Chance*, p. 30.

a questionable spiritual nature: during the collection he and a contemporary sang the materialistic jingle: 'Hear the pennies dropping, Listen how they fall, Every one for Jesus, He shall have them all.'[12]

Callaghan remained a Sunday-school teacher until he left Portsmouth to begin work at the age of 17. On his departure, he was presented with a large Bible signed by the minister and Sunday-school superintendent and a framed copy of the Scripture verse: 'The steps of a good man are ordered by the LORD: and he delighteth in his way' (Psalm 37.23). He retained the Bible and had it rebound in his old age.[13]

Intellectual socialism versus 'fundamentalist religion'

Having passed his Civil Service exam, Callaghan started work as a tax officer in the Maidstone Inland Revenue Office in 1929. He was a young man alone and a long way from home. He wrote:

> We knew no one in Maidstone, but the Baptist Chapel rallied round and I was found lodgings . . . I had transferred, as it were, from the bosom of one Church to the care of another, and I found myself in a familiar and stable background.[14]

He was already critical of the Baptist faith in which he had been raised in Portsmouth. His biographer wrote: 'He lost his religious views altogether when he moved to Maidstone.'[15] Initially that did not appear inevitable. He attended the Knightrider Street Baptist Church and taught in its Sunday school. Callaghan was already a Labour Party supporter when he arrived in Kent, where he began to study socialist philosophy systematically, encouraged by a senior colleague in the tax office. He read extensively: George Bernard Shaw, H. G. Wells, H. N. Brailsford, G. D. H. Cole and Harold Laski. Evening classes of the Workers' Educational Association

12 JC, *Time and Chance*, p. 25; Morgan, *Callaghan*, p. 14.

13 JC, *Time and Chance*, p. 30; Morgan, *Callaghan*, p. 14.

14 JC, *Time and Chance*, pp. 36, 39.

15 Morgan, *Callaghan*, p. 15.

introduced him to Karl Marx's *Das Kapital.* The intellectual socialism he discovered 'seemed much more real and true than the fundamentalist religion in which I had been brought up'. In the perceived conflict between his adopted political creed and his inherited faith, he abandoned the latter.

Many in his position would simply have lapsed, ceasing to attend Sunday chapel. Callaghan had too much integrity to slip away quietly. With the assurance of youth, he penned a formal letter of resignation to the secretary of the Maidstone Baptists. An interview was arranged with a senior deacon from the church:

> He was a wise man who argued that although he disagreed with my new-found socialist beliefs, there need be no conflict between them and Church membership. Many tenets of the Christian faith were reconcilable with socialism. He rather surprised me by adding that I should not believe that every Christian subscribed to the kind of fundamentalist beliefs in which I had been brought up, and I need not fear that I would be behaving hypocritically if I remained a Church member.[16]

Callaghan's name remained on the roll of church members, but his time and allegiance were given to the Labour Party and trade union movement.

While severing the ties to the faith of his youth, Callaghan was generous in his subsequent acknowledgements: 'I never forget the immense debt I owe to a Christian upbringing, nor have I ever escaped its influence.'[17] He found his experience of chapel harsh and joyless, inculcating a sense of guilt and inadequacy,[18] and was disturbed by some of the views propounded (including by his sister), such as that a bright side to infant mortality might be that it afforded instant access to heaven.[19]

Callaghan's reservations concerning doctrines and practice did not prevent him admitting the human qualities he found among the Baptists: kindness, fellowship and practical charity. He recalled the handcart loaded with

16 JC, *Time and Chance*, p. 40.
17 JC, *Time and Chance*, p. 40.
18 Morgan, *Callaghan*, p. 14.
19 JC, *Time and Chance*, p. 40.

groceries at the chapel on the Sunday before Christmas, with sugar, sultanas and margarine to be distributed to homes in need. The Callaghans themselves benefited from this charity: after his father's death they were given accommodation by a deacon of the Brixham Baptist Church, while another chapelgoer ensured they received a regular supply of fresh fish. When the family returned to Portsmouth in 1923 life was hard. Callaghan recalled: 'It was an unsettling time in which the Chapel acted as an anchor.'[20]

He found the same kindness among the Baptists of Maidstone. One of the deacons, Frank Moulton, took pity on the young man away from home and invited him to dine with his family on Sundays. Callaghan had already met his daughter, Audrey, who taught alongside him at the Sunday school.[21] Indeed, she might have been another reason why he did not slip quietly away from the Baptist Church. Callaghan was smitten. The couple were married at the Knightrider Street Church on 28 July 1938 by the Revd R. Brunskill, assisted by another Baptist minister, the Revd Sidney Carter – his sister Dorothy's husband and Callaghan's brother-in-law. Audrey had no more attachment to her Baptist roots than her husband. The couple had three children, Margaret, Julia and Michael, but there is no evidence of the family practising faith in any form in the home or at church.

During the Second World War, Callaghan served in the Royal Navy, like his father before him. In the services, religion was compulsory and Callaghan was marched off to church on a Sunday. Befriending Hebridean fishermen, he elected to wear the same plastic tag around his neck as them, identifying him as a Scottish Presbyterian. He recalled the advantage of attending Church of Scotland services – they served a better breakfast afterwards than the other denominations.[22]

'The tide of permissiveness has gone too far'

His politics did not spring directly from his early religious beliefs, but as the deacon in Maidstone pointed out, nor were they necessarily in opposition. Increasingly, Baptists transferred their allegiance from the Liberals to the Labour Party. Callaghan knew many other Labour supporters at the

20 JC, *Time and Chance*, pp. 24, 33, 36.

21 JC, *Time and Chance*, p. 39.

22 JC, *Time and Chance*, p. 58.

Portsmouth Baptist Church. With Wilson, he re-echoed the words of Morgan Phillips, the party's General Secretary, that the Labour Party owed more to Methodism than to Marx.[23] His Nonconformist background formed a point of reference with constituents in South Wales, 1950s African nationalist leaders and the Southern Baptist US President Jimmy Carter. Callaghan's determination to reduce social inequality was based in his belief that socialism was as much an ethical as a material programme. Nevertheless, it caused some amusement when Lord Longford identified Callaghan, with other senior members of the 1964 Labour Cabinet, as a committed Christian.[24]

After the devaluation of sterling, Wilson moved Callaghan from the Treasury to the Home Office. He had supported the changes to social legislation but, unlike his predecessor, Roy Jenkins, he was not an enthusiast – with one exception. He passionately opposed capital punishment, stating that he would resign rather than authorize an execution.[25] Callaghan was uncomfortable with abortion and homosexuality – matters that simply were not discussed when he was young. He was one of the Cabinet members who saw no reason why parliamentary time should be allocated for a bill to legalize homosexuality when the proposal was first mooted. Like Thatcher, he favoured tolerance with respect to an individual's private life but 'recoiled' from the 'aggressive' promotion of these 'minority interests'. As far as he was concerned, the 'nuclear family is the most loving you can have'.[26] As Home Secretary, he tapped into a vein of popular sentiment when he declared that 'the tide of permissiveness has gone too far'.[27]

Raised in a working-class home, Callaghan was a social conservative by comparison with many in his party. Of course, he never sought to justify his views by reference to Christian teaching. Yet his biographer argued that this constitutes the most abiding legacy of his religious upbringing: he was 'surely giving voice to the fundamentalist creed of the Portsmouth Baptists, all those long years ago, shouting out in defiance, almost in despair, against what he saw as an amoral, rootless world'.[28]

23 JC, *Time and Chance*, p. 36.
24 Morgan, *Callaghan*, pp. 15–16.
25 Morgan, *Callaghan*, p. 297.
26 JC, Interview with Brian Walden (17 April 1987), cited *The Times* (18 and 20 April 1987).
27 Cited Morgan, *Callaghan*, p. 16.
28 Morgan, *Callaghan*, p. 16.

Ceding powers of patronage

Callaghan was the last Prime Minister to exercise the old powers of patronage in the appointment of Church of England bishops. Although generally consulting widely, in principle his predecessors had often been the key players in recommending the candidate who would then be formally appointed by the sovereign. That changed with the creation of the Church Appointments Commission. From 1 June 1977, this body put the names of two candidates for each vacancy before the Prime Minister, whose role was limited to either reversing the order of the two before passing the recommendation to the Crown, or requesting the commission to propose further candidates. A Prime Minister could no longer advance a candidate on his or her own initiative.

Three diocesan bishops were recommended by Callaghan under the old system. Although a sceptical Nonconformist, Callaghan took the process very seriously. Colin Peterson, the Appointments Secretary, produced information on the potential candidates. Callaghan was eager to match the qualities of the candidates with the specific needs of the Diocese. His knowledge of Anglican church politics was such that he aimed to maintain 'a balance between what I (perhaps improperly) called high or low church'. He or Peterson would then interview the preferred candidate. Referring to the change, he wrote:

> I found no real opposition from [the Queen] for a step which involved her personally, and as a Free Churchman, I felt that I should not stand in the way of the Church's desires, even if my opinion had been different.[29]

A 'fervent atheist'?

Was Callaghan an atheist? Several websites identify him as such. The evidence either way is scant. His colleague Richard Crossman labelled him

29 JC to Bernard Palmer, 19 September 1991, cited Bernard Palmer, *High and Mitred: A study of Prime Ministers as bishop-makers, 1837–1977* (London: SPCK, 1992), p. 275.

a 'fervent atheist'.[30] (Crossman, however, was not the most reliable source in these matters. Around the same time he classified Wilson as 'a perfectly sincere Sunday Methodist'.[31]) Callaghan is said to have admitted to being an atheist in an interview in the mid-1980s, but no citation is given. On the other hand, he was critical of declining respect for law and order and a weakened sense of community. The fact that he thought that, partially, this might be due to 'a materialist society with changing values' and 'a loss of faith', does not make him a believer. Kenneth Morgan noted that Callaghan prayed 'at critical moments when in government, notably in his time at the Treasury'.[32] But was this more desperation than proof of Christian belief? The better position is to categorize him from the 1930s as a *practical* atheist – whatever his personal beliefs, the existence or otherwise of God had no perceptible bearing on his behaviour.

Callaghan's experience was similar to that of hundreds of thousands of twentieth-century Britons. Their childhood and adolescent years were immersed in chapel and Sunday school, Scripture and Sabbath Day observance. Many endured worship as tedious and emotionally unsatisfying. They found any intellectual basis for Christianity lacking or unconvincing. Enjoying a degree of opportunity, affluence and mobility unknown to their forebears, they dropped the practice of faith at the earliest opportunity. They generally harboured little hostility to the Christianity in which they had been raised. It simply faded from their adult lives as something unnecessary and largely unmissed.

A Catholic ending

In his final years, Callaghan was unexpectedly brought into contact with the Catholic faith of his Irish forefathers. It began with Audrey. The couple were together for some 70 years and enjoyed a close and happy marriage. In the 1990s she was diagnosed with Alzheimer's. Callaghan was distraught when it was decided in 2001 that she required full-time care in

30 Richard Crossman, Diary, 4 October 1966, cited Crossman, *The Diaries of a Cabinet Minister*, Vol. 2 (London: Hamish Hamilton, 1976), p. 63.

31 Crossman, Diary, 11 December 1966, cited Crossman, *The Diaries of a Cabinet Minister*, Vol. 2, p. 160.

32 Morgan, *Callaghan*, p. 32.

a nursing home. The family selected St George's Retreat outside Burgess Hill, 12 miles from the small farm Callaghan had purchased at Ringmer in Sussex. He was assiduous in the care he showed Audrey, visiting every day for the remaining three and a half years of her life.[33]

St George's enjoyed an excellent professional reputation. It was owned by Catholic Augustinian nuns, who at the time were much involved in its daily management. Callaghan struck up a good relationship with the sisters and also provided practical help, attending planning meetings to lend support for their development proposals. They in turn witnessed to him a joy in the Christian faith that had been lacking in his own childhood. He told one of the sisters he 'wished he had got involved with them earlier in his life'. But although well disposed towards them and their faith, there is no evidence this changed his personal beliefs, about which he remained reticent.

Audrey died on 15 March 2005. Her funeral was celebrated in the chapel at St George's by the local Catholic priest. It was the last event Callaghan attended. Having been together throughout their adult lives, the couple were not long separated in death. He asked to be admitted to the same room Audrey had occupied and died just 11 days after his wife, the day before his ninety-third birthday. His own funeral was also held in the chapel at St George's. In his case, however, an Anglican clergyman from a Sussex parish presided.[34]

After the funeral, Callaghan was cremated. His ashes were scattered with those of Audrey at the base of the Peter Pan statue at Great Ormond Street Hospital, whose board of governors she had chaired. A memorial service for both, held at Westminster Abbey on 28 July 2005, was attended by the great and the good, and also by the Augustinian sisters from St George's.

33 Cherie Booth and Cate Haste, *The Goldfish Bowl: Married to the Prime Minister, 1955–97* (London: Chatto & Windus, 2004), p. 181.

34 Private information communicated to the author.

Margaret Thatcher (1979–1990)

'Where there is doubt, may we bring faith'

Margaret Hilda Roberts was born in Grantham, Lincolnshire, on 13 October 1925. She attended Kesteven and Grantham Girls' School and graduated from Somerville College, Oxford.

She fought Dartford as the Conservative candidate in the general elections of 1950 and 1951. After marrying Denis Thatcher in 1951, she requalified as a barrister. She was elected for Finchley in 1959, representing the constituency until her retirement from the Commons in 1992.

Thatcher was appointed Undersecretary at the Ministry of Pensions in 1961, earning a reputation for hard work, mastery of detail and forceful presentation. She held the pensions brief in Opposition, then spoke on housing, tax, fuel and education. In 1970, Thatcher entered the Cabinet as Secretary of State for Education and Science. She gave local authorities greater freedom to determine secondary education policy but failed to stem the general move from grammar schools to comprehensives. Back in Opposition she was Shadow Environment Secretary, then an effective deputy to the Shadow Chancellor.

Dissatisfaction with Heath's leadership grew as he lost three out of four general elections. When others proved unwilling, Thatcher challenged him for the leadership and, to the surprise of most, defeated him on the first ballot on 4 February 1975. Urging a return to robust Conservative values, she won the second ballot the following week. Despite the Labour government's precarious parliamentary position, she had to wait four years for a general election and was perceived as inexperienced and shrill – Labour's defeat on 3 May 1979 was largely the consequence of the 'winter of discontent'. Winning a majority of 43 seats, Margaret Thatcher was appointed Prime Minister on 4 May 1979.

Thatcher identified herself as a 'conviction politician', rejecting the postwar consensual style of government. Determined to roll back the frontiers of the state and encourage private enterprise, she cut rates of personal taxation and pursued monetarist policies to curb inflation. The results were dramatic: the country plunged into recession, manufacturing industry declined and unemployment rose, peaking subsequently at 3.3 million. Opposed by 'wets' in her own Cabinet, Thatcher held her nerve, but her popularity plummeted.

The Argentinian invasion of the Falkland Islands in April 1982 and its defeat by the British task force led to the reversal of her political fortunes. Helped also by a recovering economy, at least in London and the south, and an Opposition split between a left-leaning Labour Party and the Liberal-SDP Alliance, Thatcher led the Conservatives to a landslide victory in the general election on 9 June 1983, winning a majority of 144.

Appointing a Cabinet more aligned to her own vision, she pressed ahead with the privatization of nationalized industries and public utilities. Council-house tenants had already been given the right to buy their own homes. Determined to curb trade union power, she defeated Arthur Scargill's National Union of Miners in a costly and violent strike in 1984–5. Strikes ceased to be a regular feature of national life. She escaped an assassination attempt when the IRA bombed her Brighton hotel during the 1984 Conservative Party conference.

Thatcher passionately opposed Communism as inimical to freedom, rejoicing in the title of 'Iron Lady' accorded her by the Soviet Union. She shared Ronald Reagan's determination to win the Cold War. The UK's nuclear deterrent was renewed despite unilateralist opposition from the Labour Party and the Campaign for Nuclear Disarmament (CND). When Mikhail Gorbachev assumed office in the Soviet Union, she recognized him as someone with whom she could do business.

A strong economy and a weak Opposition allowed Thatcher to win a historic third general election victory on 11 June 1987 with a majority of 102.

Although a supporter of UK membership of the EEC, Thatcher's tough negotiating stance resulted in rebates of the British contribution to the European budget. She strongly resisted moves towards political federalism and monetary union, promoting her own vision of a free-trade alliance of sovereign states. She reluctantly agreed to sterling joining the Exchange Rate Mechanism in 1990.

Tensions over Europe, Thatcher's use of special advisers and her abrasive treatment of Cabinet colleagues led to growing unease as she refused to contemplate retirement. The introduction of the Community Charge (poll tax) proved hugely unpopular. The resignation speech of Sir Geoffrey Howe, the Deputy Prime Minister, opened the way for the challenge to her leadership by Michael Heseltine (who had resigned acrimoniously as Secretary of State for Defence in January 1986). Thatcher won the vote on 20 November 1990, but by an insufficient margin to avoid a second ballot. Reluctantly convinced by colleagues that she could not win, she resigned on 28 November 1990. She was the longest-serving Prime Minister in the twentieth century, and one of the most influential and controversial.

In December 1990 she was awarded the Order of Merit and became Lady Thatcher as Denis was created a baronet. Standing down as an MP, she was granted a life peerage as Baroness Thatcher of Kesteven in 1992 and created a Lady Companion of the Garter in 1995. She continued to speak on issues she cared passionately about, opposing European federalism, to the irritation of her successor.

Following Denis's death in 2003, Lady Thatcher suffered increasing ill health. She died in a private suite at the Ritz Hotel, London, on 8 April 2013 and was accorded a state funeral at St Paul's Cathedral on 17 April 2013.

* * *

She owed everything to her father

At the time, it was perceived as an event of great significance. The UK had elected its first female Prime Minister. Only hindsight would reveal how seismic the change actually was. On entering Downing Street on 4 May 1979, convinced that she was called to change the country beyond the narrowly political and economic, Margaret Thatcher recited the prayer of Saint Francis of Assisi:

> Where there is discord, may we bring harmony.
> Where there is error, may we bring truth.

Where there is doubt, may we bring faith.
And where there is despair, may we bring hope.[1]

Her choice of words was criticized then and subsequently. It was claimed she was mistaken, even hypocritical, to present herself as a force for conciliation. Thatcher retorted in her autobiography that Saint Francis did not just pray for peace, but also for an end to error and doubt.[2] The aptness of the text may be disputed; the fact that Thatcher chose to begin her premiership with words of faith, however, should have surprised no one.

After reciting the prayer, she was asked for her thoughts about her mentor, her own father. She declared she owed everything to him. (It was always her father of whom she spoke, never her mother.) Through thrift and hard work, Alfred Roberts had built up a grocer's business from nothing. An alderman and councillor in Grantham, he introduced his daughter to the political life. Prior to this, he had introduced her to the Christian faith.

Thatcher's parents were Wesleyan Methodists who met at the Bridge End Road Chapel, Grantham, marrying there in May 1917. Early twentieth-century Methodists in Grantham had various options in terms of worship. Wesleyans, Primitive Methodists and Free Methodists all had their own chapels. The differences were not simply doctrinal. Wesleyans tended to be from a slightly higher social background, such as shopkeeping and farming, and more likely to vote Conservative. Nationally, moves were afoot to unite Methodism, resulting in the Methodist Union of 1932. Grantham Methodists, however, maintained their separate traditions until after Margaret had left the town.

The newly wed Alfred and Beatrice Roberts chose not to attend their closest chapel but rather the Wesleyan Finkin Street Church in the town centre. It is an imposing stoneclad edifice, built in 1840, seating 600 (though even in the interwar years there were concerns about debt and declining membership).[3] There was no doubt as to the focus of worship. The congregation's eye was drawn not to an altar but to the central pulpit and organ.

---

1 Although attributed to the thirteenth-century saint, the prayer first appeared in a French Catholic journal in the early twentieth century.

2 Margaret Thatcher, *The Downing Street Years* (London: HarperCollins, 1993), p. 19.

3 Indicative of the decline of English Nonconformity, all the other chapels have closed; the Methodists at Finkin Street merged with the United Reformed Church in 2008.

Services assumed the typical Methodist 'hymn sandwich' format: hymns alternating with prayers, Scripture readings and sermon. The chapel enjoyed a reputation for good preaching.

Alfred Roberts was a regular lay preacher at the Finkin Street Church and in the surrounding village chapels in the Grantham Circuit. As a circuit steward, he was responsible for organizing the rota of preachers. The young Margaret often accompanied him. She recalled that he

> was a powerful preacher whose sermons contained a good deal of intellectual substance. But he was taken aback one day when I asked him why he put on a 'sermon voice' on these occasions. I don't think that he realized that he did this. It was an unconscious homage to the biblical message.[4]

Thatcher's biographers differ radically in their interpretation of Alfred Roberts's faith. For John Campbell, his preaching

> was fundamentalist, Bible-based, concerned with the individual's responsibility to God for his own behaviour. It was not a social gospel, but an uncompromisingly individualistic moral code which underpinned an individualistic approach to politics and commerce. A man's duty was to keep his soul clean, mind his own business and care for his own family.[5]

Jonathan Aitken dated Thatcher's daughter, Carol. After a spell in the Cabinet (and in prison), he was ordained to Anglican ministry. For Aitken, Roberts's preaching displayed 'a theological understanding that was broadminded and original. He was liberal in his doctrine, claiming no monopoly of wisdom for Methodism, and quoting from a wide range of secular writers.'[6] Aitken followed the line developed by Antonio Weiss in his paper on Thatcher's religion, which strongly rejected Campbell's

4 Margaret Thatcher, *The Path to Power* (London: HarperCollins, 1995), p. 5.

5 John Campbell, *Margaret Thatcher: The grocer's daughter* (London: Jonathan Cape, 2000), p. 16.

6 Jonathan Aitken, *Margaret Thatcher: Power and personality* (London: Bloomsbury, 2013), p. 22.

analysis. Weiss argued that Roberts was doctrinally liberal and ecumenical – a stance he transmitted to his daughter.[7]

Some of Roberts's sermon notes survive. They suggest neither a theological fundamentalist nor an ecumenical liberal. He was a product of his age and background. What distinguished him from his fellow lay preachers was the intellectual structure and content of his sermons. A self-educated man, he was widely read. His daughter recalled the amount of time he spent preparing sermons.[8] Roberts insisted on the preacher's duty to study and live out what he preached. The sermons contain historical and literary allusions, but mainly they relay the scriptural quotations, hymn verses and homely teaching familiar to Methodists.

Preaching close to Isaac Newton's birthplace, Roberts saw no conflict between science and religion. He was willing to interpret the Old Testament. He asserted: 'To make uniformity of doctrine the only basis of a church is a return to the old fundamentalism which has hindered and splintered the Christian Church probably more than any other one thing.' His objection was to making uniformity the *only* basis of the Church. Doctrinal fundamentalism was wrong if it impeded the spiritual life, a personal relationship with Christ and human freedom. Doctrine per se was not wrong. Nothing in Roberts's preaching challenged the Methodist and Protestant orthodoxy of his day. He gave no succour to liberalism: 'The Gospel is not for an age but for all time'; 'There is no by-pass road round Calvary.' His faith was Christocentric; he preached a message of hope in the blood of Christ that had delivered us 'from the power of sin that destroys everything that is most precious in human experience'.

Roberts advised his congregation to 'avoid the principle of a denominational "closed shop"'.[9] In doing so he was faithful to the Methodist Catechism, which taught that 'there are many communions of Christians throughout the world . . . [forming] one Church.'[10] Unlike the historic

7 Antonio E. Weiss, 'The Religious Mind of Mrs Thatcher' (2011), <www.margaretthatcher.org/document/112748>, accessed 19.11.20.

8 Margaret Thatcher, Interview, Royal Marsden Hospital Radio, 12 April 1989, <www.margaretthatcher.org/document/107638>, accessed 19.11.20.

9 Alfred Roberts, Sermon Notes, <www.margaretthatcher.org/document/109898>, accessed 19.11.20.

10 *The Catechism of the Methodist Church*, <www.margaretthatcher.org/document/109910>, accessed 19.11.20.

churches, John Wesley's followers made no claim to universality nor exclusivity. That was the theory. In practice, Roberts's 'ecumenism' did not extend to Roman Catholics, nor perhaps even to his separated Methodist brethren. Thatcher recalled the Grantham churches in that pre-ecumenical age as 'competitive and fuelled by a spirit of rivalry'.[11]

Their 'lives revolved around Methodism'

This was the faith Alfred Roberts believed and preached, and in which Margaret and her elder sister, Muriel, were raised: to *know* God and to live out this relationship in one's daily life. Margaret was baptized in the Finkin Street Church on 20 December 1925.

Children are more likely to be conscious of the practice of religion than of its doctrinal content, and Margaret was fully aware of the practical consequences of her parents' faith. Home was 'intensely religious'; their 'lives revolved around Methodism'.[12] Sundays were virtually lived in the chapel. Margaret was taken to Sunday school at 10 a.m., followed by the morning service at 11 a.m. At 2.30 p.m. she was back at Sunday school, where from the age of 12 she played hymns on the piano for the younger children. Then the family might well return for the 6 p.m. evening service. Her parents frequently brought home other chapelgoers for refreshments and discussion.[13] Nor was religion simply for Sundays: 'We attended a number of Church activities during the week.'[14] One of her greatest childhood excitements was a trip to London. Her hosts, a Methodist minister and his wife, took her to St Paul's Cathedral, where John Wesley had prayed on the morning of his conversion (though being taken to a musical featured more prominently in her memory).[15]

School was her first substantive exposure to non-Methodists. In 1930, Alderman Roberts sent Margaret to Huntingtower Road Council School,

11 MT, *The Path to Power*, p. 8.

12 MT, *The Path to Power*, p. 5.

13 MT, Interview with Cliff Michelmore, BBC1, *A Chance to Meet*, 21 March 1971, <www.margaretthatcher.org/document/101894>, accessed 20.11.20; MT, *The Path to Power*, p. 6.

14 MT, 'I Believe: A speech on Christianity and politics', St Lawrence Jewry, 30 March 1978, <www.margaretthatcher.org/document/103522>, accessed 20.11.20.

15 MT, *The Path to Power*, pp. 9–10.

selected partly for its non-denominational character. Not that he was seeking a secular education for his daughter but rather simple Bible teaching unadulterated by Anglican creeds and rites. Margaret later attended Kesteven and Grantham Girls' School. At school, she came to appreciate how atypical her home was even in a 1930s East Midlands town where churchgoing was still the norm: 'I was the only person at school who went to church quite as often.'[16] Forty years later, the passion was still evident: her family's religiosity had the effect 'of marking one out from one's fellows, which is very difficult for a child . . . One of the most difficult things for a child is to be made conspicuous among the child's friends.'[17]

She reacted in a limited way, on occasion attempting to avoid chapel, and resented being refused permission to walk with a friend on Sunday evenings. She disagreed with her father's opposition to the relaxation of regulations enforcing Sunday observance on local residents.[18] Muriel resented the constraints even more keenly: 'It was all church, church, church. We had an uncle every Christmas who sent us religious books. Oh God how we hated it. You weren't allowed to play games. That really is bigoted, isn't it?'[19]

Why did this not lead to Margaret's outright rejection of her parents' Methodism? Certainly she wished to avoid causing her father any distress. There is the suggestion that, initially at least, Roberts was not entirely master of his own home. Muriel believed it was her mother who was the 'bigoted Methodist',[20] her fundamentalist approach reinforced by her own mother, Phoebe Stephenson, who lived with the family for ten years until her death in 1934. Only then were the prohibitions against possession of a wireless or attendance at a musical relaxed.[21] Muriel endured this puritanical regime longer than her sister.

Despite the constraints, there was much Margaret found positive in Methodism. The preaching was 'intellectually stimulating. The ministers

16 MT, Wesley's Chapel, 9 April 1993, cited Eliza Filby, *God and Mrs Thatcher: The battle for Britain's soul* (London: Biteback Publishing, 2015), p. 15.

17 MT, Interview with Cliff Michelmore, 21 March 1971.

18 MT, *The Path to Power*, pp. 6–7; MT, Interview with Cliff Michelmore, 21 March 1971.

19 Muriel Cullen, cited Charles Moore, *Margaret Thatcher: Not for turning* (London: Allen Lane, 2013), p. 7.

20 Muriel Cullen, cited Moore, *MT: Not for turning*, p. 9.

21 Aitken, *MT*, p. 14.

were powerful characters with strong views.' Even in youth she listened carefully to sermons. She recalled being challenged and persuaded by a Congregationalist minister who urged equality of treatment for illegitimate children, not visiting the sins of their parents on them.[22] The chapel also provided a glimpse of a world beyond a small provincial town, offering the opportunity to meet preachers of national repute as well as overseas missionaries.[23]

Then there was music. She was an archetypal Methodist, revelling in Charles Wesley's rousing hymns, including 'Lo, He comes with clouds descending' and 'Can it be that I should gain'.[24] She confided that it was 'the musical side of Methodism which I liked best. We sang special hymns on the occasion of Sunday School anniversaries . . . Our church had an exceptionally good choir.'[25]

'She was a preacher before she was a politician'

In 1943, Margaret went up to Oxford to read Chemistry. She went to the non-denominational Somerville College rather than the Anglican foundation, Lady Margaret Hall. Nor did she leave her Methodism behind in Grantham: 'There are many tales of young people entering university and, partly through coming into contact with scepticism and partly for less wholesome reasons, losing their faith. I never felt in any danger of that.' Occasionally she attended her own college chapel or the University Church of St Mary the Virgin ('a somewhat cold place of worship') to hear a good sermon. Normally, however, she would be found on Sundays at the Wesley Memorial Church.[26]

Her practice was far from perfunctory. She was an active member of the John Wesley Society, a Methodist student group that met in the minister's

22 MT, *The Path to Power*, pp. 10–11.

23 MT, Interview with Miriam Stoppard, Yorkshire Television, *Woman to Woman*, 2 October 1985, <www.margaretthatcher.org/document/105830>, accessed 20.11.20.

24 Aitken, *MT*, p. 14.

25 MT, *The Path to Power*, pp. 8–9.

26 MT, *The Path to Power*, pp. 39–40.

house after the Sunday evening service, engaging in vigorous religious debates. Thatcher joined those undergraduates who went out in pairs to visit the chapels in the Oxford Circuit, occasionally preaching herself. One contemporary recalled an 'outstanding' sermon she preached on the text: 'Seek ye first the kingdom of God; and all these things shall be added to you.' John Campbell observes: 'She was a preacher before she was a politician.' In her final year, involvement in Conservative student politics came to predominate, but she never entirely abandoned her participation in the Methodist prayer and discussion groups.[27]

She was captivated by C. S. Lewis's wartime broadcasts, 'Christian Behaviour' (later published in his *Mere Christianity*), and acknowledged him as the foremost influence on her religious intellectual formation. Lewis answered many of her questions concerning the Christian faith. She discussed his thought at the Wesley Society and devoured his works, including *The Screwtape Letters* and *The Abolition of Man*, returning to them later in life. They gave her an understanding of the natural law – the morality that, Lewis argued, was innate and accessible to all humanity due to our common created nature.[28] Although an Anglican, Lewis avoided confessional controversies, focusing on basic Christian apologetics and practical morality. One of the most significant and popular Christian writers of the century, his gentle wit and simple language conveyed real theological depth. His books, which included *The Chronicles of Narnia*, sold tens of millions of copies. It is surprising that Thatcher was the only twentieth-century Prime Minister to mention him.

On graduating, Thatcher found work as a research chemist in Essex. Her heart, however, was set on a parliamentary career. Weekends were often spent travelling, attending political gatherings and selection conferences. Nevertheless, when in Colchester on Sundays she attended the Culver Street Wesleyan Church. There she read the lesson and, as at Oxford, joined other young Methodists in visiting the surrounding village chapels.[29]

27 MT, *The Path to Power*, p. 40; Campbell, *MT: The grocer's daughter*, pp. 47–8.
28 MT, *The Path to Power*, p. 40.
29 Campbell, *MT: The grocer's daughter*, p. 68.

A 'middle-stump Anglican'

At her adoption meeting as the Conservative candidate for Dartford in 1949, she met Denis Thatcher, a businessman. It took a while for the romance to flourish. She had other romantic interests and was busy establishing herself in the constituency. Denis was ten years her senior. Another factor caused her to hesitate – Denis had been married previously and was divorced. It had been a wartime romance. Returning from military service overseas, he found his wife in a relationship with another man.

Divorce was still frowned on socially in post-war Britain. Most Christians considered themselves bound by Christ's teaching on the subject, allowing only limited, if any, exceptions. The Methodist Church changed its stance only in 1948, permitting the remarriage of the innocent party in chapel – at the discretion of the minister. Speaking in later years, Thatcher expressed her unease about soaring divorce rates. She was sufficiently troubled to seek her father's advice. Where his own daughter was concerned, Roberts took a surprisingly relaxed and pragmatic approach. He approved of Denis personally. The fact that he was 'very comfortably situated financially' helped. Roberts gave his blessing: 'I told Margaret that she could disregard [Denis's divorce] as he was in no way at fault.'[30]

The couple married on 13 December 1951 in Wesley's Chapel close to the City of London. They argued that it was more convenient for their London-based friends. Denis's divorce, however, may also have been a factor. Grantham Methodists might not have held such advanced views. Alfred and Beatrice Roberts' tolerance was severely tested. The London chapel was liturgically much higher than Finkin Street, in their view 'halfway to Rome'.[31]

There have been varied and mistaken attempts to identify Denis's religious affiliation. Andrew Thomson, Thatcher's constituency agent, thought Denis 'a Methodist like her'.[32] Nick Spencer was wide of the mark when he

30 Alfred Roberts to Muriel Cullen, 25 September 1951, cited Moore, *MT: Not for turning*, p. 105.

31 Cited Moore, *MT: Not for turning*, p. 109.

32 Andrew Thomson, *Margaret Thatcher: The woman within* (London: W. H. Allen, 1989), p. 121.

claimed that Denis 'was, to all intents and purposes, a non-believer'.[33] Cynthia Crawford, Thatcher's personal assistant, was slightly closer when she said, 'Denis was quite a high Anglican.'[34]

He described himself as a 'middle-stump Anglican'.[35] His family were originally Anglican farmers from Berkshire who emigrated to New Zealand. Denis was more than a cultural Anglican. His father, a committed Freemason, deliberately sent him to a non-Anglican school. Denis consciously opted to attend Church of England services with his mother and sister.[36] He happily took Catholic guests at Chequers to Mass at Great Missenden, mischievously suggesting that he might convert to Catholicism as their churches were better heated.[37] His faith was non-demonstrative and traditional, but it was real. This is important because, on occasion, it was Denis who took the initiative regarding family religious practice.

'Something a little more formal'

Eliza Filby has written that

> it was precisely at this time [after her marriage to Denis] that Margaret Thatcher moved away from Methodism and became an Anglican, albeit of a 'low church' variety . . . the strict and sober Nonconformity into which she had been raised did not complement the new world Thatcher was now operating in.

The implication is that such a move was made for reasons of social and political 'expediency',[38] which is neither entirely fair nor accurate. It was not that straightforward or sudden – or definitive.

33 Nick Spencer, 'Margaret Thatcher (1979–90)', in ed. Nick Spencer, *The Mighty and the Almighty: How political leaders do God* (London: Biteback Publishing, 2017), p. 2.

34 Cited Charles Moore, *Margaret Thatcher Herself alone* (London: Allen Lane, 2019), p. 819.

35 Cited Aitken, *MT*, p. 684.

36 Carol Thatcher, *Below the Parapet: The biography of Denis Thatcher* (London: HarperCollins, 1996), p. 29.

37 Carol Thatcher, *Below the Parapet*, p. 241.

38 Filby, *God and Mrs Thatcher*, p. 67.

Thatcher admitted to being more attracted to Anglicanism from her time at Oxford, but continued to practise as a Methodist.[39] When they returned from their honeymoon, she took Denis to a Methodist chapel dedication service on the Saturday and went back to Wesley's Chapel the following day for Sunday service.[40] She gave birth to twins, Mark and Carol, in August 1953, and four months later had them baptized at Wesley's Chapel. Aged nine, Carol was sent to Queenswood School in Hertfordshire, which began life as a school for Wesleyan ministers' daughters.[41] As Prime Minister, Thatcher was a member of the Methodist Parliamentary Fellowship.[42]

The move to Anglican practice was gradual and, largely, pragmatic. In 1957, the Thatchers moved to Farnborough in Kent. There they attended the family service at the parish church. Beatrice Roberts objected when she discovered that her grandchildren were being raised as Anglicans.[43] Thatcher gave her rationale: 'We both felt that it would be confusing for the children if we did not attend the same church. The fact that our church was Low Church made it easier for the Methodist in me to make the transition.' She further justified herself, referring on numerous occasions to the fact John Wesley considered himself a member of the Church of England until his dying day.[44] That may be true but, by the mid twentieth century, Methodists were conscious and proud of their distinct identity.

Thatcher was genuinely horrified by suggestions that her transition to Anglicanism was politically motivated.[45] Andrew Thomson's explanation that she preferred the 'less emotional' style of worship in the Church of England is more accurate.[46] She sought something else she felt Anglicanism better able to provide:

> You sometimes feel the need for a slightly more formal service and perhaps a little bit more formality in the underlying theology too. So

39 MT, Interview with Chris Ogden, 16 January 1989, <www.margaretthatcher.org/document/107438>, accessed 22.11.20.

40 Moore, *MT: Not for turning*, p. 125.

41 Carol Thatcher, *A Swim-on Part in the Goldfish Bowl: A memoir* (London: Headline Review, 2008).

42 Filby, *God and Mrs Thatcher*, p. 144.

43 Moore, *MT: Not for turning*, p. 8.

44 MT, *The Path to Power*, p. 105.

45 MT, Interview with Chris Ogden, 16 January 1989.

46 Thomson, *MT*, p. 66.

throughout my life I have felt the need for both things, to some extent for the informality, for the works you do; but always I found myself groping out for more of the actual teaching of the religious basis. As I say, I went for something a little more formal.[47]

Thatcher was never officially received into the Anglican Church. Not being confirmed, she always declined to receive Holy Communion.[48]

Speaking in a City church in 1978, she shared her view that 'the majority of English parents want their children to be brought up in what is essentially the same religious heritage as was handed to me.' It was not something she herself put into practice.[49] As they grew older, Mark and Carol were not required to attend church because, Thatcher commented: 'I'd had so much insistence myself.'[50] It was a right the children quickly chose to exercise, after which Carol remembers that her parents continued to attend only 'irregularly'.[51] The sight of the couple in church was not calculated to infuse the vicar with joy. Denis narrated one encounter: 'Woke up. Lovely morning. Sun shining. I said: "Come on, love. Let's go to church." Do you know the vicar was anti-South Africa and anti-Rhodesia! Came out. Said "Thanks very much padre." Never went back!'[52]

'I am in politics because of the conflict between good and evil'

From the 1950s, as a Conservative candidate and then MP, Thatcher spoke often to church groups and in church venues. She was a regular at the Finchley Women's Inter-church Luncheon Club. Even as Prime Minister, the Finchley Women's Day of Prayer meetings were a fixture in her diary. There was, however, little out of the ordinary in these commitments or the speeches delivered.

---

47 MT, Interview with Richard Dowden, *Catholic Herald*, 22 and 29 December 1978, <www.margaretthatcher.org/document/103793>, accessed 22.11.20.

48 Filby, *God and Mrs Thatcher*, p. 145.

49 MT, 'I Believe'.

50 Cited Campbell, *MT: The grocer's daughter*, p. 29.

51 Carol Thatcher, *Below the Parapet*, p. 22.

52 Denis Thatcher, Interview, cited Moore, *MT: Not for turning*, p. 176.

In the 1970s she began to speak with greater conviction on what she saw as essential Conservative values, distinct from both socialism and a more consensual approach within her own party. Increasingly, she associated this with Christianity – while never denying that political opponents could also be sincere Christians. She viewed life and politics in dualistic terms: 'I am in politics because of the conflict between good and evil, and I believe that in the end good will triumph.'[53] For her, public office was necessarily a spiritual vocation: 'Economics is the method; the object is to change the soul.' Notwithstanding the vocabulary, she was not preaching personal salvation. She was talking of 'the heart and soul of the nation', of her passionate desire to redress the balance between 'personal society' and 'collectivist society', to restore a sense of meaning and purpose to the individual.[54]

Thatcher could be surprisingly open to other faiths, according a favoured status to Judaism, but Christ and Christianity held an exclusive position. It was not possible, she wrote 'for society to exclude or eliminate Christ from its social and political life without a terrible consequence'.[55] Democratic society was founded on concepts of human dignity and human rights that derived from the Bible and Christianity.[56] She could not 'imagine that anything other than Christianity is likely to resupply most people in the West with the virtues necessary to remoralize society in the very practical ways which the solution of many present problems requires'.[57]

Her first tentative steps in this direction were contained in the Iain Macleod Memorial Lecture, which she delivered to Young Conservatives in 1977. (In her speeches and writings, Thatcher was often assisted by a team of advisers. No one would claim, however, that she articulated ideas of which she was not personally convinced.) Religion, she asserted, gave the Conservative Party its distinctive character. Faith taught that the individual was unique, with a duty to cooperate with God in working out his or her own salvation. Conservatives, therefore, always began with the person

53 MT, Interview, *Daily Telegraph*, 18 September 1984, cited Hugo Young, *One of Us: A biography of Margaret Thatcher* (London: Macmillan, 1989), p. 352.

54 MT, Interview, *Sunday Times*, 3 May 1981, <www.margaretthatcher.org/document/104475>, accessed 24.11.20.

55 MT, 'Preface', in eds Michael Alison and David L. Edwards, *Christianity and Conservatism: Are Christianity and Conservatism compatible?* (London: Hodder & Stoughton, 1990).

56 MT, Interview with David Frost, TV-AM, *Frost on Sunday*, 1 January 1989, <www.margaretthatcher.org/document/107022>, accessed 26.11.20.

57 MT, *The Path to Power*, p. 554.

for whose benefit economic and social policies should be moulded – and not vice versa. Christianity was a moderating force. It valued the creation of wealth 'but warns against obsession with it, warns against putting it above all else. Money is not an end in itself, but a means to an end.'[58]

'We do not achieve happiness or salvation in isolation'

Her next foray into the field was more substantive. Thatcher accepted the invitation to give a Lenten talk, 'I Believe: A speech on Christianity and politics', in the City church of St Lawrence Jewry on 30 March 1978. Alfred Sherman, Simon Webley and the journalist T. E. Utley assisted with the drafting. She reaffirmed the importance of politics as 'one of the ways in which individuals could discharge that duty to their neighbours which God has enjoined on mankind'. Christianity, for her, was practical morality, not 'political philosophy'. It provided those 'standards to which political actions must, in the end, be referred'. It was a reminder of the provisional nature of this life, teaching that politics was 'about establishing the conditions in which men and women can best use their fleeting lives in this world to prepare themselves for the next'.

She refused to disown her own 'rather pious' upbringing. With more enthusiasm than precision, she nailed her colours to the traditionalist mast, disparaging those 'sophisticated theologians' who had stripped religion 'of its supernatural elements'. Implicitly, Thatcher included herself among the 'ordinary people' to whom 'heaven and hell, right and wrong, good and bad, matter'. She reverted in the speech to battles while at the Department of Education and Science to prevent the dilution of 'the specifically Christian content of teaching and corporate life in our schools'.

Thatcher condemned the claim of any political system to offer a panacea for the human condition. There is 'some evil' in all of us, she insisted, and 'it cannot be banished by sound policies and institutional reforms', nor by the free-enterprise system and certainly not by Marxist collectivism. She

58 MT, Iain Macleod Lecture, 'Dimensions of Conservatism', Young Conservatives, 4 July 1977, <www.margaretthatcher.org/document/103411>, accessed 26.11.20.

challenged 'bad theology' – 'the Devil is still with us' and would not be exorcized by increased affluence:

> There is another dimension – a moral one . . . people need a purpose and an ethic. The State cannot provide these – they can only come from the teachings of a Faith. And the Church must be the instrument of that work.

She was not, of course, impressed when in the following decade the Church of England took her at her word and sought to provide that purpose and teaching – at variance with her own beliefs.

In this early speech, Thatcher developed a theme that fascinated Tony Blair: the relationship between the community (she preferred the term 'society') and the individual, and the role of religion in furthering that relationship. Her first point might surprise her detractors. It was quoted by the Bishop of London at her funeral:

> There is that great Christian doctrine that we are all members one of another expressed in the concept of the Church on earth as the body of Christ. From this we learn our interdependence, and the great truth that we do not achieve happiness or salvation in isolation from each other but as members of society.

Her second point was more predictable: the individual human capacity, as created beings, for moral choice between good and evil. She concluded by stating that almost 'the whole of political wisdom consists in getting these two ideas in the right relationship to each other'. They might have placed the emphases differently, but in this instance at least there is similarity in the approach of Thatcher and Blair.[59]

Of course, there was criticism. There is bound to be when any English politician makes public reference to religion. That criticism, however, was relatively muted. It had been a considered reflection in which Thatcher explicitly acknowledged that 'many sincere Christians' would disagree with her 'practical conclusions'. Her other major speech on the subject of

59 MT, 'I Believe'.

Christianity and politics was deemed more strident, and created a massive furore.

The Sermon on the Mound

'An unmitigated disaster and she should never have done it'[60] was the assessment of Charles Powell, her foreign-policy aide, on the speech Thatcher delivered on 21 May 1988 to the Church of Scotland's General Assembly. She was not naïve. She was aware of the pitfalls associated with 'politicians preaching sermons' – and generally disapproved of the attempt. However, when so many clerics preached politics, she mischievously argued, there was no room for 'restrictive practices' in this regard.[61] The naïvety was rather on the part of the Presbyterians. By the late 1980s, Scotland was hostile territory for the Conservatives. The Church of Scotland issued the invitation. After almost a decade in office, Thatcher was not an unknown quantity. She had a message to deliver to a religious establishment critical of her economic and social policies, and proceeded to do so with more courage than tact.

Brian Griffiths, Director of Thatcher's Policy Unit in the late 1980s, was a committed Christian. Originally an independent Welsh Congregationalist, he came to find his spiritual home in evangelical Anglicanism. Some of her more secular colleagues were highly suspicious of his religious influence on the Prime Minister. Griffiths regarded the first draft of her Edinburgh speech as 'appalling – wishy-washy in the extreme'. At short notice, Thatcher sought his help to redraft it. He described himself as sorting 'out the soundness of her theology and [finding] the right biblical quotations to make her points'.[62] The thought might have owed much to Griffiths but, in the face of subsequent criticism, Thatcher stood resolutely by the content: 'I said what I believed.'[63]

In her 'Sermon on the Mound', named after the Edinburgh venue at which it was delivered, Thatcher began forthrightly: 'Christianity is about

60 Cited Filby, *God and Mrs Thatcher*, p. 238.

61 MT, *The Path to Power*, p. 555.

62 Brian Griffiths, Interview, cited Moore, *MT: Herself alone*, pp. 399, 402.

63 MT, Interview with Robin Oakley, *The Times*, 26 October 1988, <www.margaretthatcher.org/document/107018>, accessed 28.11.20.

spiritual redemption, not social reform.' As the two cannot be separated, she sought to nuance the comment: 'Most Christians would regard it as their personal Christian duty to help their fellow men and women.' Yet, she continued, this was not a specifically Christian trait.

It was the spiritual rather than the social side of our nature that made Christianity distinctive. For an audience of Presbyterian ministers and elders, that ought not to have been contentious. It was where Thatcher went from there that caused the controversy. For her, three of the most important Christian beliefs were

1 the God-given capacity 'to choose between good and evil';
2 the duty 'to use all our power of thought and judgement in exercising' that capacity; and
3 Christ freely *choosing* 'to lay down his life that our sins may be forgiven'.

It appeared an implicit judgement on her audience when she criticized those who went to church simply because they sought 'social reforms and benefits or a better standard of behaviour'. She lectured them on the true basis of the Christian faith: acceptance of 'the sanctity of life, the responsibility that comes with freedom and the supreme sacrifice of Christ'.

She employed Griffiths's scriptural citations to justify 'Thatcherism'. There was a fleeting reference to the duty to love one's neighbour, but she passed rapidly on to Saint Paul: 'If a man will not work, he shall not eat' – a citation unlikely to be well received in the circumstances.[64] The Bible imposes a duty to 'work and use our talents to create wealth'. Thatcher returned to a point made earlier at St Lawrence Jewry, that Christ does not condemn wealth creation: 'The spiritual dimension comes in deciding what one does with the wealth.'

She risked patronizing her audience, reminding them of the scriptural injunction to support one's family. Her robust defence of traditional Christian religious education seemed to imply that the Scots had failed in this regard also. People could take from the speech what they liked. She insisted: 'There is no place for racial or religious intolerance in our creed.' Her critics, however, were more likely to hear her assertion of 'absolute moral

64 2 Thess. 3.10, NIV 1984.

values'. She concluded: 'We Parliamentarians can legislate for the rule of law. You, the Church, can teach the life of faith.'[65] She intended this as an acknowledgement of the higher ecclesiastical vocation. It was more likely interpreted as a reprimand for perceived failings and errors.

The liberal author and broadcaster Ludovic Kennedy lambasted Thatcher for her 'effrontery, not to say insensitivity' in preaching 'a weird amalgam of fundamental Conservativism and simplistic Sunday school homilies'.[66] Jonathan Raban contended that the speech amounted to an attempt to enlist:

> Christianity to provide a theological legitimization for the individual's *right to choose* . . . Christ dying on the Cross joins those folk who exercised their right to choose – to buy their own council houses, to send their children to private schools, to occupy 'paybeds' in NHS-funded hospitals.[67]

Not all reaction was hostile. Downing Street was inundated with requests for copies of the speech. Graham Leonard, the Bishop of London, thanked the Prime Minister, distancing himself from the negative response of the Church of England's Board of Social Responsibility.[68] Much of the reaction was disproportionate. The speech was a sincere contribution to a debate, but lacked theological depth and sensitivity.

'The right to choose is the essence of Christianity'

Raban identified the central issue. In theology, as in politics, what was most important to Thatcher was freedom. During the 1987 general

65 MT, Speech to the General Assembly of the Church of Scotland, 21 May 1988, <www.margaretthatcher.org/document/107246>, accessed 28.11.20.

66 Ludovic Kennedy, cited John Campbell, *Margaret Thatcher: The Iron Lady* (London: Jonathan Cape, 2003), p. 392.

67 Jonathan Raban, *God, Man and Mrs Thatcher: A critique of Mrs Thatcher's address to the General Assembly of the Church of Scotland* (London: Chatto & Windus, 1989), p. 33.

68 Rt Revd Graham Leonard to MT, 1 June 1988, <www.margaretthatcher.org/document/209630>, accessed 28.11.20.

election campaign, she stated her belief: 'The right to choose is the essence of Christianity.'[69] She was challenged by the bishops of the Church of England, and by the presenter John Humphrys on BBC Radio 4's *Today* programme the following morning. Surely, they asked, the essence of Christianity was Christlike love. Thatcher defended herself: 'How can you express unselfish love if you have no choice?' There can be no personal responsibility without the possibility of choice.[70]

The situation cried out for dialogue. Thatcher made legitimate points, requiring refinement perhaps but deserving to be taken seriously. If the bishops had been more generous in engaging with her, if she had been more willing to listen, there would have been ground for a fruitful exchange. She was not as theologically unformed as some asserted. Interviewed by David Frost on New Year's Day 1989, she delivered a masterly exposition of human nature understood from the perspective of faith. She correctly identified that humanity is distinguished from the rest of the animal kingdom by a 'capacity to decide what to do, to think – more than an instinct – to think. [Humanity] was given, therefore, the right to choose between good and evil . . . if we had not the right to choose we would not be human beings.' It is the consequence of our being created in the image and likeness of God, who is pure mind, pure spirit. Again, if in the face of tragedies and wrongdoing God continually interfered and changed everything, 'then we should not be human beings with this God-given right to choose'.[71]

Thatcher was right: freedom is logically prior to love. Freedom presupposes genuine options, love or hate, good or evil. The bishops failed to give adequate recognition to the place of freedom in a Christian anthropology. Simultaneously, however, Thatcher needed to develop further the purpose of freedom in Christian theology: to be compassionate like Christ, to reflect in the world the God who is love and in whose image we are made.

She certainly did not sanction unrestrained licence. However, in Edinburgh as elsewhere she formulated freedom in terms of duty, not love:

69 MT, Interview with Jimmy Young, BBC Radio 2, *Jimmy Young Programme*, 5 June 1987, <www.margaretthatcher.org/document/106645>, accessed 28.11.20.

70 MT, Interview with John Humphrys, BBC Radio 4, *Today*, 6 June 1987, <www.margaretthatcher.org/document/106646>, accessed 28.11.20.

71 MT, Interview with David Frost, 1 January 1989.

> Freedom will destroy itself if it is not exercised within some sort of moral framework, some body of shared beliefs, some spiritual heritage transmitted through the Church, the family and the school. It will also destroy itself if it has no purpose . . . My wish for the people of this country is that we shall be 'free to serve'. So we must have freedom and we must have a morality.[72]

Reflecting her practical nature, Thatcher emphasized morality more than doctrine.

'Would I have voted differently on any of these matters?'

The legislation introduced during Wilson's second term in office began the process of decoupling laws relating to social and personal mores from traditional Christian teaching. There were those who expected Thatcher to roll back the liberal, permissive society in moral matters as she did the power of the state in the political and economic sphere. She surprised some and disappointed others, viewing much of that legislation as necessary reform designed 'to deal with specific problems, in some cases cruel or unfair provisions'. Her personal response was invariably pragmatic, 'strongly influenced by my own experience of other people's suffering'.[73]

She supported the Liberal MP David Steel's 1967 Abortion Act (introduced as a Private Member's bill), permitting abortion subject to certain conditions, wishing to end the practice of back-street abortions. She thought there was little worse than bringing an unwanted child into the world – the child started life subject to a great handicap.[74] Neither the arguments of faith nor science convinced her that a new human life existed from the moment of conception. Without giving her reasons, Thatcher

72 MT, Speech to the General Assembly of the Church of Scotland, 21 May 1988.

73 MT, *The Path to Power*, p. 150.

74 MT, Interview with Joan Yorke, BBC Radio 4, *Woman's Hour*, 9 April 1970, <www.margaretthatcher.org/document/101845>, accessed 29.11.20.

believed that it was only 'after a few months of pregnancy the foetus took on the characteristics of a human being'. She later supported limited moves to reduce the age limit for abortions as medical advances made it increasingly possible to save the lives of premature babies,[75] but gave little succour to the pro-life movement. Her pragmatic approach was uninfluenced by the teachings of faith.

Her position concerning divorce was more complex. She spoke on the subject relatively frequently, given her own marriage to a divorcee. She was not opposed to divorce in principle, unsurprisingly. Where there was marital violence, she considered divorce 'not just permissible, but unavoidable'.[76] Yet she opposed 'no-fault' divorce, concerned both by the plight of deserted wives and the prospect of young people taking their marriage vows less seriously.[77] In 1968 she voted against the relaxation of the divorce laws, but in 1984 her government reduced the period for finalizing divorce from three years to one. Her motivation was the social cost of divorce. There was no reference to Christ's teaching on the indissolubility of marriage.

Likewise, her voting record on legislation relating to homosexuality was inconsistent. She supported the bill that led to the decriminalization of homosexual acts between consenting adults in 1967. Yet she adopted a Private Member's bill that became Section 28 of the Local Government Act 1988, preventing local authorities promoting homosexuality in schools or elsewhere. Despite personal reservations, she approved the government's advertising campaign during the AIDS crisis, leading to a further liberalization of attitudes towards homosexuality – then criticized the Church for not expounding traditional moral teaching.[78] Thatcher herself saw no inconsistency in her approach, arguing that people should be 'free to live their own lives in private' but not expect the taxpayer to fund that lifestyle.[79] There was no reference to the Christian understanding of marriage being between a man and a woman for the purpose of raising children.

---

75 Health Committee Minute, 25 October 1985, <www.margaretthatcher.org/document/144072>, accessed 29.11.20.

76 MT, *The Downing Street Years*, p. 630.

77 MT, Speech, Finchley Women's Inter-church Luncheon Club, 17 November 1969, *Finchley Press*, 21 November 1969, <www.margaretthatcher.org/document/101704>, accessed 29.11.20.

78 Young, *One of Us*, p. 421.

79 MT to Mr and Mrs Dennison, 3 April 1988, cited Moore, *MT: Herself alone*, p. 55.

On the question of Sunday trading, she was more consistent, but her approach distanced her still further from her Methodist roots. In her youth she had disagreed with her family's strict sabbatarianism. As Prime Minister she supported proposals in 1986 to extend Sunday trading. In doing so she placed herself alongside libertarians and big business, and against her own Christian Evangelical advisers.

Ironically, the issue on which she was uniformly socially conservative was the very one on which Christians were most likely to oppose her. Thatcher never wavered in her support for the death penalty: 'I believe', she wrote, 'that capital punishment for the worse murders is morally right as retribution and practically necessary as a deterrent.'[80]

Eliza Filby's observation is accurate: 'When faced with the choice between social conservatism and libertarianism, Margaret Thatcher seemed to prioritize the latter.'[81] Can her record be reconciled with her Christian background and beliefs? What happened to the 'absolute moral values' espoused in Edinburgh? In fairness, could she be expected to be the standard-bearer for traditional Christian moral values when Anglican bishops and others gave, at best, a divided and hesitant lead? Of course, this did not prevent her from denouncing them as weak.

In the interplay of freedom and authority, Thatcher was always likely to come down on the side of freedom. While hoping that people would exercise their freedom to choose the more moral option, in the private sphere she felt unable to impose her views on others. She believed that 'a functioning free society cannot be value-free',[82] but it was the role of the family and the Church, not government, to inculcate those values.

In later life, however, she gave indications of rethinking her earlier support for social liberalization: 'As regards abortion, homosexuality, and divorce reform it is easy to see that matters did not turn out as was intended.' Abortion had become, for many, simply a backup for contraception. She had advocated 'the right of privacy' for homosexuals, not the equivalence of 'the gay lifestyle' and heterosexual marriage. 'Knowing how matters have turned out, would I have voted differently on any of these matters?'[83]

80 MT, *The Downing Street Years*, p. 308.
81 Cited Filby, *God and Mrs Thatcher*, p. 232.
82 MT, *The Path to Power*, p. 553.
83 MT, *The Path to Power*, p. 152.

Tantalizingly, she failed to answer her own question. Lacking a clear moral theology, she responded to such important matters ad hoc on purely pragmatic grounds.

Thatcher was a committed proponent of compulsory religious – by which she meant Christian and scriptural – education in schools, with a right of withdrawal for those of other faiths. She regretted that some schools were failing to provide this but backed down from enforcing exclusively Christian religious education when advised it might lead to more parents withdrawing their children from lessons. She argued that religious education would impart a proper grasp of British history and literature, an understanding of the basis of human rights.[84] There is no suggestion it might develop the spiritual life or a personal relationship with God.

Thatcher's Evangelicals

Her constituency agent, himself an elder of the Church of Scotland, noted that Thatcher liked to surround herself with 'politicians and aides who are deeply religious'.[85] There is no evidence she deliberately sought out fellow believers or excluded non-believers. She obviously felt comfortable, however, in the company of Christians – and Jews – of sincere, even fervent faith.

Michael Alison was Thatcher's Private Parliamentary Secretary from 1983 to 1987. A committed Evangelical, he had attended theological college with a view to ordination. He regularly attended prayer meetings and brought his faith into politics. When travelling with the Prime Minister, he read to her from the Bible and C. S. Lewis.[86] Utterly devoted to her, he compared Thatcher to Moses leading God's people to the Promised Land and succeeding by dint of her faith.[87] She drew the line at some of his more charismatic practices but appreciated his spiritual input, writing the preface

84 MT, Interview with Joe Steeples, *Woman*, 13 April 1988, <www.margaretthatcher.org/document/107051>, accessed 30.11.20.

85 Thomson, *MT*, p. 25.

86 Charles Moore, *Margaret Thatcher: Everything she wants* (London: Allen Lane, 2015), p. 73.

87 Michael Alison to MT, 30 July 1985, <www.margaretthatcher.org/document/142264>, accessed 01.12.20.

for *Christianity and Conservatism*, a 1990 collection of essays he co-edited with David L. Edwards, the Provost of Southwark.[88]

Brian Griffiths, the Director of her Policy Unit, was the other prominent Evangelical in Downing Street. Others felt that her Edinburgh speech and its adverse reception justified their view that Griffiths encouraged Thatcher to engage in religious controversies she would have done better avoiding entirely. Griffiths maintained, however, that she understood such risks perfectly well and 'never wanted to make the Christian faith an issue in party politics'.[89] Harvey Thomas was her public relations adviser throughout her premiership. Previously, he had worked for Billy Graham for 15 years. Graham visited Downing Street as Thatcher's guest and was invited to the dinner President Reagan hosted for her on his retirement in 1988.

'Rome never seemed closer to Grantham'

Evangelicals were in the ascendancy but they did not constitute the only Christian influence. John Gummer, one of Thatcher's speechwriters and later party Chairman, was an Anglo-Catholic member of the Church of England General Synod who subsequently converted to Roman Catholicism. John O'Sullivan was another Downing Street speechwriter and Robin Harris was a former Director of the Conservative Research Department. Both were committed Catholics who helped ghost Thatcher's memoirs. This helps explain why those memoirs conclude with her near apotheosis at a Catholic Mass in Warsaw in 1993.[90]

The early years of her premiership were dominated by economic affairs and industrial relations. In the mid-1980s she gave more time to international relations. In her third term, Europe assumed an increasing prominence but Thatcher also devoted herself more to social policy. Seeking an ethical basis for free market economics, she became fascinated with 'the relationship between Christianity and economic and social policy'.[91] Religion was needed, she believed, to induce self-restraint, to teach that one was accountable to God. Faith 'reinforces man's sense of responsibility to

88 MT, 'Preface', Alison and Edwards, *Christianity and Conservatism*.

89 Brian Griffiths, Interview, cited Moore, *MT: Herself alone*, p. 21.

90 MT, *The Path to Power*, pp. 602–3.

91 MT, *The Path to Power*, p. 556.

his neighbour, of trusteeship towards the next generation, and of respect towards society's institutions and achievements'.[92]

Her interest in the subject was aided and abetted by Alison and Griffiths. Committed, like Thatcher, to individual freedom, Griffiths argued that neither unrestrained capitalism nor coercive collectivism provided the answer. He promoted the concept of the 'social market economy', with greed and injustice tempered by a sense of social responsibility. This in turn was based on biblical principles: the right to private property; the distinction between wealth creation (a good thing) and the worship of mammon (a bad thing); and the obligation of charity.[93]

Thatcher cited approvingly Pope John Paul II's 1991 encyclical, *Centesimus Annus*, in which he denounced the collectivist state as stifling people's initiative and failing to provide for their real needs.[94] 'Rome never seemed closer to Grantham'[95] she opined, without reflecting whether the Pope was really equating the British welfare system with Soviet Bloc planned economies. Nor did she note the Pope's teaching that the market be subject to state control to protect vulnerable members of society. Another Catholic of whom Thatcher approved was the American lay theologian Michael Novak. She applauded *The Spirit of Democratic Capitalism*, in which he extolled capitalism as a spiritual as well as an economic system. She agreed with Novak that capitalism rather than socialism 'encouraged a range of virtues and that it depended upon co-operation not just "going it alone"'.[96]

Faith in the City

The media chose to characterize Thatcher's relationship with the Established Church in terms of conflict. There was truth in that. When York Minster was struck by lightning in 1984, she commented that some attributed the damage caused to 'divine punishment . . . for the wayward

92 MT, 'Reason and Religion: The moral foundations of freedom', James Bryce Lecture, 24 September 1996, <www.margaretthatcher.org/document/108364>, accessed 02.12.20.

93 Filby, *God and Mrs Thatcher*, p. 236.

94 John Paul II, *Centesimus Annus* (Vatican: Libreria Editrice Vaticana, 1991), <www.vatican.va/content/john-paul-ii/en/encyclicals/documents/hf_jp-ii_enc_01051991_centesimus-annus.html>.

95 MT, *The Path to Power*, p. 556.

96 MT, *The Downing Street Years*, p. 627; Michael Novak, *The Spirit of Democratic Capitalism* (New York: Simon & Schuster, 1982).

theology of leading Anglican clerics'.[97] She had no inhibitions in telling a 'socialist CND-promoting vicar in Finchley' that his political views might account for his lack of a congregation.[98] She felt that she had defeated the Left at the polls, only for its votaries to emerge in the pulpit. 'It's so difficult to hear a good strong teaching sermon these days,' she complained. 'I'd like to listen to a preacher tackling a challenging text like "the fear of the Lord is the beginning of wisdom" for twenty-five fiery minutes.'[99]

Archbishop Robert Runcie's tenure at Lambeth Palace largely coincided with Thatcher's time in Downing Street. She would ask him: 'Why can't we have any Christian bishops?'[100] Did she use her patronage to achieve her objective? Her scope, as it had first been for Callaghan, was limited to reversing the order of the two names submitted to her or rejecting both and asking for two more. She took her role in episcopal appointments seriously. Runcie recalled that she regretted that her powers were so circumscribed, but that she acted perfectly properly and within her rights.[101]

It is believed that in her recommendations to the Crown, Thatcher only twice reversed the order of the candidates submitted by the Crown Appointments Commission. In 1981 she preferred Graham Leonard to John Habgood for the Diocese of London. An Anglo-Catholic who converted to Roman Catholicism in retirement, Leonard might have seemed an odd choice for her Low Church tastes. He was a theological and social conservative, however, willing to criticize the liberal Establishment, represented by Habgood. In 1987 she put Mark Santer's name before that of Jim Thompson for the Diocese of Birmingham. It served little purpose from her perspective; both were of a similar political hue. Although finalized after her departure from office, it is alleged that Thatcher was influential in George Carey's appointment as Archbishop of Canterbury, having placed an Evangelical, Lord Caldecote, to chair the Appointments Commission. She is understood, however, to have been disappointed by Carey's failure to meet her

97 MT, *The Downing Street Years*, p. 365.

98 Thomson, *MT*, p. 66.

99 MT, cited Aitken, *MT*, p. 684.

100 Archbishop Robert Runcie, Interview, cited Moore, *MT: Herself alone*, p. 406.

101 Humphrey Carpenter, *Robert Runcie: The reluctant archbishop* (London: Hodder & Stoughton, 1996), p. 215.

expectations during his time at Lambeth.[102] Thatcher was not fortunate in her bishops.

It is claimed that the rift between Downing Street and the bench of bishops crystallized in the aftermath of the Falklands campaign. On 26 July 1982, a Service of Thanksgiving – even the name was contentious – was held in St Paul's Cathedral. It was rumoured that the Prime Minister strongly disapproved of Runcie's measured sermon, in which he asked the congregation to remember the grief of both British and Argentinian families. She was more concerned, however, that the armed forces were not accorded the recognition that was their due, at least by some of the clergy at St Paul's. She was scrupulously correct as to her own role, determining that neither she nor any other politician should read a lesson.[103]

The real divergence between the Church and Downing Street related to the government's economic and social policies which, it was asserted, lacked concern and compassion for the poor and marginalized. Matters came to a head in 1985 with publication of the Church of England report, *Faith in the City*. Critical of the Church's own failings, it was interpreted as a condemnation of government-promoted greed. Denounced as Marxist-inspired in some quarters, Thatcher's public response was more balanced. She read the report 'with the greatest possible interest' but was disappointed by its lack of recommendations for individuals and families. She was 'absolutely shocked' at the Church's belief that families could not be expected to set standards and discipline their children.[104]

Despite her disapproval of ecclesiastical liberalism, Thatcher did not seek conflict with the Church. Unrealistically, she hoped for the Church's moral support for her policies. Extending an olive branch, in November 1987 she invited a group of Anglican bishops to lunch at Chequers. Rather than revisit recent controversies, they agreed to a general discourse on the role of Church and state. It did not end well. Even his brother bishops felt that Runcie was unfocused, a stance unlikely to endear him to Thatcher. She

102 Filby, *God and Mrs Thatcher*, pp. 148–9.

103 MT, Annotation, Coles Minute to Whitmore, 2 July 1982, <www.margaretthatcher.org/document/124449>, accessed 03.12.20.

104 MT, Interview with Michael Charlton, BBC Radio 3, 17 December 1985, <www.margaretthatcher.org/document/105934>, accessed 03.12.20; Church of England, Commission on Urban Priority Areas, *Faith in the City: A call for action by church and nation* (London: Church House Publishing, 1985).

was predictably assertive, engaging fiercely with David Jenkins, Bishop of Durham, and David Sheppard, Bishop of Liverpool, on the very issues they had agreed to avoid. Michael Baughen, Bishop of Chester, intervened to assert the primacy of love over freedom in Christianity – precisely the sort of point that ought to have been constructively explored. Thatcher was not listening. There was no convergence. Richard Harries, Bishop of Oxford, graciously acknowledged that the fault was not entirely that of the Prime Minister: 'We bishops didn't make a great deal of effort to enter sympathetically into her position.'[105]

'One soul among many in a fellowship of believers'

Unlike Macmillan, Margaret Thatcher had no interest in internal church politics. She was rather thrown in 1978 when asked for her views on the ordination of women. Unsurprisingly, given her background and lack of sacramental theology and ecclesiology, she seemed in favour. It was necessary to be 'in touch with and in tune with the times'; but she urged caution. She recognized the need to move at a pace acceptable to church members.[106] It was a purely pragmatic response. Her position did not change significantly over the subsequent decade: support in principle; concern for the consequences.[107]

Thatcher was very much a child of Protestant Nonconformity. Curiously, her early years were spent in the shadow of Rome. The grocer's shop in Grantham was opposite St Mary's Catholic Church. The young Margaret envied the First Communion girls their white dresses, ribbons and flowers. At Oxford, her neighbours were the Jesuits at St Aloysius. Personally, Alfred Roberts enjoyed friendly relations with the local Catholic priest but refused categorically to set foot in a Catholic church. He warned his fellow Methodists: 'We must never believe that a priest is an indispensable intermediary between the soul and God – an idea which is destitute of New Testament authority and also of the apostolic Gospel. Nor is absolution

105 Interview with Lord Harries, cited Moore, *MT: Herself alone*, p. 400.

106 MT, Interview with Richard Dowden, 22 and 29 December 1978.

107 Filby, *God and Mrs Thatcher*, p. 147.

dependent upon priestly performance.'[108] Roberts made himself ill with worry when his younger daughter took up with a Catholic friend, Mary Rohan, in Dartford. Fearing she was about to convert, he wrote to Muriel:

> I should be grieved beyond all measure if the R/Cs got hold of Margaret. She would no longer be free, and they might cause untold family misery. As you know I left you both free in regard to religion, as a parent must and does who trusts his children, but R/C is Spiritual Totalitarianism with all its damning intolerance for others.[109]

Muriel knew her sister far better. If anyone was at risk of undue influence, she replied, it was Mary Rohan.

Thatcher did not share her parents' anti-Catholic prejudice. Conversion was never considered; she possessed only a rudimentary grasp of Catholic doctrine and practice. Nevertheless, she developed a sincere respect for Catholicism. She regarded the election of John Paul II in 1978 as 'providential'. At a private audience with the Pope on 24 November 1980, in addition to Northern Ireland they discussed 'the irreligious nature of communism'. She wrote subsequently:

> It is no secret that I greatly admire the role played by John Paul II in the liberation of his country, Poland, and of the other countries of Eastern Europe from the legions of communists that proved no match to his spiritual authority.[110]

She was Prime Minister during the first papal visit to Britain in 1982. Concern for the Established Church caused her to tread cautiously, advising against a papal address to the joint Houses of Parliament.[111] In the event, the Falklands War meant she did not meet the Pope during his visit – 'a great opportunity missed',[112] opined one adviser. In 2009 she met

108 Alfred Roberts, Sermon Notes.

109 Alfred Roberts to Muriel Cullen, 8 August 1951, cited Moore, *MT: Not for turning*, p. 104.

110 MT, *The Path to Power*, pp. 345–6.

111 MT, Annotation, Colin Peterson Minute, 20 March 1981, <www.margaretthatcher.org/document/127320>, accessed 04.12.20.

112 John O'Sullivan, *The President, the Pope and the Prime Minister: Three who changed the world* (Washington DC: Regnery Publishing, 2006), p. 166.

Pope Benedict XVI, whose clarity of thought and critique of liberalism she also admired.

Catholic liturgy was alien territory. In May 1993 she attended Mass at the Holy Cross Church in Warsaw. The crowds, intense devotion and elaborate ceremony were far removed 'from the restrained piety of Anglican services and the resolutely simple Methodism of Grantham'. She allowed herself, however, to be swept along by the praise she received in the sermon and the tumultuous applause accorded her at the end of Mass, feeling she 'was one soul among many in a fellowship of believers that crossed nations and denominations'.[113] Orthodoxy was even more perplexing. In 1987, Thatcher attended the liturgy at the monastery at Zagorsk, outside Moscow. She failed to recognize that 'the apparently endless ritual' constituted a service with a congregation, as she understood it. Rather it seemed just 'a matter of private prayer'. She lit a candle and withdrew – but it had been important for her to show solidarity with Russian Christians.[114]

Thatcher was very comfortable with Judaism. Some 20 per cent of her Finchley constituents were Jewish. The number of Jewish Cabinet ministers she appointed caused comment. She admired the Jewish values of family, hard work and individual responsibility. The Chief Rabbi, Immanuel Jakobovits, was a great favourite – her model of a religious leader whom she wished Christians might imitate.[115] He shared her rejection of the Church of England report *Faith in the City*, believing it should have emphasized work, not welfare. Thatcher recommended Jakobovits for a knighthood and then a peerage – and she is even reported to have wished she could appoint him Archbishop of Canterbury.[116]

She spoke frequently of 'Judaeo-Christian values', believing the basis for individual human dignity and freedom was ultimately religious. She recognized Christianity's debt to Judaism, insisting that the Old Testament and New Testament constituted one, not two separate religions.[117] Yet she was quite clear that she was a Christian, and why: 'The Old Testament – the

---

113 MT, *The Path to Power*, pp. 602–3.

114 MT, *The Downing Street Years*, pp. 478–9.

115 MT, *The Downing Street Years*, p. 510.

116 Moore, *MT: Herself alone*, p. 448.

117 MT, Interview with Chris Ogden, 16 January 1989.

history of the Law – [cannot] be fully understood without the New Testament – the history of Mercy.'[118]

Thatcher was also willing to find elements of truth in Islam. Unlike the religions and philosophies of the Far East, it too, she held, was 'at least based on the common God'.[119] She was among the earliest and strongest champions of Bosnian Muslims when they were subject to ethnic cleansing at the hands of Orthodox Christians.

'Not too much enthusiasm, y'know'

When at Chequers the Thatchers regularly attended the parish church of St Peter and St Paul, Ellesborough. She wrote to the rector telling him how 'much comfort she derived' from doing so.[120] Their London churchgoing during her time in office was rather more sporadic. After her departure from Downing Street, when they went to church it was to the 11 a.m. service at St Margaret's, Westminster, next to the abbey and across the road from the Houses of Parliament. The sung Eucharist, however, was rather too high for her taste.

After three years they moved to St Michael's, Chester Square, a stone's throw from their Belgravia home. Brian Griffiths was a prominent member of the congregation. Denis endured its Evangelical worship for a while but finally drew the line at the 'happy-clappy' liturgy and guitar choruses. Michael Alison tried to persuade Thatcher to attend the Evangelical stronghold of Holy Trinity, Brompton, where he was churchwarden and the Revd Sandy Millar was vicar. She approved of Millar's sermons, copies of which were supplied by Alison, but was perturbed by press reports of 'the Toronto Blessing' there, in which worshippers fell to the ground slain by the Spirit. They would not be attending 'HTB', she announced – 'Denis couldn't stand it. We like to reflect on religion privately. Not too much enthusiasm, y'know.'

---

118 MT, *The Downing Street Years*, p. 510.

119 MT, Interview with Trevor Grove, *Sunday Telegraph*, 4 April 1990, <www.margaretthatcher.org/document/107906>, accessed 06.12.20.

120 MT to Revd Norman White, 2 January 1981, <www.margaretthatcher.org/document/121575>, accessed 06.12.20.

In 1998, Denis decided they needed to find a permanent spiritual home in which both felt comfortable. They went church-shopping, trying out the Guards Chapel and the Chapel Royal. It was the Royal Hospital Chapel, Chelsea, however, that best satisfied their needs. Built by Sir Christopher Wren for the Chelsea Pensioners, it offered the dignified worship of the Book of Common Prayer, familiar hymns and military tradition in abundance. Both attended matins each Sunday while health permitted. The chaplain, the Revd Dick Whittington, a former soldier himself, was conscious of the attention Thatcher paid to his sermons. He was present at Denis's death in 2003 and brought spiritual consolation to his widow.[121]

'Living faith' or 'cut-flower' religion?

When Eliza Filby's book *God and Mrs Thatcher* appeared in 2015, its title promised the first full-scale spiritual biography of a twentieth-century Prime Minister. Reviewing the work for the magazine *Third Way*, the Christian Labour MP Stephen Timms complained that he ended none the wiser as to what Thatcher actually believed.[122] In her Preface, Filby made clear that her book was 'chiefly about the conflict between the Established Church and the Conservative Party . . . Margaret Thatcher's life and times are used as narrative hinges.'[123] It was not intended as an account of her personal faith.

So what did Thatcher actually believe? Some maintain she was the most explicitly religious Prime Minister since William Gladstone or Lord Salisbury,[124] others that she was not religious at all. In this she resembled Balfour – a politician identified as profoundly interested in religion but dividing contemporaries as to the exact nature, even existence, of his or her personal faith.

Nicholas Ridley, a Cabinet colleague, wrote: 'I doubt if she was a very religious person in terms of strong beliefs, but she believed passionately

121 Aitken, *MT*, 679–82; Moore, *MT: Herself alone*, p. 819.

122 Stephen Timms, <https://thirdway.hymnsam.co.uk/editions/july-2015/reviews/god-and-mrs-thatcher-the-battle-for-britain's-soul.aspx>, accessed 06.12.20.

123 Filby, *God and Mrs Thatcher*, pp. xix, xxi.

124 Nick Spencer, 'MT (1979–90)', p. 1; Thomson, *MT*, p. 64.

in the Christian morality.'[125] Such a comment might be dismissed on the grounds that the two, although politically close, were unlikely to have shared spiritual intimacies. It is harder to deflect the criticism of those serious about faith. John Gummer rather unkindly employed a phrase of his clerical father's: Thatcher's religion was of the 'cut-flower' variety – 'neatly preserved and presented, but no longer alive'.[126] Thatcher approved of the Anglican academic Edward Norman. His judgement of her was less complimentary: 'Lady Thatcher was not, at least externally, especially religious. All those services which she attended at Grantham had left an enduring disposition, however, to associate Christianity with hard work and a provident use of time.'[127]

Robin Harris agrees that Thatcher was 'extremely moral', though in his biography he went to considerable lengths to establish that she was not 'an obviously spiritual person'. She was interested in the social and political aspects of religion rather 'than for its own sake'. He marshalled his evidence: Thatcher failed 'to talk of God or the afterlife in a personal way'; she did not practise the Christian virtue of forgiveness; she had a complete 'disregard for systematic theology'; her knowledge of Scripture was poor.[128] Harris's comments must be taken seriously – he worked closely with her for a decade, remained on good terms with her after her resignation and assisted in the writing of her memoirs. (He himself is a committed Catholic.)

Alfred Sherman, the son of Jewish immigrants, was a political collaborator in Thatcher's early years as party leader. He arrived at a diametrically opposed conclusion: 'For her, God was a real presence.'[129] The Evangelicals around her were eager to claim Thatcher as one of their own. Harvey Thomas's assessment admitted of no doubt: 'Good, straightforward, practical evangelicalism. It was quite a driving thought in her mind.'[130] Griffiths was equally adamant: Thatcher's was 'a living faith, not a merely cultural Christianity'; she enjoyed a 'real and meaningful personal faith in Christ'.

125 Nicholas Ridley, cited Campbell, *MT: The Iron Lady*, p. 389.

126 John Gummer, cited Moore, *MT: Everything she wants*, p. 18.

127 Edward Norman, Obituary: 'Lady Thatcher of Kesteven', *Church Times*, 12 April 2013.

128 Robin Harris, *Not for Turning: The life of Margaret Thatcher* (London: Bantam Press, 2013), pp. 20–3.

129 Alfred Sherman, *Paradoxes of Power: Reflections on the Thatcher interlude* (Exeter: Imprint Academic, 2005), p. 86.

130 Harvey Thomas, cited Filby, *God and Mrs Thatcher*, p. 146.

Without having discussed this with her, he concluded that she underwent a 'conversion experience' prior to her arrival in Oxford.[131] George Carey lent his support to this interpretation. Contrasting her with Blair, he believed, 'Her faith was quite real to her . . . Margaret's [faith] appealed to me much more than Tony's. I couldn't see where his was going . . . whereas I could sense her thinking was quite theological in many senses.'[132]

How to make sense of such divergent views? Those who queried Thatcher's religion simply failed to see in her faith one that resembled their own – her understanding of Christianity was significantly different from that of Gummer and Norman. Her copy of the Methodist Catechism taught that baptism and the Lord's Supper 'were appointed by Christ Himself to be outward signs and means of inward grace and spiritual blessing'. Sacraments, however, meant little to her. She was baptized herself and had both her children baptized, but her grasp of the rite and theology was shaky. When the journalist and editor – and later her authorized biographer – Charles Moore asked about her children's baptism, she replied: 'Oh well, they were christened but they didn't have the water.'[133] Thatcher never received Holy Communion in the Church of England, apparently feeling no need to do so. She displayed no interest in ecclesiology or church politics. Her 'systematic theology' may have failed Harris's standard, but English churches would be very empty if this were a condition of membership.

Harris maintains that Thatcher's 'failure to talk of God or the afterlife in a personal way . . . seemed to go beyond the traditional reserve'.[134] He underestimates the English sense of reserve. Emotions were rarely externalized in interwar Lincolnshire Wesleyanism – one simply did not talk about the spiritual life. Thatcher's upbringing is evident in the answers she gave in interviews. Asked after her notorious Edinburgh speech whether religion was becoming more important to her, she was unwilling to be drawn: 'One is very, very careful, as a politician, to speak about religion because it is a personal thing – very, very careful indeed.'[135] She began on a similar tack with David Frost: 'I am very wary of talking about personal belief,

131 Brian Griffiths, cited Moore, *MT: Herself alone*, p. 402.

132 Archbishop George Carey, cited Filby, *God and Mrs Thatcher*, p. 145.

133 Cited Moore, *MT: Not for turning*, p. 8n.

134 Harris, *Not for Turning*, p. 20.

135 MT, Interview with Robin Oakley, 25 October 1988.

because it could so easily be misinterpreted.' Such reticence, however, does not mean her faith was superficial or insincere.

'Believing there is a God is knowing there is a God . . . I believe'

Christian faith involves belief in the Trinitarian God, the divinity and humanity of Jesus Christ, his crucifixion for the forgiveness of sin and his resurrection in which his disciples hope to share. It is manifest in public worship, private prayer and the attempt to live moral and charitable lives according to Christ's teaching. Protestants were more likely to turn to Scripture than the teaching authority of the Church for such guidance. How does Thatcher fare on these criteria?

Unless her honesty is to be questioned – and even her political enemies seldom did that – one must accept Thatcher's belief in the existence of God. This was more than intellectual assent. She was emphatic: 'Believing there is a God is knowing there is a God . . . I believe.'[136] It was the Christian God in whom she believed, and she never departed from the core beliefs she had been taught in Grantham. That did not mean she did not question – after all she was a scientist – but the result of that questioning 'was to enlarge one's ideas of God and not to reduce them in any way'.[137] She admitted to doubts, which she thought a necessary part of the process to reconvince oneself. Natural disasters caused her to question, but she reflected that such occurrences were inevitable given the immutable laws of physics.[138]

The Methodist Catechism taught the doctrines of personal survival and judgement after death: 'Death is not the end for any man, but that there is a life of the world to come – for the good, blessedness with God; for the evil, misery without Him.' Thatcher made occasional references to heaven and hell. She believed 'that we are ultimately accountable'; this belief gave purpose to life in this world.[139] She expanded on this in 1996:

136 MT, Interview, David Frost, 1 January 1989.
137 MT, Interview with Cliff Michelmore, 21 March 1971.
138 MT, Interview with Miriam Stoppard, 2 October 1985.
139 MT, Interview with David Frost, 1 January 1989.

> The idea of an omnipotent God who not only judges but may mete out punishment in the next life for transgressions in this one bolsters man's rational impulse toward civil society and obedience to the positive law. That one might commit crimes in this world and elude punishment by the civil authorities, but still have to face one's Maker in the next, tends to focus one's attention.

It was, she claimed, one of the greatest contributions of the Judaeo-Christian tradition to Western civilization.[140]

Thatcher was a person with very decided convictions and a busy schedule – she would not attend church simply from habit or convention. Chapel was a constant for her first two decades. With a young family and during her premiership, she practised intermittently as an Anglican, but church again became a regular feature of her life in retirement. Jonathan Aitken remembered her as 'an assiduous attender of services, a thoughtful critic of the sermons she heard'.[141] When church attendance was no longer possible, she listened at home to gospel choirs and sang along to BBC television's *Songs of Praise*.[142]

'Prayer', according to the Methodist Catechism, 'is communion with God in Christ.' As it is one of the most intimate aspects of faith, it is unsurprising that Thatcher made few references to her prayer life. We do not know whether prayer was part of her daily routine – probably not. When asked, she replied that she prayed 'when she had need of it'.[143] This she certainly had in the aftermath of the 1984 Brighton bombing. Ignorant of the full extent of the casualties, she was whisked away to a secure location: 'I could only think of one thing to do. Crawfie [Cynthia Crawford, her personal assistant] and I knelt by the side of our beds and prayed for some time in silence.'[144] (Unlike Ronald Reagan and John Paul II, she did not attribute her deliverance to divine intervention, God sparing her for a particular purpose.[145]) It is known that the Labour MP Frank Field visited Thatcher

140 MT, 'Reason and Religion'.

141 Aitken, *MT*, p. 680.

142 Moore, *MT: Herself alone*, p. 838.

143 MT, Interview with Terry Coleman, *The Guardian*, 2 November 1971, cited Campbell, *MT: The Iron Lady*, p. 388.

144 MT, *The Downing Street Years*, p. 381.

145 O'Sullivan, *The President, the Pope and the Prime Minister*, p. 85.

in Downing Street the night before her resignation to persuade her to go, and spare herself public humiliation. Field, a practising Anglican, recounted privately how Thatcher had willingly agreed to his suggestion that they kneel and pray together before he left.[146]

Generally, however, Thatcher believed that church was the proper venue for prayer. Donald Gray, Rector of St Margaret's, Westminster, expressed frustration that she invariably arrived early for grand occasions there. Her put-down was immediate: 'Yes, Canon Gray. I like to be here in good time – to say my prayers.'[147] And that apparently is how she regarded the spiritual life – the rather formal act of *saying* one's prayers.

'I measure myself by my imperfections'

No one disputes the importance Thatcher attached to the moral life, the duty of daily living out faith. Her religion was practical not mystical. She cited the influence of Wesley: 'He inculcated the work ethic. You worked hard, you got on by the result of your own efforts. Then, as you prospered, it was your duty to help others to prosper also.'[148] Those who alleged, however, that morality was the sole residue of Christian faith are wrong. Years before Gummer's 'cut-flower' quip, a local paper summarized a speech of hers at the Finchley Women's Inter-church Luncheon Club: 'People had come to take for granted the good that sprang from Christianity, but she thought that the Christian ethic without a real belief would not continue indefinitely alone – it would be like a flower without a root.'[149] Thatcher later reiterated this:

> Christianity is about more than doing good works. It is a deep faith which expresses itself in your relationship to God . . . Good works are not enough because it would be like trying to cut a flower from its root.[150]

146 Private information communicated to the author.

147 Aitken, *MT*, p. 681.

148 MT, cited Young, *One of Us*, p. 421.

149 MT, Speech to Finchley Churchwomen, 16 January 1967, *Finchley Times*, 27 January 1967, <www.margaretthatcher.org/document/101298>, accessed 09.12.20.

150 MT, Interview with Richard Dowden, 22 and 29 December 1978.

Methodists maintain: 'The Holy Scriptures are for Christians the sufficient rule of faith and practice.'[151] Harris's criticism of Thatcher not knowing Scripture is contested. Her policy adviser and successor as Finchley MP, Hartley Booth, recalls the Bible by her bedside,[152] and Aitken states: 'She did a great deal of Bible reading, even in her busiest years at No. 10.'[153] In 1988 she set out to reread the Old Testament in its entirety – an objective she did not fulfil – but she quizzed her staff on its contents.[154] She was struck by its account of 'really quite terrible things', but at the same time felt it 'the most fascinating story of the world and its development'. It was a text requiring interpretation. Unlike some politicians, when asked she had no trouble reciting her favourite scriptural verses: Psalm 139 ('O Lord, thou hast searched me and known me') and Psalm 46 ('God is our refuge and strength').[155]

It was not just the Bible. She reread C. S. Lewis and much else besides – spiritual works by Graham Leonard and Cardinal Hume, *The Ten Commandments* by Stuart Blanch, Archbishop of York.[156] She told the journalist Hugo Young (who would later write a critical biography): 'I am always trying to read a *fundamental* book. I read quite a lot of theological work.'[157] Werner Keller's 1955 bestseller *The Bible as History* made a deep impression.[158] She read Morris West's *The Devil's Advocate*, an account of raw passion and the quest for sanctity set in southern Italy.[159] The conflict between two absolute value systems, Communism and Catholicism, in which the latter wins out, is likely to have commended the novel to her.

Harris noted Thatcher's incapacity to forgive those, like Michael Heseltine, she believed had gravely wronged her. Even Michael Alison conceded her failing in this respect.[160] It was incompatible with the Christian ideal. In her claim to be a Christian, Thatcher admitted her failings: 'I would still

151 *Methodist Catechism.*

152 Moore, *MT: Herself alone*, p. 22.

153 Aitken, *MT*, p. 679.

154 Young, *One of Us*, p. 425.

155 MT, Interview with David Frost, 1 January 1989.

156 Stuart Blanch, *The Ten Commandments* (London: Hodder & Stoughton, 1981).

157 MT, Interview with Hugo Young, 27 February 1983, cited Young, *One of Us*, p. 420.

158 Werner Keller, *The Bible as History: Archaeology confirms the book of books* (London: Hodder & Stoughton, 1956; originally published in German, 1955).

159 Morris West, *The Devil's Advocate* (London: Heinemann, 1959).

160 Aitken, *MT*, p. 680.

regard myself as a religious person, although very, very much, very much less perfect than I would wish to be. I measure myself by my imperfections.'[161] Taking the evidence as a whole, one must conclude that Thatcher was a sincere Christian believer. She reflected on the attempt on her life made by the IRA: 'It would have been difficult to have gone through last weekend without a strong faith.'[162] After Denis's death, suffering depression and ill health, she plaintively declared: 'It's so lonely at night with no one to come back to. Without my faith, I don't know how I would keep going.'[163]

'That's not for me'

What kind of Christian was she? Thatcher herself eschewed denominational labels. For her, the distinctions between Methodism and (Low Church) Anglicanism were not pronounced – she made the transition from one to the other relatively seamlessly. Certain of her former colleagues and advisers have claimed her as an Evangelical. Some biographers have gone along with this. Hugo Young concluded: 'Even considered as an Anglican, she was firmly of the Evangelical persuasion.'[164] One MP and former staff member queried the attribution.[165] So did her constituency agent: 'Her belief in God has a practical expression, unlike the fervour of some of the "born-again" Christians who inhabit Conservative Central Office and other posts close to the Prime Minister.'[166]

The difficulty is that Evangelicalism is understood differently in different contexts and periods. Traditionally, it has been viewed as a Protestant expression of Christianity emphasizing new birth and conversion, the centrality of Christ, life in the Spirit, Scripture and preaching, personal salvation, fellowship and perhaps a more emotional experience of faith. Thatcher would, of course, have identified with the focus on personal salvation, and good preaching was important to her. She also approved of

161 MT, Interview with Cliff Michelmore, 21 March 1971.

162 MT to Harvey Thomas, October 1984, cited Filby, *God and Mrs Thatcher*, p. 146.

163 MT, cited Moore, *MT: Herself alone*, p. 832.

164 Young, *One of Us*, p. 419.

165 Sir Edward Leigh to the author, 2 December 2020.

166 Thomson, *MT*, p. 64.

those Evangelicals who, rejecting liberalism, upheld Scriptural and moral truths – although she also respected Catholics who did the same.

More recently, Evangelicalism has become associated with charismatic forms of worship. That she was decidedly uncomfortable with – hence her declining the invitation to Holy Trinity, Brompton. She was taken aback to be offered a handshake at the sign of peace during George Carey's enthronement in Canterbury Cathedral in 1991. Modern Evangelicals are more likely to favour personal and extempore prayer. Sensing her bitterness following her departure from office, Michael Alison offered to pray with her. She was having none of it. 'That's not for me,' was her firm response.[167]

It is more accurate to describe Thatcher as a Low Church Anglican, heavily influenced by her Wesleyan background. Her faith was not sacramental, ecclesial nor particularly doctrinal. Her taste in worship was more conservative than that of many modern Evangelicals. She appreciated the dignity and cadences of the King James Bible and the Book of Common Prayer.[168] She loved rousing hymns and choral music. Her religion was similar to that of most mid-twentieth-century English Protestants.

'And soul by soul and silently her shining bounds increase'

All this was reflected in her funeral service held in St Paul's Cathedral on 17 April 2013. Richard Chartres, Bishop of London, gave the address. It was Thatcher's express request, he noted, that it should be a Christian funeral and not a memorial service eulogizing the deceased. She had chosen the music and readings herself. Wesley's hymn 'Love Divine' was a concession to her Methodist origins and the music included the Anthem from Brahms's *German Requiem* and the In Paradisum from Fauré's *Requiem*. Otherwise, everything spoke of traditional Anglicanism. The service began with the Prayer Book Sentences proclaiming faith in the resurrection. The final hymn was 'I vow to thee, my country', including the verse she was wont to quote in support of her contention that salvation

167 MT, cited Aitken, *MT*, p. 680.

168 Moore, *MT: Herself alone*, p. 843.

was personal and not collectivist: 'And soul by soul and silently her shining bounds increase.'

Her ashes were interred beside those of Denis in the grounds of the Royal Hospital, Chelsea.

John Major (1990–1997)

'A believer at a distance'

John Roy Major[1] was born in Carshalton on 29 March 1943 and raised in Worcester Park and Brixton in south London. Having left Rutlish Grammar School, Merton, with three O levels, he had a number of jobs and a period of unemployment before establishing himself in banking.

Elected a Conservative councillor in Lambeth in 1968, Major fought St Pancras North in the two general elections of 1974. In 1979 he won the safe seat of Huntingdonshire (renamed Huntingdon in 1983 following boundary changes), and represented the constituency until his retirement from the Commons in 2001.

Promotion came rapidly. Major was appointed Parliamentary Private Secretary to Ministers in the Home Office in 1982, assistant whip in 1983, Parliamentary Undersecretary for Social Security in 1985 and Minister of State for Social Security in 1986. Having gained a reputation for financial competence, he entered the Cabinet in 1987 as Chief Secretary to the Treasury. In July 1989, Margaret Thatcher appointed him Foreign Secretary, believing him closer than Geoffrey Howe to her position on Europe. When Nigel Lawson resigned three months later, Major replaced him as Chancellor of the Exchequer. Ironically, given her dispute with his predecessor, Major persuaded Thatcher to join the Exchange Rate Mechanism. Sterling's alignment with other European currencies was announced on 5 October 1990.

He was out of London recovering from dental surgery when Michael Heseltine challenged Thatcher for the party leadership. (Heseltine had been Secretary of State for Defence from 1983 to 1986.) Subsequently, Major's support for her fight to retain the premiership was questioned. When she

1 To the irritation of his father, 'Roy' was added by his godmother at his baptism. The name was later dropped.

decided not to contest the second ballot, he was one of the candidates to succeed her. Having rejected the Prime Minister who had won them three election victories, the Conservatives arguably suffered a sense of collective guilt and opted for the person they believed closest to her political position. Major narrowly failed to win the requisite majority in the first ballot, but Heseltine and Douglas Hurd withdrew from the field and he was appointed Prime Minister on 28 November 1990.

Major's government was less ideological than his predecessor's, and his leadership rivals joined the Cabinet. He promised to promote opportunity for all. Central government funding was used to reduce people's bills for the Community Charge (poll tax), which was replaced by the Council Tax. Military operations in the First Gulf War commenced in January 1991 and ended five weeks later. Kuwait was liberated but Saddam Hussein was left in power in Iraq. In an attempt to improve public services, Major launched the Citizens' Charter, publishing league tables for schools and performance tables in other areas of the public sector.

The government entered the 1992 general election campaign with the country in recession and the Labour Party ahead in the opinion polls. With the Labour leader Neil Kinnock running a slick media campaign, Major resorted to the more traditional methods of personal contact and speeches delivered from a soap box. The electorate still distrusted Labour and reacted badly to their final triumphalist rally. Major led the Conservatives to a record fourth successive victory, winning a majority of 21 in the general election on 9 April 1992.

Subsequently, circumstances seemed to conspire against the government. Interest-rate increases to support sterling damaged the economy while failing in their objective. Sterling crashed out of the Exchange Rate Mechanism on 16 September 1992, destroying the Conservatives' reputation for fiscal competence. In December 1991, Major had committed the UK to the Maastricht Treaty (the founding agreement of the European Union), negotiating exclusions from the 'Social Chapter' and currency union. Mounting Euro-scepticism and opposition from his predecessor led to the party tearing itself apart. The Commons only approved the treaty after he made it an issue of confidence.

Major attempted to regain the initiative by resigning as leader of the Conservative Party and submitting himself for re-election. His defeat of the challenger, John Redwood, by 218 votes to 89 in the ballot on 4 July 1995 was scarcely a resounding victory. The government's parliamentary majority dwindled with by-election losses and the removal of the whip from Euro-rebels. Financial and sexual scandals created an atmosphere of sleaze, not helped by Major's previous 'back to basics' campaign, interpreted by the press as a moral crusade.

On 7 February 1991, the IRA had launched a mortar attack on Downing Street. Although there were no casualties, Major made ending the conflict in Northern Ireland a priority. The Joint Declaration of 15 December 1993 committed London and Dublin to obtaining the consent of the Northern Irish people to any constitutional change. The IRA renounced violence and the British government engaged in talks with Unionists, Sinn Fein and the IRA. No agreement was reached but much of the ground was laid for subsequent progress.

The economy was performing strongly by the time of the general election on 1 May 1997, but Major faced a resurgent Labour under Tony Blair, and the consensus was that after 18 years of Conservative government, it was 'time for a change'. Still badly divided over Europe, the Conservatives were reduced to 165 MPs – to Labour's 418 – and their lowest share of the popular vote in modern times. Major resigned as Prime Minister on 2 May and was replaced as party leader by William Hague on 19 June.

Major was created a Knight of the Garter in 2005. Since leaving office, he has pursued various business interests and actively supported a number of charities. He was vocal in his opposition to the UK's departure from the European Union.

* * *

'God is in our house. We don't have to go to his'

The Prime Ministers' spouses have been neglected almost as much as the Prime Ministers' faith. Cherie Blair set out to rectify this omission in her book *The Goldfish Bowl*, telling the story of the six wives and one husband who had occupied the role in the 40 years before she and Tony

Blair entered Downing Street. She suggested there had been a significant change by the 1990s: whereas the spouses had formerly often possessed a strong religious faith, she detected a 'sense of duty and social conscience' in her immediate predecessor, Norma Major. This was, however, 'more contemporary, reflecting our more secular times'.[2] Even if true of Norma, was it also true of her husband? Was John Major the first secular Prime Minister – not in the sense of hostility to religion but in its not featuring large in his background and personal life?

Major's background was different from that of his predecessors. No Prime Minister since the early 1960s had enjoyed the advantages of social privilege and wealth from birth, but all had rapidly fitted into the political establishment either by virtue of an Oxbridge education or holding office in the trade union movement. Major's path to power differed significantly.

At the time of Major's birth, his father was already 63. Tom Ball – 'Major' was his stage name – had been born in the Midlands in 1879 and made a career for himself as an entertainer in the USA. Returning to Britain, he married his second wife, Gwen, in 1929. A dancer, she was 26 years his junior. They settled in Worcester Park, where they raised their three surviving children, Pat, Terry and John, and Tom ran a garden ornament business.

In the post-war Britain in which Major grew up, the Church of England held for the final time a prominent and assured position in much of English society. The Church, however, played little part in the life of his family – Terry's memoirs, for example, contain no reference to religion.[3] Neither it nor politics were ever discussed at home, although Major never doubted both his parents were believers. For them, 'the Church was something rather quaint, an honoured but distant institution'. There was no animosity – they simply felt no need for organized religion. Major speculated that perhaps they 'had got out of the habit' as they continuously travelled the country in the entertainment business – 'God is in our house. We don't have to go to his' was his mother's attitude. She criticized neighbours who donned

2 Cherie Booth and Cate Haste, *The Goldfish Bowl: Married to the Prime Minister, 1955–97* (London: Chatto & Windus, 2004), pp. 266–7.

3 Terry Major-Ball, *Major Major: Memories of an older brother* (London: Duckworth, 1994).

their Sunday best and appeared pious in the presence of others – 'She's got religion,' she would comment.[4]

An Anglican at a distance

Baptized but never confirmed, Major always considered himself a member of the Church of England. During his youth, contact with the Church consisted of no more than attendance at Christmas and Easter services and church fêtes and jumble sales. Christian values were imbibed from his parents' daily example rather than their Sunday practice. His mother had 'a puritanical side' but nevertheless 'her God was a forgiving God'. It was this God in whom Major believed. He always had the desire to take the Church more seriously than his parents, but it was a desire that went largely unfulfilled.[5]

With his parents' health and business failing, Major did not enjoy his schooldays, other than the cricket and rugby. Religious education was a rare bright spot among the academic subjects. His general approach to life was to search for facts, yet he enjoyed a subject that raised questions admitting of no easy answers.

Having left school at the age of 16, Major set out in his late teens to provide himself with an education. He read the classics, ethics and philosophy extensively but did not consciously seek out spiritual works. With hindsight, however, he could see that he 'favoured books that carried a Christian message'. Like Macmillan and Blair, he too read John Robinson's *Honest to God* – no easy read, so it was a testimony to a certain commitment on his part to exploring existential questions.[6]

Major met Norma Johnson through their mutual involvement in local government politics. Norma taught domestic science at an Anglican secondary school in Camberwell. The two were married at St Matthew's, Brixton, on 3 October 1970. Notwithstanding Cherie Blair's secular label, Norma, like her husband, was a member of the Church of England. Sympathetic

4 John Major, *The Autobiography* (London: HarperCollins, 1999), pp. 13–14; John Major to the author, May 2021.

5 JM, *The Autobiography*, pp. 13–14; JM to the author, May 2021.

6 JM to the author, May 2021; John A. T. Robinson, *Honest to God* (London: SCM Press, 1963).

to other faiths, she was a proponent of tolerance, echoing Elizabeth I's comment that one should not seek to make a window into the souls of others. Their children, Elizabeth and James, were baptized – 'It would never have occurred to me or Norma not to have done so.'[7]

Wanting the Church 'to connect'

Britain was on the brink of entering the First Gulf War when John Major became Prime Minister in November 1990. It mattered enormously to him that the proposed military action satisfied the criteria for a 'just war'. Therefore he met privately with Robert Runcie, Archbishop of Canterbury, and Basil Hume, Cardinal Archbishop of Westminster, in the Cabinet Room. Both assured him of their support, which was 'immensely important' to him: he wrote that he 'would have been uneasy' proceeding without it. At the launch of Operation Desert Storm, he concluded his broadcast to the nation with an impromptu 'God bless' because it came instinctively to him – it was what he would have said to his son, had he been a combatant.[8] The subsequent Service of Thanksgiving held in Glasgow Cathedral proved far less controversial than the Falklands War service at St Paul's Cathedral in 1982.

It was not just during the Gulf War that Major maintained contact with faith leaders and benefited from their advice. It was difficult, he acknowledged, to overemphasize the importance of the support, both spiritual and practical, he received from the churches during the Northern Irish Peace Process in the early 1990s.[9] George Carey, who succeeded Runcie in April 1991, recalled how he met informally with Major 'every six months for a quiet tête-à-tête'.[10]

In his youth, 'the Church as an institution seemed very remote' to Major. Neither its voice nor its tone had appealed to him. He continued to believe that it struggled to connect with people, internal theological disputes making it seem irrelevant. Yet he longed for the Church to find its voice in

7 JM to the author, May 2021.

8 JM, *The Autobiography*, pp. 232, 234; JM to the author, May 2021.

9 JM to the author, May 2021.

10 George Carey to Tony Blair, 19 October 1994, cited Anthony Seldon, *Blair* (London: Free Press, 2004), p. 523.

addressing modern problems, to 'speak out about injustice, prejudice, poverty', as Jesus had done. It should ignore criticism of straying into politics, provided it did not engage in *party* politics. He wanted the Church 'to connect with people by stating its views clearly on matters of compassion, or conscience or social equity'. Unless it used its influence, the Church would lose it.[11] It is easy to sympathize with Major's desire to see the Church exercise more effectively its prophetic role and to become more countercultural. Jesus was concerned with social justice, but any close reading of Scripture reveals his concern also for personal morality, authentic worship and eternal salvation.

Major always distinguished the Church as an institution from the individual clergy he encountered. He found many faith leaders appealing and impressive. The Revd John Franklin Cheyne, Vicar of St James's, Brixton, offered the family solace at the time of Major's father's death in 1962. Major remembered him affectionately as 'warm, compassionate and kind', 'a wonderful advertisement for the Church'.[12] The Huntingdon constituency lay within the Diocese of Peterborough. Major found in its bishop, Bill Westwood, 'a firm friend, one of the best pastoral bishops I've ever come across'.[13] Although Jesus enjoined the evangelical counsel of poverty upon his apostles, Major made an impassioned plea on behalf of the clergy, believing them to be 'miserably underpaid'. In his view, especially in relation to married clergy, 'poverty or near-poverty is not a virtue'.[14]

For someone presenting himself as primarily interested in facts and calling for the Church to engage with modern issues, Major could sometimes take a rather romantic or whimsical view of faith. Quoting George Orwell, together with cricket, warm beer, green suburbs and dog-lovers, 'old maids bicycling to Holy Communion through the morning mist', embodied quintessential England for him.[15] Macmillan was famously a devotee of Anthony Trollope. It is more surprising to find Major advancing the Revd Septimus Harding from the Chronicles of Barsetshire as his model

11 JM to the author, May 2021.

12 JM to the author, May 2021.

13 JM, *The Autobiography*, p. 72.

14 JM to the author, May 2021.

15 JM, Speech to Conservative Group for Europe, 22 April 1993, <https://johnmajorarchive.org.uk/1993/04/22/mr-majors-speech-to-conservative-group-for-europe-22-april-1993>, accessed 05.06.21.

Christian.[16] Harding was indeed tolerant and good-natured, humble and patient in adversity – but he was also a fictional character from novels set in a time and society that can appear as remote to contemporary sensibilities as the Dark Ages.

'Balm on a troubled mind'

Regular churchgoing did not feature in Major's youth. This was not something that changed significantly in later years. In the late 1960s he was sent by Standard Bank to work in Nigeria. His house steward there was struck by his non-attendance at church.[17] Echoing earlier Prime Ministers' reaction against puritanism, Major pondered whether his attitude was influenced by 'childhood memories of thoroughly dreary Sundays – when everything was closed, and any kind of amusement was forbidden'. Living by Christian values was, for him, more important than regular churchgoing.

As a member of the Church of England, Major felt he *should* have attended church more often. The demands of office, especially the travel commitments of a Prime Minister, militated against the possibility. He acknowledged that other Prime Ministers had found a solution but that, for him, 'the impetus to overcome the obstacles was clearly not there'. In retirement he has only very rarely attended his local church, and felt 'conflicted' about this. Nevertheless, when diary commitments permitted, he would slip quietly into St George's, Windsor, or, more likely, Westminster Abbey for evensong. After a particularly fraught or worrying day, he found that the experience poured 'balm on a troubled mind'.[18]

Major, although politically Conservative, tended like Thatcher and Heath towards social liberalism. He took 'a tolerant view of personal misdemeanours' – a tolerance tested by the allegations of sleaze that beset the latter years of his government. With Blair, in 1990 he voted against proposals to reduce the time limits for abortion, and did not regard homosexuality

---

16 JM to the author, May 2021.

17 Edward Pearce, *The Quiet Rise of John Major* (London: Weidenfeld & Nicolson, 1991), p. 11.

18 JM to the author, May 2021.

as 'a social evil',[19] supporting plans to allow the celebration of same-sex marriages in church. There was no reference to faith in his rationale for these positions.

On the other hand, Major felt extremely strongly about *Visions of Ecstasy*,[20] a sexually explicit short portraying Christ that had been banned on the grounds of blasphemy. He found the film director's appeal to the European Court of Human Rights on the grounds of breach of freedom of expression 'wholly unacceptable', to the extent that he contemplated opting out of the European Convention on Human Rights if the Court required the UK to grant a certificate to this or similar films. Major wrote warmly to Mary Whitehouse on her retirement as President of the National Viewers' and Listeners' Association, praising her long-standing campaign to protect standards as to what constituted acceptable viewing.[21]

'A believer nonetheless'

Major was reluctant to discuss matters of faith, preferring 'a little English reserve on the subject'. In this respect he was similar to the great majority of twentieth-century Prime Ministers. During the 1990 leadership campaign, he was invited on to BBC Radio 4's *Sunday* programme to discuss his religious faith. His preference was to decline but he was told by his team that then 'the view would be put about – wrongly – that I was a non-believer'. He was 'mortally embarrassed' by the experience of being asked personal questions he felt unable to answer 'without sounding sanctimonious'.[22] Major's Cabinet contained a number of committed Christians but faith was rarely discussed, even with friends such as Chris Patten, John Gummer and Peter Brooke. Most considered it a private matter; others respected that.[23]

In his autobiography, Major stated: 'I am a believer in the message more than in the rituals of the Church.'[24] What did he understand that message

19 JM, *The Autobiography*, pp. 551, 213.

20 Dir. Nigel Wingrove, Axel Films Ltd, 1989.

21 <https://premierchristian.news/en/news/article/john-major-supported-banning-film-censored-in-uk-for-blasphemy>, accessed 06.06.21.

22 JM, *The Autobiography*, p. 195.

23 JM to the author, May 2021.

24 JM, *The Autobiography*, p. 195.

to be? It was moral, rather than doctrinal, embodied in Jesus' teaching in the Sermon on the Mount: 'Do unto others as you would have them do unto you' (Matt. 7.12). For Major, this meant compassion towards the less fortunate, tolerance, forgiveness and generosity with money, time and deeds. When faith failed wholly to convince, there remained an appreciation of the compassion that faith engendered.[25]

Of course, this call to personal and social action is part of the gospel message. There is no authentic Christianity unless belief is reflected in daily life. What, however, of the supernatural claims of Jesus that give particular force to the gospel imperative, which enable believers to fulfil that duty and promise life beyond this world?

Faced with the question of belief in the fundamental Christian doctrines of the Trinity, the Incarnation and the resurrection, Major wished he could answer yes but struggled intellectually with these propositions. Increasingly, he is asked to deliver memorial addresses for those who have died. The pondering of one's own mortality and faith this entails he finds 'a deeply spiritual experience'. He hopes for an afterlife but finds it difficult to convince himself of this. On the other hand – and it would be interesting to know what he considers the distinction to be – he does believe that the soul 'lives on in a tangible way'. In some way we are conscious in our hearts, in our souls, of what our deceased loved ones would wish us to do or say. Is this just wishful thinking? Major may be closer to the fullness of belief than he admits, simply requiring the doctrinal underpinning for the intimations of the heart.

Prayer is important to him. He finds it certainly brings comfort 'most especially in times of distress'. What appears unfocused – the question of whether one is 'directing one's prayers to a higher being (or an inner soul)' – is, of course, consistent with some Christian traditions that believe God is to be found in the inner soul. Major entertains the clear hope that 'someone might be listening'.[26]

There is a touching sense of self-deprecation about his description of his spiritual life. Humility, of course, is among the virtues most commended by Jesus – but so is perseverance in the search for God. Here there seems

25 JM to the author, May 2021.
26 JM to the author, May 2021.

an unresolved tension between diffidence and reserve on the one hand, and a desire for the assurance of the realities of faith on the other. Despite his professed admiration for English reserve in these matters, Major did want to know what his colleagues believed.[27] However, to make full sense of Christianity, to experience it as a lived reality, requires active membership of a community, the Church. It is the Church that transmits faith both as revealed knowledge of God and as lived reality, to attain this conviction that we are loved and created for something that transcends the immediate and the temporal.

Major regretted never having been confirmed but worried his motives would be questioned were it to take place after he became a public figure. He likewise regretted that the Church 'never reached out' to him.[28] Sadly, it failed to reach out effectively to many of the twentieth-century Prime Ministers. There remains a duty on the part of the individual, however, to respond to the call of faith, even when inadequately proclaimed by the Church.

Was Major the first secular Prime Minister? Eighteen years younger than his predecessor, he was in many ways the first to be raised outside an environment in which the practice of Christian faith and the presence of its institutions were taken for granted and, for better or worse, indelibly marked former holders of the office. It is clear, however, that interest in faith remained a live issue and that the attempt to live a Christian life was sincere. He was not a secular Prime Minister. His self-assessment is accurate: 'Chance and circumstance left me a believer at a distance, but a believer nonetheless.'[29]

27 Edwina Currie, Diary, 25 December 1987, cited Edwina Currie, *Diaries, 1987–1992* (London: Little, Brown, 1992), p. 26.

28 JM, *The Autobiography*, p. 13.

29 JM, *The Autobiography*, p. 14.

Tony Blair (1997–2007)

'Jesus was a moderniser'

Anthony Charles Lynton Blair was born in Edinburgh on 6 May 1953. He was educated at Fettes College, Edinburgh, and St John's College, Oxford. Having graduated in law, he practised at the Bar.

Blair fought the 1982 Beaconsfield by-election as the Labour candidate. In 1983 he was elected for Sedgefield, County Durham, a seat he held until his resignation in 2007.

Blair was a modernizer, recognizing that Labour's chances of re-election required significant changes in policy and presentation. Appointed to the Shadow Treasury team in 1984, he proved himself articulate, capable and a good media performer. He joined the Shadow Trade and Industry team in 1987, was appointed Shadow Energy Secretary in 1988 and Shadow Employment Secretary the following year. Shadow Home Secretary from 1992, his message, 'Tough on crime, tough on the causes of crime', resonated with the public.

Following John Smith's early death, Blair was elected Labour Party leader on 21 July 1994. He persuaded the party to amend its constitutional commitment to public ownership of the means of production. Under Blair, 'New Labour' ruled out a return to high taxation and nationalization. He appealed to the electorate's legitimate aspirations for self-improvement while promising compassion for the poorest and those in need. He successfully wooed the City and the media. In contrast to the youthful Blair, Major's Conservatives appeared tired, divided and immersed in sleaze. Labour won a landslide victory with a majority of 179 in the general election on 1 May 1997. The following day, Blair was appointed Prime Minister.

The Chancellor, Gordon Brown, made a commitment to fiscal prudence and gave the Bank of England independence from the government. Blair had to manage the crisis that threatened the monarchy on the death of Diana, Princess of Wales, and was felt to have captured the mood of the nation. His enthusiasm for constitutional reform might have been limited, but the consequences were significant: devolved assemblies for Scotland and Wales, an elected mayor and assembly for London. Foxhunting was outlawed and (most) hereditary peers were removed from the House of Lords.

Not everyone was enamoured of the new administration. Blair was criticized for his reliance on special advisers. It was claimed that 'spin' prevailed over substance, with presentation tightly controlled by his Press Secretary, Alastair Campbell. The Conservatives, however, remained weak and divided. Labour won a second landslide victory with a 167 seat majority in the general election on 7 June 2001, albeit on a much lower turnout.

In his second term, Blair aimed to focus on domestic reforms. His 'Third Way' sought to improve public services, especially health and education, encouraging the cooperation of public and private sectors. Academy schools and foundation hospitals were given significant autonomy and access to private funding, while remaining within the state sector.

The international situation was transformed by the 9/11 terror attacks on the USA in 2001. Blair immediately assured President Bush of British support and backed the removal of the Taliban regime in Afghanistan by a US-led coalition. The attack on Iraq in March 2003 was more controversial. There were claims that Blair misled Parliament and the country about the existence of weapons of mass destruction, and accusations of inadequate planning for the reconstruction of Iraq, leading to chaos and killing on a massive scale. Blair was unrepentant, believing that Saddam Hussein's human rights record as Iraqi leader amply justified military intervention.

Labour won a third successive victory and a majority of 66 seats in the general election on 5 May 2005, but with just 36 per cent of the popular vote. London was subject to Islamicist terror attacks on 7 July 2005.

Blair's relationship with his Chancellor was already tense. Brown accused him of failing to honour an agreement to hand over the leadership in return for his support back in 1994. Blair was an enthusiastic European; Brown blocked his attempts to commit the UK to joining the Euro. Doubts as to Brown's electoral appeal and commitment to the reform programme caused Blair to defer his departure. When Israel invaded Lebanon in the summer of 2006, he again followed Bush's lead and refused to call for a ceasefire, angering many in his own party. In September 2006, Labour

MPs' calls for his resignation compelled him to announce that the party conference that autumn would be his last as leader.

Blair spent his final months in office attempting to secure his legacy at home and overseas. He strove to coordinate the international effort for aid for Africa and to combat climate change. This time was overshadowed, however, by the 'cash for honours' police inquiry. Building on Major's initiative, one of Blair's greatest successes had been the 1998 Good Friday Agreement that brought peace to Northern Ireland. He succeeded largely due to his charm, tenacity and negotiating skills. His continuing commitment to the Northern Irish peace process led to the power-sharing arrangement between Unionists and Sinn Fein announced on 8 May 2007. Efforts to promote peace in the Middle East were less successful.

Blair resigned as Prime Minister and as an MP on 27 June 2007. A controversial figure, he was reviled by many for the Iraqi war but was unquestionably Labour's most electorally successful leader, with an impressive record of legislative reform. Only 54 when he left office, he committed himself to the causes he cared most about: the Middle Eastern peace process, Africa, the environment and interfaith relations. Controversy continued, with criticism of his financial dealings and contact with foreign leaders. He was created a Knight of the Garter in 2022.

* * *

'More interested in religion than politics'

In June 2003, Tony Blair was interviewed by the magazine *Vanity Fair*. When the talk turned to religion, Alastair Campbell pre-empted further discussion, insisting firmly: 'We don't do God.'[1] Both Blair and Campbell subsequently clarified that this was not intended as an anti-religious remark, rather a demarcation of boundaries: a politician's faith is a private

1 Alistair Campbell, cited Tom Bower, *Broken Vows: Tony Blair – the tragedy of power* (London: Faber & Faber, 2016), pp. 329–30.

matter, not for public consumption. 'It was always a packet of trouble to talk about it', Blair later commented.[2]

The one thing everyone knew about Blair was that 'he did God'. When political biographers and journalists discover to their surprise – and occasional horror – that their subject is a committed Christian, they turn to Gladstone as their benchmark. Why Salisbury is overlooked is not entirely clear – or Baldwin, Macmillan and Douglas-Home. Philip Stephens has a long paragraph in his biography of Blair comparing him to Gladstone.[3] For John Rentoul, Blair was 'the first Prime Minister since Gladstone to read the Bible habitually'.[4] Anthony Seldon claims that no other Prime Minister since Gladstone 'has been so influenced by his religion'.[5] Peter Oborne has him as 'the most religious prime minister since Gladstone'.[6] Anthony Connell states: 'In the public mind, Blair was probably more closely associated with Christianity than any Prime Minister since Gladstone.'[7] It is this public consciousness that connects Gladstone and Blair. Other Prime Ministers successfully deflected interest in their religious beliefs and practice – and lived in an age when this was possible.

Blair once protested: 'I can't stand politicians who go on about religion.'[8] His PR team were generally successful in keeping him off the subject during his years in office, but he needed little persuasion to talk about his Christian faith, and did so extensively before and after his occupancy of Number 10. It came naturally to him. He wrote in his autobiography: 'I have always been more interested in religion than politics.'[9] What caused this interest?

2 Alastair Campbell, *Diaries: Outside, Inside, 2003–2005*, Vol. 5 (London: Biteback Publishing, 2016), pp. 492–3; Tony Blair, 'Faith and Globalization', The Cardinal's Lectures 2008, 3 April 2008, <https://sewauk.org/tony-blair-speech-on-faith-and-globalisation>, accessed 21.10.20.

3 Philip Stephens, *Tony Blair: The making of a world leader* (London: Viking, 2004), p. 16.

4 John Rentoul, *Tony Blair: Prime Minister* (London: Faber & Faber, 2013), p. 351.

5 Anthony Seldon, *Blair* (London: Free Press, 2004), pp. 516–17.

6 Peter Oborne, 'The Special Relationship between Blair and God', *Spectator*, 5 April 2003.

7 Anthony Connell, 'Tony Blair (1997–2007)', in ed. Nick Spencer, *The Mighty and the Almighty: How political leaders do God* (London: Biteback Publishing, 2017), p. 87.

8 Tony Blair, *Vanity Fair*, March 1995, cited Rentoul, *TB*, p. 236.

9 Tony Blair, *A Journey* (London: Hutchinson, 2010), p. 690.

'Not a church-going family'

Compared to other Prime Ministers, Blair was not from an overtly religious home. According to Cherie, 'The Blairs were not a church-going family.'[10] His father, Leo Blair, the illegitimate son of English actors, was raised by a working-class Glaswegian couple, James and Mary Blair. Initially a Communist, Leo's political views developed after he was commissioned during the Second World War. He went on to work as a tax inspector, then qualified as a law lecturer and barrister, seeking to enter Parliament as a Conservative. There was no comparable change in Leo's religious views. His son recalled: 'Dad wasn't religious at all and after my mum died he was firmly anti-religious.'[11] Later he described his father as 'a militant atheist'.[12]

It is often assumed that Blair is an anglicized Scot. Although never something he sought to conceal, he is in fact half-Irish. It may partly account for his predilection for matters of faith, if not the specific direction in which this was ultimately channelled. Leo Blair married Hazel Corscaden at the Presbyterian Barony Church, Glasgow, in November 1948. Hazel had a definite religious identity. Her family were originally Protestant farmers from Donegal and her father had been Grand Master of the local Orange lodge. Although Hazel was raised in Glasgow, Ulster coloured the family's perspective on the world. Until 1969, Blair's summers were spent in Donegal. Visits to cousins in Dungannon across the border in Northern Ireland afforded direct experience of sectarian divisions. With the outbreak of the Troubles, those holidays ceased, but Irish friends maintained contact, relaying their anti-Catholic fears. Blair recounts his maternal grandmother's deathbed wish on a final visit in the 1970s: 'Whatever else you do, son, never marry a Catholic.'[13]

Blair was particularly close to his mother, who died shortly after his graduation. Hazel's religious identity was clear, her practice less so. In one interview, Blair stated: 'Mum took us to church but not as regularly as I go with my kids now.' In view of Cherie's comment, it appears that

---

10 Cherie Blair, *Speaking for Myself: The autobiography* (London: Little, Brown, 2008), p. 82.

11 TB, Interview with Lynda Lee-Potter, *Daily Mail*, 26 October 1996.

12 TB, Interview with John Geiger, *The Globe and Mail*, 29 November 2010.

13 TB, *A Journey*, pp. 154–6.

churchgoing was neither regular nor frequent. Elsewhere, Blair said that his mother 'wasn't especially religious'. Her most important influence on her son's life of faith was the introduction to prayer: 'Mum taught us all our prayers and said them with us.'[14]

'Tony did not really have an interest in religion'

Leo's academic career took the family first to Australia and then to Durham. Blair followed his elder brother to Durham Cathedral's Chorister School. Although not a chorister himself, it would be difficult to remain indifferent to being educated in the shadow of the imposing Norman cathedral. He acknowledged that he 'imbibed a certain amount of religion there'.[15] His most abiding religious memory from his time at his prep school occurred in 1964. Summoned to the study of the headmaster, Canon John Groves, he was told that his father had suffered a stroke. Headmaster and pupil knelt and prayed together.[16] Groves felt that, even at the age of eleven, Blair was a believer.[17]

In 1966, Blair was sent to Fettes College, Edinburgh. It was not a positive experience and he developed a reputation as a rebel. He chose not to be confirmed at Fettes and was under no parental pressure to be. Peter Thomson, his spiritual mentor at Oxford, felt that Blair's experience was similar to that of many public schoolboys – 'school chapel and chaplains hadn't inspired him'. Blair did not, however, ridicule the chapel, as he did most school institutions. At Fettes, as at Durham, religion provided one bright spot.[18] Opting out of the Combined Cadet Force, he undertook voluntary community work. As a result, he met the Revd Ronald Selby Wright, minister of the city's Canongate Kirk and previously a chaplain at Fettes. Selby Wright was a charismatic figure, a former military chaplain and religious

14 TB, Interview with Lynda Lee-Potter, 26 October 1996; TB, Interview with John Geiger, 29 November 2010.

15 TB, Interview with John Geiger, 29 November 2010.

16 TB, Interview with Lynda Lee-Potter, 26 October 1996.

17 Rentoul, *TB*, p. 30.

18 Peter Thomson, Interview, cited Seldon, *Blair*, p. 41.

broadcaster, a chaplain to the Queen and future Moderator of the Church of Scotland. Blair assisted at his Boys' Club summer camp. It is suggested that Selby Wright intervened to prevent his expulsion from Fettes. Selby Wright, however, discerned no spiritual motivation in Blair's voluntary work: 'Tony did not really have an interest in religion.'[19]

For someone with no real interest in religion, Blair had an uncanny ability to encounter its personnel and institutions from an early age. His gap year was spent in London setting up a rock band with his business partner Alan Collenette. Church halls offered cheap potential venues for concerts but few were willing to rent to rock bands. An exception was the Vineyard Congregational Church in Richmond, attended by Harold Wilson a generation earlier. In return, the two young musical entrepreneurs assisted Norman Burt, a teacher and deacon at the church, with the youth club he ran in the crypt. His involvement appears more than a cynical ploy on Blair's part – he lodged with Burt and visited his Norfolk cottage. Blair remained friends with Collenette, who may possibly be transposing memories of a later period when he claims that even then Blair 'was God-fearing and that was unusual at that time in that circle of people. I respected him greatly for it.'[20]

Blair arrived at St John's College, Oxford, to read law in October 1972. He considered himself a Christian but did not see the point of religion. He did not practise his faith and it had no appreciable impact on his life. Later he reflected: 'I had always believed in God but I had become slightly detached from it. I couldn't make sense of it.'[21]

Peter Thomson: 'my friend, teacher, mentor and guide'

That changed as Blair, an early riser, engaged in conversation over breakfast with an Australian Anglican cleric coming in from morning service in the college chapel. He acknowledged that Peter Thomson was 'probably the most influential person in my life', and paid tribute to him after his

19 Revd Ronald Selby Wright, Interview, cited Rentoul, *TB*, p. 19.

20 Alan Collenette, Interview, cited Rentoul, *TB*, p. 30.

21 TB, Interview with Martin Jacques, *Sunday Times Magazine*, 17 July 1994.

death in January 2010: 'There are very few people of whom you can say: he changed my life. Peter changed mine . . . He was my friend, teacher, mentor and guide.'[22] One priest recollected that Blair always attributed 'his Christianity to Peter, never to his parents'.[23]

A charismatic figure, Thomson divided his ministry between educating privileged children, social activism and landing himself in trouble with the church authorities.[24] Aged 36, he was a mature student studying theology. Blair was drawn to Thomson's circle, which engaged in endless discussion of politics and religion – subjects that had never interested him previously. His intellect and passion were fully engaged – 'My Christianity and my politics came together at the same time.'[25] Blair was won over by Thomson's conviction that Christianity was about building up community and making a difference in the world. 'What I took away from Peter Thomson,' he wrote, 'is the idea that your religious beliefs aren't something that you shut away from the world, but something that meant you had to go out and act.'[26] He discovered 'religion as something living, that was about the world around me rather than a special one-to-one relationship with a remote being on high. Suddenly I began to see its social relevance. I began to make sense of the world.'[27]

Simultaneously with this discussion of radical theology and its social application, Blair was drawn to a more conventional practice of faith. The Ugandan Olara Otunnu was also a member of Thomson's circle and a practising Christian. Blair began to attend the college chapel with him. In his second year he asked to be confirmed as an Anglican. The assistant chaplain, Graham Dow, later Bishop of Carlisle, was delighted. Blair was fun and normal, different from the pious Evangelicals and intense intellectuals he generally encountered: 'He gave the impression of someone who had just discovered something exciting and new – he didn't know it all.'[28]

---

22 TB, *A Journey*, p. 79.

23 Fr John Caden, Interview, August 2008, cited John Burton and Eileen McCabe, *We Don't Do God: Blair's religious belief and its consequences* (London: Continuum, 2009), p. 35.

24 Andrew Mawson, Obituary: 'Rev Peter Thomson', *The Guardian*, 25 January 2010.

25 TB, *News of the World*, 29 October 1995, cited Rentoul, *TB*, p. 43.

26 TB, *Evening Standard*, 18 July 1994, cited Seldon, *Blair*, p. 44.

27 TB, *Third Way Magazine*, cited *The Observer*, 23 December 2007.

28 Rt Revd Graham Dow, Interview, cited Rentoul, *TB*, p. 43.

Dow recalled that Blair 'was less concerned to save his own soul, still less those of others, than to make the world a better place'.[29] He pulled no punches about the commitment required by faith: Blair 'didn't disagree' with his presentation of Christianity as a personal relationship with Christ aimed at building up the kingdom of God. Dow did not judge Blair an original thinker but neither did he doubt his sincerity.[30] The confirmation took place in the spring of 1974.

While there was no 'one moment of conversion', Blair dated the beginning of his 'spiritual journey' to those undergraduate days.[31] Visiting his friend at Oxford, Collenette noted Blair's active social life but also the Bible by his bedside.[32] Inevitably, when faith is embraced in youth with such enthusiasm, the question of ordained ministry is raised. Thomson felt that Blair 'could easily have gone into the Church'.[33] According to Otunna, it was something he considered: 'It was at one point very much on his mind. It was certainly one of the options that he talked about seriously.'[34] Questioned subsequently about a possible vocation, Blair sought to deflect interest. He was not, he maintained, 'a good enough person to assume that type of role'. He was captivated rather by 'the power of politics to change the world'.[35]

John Macmurray: religion as action

Blair read widely on religion and philosophy, including Søren Kierkegaard, Carl Jung and Immanuel Kant.[36] He returned, however, to one particular author. At the time of his election as Labour Party leader, Blair suggested: 'If you really want to understand what I'm really about, you

29 Dow, Interview, 19 July 2003, cited Seldon, *Blair*, p. 516.

30 Dow, Interview, cited Rentoul, *TB*, p. 43.

31 TB, Interview with John Geiger, 29 November 2010.

32 Collenette, Interview, cited Rentoul, *TB*, p. 33.

33 Peter Thomson, Interview, Michael Cockerell, Documentary, *What Makes Tony Tick?* (BBC, 2000).

34 Olara Otunna, Interview, cited Rentoul, *TB*, p. 44.

35 TB, Interview with John Geiger, 29 November 2010.

36 TB, Interview with Matthew d'Ancona, *Sunday Telegraph*, 7 April 1996.

have to look at a guy called John Macmurray. He was influential – very influential, not in the detail but in the general concept.'[37]

John Macmurray, a Scottish philosopher who had taught at Oxford, University College London and Edinburgh, was no longer widely read when Blair discovered him in the 1970s. From a strict Presbyterian family, Macmurray rejected institutional religion, ritual and dogma during the First World War, becoming a Quaker towards the end of his life. Deeming the churches irrelevant, he sought to recreate Christianity, reawakening a sense of moral purpose and duty. He was deeply critical of individualism – human beings, he held, are formed in relationship. He also opposed idealism:

> If it were to be cured of idealism, religion would be about this world, and not about any other world . . . Our religion would cease to be for our comfort or consolation, a compensation for the futilities and failure of our material life, and become power and knowledge for the salvation of the world through us, and even at our expense.[38]

Action not idealism was the essence of true religion. Macmurray taught that, contrary to its contemporary manifestation: 'Christianity is inherently a *revolutionary* religion seeking the achievement of a world community.'[39]

Blair was introduced to Macmurray's work by Thomson. It had had an impact on him too:

> Macmurray taught me how to think through the whole notion of religion in relationship to action. Here, we had been from the time of our theological days, involved in reflective thinking and contemplating our navels and all that type of thing, trying to get yourself right with God and of course there is an important part of

37 TB, *New Statesman*, 13 July 1994, cited Burton and McCabe, *We Don't Do God*, p. 11.

38 John Macmurray, *Idealism Against Religion* (London: Lindsey Press, 1944), p. 18 ff., cited ed. Philip Conford, *The Personal World: John Macmurray on self and society* (Edinburgh: Floris Books, 1996), pp. 189–90.

39 John Macmurray, *Challenge to the Churches: Religion and democracy* (London: Kegan, Paul, 1941), p. 42, cited ed. Conford, *The Personal World*, p. 210.

all that. But what became real for me was every time I was involved in action, everything came alive.[40]

Thomson shared Macmurray's thought with those around him at Oxford: religion as a call to action, and its importance in forming community.

Blair acknowledged Macmurray's influence on his own political thought: 'I developed a theory about the basis of socialism being about "community."'[41] Commentators challenged how much Blair's 'communitarianism' in fact owed to Macmurray.[42] They cited Sarah Hale's claim that he failed to grasp Macmurray's fundamental distinction between 'society' (an external construct based on mutual dependence), which was destructive of the 'community' (based on shared values and 'personal' life), which Macmurray promoted. Those commentators omitted to mention, however, Hale's conclusion that if Macmurray's influence on Blair's political philosophy is questionable, it is certainly discernible with respect to his religion.[43]

Writing the preface for an anthology of Macmurray's work in 1996, Blair paid tribute to the importance of his thought in understanding 'the relationship between individual and society' and for locating spirituality 'in the world' rather than its being 'an abstraction from it'.[44] John Burton was Blair's constituency agent, friend and fellow believer. The two discussed faith at length. Burton recognized Macmurray's influence on Blair: 'Once he realized that religion wasn't just about getting down on your knees and praying, but about action, about community, he saw the sense in it.'[45]

What, however, of the content rather than the consequences of faith? Blair read *Honest to God* by John Robinson, Bishop of Woolwich. No theological conservative, Robinson queried Macmurray's concept of God. He left 'one wondering whether there is anything distinctive about religion at all . . . The question inevitably arises, if theology is translated into

---

40 Peter Thomson, Interview, Australian television, *Keys of the Kingdom*, 29 June 2000, cited Burton and McCabe, *We Don't Do God*, pp. 5–6.

41 TB, *A Journey*, p. 79.

42 Francis Beckett and David Hencke, *The Blairs and Their Court* (London: Aurum Press, 2004), pp. 30–1; Connell, 'TB (1997–2007)', in ed. Spencer, *The Mighty and the Almighty*, p. 91.

43 Sarah Hale, *Blair's Community: Communitarian thought and New Labour* (Manchester: Manchester University Press, 2006), pp. 86, 84n.

44 TB, 'Preface', in ed. Conford, *The Personal World*, pp. 9–10.

45 Burton and McCabe, *We Don't Do God*, p. 9.

anthropology, why do we any longer need the category of God?'[46] Macmurray denied the charge of pantheism but he was not an orthodox Christian. The kingdom of heaven was 'the universal community of mankind, based on the sense of unity between man and man'. The possibility of an afterlife is downplayed. There is no sense of the divinity of Christ:

> Jesus was the man in whom the religious significance of the world was revealed in a definitive and complete form . . . Jesus discovered the significance of human life . . . Jesus became conscious of the intention of God in human history.[47]

To what extent did Blair buy into this? He conceded that at one point he 'almost rebelled against the church and saw Christianity almost in humanist terms'. His thinking developed, however, combining aspects of Macmurray's philosophy with a more personal relationship with God.[48] The Church and corporate worship came to assume an importance for him completely lacking for Macmurray. Burton claimed, however, that Blair 'certainly wasn't orthodox in either his politics or his religion'.[49] In view of Blair's subsequent spiritual journey, it is intriguing to note Macmurray's denunciation of 'the priestly type of religion', contrasting it unfavourably with a personal 'prophetic' religion.[50]

'Whatever else you do, son, never marry a Catholic'

Having graduated from Oxford, Blair followed his father and brother into the legal profession. While training to be a barrister at Lincoln's Inn in early 1976, he met a fellow pupil who was to be his companion on his spiritual journey.

46 John A. T. Robinson, *Honest to God* (London: SCM Press, 1963), p. 51.

47 Macmurray, cited ed. Conford, *The Personal World*, pp. 205, 111, 135, 209.

48 TB, Interview with Roy McCloughry, *Third Way*, October 1993.

49 Burton and McCabe, *We Don't Do God*, p. 9.

50 Macmurray et al., *Adventure: The faith of science and the science of faith* (London: Macmillan, 1927), pp. 195–8, cited ed. Conford, *The Personal World*, pp. 178–9.

Cherie Booth's childhood was very different from Blair's. Her father was the actor Tony Booth. Her parents separated when she was young and she was raised in Crosby by her non-Catholic mother and Catholic grandmother. Cherie's childhood experience was that of the pre-Conciliar Catholic Church on Merseyside. Sunday Mass was both communion with God and the gathering of the wider family community. The parish priest was her grandmother's cousin. Two cousins were priests. Cherie attended Seafield Convent Grammar School, where the Sacred Heart of Mary sisters began every lesson with a prayer. She rejected, however, any suggestion that an intelligent woman's options were restricted to a teaching career and marriage.[51]

The changes of the Second Vatican Council began to make themselves felt at a local level during Cherie's teens. As part of her religious studies programme, she ventured beyond her Catholic parish, visiting Anglican and Congregationalist churches. The Catholic Church in Liverpool remained close to its working-class parishioners. There was often a left-wing political expression to faith. Cherie recalled her involvement with the liberation theology espoused by the Young Christian Students:

> We'd play our guitars and have Masses in the round or outdoors which were full of sharing and 'Bridge over Troubled Water'. We thought we were very radical and would change the world. We put on 24-hour fasts in the city centre for the Third World, and over the summer holidays would organize a playgroup on a housing estate.[52]

As a student at the London School of Economics, Cherie ceased to attend Mass, except on visits home, but Catholicism remained part of her identity.

Pre-Conciliar piety coexisted with a radical questioning of the institution. Cherie made no secret of her disagreement with church teaching on issues such as contraception and the ordination of women. She brought to the Church the same attitude she and her future husband would bring to the 1980s Labour Party – the determination to stay and fight for change

51 Cherie Blair, *Speaking for Myself*, pp. 31–2.

52 Cherie Booth, 'A Little Bit of Grit', in ed. Peter Stanford, *Why I Am Still a Catholic: Essays in faith and perseverance* (London: Continuum, 2003), pp. 23–4.

from within. This was combined with devotion to the Virgin Mary: 'I admire her self-sacrifice, her ability to accept God's will and her trust in Him.'[53] While Blair underwent heart surgery in 2004, Cherie was on her knees praying the rosary throughout the operation.[54] Despite her disagreement with aspects of church teaching, her veneration for the office and holders of the papacy was palpable at the Vatican audiences she attended. The space for reflection afforded by weekly Mass and the strong 'sense of community' anchored Cherie to the Catholic Church.[55]

Although Tony was Anglican and Cherie Catholic, religion was a bond that brought them together. On her first visit to the Blair home in Durham, he spoke about his mother's death the preceding year and also about his faith: 'Even at that very early stage in our relationship, Tony and I would spend hours talking about this kind of thing, about God and what we were here for.' Cherie felt that 'religion was more important to him than anyone else I had ever met outside the priesthood'.[56]

Tony and Cherie married on 29 March 1980 in the chapel of St John's College, where he had been confirmed six years earlier. They were married by the chaplain, Canon Anthony Phillips, who found them both 'devout in their Christianity'.[57] As a Catholic, it would have been relatively easy for Cherie to have had the marriage recognized by her own Church. She felt it impolite, however, to ask the Established Church if her priest cousin could participate in the marriage ceremony.[58]

Normal parish life

Two things increased the Blairs' commitment to their faith. The first was their involvement with the community in Sedgefield, where Blair was elected MP in 1983. Catholics were prominent in the local Labour Party. The Sedgefield parish priest, Fr John Caden, an independent county councillor, was influential in local politics. Blair told Caden that his wife was

53 Cherie Booth, 'A Little Bit of Grit', pp. 21–2, 25–6.

54 Cherie Blair, *Speaking for Myself*, p. 371.

55 Cherie Blair, *Speaking for Myself*, p. 359; Cherie Booth, 'A Little Bit of Grit', p. 26.

56 Cherie Blair, *Speaking for Myself*, pp. 82, 95.

57 Canon Anthony Phillips, cited Seldon, *Blair*, p. 66.

58 Cherie Blair, *Speaking for Myself*, p. 108.

a Catholic and asked if he could bring her to Mass. Of course, Caden replied. The two became firm friends and tennis partners, discussing religion and politics between games. It helped that Caden shared Thomson's interest in liberation theology and the Church's social teaching. He asked Blair to become a reader at Mass at St John Fisher Catholic Church,[59] and baptized all four of the Blair children.

The second factor was the arrival of those children. Cherie 'was always insistent that the children be brought up as Catholics'. Both parents wanted the family to experience normal community life away from the Westminster political bubble. Cherie knew that in London one of the most effective ways of ensuring this was through participation in the local parish. Moving to Islington in 1986, the Blairs attended the Sunday morning family Mass at St Joan of Arc Catholic Church, Highbury, 'a genuinely warm and friendly affair, if a little chaotic'. The elder three children received their First Holy Communion there and attended the parish primary school.[60] Cherie counted this 'time in a parish in north London as among the happiest in our family life'.[61]

Blair accompanied his wife and children to Mass. It was inconceivable to him that he might attend church elsewhere by himself. There was an added advantage: 'Going to church is one of the few times we get out and actually mix with people.'[62] As at Sedgefield, he read the lessons at Mass at St Joan of Arc.

Christianity and socialism

Graham Dow, his college chaplain from undergraduate days, had remarked that Blair was not a proselytizing type of Christian. While he believed and practised his faith, many of his political colleagues were unaware of the fact throughout the 1980s. He would disconcert friends by asking the location of the closest church on a Sunday. 'It's not a sin, is it?' was his response to their surprise.[63]

59 Caden, Interview, August 2008, cited Burton and McCabe, *We Don't Do God*, p. 26.
60 Cherie Blair, *Speaking for Myself*, pp. 142, 196.
61 Cherie Booth, 'A Little Bit of Grit', p. 28.
62 TB, Interview, *Daily Record*, 6 March 1998, cited Rentoul, *TB*, p. 351.
63 Rentoul, *TB*, p. 44.

Blair acknowledged his Christianity on BBC television's *Question Time* in 1991. The election of John Smith, a Christian socialist, as Labour leader in 1992 encouraged him to testify more publicly to his faith. He followed Smith in joining the Christian Socialist Movement (CSM). Blair wrote the Foreword for the 1993 book, *Reclaiming the Ground: Christianity and socialism*, although the editor, Chris Bryant, the CSM chairman, recalled the effort required to obtain the piece.[64] When written, it was a bland commitment to equality, compassion and freedom, with a reference to Blair's interest in the relationship between the individual and the community. There was no mention of God or Christ.[65] Nevertheless, Blair certainly viewed his political involvement in terms of faith. The memorandum he produced during his bid for the Labour Party leadership in 1994 stated his vision: 'Traditional principles but modern application . . . strong convictions based around Christian socialism . . . family; more to life than politics.'[66]

He told the 1992 Labour Party Conference:

> We are trying to establish in the public mind the coincidence between the values of democratic socialism and Christianity. There's a desire in the Labour Party to rediscover its ethical values, the ethical code that most of us really believe gave birth to the Labour Party.[67]

His 1995 Conference speech was replete with scriptural references:

> Socialism for me . . . is a moral purpose to life, a set of values, a belief in society, in co-operation, in achieving together what we cannot achieve alone. It is how I try to live my life, how you try to live yours – the simple truths – I am worth no more than anyone else, I am my brother's keeper, I will not walk by on the other side.[68]

64 Seldon, *Blair*, pp. 516–17.

65 TB, 'Foreword', in ed. Chris Bryant, *Reclaiming the Ground: Christianity and socialism* (London: Spire, 1993), pp. 10–11.

66 Rentoul, *TB*, p. 236.

67 Cited Burton and McCabe, *We Don't Do God*, p. 39.

68 TB, Speech, Labour Party Conference, 1995 <www.britishpoliticalspeech.org/speech-archive.htm?speech=201>, accessed 21.10.20.

The Blairs attended the non-denominational church service organized by the CSM at the beginning of each conference. In 1997 he asked for the format to be changed to a eucharistic celebration, with Anglican, Methodist and Catholic representatives participating.[69]

'I shouldn't have done it and I won't do it again'

The British public is not accustomed to political leaders discussing their religion in the national press. Blair's article in the Easter edition of the *Sunday Telegraph* on 7 April 1996 caused quite a stir. He gave a curious reflection on the figure of Pontius Pilate, whom he regarded as 'a timeless parable of political life'. (Pilate fascinated him – he had recently described him as 'the second most interesting character in the New Testament', arguing that the politically powerful were also deserving of sympathy.)[70] Other characters from the Passion narrative – Judas and Peter, even Christ – received less attention.

Blair also described how his faith was manifest: prayer was 'a source of solace'. He read the Bible daily, both Old and New Testaments. The gospel was, for him, 'the most extraordinary expression of sensitive human values'. Christianity had helped him to reject Marxist determinism. Human nature was about 'free will, individual responsibility', about the capacity to choose and decide.

Sin was acknowledged in the article, as a theological reality as 'alienation from God'; in daily life as 'the acknowledgement of right and wrong'. It was a concept Blair harnessed to his political philosophy. The Christian understanding of sin was a rejection of libertarianism, a shared recognition 'of values, of common norms of conduct'. Christianity was about 'mercy and compassion' but it was realistic about the human condition: 'It can identify what is good, but knows the capacity to do evil. I believe that the endless striving to do the one and avoid the other is the purpose of human existence. Through that comes progress.'

69 Rentoul, *TB*, p. 352.

70 Cited Rentoul, *TB*, p. 353.

Secularists and atheists might have felt uncomfortable with the leader of the Opposition articulating such a candidly theological message. To others, these aspects of the article were unexceptional. Blair stated his belief that Christians need not necessarily vote Labour. He then proceeded to cause considerable offence by saying that Christianity had led him to oppose 'the narrow view of self-interest that Conservatism – particularly in its modern, more right-wing form – represents'. Only the Left, he implied, understood Christianity as 'more than a one-to-one relationship with God', involving also a relationship 'with the outside world'.[71] Potentially even more explosive was Blair's off-the-record comment, not published at the time, that 'Jesus was a moderniser.'[72] Critics alleged he was claiming the Labour Party to be the authentic contemporary expression of Christianity, that he shared the same mission as Christ.

Blair later regretted the *Sunday Telegraph* article: 'I shouldn't have done it and I won't do it again.'[73] It may account for Campbell's subsequent determination to keep Blair off the subject of religion.

Faith influencing politics

In the article, Blair said of his religious beliefs: 'Of course, they influence my politics, but I do not wish to force them on anyone else.'[74] Religion was responsible for his initial involvement in politics, seeking to effect a change for the good in the world. Recognizing that there was no absolute separation, Blair held that religion was concerned with values, and politics with changing society. Religion led him to adopt as his starting point human beings, not ideologies.[75] It led him to understand the apparent 'coincidence between the philosophical theory of Christianity and left-of-centre politics'.[76] Burton argued that the influence was much more specific: 'Tony's Christian faith is part of him, down to his cotton socks. How can you understand his thinking on any front if you don't understand his

71 TB, Article, *Sunday Telegraph*, 7 April 1996.

72 Rentoul, *TB*, p. 354.

73 Cited Burton and McCabe, *We Don't Do God*, p. xviii.

74 TB, Article, *Sunday Telegraph*, 7 April 1996.

75 TB, *A Journey*, p. 79.

76 TB, *Evening Standard*, 18 July 1994, cited Rentoul, *TB*, p. 42.

core beliefs?' It was Campbell, fearing adverse electoral consequences, who vetoed that influence being made more explicit.[77]

One area in which Blair's religious beliefs had a clear influence on policy was his commitment to faith schools, in which he chose to have his own children educated. The Church was encouraged to open new schools; other faiths were permitted schools of their own. The contribution towards capital costs faith schools were required to pay was reduced from 15 per cent to 10 per cent. A proposal to cap the proportion of admissions from a particular faith at 75 per cent was dropped following opposition from the Catholic Church. Blair maintained that children should be taught about faiths and beliefs other than their own. In the face of significant criticism, he was consistently supportive of faith schools: 'Here in the UK we should be proud of the work of the churches; proud of the commitment of the British people. I think that faith schools have a strong role to play.'[78]

Iraq, the premier and the Pope

In the mind of many, the Blair premiership is defined by his decision to support the US-led invasion of Iraq in 2003. He had already shown himself willing to adopt an interventionist policy in Kosovo and Sierra Leone. For Burton, this too was a direct consequence of his faith. It was

> part of the Christian battle; good should triumph over evil, making lives better, not necessarily because of religion itself but because of shared universal values that could be a guide in a troubled world going through the most difficult times.[79]

When asked whether his moral certainty concerning intervention in Iraq derived from his Christian faith, Blair himself neither confirmed nor denied it. He spoke rather of the 'values' and 'perspectives' required to con-

77 Cited Burton and McCabe, *We Don't Do God*, p. xviii.

78 TB, Speech to Evangelical Christians, Faithworks, 2005, cited Burton and McCabe, *We Don't Do God*, p. 157.

79 Cited Burton and McCabe, *We Don't Do God*, pp. xv–xvi.

front the Iraqi regime's human rights abuses.[80] Blair's own values and perspectives were, however, inseparable from his Christianity.

The Apostolic Nuncio in London at the time was a Spaniard, Archbishop Pablo Puente. His role in the prelude to the invasion of Iraq has gone unremarked. Puente was steeped in the Arab and Middle Eastern world, having previously served as Nuncio to Lebanon and Kuwait and Apostolic Delegate to the Arabian Peninsula. He played a much more political role than is normal for nuncios and visited the Blairs in their private flat at Downing Street on several occasions in 2002 and 2003. It was Puente who was instrumental in arranging the audience Blair had with Pope John Paul II in February 2003, just one month before the invasion.

The Polish Pope was one of the strongest opponents of military action in Iraq. He had recently seen Tariq Aziz, the Iraqi foreign minister and a Chaldean Catholic. Blair was visiting the Italian Prime Minister, Silvio Berlusconi. His advisers sought to dissuade him from meeting the Pope, failing to see what might be gained in such diplomatically sensitive times. Blair was not to be deflected. John Paul II was compassionate and polite at the audience, but he remained uncompromising in his opposition to military intervention.

Most Christian leaders believed that military action in Iraq failed to satisfy the 'just war' criteria. Like the Pope, the Archbishop of Canterbury and the Archbishop of Westminster spoke out against the war. Blair ultimately disagreed with them. One adviser said of him:

> This is a man who, in terms of judgement of right and wrong, would think that his own judgement was at least as good as that of the Archbishop of Canterbury, of the Cardinal of Westminster and the Pope combined.[81]

Graham Dow felt that, for Blair, Iraq was about responsibility to God for putting faith into action.[82] Some judged his action as characteristic of a certain type of Evangelical, confident of his unmediated access to God.

---

80 Stephens, *TB*, p. 246.

81 Sir Stephen Wall, Interview, 6 March 2007, cited Anthony Seldon, *Blair Unbound* (London: Simon & Schuster, 2007), pp. 154–5.

82 Connell, 'TB (1997–2007)', in ed. Spencer, *The Mighty and the Almighty*, p. 96.

Others concluded differently, seeing him not as a self-righteous politician dismissive of the Pope's intervention but as someone deeply troubled on the day of his papal audience.

Blair and Paisley

By contrast, the creation of a power-sharing administration in Northern Ireland in 2007 was one of Blair's greatest successes. His interest in religion was not necessarily an advantage. Personally he viewed differences between Catholics and Protestants as incomprehensible and irrelevant, although many in Northern Ireland still defined themselves by such distinctions. Many Unionists looked askance at Blair's Catholic wife and Mass attendance. The success of the peace process was testimony to his tenacity, commitment and negotiating skills.

Religion, however, also contributed to the achievement. Drawing on the experience and vocabulary of his maternal Irish Protestant ancestry, he secured an unlikely friend and ally in the person of the Revd Ian Paisley, the Democratic Unionist politician and former demagogue. Blair found him 'a genuine and committed Christian, a true God-fearing man'. Blair and Paisley 'were both fascinated by religious faith'. Discerning and implementing God's will mattered to both of them.[83] They spoke at length on spiritual matters, exchanging reading material.[84] In the peace process, when the outcome so often hung by a thread, the significance of this relationship, based on shared faith, should not be discounted.

'His own man'

In 1993, Blair was asked whether there were issues on which his Christian beliefs might cause him to defy the parliamentary whip. He agreed there might be. When pressed, he identified two possible difficulties: 'measures which were very oppressive in terms of gay rights or . . . if we were to vote for the restoration of capital punishment'.[85] Together with Iraq, it was

83 TB, *A Journey*, pp. 195–6.

84 Revd Ian Paisley, Interview, *The Guardian*, 14 March 2007.

85 TB, Interview with Roy McCloughry, October 1993.

Blair's stance on social issues that brought him into greatest conflict with traditional Christian teaching.

Speaking in April 2008, Blair declared that faith 'says there are absolutes – like the inalienable worth and dignity of every human being – that can never be sacrificed'.[86] Pro-life Christians and others may ask why this absolute protection did not extend to the unborn child. Abortion was an issue Blair agonized over. He told the Sedgefield parish priest, who lobbied him on the subject, that 'though he was personally against abortion, legislating was something else again, and he believed that politicians should never use their ethical views to obstruct action or change'.[87] Blair consistently voted against the pro-life lobby.[88] He supported embryonic stem-cell research and extending the time limits for abortion on the grounds of handicap.[89]

Similarly, his views on same-sex relationships placed him at odds with traditional Christian teaching that marriage is between a man and a woman. In 1994 he supported the lowering of the age of consent for homosexuals to 16. The Civil Partnership Act 2004 was one of the government's legislative acts of which he was most proud.[90] In 2007 he made clear his personal support for adoption by same-sex couples, while simultaneously seeking to negotiate an exemption for Catholic adoption agencies.[91] He failed. While acknowledging the existence of difficult and complex issues, particularly when revealed religion was confronted by secularism's rights-based demands, Blair believed them capable of rational resolution by reasonable people such as himself.

Departure from office freed Blair to acknowledge those influences most important to him:

> One of the oddest questions I get asked in interviews . . . is: is faith important to your politics? It's like asking someone whether their health is important to them or their family. If you are someone 'of

86 TB, 'Faith and Globalization'.

87 Caden, Interview, August 2008, cited Burton and McCabe, *We Don't Do God*, pp. 208–9.

88 Burton and McCabe, *We Don't Do God*, p. 211.

89 Oborne, 'The Special Relationship between Blair and God'.

90 TB, *A Journey*, p. 581.

91 *The Guardian*, 25 January 2007.

faith' it is the focal point of belief in your life. There is no conceivable way that it wouldn't affect your politics.[92]

As his stance on social issues indicates, the position could be complicated but the significance of faith is undeniable. Anthony Connell's analysis is accurate: 'It is possible to imagine other leaders doing similar things for different reasons. But to understand why *he* chose to act in the way he did, his faith and the moral framework which he derived from it, is crucial.'[93]

Blair's entry into Downing Street was a heaven-sent opportunity for the satirical magazine *Private Eye*. It introduced a regular feature, 'St Albion Parish News', in the format of a parish newsletter written by the trendy vicar, who insisted on being called 'Tony'. Blair's demeanour and style inspired *Private Eye*'s editor, Ian Hislop, to write letters, sermons and songs for the young, reforming cleric. Others took Blair's Christianity extremely seriously, believing that it went to the substance of his time in office. Burton was one of those:

> I've spent hours and hours in his company . . . I truly believe that his Christianity affected his policy-making on just about everything from aid to Africa, education, poverty, world debt and intervening in other countries when he thought it was right to do it.

Religion was key to understanding him politically but Blair was always 'his own man', never beholden to hierarchies or doctrine. Religion gave him a self-confidence that meant 'he didn't always listen to advice'. Burton portrayed this as an advantage – what made Blair a leader.[94] He made no mention, however, of the Christian's primary calling to discipleship.

A 'Robinson Crusoe believer'

Attracted by its inclusive nature, Blair was committed to retaining the established status of the Church of England.[95] He displayed a greater

92 TB, 'Faith and Globalization'.

93 Connell, 'TB (1997–2007)', in ed. Spencer, *The Mighty and the Almighty*, p. 100.

94 Cited Burton and McCabe, *We Don't Do God*, pp. 218–19.

95 Rentoul, *TB*, p. 348.

interest in episcopal appointments than any Prime Minister since Macmillan: only four months in office, he disturbed ecclesiastical sensibilities by rejecting both candidates for the vacancy at Liverpool – the first to exercise this power since Callaghan had established the new appointments procedure.[96] He also reputedly disagreed with the Archbishop of Canterbury, George Carey, over the choice of his successor: Carey preferred the conservative Evangelical Michael Nazir-Ali, Bishop of Rochester, while Blair recommended Rowan Williams, Archbishop of Wales. Williams may have been the more progressive candidate but he did not, as claimed, share Blair's liberal views on abortion.[97] He also became a fierce critic of his policy in Iraq.

Carey initially entertained high hopes of a Blair premiership: 'You have a strong Christian conscience and . . . Christian philosophy which is a marvellous basis upon which to create a vision for our society.' He proposed regular informal meetings and the opportunity to receive Holy Communion at Lambeth Palace.[98] They discussed matters of faith, relations were amicable, but Carey began to cool when Blair did not take up his offer of spiritual guidance or give the Church of England the public support he had hoped for.[99] Praise turned to puzzlement. He felt Blair was a 'Robinson Crusoe believer. He is an island who doesn't have Christian believers around him to nourish him.'[100] Margaret Thatcher's uncomplicated faith was more akin to his own Evangelical beliefs, whereas concerning Blair's, he confessed, 'I couldn't see where his was going.'[101]

'I wonder what Jesus would have made of it'

The fact that Blair, an Anglican, regularly attended Mass at a Catholic church attracted little attention while he was a Shadow Cabinet member. Fr John Caden in Sedgefield stated that he 'never received Communion at

96 Rentoul, *TB*, p. 24.

97 Seldon, *Blair*, pp. 524–5.

98 George Carey to TB, 18 March 1997 and 19 October 1994, cited Seldon, *Blair*, p. 523.

99 Seldon, *Blair*, pp. 523–4.

100 George Carey, Interview, 17 September 2003, cited Seldon, *Blair*, p. 520.

101 George Carey, Interview, cited Eliza Filby, *God and Mrs Thatcher: The battle for Britain's soul* (London: Biteback Publishing, 2015), p. 145.

my church or expected to'.[102] Perhaps Caden was more attentive to matters of sacramental discipline or perhaps in a tight-knit community in the north-east, parishioners were more aware of their MP's Anglican identity. It was different in London. Cherie wrote that at St Joan of Arc, Highbury: 'Tony used to take communion on a regular basis . . . He was a member of our church community. Few, if anyone, in the congregation knew he wasn't a Catholic.'[103]

All that changed when Blair became leader of the Opposition. In 1996 his daughter, Kathryn, received her First Holy Communion at St Joan of Arc. Blair joined her at the altar in receiving the sacrament. An angry member of the congregation complained that, when it came to non-Catholics receiving Communion, it seemed 'that there was one law for the Blairs and one law for the rest'. The press took up the story. When the parish priest sought guidance, Cardinal Hume wrote to Blair in June 1996 asking him to refrain from receiving Communion. Blair made it clear he would comply but disagreed with the Cardinal's decision. 'I wonder what Jesus would have made of it', he remarked pointedly to the Cardinal. (Jesus might have thought that he had appointed apostles and bishops as stewards of his sacraments precisely to make such decisions.) Caden recalled that 'Tony was hurt but understood.'[104] Peter Thomson believed 'that Blair felt far more angry than his letter suggested'.[105] He continued to attend Mass but no longer received Communion publicly in Britain, but could overseas, Hume had explained, if there was no Anglican church in the vicinity. Hence American Augustinians at San Gimignano said Mass for the Blairs during their Tuscan holidays.

'Well on his way to joining the Catholic communion'

Blair's visit to the Holy See in February 2003 was highly unusual. He visited the Vatican three times in 24 hours. There was his audience on Saturday morning to discuss Iraq, a private tour with his family on Saturday after-

102 Caden, Interview, August 2008, cited Burton and McCabe, *We Don't Do God*, p. 35.
103 Cherie Blair, *Speaking for Myself*, p. 196.
104 Caden, Interview, August 2008, cited Burton and McCabe, *We Don't Do God*, pp. 211–12.
105 Beckett and Hencke, *The Blairs and Their Court*, p. 41.

noon and Mass with the Pope on Sunday morning. The family stayed at the Irish College to emphasize that this was a private 'pilgrimage' not an official visit. John Paul II insisted that the Blairs brought their youngest child, Leo, then just a toddler, to Mass. At the last moment, Blair was invited to read and receive Communion at Mass. Archbishop Puente was instrumental in this too, having assured the Pope that Blair was effectively a Catholic, only prevented from converting while in office by political considerations. Due to the John Paul II's frailty, his secretary, Bishop Stanislaw Dziwisz, administered Communion – but the decision was the Pope's.

There was controversy in March 1998 when the Press Association reported that Blair had been observed attending Mass at Westminster Cathedral alone. George Carey contacted the Prime Minister with his concerns. He understood, he wrote, that Blair might attend Catholic services with his wife and children, but he was afraid that such stories would fuel speculation about his possible conversion to Catholicism. Could he not occasionally be seen attending Anglican or Free Church services?[106] Blair reassured the Archbishop. He was not about 'to defect' from the Church of England to Catholicism. The plan had been to meet his family at Mass at the Cathedral but circumstances had prevented their attendance.[107]

There was, however, substance to the press report and Carey's fears. Blair did regularly attend the 5.30 p.m. Mass at Westminster Cathedral on Sundays when he was in London – sometimes with Cherie and the children; sometimes alone.[108] It was a similar story in the country. When the staff at Chequers discovered that the new Prime Minister was a practising Christian, they offered to make arrangements: 'We'll get a vicar to come and take a family service so you don't have to go out.' Blair was having none of it.[109] Instead, he attended the closest Catholic church, the Immaculate Heart of Mary at Great Missenden. The parish priest, Canon Timothy Russ, recalled: 'He was extremely diligent in attending Mass. He came on his own a lot.' Blair was surprised to find a diverse and socially engaged congregation

106 George Carey to TB, 5 March 1998, cited Seldon, *Blair*, p. 521.

107 TB to George Carey, 6 March 1998, cited Seldon, *Blair*, pp. 521–2.

108 Michael Seed, *Saints and Sinners: The irreverent diaries of Britain's most controversial priest* (London: Metro Publishing, 2009), p. 40.

109 TB, Interview, *Daily Record*, 6 March 1998, cited Rentoul, *TB*, p. 351.

in the midst of the Buckinghamshire countryside. Russ thought that Blair 'was well on his way to joining the Catholic communion even before he came here'.[110]

The family relished the normality afforded them as ordinary parishioners attending Sunday Mass at Westminster Cathedral and Great Missenden. That ended with the security concerns raised in the wake of the 2001 US terror attacks. For a time, the Prime Minister visited various central London churches on a random basis but a more permanent solution was sought. Fr Michael Seed was a Franciscan friar living by Westminster Cathedral, an improbable combination of unworldliness and social connectivity. Known for his spiritual accompaniment of politicians and royalty into the Catholic Church, he first visited the Blairs in Downing Street to take Communion to Cherie after the birth of Leo. For six years after 9/11, he and other priests from the cathedral celebrated Mass for the family in Downing Street.[111] When at Chequers, Mass was celebrated for the family on Saturday evenings by Canon Russ and then from 2004 by Mgr John Walsh, chaplain at RAF Halton. A priest of the Diocese of Liverpool, Walsh knew well Cherie's clerical cousins.[112]

As an Anglican practising faith as a Catholic, speculation was inevitable. Initially, conversion to Catholicism was not something he saw the need for. He dismissed all questions on the subject – 'Surely, being a Christian is what is important,' he told the *Sunday Telegraph*.[113] Asked after his first general election victory whether he would become a Catholic, he was even more blunt: 'I am not proposing to do that.'[114]

Blair's intention of being received into the Catholic Church was made public as he left office in 2007. Were there restraints on his becoming a Catholic as Prime Minister? Although the Church of England remained established by law, there had been at least half a dozen non-Anglican Prime Ministers since Campbell-Bannerman almost a century earlier. John Burton, however, felt that 'there was no way he could have converted while

110 Canon Timothy Russ, cited *The Observer*, 23 December 2007.

111 Seed, *Saints and Sinners*, pp. 40–1.

112 Mgr John Walsh to the author, 31 March 2021.

113 TB, Interview, *Sunday Telegraph*, 7 April 1996, cited Rentoul, *TB*, p. 351.

114 TB, Interview, *Birmingham Evening Mail*, 13 June 1997, cited Rentoul, *TB*, p. 351.

still Prime Minister.'[115] There was the relationship with the Queen in her capacity as Supreme Governor of the Church of England. The provisions of the Catholic Relief Act 1829 arguably still applied, preventing a Catholic advising the monarch on ecclesiastical appointments. The Northern Irish peace process was another reason for delay. The situation was sufficiently delicate without the Prime Minister being compromised in Unionist eyes by conversion to Catholicism.

Blair claimed that he did not delay his reception into the Catholic Church 'for reasons of religious controversy'. By 2010, however, he could speak more openly and candidly admitted his pragmatism. As Prime Minister he had simply been too busy; there were too many issues to deal with. Conversion to Catholicism would have proved an unnecessary complication and distraction. It would have invited all manner of 'conspiracy theories' and required 'endless explanations'. He 'just literally decided it was something I didn't want to have as an additional issue alongside all the other issues I had'.[116]

'A completely logical step'

So why did he become a Catholic? Blair identified the person he felt primarily responsible: 'Frankly, this all began with my wife. I began to go to Mass and we went together. We could have gone to the Anglican or Catholic church – guess who won?' He made the same point speaking in Italy in August 2009, noting that Cherie had been the driving force behind his reception into the Catholic Church.[117] Burton was also clear that the family constituted Blair's principal motive. At Communion, he felt 'excluded from something that was very important to him . . . Without the family, I reckon he would have carried on as he was – a High Anglican churchgoer who wasn't far from the Catholic Church anyway.'[118]

Blair told an Italian audience: 'There was something, not just about the doctrine of the Church, but of the universal nature of the Catholic Church.' Canon Russ recognized the attraction: 'Tony is an idealist. And he found,

115 Cited Burton and McCabe, *We Don't Do God*, p. 211.

116 TB, Interview with John Geiger, 29 November 2010.

117 TB, cited *The Guardian*, 28 August 2009.

118 Cited Burton and McCabe, *We Don't Do God*, pp. 211, 220.

in the English Catholic parish, what the Labour Party should ideally be: a place where everyone, no matter what their colour or race, should feel at home.'[119] Community was important to Blair, and he wished to be a member of the ecclesial community that embraced the world and the centuries. Some suggested his action was a manifestation of his rebellious streak – his Catholicism represented the ultimate act of defiance against the Orange intolerance he had encountered in his maternal family many years earlier. Did he also relish the reaction of his atheist father?

Intellectual reasons are important but not always decisive. A sense of relationship and belonging are often more compelling. Blair articulated it thus: this 'is now where my heart is . . . I felt this was right for me.'[120] After a further year's reflection he summarized his position: 'I've been attending Mass for 25 years and it was a completely logical step for me to be able to take Communion in a Catholic church along with my family.'[121]

Reception into full communion

In September 2006, Blair was finally persuaded to announce a timetable for his resignation from the premiership. Early in 2007 he raised with Mgr Walsh at Chequers his desire to enter full communion with the Catholic Church. After further discussions with Walsh, Blair met with Cardinal Murphy-O'Connor, Archbishop of Westminster.[122] He requested that, as far as possible, he follow the normal procedure for reception into the Catholic Church. It was agreed that there would be a formal period of preparation after he left office on 27 June 2007.[123]

It is difficult to believe that the decision to convert was made suddenly in 2007. More likely, it was the culmination of a process stretching back two decades. The Downing Street meetings with Puente and the 2003 papal audience appear to be significant milestones. In 2005, Blair told Prince Charles of his determination to attend John Paul II's funeral, despite the

119 Canon Timothy Russ, 2008, cited Obituary: 'Canon Timothy Russ', *The Tablet*, 3 August 2013.

120 TB, cited *The Guardian*, 28 August 2009.

121 TB, Interview with John Geiger, 29 November 2010.

122 Mgr John Walsh to the author, 31 March 2021.

123 Bishop Mark O'Toole to the author, 5 March 2021.

clash with the date originally set for Charles's marriage to Camilla. There were to be further papal audiences in 2005 and 2007.

It was hugely significant that Blair's final overseas engagement as Prime Minister was his Vatican audience on 23 June 2007. He was well advised, giving three framed prints of John Henry Newman to Benedict XVI, who would beatify the convert English Cardinal in 2010. Blair spent 25 minutes with the Pope before Murphy-O'Connor was summoned to join them. This in itself was highly unusual. The Vatican observes protocol in ensuring that such audiences are strictly meetings between governments without accompanying bishops. Murphy-O'Connor's presence indicated a definite pastoral dimension. *The Observer* reported that the subject of conversation was not the possibility of Blair's conversion, rather its timing.[124] After the audience, Murphy-O'Connor hosted a lunch for the Blairs at the English College, the national seminary in Rome.

Blair was accustomed to discussing Catholic theology and practice with Caden, Russ and Walsh. On his departure from office, the process was formalized. Michael Seed had been a regular visitor to Downing Street and became a family friend, but it was decided that 'a less well-known, and more discreet' spiritual guide was required.[125] Murphy-O'Connor was determined to minimize press coverage of a private spiritual matter. Mgr Mark O'Toole, his private secretary, had known the Blairs from his time as a deacon at St Joan of Arc. O'Toole was delegated to meet Blair regularly for 'doctrinal and spiritual preparation' from July to December 2007, when it was felt that Blair was ready to be received.

His reception into the Catholic Church and confirmation occurred within a Mass in the Cardinal's private chapel at Archbishop's House, Westminster on the evening of 21 December 2007. It was a quiet affair with only family and a few friends present. All semblance of triumphalism was avoided, the Cardinal giving thanks for Blair's Christian faith, which had brought him to this point.[126]

Archbishop Rowan Williams offered his best wishes to Blair and his family. Not all Catholics, however, were delighted by their new coreligionist. Those in the pro-life movement and others called for an explicit

124 *The Observer*, 23 December 2007.

125 *The Guardian*, 22 June 2007.

126 O'Toole to the author, 5 March 2021.

repudiation of his former voting record on ethical issues. Blair himself described the moment as the sensation of 'coming home'.[127]

'How can he suddenly start believing in that?'

Four months after becoming a Catholic, Blair was invited by Murphy-O'Connor to speak at one of the 2008 Cardinal's Lectures. Blair warned against religious extremism, spoke of faith organizations' commitment to social justice and their humanitarian work, referred to the essential compatibility of science and faith, reason and religion, and noted the need to transcend self and seek God's forgiveness. It was striking, however, that while he praised Gandhi and 'the radical and brave liberation priests of South America', he made no mention of either Jesus Christ or the Church.[128]

The Cardinal's guests might have been surprised to hear Blair extol the ex-nun and populist religious writer Karen Armstrong. He took the opportunity to promote 'her remarkable book', *The Great Transformation*. Was he identifying with her criticism of orthodoxy and 'misplaced certainty and clarity'? Armstrong admired the life of Jesus but regarded him neither as divine nor the founder of a new religion. Rather he was 'a Galilean faith healer' who simply offered 'a new way of being Jewish'.[129]

Blair was a great enthusiast of another controversial writer. Thomson had introduced him to the works of Hans Küng, a Swiss priest and professor at the University of Tübingen whose authorization to teach as a Catholic had been withdrawn by the Vatican. Blair rated Küng's *On Being a Christian* as 'a great work'.[130] The style was engaging and direct if often polemical. Küng purported to offer a third way between conservative obscurantism and liberal scepticism. He presented Jesus as a moderate, 'neither a supporter of the system nor a politico-social revolutionary'. Christianity

127 TB, cited *The Guardian*, 28 August 2009.

128 TB, 'Faith and Globalization'.

129 Karen Armstrong, *The Great Transformation: The world in the time of Buddha, Socrates, Confucius and Jeremiah* (London: Atlantic Books, 2007), pp. 264, 382.

130 TB, *A Journey*, p. 279.

was to be neither 'contemplated' nor 'theorized', rather 'done' and 'practised'. Faith was concerned less with an afterlife than 'changing life and social conditions here and now *before* death'.[131] All this was familiar to Blair from his reading of Macmurray and discussions with Thomson. In June 2000, at Thomson's instigation, Küng invited Blair to speak at his Global Ethics Foundation in Tübingen.[132]

From a Catholic perspective, Küng was problematic. He breezily dismissed doctrinal issues such as the Trinity, the divinity of Christ and the nature of miracles as 'not meaningful to modern man'. Much of the New Testament was rejected as 'legendary' or a later development, for no more obvious reason than it did not fit with Küng's views on the Church or the priesthood. Strongly anti-Roman, there is little sense of Küng seeking to situate his work within the broader Catholic tradition.

On becoming a Catholic, Blair declared: 'I believe and profess to be true all that the Catholic Church believes, teaches and proclaims to be revealed by God.' Russ had commented earlier that he still had 'some way to go' in aligning his views on moral issues such as abortion and stem-cell research with the Church's teaching.[133] Burton also queried this:

> I still can't see how he can have changed his views completely. I can't imagine that he's bound totally by Catholic doctrine, and obviously disagrees with some of it . . . he always voted against the pro-life lobby. Same with homosexuality and same-sex marriage. And you can't suddenly change your mind on these issues although he's had to reconcile himself to some of them. Again the Vatican believes that all life is sacred and opposes birth control even in Africa where AIDS is rife. How can he suddenly start believing in that?[134]

If Blair struggled with aspects of church teaching, he kept his doubts mostly to himself. Speaking to the magazine *Attitude*, however, he

---

131 Hans Küng, *On Being a Christian* (London: SCM Press, 1977), pp. 167, 410, 400.
132 Seldon, *Blair*, p. 527; TB, *A Journey*, p. 279.
133 Cited *Daily Telegraph*, 15 October 2004.
134 Cited Burton and McCabe, *We Don't Do God*, pp. 210–11.

distanced himself publicly from the Catholic Church's position on homosexuality, calling on the Vatican to rethink its 'entrenched' attitudes.[135]

Truth and relativism

Contrary to popular belief, Catholics are not called to accept unthinkingly all statements proposed by the Church on every matter in every detail. In 2008, Blair told his audience: 'Faith is a living and growing belief, not stuck in one time in history.'[136] Doctrine may, of course, 'develop'. As understood by Catholics, this is never a departure from fundamental truths and always occurs under the guidance of the Holy Spirit and the teaching authority of the Church. Catholics follow their conscience, which they seek to inform and align to the truth. It is difficult to define Blair's ecclesiology. While the concept and reality of community were of great importance, where did community feature in his search for truth? For a Catholic, that search is undertaken not only with the immediate ecclesial community but also with the universal community of the Church and the community of previous generations of believers.

It is not as if Blair promoted a 'soft' Christianity devoid of content and consequence. He stressed that in the early 1990s:

> Christianity is a very tough religion. It may not always be practised as such. But it is. It places a duty, an imperative on us to reach our better self and to care about creating a better community to live in . . . It is judgmental. There is right and wrong. There is good and bad.[137]

Against what criteria are Christians supposed to judge? By what standards is something deemed right or wrong, good or bad? These were questions he did not address.

'For most people of faith,' Blair recognized, 'religious belief is quintessentially about truth.' He spoke of faith as a necessary corrective to the human tendency to relativism.[138] Asked whether there was a hierarchy of

135 *The Guardian*, 8 April 2009.

136 TB, 'Faith and Globalization'.

137 TB, 'Foreword', in ed. Bryant, *Reclaiming the Ground*, p. 12.

138 TB, 'Faith and Globalization'.

moral truths or whether all were essentially the same, he replied: 'Even if I have my own belief, I can still respect not just the right of the person to hold that different belief but also respect that belief.'[139] Interpreted in one sense, that sounded like relativism. With Rowan Williams and Charles Moore, Blair was a member of the panel in the 2012 Westminster Faith Debate. Cormac Murphy-O'Connor asked about the challenges of 'militant secularism' and 'militant relativism', which undermined the very possibility of dialogue if there was no acceptance of 'objective truth, which is true for everyone'. Williams strongly affirmed the Cardinal's concern about relativism; Moore also dealt with the point. Acknowledging aspects of the dignity of the human person 'which cannot be relativized away', Blair did not touch on the question of objective truth.[140]

John Rentoul was disconcerted by the announcement of Blair's conversion. With others, he struggled to understand how a liberal, inclusive politician could be a member of a Church making exclusive claims to truth and whose teaching he disagreed with in certain areas. He had defined Blair as 'an ecumenical Christian' and thought he accepted that label.[141] A decade earlier, Blair had stated: 'I am an ecumenical Christian. I find many of the angry debates between Catholic and Protestant completely baffling.'[142] The CSM chairman, Chris Bryant, recalled the need to find a local church at which Blair could worship when travelling on a Sunday. If accompanied by Cherie it would be a Catholic church. Otherwise, at least prior to his conversion, 'Blair would indeed be happy to worship in any denomination of church, as long as it was not aggressively fundamentalist.'[143]

Possibly the attraction of the sacramental and mystical aspect of Catholicism grew as the years progressed. No doubt Blair was influenced by Küng and Cherie. Yet as commentators have pointed out, there is a difference between being raised in a certain church from birth and deliberately choosing to join it as a mature adult. They have also referred to Blair's 'evangelical' style – the emphasis on individual responsibility, private judgement, a

---

139 TB, Interview with John Geiger, 29 November 2010.

140 TB, Westminster Faith Debate, 'Religion in Public Life', 24 July 2012, <www.youtube.com/watch?v=evDIBRcvb6o&t=3990s>, accessed 27.03.21.

141Rentoul, 'The Mystery of Blair the Convert', *The Independent*, 23 December 2007.

142 TB, Interview, *Sunday Telegraph*, 7 April 1996.

143 Chris Bryant, Interview, 30 January 2004, cited Seldon, *Blair*, p. 521.

strongly personal relationship with God and unmediated access to him.[144] It would be fascinating to investigate how this fits with the Catholic emphasis on priesthood, tradition and the teaching authority of the Church.

Interfaith relations

Blair's ecumenism was mirrored by his commitment to interfaith relations. 'I am passionate about the importance of faith to our modern world,' he declared, 'and about the need for people of faith to reach out to one another.'[145] He believed that, beneath the ritual and dogma, the main world religions shared common values. He admired Küng's role in interfaith relations and was influenced by his belief that to secure peace among nations, it must first be established among religions. Blair relished the religious pluralism existing in Britain and was the first Prime Minister to greet different faiths on their religious festivals.[146]

He was more akin to the early twentieth-century Prime Ministers in the emphasis he placed on the Old Testament, finding it 'in some ways more detailed and vivid' than the New.[147] He held the Chief Rabbi, Jonathan Sacks, in great affection, admiring him as a teacher, friend and hero. Their first extended conversation occurred on the return flight from Yitzhak Rabin's funeral in Jerusalem in 1995. Blair expressed curiosity when he noticed Sacks reading Scripture and a commentary. The Chief Rabbi offered an impromptu lesson in biblical exegesis to Blair and to Prince Charles, sitting on the other side of the aisle. After Blair became Prime Minister, when the two had official business they took time subsequently to study the Old Testament together, taking as their text whatever passage Blair had been reading the previous night. Sachs judged Blair 'a deeply religious man' with 'an abiding love for the Bible'.[148]

His relationship to Islam was more complex given the invasion of Iraq, the consequent regional instability and terror attacks in the West. Blair

144 Connell, 'TB (1997–2007)', in ed. Spencer, *The Mighty and the Almighty*, pp. 97–8; Oborne, 'The Special Relationship between Blair and God'.

145 TB, 'Faith and Globalization'.

146 Seldon, *Blair*, p. 525.

147 TB, Interview, *Sunday Telegraph*, 7 April 1996.

148 Jonathan Sacks, *Covenant and Conversation: Exodus, the book of redemption* (Jerusalem: Maggid Books, 2010), pp. 289–90.

praised Islam, properly understood and practised: 'If you read the Koran it is so clear . . . the concept of love and fellowship as the guiding spirits of humanity . . . [Islam is] a deeply reflective, peaceful, very beautiful religious faith.'[149] He told the Labour Party Conference: 'It is time the West confronted its ignorance of Islam. Jews, Muslims and Christians are all children of Abraham.'[150] He himself had read the Qur'an three times and extolled Islam's original peaceful intentions and its cultural and scientific achievements, contrasting it favourably with Christianity.

He revised his views following the murder of the soldier Lee Rigby by Islamist terrorists on the streets of Woolwich in 2013:

> But there is a problem *within* Islam, and we have to put it on the table and be honest about it . . . I am afraid that the problematic strain within Islam is not the province of a few extremists. It has at its heart a view of religion – and of the relationship between religion and politics – that is not compatible with pluralistic, liberal, open-minded societies. At the extreme end of the spectrum are terrorists, but the worldview goes deeper and wider than it is comfortable for us to admit. So, by and large, we don't admit it.[151]

Such incidents reinforced Blair's commitment to interfaith dialogue as a means of combating extremism.

Following his departure from office, interfaith relations were one of the main areas in which Blair focused his energy and attention. His Faith Foundation was launched in New York in May 2008. Its aims were ambitious: to rescue religion from the dangers of irrelevance and extremism, and to ensure it was a force for peace and unity. At the foundation's launch, he outlined the risks faced in the world: 'Globalization is pushing people together. Interdependence is reality. Peaceful co-existence is essential. If faith becomes a countervailing force, pulling people apart, it becomes destructive and dangerous.'[152] Working with the six main world religions

149 TB, *Muslim News*, 31 March 2000, cited Rentoul, *TB*, p. 351.

150 TB, Speech, Labour Party Conference, 2 October 2001, cited Rentoul, *TB*, p. 648.

151 TB, *Mail on Sunday*, 1 June 2013.

152 TB, Launch, Faith Foundation, May 2008, cited Burton and McCabe, *We Don't Do God*, p. 200.

(Christianity, Islam, Judaism, Hinduism, Buddhism and Sikhism), the Foundation sought to counter that threat through education. It aimed to teach children respect for and the truth about other faiths. A course on faith and globalization was offered at Yale, later extended to eight other universities.[153]

Blair rejected accusations of syncretism, that his project was 'about chucking faith into a doctrinal melting pot': 'It is not about losing our own distinctive faith. It is about learning about, living and working with others of a different faith.' Faith, he believed, could 'transform and humanize the impersonal forces of globalization, and shape the values of the twenty-first century'.[154]

In its first year, £4 million was raised for the foundation. The presence on its Advisory Council of Jonathan Sacks and Richard Chartres, the Bishop of London, gave the foundation a certain gravitas in establishment eyes. Otherwise, it was weighted in an evangelical direction. Given Blair's recent conversion, the lack of Catholic representation at this level was telling. His involvement having been announced on the foundation's website, Murphy-O'Connor declined an invitation to join.[155] Possibly this relates to Blair's lecturing the Catholic Church on the subject of homosexuality in his interview with *Attitude* magazine. The foundation's work was subsumed into that of the Tony Blair Institute for Global Change in 2016.

'Blair's relationship with God is more important than any other'

Blair's personal faith was rooted in the person of Jesus. Speaking in Italy after his conversion, he stated: 'I am and remain a Christian, seeking salvation through our Lord, Jesus Christ.'[156] While recognizing that there was a discussion to be had concerning the category of risen life, Blair fully acknowledged the centrality of the Easter event: 'For me the Resurrection, in the sense of someone reborn, is very important, indeed the essential

153 TB, *A Journey*, p. 690.

154 TB, 'Faith and Globalization'.

155 *The Guardian*, 1 June 2009.

156 TB, cited *The Guardian*, 28 August 2009.

part of the Christian faith.'[157] He was less certain, when asked, about redemption. Other than commenting that it caused him to 'think about the degree to which I fall short from the best that I could be', he rapidly retreated into generalizations about the importance of faith in the modern world.[158] There was no reflection on the need for, and the purpose of, the cross.

If prayer is testimony to a strong personal faith, then Blair emerged with flying colours. He accepted that prayer did not provide simplistic solutions; he did not expect God to tell him what to 'think of City Academies or Health Service reform or nuclear power'. Prayer did not abnegate the need for the use of human reason.[159] The importance of prayer consisted less in establishing 'a hotline to God' to be told the right thing to do, but more in receiving 'the strength to do it'.[160] He admitted to being a practitioner of meditation but claimed no proficiency in the field.[161]

Blair was quite open about the place of prayer in his own life, confessing to praying about both 'political decisions' and 'the more personal side of things'.[162] He prayed in Durham Cathedral before his selection meeting at Sedgefield.[163] He prayed regularly at times of major decisions. The insistent questions about whether he had prayed together with President Bush were an irrelevance obscuring the more important fact of the centrality of prayer in his life. Such an instance of spiritual communion between the two leaders did not occur – that type of prayer was not Blair's style.[164]

As prayer provided solace at moments of stress, so too did reading – Scripture and books on religion. His reading material was eclectic. He advertised his admiration for Küng and Armstrong. There were popular accounts of church history and more challenging works such as Rowan Williams's book on the fourth-century heresiarch Arius. Blair also read widely on the

157 TB, Westminster Faith Debate, 'Religion in Public Life', 24 July 2012.

158 TB, Interview with John Geiger, 29 November 2010.

159 TB, 'Faith and Globalization'.

160 TB, *Time* magazine, 29 May 2008, cited Burton and McCabe, *We Don't Do God*, p. 206.

161 TB, Interview with Decca Aitkenhead, *Sunday Times*, 28 June 2020.

162 TB, Interview with Roy McCloughry, October 1993.

163 Lily Burton, August 2008, cited Burton and McCabe, *We Don't Do God*, p. 24.

164 Bryant, Interview, 30 January 2004, cited Seldon, *Blair*, pp. 521, 623.

origins of Islam.[165] The only apparent omissions are more orthodox works of Catholic theology and the writings of the spiritual masters.

What is less obvious is the importance of the sacramental life to Blair. The Eucharist has both a vertical and horizontal dimension. It was the latter that Blair stressed. Speaking to the *Sunday Telegraph* in 1996, he said:

> We can choose and decide . . . it is from a sense of the individual duty that we connect to the greater good and the interests of the community – a principle the Church celebrates in the sacrament of communion.[166]

He repeated this understanding of the sacrament elsewhere:

> Christianity means we are not stranded in helpless isolation but owe a duty both to ourselves and to others. The act of Communion is symbolic of that message. It acknowledges that we do not grow up in total independence but interdependently.[167]

Such an interpretation was unexceptional for an Evangelical. It did not – understandably, given that he was speaking prior to his conversion – reflect the fullness of Catholic teaching, which understands the Eucharist to be the body and blood of Christ, his real presence, the reception of which gives communion with Christ and with fellow believers. In declaring that the Eucharist is simply a meal and using the terms 'sacrifice of the Mass' 'misleading' and to 'be avoided',[168] Küng placed himself at odds with official Catholic teaching. For Catholics, the sacraments in general and the Eucharist in particular are the principal means of grace, access to the very life of God, instituted by Christ himself. What the new convert characterized in the Cardinal's Lecture as 'empty ritualism' and 'arid ritual',[169] many of his audience would have cherished as lifegiving liturgy.

165 TB, Interview with John Geiger, 29 November 2010.

166 TB, Interview, *Sunday Telegraph*, 7 April 1996.

167 TB, cited Stephens, *TB*, p. 19.

168 Küng, *On Being a Christian*, pp. 406–7.

169 TB, 'Faith and Globalization'.

Balfour and Blair provide the bookends for this study. One was a grandee and an electoral disaster, the other thoroughly middle class and, electorally, the most successful Labour leader ever. They held more in common, however, than birth in the Scottish Lothians. Both were fascinated by religion – and widely known to be so. That interest took very different forms: for Balfour it was largely academic; for Blair overwhelmingly practical. Both resist simplistic categorization in terms of faith.

In many ways, Blair is the more intriguing of the two. Prime Ministers at the beginning of the twentieth century were expected, at least externally, to conform in terms of religious practice. In Balfour's day, it was impossible to avoid taking a stance on religious issues that divided Parliament and the country. When Blair was elected in 1997, Britain was largely a secular country. There was no electoral advantage to be gained by a public manifestation of faith and, arguably, some risk in doing so. This willingness to oppose the zeitgeist was a mark of integrity and considerable courage. The emphasis may have been muted during the years in office, and questions remain about the nature of Blair's beliefs, yet the sincerity of his faith is undeniable.

Anthony Seldon structured his biography of Blair around the key events and people who influenced him, and had no hesitation in concluding: 'Blair's relationship with God is more important than any other described in this book.'[170] A century after Balfour, Prime Ministers were still definitely doing God.

170 Seldon, *Blair*, p. 515.

Conclusion

'The foolish man has said in his heart there is no God'

Going against the flow

No Prime Ministers have been harmed in the writing of this book. It is not the intention to hold them to account with respect to their spiritual lives but rather to examine a neglected factor significant to the formation of virtually all the premiers and a continuing influence in the lives of most.

The twentieth-century Prime Ministers constitute a surprisingly decent set of individuals – although an exception might be made for Lloyd George. As a group, they were honest, hard-working and public-spirited. Arguably, these values reflect their Christian backgrounds. Given that the majority were not practising Anglicans, it is also noteworthy that most were diligent and scrupulously fair in the exercise of their powers of patronage with regard to appointments in the Church of England.

One of the most striking changes over the century is the extent to which the Prime Ministers became more believing – an unexpected finding given that Britain has become a more secular country. Until 1960, the national religious practice remained relatively stable in absolute terms, although declining proportionately given the growth in population. Since 1960, that decline has become precipitous. The opposite is true of the Prime Ministers. In the first half of the period, perhaps only Baldwin was an uncomplicated orthodox Christian. (Campbell-Bannerman was more orthodox than his contemporaries suspected, but hid it well.) From Macmillan's appointment in 1957, the contrast is clear. Of the final eight premiers, only Callaghan did not claim to be a believing Christian. Macmillan, Douglas-Home, Heath, Thatcher and Blair took their Christian faith seriously – intellectually and in terms of practice.

Why was this? A superficial answer would be that the occupants of 10 Downing Street became more bourgeois – the class most likely to be found in church or chapel on a Sunday. This does not bear close scrutiny: two of the most committed Christians, Douglas-Home and Macmillan, were Old Etonian grandees; some of the least believing, or least orthodoxly Christian, were from the least privileged backgrounds – Lloyd George, Ramsay MacDonald and Callaghan. Heath and Thatcher were not from significantly more exalted backgrounds but both identified as people of faith. For these 19 Prime Ministers, social class provides little indication of the likelihood of belief.

Was the advance of scepticism checked by a diminished belief in liberal progress as a consequence of the world wars and ideologies of the twentieth century? While possibly true at a national level, it does not explain this group of individuals. Churchill, Atlee, Eden and Macmillan all endured the horrors of the First World War but held very different religious views. Macmillan's deep Christian faith survived the trenches of the Western Front but was not formed there. Heath and Callaghan both served in the Second World War yet their respective positions as orthodox Anglican and practical atheist were unchanged by their experience of conflict.

Reasons for disbelieving

It is more instructive to analyse the influences on the earlier Prime Ministers militating against belief, and to examine the specific dogmas and practices against which they were reacting. The Prime Ministers of the first half of the twentieth century were raised in the late Victorian period, which Anthony Seldon describes, with justification, as 'a deeply religious time'.[1] The churches appeared vibrant and expanding. Yet scepticism was already widespread among the educated and political classes.

Charles Darwin's *On the Origin of Species* was published in 1859.[2] Darwin did not formulate the theory of evolution but did help to popularize

1 Anthony Seldon, *The Impossible Office? The history of the British Prime Minister* (Cambridge: Cambridge University Press, 2021), p. 110.

2 Charles Darwin, *On the Origin of Species by Means of Natural Selection, or the Preservation of Favoured Races in the Struggle for Life* (London: John Murray, 1859).

it. Together with geological discoveries, the theory of evolution rendered a literal interpretation of the book of Genesis untenable at a time when Protestant England was still a Bible-reading nation. However, modern scientific discoveries did not destroy the Christian faith of the earlier Prime Ministers in our period. Balfour arrived at Cambridge a decade after the publication of Darwin's magnum opus. He devoted his life to reconciling the claims of religion and science, and did not consider the theory of evolution an insurmountable obstacle to belief. The conventionally Anglican Attlees had accommodated evolution into their belief system before Clem rejected Christianity wholesale.

More damaging to orthodox Christianity were the claims of contemporary biblical criticism. If science refuted the traditional chronology of the Old Testament, liberal scriptural criticism appeared to negate the content of the Gospels, the very heart of Christianity.

Balfour and MacDonald were familiar with the works of the pioneers of this school, Friedrich Schleiermacher, David Strauss and others, but it is the popularizer Ernest Renan who recurs continually in the earlier Prime Ministers' reading material. It is difficult today to appreciate the damage caused by his *Life of Jesus*. Within a few decades of its publication in Paris in 1863, it had run through 52 editions – an English translation had appeared within months.[3] Almost all the early twentieth-century Prime Ministers referred to it. Retaining a religious aura, it deceived many because the author wrote well, with apparent moderation, and was immersed in the country and culture of Christ. Yet it systematically stripped the Gospels of any claim to supernatural authority. The Incarnation, the divinity of Christ, his resurrection, miracles and dogma were all dismissed a priori, without the author producing any substantive evidence. Renan's anti-Catholicism and anti-clericalism further recommended him to an English Protestant audience.

Renan reduced Jesus to a teacher of morality. To claim more than this was to be convicted of obscure fundamentalism. The *Life of Jesus* was comprehensively denounced by all denominations in England on its appearance, though there was little attempt to produce a rigorous academic

3 Ernest Renan, *Histoire des origines du christianisme, tome 1: Vie de Jésus* (Paris, Michel Lévy frères, 1863); *Life of Jesus*, trans. Charles E. Wilbour (London: Trübner, 1863).

critique, and subsequently they hardly mentioned it at all. At first, Oxford and Cambridge, and therefore most Anglican clergy, remained largely immune to the influence of German biblical scholarship and Renan. Yet intellectual complacency led to a rapid acceptance of modern criticism by the Established and Free Churches from the 1880s. The Bible was still read for spiritual and moral guidance but many abandoned the traditional acceptance of scriptural inerrancy.[4] If the Bible was uncertain as a source of history and doctrine, the intelligent layman was left wondering at its claim to spiritual and moral authority.

Rarely from the pulpit or in print did the earlier Prime Ministers receive an adequate defence of traditional Christian doctrine, while prejudice prevented them seeking solutions from High Church Anglicanism or Roman Catholicism. Interviewing Geoffrey Fisher for the vacancy at Canterbury, Churchill asked a reasonable question: had he read Renan? Fisher had not. Churchill expressed surprise, finding it 'quite unthinkable' that a senior prelate was unacquainted with one of traditional Christianity's most trenchant critics.[5] Had the clergy been reading the same material as the educated and ruling classes, they would have been better placed to counter the scepticism engendered by Modernism.

A recovery of belief later in the twentieth century is not necessarily indicative of a higher quality of apologetical works. Macmillan was disappointed by the lack of books providing a convincing intellectual basis for faith in the light of modern thought and science. Heath, too, regretted the lack of a credible apologetic. Thatcher was the exception among the Prime Ministers in discovering C. S. Lewis's rationale for Christianity. Rather than confronting Renan and his like, modern liberal theology simply conceded ground. The heat went out of the intellectual battle. Prime Ministers might look to religion for spiritual solace or the motivation to engage in social reform, but they rarely discovered there a credible answer to existential issues.

Even when a convincing Christian apologetic was lacking, few if any of them were doctrinaire atheists in the sense of having constructed for

4 Daniel L. Pals, *The Victorian 'Lives' of Jesus* (San Antonio, TX: Trinity University Press, 1982).

5 W. F. Purcell, *Fisher of Lambeth: A portrait from life* (London: Hodder & Stoughton Ltd, 1969), pp. 20, 110.

themselves a materialist mindset that definitively denied the existence of God. Rather, faith was damaged or destroyed by practical considerations. Sabbatarianism and puritanism have much to answer for. It is difficult today to imagine the sheer tedium of the Victorian Sunday, which survived well into the twentieth century. Asquith, Lloyd George, Attlee and others were bored to distraction by lengthy services and the absence of secular pleasures. The relaxation of Victorian mores may be partly why later Prime Ministers were more likely to be practising Christians. The most obvious exception, Callaghan, was subjected to a strict Baptist upbringing. Thatcher, who displayed early signs of rebellion, might have had her faith saved by the milder regime introduced after her grandmother's death.

It has been claimed that the loss of morals often precedes the loss of faith. People do not wish to feel constrained by a divinely instituted code of conduct, nor be reminded they will account in a future life for misdemeanours committed in this. Such considerations might have coloured the attitude towards Christianity of Lloyd George and MacDonald, and possibly of Asquith and Eden. Baldwin, Douglas-Home and Thatcher were committed believers who enjoyed long and happy marriages. There is, however, no strict correlation between Christian belief and moral behaviour. Bonar Law, Chamberlain, Attlee and Callaghan – all agnostics or atheists – were upright individuals, devoted husbands and exemplary fathers.

What remains?

The American historian of ideas Gertrude Himmelfarb charted the abandonment of Christian doctrine and belief in the afterlife in late Victorian England. She noted, however, a commitment remained, at least in principle, to morality and duty after the rejection of doctrine.[6] This was the conception of Christianity presented by Renan: a 'pure religion' devoid of ritual and dogma, residing in the individual conscience. It can be detected in Law's devotion to duty and MacDonald's ethical socialism. Attlee admired Christian ethics while simultaneously rejecting the 'mumbo jumbo'.

6 Gertrude Himmelfarb, *Victorian Minds* (Chicago, IL: Ivan R. Dee, 1968).

Even when they abandoned Christian doctrine, most of the early Prime Ministers still strove to discover the purpose to life and answers to existential questions. They yearned especially for the assurance of personal survival beyond death. Deprived by Renan and modern biblical criticism of a firm faith in the resurrection, they proved susceptible to real 'mumbo jumbo'. Balfour affected an intellectual curiosity towards spiritualism; MacDonald allowed it to prey on his emotional needs. For a generation demanding rational proof for Christianity, it was surprisingly credulous when it came to the paranormal. Churchill gave encouragement to his astrologer; Eden's mother and Attlee's wife dabbled with the spirit world. The aphorism once attributed to G. K. Chesterton comes readily to mind: when we stop believing in God we don't then believe in nothing; we believe in anything.

'Faith of the Fatherless'

Being orphaned in infancy was a common phenomenon in the nineteenth and early twentieth centuries. Nevertheless, the proportion of Prime Ministers losing fathers during childhood is striking: Balfour, Asquith, Lloyd George and Callaghan. Law was separated from his father at an early age; MacDonald never knew his; Chamberlain and Churchill idolized their famous fathers but suffered from a lack of paternal presence and affirmation; Eden's relationship with his father was tumultuous.

Is there a correlation between the father–child relationship and belief in God? Sigmund Freud proposed such a link:

> Psychoanalysis, which has taught us the intimate connection between the father complex and belief in God, has shown us that the personal God is logically nothing more but an exalted father, and daily demonstrates to us how youthful persons lose their religious beliefs as soon as the authority of the father breaks down.[7]

Without necessarily accepting his conclusion, the observation merits further investigation. A damaged relationship with the biological father may well affect one's perception of the heavenly Father. (This was true for

7 Sigmund Freud, *Leonardo da Vinci* (New York: Vintage/Random House, 1947), p. 98.

Freud himself.) While not disproving the existence of God, it may help to explain an individual's rejection of or distorted belief in God.

The American psychologist Paul Vitz turned Freud's projection theory of religion as a human construct on its head. He argued persuasively that if psychological factors can account for belief in God, then similar explanations for atheism are plausible. His book *Faith of the Fatherless* examined the lives of prominent atheists, concluding that in each case a weak, dead or abusive father contributed to the individual's rejection of God. Conversely, he demonstrated that many well-known theists enjoyed good relations with their fathers.[8]

Our 19 Prime Ministers constitute a small and unrepresentative sample, yet they lend strong support to Vitz's hypothesis. The nine Prime Ministers[9] who lost their fathers or were physically or emotionally distanced from them were all atheists, agnostics or lacking a firm faith in the Christian God. By contrast, Baldwin, Douglas-Home, Thatcher and Blair enjoyed good relations with their fathers and were uncomplicated believing Christians. Vitz's summary should not surprise: to a far greater extent than today, when religion has become more a matter of individual choice, faith was primarily mediated through the family during these leaders' formative years.

Psychology can go some way to explaining powerful influences but religious faith is not a determinist construct. Attlee enjoyed a perfectly good relationship with his devoutly Anglican father but went on to become a practical atheist. Macmillan and Heath were much closer to their mothers than their fathers; both were committed Christians. Ultimately, faith remains a matter of free will and personal choice.

If the influence of parents, particularly a father, was one formative factor, it is unsurprising that the presence of a spiritual mentor in youth was another. For Baldwin, Douglas-Home and Thatcher, their fathers constituted just such mentors in their religious awakening. Macmillan was fortunate to encounter Ronnie Knox as a private tutor and again at Oxford. Douglas-Home benefited also from the preaching and witness of Cyril Alington at Eton. Blair acknowledged Peter Thomson's role in making sense of

8 Paul C. Vitz, *Faith of the Fatherless: The psychology of atheism* (San Francisco, CA: Ignatius Press, 2013).

9 Balfour, Asquith, Lloyd George, Law, MacDonald, Chamberlain, Churchill, Eden and Callaghan.

Christianity for him as an undergraduate. Heath adopted Archbishop William Temple as a spiritual mentor at a distance but lacked anyone to fulfil the function more directly. The religious development of Balfour, MacDonald, Churchill and Major might have been different had they encountered convincing spiritual mentors during their youth.

Denominational fluidity

Another feature is striking. Party lines were firmly drawn in the twentieth century. (Only Churchill transgressed and never felt comfortable within them.) It is fascinating to note, therefore, how few Prime Ministers were entirely loyal to *confessional* divides at a time when such matters were taken extremely seriously.

Balfour and Campbell-Bannerman happily worshipped both as Anglicans and Presbyterians. Asquith left Congregationalism for Anglicanism. Lloyd George publicly sported his Baptist credentials but privately was happy with the Church of England or non-practice. Baldwin was an Anglican who could appear more comfortable in the company of Free Churchmen. When MacDonald felt the need for organized religion, he chose between Presbyterians, Baptists, Quakers, Unitarians and Low Church Anglicans. Douglas-Home expressed his frustration with denominational differences. Wilson was raised among Baptists and Congregationalists but, if at all, practised later in life with Methodists and Anglicans. Thatcher was a Methodist who practised as an Anglican. Blair was 'an ecumenical Christian' who converted from Anglicanism to Catholicism.

Macmillan was almost the only Prime Minister who obviously retained a steadfast lifelong ecclesial allegiance – and even he wobbled significantly in the direction of Rome as a young man. The others who were less religiously promiscuous – Law, Eden and Heath – possessed a weaker or low-key faith. The Prime Ministers studied here derived their sense of identity from party politics rather than denominational allegiance.

Christianity and other faiths

If, despite its rejection of certain core doctrines, Unitarianism is understood as a form of Christianity – and Chamberlain saw himself within the Protestant Nonconformist tradition – then all the Prime Ministers came from Christian homes and were raised as Christians. They identified as Christians in their youth, when virtually all attended church and received some Christian instruction at home, at school or within their denomination.

In a more homogenous culture, that is not surprising. Trade and empire, however, exposed the British to other cultures. Lloyd George, Churchill and Eden took an interest in Islam and Judaism (though such otherwise liberal and tolerant figures as Asquith and Macmillan occasionally displayed the endemic anti-Semitic prejudice of their age). Recognition of non-Christian religions was, however, limited to the other Abrahamic faiths. Blair was the first Prime Minister to display an interest in other world religions. An agnostic or atheist in Downing Street attracted little comment, but even at the end of the twentieth century it was barely conceivable that a Prime Minister might be a non-Christian believer – now a real possibility in the contest to replace Boris Johnson.

Chamberlain was nominally the only lifelong Unitarian, but Unitarian influence was far more widespread: Lloyd George was attracted to its tenets in youth; MacDonald was a Unitarian lay preacher for many years; Balfour's theism and Churchill's deism bore a certain resemblance to the Unitarian position. With the exception of Baldwin, only from the time of Macmillan did most Prime Ministers actively subscribe to traditional orthodox Christianity in terms of belief in the doctrines of the Trinity, Incarnation and resurrection.

Among those who professed themselves Christian, little value was attached to the practice of corporate worship. Many were prejudiced by the excesses and bad experiences of youth. When they did attend, church services were rated on the quality of the preaching and the music. Some, like Asquith, appreciated the cadences of the King James Bible and the Book of Common Prayer. Others spoke occasionally of benefiting from a sense of interior peace. Douglas-Home made the valid point that it did no harm to sublimate one's own desires for one hour of the week. These were very Protestant responses. With the exception of Macmillan, introduced as an Anglican by Ronnie Knox to 'the Catholic system', there was little comprehension of the sacraments as an extension of the Incarnation, as vehicles of grace with the power to transform the life of the believer.

The Premier League

Ranking the Prime Ministers in order of success has become something of an obsession for historians and political commentators. It would be invidious, and inevitably inaccurate, to attempt a table of all 19 in terms of religious belief. What exactly would the criteria be? Is there sufficient information to make such a judgement?

The temptation is too great, however, to avoid speculation as to which twentieth-century premier should head the list. Two names suggest themselves. First, Blair as the most 'religious'. Balfour displayed a similar interest in religious questions and expended much time and commitment pursuing answers, but for him the conclusions always remained tentative. Blair's personal commitment went beyond mere intellectual curiosity and was translated into practice, prayer and policy. Macmillan might be proposed as the most 'Christian' Prime Minister, though claims could also be made for Baldwin and Douglas-Home. The distinction consists in the fact that Macmillan was more Christocentric. His theological and historical knowledge allowed him to contextualize Christianity and his own personal faith more than any other Prime Minister.

The twenty-first century

This study concludes with the end of the Blair premiership in 2007. From the perspective of the third decade of the twenty-first century, the faith of the late twentieth-century Prime Ministers does not appear to be an aberration. Gordon Brown was a 'son of the manse', his father a Church of Scotland minister. Evidence of personal faith in his earlier years is scarce. Some questioned the authenticity of his scriptural allusions, and he was far more reticent in referring to religion than his predecessor. Yet he devoted a whole chapter of his autobiography to 'Faith in the Public Square?' It was something in which he believed passionately. He collaborated with religious leaders in combating want and injustice at home and overseas. What, however, of personal faith? Brown spoke movingly of his daughter's baptism before her death days after her premature birth in 2001. In his autobiography he declared himself a member of the Church of Scotland

and referred to his 'strong religious beliefs'.[10] One who knew him judged Brown the most religious of all recent Prime Ministers.[11]

No similar claim has been made for David Cameron. Culturally Anglican and an occasional churchgoer, he employed self-deprecation, confessing to vagueness as to doctrinal detail, identifying as 'a wishy-washy Christian'.[12] This unthreatening self-presentation allowed him to refer repeatedly to Britain as 'a Christian country' – at a time when that was manifestly less true – and to claim religious inspiration for his concept of the Big Society. It was not simply rhetoric. Although Cameron angered many Christians by his promotion of same-sex marriage, he intervened in other areas to delay the secularist tide.

Theresa May was much more than just a cultural Anglican. She did not flaunt her Christianity but acknowledged: 'It is part of me. It is part of who I am and, therefore, how I approach things.'[13] When she appeared on BBC Radio 4's *Desert Island Discs*, one of her musical selections was the hymn 'When I survey the wondrous cross'. Another was Saint Thomas Aquinas' eucharistic hymn 'Pange lingua'. No other Prime Minister could have made such a choice. In her youth she had been accustomed to singing the hymn kneeling in church with her parents. (Her father was an Anglo-Catholic clergyman.) She has remained a committed Anglican and regular communicant.

Anthony Seldon noted that Boris Johnson was 'not known to be devoutly religious'.[14] Many may think that a considerable understatement – that he lacked any moral compass. Yet Johnson embodied religious diversity more than any other Prime Minister. One great-grandfather was a Turkish Muslim; another a Lithuanian Jew. An aunt was a nun. Baptized a Catholic, Johnson was confirmed as an Anglican at Eton. His 2021 Easter message was explicitly Christian: 'Jesus Christ is the way, and the truth and the life, not just today but every day. His teachings and the message of his death and resurrection permeate through every aspect of daily life.'[15] Johnson refuted

10 Gordon Brown, *My Life, Our Times* (London: The Bodley Head, 2017), pp. 160, 429.

11 Private information communicated to the author.

12 *Church Times*, 5 May 2011.

13 Theresa May, Interview with Kirsty Young, BBC Radio 4, *Desert Island Discs*, 23 November 2014.

14 Seldon, *The Impossible Office?*, p. 19.

15 <www.youtube.com/watch?v=t1oXVlu9PRw>, accessed 14.08.21.

the claim that he was a pre-Christian pagan, counting himself rather 'a kind of very, very bad Christian'. Christianity was 'a superb ethical system' and made 'a lot of sense' to him.[16]

Religion mattered sufficiently for Johnson's youngest children, Wilfred and Romy, to be baptized and his marriage to Carrie Symonds to be celebrated in Westminster Cathedral – arousing considerable controversy as to how a man twice divorced could marry in a Catholic church. He refused to be drawn when Robert Peston asked subsequently whether he was now a practising Catholic. When Peston contrasted this with Keir Starmer's willing self-identification as an atheist, Johnson parried immediately, citing Psalm 14.1: 'The foolish man has said in his heart there is no God.'[17]

Even in twenty-first-century Britain, religious belief cannot be summarily dismissed. Allow Tony Blair the final word:

> Faith plays a far greater role in political leaders than you might think . . . I would say that even if you're not the slightest bit religious you can't really understand the modern world unless you know something about the faith community. And the great prediction that was made when I was growing up and at university that as society developed, so religion would fall away, has proven to be one of the many wrong predictions that were made. The truth is religious belief is still very much with us and very alive.[18]

With respect to the British Prime Ministers, that remains an accurate observation.

16 Boris Johnson, Interview with Tom McTeague, *Atlantic*, July/August 2021.

17 <www.itv.com/news/2021-06-12/why-did-the-prime-minister-refuse-to-discuss-his-faith>, accessed 14.08.21.

18 Tony Blair, Interview with John Geiger, *The Globe and Mail*, 29 November 2010.

Sources and select bibliography

Primary sources

Papers	*Depositories*
Asquith Papers	Bodleian Libraries, Oxford
Margot Asquith Papers	Bodleian Libraries, Oxford
Attlee Papers	Bodleian Libraries, Oxford
Attlee Papers	Churchill College Archives Centre, Cambridge
Avon Papers	Cadbury Research Library, Birmingham
Baldwin Family Papers	Worcestershire Archive & Archaeology Service
Baldwin Papers	Cambridge University Library
Balfour Papers	British Library
Balfour Papers	National Records of Scotland
Bell Papers	Lambeth Palace Library
Campbell-Bannerman Papers	British Library
Chamberlain Papers	Cadbury Research Library, Birmingham
Churchill Papers	Churchill College Archives Centre, Cambridge
D. R. Daniel Papers	National Library of Wales
Davidson Papers	Lambeth Palace Library
Fisher Papers	Lambeth Palace Library
William George Papers	National Library of Wales
Mary Gladstone Papers	British Library
Horner Archives	Private collection
Thomas Jones Papers	National Library of Wales

Ronald Knox Papers	Private collection
Lang Papers	Lambeth Palace Library
Bonar Law Papers	Parliamentary Archives
Lloyd George Papers	National Library of Wales
Lloyd George Papers	Parliamentary Archives
James Ramsay MacDonald Papers	National Archives
Macmillan Papers	Bodleian Libraries, Oxford
Ramsey Papers	Lambeth Palace Library
Margaret Sackville Papers	National Archives
Thatcher Papers	Churchill College Archives Centre, Cambridge

Select bibliography

R. J. Q. Adams, *Balfour: The last grandee* (London: John Murray, 2008).

R. J. Q. Adams, *Bonar Law* (London: John Murray, 1998).

Jonathan Aitken, *Margaret Thatcher: Power and personality* (London: Bloomsbury, 2013).

Herbert Henry Asquith, *Memories and Reflections, 1852–1927*, 2 vols (London: Cassell & Co., 1928).

Margot Asquith, *The Autobiography of Margot Asquith*, 2 vols (London: Thornton Butterworth, 1920, 1922).

C. R. Attlee, *As It Happened* (London: William Heinemann, 1954).

C. R. Attlee, *The Labour Party in Perspective* (London: Victor Gollancz, 1937).

A. W. Baldwin, *My Father: The true story* (London: George Allen & Unwin, 1956).

Stanley Baldwin, *On England and Other Addresses* (London: Philip Allen & Co., 1926).

Stanley Baldwin, *Service of Our Lives: Last speeches as Prime Minister* (London: Hodder & Stoughton Ltd, 1937).

Stanley Baldwin, *This Torch of Freedom: Speeches and addresses* (London: Hodder & Stoughton, 1935).

A. J. Balfour, *Chapters of Autobiography* (London: Cassell & Co., 1930).

A. J. Balfour, *A Defence of Philosophic Doubt: Being an essay on the foundations of belief*, 2nd edn (London: Hodder & Stoughton Limited, 1920).

A. J. Balfour, *The Foundations of Belief: Being notes introductory to the study of theology* (London: Longmans, 1895).

A. J. Balfour, 'Introduction', in ed. Joseph Needham, *Science, Religion and Reality* (London: Sheldon Press, 1925).

A. J. Balfour, *Theism and Humanism: Being the Gifford Lectures delivered at the University of Glasgow, 1914* (London: Hodder & Stoughton, 1915).

A. J. Balfour, *Theism and Thought: A study in familiar beliefs – being the second course of Gifford Lectures delivered at the University of Glasgow, 1922–23* (London: Hodder & Stoughton, 1923).

A. J. Balfour (ed.), *Papers Read before the Synthetic Society, 1896–1908* (London: Spottiswoode & Co., 1908).

Lady Frances Balfour, *Ne Obliviscaris: Dinna forget*, 2 vols (London: Hodder & Stoughton, 1930).

Clyde Binfield, *A Congregational Formation: An Edwardian Prime Minister's Victorian education* (London: Congregational Memorial Hall Trust, 1996).

Augustine Birrell, *Things Past Redress* (London: Faber & Faber, 1937).

Cherie Blair, *Speaking for Myself: The autobiography* (London: Little, Brown, 2008).

Tony Blair, *A Journey* (London: Hutchinson, 2010).

Robert Blake, *The Unknown Prime Minister: The life and times of Andrew Bonar Law, 1858–1923* (London: Eyre & Spottiswoode, 1955).

Cherie Booth and Cate Haste, *The Goldfish Bowl: Married to the Prime Minister, 1955–97* (London: Chatto & Windus, 2004).

John Burton and Eileen McCabe, *We Don't Do God: Blair's religious belief and its consequences* (London: Continuum, 2009).

James Callaghan, *Time and Chance* (London: Collins, 1987).

John Campbell, *Edward Heath: A biography* (London: Jonathan Cape, 1993).

John Campbell, *Margaret Thatcher: The grocer's daughter* (London: Jonathan Cape, 2000).

John Campbell, *Margaret Thatcher: The Iron Lady* (London: Jonathan Cape, 2003).

Owen Chadwick, *Michael Ramsey: A life* (Oxford: Oxford University Press, 1991).

Randolph S. Churchill, *Winston S. Churchill*, Vols 1 and 2 and Companion Vols (London: Heinemann, 1966–69).

Winston S. Churchill, *My Early Life: A roving commission* (London: The Reprint Society, 1944).

Winston S. Churchill, *Thoughts and Adventures* (London: Thornton Butterworth, 1932).

John Colville, *The Fringes of Power: Downing Street diaries, 1939–1945* (London: Hodder & Stoughton, 1985).

Anthony Connell, 'Tony Blair (1997–2007)', in ed. Nick Spencer, *The Mighty and the Almighty: How political leaders do God* (London: Biteback Publishing, 2017).

Jane Cox (ed.), *A Singular Marriage: A Labour love story in letters and diaries* (London: George G. Harrap, 1988).

Andrew Crines and Kevin Hickson (eds), *Harold Wilson: The unprincipled Prime Minister?* (London: Biteback Publishing, 2016).

Colin Cross (ed.), *Life with Lloyd George: The diary of A. J. Sylvester, 1931–45* (London: Macmillan, 1975).

David Dilks, *Neville Chamberlain: Pioneering and reform, 1869–1929* (Cambridge: Cambridge University Press, 1984).

Blanche Dugdale, *Arthur James Balfour: First Earl of Balfour, KG, OM, FRS, 1848–1905* (London: Hutchinson & Co., 1939).

Blanche Dugdale, *Arthur James Balfour, First Earl of Balfour, KG, OM, FRS, 1906–1930* (London: Hutchinson & Co., u/d [1936]).

Anthony Eden, *Another World, 1897–1917* (London: Allen Lane, 1976).

Clarissa Eden, *A Memoir: From Churchill to Eden* (London: Weidenfeld & Nicolson, 2007).

Timothy Eden, *The Tribulations of a Baronet* (London: Macmillan, 1933).

Max Egremont, *Balfour: A life of Arthur James Balfour* (London: Phoenix, 1998).

Lord Elton, *The Life of James Ramsay MacDonald, 1866–1919* (London: Collins, 1939).

Keith Feiling, *The Life of Neville Chamberlain* (London: Macmillan, 1946).

Eliza Filby, *God and Mrs Thatcher: The battle for Britain's soul* (London: Biteback Publishing, 2015).

A Gentleman with a Duster [Edward Harold Begbie], *The Conservative Mind* (London: Mills & Boon, 1924).

William George, *My Brother and I* (London: Eyre & Spottiswoode, 1958).

B. B. Gilbert, *Lloyd George: A political life – the architect of change, 1863–1912* (Columbus, OH: Ohio State University Press, 1987).

Eldon Griffiths (ed.), *Peaceful Change: A selection of speeches by Sir Alec Douglas-Home* (London: Arthur Baker, 1964).

John Grigg, *Lloyd George: From peace to war, 1912–1916* (London: Methuen, 1985).

John Grigg, *Lloyd George: The people's champion, 1902–1911* (London: Eyre Methuen, 1978).

John Grigg, *Lloyd George: War leader, 1916–1918* (London: Allen Lane, 2002).

John Grigg, *The Young Lloyd George* (London: Eyre Methuen, 1973).

Kenneth Harris, *Attlee* (London: Weidenfeld & Nicolson, 1982).

Kenneth Harris, *Conversations* (London: Hodder & Stoughton, 1967).

Robin Harris, *Not for Turning: The life of Margaret Thatcher* (London: Bantam Press, 2013).

Edward Heath, *The Course of My Life: My autobiography* (London: Hodder & Stoughton, 1998).

Lord Home, *Letters to a Grandson* (London: Collins, 1983).

Lord Home, *The Way the Wind Blows* (London: Collins, 1976).

William Douglas Home *Mr Home Pronounced Hume: An autobiography* (London: Collins, 1979).

Alistair Horne, *Macmillan, 1894–1956* (London: Macmillan, 1988).

Alistair Horne, *Macmillan, 1957–1986* (London: Macmillan, 1989).

George Hutchinson, *Edward Heath: A personal and political biography* (London: Longman, 1970).

Robert Rhodes James, *Anthony Eden: A biography* (New York: McGraw-Hill, 1987).

John Jolliffe, *Raymond Asquith: Life and letters* (London: Collins, 1980).

Thomas Jones, *A Diary with Letters, 1931–1950* (London: Oxford University Press, 1954).

Thomas Jones, *Whitehall Diary, Vol. 1: 1916–1925* (London: Oxford University Press, 1969).

Thomas Jones, *Whitehall Diary, Vol. 2: 1926–1930* (London: Oxford University Press, 1969).

Ernest Kay, *The Pragmatic Premier: An intimate portrait of Harold Wilson* (London: Leslie Frewin, 1967).

R. A. Knox, *A Spiritual Aeneid* (London: Longmans, Green & Co., 1918).

Frances Lloyd George, *The Years that Are Past* (London: Hutchinson, 1967).

Richard Lloyd George, *Lloyd George* (London: Frederick Muller, 1960).

J. Ramsay MacDonald, *Margaret Ethel MacDonald*, 2nd edn (London: Hodder & Stoughton, 1912).

J. M. McEwen (ed.), *The Riddell Diaries, 1908–1923* (London: Athlone Press, 1986).

Harold Macmillan, *War Diaries: Politics and war in the Mediterranean, January 1943–May 1945* (London: Macmillan, 1984).

Harold Macmillan, *Winds of Change, 1914–1939* (London: Macmillan, 1966).

John Major, *The Autobiography* (London: HarperCollins, 1999).

David Marquand, *Ramsay MacDonald*, 2nd edn (London: Jonathan Cape, 1997).

Lucy Masterman, *C. F. G. Masterman: A biography* (London: Nicholson & Watson, 1939).

Keith Middlemas and John Barnes, *Baldwin: A biography* (London: Weidenfeld & Nicolson, 1969).

Charles Moore, *Margaret Thatcher: Everything she wants* (London: Allen Lane, 2015).

Charles Moore, *Margaret Thatcher: Herself alone* (London: Allen Lane, 2019).

Charles Moore, *Margaret Thatcher: Not for turning* (London: Allen Lane, 2013).

Lord Moran, *Churchill: The struggle for survival, 1945–65* (London: Robinson, 2006).

Lord Moran, *Churchill at War, 1940–45* (London: Robinson, 2002).

Kenneth O. Morgan, *Callaghan: A life* (Oxford: Oxford University Press, 1997).

Janet Oppenheim, *The Other World: Spiritualism and psychical research in England, 1850–1914* (Cambridge: Cambridge University Press, 1988).

Bernard Palmer, *High and Mitred: A study of Prime Ministers as bishop-makers, 1837–1977* (London: SPCK, 1992).

Lord Pentland (ed.), *Early Letters of Sir Henry Campbell-Bannerman to His Sister Louisa* (London: T. Fisher Unwin, 1925).

Ben Pimlott, *Harold Wilson* (London: HarperCollins, 1992).

John Rentoul, *Tony Blair: Prime Minister* (London: Faber & Faber, 2013).

Andrew Roberts, *Churchill: Walking with destiny* (London: Allen Lane, 2018).

Jonathan Sandys and Wallace Henley, *God and Churchill: How the great leader's sense of divine destiny changed his troubled world and offers hope for ours* (London: SPCK, 2015).

Anthony Seldon, *Blair* (London: Free Press, 2004).

Anthony Seldon, *Blair Unbound* (London: Simon & Schuster, 2007).

Robert Self, *Neville Chamberlain: A biography* (London: Routledge, 2016).

Leslie Smith, *Harold Wilson: The authentic portrait* (London: Hodder & Stoughton, 1964).

Nick Spencer (ed.), *The Mighty and the Almighty: How political leaders do God* (London: Biteback Publishing, 2017).

J. A. Spender, *Life of the Right Hon. Sir Henry Campbell-Bannerman, GCB*, 2 vols (London: Hodder & Stoughton, 1923).

J. A. Spender and Cyril Asquith, *Life of Herbert Henry Asquith, Lord Oxford and Asquith*, 2 vols (London: Hutchinson & Co., 1932).

A. J. Sylvester, *The Real Lloyd George* (London: Cassell and Co., 1947).

A. J. P. Taylor (ed.), *Lloyd George: A diary by Frances Stevenson* (London: Hutchinson & Co., 1971).

A. J. P. Taylor (ed.), *My Darling Pussy: The letters of Lloyd George and Frances Stevenson* (London: Weidenfeld & Nicolson, 1975).

H. A. Taylor, *The Strange Case of Andrew Bonar Law* (London: Stanley Paul & Co., 1932).

Carol Thatcher, *Below the Parapet: The biography of Denis Thatcher* (London: HarperCollins, 1996).

Margaret Thatcher, *The Downing Street Years* (London: HarperCollins, 1993).

Margaret Thatcher, *The Path to Power* (London: HarperCollins, 1995).

R. W. Thompson, *Churchill and Morton: The quest for insight in the correspondence of Major Sir Desmond Morton and the author* (London: Hodder & Stoughton, 1976).

Andrew Thomson, *Margaret Thatcher: The woman within* (London: W. H. Allen, 1989).

D. R. Thorpe, *Alec Douglas-Home* (London: Sinclair-Stevenson, 1996).

D. R. Thorpe, *Eden: The life and times of Anthony Eden, First Earl of Avon, 1897–1977* (London: Chatto & Windus, 2003).

D. R. Thorpe, *Supermac: The life of Harold Macmillan* (London: Chatto & Windus, 2010).

Evelyn Waugh, *The Life of Ronald Knox* (London: Chapman & Hall, 1959).

Philip Williamson, *Stanley Baldwin: Conservative leadership and national values* (Cambridge: Cambridge University Press, 1999).

Philip Williamson and Edward Baldwin (eds), *Baldwin Papers: A Conservative statesman, 1908–1947* (Cambridge: Cambridge University Press, 2004).

Harold Wilson, *Memoirs: The making of a Prime Minister, 1916–64* (London: Weidenfeld & Nicolson, 1986).

John Wilson, *CB: A Life of Sir Henry Campbell-Bannerman* (London: Constable, 1973).

Hugo Young, *One of Us: A biography of Margaret Thatcher* (London: Macmillan, 1989).

Kenneth Young, *Arthur James Balfour: The happy life of the politician, Prime Minister, statesman and philosopher, 1848–1930* (London: George Bell & Sons, 1963).

Kenneth Young, *Sir Alec Douglas Home* (London: J. M. Dent & Sons, 1970).

Kenneth Young, *Stanley Baldwin* (London: Weidenfeld & Nicolson, 1976).

Philip Ziegler, *Edward Heath: The authorised biography* (London: HarperCollins, 2010).

Philip Ziegler, *Wilson: The authorised life of Lord Wilson of Rievaulx* (London: Weidenfeld & Nicolson, 1993).

Index

Note: the subentries under the names of people are given in chronological rather than alphabetical order.

Index